Background Readings

for Teachers of American Literature

Second Edition

Venetria K. Patton

Purdue University

Bedford/St. Martin's   Boston ◆ Ne

In memory of Emory Elliott, for shaping my love of American literature

For Bedford/St. Martin's
Assistant Director of Development: Maura Shea
Developmental Editor: Shannon Walsh
Assistant Production Editor: Lidia MacDonald-Carr
Senior Production Supervisor: Steven Cestaro
Marketing Manager: Stacey Propps
Editorial Assistant: Sherry Mooney
Project Management: Jouve North America
Copy Editor: Wesley Morrison
Text Researcher: Barbara Hernandez, Bookworm Permissions
Senior Art Director: Anna Palchik
Cover Design: Billy Boardman
Composition: Jouve North America
Printing and Binding: RR Donnelley & Sons

Manufactured in the United States of America.

9 8   7   6   5   4
f   e   d   c   b   a

For information, write: Bedford/St. Martin's, 75 Arlington Street, Boston, MA 02116
(617-399-4000)

ISBN 978-1-4576-7637-6

Acknowledgments
Margaret D. Bauer. Reprinted by permission of copyright owner, the Modern Language Association of America from "From Gilded Garden to Golden Anniversary: Teaching Hurston's 'The Gilded Six-Bits,'" *Approaches to Teaching Hurston's Their Eyes Were Watching God and Other Works*, pages 164–74.
Shari Benstock, Suzanne Ferriss, and Susanne Woods. "Feminist Literary Criticism and Theory" (pp. 153-178) from *A Handbook of Literary Feminisms* by Shari Benstock, Suzanne Ferriss, and Susanne Woods. Copyright © 2002. Reprinted by permission of Oxford University Press, USA.
Lawrence Buell. "American Literary Emergence as a Postcolonial Phenomenon" by Lawrence Buell from *American Literary History*, Vol. 4, No. 3 (Autumn, 1992): pp. 411–442. Copyright © 1992. Reproduced with permission of Oxford University Press in the format reuse in a book/e-book via Copyright Clearance Center.

Preface

Anthologies are a mainstay for many literature instructors, but it can be difficult to find a suitable selection for our courses. Many of the current anthologies have become almost unwieldy in their attempt to include everything that an instructor might wish to teach. However, *The Bedford Anthology of American Literature*, Second Edition, takes a very different approach by aiming for representation rather than comprehensive coverage. The anthology includes frequently taught writers while also reflecting the gender and ethnic diversity of American literature. The editors also seek to provide crucial historical context for the selections by including brief introductions to the periods and writers. Yet, what I find most attractive about the anthology is the inclusion of clusters of related works found in the American Contexts sections and the brief Writers on Writers features, which put later writers in conversation with their predecessors. Because of my excitement about this new anthology, I was pleased to be asked to edit this companion essay collection, *Background Readings for Teachers of American Literature*, on the challenges of teaching American literature.

In an era of canon expansion and even destruction, one of the clearest challenges is determining what constitutes American literature. With the increased emphasis on diversity, scholars are questioning why certain women and ethnic writers have been undervalued. Critics are also insisting that issues of sexuality and class be addressed in discussions of literature. The landscape has clearly changed, and many instructors lack formal training in more recent critical approaches. While many of us use conferences and professional journals to keep up with the changing times, it can be hard to find time for such professional development. In addition to a more diverse body of literature, instructors are also faced with a more diverse student body, and instructors often require a variety of teaching methodologies in order to be successful in the classroom. This collection speaks to these challenges. While one book cannot provide all of the answers, I do believe that this set of essays addresses some of the most pressing issues in the field and provides essential resources for teaching in the trenches.

I think many teachers are, like me, collectors. I am always looking for good ideas and resources for my classes. I have a sizeable collection of books related to teaching American and African American literature, but the vast majority is devoted to how to teach a particular text or provides contextual material to assist in the teaching of a particular text. I h nothing on my bookshelves that approaches the collection gathered here. My hope is that this text will fill a hole in the bookshelves of many American literature instructors.

In thinking about how to approach this collection and how to organize the materials, I reflected on the numerous conversations I have had with colleagues over lunch, in the hallways, or even on the phone after a particularly rough class. My colleagues were struggling with many of the same teaching dilemmas that I faced: what should I include on the syllabus, how can I break the monotony of the classroom, how do I make the text accessible, how do I get students to talk about the reading, and what type of assignments should I use? As instructors, we like to appear calm and collected in front of our students, but amongst ourselves we often shake our heads, frown, and grimace about our teaching. Of course there are times when we beam with joy because a class went exactly as we had planned or even better, but I have found that my colleagues tend to be type-A personalities, who while pleased with success are troubled by the one student they did not reach.

Before discussing the aims of this collection, I would like to share a bit about some of my initial experiences teaching American literature courses. During my Ph.D. studies, while teaching composition at a nearby junior college, I was asked to substitute for an ill instructor who had been assigned to teach American Literature: 1865 to Present. Since I entered the class *in medias res*, I did not have to worry about how to cram a century of literature into sixteen weeks. My main concern was keeping the attention of my students and keeping the discussion flowing. In fact, my initial difficulty engaging students in discussion inspired me to assign study questions on a fairly regular basis. The questions served as both a reading check and a starting point for in-class discussion of the reading. My next foray into teaching American literature was the American Novel to Dreiser course, now known as American Novel I. Although I realized that my predecessors had tended toward a rather traditional approach to the class, I was not dissuaded from offering a more colorful approach to the American novel. I consciously selected more women and African American writers for my syllabus. While I wanted to shake up my students a bit by highlighting issues of race, gender, and nation building, I did not abandon the canon. However, I think some of my students suspected I had gone off the deep end; they questioned my notion of the American novel because I was not teaching what was expected.

Looking back on this experience, I suspect that I could have set things up better in order to build a case for the approach I was using. The course was essentially based on the primary texts, and it could have benefited from some secondary sources. I had a vision for the course, but I didn't know how to share it with my students. I spent many a lunch hour with my colleagues moaning and groaning about that course. The moaning and groaning had a cathartic effect, but what I really needed was guidance—I needed this book.

Background Readings for Teachers of American Literature, Second Edition, is the resource I needed as a beginning teacher, and can still use even as a seasoned, award-winning teacher. My intent was to create a book that would be essential for new teachers but also beneficial for veteran teachers. Moreover, I kept in the forefront of my mind the fact that we all have holes in our training, so someone completely at home with the Puritans might be at sea with the modernists. I have also found that sometimes instructors get into a bit of a rut once they discover what works for them, and they do not try new things. While I am open to trying what has worked for my colleagues, if I have not had success with something I am loathe to tweak it and try again. So this is why I have pulled together a mix of informative background readings as well as practical teaching suggestions for this book. There is no other collection quite like this, as most books on teaching focus on a particular text or type of text, while this volume seeks to address a variety of concerns related to the American literature survey.

Chapter 1, Challenges of Teaching American Literature, serves as an overview of ongoing concerns within the field of American literary studies. The first two essays, by Cecelia Tichi and Philip Fisher, provide a nice overview of the two main periods of American literature, while Gregory S. Jay's essay addresses the impact multiculturalism has had on the field. Chapter 2, Considering Literary and Social Movements, highlights some of the movements that are reflected in American literature survey courses. This is the section that I imagine filling in the gaps for instructors teaching outside of their specialty.

The emphasis on multiculturalism has become so ingrained in Ph.D. programs that references to race, gender, and sexuality have become expected. In fact, some are beginning to argue that we need to move beyond identity politics. Regardless of one's particular position, Chapter 3, Considering Identities, includes a wealth of information. David Palumbo-Liu's "Assumed Identities" sets the stage with regard to the continuing importance of considering identities. The essays that follow all address some aspect of race, gender, or sexuality. The essays on ethnic literature are meant to provide a broad overview for those who are less familiar with the particular fields. The essays on gender provide a nice balance to each other because one focuses on feminism while the other addresses manhood. This construction destabilizes the notion that discussions of gender only pertain to women. The chapter concludes with an excerpt from Michael Ryan that addresses the intersection of gender studies and the study of sexuality.

Chapter 4, Considering the Geopolitical, looks toward recent concerns regarding the impact of political, geographic, demographic, and economic issues on our approach to American literary studies. Since this is a relatively new direction in the field, many instructors will benefit from reading these very different approaches to the geopolitical. These essays may inspire instructors to structure their courses differently or incorporate some different material.

The final chapter turns to the practical concerns of classroom practices. Chapter 5, Approaches in the Classroom, brings together a set of essays that provide very specific examples of classroom activities. While some might think that this section is meant for novice instructors, I encourage more senior instructors to peruse these pages as well. I found that I learned quite a bit during the process of selecting the material, and I am looking forward to trying out some of these practices. I hope that readers of this collection will find it useful and informative.

In closing, I must acknowledge that this collection has benefited from the contributions and expertise of many people. The editors of *The Bedford Anthology of American Literature*, Susan Belasco and Linck Johnson, provided extensive and invaluable suggestions for this collection. I must thank my editor, Shannon C. Walsh, for her excellent guidance throughout this process. I would also like to recognize other members of the Bedford/St. Martin's staff for their hard work on this project: Steve Scipione, Executive Editor; Maura Shea, Assistant Director of Development; and Sherry Mooney, Editorial Assistant. I must also extend my sincere thanks to the many reviewers who provided detailed feedback regarding the initial plans for this project: Joseph Alkana, University of Miami; Elizabeth Ammons, Tufts University; Scott Ash, Nassau Community College; Peter J. Bellis, University of Miami; Robert Bergstrom, University of Nebraska–Lincoln; Donna Campbell, Washington State University; David J. Carlson, California State University, San Bernadino; David Chinitz, Loyola University Chicago; Matt Cohen, University of Texas at Austin; Patty Cowell, Colorado State University; Michael Coyle, Colgate University; Paul Crumbley, Utah State University; William Merrill Decker, Oklahoma State University; Robert Donahoo, Sam Houston State University; Heather Duda, University of Rio Grande & Rio Grande Community College; Thomas C. Gannon, University of Nebraska, Lincoln; Ivonne M. García, Kenyon College; Sharon M. Harris, University of Connecticut; Carole E. Henderson Belton, University of Delaware; Desiree Henderson, University of Texas at Arlington; Chuck Johanningsmeier, University of Nebraska, Omaha; Patricia L. Kalayjian, California State University, Dominguez Hills; AnaLouise Keating, Texas Woman's University; Peggy Pritchard Kulesz, University of Texas at Arlington; Linda Leavell, Oklahoma State University; Lisa Logan, University of Central Florida; Tom Lynch, University of Nebraska, Lincoln; Beth Maxfield, Henderson State University; Laura L. Mielke, University of Kansas; Richard M. Millington, Smith College; Sally Mitchell, Temple University; James Nagel, University of Georgia; Sandra Oh, University of Miami; Patricia Okker, University of Missouri, Columbia; Leland S. Person, University of Cincinnati; Connie L. Richards, Salisbury University; Sarah Robbins, Texas Christian University; Paul Sorrentino,

Virginia Tech; Michael Soto, Trinity University; Susan Tomlinson, University of Massachusetts, Boston; Nicole Tankovich, University of California, San Diego; Joseph Urgo, University of Mississippi; Lara Vetter, University of North Carolina, Charlotte; Eric A. Weil, Shaw University; Cindy Weinstein, California Institute of Technology; Gary Williams, University of Idaho; and Susan Williams, Ohio State University. In addition, I would like to recognize my administrative assistant, Matilda Stokes, who helped me in innumerable ways throughout this endeavor. Finally, I must acknowledge the support of my son, Hollis, and my partner, Ronald, who endured my long hours when necessary, but also reminded me of the importance of family time.

Venetria K. Patton

Contents

Ed Folsom
Portrait of the Artist as a Young Slave: Douglass's Frontispiece Engravings 419

I tell the students I'd like them to *read* this portrait, to view it not only as a key physical element of the *book* that appeared in 1845, but also as an important component of the *text*. . . .

Martha Nell Smith
Enabling Undergraduates to Understand Advanced Humanities Research: Teaching with the *Dickinson Electronic Archives* 431

[I] do not build software, I am not an advanced specialist in text encoding, and . . . I do not think one needs to be either of those things to use technology, and use it well, in teaching and research.

Margaret D. Bauer
From Gilded Garden to Golden Anniversary: Teaching Hurston's "The Gilded Six-Bits" 441

[I] try to coax students from their usual initial response to Missie May's affair with Otis D. Slemmons as an unforgivable betrayal of her husband, Joe, to a more compassionate response to this young woman's fall.

SueEllen Campbell
Asking Ecocritical Questions 449

If questions are carefully handled, I have learned, even the simplest ones will open up into layered mazes of complications—and into unexpected illuminations.

Challenges of Teaching American Literature

One of the biggest challenges of teaching is determining what to teach—there always seems to be more material than time. However, this concern has been exacerbated since the 1970s, as the nature of American literary studies has been questioned. Just what is American literature? As Cecelia Tichi points out in "American Literary Studies to the Civil War," it is no longer just the literature of white men. Scholars have broadened our notion of canonical American literature by including the literature of women and people of color. However, this expansion of the canon was just the beginning of a major revolution within American literary studies. New theoretical approaches were developing, and some scholars were even talking about the end of American literature. The essays included in this section should put these changes in perspective.

Canonical shifts are apparent in recent anthologies that include more than the perfunctory woman author and slave narrative. Many newer anthologies are beginning with the oral traditions of Native Americans and include a much more representative sampling of African American, Asian American, and Latino/a literature. This greater inclusiveness is also apparent with regard to women writers of all ethnicities. Of course, for the instructor the more representative anthologies are a double-edged sword. While there is more great material to teach, there is also more to exclude, since our semesters or quarters have not been lengthened to accommodate these additional options.

Even after instructors have risen to the challenge of deciding what to teach, there is still the question of how to teach it. Should students be introduced to newer critical approaches, or would they be better served by more traditional approaches? Or might they benefit from studying very different readings of the same text? In "American Literary Studies to the Civil War," Tichi notes the deceptively constant use of this rubric in what has become an ideologically complex understanding of American literary studies. In other words, we continue to maintain traditional trappings such as the existence of a literary canon and major wars as demarcations of literary periods, but their significance has changed. Not only are we reading women's texts, but we are often using feminist or gender theory. The study of oral traditions is enhanced by the use of rhetorical theory. However, as Tichi points out, these newer methodologies "have not come to the fore without a degree of resistance and hostility" (p. 22). Tichi concludes by noting the cyclical nature of literary studies.

Philip Fisher takes a slightly different approach in his essay, "American Literary and Cultural Studies since the Civil War." According to Fisher, the new generation of American studies scholars is moving from myth, a singular story, to rhetorics, a plural approach to culture. This pluralistic, dynamic approach to culture is reflected in what he terms "episodes of regionalism" (p. 39). Although Fisher and Tichi approach the changing theoretical terrain in different ways, they both point to the challenge for instructors who are typically not versed in all of the available critical approaches.

While many of us are still grappling with the changes within the field of American literary studies, some scholars have begun to question the very nature of the term *American*. Gregory S. Jay begins "The End of 'American' Literature: Toward a Multicultural Practice" by saying, "It is time to stop teaching 'American' literature" (p. 49). Jay argues for not just a revision of curriculum and pedagogy, but a dismantling of what he considers to be an "oppressive nationalist ideology" (p. 50). Jay would like the borders between the United States, Canada, and Mexico to be seen as the products of our history and not its origins. This revised approach to American literary studies would address the role of assimilation and translation within American literature and allow more cultural exchange between cultural groups.

These essays by Jay, Fisher, and Tichi do not solve the challenges associated with teaching American literature, but they do contextualize major issues within the field. Fisher and Tichi make important connections between content and approach. The incorporation of new topics of study has necessitated new approaches and calls into question one-size-fits-all notions of literary criticism. The heterogeneity of the field demands a variety of methodologies. This may at times be disconcerting to students who often want "the" answer rather than several possibilities, but it can also be empowering as students are taught to engage the literature. Jay's essay includes a practical discussion of how his ideas might be transferred to the classroom. I can imagine an interesting unit on assimilation that would bring together a wide range of readings and perspectives. This might include an excerpt from Phillis Wheatley's "On Being Brought from Africa to America," Sojourner Truth's, "Speech to a Women's Rights Convention, 1851," Frederick Douglass's "Men of Color, to Arms!," Paul Laurence Dunbar's "We Wear the Mask," José Martí's "Impressions of America, I and II," Zitkala-Sä's "The School Days of an Indian Girl," Hisaye Yamamoto's "Seventeen Syllables," and an excerpt from Jane Addams's *Twenty Years at Hull-House*. I might begin this unit with an excerpt from W. E. B. Du Bois's *The Souls of Black Folk*, using his concept of double consciousness as a starting point for our discussion of how one becomes an American. In an oft-quoted passage from the first chapter of his landmark book, Du Bois describes double consciousness as seeing oneself through the eyes of another and relates this to the African American's sense of "twoness"—of being African *and* American. Du Bois's notion of two ideals in one body serves as a nice introduction to a discussion of American identity construction. Students may be able to easily relate this concept to ethnic identities because these are often thought of as hyphenated, but with some prodding students should also be able to link double consciousness to other forms of identity formation.

American Literary Studies to the Civil War

Cecelia Tichi

Taken from the collection Redrawing the Boundaries *(1992), Tichi's essay observes that beginning in the 1970s, scholars noticed that texts taught in American literature courses tended to focus on the Anglo-American experience to the exclusion of the perspectives of ethnic groups, women, and non-Anglo colonial powers. This recognition led to more representative anthologies, broader literary histories, and different literary approaches. These changes have prompted not only the study of new material, but also a rethinking of canonical works. For example, despite the revision of the American literary canon, New England Puritanism remains a hot topic for scholars. Thus Mary Rowlandson's captivity narrative remains a staple on Early American literature syllabi; however, Tichi asserts that since the 1990s Rowlandson's text has been "reread as an ethnographic juxta-positioning" (p. 9) of Anglo-American and Native American cultures rather than merely as an exemplar of Puritan doctrine. According to Tichi this change in approach is in part related to poststructuralism's interest in gender, race, and class as categories of inquiry. She argues that*

From *Redrawing the Boundaries: The Transformation of English and American Literary Studies*, ed. Stephen Greenblatt and Giles Gunn (New York: MLA, 1992) 209–31.

New Historicism has led to a rereading of "classic" American authors as complicit with marketplace values rather than as critics of culture. Thus the contemplative attitudes of transcendentalists such as Emerson and Thoreau become products of economic history, and their visionary think- ing is seen as the necessary outcome of capitalist alienation. Tichi notes that another recent trend in American literary studies is the application of reader-response theory to ask questions about the cultural shaping of interpretation and assessment.

Tichi concludes with the caveat that recent changes in scholarship have not come without resistance and hostility from scholars trained in New Criticism. She considers the controversy associated with newer meth- ods as a political struggle to control the meaning of literary works. Tichi cautions both camps to be aware of the shortcomings of their respective approaches, as neither historicism nor formalism is without blind spots.

For some twenty-five years, from the close of World War II through the 1960s, American Literary Studies to the Civil War seemed to be a clear, straightforward rubric. It performed—as it continues to per- form—taxonomic service in classroom texts and in college texts and in college and university catalogs. Within the rubric a certain evo- lutionary literary coherence, even progress, was presumed to be demonstrable, as instructors and critics located in prose and poetry the growing expressions of democratic consciousness and of such values as individualism and self-reliance. Certain topics and themes were shown to undergo development—for instance, in the *from-to* model based on the notion of aesthetic or thematic incipience leading to ful- fillment (e.g., from nature in Jonathan Edwards's *Personal Narrative* to Emerson's *Nature*). Thus it was in no way considered disruptive for teaching or scholarship to subdivide American literature to the Civil War into such areas as colonial, revolutionary, early national, tran- scendental, American Renaissance.

And if few scholars assented to the simplicity of the homogeneous melting pot, the acceptance of such formulations as the American Adam (Lewis) or the American Renaissance (Matthiessen) reinforced the im- portance of certain patterns of texts considered to be major because they demonstrated salient parts of the American identity and its aes- thetic expression. "American" in those years seemed synonymous with "United States," and teachers and students were in the main un- troubled by conceptual problems implied in a body of literature repre- senting a developing nation-state but claiming the whole of two continents as its purview.

This postwar epoch in American literary study, however, began to undergo major revaluation in the 1970s, when scholars pointed out that the canonical texts thought to constitute American literature excluded the cultural record of indigenous peoples, ethnic and minority groups, women, and non-Anglo colonial powers. A post-1960s generation of scholars and editors, moreover, invoked the terms of this rubric with growing awareness of myriad complexities embedded in virtually every word. The term *American* began to seem hegemonic and inaccurately univocal, while the largely Marxist challenge to the belletristic tradition made *literary studies* itself a problematic category. If *Civil War* has often been read as a contradiction in terms, newer scholarship additionally would point out that, given Michel Foucault's arguments on social discipline, the phrase is a tautology. Suffice it to say that for the past twenty-five years, every term in the title of this essay and every ramifying subcategory has undergone dynamic, radical change.

"Always historicize!" begins Fredric Jameson's *Political Unconscious*. And that is one crucial heuristic enterprise of contemporary critics of American literature from the colonial era through the mid-nineteenth century. The other is a change of subject positions. The two are of course related. Historicizing, as Jameson comments, can follow two paths, of the object and of the subject (9). Critical theory, particularly deconstruction, has let critics do both. The critical byword has become "the social construction of —," the prepositional object of that phrase including not only texts but temporal periods, authorial careers, and scholars' own argumentative positions. No category of literary text, period, approach is considered to be a natural one, from Puritan New England to the reputation of Nathaniel Hawthorne to the mid-nineteenth-century American Renaissance; and the inquiry into the process of naturalization necessarily results in the vigorous decentering of all literary categories.

The classroom anthologies show this new decentering, from the once-standard *American Tradition in Literature* (Bradley, Beatty, and Long), which as recently as 1974 opened with a section called "The Puritan Culture," down to *The Harper American Literature* (McQuade et al., 1986), which repositioned the literary origins with the Renaissance discovery narratives, and now *The Heath Anthology of American Literature* (Lauter et al., 1990), which, committed to a multiethnic, multiracial, and doubly gendered canon, opens with a section entitled "Native American Traditions" and boasts the work of "time-honored favorite authors placed alongside the writings of women and minority authors whose importance is only now being recognized" (iii). And just as the anthologies measure the shift in the canon, the literary history compendiums reveal the changed census of those considered qualified to form it and comment on it. Of the contributors to *Literary History of the United States*, edited by Robert Spiller et al. (1946; rev. ed. 1953), all fifty-five were white men, while *The Columbia Literary History of the United States*, edited by Emory Elliot (1986), lists seventy-four contributors, sixteen of whom are women and at least four of whom are specialists in ethnic or minority American texts.

The simple rubric American Literature to the Civil War is thus deceptively constant in its continuing use in classroom texts, in course titles, and even in journal titles (*American Literature, Early American Literature, Studies in American Fiction, American Literary History*). A post-1960s generation of scholars and editors by no means invokes the term without awareness of its ideological complexities.

For the colonial period, New England Puritanism continues to be a scholarly force field. And though the issue of New England's exceptionalism will concern us momentarily, suffice it to say here that books beget books, and arguably the sheer quantity of studies of seventeenth-century New England (by one estimate, a book or article for every one hundred persons alive in New England in 1650) engenders vigorous continuing scholarship (Wood 26). A 1986 investigation, for instance, of John Cotton's rhetoric and the ways in which the spoken word was aural sculpture for the New England Puritans is indebted to Larzer Ziff's 1962 biography of John Cotton (Kibbey), while a 1990 study of identity formation in colonial New England acknowledges its paternity in Perry Miller's *New England Mind*: "My primary scholarly inspiration came from that prime inspirer of American Puritan studies, Perry Miller" (Canup vii).

Miller's position as founder of contemporary colonial studies continues secure (Wood). His two-volume *New England Mind* (*The Seventeenth Century*, 1939; *From Colony to Province*, 1953) had located in colonial Puritanism what he termed "the meaning of America," a heroic and individualistic mission. From a congeries of Puritan texts, Miller configured a paradigmatic univocal construct, the Puritan mind. His Puritans struggled with anxieties and fears and with their human scale as motes in the cosmos, but they were intellectual heroes in the New World wilderness, tough-minded, courageous, bold, robust, and central to Western civilization: "Puritanism was one of the major expressions of the Western intellect [and] achieved an organized synthesis of concepts which are fundamental to our culture." Committed to the idea of a Puritan "single intelligence," Miller was a self-identified cartographer and anatomist, "map[ping] the intellectual terrain of the seventeenth century" and "the anatomy of the Puritan mind" (*New England* 1: viii, vii).

Miller's drive, as he put it, to expound "the innermost propulsion of the nation" (*Errand* viii) rhetorically suited midcentury industrial America, and his insistence on a purely intellectual formulation for the founding psyche doubtless served the position of the United States as the democratically triumphant nation of World War II. The nation that twice used the atomic bomb needed vindication as democratic *and* rational, impervious to raging passions. According to Miller, the New England mind, struggling to exploit the triad of reason-will-understanding, the best of the postlapsarian mental components, strove not only to apprehend God's will but also to contain the unruly and wayward passions: "Reason, free and independent, is the king and ruler of the faculties, and its consort, the will, is queen and mistress. . . .

[L]ogic was a corrective of sinful passions." Miller offered a heroically cerebral American paternity that put passion into the service of the intellect, where it was contained. Puritan "regeneration would take the form of a reinvigoration of rational discourse" (*New England* 1: 247, 263). There is no nuclear-age demonic Dr. Strangelove among Miller's rational, national founders.

Puritan passions, however, have been the unabated focus of subsequent scholarship, beginning in the early 1970s with the inversion of Miller's interpretation of the Puritan "errand into the wilderness," the phrase from a sermon by John Danforth and one centered on the lamentations of the Old Testament prophet Jeremiah. Miller considered the sermon to be testimony to the crisis of diminished piety and zeal on the part of the second-generation Puritans. Subsequent critics began to see eschatological affirmation where Miller read Puritan self-admission of decline. The newer scholarship, in a tradition initiated by Ernest Lee Tuveson, Aletha Joy Bourne Gilsdorf, and others but developed most fully by Sacvan Bercovitch, redirected colonial studies away from the previously dominant exegesis on the Puritan intellect. In a move that upended the heuristic subject position, it argued that the Puritan glass, or perhaps tankard, was not half empty but half full. Exegesis of Puritan millennialism enabled the formulation of the American self and its Christic mission in the New World (Bercovitch, *Puritan Origins*). This approach also located in Puritan lamentation a covert imperative for national renewal that, in literature, took the form of a recurrently inscribed sense of national mission extending from the seventeenth century into the presidential rhetoric of the television age (Bercovitch, *American Jeremiad* and "Horologicals"). "The New World ministers, already committed to a scheme which would not admit of failure, compensated for their thwarted errand by constructing a legendary past and prophetic future for the country. . . . The popular aspect of the legacy [of the Jeremiad] consists in the exuberant national eschatology embodied in the American Dream" ("Horologicals" 43, 75).

Identified as a middle-class culture, America in this configuration embodies a myth leading the country into the millennium prophesied in the New Testament book of Revelation. From the early 1970s into the later 1980s, colonial American literary study flourished via scholarly exegesis on eschatology, especially on the ways in which the Puritan American self and the United States are susceptible to recurrent renewable commitment to the national destiny. During those years, most of us working in the area of Puritan studies exploited the schema in our own scholarship, whether it focused on, say, biography or the American landscape (Middlekauff; Tichi, *New World*).

As presentism is invariably a part of scholarly findings, it is the case that just as the idea of the Puritan mind should find favor in a particular postwar climate, so should the millennialist arguments be enabled by the cultural moment of the 1960s (roughly 1965–75), the Vietnam War era, in which many in literary studies perceived the United States not as a global democratic benefactor but as a militaristic empire. Responding in the late 1970s to a question from the audience after a talk at the Boston Public Library, Bercovitch spoke for scholarly cohorts when he asserted that it is precisely the critic's situation in contemporary history that promotes scholarly insights, customarily by turning presumed truth into exposed myth. Because ideology discloses itself as a result of historical processes, he remarked, the eschatological literary discourses had become particularly accessible as the United States began to decline as a global imperial power.

The continuing diminution of United States imperial authority, together with its economic decline, is plausibly the historical basis for yet another change in colonialists' critical subject positions. Continuing the investigation of the literary history of the seventeenth-century emigrants' emotional lives, recent scholarship now concerns itself not with messianic passions but with those of anguish, grief, and mourning. Thus Anne Bradstreet, the Puritan poet who admitted that the sight of the New World made her nauseous, comes to the fore as a poet of feminist sensibilities at odds with patriarchal Puritanism (W. Martin 15–76). The discourses, moreover, of intellectual heroism and of imperial millennialism, other scholars argue, occlude another kind of discourse, that of the anguished Puritan as immigrant. Recent work emphasizes the dreadful ordeal of the errand, the psychological deracination of a people caught in a double bind, their native land in chaos, their alternative the upheaval of dislocation in the New World (Delbanco).

This newer position calls into question the kinds of Puritan colonial texts accorded privileged status over the past quarter-century. The premise of a paradigmatic masculine mind permits the scholar to construct a composite *Ur*-text from fragments of many kinds of writings, including sermons, diaries, and tracts. (Deconstructive theory, in fact, has come relatively late to colonial American literary studies, probably because one element necessary to its operation—the antecedent New Critical presumption of textual integrity—has always been a tenuous proposition in a field of study so dependent on the pastiche, or composite text.) Yet even the intact text, such as the Danforth sermon "Errand into the Wilderness," has been positioned as inclusively corporate, representative of a group of visible saints (as the Puritan church members were called). And the spiritual biography, such as Cotton Mather's "Nehemiah" on Governor John Winthrop (in the *Magnalia Christi Americana* [1702]), has been presented as representative of the univocal middle-class "American self" (Bercovitch, *Puritan Origins*). In all of these, the literary text is exclusively self-referential to one presumably homogeneous group, the Puritans, and is emphatically masculine even as it subsumes two genders. Reference to all others, whether Satanic Indians, heretics, or those outside the circle of church membership, essentially reinforces both Puritan centrality and the otherness—the alien status—of non-Puritans.

The poststructuralist moment, however, in colonial studies currently reveals itself in scholarly claims for a different kind of representative text. Such a text extends beyond the patriarchal male realm to bring into juxtaposition the newer categories of critical inquiry, gender and race and, implicitly, class. Gender was a salient issue in the 1637–38 antinomian controversy in which the Puritan wife and mother Anne Hutchinson, in her lay preaching, contested the spiritual authority of Puritan patriarchy and became a "disturber in Israel" with her female narrative of dissent (Lang, *Prophetic Woman*). Hutchinson left no written text (her voice recorded only in the transcript of her trial on charges of heresy), although her story, obsessively retold by others, was to ramify into, and to problematize, nineteenth-century American fiction and the essay (Lang).

Seventeenth-century studies have now identified the work that lends itself to considerations not only of gender but of the heuristics of race and class, resisting the totalizing tendencies indicated in such a term as *American self.* It is Mary White Rowlandson's *True History of the Captivity and Restoration of Mrs. Mary White Rowlandson* (see Lang, "Introduction"). The narrative describes the months during which Rowlandson, a mother and a Puritan minister's wife, was held captive by the Algonquians during King Philip's War (mid-1670s), as the colonists called it, when a confederation of Indian tribes led by their chief, Metacom ("King Philip"), fought the colonists because they feared loss of lands and tribal annihilation. Rowlandson's account began what has been called the first American literary genre, the captivity narrative. For the past three decades it has been, in excerpts, a staple of the classroom anthologies, in which interpretive headnotes customarily emphasized its importance in depicting Puritan trials and doctrinal orthodoxy on the colonial frontier.

Yet in the 1990s Rowlandson's text is being reread as an ethnographic juxtapositioning of two cultures, colonial whites and the indigenous Americans, and involving two genders, even as it presumes that the central experience of New England Puritanism is that of mourning (Breitwieser; Lang, "Introduction"). The title of a 1990 critical study devolving from Rowlandson's narrative is indicative: *American Puritanism and the Defence of Mourning: Religion, Grief, and Ethnology in Mary White Rowlandson's Captivity Narrative* (Breitwieser). It argues that the fundamental Puritan experience is loss at every level (social, economic, personal) and that the most profound psychological impulse, accordingly, is grief and mourning. The mandate of the clerical leadership becomes, essentially, a valediction forbidding mourning, a channeling of thought and feeling away from grief into a spiritual utilitarianism. Loss is identified as the central ethos of Puritanism, though it is suppressed and repressed everywhere in the official culture. Loss becomes overwhelmingly present in its absence, and the Puritans become one ethnic group over and against another, the Algonquians. In this configuration, Rowlandson's text is dissonant, not only because its author was a woman whose intrinsic aggression was to write but because it is about mourning and because, as a captivity narrative of cross-cultural encounter, it becomes as well an ethnographic text of a kind dangerous to establishment Puritanism. Cultural relativity inadvertently comes into play: "If what seems white can turn out to be red . . . it is also the case that what has been thought red can turn out to be analogous to white. . . . Thus reversibility . . . reappears as a property of relative cultures" (Breitwieser 170–71). An understanding of what constitutes a rhetoric of dissonance in Puritan texts becomes the scholarly imperative. And the opening of ethnological rhetoric to discussion enables scholars to exploit ethnographers' and ethnographic historians' findings.

One critic asks, "What explains this remarkable scholarly attention [to New England Puritanism]?" and answers that it is "what" Puritanism seems to say about contemporary America, that there is "something" in it that still resonates in the late twentieth century, that in "some way or another" Puritanism has been, as Miller called it, an "ideal laboratory" for the study of America. The ineffable "what" and "something" both work ineffably, "some way or another" (Wood 26). Even though the Puritans themselves promulgated the myth of their exceptionalism (Gura 215–34), it may be surprising to find late-twentieth-century scholarly assent to the notion even by those historicizing the construction of New England Puritan studies: "The originating, generative power of the Puritan imagination continues to shape the way we tell the American literary story, indeed the way we explain the development of American culture" (D. Weber 101).

As some scholars recognize, the presumption of New England Puritan literary exceptionalism is, strictly speaking, neither a colonialist concern nor an antiquarian one, ramifying as it does directly into the nineteenth-century "classic" American literature, the canonical texts of Emerson and Thoreau, Hawthorne and Melville. The notion of a sui generis originating power is under challenge as research discloses the social construction of literary New England long represented as if it were a natural phenomenon (Baker, "Figurations" 148–49; Baym, "Early Histories," *Novels*, and *Women's Fiction*; Buell 193–250; Tompkins 3–39). Historically, one study finds, a kind of New England academic interlocking directorate "made literary works and authors display the virtues and achievements of an Anglo-Saxon United States founded by New England Puritans." That New England's exceptionalism emerges in such research shows the extent to which the literature of the South was systematically excluded from schoolbooks on American literature, just as New England was systematically privileged as *the* literature of this nation. "When in the second decade of the twentieth century, academics defined . . . 'American literature,' they did so by appropriating and sophisticating a narrative already constructed in the plethora of American literary history textbooks" that "encouraged respect, veneration, and gratitude toward these men who had achieved American literature on behalf of the rest of us" (Baym, "Early Histories" 459–60).

The argument that New England is a regional literature (Buell) with a literary history of intraregional responses (Bell), and that its putative national scope is the result of its social construction by academic-publishing elites rooted in Boston (Baym, "Early Histories," *Novels*, and *Women's Fiction*; Tompkins) may renew scholarly efforts to historicize and to develop theoretical positions toward the literature of other regions. The South, despite prodigious scholarship (e.g., R. B. Davis's three-volume intellectual history of the colonial South), to date has not commanded such attention. Yet the articulation of the idea of the South as an Eden from which the inhabitants are dispossessed because of the inherently corruptive institution of slavery establishes the theoretical basis on which Southern colonial studies might proceed (see L. P. Simpson). Lewis Simpson's work points up the need for a multivalent theoretics of regional Americas. The recent conception, moreover, of four distinct sets of English folkways disseminated in North America (see Fischer) and persisting in the subcultures of the United States may renew interest in a moribund regional American literary studies.

As of now, the paradoxical centrality of the marginal text has become a fruitful approach to earlier American literature and marks a distinct change in scholarly direction. For the revolutionary and postrevolutionary–early national periods, for instance, traditional scholarship has focused on the texts that explicitly expound the problematics and potential of republican political principles—texts such as the Declaration of Independence, the *Federalist* papers, or the verse of the Connecticut Wits, Timothy Dwight, Joel Barlow, David Humphreys, Jonathan Trumball (e.g., L. Howard). Recently, however, critical theory has concentrated on other categories of texts, heretofore considered at most obliquely concerned with issues central to the formation of the Republic. These reveal their "cultural work . . . redefining the social order" (Tompkins xi). Early American fiction is one such textual category: "Because the novel as a form was marginalized by social authorities [including clergy, educators, political figures], because novelists could neither support themselves by their trade nor claim a respectable position within society because of it, the early American novel . . . was ideally suited to evaluate American society and to provide a critique of what was sorely missing in the exuberant postrevolutionary rhetoric of republicanism" (Davidson 218).

The Gothic novel, in this scheme, is particularly important as a social critique. Charles Brockden Brown's *Wieland*, for instance, in which an idyllic Philadelphia country-house life is disrupted by the arrival of a ventriloquist whose multiple voices are the catalyst for murder and mayhem—this text becomes engaging not for the solution of formal and thematic problems thought to be intrinsic to a "primitive" American fictional form nor for its psychoanalytical probings, but instead for the ways in which it pleads for the restoration of civic authority in a tumultuous postrevolutionary movement (Tompkins 40–61). Gothic novels can be seen, additionally, as criticisms of a hierarchical traditional society and of "the excesses of individualism" (Davidson 212–53).

Marxist and feminist approaches have also led to reconfigurations and revaluations of revolutionary and postrevolutionary–early national canonical and noncanonical texts—for instance, in work asserting the apposition between the narrative and the legal brief (R. A. Ferguson) and thus breaking the generic barrier between the belles lettres and documentary texts by insisting on the conceptual, structural, and argumentative enmeshment of letters and legal texts. And feminism has forced into unprecedented focus the patriarchal premises and presumptions of the canonical texts of the era, from Franklin's *Autobiography* to Jefferson's *Notes on the State of Virginia* (C. Jordan; Kerber). Feminist heuristics have so rigorously exposed patriarchy in the literature of this period and so thoroughly critiqued its arrogation of the power of social control by white males that the recent scholarly apologia for the revolutionary writers finds itself repudiating or redefining the nature and contingent status of patriarchy itself (Fliegelman).

Studies of the mid-nineteenth-century American Renaissance are also decentering the literary canon both by the reinterpretation of "major" texts and by the inclusion of those texts long thought to be marginal. Though the term was coined in 1829 by Samuel Knapp (see Gunn, "Kingdoms" 222), the rubric, as all Americanists know, was forcefully renewed by F. O. Matthiessen's *American Renaissance: Art and Expression in the Age of Emerson and Whitman*, itself a monumental act of canon formation, one that displaced the genteel "fireside" writers (Henry Wadsworth Longfellow, James Russell Lowell, John Greenleaf Whittier, Oliver Wendell Holmes) and instated a new constellation of major literary figures, among them Emerson, Thoreau, Hawthorne, Melville, and (as Emerson's designated poet-literatus) Whitman. In Matthiessen, the New England literary hegemony would remain intact, revivified—and also vivifying, as a vigorous post–World War II American literary criticism took flight from his scholarship (see Gunn, *Matthiessen*; Cain; Arac). As Charles Feidelson Jr. remarked at the outset of his own influential *Symbolism and American Literature*,

"The first large-scale attempt to define the literary quality of American writing at its best was Matthiessen's *American Renaissance*" (3).

The central postwar critical texts—Henry Nash Smith's *Virgin Land: The American West as Symbol and Myth*, Feidelson's *Symbolism and American Literature*, R. W. B. Lewis's *American Adam*, Richard Chase's *American Novel and Its Tradition*, Daniel Hoffman's *Form and Fable in American Fiction*, Leo Marx's *Machine in the Garden*, and, towering above these, Matthiessen's *American Renaissance*—all emphasized the United States as a country of democratic values encoded in a "classic" mid-nineteenth-century literature centered in New England, itself implicitly a synecdoche of the nation. This generation of theorists, moreover, was the first to incorporate New Criticism in approaches to American literature. They brought the social dimensions of New Criticism into organicist reading of individual texts. "The theorists of American literature conceived the social structure of the literary work as a microcosm of collective psychology or myth and thus made New Criticism into a method of cultural analysis" (Graff, "Promise" 217). It is no coincidence that the myth-symbol school of American studies flourished at this time (H. N. Smith; L. Marx), based on the premise that patterns of symbol embedded in the literary text manifest the ethos of the nation. By precept and example, the work of these scholars has continued to influence the terms and the design of scholarship; for instance, one study presumes that "the problems of American politics and the problems of American literary genius may be said to belong to the same family of problems" (Marr 39; see also Porte).

The newer scholarly subject positions, however, reject as invalid any claims to the organicism implied in the term *family of problems.* Accordingly, they have approached antebellum American literature very differently. It may well be that the nickname *cold war criticism* will become the term by which post–World War II studies are known in retrospect. The "cold war consensus" (Pease, *Visionary Contacts*) is being defined as ideological in its very contention that the major American literary texts (those of indigenous "genius") transcend ideology. Recent scholarship finds that cold war consensus to be earmarked by its argument and its presumption that the "classic" texts enact democratic freedom in their structural openness and thus oppose (and repudiate) the closed systems denoting totalitarianism (Pease, *Visionary Contacts*; Bercovitch and Jehlen).

Such retrospect is possible, in fact inevitable, when critical subject positions change to the extent that both culture and text are seen as a field in which power is contested and in which the text inscribes the contention of competing and combative forces. From Roland Barthes's essay "The Death of the Author" and Michel Foucault's "What Is an Author?" the very conception of authorship has undergone the process of historicization that discloses how problematic is the term, how coordinate through the centuries with the unprecedented rise of individualization and private property. The *author* cannot now be presumed to stand outside a situated world of roiling forces—political, economic, ideological, cultural. The premise of transcendent democratic truths embodied in texts of aesthetic genius is thus reassessed as ideologically self-serving to certain groups, especially to white male elites, and enactive of its own historical moment, such as the cold war.

In New-Historicist terms, then, the criticism of the 1940s through 1960s becomes cold war criticism, an ideological construct, "a holistic master story of large-scale structural elements directing a whole society," when in actuality "selves and texts are defined by their relation to hostile others," such as "despised and feared Indians, Jews, Blacks" (Veeser xiii), and to disciplinary power represented in figures of institutional authority, such as Hawthorne's judge, Jaffrey Pyncheon, in *The House of the Seven Gables* or Melville's Captain Ahab. Previous criticism is seen to be flawed because of its evasion of these matters. Thus Matthiessen's treatment of mid-nineteenth-century American texts is condemned for its "most extravagant idealization: the diminishment of the Civil War. . . . Rather than facing up to divisions within the renaissance, Matthiessen divided the renaissance from the war. . . . His wish for wholeness led to disconnection" (Arac 97–98).

While American Renaissance has served for decades as a course title in countless colleges and universities, current scholarship is reconfiguring the terms of the rubric. Studies of antebellum American literature bring texts previously excluded or marginalized onto the field; they reread the "renaissance" texts in light of the proposition that the written text, the author, and his or her culture coexist in a dynamic interplay of contending forces—a point demonstrable in work on Hawthorne.

For decades, scholars demonstrated Hawthorne's indebtedness to *The Faerie Queene* as a source for the character Pearl in *The Scarlet Letter*, citing as one instance Hawthorne's naming his daughter, Una, after Spenser's allegorical character. Currently, however, Hawthorne, Una, and *The Scarlet Letter* are positioned as "interactive, contingent and interdependent participants in a collective process" (Herbert 287). *The Scarlet Letter* does not, in these terms, become the transmuted form of autobiographical or sociocultural and literary influences on Hawthorne, much less the work of art transcendent of these forces. Indeed, the presumption of such transcendence is discredited, downgraded into mere reification. "Instead of reifying Hawthorne's entangled brooding on Una's character into transcendent aesthetic terms, *The Scarlet Letter* extends that brooding and complicates the entanglement" (287).

Melville, to cite another canonical example, is similarly recontextualized, approached as a participant in a network of dynamic associations—familial, political, cultural, economic—in all of which he becomes a figure of historical contingency. The conception of Melville as author, recent critics assert, has been reified in scholarly emphasis on his separateness from his sociocultural contexts. To call Melville a genius or great author is emphatically to remove him from his cultural milieu. To enshrine him (or, for that matter, Emerson or Thoreau or Poe) in a fraternal pantheon of singular cohorts is to stress his separateness, his distinctness from the society he inhabited, which inscribes itself in his texts. Selfhood becomes not an index of singularity but a term referring to the historical process of which any individual, including the writer, is necessarily a part. The text, accordingly, is not seen to be an entity transcendent of its time but one inscriptive of it. In this sense, author, text, and context merge. And to approach Melville or any other canonical author in this way is not to be iconoclastic but to reclaim that figure and the texts from reification—and to rescue scholars from their roles as monument makers, agents of reification. Thus Melville is viewed as being involved in nineteenth-century American imperialism even in his family relationships, those of "subversive genealogy," and *Moby-Dick* is revealed to enact the politics of imperialism, with Ahab exploiting Third World labor to plunder the globe's natural resources (Rogin; Dimock).

The "renaissance," not surprisingly, becomes a historical moment in which unexamined literary-cultural associations, in particular the economic, are investigated, as scholars draw from the work of Marx, Georg Lukács, and Raymond Williams to explore the ways in which the commodification of labor and the permeation of social relations by a market economy manifest themselves in literary texts previously thought impervious to such matters. The study of industrial capitalism in the United States reveals its development to be considerably earlier than once was thought, not a post–Civil War phenomenon but one occurring in the antebellum decades (Gilmore; Porter, *Seeing* and "Reification"; Shulman). According to the premises of New Historicism, the "classic" American writers are no longer simply oppositional critics of marketplace values but inevitably, if inadvertently, complicitous with them.

Their response to an insurgent corporate capitalism is shown to be formal, not only discursively resistant to the market system for its exploitation of workers' wage slavery but participating in—in fact, enacting—the presumptions of the new economic order. Although Melville's "Tartarus of Maids" has long seemed a trenchant critique of the evolving industrialism—testimony to his opposition to systematic murder by wage slavery—his acquiescence in the new order has lately come to light. For instance, the cetology chapters in *Moby-Dick*, in which Melville's sources on whales and whaling are printed verbatim, are read as the writer's raw materials that, when processed through the imagination, emerge as a finished product, a literary symbol, to be marketed as fiction for profit (Gilmore). The novel thus takes on the character of a factory. And the domestic novel, in which the sacrosanct home is customarily thought to be exempt from commercial values, instead reveals the infiltration of the market at its worst: *Uncle Tom's Cabin* "show[s] the involvement of the home and its keeper in the practice of slavery . . . slavery as itself a domestic institution [with] an intrusion of the marketplace into the home" (Lang, *Prophetic Woman* 197–98).

Even the most visionary of nineteenth-century literary symbols, Emerson's "transcendent eyeball," when examined in the context of industrial capitalism becomes the signifier of a society that alienates individuals from themselves and their work and insinuates itself within the social consciousness. Such a society "generates people who assume a passive and 'contemplative' stance in the face of objectified and rationalized reality — people who seem to themselves to stand outside that reality because their own participation in producing it is mystified" (Porter, "Reification" 189). Emerson and Thoreau, from this viewpoint, become figures whose contemplative stance and visionary attributes are products of nineteenth-century economic history. In fact, the visionary is redefined as the inevitable outcome of capitalist alienation, and transcendentalism thus takes its place as a phenomenon grounded in economic history.

With increasing aggressiveness, critics have repudiated the once-eulogized American individualism, its major exponent being the Emerson of "Self-Reliance." Of course, the postwar critics had drawn careful distinctions among writers with claims to individualism, especially juxtaposing Captain Ahab against the Thoreau of *Walden*. The two are individualist antitheses, with Ahab portrayed as the nemesis of the ideal, the very "embodiment of his author's most profound response to the problem of the individual free will *in extremis*. . . . He can see nothing but his own burning thoughts since he no longer shares in any normal fellow-feelings [and] refuses to be deflected from his pursuit by the stirring of any sympathy for others" (Matthiessen, *American Renaissance* 447–51). Ahab thus became a "fearful example of the self-enclosed individualism that . . . brings disaster both upon itself and upon the group of which it is a part" (459). In postwar critical terms, he is "a false culture-hero, pursuing a private grievance (rather than a divine behest) at the expense of the mankind in his crew . . . a Satan, a sorcerer, an Antichrist" (Hoffman 234). Investigators who take this approach read *Moby-Dick* as "a book about the alienation from life that results from an excessive or neurotic self-dependence," one in which Ahab is "guilty of or victimized by a distorted 'self-reliance'" (Lewis 105). The critic who celebrates *Moby-Dick* for embodying the "great cultural heritage" of the United States warns nonetheless that Melville must not be seen to approve Ahab's "intensity, power, and defiant spirit" because he represents the deformation of individualism and self-reliance (L. Howard, *Literature* 176–77). And if the cold war version of Captain Ahab echoes the horrors of Hitler and totalitarianism (and, retrospectively, in U.S. history, indicts the unchecked predations of the robber barons, as Matthiessen remarked), he also stands interpretively as an alienated anti-individualist.

Thoreau, on the contrary, was presented in the postwar era as the exemplar of the democratic common person, recommitting himself to American traditions of hard work and artisanship, his *Walden* also making a claim for "communal security and permanence," for "order and balance" (Matthiessen, *American Renaissance* 172–73). He was a "visionary hero" who "demonstrates his freedom in the liberation of others," thus working on behalf of other human beings to further the greatest cause of freedom (Lewis 21). Thoreau's "aggressiveness," though regrettably "excessive" for his time, is vindicated when his democratic "symbol of the hermitage" is exported to India for Mahatma Gandhi's successful struggle for independence (L. Howard, *Literature* 158–60). Thoreau, then, becomes the democratic heroic individualist precisely because he represents the dutiful and responsible postwar American working person committed to communal security and stability, and also to social order. In postwar criticism, then, the individualist must either be brought within the democratic fold, as was Thoreau, or, failing that, be consigned to un-American realms beyond—that is, to the alienationist domains of insanity, abnormality, deformity.

Beginning in the 1970s, however, a challenge to the ideal of American individualism as hostile to human interests and pernicious in its effects was undertaken. Narratives on American environmentalism were shown to endorse violence against the self and others; representations of life on the frontier were felt to be tributes not to personal and national independence and courage but to deracinative isolation and alienation. Regenerative energies were seen to be aroused precisely in violent, aggressive action (Kolodny, *Lay of the Land*; Slotkin).

Critics have continued to challenge individualist ideals. Studies of eighteenth-century commodity capitalism and the concomitant picaresque novel, both in England and America, reveal the imperative of incessant social upheaval that defines individualism as "change, difference, possibility, mobility, restlessness, flux," qualities that thwart stable cultural relationships and, when convergent, represent "the excesses of individualism" (Davidson 167, 219). And one recent study of individualism in the United States, *Habits of the Heart*, acknowledges in brief that "sometimes the flight from society is simply mad and ends in general disaster," offering Ahab as the consummate example of "asocial individualism" unredeemed by the postwar critics' solace of a democratically pervasive and enduring Ishmael (Bellah et al. 144–45). In this sense, Thoreau becomes not the exemplar of visionary democracy but the isolate in whom the potential to be an "inspiring friend replaces the need for any actual friendship" and who "etherealizes friendship to the point of mutual evanescence" (Pease, *Visionary Compacts* 263). "Thoreau did not want a friend of his own. . . . what he wanted in a friend was a confirmation of the self" (J. W. Warren 59). The masculine ethos of individualism in Thoreau, as well as in Cooper, Emerson, and Melville, is reidentified as egocentric narcissism: "The American myth of the individual has encouraged the development of narcissism, not only in the psychological sense of an individual's unsuccessful resolution of an early failure in identity but in a cultural sense. . . . The male individualist . . . sees himself as all-powerful and all-encompassing, and he sees only himself" (J. W. Warren 13).

If marketplace capitalism is one heuristic by which to critique the development of individualist ideology and its literary consequences, another is the inverted subject position focused on the founding of the New World. According to a line of argument that bypasses the colonial New England tradition, the dominant nineteenth-century canonical texts devolved from the European Enlightenment's projection of a mythic, pristine New World, the crucial concept being that of the *discovery* of America. This is not the nation understood to have developed through historical processes but instead perceived to be a world come upon intact, existing essentially outside of history. And the kinds of literary production emerging from that position were predetermined by it: the discovered, pristine America, existing primarily in a state of perfection, but its very definition admits of no change; literary representations of social or personal change in a fluid context were thus precluded. The literary opportunity is one of entitlement—and of tremendous constraint. It is chiefly one of ratification and celebration of the quotidian world whose representative American incarnates the continent itself (thus the scholarly title *American Incarnation*, with its pun on *nation*). "The American, and therefore the American artist, is identical with America and sufficient unto all of it. He incarnates America and encompasses its entire consciousness" (Jehlen, *American Incarnation* 132). Thus the novel—the genre central to historical process—is excluded because it is precluded, since nineteenth-century American genre and ideology must be inextricably connected in the dominant literary forms. What remains is nonfiction and the romance: the Emersonian or Thorovian essay and the likes of *The Scarlet Letter.* Literary efforts at the novel as a historical narrative (e.g., Hawthorne's *The Marble Faun* or Melville's *Pierre*) are doomed to fracture because they attempt the intervention of history into an America that is conceptually ahistorical.

Other reassessments of antebellum American literature resist the notion of dominant literary forms and inject the traditional rubrics— the Age of Emerson and Whitman, the American Renaissance—with irony as they redefine the period by widening its scope to include texts previously marginalized or excluded altogether, especially those categorized as belonging to popular culture or to sentimental (i.e., women's) fiction. While Matthiessen traced a trajectory "from Coleridge to Emerson" (*American Renaissance* 133), writers such as David S. Reynolds now argue that popular culture, particularly vernacular religious rhetoric, was at least as important a source for Emerson and his major-figure cohorts. Colloquial revivalism is now asserted to be an integral part of the formation of Emerson's discourse (as well as that of Whitman and Poe), and the "renaissance" shown to be so riddled with "subversive" works that "the major texts [become] artistic renderings of irrational or erotic themes predominant in a large body of overlooked sensational writings of the day" (169).

The sensational, mass-market press filled with ghoulish crimes, sex scandals, felonies, celebrity criminals, and the like becomes permeable with the previously sacralized literary productions of the canonical figures, and scholarly rubrics indicate this newer high culture–low culture inclusivity: Poe and Popular Irrationalism, Hawthorne and Crime Literature, *The Scarlet Letter* and Popular Sensationalism (Reynolds). Robert S. Levine argues that a pervasive cultural paranoia, much of it anti-Catholic and extending from the colonial era through the nineteenth century, recurrently engendered texts centered in anxiety about conspiratorial subversion. In this sense literary studies become cultural studies, diminishing the possibility of sensationalist, even prurient exposés of canonical figures. "Beneath" the American Renaissance, in Reynolds's phrase, may be an unfortunate and misleading preposition when criticism shows the more accurate term to be "within."

Locating diverse kinds of texts *within* the period, moreover, investigators looking at the sentimental tradition most closely identified with women writers and readers have taken a prominent position over the past decade. The *feminine*, a word disparaged in Hawthorne's dismissal of the "damned mob of scribbling women" (meaning his commercially successful woman-author rivals), and sustained in the title of Fred Lewis Pattee's historical examination *The Feminine Fifties* (1940), had continued to be a term of opprobrium even in the scholarship that, in the 1970s, initiated the revaluation of the sentimental (see Ann Douglas, *Feminization*).

The long-forgotten body of popular texts written by and for nineteenth-century women has now come to the fore in analysis that earns the title "sentimental power" (Tompkins 122–201). Such examinations, begun originally as bibliographic study to determine authors, titles, sales figures, and audiences for nineteenth-century sentimental fiction (Baym), utilize that data to formulate arguments on the sociocultural power of these texts, whose authors include Susan Warner, E. D. E. N. Southworth, Elizabeth Stuart Phelps, Louisa May Alcott, and especially Harriet Beecher Stowe. If a positivist, materialist, and scientific-technological bent dominated later nineteenth- and twentieth-century American history, feminist criticism argues, that direction nonetheless must not conceal a mid-nineteenth-century ethos of evangelistic piety — much less prevent the study of it. The terms of the mid-nineteenth-century moral universe now demand exegesis, and the texts that represent that universe should be included in any configuration of American antebellum literature. No longer can these texts be dismissed as naive or ingenuous, such dismissal itself understood as having served a particular critical-political agenda in postwar literary criticism (Baker, "Figurations"; Tompkins).

Nor is sentimental, domestic American fiction divided along gender lines exclusively. The sentimental tradition is currently understood to include both the women writers and the canonical Hawthorne. Jane Tompkins (11) points out that Hawthorne was most valued in the mid-nineteenth century not for the ironic dark fiction the era of T. S. Eliot came to value but rather for the tales that moralize on domestic topics ("Sunday at Home," "A Rill from the Town Pump," "Little Annie's Ramble"). In interdisciplinary cultural studies, still best known as American studies, the study of sentimental fiction has been extended into cognate forms, especially into nineteenth-century American sculpture; for example, such objects as Hiram Powers's *Greek Slave* are only ostensibly classically derivative and, like the sentimental tradition itself, have been too long dismissed as vapid. Instead, as Joy S. Kasson shows, such sculpture enacts the tensions and political divisions of its antebellum era, including slavery, feminism, class divisions, the developing capitalist and marketplace economics.

The sentimental, moreover, is not solely a category for the scrutiny of domesticity and evangelistic piety. For instance, scholarship involving the "hard facts" of American literary culture, including the rhetoric of extirpation of the Indians in James Fenimore Cooper's fiction, includes an extended discussion of Stowe's *Uncle Tom's Cabin* under the heading "The Sentimental Novel and Slavery" (Fisher 87–127). And the legacy of Hutchinson, the "prophetic woman," is shown to be the narrative paradigm splaying into the texts of Emerson, Hawthorne, and Stowe (Lang). Beyond the issue of the social construction of gender and text lies the related but separate matter of sexuality and its construction over time. The seemingly "exaggeratedly male" Walt Whitman proclaiming his virility and phallic power becomes, in recent analysis of his poetic persona, a figure who is alternately female and transsexual, just as Poe is reread as a writer whose heroes are androgynous, embodied pleas for the human wholeness that must encompass the male and the female (Gilbert; C. Jordan 133–51). American literary studies, long dominated by an overarching presumption of masculinity in its primary and critical texts, may well continue to elicit kindred studies of sexuality and gender like that on Whitman (and like those currently appearing on Hemingway).

Another recent direction in American literary study involves the role(s) of the reader in the formulation of the text. The process of interpretation in which readers are thought to construct a text has also come in for particular attention as reader-response theory is applied to American literary study that asks, What are the cultural or political shapings of reading and what a priori literary conventions affect interpretation and assessment? Answers to such inquiry reveal that the reception of texts differentiates according to national-cultural patterns. *Moby-Dick*, for instance, was received differently in England and the United States. The British, preoccupied with literary conventions, evaluated the novel according to prescriptive rules for fiction and found it wanting because it defied taxonomic convention; American reviewers, less constrained by normative rules, were less exasperated by Melville's mix of genres (Mailloux 169–78). And the reader-response theorist now takes us through a Hawthorne story like "Rappaccini's Daughter" to disclose the process of the time flow of reading, its constraints and liberations, while the scholar of African American literature finds this methodology to be particularly useful for texts in which "the distinctions between telling and writing on the one hand, and hearing and reading on the other, are far more profound than they usually are determined to be in those interpretive groupings constituted by other types of fictive narrative" (Mailloux 80–92; Stepto, "Distrust" 306).

Those students of American literature conversant largely (or solely) with the traditions of Western civilization, moreover, are increasingly impaired, as scholars of ethnic and racial literary traditions explore the intratextual functioning of cultural-rhetorical patterns indigenous to non-Western groups. As one states, "It is well worth it to interpret America not narrowly as immigration but more broadly as ethnic diversity and include the pre-Columbian inhabitants of the continent, the kidnapped Africans and their descendents, and the Chicanos of the Southwest" (Sollors, *Beyond Ethnicity* 8). (It would be interesting to hear the postwar critics reevaluate their major studies in this light, as Henry Nash Smith did, acknowledging that *Virgin Land* ignored the populations of indigenous groups on the North American continent, whose very existence gives an ironic dimension to the term *Virgin* [see "Symbol and Idea"].)

The civil rights movement of the 1960s gave impetus to the study of African American literature, beginning with the examination of figures and images of the black in the literature and culture of the United States (Yellin; Boskin) and proceeding with an analysis of the ways in which American literary history excluded African American texts from "traditional, orthodox patterns of a spiritually evolving American literature" (Baker, "Figurations" 149). Studies of canonical texts have disclosed their criticism of racism—for instance, Melville's *Benito Cereno*, the story of the suppression of a slave mutiny, has been the focus of scholarship revealing Melville's scathing critique of the paternalistic white male, a type prominent in antebellum political life of the North and South, and his prescience in blasting the plantation myth as politically and psychologically repressive (Sundquist; Rogin 210–15).

More recently, African American literature has been subjected to theoretical analysis of its rhetorical structures (Gates, *Signifying Monkey*). Generations of Western writers have exploited their literary innovations to surpass or to destroy the work of their predecessors, this argument says, but the African American tradition operates very differently and needs to be understood in its development from the sophisticated folk cultures of Africa. (According to one scholar, the marginalization of those traditions in the hegemonic development of the West via classical Greece and the Hebrews had profoundest impact in nineteenth-century concepts of race and therefore has special bearing on the period under discussion here; see Appiah, "Race.") "Black people," then, have embraced "a system of rhetorical strategies peculiar to their own vernacular tradition," in which "the Signifyin(g) Monkey is the figure of a black rhetoric in the Afro-American speech community," existing to "embody the figures of speech in the black vernacular," and as the principle of self-consciousness in that vernacular, becoming "the meta-figure itself" (Gates 53). The African American text, moreover, is not fixed in a determinate sense but works by indeterminacy and uncertainty, so that simultaneous plurality of meanings is possible: "The ironic reversal of a received racist image of the black as simianlike, the Signifying Monkey, [is] he who dwells at the margins of discourse, ever punning, ever troping, ever embodying the ambiguities of language." In African American texts he becomes the "trope for repetition and revision, indeed [the] trope of chiasmus, repeating and reversing simultaneously as he does in one deft discursive act" (52). (The opening of ethnically and racially diverse traditions continued and was accelerated by the Columbian quincentennial year, 1992, in which academic conferences and scholarly publications focused on earlier Caribbean American literature and the literature of New World cross-cultural encounter. This work departs from the perspectives of the Mexican historian Edmundo O'Gorman, who emphasizes the "invention" of America, as well as from Tzvetan Todorov's argument on the Western European "conquest" of Mexico.)

The kinds of scholarship discussed in this essay have not come to the fore without a degree of resistance and hostility on the part of a generation of Americanists educated in the New Criticism, well trained in bibliographic and research methods and plying these skills to excellent results in the college classroom, in journal articles, and in books. One can point, moreover, to the continuation of exemplary scholarship of a traditional design in this poststructuralist moment—for instance, in studies of national character in Hawthorne and Melville, of democratic ideals pursued in the praxis of rhetoric, of Cooper's politics or of Thoreau's classical influences, or of the relation of popular historical romance to Hawthorne's fiction (McWilliams, *Political Justice*; Dauber; Richardson; Bell).

The controversy over the newer methodologies, however, is essentially one of epistemology and of its political orientation as a struggle for the control of meaning. Professional, collegial, and scholarly endeavor are all seen at this point as overtly political. Editorial succession—for instance, for the journal *American Literature*—becomes a matter not only of the maintenance of scholarly scrupulousness but of ideological positioning, as groups of researchers perceive their interests to be potentially furthered or frustrated by a likely appointee. Disagreement about the openness of the long-established "flagship" journal to newer viewpoints has had the market-economy effect of the formation of a new, competing periodical, *American Literary History*, which is explicitly hospitable to articles on "theoretical problems" (perhaps implying lack of receptivity to such work in other, established journals).

At this juncture, as groups of Americanist scholars contend for interpretive legitimation and critical assent, those cognizant of both the postwar and post-1960s scholarship can point out certain as-yet unresolved (and even unacknowledged) problems in criticism. This is to say that the practitioners of the newer critical approaches can find themselves unwittingly in a vexed relation to the scholarship of their predecessors, the very scholarship they are challenging. Suppose one were to read Leo Marx's *Machine in the Garden*, for instance, as a cold war fable on a pastoral America threatened with the nuclear invasion figured in the machine and therefore to historicize that text as a critical act of the nuclear age mentality. To do so would require the elucidation of the American literary pastoralism so closely defined in *The Machine in the Garden*. Thus one historicizes the very texts whose data and argumentative shape are necessary for the foundations of one's own argument. The risk is one of simultaneous exploitation and reification, the latter an act that contemporary scholarship deplores.

The community most receptive to the New Historicism, moreover, awaits the cogent theoretics who would justify and guide its assimilative practices. If the New Historicist faults the New Critic predecessor for explaining away the irreconcilable and the contradictory in the sacralizing name of paradox and irony, for example, then the New Historicism must bring to visibility—and account for—those lines of cultural and literary contention that pose challenge to—even threaten to subvert the plausibility of—the New Historicist's own disclosures. As it is, New Historicism implies a territorial comprehensiveness that functions to exclude realms fraught with oppositional possibility.

Those trained in traditional methods, at the same time, must be aware that literary study cannot be unaffected by historical process, that every literary critic belongs to an incessantly changing intellectual-cultural world, that no position, argument, stance can be impervious to change, as those scholars currently historicizing the discipline of literary studies have so well revealed. New Criticism was certain to have a limited shelf life, but so will any other "ism," though it remains to be seen whether poststructuralists will be any more prepared for what succeeds them—perhaps some neocanonicalism marshaled in arguments as yet unforeseen as the category of the aesthetic begins to reinsinuate itself in literary study. Any examination of changing patterns in American literary study ought to take notice of scholarship reflecting on the history of the profession, including Giles Gunn's *Culture of Criticism and the Criticism of Culture*, Jonathan Culler's "Literary Criticism and the American University," and Gerald Graff's *Professing Literature: An Institutional History*.

Those who may feel that the insurgence of newer approaches represents certain professional betrayal might, in fact, find it useful to survey the social construction of an anthropological text considered especially congenial to literary study. Clifford Geertz's "Deep Play: Notes on the Balinese Cockfight" has been taken up virtually as a fable for critics, appearing as it did at the point in the history of New Criticism at which every possible interpretation of any given canonical text seemed already to have been published, ultimately with diminishing returns, and few could conceive of the usefulness of yet another interpretive refinement of a Hawthorne tale or Thorovian essay—in sum, when younger scholars could but feel themselves relegated to roles of acolytes to the preceding generations, producing secondhand versions of the arguments of their own scholarly parents.

At that point, enter Bali, in Geertz's term "the well-studied place" whose mythology, art, ritual, social organization, law, and child-rearing practices had all been "microscopically" examined by the authoritative master scholars (Gregory Bateson and Margaret Mead) but that now could suddenly yield itself anew as a text. Long overlooked as mere cultural minutiae, the Balinese cockfight, the heretofore marginal text, discloses previously unnoticed dimensions of intrapsychic struggle, social status, hierarchy, morality. The authorities had somehow missed these important dimensions, just as the master scholars of American and other literatures had undertaken massive studies but somehow overlooked crucial heuristics that would reopen the texts, especially to the researchers of the succeeding generation. Though Geertz has recently been attacked for splitting language from reality (Bercovitch and Jehlen 12–13), the motives for literary scholars' affinity with his work are self-evident. The lesson of the cockfight is that the imprint of august scholars need not deter one, that "exhaustive" or "microscopic" examinations are only spuriously so, that the seemingly marginal text can yield insights of central importance, that the canonical text holds surprises if only one knows how to look for them. The lesson is cyclical and applicable to American literary study.

Selected Bibliography

Baym, Nina. "Early Histories of American Literature: A Chapter in the Institution of New England." *American Literary History* 1 (1989): 459–88.

———. *Novels, Readers, and Reviewers: Responses to Fiction in Antebellum America*. Ithaca: Cornell UP, 1984.

Two titles that survey the range of antebellum fiction, its market and audiences, and historicize the literary hegemony of New England.

Bercovitch, Sacvan. *The American Jeremiad*. Madison: U of Wisconsin P, 1978.

A literary theory of nationalism rooted in Puritan eschatology.

———, ed. *Reconstructing American Literary History*. Cambridge: Harvard UP, 1986.

Revaluative essays on the early republican era through the mid-nineteenth century and beyond.

Bercovitch, Sacvan, and Myra Jehlen, eds. *Ideology and Classic American Literature*. New York: Columbia UP, 1986.

Language and politics of mid-nineteenth-century texts examined by diverse groups of scholars.

Breitwieser, Mitchell. *American Puritanism and the Defence of Mourning: Religion, Grief, and Ethnology in Mary White Rowlandson's Captivity Narrative*. Madison: U of Wisconsin P, 1990.

A new theory of New England Puritanism based on a heuristics of race, gender, and, implicitly, class.

Buell, Lawrence. *New England Literary Culture: From Revolution through Renaissance*. New York: Cambridge UP, 1986.

A reconceptualization of New England literature.

Davidson, Cathy N. *Revolution and the Word: The Rise of the Novel in America*. New York: Oxford UP, 1986.

A study of the rise of the novel and its relation to political life of the early Republic.

Dimock, Wai-chee. *Empire for Liberty: Melville and the Poetics of Individualism*. Princeton: Princeton UP, 1989.

A New-Historicist consideration of the Melville oeuvre.

Gates, Henry Louis, Jr. *The Signifying Monkey: A Theory of African-American Literary Criticism*. New York: Oxford UP, 1988.

A theory of language and signification in African American literature.

Gilmore, Michael T. *American Romanticism and the Marketplace*. Chicago: U of Chicago P, 1985.

An analysis of the insurgence of industrial capitalism in mid-nineteenth-century America and the response of Emerson, Hawthorne, and Thoreau.

Jameson, Frederic. *The Political Unconscious: Narrative as a Socially Symbolic Act*. Ithaca: Cornell UP, 1981.

Jehlen, Myra. *American Incarnation: The Individual, the Nation, and the Continent*. Cambridge: Harvard UP, 1986.

On the European projection of an America extrinsic to historical processes and the literary result of that conception of a nation whose citizens are its incarnation.

Jordan, Cynthia. *Second Stories: The Politics of Language, Form, and Gender in Early American Fictions*. Chapel Hill: U of North Carolina P, 1989.

Two generations of patriarchal texts and the permutations of language of gender.

Kasson, Joy S. *Marble Queens and Captives: Women in Nineteenth-Century American Sculpture.* New Haven: Yale UP, 1990.
Cultural study of sculpture, contemporary medicine, feminism, and social practices in the arts.

Lang, Amy Schrager. *Prophetic Woman: Anne Hutchinson and the Problem of Dissent in the Literature of New England.* Berkeley: U of California P, 1987.
The culturally obsessive narrative of the seventeenth-century Puritan woman as it reemerges in Emerson, Hawthorne, Stowe.

Mailloux, Steven. *Interpretive Conventions: The Reader in the Study of American Fiction.* Ithaca: Cornell UP, 1982.
Reader-response theory in the interrogation of American texts.

Michaels, Walter Benn, and Donald E. Pease, eds. *The American Renaissance Reconsidered: Selected Papers from the English Institute, 1982–83.* Baltimore: Johns Hopkins UP, 1985.
Revaluation of canonical texts and arguments for the inclusion of popular, sentimental, and ethnic texts.

Reynolds, David S. *Beneath the American Renaissance: The Subversive Imagination in the Age of Emerson and Melville.* New York: Knopf, 1988.
The permeability of popular and canonical texts in antebellum America.

Rogin, Michael Paul. *Subversive Genealogy: The Politics and Art of Herman Melville.* Berkeley: U of California P, 1979.
A New-Historicist and psychoanalytical study of Melville and his culture.

Shulman, Robert. *Social Criticism and Nineteenth-Century American Fictions.* Columbia: U of Missouri P, 1987.
A discussion of the impact of capitalism on canonical texts of the American Renaissance.

Tompkins, Jane. *Sensational Designs: The Cultural Work of American Fiction, 1790–1860.* New York: Oxford UP, 1985.
Examines the social power of the sentimental and the social construction of literary careers, principally that of Hawthorne.

Warren, Joyce W. *The American Narcissus: Individualism and Women in Nineteenth-Century American Fiction.* 1984. New Brunswick: Rutgers UP, 1989.
Argues that male narcissism in the guise of individualism precluded the participation of women in canonical texts.

Works Cited

Appiah, Kwame Anthony. "Race." *Critical Terms for Literary Study.* Ed. Frank Lentricchia and Thomas McLaughlin. Chicago: U of Chicago P, 1990. 274–87.

Arac, Jonathan. "F. O. Matthiessen: Authorizing an American Renaissance." Michaels and Pease 90–112.

Baker, Houston, Jr. "Figurations for a New American Literary History." Bercovitch and Jehlen 145–71.

Barthes, Roland. "The Death of the Author." *Image-Music-Text.* Trans. Stephen Heath. New York: Hill, 1977. 142–48.

Baym, Nina. *Women's Fiction: A Guide to Novels by and about Women in America, 1820–1870.* Ithaca: Cornell UP, 1978.

Bell, Michael Davitt. *The Development of American Romance: The Sacrifice of Relation.* Chicago: U of Chicago P, 1986.

Bellah, Robert N., Richard Madsen, William M. Sullivan, Ann Swidler, and Steven M. Tipton. *Habits of the Heart: Individualism and Commitment in American Life.* 1985. New York: Harper, 1986.

Bercovitch, Sacvan. "Horologicals to Chronometricals: The Rhetoric of the Jeremiad." *Literary Monographs.* Vol. 3. Ed. Eric Rothstein. Madison: U of Wisconsin P, 1970. 1–124.

———. *Puritan Origins of the American Self.* New Haven: Yale UP, 1975.

Boskin, Joseph. *Sambo: The Rise and Demise of an American Jester.* New York: Oxford UP, 1986.

Bradley, Scully, Richard Croom Beatty, and E. Hudson Long, eds. *The American Tradition in Literature.* 3rd ed. New York: Norton, 1967.

Cain, William E. *F. O. Matthiessen and the Politics of Criticism.* Madison: U of Wisconsin P, 1988.

Canup, John. *Out of the Wilderness: The Emergence of an American Identity in Colonial New England.* Middletown: Wesleyan UP, 1990.

Chase, Richard Volney. *The American Novel and Its Tradition.* Garden City: Doubleday, 1957.

Culler, Jonathan. "Literary Criticism and the American University." *Framing the Sign: Criticism and Its Institutions.* Norman: U of Oklahoma P, 1988. 3–40.

Dauber, Kenneth. *The Idea of Authorship in America.* Madison: U of Wisconsin P, 1990.

Davis, Richard Beale. *Intellectual Life in the Colonial South, 1585–1763.* 3 vols. Knoxville: U of Tennessee P, 1978.

Delbanco, Andrew. *The Puritan Ordeal.* Cambridge: Harvard UP, 1989.

Douglas, Ann. *The Feminization of American Culture.* New York: Knopf, 1977.

Elliot, Emory, ed. *The Columbia Literary History of the United States.* New York: Columbia UP, 1986.

Feidelson, Charles, Jr. *Symbolism and American Literature.* Chicago: U of Chicago P, 1953.

Ferguson, Robert A. *Law and Letters in American Culture.* Cambridge: Harvard UP, 1984.

Fischer, David Hackett. *Albion's Seed: Four British Folkways in America.* New York: Oxford UP, 1989.

Fisher, Philip. *Hard Facts: Setting and Form in the American Novel.* New York: Oxford UP, 1987.

Fliegelman, Jay. *Prodigals and Pilgrims: The American Revolution against Patriarchal Authority, 1750–1800.* New York: Cambridge UP, 1982.

Foucault, Michel. "What Is an Author?" Trans. Josué V. Harari. *Foucault Reader.* Ed. Paul Rabinow. New York: Pantheon, 1979. 101–20.

Geertz, Clifford. "Deep Play: Notes on the Balinese Cockfight." *Interpretation* 412–53.

Gilbert, Sandra M. "The American Sexual Poetics of Walt Whitman and Emily Dickinson." Bercovitch, *Reconstructing* 123–54.

Graff, Gerald. *Professing Literature: An Institutional History.* Chicago: U of Chicago P, 1987.

———. "The Promise of American Literature Studies." *Professing* 209–25.

Gunn, Giles. *The Culture of Criticism and the Criticism of Culture.* New York: Oxford UP, 1987.

———. *F. O. Matthiessen: The Critical Achievement.* Seattle: U of Washington P, 1975.

———. "The Kingdoms of Theory and the New Historicism in America." *Yale Review* 76 (1987): 207–36.

Gura, Philip P. *A Glimpse of Sion's Glory: Puritan Radicalism in New England, 1620–1660.* Middletown: Wesleyan UP, 1984.

Herbert, T. Walter, Jr. "Nathaniel Hawthorne, Una Hawthorne, and *The Scarlet Letter:* Interactive Selfhoods and the Cultural Construction of Gender." *PMLA* 103 (1988): 285–95.

Hoffman, Daniel. *Form and Fable in American Fiction.* 1961. New York: Oxford UP, 1965.

Howard, Leon. *The Connecticut Wits.* Chicago: U of Chicago P, 1943.

———. *Literature and the American Tradition.* Garden City: Doubleday, 1960.

Kerber, Linda. *Federalists in Dissent: Imagery and Ideology in Jeffersonian America.* Ithaca: Cornell UP, 1970.

Kibbey, Ann. *The Interpretation of Material Shapes in Puritanism: A Study of Rhetoric, Prejudice, and Violence.* New York: Cambridge UP, 1986.

Kolodny, Annette. *The Lay of the Land: Metaphor and Experience in American Life and Letters.* Chapel Hill: U of North Carolina P, 1975.

Lang, Amy Schrager. "Introduction to *The Captivity and Restoration of Mrs. Mary Rowlandson.*" *Journeys in New Worlds: Early American Women's Narratives.* Ed. Daniel B. Shea. Madison: U of Wisconsin P, 1990. 13–26.

Lauter, Paul, et al., eds. *The Heath Anthology of American Literature.* Lexington: Heath, 1990.

Lewis, R. W. B. *The American Adam: Innocence, Tragedy, and Tradition in the Nineteenth Century.* Chicago: U of Chicago P, 1955.

Marr, David. *American Worlds since Emerson.* Amherst: U of Massachusetts P, 1987.

Martin, Wendy. *An American Triptych: Anne Bradstreet, Emily Dickinson, Adrienne Rich.* Chapel Hill: U of North Carolina P, 1984.

Marx, Leo. *The Machine in the Garden: Technology and the Pastoral Ideal in America.* New York: Oxford UP, 1964.

Matthiessen, F. O. *American Renaissance: Art and Expression in the Age of Emerson and Whitman.* New York: Oxford UP, 1941.

McQuade, Donald, et al., eds. *The Harper American Literature.* New York: Harper, 1986.

McWilliams, John P. *Political Justice in a Republic.* Berkeley: U of California P, 1972.

Middlekauff, Robert. *The Mathers: Three Generations of Puritan Intellectuals, 1596–1728.* New York: Oxford UP, 1971.

Miller, Perry. *Errand into the Wilderness.* Cambridge: Harvard UP, 1956.

———. *The New England Mind.* 2 vols. Vol. 1: *The Seventeenth Century.* 1936. Vol. 2: *From Colony to Province.* 1953. Boston: Beacon, 1953.

O'Gorman, Edmundo. *The Invention of America: An Inquiry into the Historical Nature of the New World and the Meaning of Its History.* Westport: Greenwood, 1972.

Pease, Donald E. *Visionary Compacts: American Renaissance Writings in Cultural Context.* Madison: U of Wisconsin Press, 1987.

Porte, Joel, ed. *Emerson: Prospect and Retrospect.* Harvard English Studies 10. Cambridge: Harvard UP, 1982.

Porter, Carolyn. "Reification and American Literature." Bercovitch and Jehlen 188–217.

———. *Seeing and Being: The Plight of the Participant Observer in Emerson, James, Adams, and Faulkner.* Middletown: Wesleyan UP, 1981.

Richardson, Robert D. *Henry Thoreau: A Life of the Mind.* Berkeley: U of California P, 1986.

Simpson, Lewis P. *The Dispossessed Garden: Pastoral and History in Southern Literature.* Athens: U of Georgia P, 1975.

Slotkin, Richard. *Regeneration through Violence: The Mythology of the American Frontier.* Middletown: Wesleyan UP, 1973.

Smith, Henry Nash. "Symbol and Idea in *Virgin Land.*" Bercovitch and Jehlen 21–35.

———. *Virgin Land: The American West as Symbol and Myth.* Cambridge: Harvard UP, 1950.

Sollors, Werner. *Beyond Ethnicity: Consent and Descent in American Culture.* New York: Oxford UP, 1986.

Spiller, Robert, et al. *Literary History of the United States.* 1949. New York: Macmillan, 1953.

Stepto, Robert. "Distrust of the Reader in Afro-American Narratives." Bercovitch, *Reconstructing* 300–22.

Sundquist, Eric J. "*Benito Cereno* and New World Slavery." Bercovitch, *Reconstructing* 93–122.

Tichi, Cecelia. *New World, New Earth: Environmental Reform in American Literature from the Puritans through Whitman.* New Haven: Yale UP, 1979.

Veeser, H. Aram, ed. *The New Historicism.* New York: Routledge, 1989.

Weber, Donald. "Historicizing the Errand." *American Literary History* 2 (1990): 101–18.

Wood, Gordon S. "Struggle over the Puritans." *New York Review of Books* 9 Nov. 1989: 26+.

Yellin, Jean Fagan. *The Intricate Knot: Black Figures in American Literature, 1776–1863.* New York: New York UP, 1972.

American Literary and Cultural Studies since the Civil War

Philip Fisher

Fisher's essay is framed by recent changes in American studies. In addressing the critical shifts within the field, Fisher conceives of the new generation as moving from myth, *a singular, static story, to* rhetorics, *a*

From *Redrawing the Boundaries: The Transformation of English and American Literary Studies*, ed. Stephen Greenblatt and Giles Gunn (New York: MLA, 1992) 232–50.

*plural, dynamic view of culture. Fisher begins by discussing the develop-
ment of American studies and its myth of American national identity. Despite the determination of Americanists to identify a grand unifying myth,
reality is complicated by the pluralistic aspect of American culture. According to Fisher, diversity resists being subsumed by myth and thus often
creates what he terms "episodes of regionalism in American cultural history" (p. 39). These regionalisms include geography, ethnicity, race, gender,
and sexuality. Fisher describes American culture as a pendulum swinging
between regionalisms and unifying projects.*

*According to Fisher, the new American studies provides an alternative
to regionalism by identifying a set of national facts, such as democratic
culture and the culture of freedom, around which identities are formed.
This allows for analysis within American studies to focus on sectors of a
diverse culture rather than on a monopoly of power, recognizing rhetorics
rather than ideology. Fisher's essay originally appeared as an introduction
to his* The New American Studies *(1991). The version here was adapted
for inclusion in the collection* Redrawing the Boundaries *(1992), edited
by Stephen Greenblatt and Giles Gunn.*

From Myth to Rhetorics

The essential books of the last fifteen years in the literary and cultural study of American life represent the work of a new generation
within American studies, and they represent, at the same time, a new
idea of what it might mean to do American studies and how one would
go about doing it. In combination they also represent the rich diversity
of explanations and materials in the study of American culture. Films
and photographs, Supreme Court decisions and industrial manuals,
educational and domestic theory, the popular culture of Horatio Alger
and the standard genres of domestic fiction: a culture in its full institutional and individual variety has been brought into play.

One way to characterize this newness would be to say that, in this
generation of American studies, interest has passed from myth to rhetorics. *Myth* in this perhaps too simple formula is always singular, *rhetorics* always plural. Myth is a fixed, satisfying, and stable story that is
used again and again to normalize our account of social life. By means
of myth, novelty is tamed by being seen as the repetition or, at most,
the variation of a known and valued pattern. Even where actual historical situations are found to fall short of myth or to lie in its aftermath, the myth tames the variety of historical experience, giving it
familiarity while using it to reaffirm the culture's long-standing interpretation of itself.

Rhetoric, in contrast, is a tactic within the open questions of culture. It reveals interests and exclusions. To look at rhetorics is to look
at the action potential of language and images, not just their power or
contrivance to move an audience but the location of words, formulas,
images, and units of meaning within politics. Rhetoric is the place where

language is engaged in cultural work, and such work can be done on, with, or in spite of one or another group within society. Rhetorics are plural because they are part of what is uncertain or potential within culture. They are the servants of one or another politics of experience. Where there is nothing openly contested, no cultural work to be done, we do not find the simplification into one and only one rhetoric. Instead we find the absence of the particular inflammation and repetition that rhetoric always marks. We find no rhetoric at all, only the ceremonial contentment of myth. Rhetorics are also distinct from ideology. Within the term *ideology* we are right to hear a combination of calculation, cynicism about social truth, a schoolteacher's relation to the pupils, indoctrination, and propaganda. Whether as reality or hope, ideology implies that one part of the legitimacy of authority is a monopoly on representation, and this is exactly the condition in which rhetorics become irrelevant.

To understand what a move from myth to rhetorics might involve, it is useful to look at two things: first, how the claim of a unitary myth worked and was used during the period that we might call the transfer of literature to the American university; second, the counterelement to central myths within American studies—the force of regionalism.

Myths and the University

The new field of American studies came to maturity in the years just before and after the Second World War. Its description of American experience had as its audience both Americans themselves and, even more important, a wider world in which American culture had begun to work as a kind of world culture. Both Europeans and Americans were asked to consider in mythic terms a prior state of American experience, one whose essence and importance lay in the fact that it no longer existed but had generated the cultural heart of American experience. But to this prior culture of Puritan mission, frontier, wilderness, garden, and innocence, contemporary Americans were just as much outsiders as Europeans and Asians were.

In this charged pre- and postwar atmosphere of cultural victory and cultural defeat, Americanists undertook the search for a central myth of America. Such key works as Henry Nash Smith's *Virgin Land*, Leo Marx's *Machine in the Garden*, R. W. B. Lewis's *American Adam*, and Richard Slotkin's *Regeneration through Violence* encouraged a study of literature, everyday culture, and history around a shared mythic content that captured American uniqueness and national identity. American studies as an academic field in its first generation took this myth of America to be its central topic and its method for linking the classics of American poetry, fiction, and painting to the culture of images, newspapers, sermons, political rhetoric, and, especially, popular fiction and verse. Here the western and the sermon met.

The first of these all-encompassing myths of America had, in fact, been defined half a century earlier. This was the frontier myth of Frederick Jackson Turner, a hypothesis as Turner called it, but ultimately a story rather than a scientific speculation, and a story whose appeal lay in the curious fact that it described just those social features that had been lost forever in the formal official closing of the American frontier noted in the census of 1890. Although Turner's great myth appeared before what we might call the capture of American culture by the universities, an event that took place in the 1930s and 1940s, his strategy of discovering one fundamental fact or myth that explained the identity of America as a nation set the stage for the mythic cast of the first generation of the academic study of American culture. After the frontier myth, the most important global explanation lay in the myth of the Puritans, their mission, the unique significance of intellectuals and ideology within the Puritan experience, the primacy of New England's religious forms for American political experience, and the residue of Puritan energy, now changed to commerce and self-cultivation, that remained as a permanent trace within the national character. If the frontier myth was a myth of the West, the Puritan myth was a myth of New England culture, asserting its right to a permanent steering function in national life. Where the western myth was democratic, based on the experience of immigration and self-reliance, the New England myth was ultimately a myth of the importance of intellectuals and, with them, of the crucial role played by writing and those who provide ideology, self-description, and history—the importance, finally, of preachers and their later descendants, the intellectuals of the nineteenth century and the university professors of the twentieth.

In spite of the built-in resistance of our literature and its awkward wildness, no cultural fact is more decisive over the past fifty years than the wholesale movement of every component of our literary life, past, present, and future, into the universities. American studies and American literature have everywhere arrived at legitimacy. American poets have been signed up as writers-in-residence. Our men and women of letters, following Philip Rahv and Irving Howe, have become professors, trading in their general audience of educated adults for a classroom full of students eighteen to twenty-five years old, and a secondary audience of their professional colleagues who have now become the main readers of their opinions. Our little magazines are now subsidized by colleges, where they too are now in residence, and they find their primary guaranteed sales to the periodical rooms of university libraries. The paperback revolution of the 1950s and 1960s that promised at first to democratize our culture by making inexpensive editions widely available has ended up filling our bookstores with texts instead of books, texts designed for adoption as required reading in courses.

The high-level professional work on the new subject of American literature has been shaped to a remarkable degree by the residence of culture within the academic world. The university and the professor think, as they must, in terms of courses—that is, in terms of a coherent set of books or themes that fit into the fifteen-week semester. Such distinguished critical studies as F. O. Matthiessen's *American Renaissance*, Marx's *Machine in the Garden*, or Smith's *Virgin Land* represent our past as a set of model courses. The great interest in myths of the frontier, the machine, the Puritan errand into the wilderness (see P. Miller, *Errand*), American violence, or American individualism served to give shape to the academic year in an ordered, consecutive, schematic way with developments and oppositions. The problem of the American romance, as opposed to the novel, or the description of so arbitrary a period of our history as what is known as the Gilded Age, redesigned the past to fit the intellectual needs and temporal rhythms of the newly professionalized study of the past.

The most common thread of the first generation of the study of America has been what could be called the disappointment of myth by fact, the failure of reality to live up to the ways in which it has been imagined. America is first mythologized as the second Eden, its purpose linked to the Puritan mission, or pictured as a frontier or free space for the unbounded individual, but then, in each case, the myth is betrayed by fact. The promise is unkept. As the purity of what was imagined grew stained over time, American reality, by means of the apparatus of myth, took on the look of a fallen state. The frontier had been closed. The high moral purpose of the Puritans had given way to commerce and commercial purpose. The innocence had blood on its hands. What was there had the look of heavily discounted possibility; what might have been had been disappointed in the act of making. Significantly, one of the master texts of a whole generation of American study was Henry James's *The Ambassadors*, perhaps from an academic point of view the most perfect book ever written by an American. James's hero Strether creates a myth of Paris, a myth of his charge, Chad, a myth of Chad's relation to Mme. de Vionnet. Each myth is betrayed by fact, stained by the complexity of the real world. An entire academic generation saw its own love of criticism, observation, nuance, disappointment, myth, and defeat in James's novel.

As the great academic popularity of James's novel made clear, if there has been one history lovingly traced by intellectuals over the past fifty years, it has been the history of intellectuals themselves. From the work of Perry Miller in the late 1930s, the explanation of America as a long history of Puritan hope and decline resulted from the fact that, looking into the past to find not necessarily its chief actors but precisely those congenial figures whose analytic and critical stance most resembled their own, the academic intellectuals discovered in Puritan writing what was for them the most intelligible feature of the past, the one mirror most filled with familiar features. The Puritans too were intellectuals, engaged in holding up a mirror of admonition or exhortation to their society. In theocratic New England they embodied one of the most secret self-images of all intellectual cultures, a world in which the critics and intellectuals of society were not marginal but actually in power.

The Puritan intellectuals had their successors in the radical critics of society from the mid-nineteenth century to the 1950s and 1960s. Utopian intellectuals of the left in the 1930s found in the radical Puritans of three hundred years earlier their own model for the role and hoped-for importance of the intellectual within politics and society. However marginal intellectuals have actually been within American culture, the study of America has reclaimed them.

Useful as the history of intellectuals as written by their own aspiring descendants might be, it amounts only to a rather timid look into the most friendly and probably most unrepresentative district of the American past. The actors in exploration and settlement, in enterprise and invention, in the making of cities and the long history of money and speculation in America, in the tangled history of black and white, Native American and settler, political and personal rebellion, have been the primary characters of the American story, even if, unlike the intellectuals, they have seldom been their own best historians.

Myth creates a fault line between what ought to have taken place and what did. It permits ideas and facts to criticize each other. Like the rebellion of an individual or like the more collective movements of reform, myths embody what Henry Adams in his *Education* called the "spirit of resistance." The search for central myths—myths that were already closed off, as the frontier was at the moment of its first description as the most vital experience for the foundation of an American identity—was inseparable from the study of resistance within culture, whether in the Gothic style of *Pierre* or in the reflective émigré style of *The Ambassadors* or the self-ironic Adams of *Education*. The appetite for resistance led Lionel Trilling to propose that all culture in the modern period was basically adversarial, at war with the commonplace or everyday social energies and beliefs. In European society of the nineteenth century, this adversarial position reflected the failure of self-belief in the emerging middle classes that had at last arrived at political and cultural power equivalent to their economic importance. But in the United States the source was quite different. It lay in a utopian or even moral radicalism combined with or concealing the resentment of artists and intellectuals at their rather small voice in a national life dominated by business and politics.

The belief in spiritual radicalism led to a focus on those writers, like Melville, who said their "No! In thunder." Such oppositional figures as the hero of Melville's *Pierre* or of "Bartleby the Scrivener" or, in real life, Thoreau defiant of Concord and moving two miles away to Walden Pond or spending a night in jail, Henry James withdrawn to England because American reality was not thick enough, the protagonist of *The*

Scarlet Letter stubborn and free: These defiant, adversarial figures, along with the challenging distance they created in standing out by standing against their world, are what the study of the tension between fact and all that resisted fact brought to the center. Within American studies the study of America had become the study of dissent. The rebels and dissidents came to the front as the leading patriots. It was the era of Thoreau, Henry Adams, and Bartleby, not of Emerson and Whitman.

By an accident of timing, American literature arrived in the university at a highly politicized moment. Its arrival coincided with the polarization between right and left or, in European terms, between fascism and communism in the period between the two world wars. The study of resistance was attractive, in part, because both the conservative right and the liberal left had rejected one key feature of what had been a synthesis in the most vital parts of nineteenth-century American culture. The right was hostile to democracy; the left to capitalism. They shared a distrust of the optimism, energy, confidence, and what might be called the surprisingly guiltless relation that figures like Emerson, Whitman, James Fenimore Cooper, or Francis Parkman had had to their own past. The lack of apology or contrition, the robust feeling of the right to be where and as they were in spite of slavery, Indian massacres, the failures of national politics to be dignified or even honest, the violence of the West, the polyglot hustle of the new cities—such guiltless self-regard seemed shallow to a left and to a right equally convinced, from different sides, of the nightmare of history. A whole new meaning of the term *innocence* had to be invented to make it seem that only some youthful unawareness of evil could explain the pride or health of Twain, Whitman, William James, or Emerson. That the greatest figures of our literature were not oppositional figures seemed almost beyond belief. But it was a fact. There is no margin of frictional energy that accounts for Emily Dickinson or Theodore Dreiser or William Faulkner. Whitman and Emerson continue to embarrass by their failure to have seen through democracy and capitalism or, rather, by their having imagined themselves to have seen into the philosophic and temperamental depths of those two systems and to have found them both profound and humane, exhilarating and enduring.

One key to the new ground claimed by critical work of the last few years has been the implicit rejection of this heroism of oppositional dissent and its replacement by collaborative and implicational relations between writer or speaker and culture. Emerson, Harriet Beecher Stowe, Twain, and William James are the masters of this new relation, not Melville and Thoreau. Richard Poirier's books on the tactics of Robert Frost within language (*Robert Frost: The Work of Knowing*) and the cultural meaning of Emerson (*The Renewal of Literature*) set out important accounts of the rich entanglement of writer and culture. In Poirier's account, the work always lives off and lives through the spaces open within the language and especially within the plural languages of culture.

The pressures of cultural life are plural and not a single hegemonic ideology that must be resisted, subverted, or surrendered to. Cultural life, in this formulation, is open to the activity of rebalancing and reconstruction that the literary work makes possible. Poirier's is an aesthetics of survival that represents at the same time a confident aesthetics of pleasure within the forces of culture and the possibility of mastery over them, what we might call the outwitting of the up-to-then apparently dead ends of language and feeling, the traps of rhetoric and commitment. In this respect, his work is remarkably similar to the claims of the major book within African American theory, *The Signifying Monkey*, by Henry Louis Gates Jr. For Gates, signifying is a way of taking over cultural formulas, living off and living within whatever is given because whatever is given can always be topped, reformulated, bent to build in whatever it was designed to place or to place out. In his theory of culture, the trickster once again displaces the victim as the essential subjectivity and actor within the cultural script. One major weakness of the theory of ideology and myth has always been its specification of subjectivity as either that of power, victim, or coopted dupe. What Gates celebrates in the trickster, Poirier had earlier called the "performing self," and the great model of this performance might be sketched out by combining the moves of Huck Finn and Whitman with those of Emerson and Frost. These tactics of freedom in the face of the givenness of reality are normative for Emersonian artists in the face of an already given set of forms, for adolescents discovering and differentiating themselves within a world of parents and parental society, and for African American culture and its practices within and yet above the surrounding culture into which they have been thrown.

A simple catalog of moves within collaboration would include boasts, lies, tricks, exaggeration, the mastery of language, even an entrepreneurial relation to language, the play with masks and roles, the caginess of Frost and Emerson, the folksy and the elusive. All are wrapped together as elements of a heightened self-consciousness and strategic style of thinking. They define the cultural location where the signifying monkey meets the performing self, when the ambiguity of Hawthorne and the glib half-serious language of Twain meet the canniness of Frost and the daring extravagance of Emerson's and Whitman's verbal bravado. Gates and Poirier have returned the study of moves within culture—the moves of the trickster—to their real importance over against the "No! In thunder" of opposition and the sentimental pathos of the many narratives of victims crushed by all-pervading scripts of power.

Sacvan Bercovitch's study of Hawthorne and what Bercovitch calls the "a-morality of compromise" interrogates and deflates the rhetoric of oppositional purity in favor of a remarkable and nuanced idea of politics, a term of extraordinary importance as an alternative to the purity of cultural dissent and protest. Politics and, along with it, the pragmatics of action and compromise within a given temporal horizon and in the face of specific counterforces that cannot be defeated but must be enlisted in a joint project define the essence of a stance beyond the merely gestural "No! In thunder" but equally beyond the various forms of radical purity—the expatriation of Henry James, the internal expatriation of Thoreau at Walden, the aloof aristocratic unemployment of Henry Adams, the utopian posture of Thoreau or the history of intellectual socialism and communism in the hundred years between the fall of the Paris Commune in 1870 and the collapse of that utopia in the face of the crisis in real-existing socialism at the end of the 1980s.

Like the texts by Poirier, Gates, and Bercovitch, but from an entirely different direction, Walter Benn Michaels's book on naturalism and the 1890s —*The Gold Standard and the Logic of Naturalism*—has demolished the oppositional simplicity in what had seemed the easiest period to locate the author automatically outside and over against the culture of capitalism. In my own book *Hard Facts*, the nineteenth-century models of cultural work are deliberately taken to be different from and more varied than the work of protest and negation or its opposite, pious complicity and conscious or unconscious propagation of a single leading ideology. In its literature a culture practices and memorizes its own self-relation, only one part of which involves its relation to what it takes to be its past, to what circumference of action and choice it holds itself accountable for in the present, and what future it takes to be its promise to itself, as opposed to the merely abstract or utopian bad infinity of possibilities. Cultural work is pragmatic, not Hegelian. Its plural objects are local, open matters, necessary cases, hard facts. One measure of cultural work is not realism but a certain decay within realism that announces that some local fact of culture has been altered or restabilized so that the work now done has made the earlier representation obsolete—that is, no longer realistic. For later periods the effectiveness of that work can be felt in what now seems like excess or exaggerated emphasis—what we sweep to the side as genre. What feels sentimental, in the bad meaning of the term, in Stowe or Wordsworth, Dickens or Dostoevsky, is exactly the marker of suffering now casually within the field of vision that once had to be forced into representation. What is now noticed as shrill in Whitman— once the work of Whitman to center the sexual and democratic self has succeeded—becomes obsolete, part of the genre or category of the egotistical sublime, the excess of Romanticism, the emotional fraud of mid-nineteenth-century boosterism, whether for land schemes, political candidates, or, in Whitman's case, self-description and construction of the role and stance of the democratic poet.

Cultural work is one concept of a cultural pragmatism, a concern with the effective strategies of culture that includes, at the level of individual psychology, such strategies as performing and signifying. Poirier's Emerson, in *The Renewal of Literature*, is a model of the tough-minded intellectual within American culture. One part of his model is that bravery of fools that Emerson shared with Whitman and Twain. Bercovitch's Hawthorne, with the notion of politics and the intriguing morality of compromise, is a second, equally important cultural model. Both are elements of the major recuperation of American philosophical pragmatism that has been a significant project of the new collaboration between American philosophy and American literary studies in the 1970s and 1980s.

The worldliness and local field of vision of pragmatism has always existed as the rough alternative both to dissent and to the spiritual purity of transcendentalism, utopianism, and Puritanism—those three overlapping radical energies within our culture. In the books of Stanley Cavell and Richard Rorty, the philosophical and literary tradition of American pragmatism has been returned to central interest in our cultural life. The easy combination of the literary and the philosophical is only one of the novelties of this recent examination of pragmatism. The contingency, irony, and solidarity that Rorty has brought together as key terms in one of his titles define a posture of liberal generosity and a dismissal of the vehemence and refusal of solidarity with one's own culture that are the classic tonal pitch of self-appointed radicalism. That Emerson and William James stand also for a genuinely popular and culturally central relation of the intellectual to society is no small part of their value and interest. They are, we might say, anti-Nietzschean models of the intellectual.

Cavell, Rorty, and Poirier have laid the basis in recent books for a profound and profoundly impure—that is, contingent and political—tradition of American intellectual culture. At the same time it is notable that Cavell and Poirier have created analyses of culture that broke the barrier between high culture and the innovative commercial and popular culture of our own time. Cavell has brought both philosophy and Hollywood into the register of literary vision. His work on film, especially on the Hollywood comedies of marriage and remarriage—*Pursuits of Happiness*—has set a new configuration in place of the older-style American studies negotiation between "major authors" and the "wider culture." Poirier's *The Performing Self* did similar decisive work in building analytic paths into the complex languages of popular music, political writing, and such authors as Frost and Norman Mailer. Gates's *The Signifying Monkey* is the key recent revision of our description of the text culture in its links to the strategies and range of everyday oral and written performance. An encyclopedic summary of what used to be called "our classic authors" in terms of this wider culture of possibilities was achieved by David Reynolds in his book *Beneath the American Renaissance.*

Regionalism and Central Culture

Alongside the search for grand unifying myths, with their inevitable narrative of a fall into imperfection and disappointment, a second element shared the stage within American studies between the 1930s and the 1970s—the claim of pluralism within American culture. This diversity, which resists the single shelter of myth or ideology, has again and again risen to dominance in what we might call the episodes of regionalism in American cultural history.

Cultural life in America swings like a pendulum between a diversity of sectional voices and an ever-new project of unity, between the representation of the nation as made up of weakly joined districts and the depiction of a central national order. A hundred and fifty years ago our then strongly sectional culture was split along geographical lines: the New England mind, the southern way of life, the West of the pioneers, with their energy and violence. Each section had its own voices and themes, its own philosophies and religions, its unique spirit and humor. A common identity was rebuilt out of these regionalisms by the Civil War, by the mythic figure of Lincoln, by the railroads and telegraph, which conquered a geography grown too large for the earlier Federalist unity of Washington and Jefferson, and by the elaboration of an American way of life made up of Singer sewing machines, Coca-Cola, Remington rifles, and Ford Model T's—a way of life created around democratically available mass-produced goods rather than by the right to vote or to own property.

Each swing to regionalism has split the country along different fault lines, and each rewon unity involves not a return to a lost identity but a new plane of association. In early twentieth-century America a regionalism that was not geographic but ethnic appeared as a result of the massive immigration that had taken place between 1870 and 1914. The local color was not that of climates and regions but of what are called, metaphorically, hyphenated Americans: Jewish Americans, Italian Americans, Irish Americans, Wasps and Chinese Americans, Poles, Swedes, and Russians. It was a regionalism of languages, folk customs, humor, music, and beliefs set over against the pull of what came to be called Americanization.

In the case of ethnic regionalism it was not the railroads and the everyday objects of a thriving economy that created the unifying force, as they had done earlier. To this regionalism was opposed the core culture of public education and the pull of economic advancement, always purchased at the price of a surrendered culture, most obviously by the requirement within the schools and business world of the English language. A third unifying force was mobility itself. Only if immigrants remained in a ghetto, the ghetto of arrival, could the coherence of language, way of life, religion, and, most important, marriage within the ethnic group be preserved. To move even once was to enter the general American condition. And the two world wars and the democratic experience of the army worked, as the Civil War and the Revolutionary War had earlier, to fuse an identity that superseded the ethnic diversity of the late nineteenth and early twentieth centuries. Thus the pots in which the melting actually occurred were the schoolroom, the offices of the business world, the new suburbs out beyond the territorial inner city, and, finally, the fields of battle. Unity within American culture has always been a postwar unity, whether Federalist, after the Revolution, capitalist, after the Civil War, or contemporary American, after, and resulting from, the two world wars.

In recent years a further episode of regionalism, neither geographical nor ethnic, has begun. The regionalism of our own times, which comes on the heels of the generation that elaborated the myth of America within the shadow and aftermath of World War II, is one of gender and race. The civil rights movement after 1954 had, as its cultural side, the debate over black identity in America. The women's movement that followed, just as the nineteenth-century suffrage movement had followed and drawn its vocabulary from the abolitionist movement against slavery, set the model for the denial of what came to be called *essentialism*, the claim to an overriding common human identity. Later gay and lesbian movements, as well as ethnic identities that were now conceived not along the model of the earlier hyphenated identities but along the more radical model of black or female identity, reopened the full spectrum of regionalized culture. Native American, Chicano, gay, black, lesbian, female: Once again, an episode of regionalism set out its claims against, in this case, a central technological culture made up of the new media—television and film—but also against the older forces of education and mass representation. The model that black or female identity set in place for regionalism was refractory in a novel way because these regional—as opposed to universal—models for identity were the first within American experience that neither mobility nor the succession of generations would alter. Earlier geographic or ethnic identities had been episodic in that the mechanisms of the culture itself would erase them over time. California, with its new "identity," was obviously composed of people who had shed—by means of the simple act of driving across the country and choosing to settle there—their prior New England, midwestern, southern, or western identities. Jewish Americans who moved to the suburbs of New York City and watched their children marry Italian Americans, German Americans, or Wasps may have seen the fading and erasure of these regionalisms in the lives of the grandchildren who went off to school in Chicago or Los Angeles. Earlier American regionalisms had been temporary and easily bargained away once the alternatives were attractive enough. The weak hold of geography could be seen in the all-purpose category "Sun Belt," which encompassed not only the states from Florida through Texas to Southern California but also, in the case of Florida, the new security of retirement and the simple desire for a warm and convenient climate that would lead Americans to desert and shed their regional identities, homes, and friends, even late in life, for a carefully calculated new start. By contrast, to be black or female was an unnegotiable identity, one that could not be dissolved by those American master plots: education, intermarriage, mobility. Insofar as other groups, including ethnic groups, took over the black model, they chose to see their own regional identity as final and began to argue for their own language, education, and culture.

In American universities the departments of American studies, established in the 1930s, 1940s, and 1950s, found themselves in the 1960s and 1970s quickly regionalized into departments of black or African American studies, Jewish studies, women's studies, Native American studies, Chicano and Asian American studies, and, in some cases, gay studies. One consequence of these new identity claims was what the proponents viewed as an aggressive unmasking of the myths of the previous generation, among other things a series of overwhelmingly white male myths of America. The pastoral, the western, the Puritan mission, the frontier experience of individualism, self-reliance, and democratic values: all had, at their center, white male actors with various supporting casts. The self-appointed task of unmasking hegemony, essentialism, and the many disguised operations of power within the culture has defined what could be called the *fundamentalism* of this third and most recent swing of regionalism. We have lived for twenty years within a scholarship that could be more and more clearly identified as, in effect, the unnegotiable regional essentialism of gender, race, and ethnicity. This new regionalism demanded and made claims for a wider membership within the university on behalf of women, blacks, and others while supplying the new members with an automatic subject matter: themselves, their own history and rights within the national array of culture.

The new American studies has grown up alongside but also as an alternative or aftermath to this regionalism, which tore apart the previous unifying and singular myths of America. The key limitation to this new phase, as well as to all earlier regionalisms, was its need to define itself and thrive only within a highly politicized atmosphere. Regionalism is always, in America, part of a struggle within representation. It is seldom or never a matter of tolerance, the blooming of a thousand, or even of three, flowers. In the regionalism of the last two decades, identity is formed by opposition: black-white, female-male, Native American–settler, gay-heterosexual. Because of this opposition, identity is located above all in the sphere of politics—that is, in the sphere of felt opposition, of movement, laws, demands, negotiations over representation, and, in the university, in struggle over curriculum and requirements. The new American studies has stood outside this regionalism by locating a set of underlying but permanently open national facts around which all identities are shaped. It is with these permanently open cultural questions that the many rhetorics of our culture are engaged. Among these permanently open, that is, never won or lost, national facts are democratic culture and its demands; the culture of freedom that permits conditions of dominance, whether economic, sexual, or cultural, and has permitted even permutations of slavery as one aspect of the nature of freedom itself; the creation of a national life that is economic rather than religious or, in the anthropological sense, cultural. This troubled utopian core of enterprise, freedom, and democratic culture, baffled by preexisting social facts while never surrendering to them, is central to much of the best recent work in American studies.

The Civil War within Representation

One consequence of the new American studies has been to replace the traditional concept of the American Renaissance with the new category of a literature located within the Civil War and driven by the particular concepts of freedom and independence, politics and compromise that the war period, with its preparation and aftermath, froze into place. Recent European historical work, particularly Reinhart Koselleck's essays on the concept of revolution in his book *Future's Past*, has brought to the center of attention the part played by civil wars in the grounding and contesting of national identity in the three hundred years between the Thirty Years' War and the English Civil War of the seventeenth century and the end of the general European civil war of 1914–45. Like the American Civil War, or the French and Russian revolutions with their phases of civil war, all such conflicts put at risk the very existence of the society itself in the name of uncompromisable values. Periods of civil war are periods without ideology, because two or more rhetorics of self-representation, national purpose, and historical genealogy are in wide enough circulation to elicit complete support, even to the point of making people willing to die for them. Civil war is the alternative condition to what we call, following Foucault's relentless analysis, the power of the centralized state, the structured, all-pervading system for stabilizing and describing a fixed social reality.

In contrast to the condition of two or more contesting powers that we can, in a shorthand way, express by the notion of civil war, the very idea of a cultural period like that of Romanticism or the American Renaissance leads us to look for a unified set of ideas and aesthetic practices. We then come to think of such concepts as the ideology of the American Renaissance or some other period. Writers can be viewed as expressing or dissenting from that ideology. Ideology, dissent, a sense of identity and of an authoritative discourse within each period are all interdependent notions. Once the idea of civil war as a normative situation within representation replaces that of ideology, the entire array of concepts falls away together.

In literary studies of the last ten years what has been called the New Historicism has, as a result of the strong influence of Foucault and modern experience of totalitarianism and its analysis by, among others, Hannah Arendt, Max Horkheimer, and Theodor Adorno, focused on the fate of representation within absolutist states or societies. The English Renaissance, taken as a glorious period of monarchy, along with its secondary pressures and exceptions, became the natural topic for New-Historicist demonstrations.

The condition of civil war can be taken to be the fundamental alternative to that of monarchical power, self-display, uniform discourse, ideology, and controlled representation. American New Historicism has its basis in the representational situation not of monarchy but of civil war. To see the central American historical episode as the civil war is to bring to the front the power of rhetorics, incomplete dominance of representation, and the borrowing or fusing of successful formulas of representation. The actual war of the 1860s stands in for the pervasive, continuously unsettled, open struggle within American culture. All cultural history in the United States is the history of civil wars.

The civil wars between contemporaries are only a local version of what, to use an Emersonian formulation, should be seen as the fundamental, permanent conflict in any society that is, as the United States is, an economy rather than a culture. That underlying civil war, as Emerson described it in his essay on Napoleon, is between the young and the old, between power that represents work done in the past and the effort of the young, who will displace all that is being defended in order to make room for themselves in the world. Railroads overthrew canals and water-based transportation, and no sooner had they succeeded than the automobile and long-distance truck overthrew the railroad. No sooner did Western Union have a monopoly on long-distance communication than the telephone industry emerged to make that monopoly worthless.

The representational topic of monarchy is the inheritance, diffusion, and protection of already-held power. The subject of civil war is the unstable contest for short-term control that is uninheritable and, in the end, undefendable. Power is not the topic of this historicism but its weak long-term expectations in a culture in which economic dominance is not located in land—that one genuinely scarce, readily transferable, and not easily variable basis of hegemony.

Print Culture without the State

The ordinary culture within which our classic authors and painters have worked has to be called a print culture, but now understood in a wider sense than the Gutenberg culture of the book. A photograph is also called a "print," as is the copy of a film. Newspapers and journals, advertisements and billboards are also, in this sense, prints, offprints, and reprints. In his book on the profession of the author in America, Michael Warner sets out the model of the printer Benjamin Franklin, with his new-made career within print culture, a culture replacing the oral culture of sermon, oratory, and statements linked to the personal presence of the speaker and the audience's identification with the spoken words. After Franklin all American authors, photographers, and filmmakers are printers.

In his important book on American photography, Alan Trachtenberg has defined the photographic print as a cultural text within the Civil War, the reform movements of the 1890s and 1930s, and the modernist aesthetic of the early twentieth century. In the photographic images of the war itself, Trachtenberg reads the rhetoric of representation as it appeared within the camera—which, like the machine gun, was one of the new instruments of this conflict. The very existence of photographs during wartime for the first time, alongside or combined with day-by-day newspaper reporting from the battlefield, set up a contest for the control and definition of this new visual genre. The photograph and newspaper did not define an ideology of the war experience and certainly not a myth. Instead, they embodied the rapidly shifting competitive rhetorics within the as-yet-unstabilized representation that would only later, with victory and time, become what we know as the "Civil" War.

Unlike myths that take on all possible historical circumstances as illustrations and by this means become universal explanations, rhetorical analysis is never universal. One important reason for the local nature of the analysis of rhetorics found in recent work is the lack of what might be called, in the European sense, the state in American experience and therefore an absence of any monopoly of either power or of violence on the part of the state. Centralization of power on the European model, and with it the centralization of the power of representation and self-conception as it has been described by Foucault, was never present in America. Unlike French schools, American education has always been local, variable, responsive, for good and ill, to local pressures and the demands of the moment. When, in the twentieth century, state control over, and funding of, culture became fundamental and deeply ideological in Europe and throughout much of the world, politicized between the radical cultural projects of the right and the left, American culture developed an almost singularly market- and consumer-based formula of funding, selection, and survival. American newspapers, music, film, radio, publishing, and television were all competitive, decentralized, and in the hands of ever-new players. Only the highly paradoxical analysis of European intellectuals, like those of the Frankfurt school, with their horror of popular or commercial culture, could have invented the claim that this unsponsored and competitive culture itself expressed an even more rigid and tricky ideology than the more obvious overt ideologies of twentieth-century European experience, the so-called ideology of capitalism (see Jay). But by 1945 no European intellectual could any longer imagine what it might mean to live in a society without a state that owned, sponsored, and used for its own purposes all the media of cultural life.

Even outside the arena of cultural conflict, or civil war per se, American culture provided the richest possible resources for escape, invisibility, and defiance. The right to "move on" or "head out west" was only one of the possibilities that limited the creation of a state. More important was the economic commitment to a rapidly changing culture of invention, with its dizzy cycles of the amassing, loss, and transfer of wealth and power. The economic commitment was far more decisive than the purely individual right to escape or move on, but even the apparently individual mobility was historically profound because it was the means of renewing the act of immigration—leaving behind and moving on—that was each individual's first drop of American identity. In fact, such an economic pressure—what has been called the "creative destruction" of the market economy—is a form of willed, collective instability, because it accepts the future as an already bankable asset that can be borrowed against to speed up the overthrow of the past. In a speculative culture, for instance, the profits of the railroads fall into an investment pool, where, since they are expected to yield the highest returns, they no longer are invested back into the railroad system itself but into the automobile industry, whose only purpose is to overthrow the railroads as the fundamental transportation system. By means of the speculative system, the past becomes the silent partner of a future that will abolish its own hold. A culture of speculation is opposite in its action to those of preservation, inheritance, and self-reproduction, which we tend to take anthropologically as the human norm. Pierre Bourdieu's *Outline of a Theory of Practice*—precisely because it is concerned with societies whose primary goal is reproduction in the widest sense of self-replication and continuation, as is, over time—can never describe an Emersonian or speculative society whose commitment to self-destruction in the name of its own next possibility is far more important than its interest in the transfer of the forms of the past to a future generation.

For these reasons analysis within American studies will always be of sectors of a diverse culture characterized by the absence of a monopoly of power. These studies will always be historical and not anthropological, because of the commitment of the culture itself to a rapid building up, wearing out, and replacement of systems of all kinds by new arrays of persons and forces. The updraft is strong, the door of immigration both to and within the country is open, the exhaustion of control is always imminent and control itself is porous. Because America had no experience of monarchy, it has a permanent democratic core working against not only the centralization of power but, more important, its inheritance or preservation over time.

In the absence of a state, we find ourselves freed of the intellectual component of the systematic state: ideology. We have rhetorics because we have no ideology, and we have no ideology because we lack the apparatus of ideology: a national religion, a unitary system of education under the control of the state, a cultural life and media monopolized by the state by means either of ownership or of subsidy. Ideology is a cultural mechanism of stabilization and transmission, neither of which is a primary topic of a culture of speculation. The study of rhetorics is our necessary alternative to the study of ideology. Rhetorics are the sign of the play of forces within cultural life, and at the same time of the power of invention and obsolescence within culture. Rhetoric is the mark of temporary location and justification. The nuances of provisional justification and defense, the opening up of newness within culture without escaping the grip of the master problems and resources of the culture: This is what is at issue within the newest writing on American literature and culture.[1]

Note

1. This essay has been adapted from the author's introduction to his volume *The New American Studies* (Berkeley: U of California P, 1991).

Selected Bibliography

Bercovitch, Sacvan, ed. *Reconstructing American Literary History*. Harvard English Studies 13. Cambridge: Harvard UP, 1986.
    A particularly thoughtful group of essays, on literary issues and texts from the eighteenth century to the present, that reflects what the editor refers to as "the self-reflexiveness that characterizes this period of critical interregnum."
Cavell, Stanley. *In Quest of the Ordinary*. Chicago: U of Chicago P, 1988.
    One of Cavell's recent collections of essays that display his efforts to recuperate the writings of Emerson and Thoreau for serious philosophical reflection and show how their pragmatist absorption with the ordinary and the familiar constitutes a profound response to the modern problem of skepticism.
Fisher, Philip. *Hard Facts: Setting and Form in the American Novel*. New York: Oxford UP, 1987.
    A study of the way cultural forms like novels transform certain of the disagreeable facts at the center of social experience—in nineteenth-century

America, the removal and destruction of Native American peoples, the enslavement of African Americans, and the later commercial objectification of all Americans—into something not only palatable but naturalized.

Gates, Henry Louis, Jr. *The Signifying Monkey: A Theory of African-American Literary Criticism.* New York: Oxford UP, 1988.
An important work that focuses on the trickster in African American literary experience, a figure whose talents for signifying, for redescription, constitute a subjectivity that can elude the structures of rhetorical and ideological closure associated with the dominant society.

Gunn, Giles. *Thinking across the American Grain: Ideology, Intellect, and the New Pragmatism.* Chicago: U of Chicago P, 1992.
A study of the renaissance of pragmatism in contemporary American intellectual culture and its application to a variety of literary and critical contexts.

Lewis, R. W. B. *The American Adam: Innocence, Tragedy, and Tradition in the Nineteenth Century.* Chicago: U of Chicago P, 1955.
A definitive study of the myth of the American Adam in the nineteenth century and of some of the tragic collisions to which its moral and spiritual pretensions were exposed in the literature of the last two centuries.

Marx, Leo. *The Machine in the Garden: Technology and the Pastoral Ideal in America.* New York: Oxford UP, 1964.
An examination of the development of nineteenth-century American literary pastoralism as a response to the social, political, and emotional threat of the rise of industrialization.

Matthiessen, F. O. *American Renaissance: Art and Expression in the Age of Emerson and Whitman.* New York: Oxford UP, 1941.
A classic study of the American literature of the mid-nineteenth century that displaced the Fireside Poets as the preeminent authors of the period with a new canon that included Emerson, Thoreau, Whitman, Hawthorne, and Melville.

Michaels, Walter Benn. *The Gold Standard and the Logic of Naturalism.* Berkeley: U of California P, 1987.
An exploration of the way literary and other cultural forms helped create value in the emergent environment of corporate capitalism at the end of the nineteenth century, as the literary romance mitigated the experience of alienation, trompe l'oeil painting served as a critique of money, and the contract became a device that eroticized slavery.

Miller, Perry. *Errand into the Wilderness.* Cambridge: Harvard UP, 1956.
A work that summarizes some of the themes that circulated in Miller's numerous and often majesterial studies of the Puritan mind, from the role of the jeremiad in American culture to the place and function of millenarianism in the American psyche.

Poirier, Richard. *The Renewal of Literature: Emersonian Reflections.* New York: Random, 1987.
A recuperation of a pragmatist tradition of American writing that runs from Emerson and the elder Henry James through William James, Gertrude Stein, Robert Frost, and Wallace Stevens to John Ashbery and, furthermore, shows how this body of writing, in addition to providing a countertradition to the high modernism of Ezra Pound and T. S. Eliot, may suggest a cultural alternative to postmodernism.

Reynolds, David. *Beneath the American Renaissance: The Subversive Imagination in the Age of Emerson and Melville.* New York: Knopf, 1988.
  A path-breaking study that rereads the work of what are here held to be the seven major writers of the middle years of the nineteenth century (in addition to Emerson, Thoreau, Hawthorne, Melville, and Whitman—Edgar Allan Poe and Emily Dickinson) against the background of a rich but little-known world of sensational and popular literature on which they drew for many of their themes, characters, settings, and even idioms.

Rorty, Richard. *Contingency, Irony, and Solidarity.* Cambridge: Cambridge UP, 1989.
  A more effective demonstration than any of his other books that Rorty has breathed new life into pragmatist motifs and concerns and resituated them at the center of contemporary cultural existence.

Ruland, Richard, and Malcolm Bradbury. *From Puritanism to Postmodernism.* London: Routledge, 1991.
  A literary history from the colonial era to the present that reflects the shift from ideological explorations of essential American myths to a pragmatic concern with the conversation between different American rhetorics and styles.

Trachtenberg, Alan. *Reading American Photographs: Images as History, Mathew Brady to Walker Evans.* New York: Hill, 1989.
  An analysis of the translation of the history of American photographs into a social text. The approach not only affords a new way of reading that history but turns it into a theory of how American culture has itself been read.

Works Cited

Bourdieu, Pierre. *Outline of a Theory of Practice.* Trans. Richard Nice. Cambridge: Cambridge UP, 1977.

Jay, Martin. *The Dialectical Imagination: A History of the Frankfurt School and the Institute of Social Research.* Boston: Little, 1973.

Kosselleck, Reinhart. *Future's Past: On the Semantics of Historical Time.* Trans. Keith Tribe. Cambridge: MIT P, 1985.

Poirier, Richard. *The Performing Self: Compositions and Decompositions in the Languages of Contemporary Life.* New York: Oxford UP, 1971.

The End of "American" Literature: Toward a Multicultural Practice

Gregory S. Jay

Jay's essay originally appeared in an issue of College English *(1991), but it sparked so much discussion that an essay collection,* The Canon in the Classroom *(1994), edited by John Alberti, was published presenting the*

From *College English* 53.3 (1991): 264–81.

essay with several responses to it. Jay begins with the radical notion that universities should no longer teach American literature. While he is pleased with recent progress in expanding the canon, he notes that these pluralistic revisions do not dismantle the "oppressive nationalist ideology" that has framed our study of American literature. Jay attempts to make visible the power dynamics and privilege that affect how cultural history and literature are reproduced and institutionalized. He believes a responsible pedagogy is multiculturalism at its best—one that seeks to foster dialogue with the Other. Jay is quick to distinguish his brand of multiculturalism from assimilationist "melting pot" rhetoric that attempts to erase difference.

Rather than promoting a literary history based on fabricated consensus, Jay proposes replacing it with a history rooted in a geographical and historical paradigm, which allows us to see the borders between the United States, Canada, and Mexico as the products of our history rather than its origins. Similarly, the lines between cultural groups within the United States would be seen as permeable borders that allow for cultural exchange. The argument for dismantling American literature and replacing it with "Writing in the United States" pushes one to question the current approach to American literary studies. According to Jay, we must not merely expand the canon but disrupt and problematize our notion of the field. This would entail addressing how assimilation and translation inform American literature. American literature must be reconceived as a study of "how various cultural groups and their forms have interacted during the nation's ongoing construction" (pp. 57–58) Jay concludes his essay with a practical discussion of what his revised Writing in the United States course might look like. For example, rather than organizing the syllabus by period or by theme, he proposes arranging the course along a list of problematics that would place texts from different cultural groups into dialogue with each other. While noting that his list of possibilities is not exhaustive, Jay recommends origins, power, civilization, tradition, assimilation, translation, bodies, literacy, and borders. Instructors interested in this approach may find it beneficial to arrange their syllabi according to a set of problematics and to base their reading selections on representative responses to these issues.

> The failure of the melting-pot, far from closing the great American democratic experiment, means that it has only just begun. Whatever American nationalism turns out to be, we see already that it will have a color richer and more exciting than our ideal has hitherto encompassed. In a world which has dreamed of internationalism, we find that we have all unawares been building up the first international nation.
>
> —Randolph Bourne

It is time to stop teaching "American" literature. The combined lessons of critical theory, classroom practice, and contemporary history dictate not only a revision of the curriculum and pedagogy of "American" literature courses, but a forceful uprooting of the conceptual model defining the field itself (Bercovitch; Elliot; Kolodny). On the one hand this means affirming the reforms that have taken hold at numerous institutions and in a number of new critical studies and anthologies, such as *Three American Literatures*, edited by Houston Baker, and the monumental achievement of Paul Lauter and his colleagues in *The Heath Anthology of American Literature*. On the other hand it means pointing out that many of these reforms have only been pluralist in character. (JanMohamed and Lloyd make the case against pluralism, while Ravitch upholds it.) They add a few new texts or authors without dismantling the prejudicial framework which has traditionally pre-scribed the kinds of works studied in "American" literature courses and the kinds of issues raised in "American" literary scholarship. That scholarship thus continues to depend upon, and reproduce, the oppres-sive nationalist ideology which is the nightmare side of the "American dream." Our goal should be rather to construct a multicultural and di-alogical paradigm for the study of writing in the United States.

The recent work of Adrienne Rich exemplifies a literary and cul-tural criticism that neither colonizes nor excludes the Other, but tries to read, think, and feel the differences that our bodily locations—in history, in geography, in ethnicity, in gender, in sexual orientation—can make. Rich's "politics of location" would begin not with the continent or nation "but with the geography closest in—the body." She would

> pick up again the long struggle against lofty and privileged abstrac-tion. . . . Even to begin with the body I have to say that from the outset that body had more than one identity [female, white, Jewish, middle-class, Southern, North American, lesbian, etc.]. . . . Two thoughts: there is no liberation that only knows how to say "I"; there is no collective movement that speaks for each of us all the way through.
> And so even ordinary pronouns become a political problem. . . .
> Once again, Who is *we*? (212–13, 215, 224, 231)

This mapping of the located body graphically resists the abstract lib-eral humanism which, for all its accomplishments, continued to force the Other to assimilate to the values and interests of an idiosyn-cratic though hegemonic Western self, and it attacks the complacency of that self in regarding its image as unitary, normative, and universal. Rich's argument closely resembles those made by postmodern anthro-pologists and ethnographers such as James Clifford, who writes that "once cultures are no longer prefigured visually—as objects, theaters, texts—it becomes possible to think of a cultural poetics that is an in-terplay of voices, of positioned utterances" (12). For Rich and Clifford multiculturalism is a dialogue among (and within) socially constructed bodies and subject positions. Students of writing in the United States will become like Clifford's "indigenous ethnographers," self-conscious both of the positions they write from and the positions they describe.

Thus I want to heed the warning of Guillermo Gómez-Peña not to "confuse true collaboration with political paternalism, cultural vampirism, voyeurism, economic opportunism, and demagogic multiculturalism" (133). I have to be self-conscious about the politics of the "we" in my own essay. In part it refers to a set of dominant groups I participate in—European-American, male, middle-class, heterosexual, US citizen, educated, institutionalized, and so on—and I speak to those groups about our need to deconstruct the basis of our own privileges. Danger (leading to "demagogic multiculturalism") lies in imagining that oppression is always someone else's responsibility. Before we get too busy celebrating our position at the forefront of the liberation of the culture, we must recognize that we are often the problem. It is our racism, our sexual prejudices, our class anxieties, our empowered desires that we must confront and resist. The unconscious character of these biases means that we cannot be complacent or comfortable even with the conscious avowal of our positions (as in this essay), for that can always be a defensive reassertion of our authority. Some who might read this essay do not belong to many of these privileged groups, so that their relation to the pronoun "we" will be different. In that case "I" and "you" and "we" may also operate performatively, in utopian fashion, as they do in the texts of Walt Whitman and of Rich—as invocations to the possibility of community. "What is it then between us?" asks Whitman: "What is the count of the scores or hundreds of years between us? . . . I too had received identity by my body" (130). In reference to our location in the United States, or the US, the problematic US indicates the specific heterogeneity of our cultural history and the difficulty of speaking for, or about, it in a univocal voice. Thus my decision to use the abbreviation for the remainder of the essay in order both to evoke and symbolically subvert the nation's identity. To play ungrammatically on Rich's question, the motto for American criticism should become: "Once again: Who is US?"

The history and literature of the US have been misrepresented so as to effectively underwrite the power and values of privileged classes and individuals. We should act on the now clichéd observation that literary judgments have always already been political; our responsibility for justice in cultural education requires more self-criticism than we have yet shown. We have to make explicit, and sometimes alter, the values at work in our schools and scholarship (see Giroux). We have to engage in struggles to change how the cultural history and writing of the US get institutionalized and reproduced. The movement toward multicultural literacy reflects more than a dedication to intellectual and historical accuracy; it expresses our sense that the legacy of nationalism must be reevaluated and that multicultural experience is our imperative reality. US multiculturalism is a living actuality we cannot escape and whose configurations we must begin to fathom, even as renascent nationalisms (here and elsewhere) pose serious political and theoretical questions. A commitment to multicultural education also belongs to our historical moment as we witness a renewed interest in democracy, and as we ask how a democratic culture might be fashioned. The contemporary failure of democracy in the US derives from oppressive social practices (material and ideological) that act against certain marked individuals, categorizing them as marginal to the interests of the nation. A responsible pedagogy requires a vigilant criticism of racism and discrimination in all their forms, aesthetic as well as political. It is the duty of educators to oppose the practices which today tolerate and even encourage cultural chauvinism and the violence of bigotry.

Aren't there dangers as well as values in multiculturalism? Diane Ravitch argues that a proper multiculturalism teaches respect for the diversity of America's "common culture" (and so is pluralistic), while a dangerous multiculturalism advocates conflicting ethnocentrisms and implies that "no common culture is possible or desirable" (and so is particularistic) (340). But the choice should not be posed as one between a common culture and chaotic ethnic rivalries. Any recourse to a notion of a national culture risks reimposing a biased set of principles or historical narratives, and Ravitch is conspicuously silent on what the content of that common culture may be. On the other hand, she is right to warn that replacing Eurocentrism with a series of ethnocentrisms would only multiply the original problem. With Elizabeth Meese I would urge that we avoid thinking of multicultural literacy as a process designed to foster or prop up an identity, whether of a person or a tradition or a nation or a school of criticism (31–32). Rather multicultural study should put people into a dialogue with the Other—with the subjects that have historically formed the boundaries of their cultural experiences. Essentialism does not have to be the result of affirmative action, especially if one understands the latter as affirmation of the Other and not of one's self. Our commonality is not a substance or essence (Americanness) but a process of social existence predicated on the espoused if not always realized principles of cultural democracy, political rights, community responsibility, social justice, equality of opportunity, and individual freedom. When these principles are subordinated to totalizing ideologies seeking to invent or impose a common culture, then the actual multicultural life of Americans suffers an oppression that is in no one's best interests.

A strong connection ties the historical development of a theory and institutional practice of American literary studies to the modern history of nationalism. The anxiety to invent an American nation and the anxiety to invent a uniquely American literature were historically coincident. As long as we use "American" as an adjective, we reinforce the illusion that there is a transcendental core of values and experiences that are essentially "American," and that literary or cultural studies may be properly shaped by selecting objects and authors according to how well they express this essence. This metaphysical approach has shaped American literary theory ever since the first attempts to invent a uniquely American literature in the 1820s, and has persisted throughout every theory that has used arguments for American exceptionalism. Current revisionary critiques show that the "American" of conventional histories of American literature has usually been white, male, middle- or upper-class, heterosexual, and a spokesman for a definable set of political and dual interests. Insofar as women, African and Asian and Native Americans, Hispanics, gays and lesbians, and others make an appearance in such histories, it is usually in terms of their also being made into spokesmen for traditional values and schemes. Their "assimilation" into American literature comes at the cost of their cultural heritage and obscures their real antagonism and historical difference in relation to the privileged classes.

The "melting pot" is a crock, as great and pernicious a myth in literary history as it is in social and political history. Today we are moving away from the myth of assimilation and into the struggle to create a just multicultural society that respects the values and practices of distinct if interdependent groups. Cultural education must aim to represent historically that ours always has been a multicultural society and that the repression of this heterogeneity (usually in the service of one group) ultimately threatens the cultural vitality and even survival of every group within it. In contrast, past histories of American literature have been active functionaries in reproducing the hegemony of culturally privileged groups. From 1882 to 1912 (and beyond), observes Nina Baym, "textbook writers made literary works and authors display the virtues and achievements of an Anglo-Saxon United States founded by New England Puritans" (459). This narrative served the purpose of "Americanizing" and assimilating the growing industrial and immigrant classes: "Paradoxically, the non-Anglo-Saxon could become American only to the extent of their agreement that only those of Anglo-Saxon lineage were really Americans" (463; see Bourne). At the level of class, the ambitions and disappointments of exploited workers could be mediated by an education in transcendentalism: "What more likely to deflect the (usually foreign-born) poor from their desire to have a substantial piece of the country's settled wealth than exposure to an idealism from whose lofty perspective the materialist struggle would seem unworthy?" (462). Literary history fabricated a symbolic consensus that papered over real social contradiction as a social practice pedagogy manufactured compliant subject positions (see Graff, *Professing* 130–32, 209–25).

I propose that we replace the idealist paradigm with a geographical and historical one. Our focus of study ought to be "Writing in the United States." The objects of study will be acts of writing committed within and during the colonization, establishment, and ongoing production of the US as a physical, sociopolitical, and multicultural event, including those writings that resist and critique its identification with nationalism. Organizing courses on the bases of national entities inevitably reproduces certain biases and fallacies, and we need to protect against these by including specific theoretical questions and methodological devices in the curriculum. Or we could simply rename our discipline "Comparative American Literature," or establish courses and programs in North American studies that would integrate the cultural history of the US with those of Canada, Mexico, the near Latin American countries, and the Caribbean, though this could end up repeating the history of colonial imperialism at the level of academic study. Still, the borders between these nations are less the origins of our history than the products of it.

Our peoples and writers have been flowing back and forth over the space these boundaries now delineate since before the colonial adventure began. These borders make little sense when one is studying the histories, say, of Native- or Hispanic- or African-American literature. This crossing of boundaries, as José Saldívar and others argue, becomes the paradoxical center of Mexican-American and Chicano literature, for example, which has been violating borders of nationality and of language since the 1500s (see Saldívar, Gómez-Peña; Rosaldo). How does one categorize a work like Rudolfo Anaya's *Bless Me, Ultima*, which crosses so many of these linguistic and cultural divides? What "Americanist" pedagogy could do justice to the traditions, historical representations, and contexts of utterance in *Black Elk Speaks* or James Welch's *Fools Crow*? Can the borders between Native-, Hispanic-, and Anglo-American literature be drawn without recalling the political treacheries that imposed a series of violated borders upon indigenous peoples and settlers from Mexico, borders that were shifted whenever white economic interest dictated, so that Hispanic- and Native-American cultures come to be an "outside" within the "inside" of "America"?

Within the boundaries of the US, the lines between cultural groups do not form impassable walls, though they often take oppressive shape. Historically these zones are an area of constant passage back and forth, as each culture borrows, imitates, exploits, subjugates, subverts, mimics, ignores, or celebrates the others. The myth of assimilation homogenizes this process by representing it as the progressive acquiescence of every other group to a dominant culture. Writers who analyze this myth often depict the experience instead under the metaphor of "passing"—as in to "pass" for white, for gentile, for straight, for American. The "object of oppression," writes Cherríe Moraga, "is not only someone outside of my skin, but the someone inside my skin" (30). Thus there are borders within, as well as between, our subject positions. This "divided consciousness" (to recall the phrasing of W. E. B. Du Bois) affects every group and individual with a specificity that must be understood and felt.

Language is a primary vehicle for passing, and literary critics should study the manner in which the formal development of genres and movements participates in its rituals and contradictions. As we highlight the politics of linguistic assimilation—of the consequences for non-English-speaking people who must learn to speak and write the master's tongue—we can exploit the pun in the phrase "Writing in the United States." "Writing" here designates not simply a static set of objects, but the process of verbal or textual production in its historical and dynamic sense, and in the sense of what a speaker or writer experiences when she or he attempts to write within the boundaries of the US (see Baker, *Journey* 1–52; Gates, *Figures* 3–58). If we replace the term "literature" with "writing" we can resist the cultural biases built into the former term and institutionalized by departments that have built their curriculum around the privileged genres developed in modern Europe. Writing, or textuality if you prefer, names events of representations, and so includes previously marginalized forms and media as well as canonical forms produced by marginalized people.

Historically, "Writing in the United States" would begin with Native-American expressive traditions and include those narratives produced by the first European explorers and colonizers, Spanish and French as well as English. This would effectively decenter histories of American literature which have always placed their origins in the Anglo-Saxon culture of Puritan New England (see Reising 49–91). That culture was a culture of the Book—of the Bible—which confronted an oral culture among the Native Americans. The cultural and literary politics of this confrontation require consideration, as does the problematic of translation it dictates. The survival of Native-American discourse henceforth began to depend on its translation into written form, often through the mediation of whites, or on the translation of native experience into white expression in the public speeches and documents produced by Native Americans in defense of their lands and rights. The literary history of the US includes the story of how the destruction of Native-American culture was essential to the literary and political invention of "America," as the struggle for culture coincided with the struggle for land. The boundaries of "Writing in the United States" could thus be drawn geographically and historically, not linguistically, through attention to the demographics of cultural populations, as we witness the dialogical interaction of succeeding generations of natives and arrivals from Europe, Africa, Asia, and Latin America. "Writing in the United States" would then be placed within the history of colonialism and imperialism, as well as nationalism, better providing a foundation for comprehending the current political and social dilemmas facing the US as it reconceives itself as a multicultural society in a multicultural world.

The nationalist biases I have referred to are built into the organization of academic literary study. For about a century we have had departments of English, French, German, Spanish, Portuguese, Italian, and so forth. These were originally conceived as the modern heirs to the tradition of classical philology, and centered on the study of language, with literature read as an illustration of the history of linguistic development. This philology, like the New Criticism that replaced it, was never entirely a formalism, for it inevitably reproduced the cultural values of the canonical texts it studied. Many language faculties advocated more cultural study in the curriculum, until a basic ambiguity haunted these departments: Were they designed to teach the history of a language or the history of a nation? (Graff, *Professing* 55–120). The question, as in the case of English, became vexing when languages crossed national borders and historical periods. When the *interpretation* of literary texts, as opposed to their philological description or use for historical documentation, became of significant institutional concern, the very rationale for language-based departments began to crumble, though we have not yet faced this fact or imagined real alternatives.

"English" is a misnomer for departments offering courses in psychoanalysis, Derrida, postcolonialism, film theory, feminism, Native-American autobiography, and Chicano poetry. "Indeed," says Annette Kolodny, "no longer can we hold to the linguistic insularity implied by the Americanist's presence in departments of *English*" (293). I would side with Kolodny against William Spengemann, who concludes that because "American" does not designate a language, we ought to abandon efforts to conceive an American literary history and instead return to the study of texts written in English, specifically those great texts that have markedly changed the language itself. Spengemann tumbles into tautology and circular reasoning when he advocates a canon based on the linguistic practices of modernism: Only those past texts that belong to modernism's history get into the canon, and modernism is the origin of the canon because past experiments in literary language lead to it.

In the study of US writing, the exclusion of texts not written in English or of authors drawing heavily on non-European sources limits the canon with pernicious results. One cannot even adequately interpret works in American English without some knowledge of the various cultures surrounding and informing them. Most writing produced here after the eighteenth century, moreover, borrows words, characters, events, forms, ideas, and concepts from the languages of African-, Hispanic-, Jewish-, Native-, and Asian-Americans. At the same time speakers and writers from these different cultures adapt the English language to create hybrid forms and texts. When analyzing writers such as Frederick Douglass, Isaac Singer, or Leslie Silko, a background in Chaucer or Restoration drama or imagist poetry may be less helpful than studying, say, the traditions of religious representation of the author's native people. The problematics of assimilation and translation inform writing in the US with a complexity that has scarcely been recognized or theorized. One could argue that the study of US writing cannot be adequately pursued within the boundaries of the English department, for this comparative project ultimately subverts the very premises of that academic organization.

Though I believe in an historical approach to writing, it will suffer the same deconstruction of boundaries as any approach that tries to impose artificial limits on language or geography. US history cannot be represented a priori as a totality, a unity, or a grand story whose plot and hero we already know. A chief model for modern literary nationalism is that historiography which represents the nation as a collective self, a figurative mind or spirit which is realizing its great soul through the unfolding progress of the national community's history. Not surprisingly, this fiction has often been compared to the *bildungsroman*, and we are familiar with the claims it makes on us, from *The Autobiography of Benjamin Franklin* to the testimony of Oliver North. The metaphorical self used to figure such national histories, of course, turns out to wear the idealized face of a very real class or group of individuals—in the West, what we now handily call white patriarchy. The spiritual story of the nation's quest to realize its dream turns out to be a set of writing practices that participates in the manipulation, exploitation, repression, and even genocide of those subjects deemed peripheral to the tale.

Of course undoing the canon doesn't just mean adding on previously excluded figures; it requires a disturbance of the internal security of the classics themselves. In gay studies, for example, cultural revision extends beyond including avowedly same-sex oriented writers in the curriculum. Gay studies extends to questioning the sexual economies of ambiguous and (supposedly) straight texts—to the ways they police their desires. According to Eve Sedgwick one "could neither dismantle" the canon "insofar as it was seen to be quite genuinely unified by the maintenance of a particular tension of homo/heterosexual definitional panic" nor "ever permit it to be treated as the repository of 'traditional' truths that could be made matter for any true consolidation or congratulation." Since "the problematics of homo/heterosexual definition, in an intensely homophobic culture, are seen to be precisely internal to the central nexuses of that culture," teasing out these contradictions in classic texts reveals the subversiveness and repression integral to them, so that "this canon must always be treated as a loaded gun" (148). Because patriarchy reproduces itself through "the stimulation and glamorization of the energies of male-male desire," it must also incessantly deny, defer, or silence their satisfaction, forming the double-bind characteristic of much male writing; thus she remaps the territory of Leslie Fiedler by exposing the ties that bind homophobia and misogyny. The mask of identity worn by the straight man covers over a split subject, from Hawthorne and Melville to James, Eliot, Fitzgerald, Hemingway, Mailer, and beyond.

The literary history of the US ought to be represented not by "*the* American" and "*his* dream," but in terms of how various cultural groups and their forms have interacted during the nation's ongoing construction. As Meese explains, once we abandon notions of literature's intrinsic value and look instead at the contingencies of writing's use values, we may stop thinking in terms of canons altogether. The "history of literature," she writes, "if it seems necessary to create such a thing, might then be a description of the uses to which texts have been put" and of the value writings have had for their subjects (33; see Smith). Such a history would have many protagonists, wearing many faces, speaking many languages, recalling divergent histories, desiring different futures. Syllabi and critical studies could be focused around contestation rather than unity, putting to work in this area the principle Graff has dubbed "teaching the conflicts." Instead of selecting a set of books and authors that express a previously agreed-upon list of characteristics that are "uniquely American," we could assemble texts that openly conflict with each other's assumptions, terms, narratives, and metaphors. These conflicts, moreover, should settle national generalities by reference to the specific pedagogical locality—to the state, region, city, area, and social group of the students, the professor, and the institution.

My own involvement in African-American literature, for example, though precipitated by the Civil Rights movement of the 1960s, received its professional impetus from my being hired—fresh from an education in California and New York—to teach the American literature survey course at the University of Alabama in 1980. I felt strongly the responsibility to develop a multicultural curriculum, with specific attention to black writers. The politics of my pedagogical location would offer me a tough but simple lesson: these students knew a lot more about racism—consciously and unconsciously—than I did. Texts and authors that I thought I knew read differently in their eyes, and to me through them. I began to juxtapose Franklin's *Autobiography* with the *Narrative of the Life of Frederick Douglass*. (The semester ended with a paper contrasting William Faulkner and Alice Walker.) Franklin's optimistic assertion that the individual can rise from poverty and obscurity to fame and power appeared both denied and confirmed by Douglass's escape from slavery and rise to international celebrity. It was intriguing that both men saw the achievement of literacy as the key to freedom, and both made their careers through the material production of books and newspapers. Could both be assimilated to "the American Dream"?

The inescapable differences between them, however, could be found when one located their writings and careers in terms of their historical bodies, especially as regards the relation of the legal system and state power to myths of individual freedom and achievement. Franklin's rise came through his genius for manipulating the legal systems of discourse; Douglass's literacy was literally a crime, and his very claim to "manhood" a violation of the dictates of the state. The ideology of individual accomplishment that Franklin has been used to promote shows up as hollow in Douglass's case, betraying even Douglass's own complicity in it. Trained in that ideology, however, as well as in the discourse of racism, the majority of my white students wanted to read both Franklin and Douglass as presenting allegories of how the individual could triumph no matter the laws or powers of the state, since that belief is precisely what allows the law and the power of the state to go unchallenged and allows the individual to continue in the complacent myth of autonomy.

For many of my black students, who were attending a recently integrated bastion of white academic racism, these materials presented an uneasy situation. They did not desire to be drawn into open hostility with their white classmates and were sensitive to the bad effects of being located in one's historical body. Many were tired of being the token black or being asked to speak for their people on every occasion, rather than for themselves. Their pride in Douglass was muted by their puzzlement over just how to express their feelings in an oppressive context, which included me—a white instructor. Ultimately we had to make these and other local tensions the subject of classroom discussion, to teach these conflicts to each other by openly questioning the relation of reading to race and of race to individual achievement. Many students began to open up, telling personal stories of their experience of racial and class difference; at that point I had to undo my position as the liberal champion, always a dangerous delusion, and reinscribe myself as another white American, one who had grown up in Los Angeles but had never heard of Watts until he watched black rioters burn it down from the cool comfort of his backyard swimming pool. Racism to me had always been someone else's problem; now I began to feel my own participation in its history. I could criticize racism, but I would never be black (just as I could criticize sexism or homophobia, yet never know them quite as women or gays and lesbians did).

At that time I also began teaching a unit of Jewish-American literature. I had to spend hours in the library researching the history of American Judaism and the details of its culture, despite the fact that my own father was a Jew and my great-grandfather an Orthodox rabbi. I was myself, I realized, the split subject of assimilation. Jewish-American literature provides a useful vantage point for multicultural study, since the Jew both belongs to the hegemony of European cultural tradition and has been the excluded Other within the body of that culture. While Jewish-American writers, critics, and intellectuals have been very successful in securing recognition in the US, they have also made the pathos and incompleteness of their assimilation a constant subject of address. (Among literary critics the classic career of assimilation is that of Lionel Trilling, whose dissertation and first book enacted an identification with Matthew Arnold.) The complexity of these realities is captured brilliantly in Tillie Olsen's *Tell Me a Riddle*, where the contrast between Jewish-American and Mexican-American assimilation unfolds a multicultural fable of the politics of recollected identities.

The autobiographical basis of my illustration may seem gratuitous, but it isn't. By bringing the writing home in this way teachers and students begin to feel the friction between ideological myths and particular histories. Anyone who has tried to teach feminism, for example, will testify to how the personal becomes the pedagogical. The dialogue can be confusing, passionate, humiliating, and transformative, demanding that everyone learn better what Teresa de Lauretis calls "the semiotics of experience" (158–86). If we are to recapture the rich diversity of life in the US, we will have to stop masquerading behind assumed poses of abstraction and generality, even if we continue—with Whitman and Rich—to use the "we" pronoun for utopian purposes. As a teacher I cannot speak on behalf of a united cultural vision or tradition, and I don't want to borrow authority from an ideology that gives me power at the cost of truth.

Historically I belong to a class and generation raised in the knowledge of one tradition, and brought by theory, history, and experience to seek a knowledge of others. My bookshelves are filling with texts and authors never mentioned to me in school. It will take years to begin to absorb them or to know how to speak or write with confidence. Of course I could go on writing about Hawthorne or James or Eliot, but that, I think, would be irresponsible. It would also be less difficult and less interesting than meeting the ethical challenge to undertake what Kolodny describes as a "heroic rereading" of those uncanonized works "with which we are least familiar, and especially so when they challenge current notions of art and artifice." Armed with the criticism and scholarship of the past twenty years, revisionists should "immerse themselves in the texts that were never taught in graduate school—*to the exclusion of the works with which they had previously been taught to feel comfortable and competent*" (302).

What practical consequences can be drawn from such a reading lesson? We should probably abandon even a reconstructed version of the American literature survey course. No one- or two-semester course can possibly live up to the implied claim of historical or representative coverage; coherence is usually bought at the cost of reductive scenarios resting on dubious premises. At best one can construct courses that take the question "What is an American?" as their only assumption and then work through close readings of texts chosen for the radically different answers they provide (for curricular alternatives see Lauter, *Reconstructing*). The result is more of a rainbow coalition than a melting pot. Facile pluralism might be avoided through demonstrations of the real conflicts between texts and cultures. I advocate courses in which the materials are chosen for the ways in which they *actively interfere* with each other's experiences, languages, and values and for their power to expand the horizon of the student's cultural literacy to encompass peoples he or she has scarcely acknowledged as real.

The socially constructed ignorance of teachers and students will be a hard obstacle to multicultural literacy, for the knowledges it requires have been largely excluded from the mainstream classroom, dissertation, and published critical study. Teachers have enough trouble trying to supply their students with information on the literary forms, historical contexts, and cultural values shaping *The Scarlet Letter* or *The Red Badge of Courage* or *The Waste Land*. Think of the remedial work for everyone when we assign David Walker's *Appeal*, Catharine Sedgwick's *Hope Leslie*, Harriet Jacobs's *Incidents in the Life of a Slave Girl*, Judith Fetterley's anthology *Provisions: A Reader from 19th Century American Women*, William Wells Brown's *Clotel*, Whitman's *Calamus*, Charlotte Gilman's *Herland*, Jacob Riis's *How the Other Half Lives*, Agnes Smedley's *Daughter of Earth*, the poetry and prose of Langston Hughes, the *corridos* of the Southwest, Scott Momaday's *House Made of Dawn*, Audre Lorde's *Zami*, Maxine Hong Kingston's *The Woman Warrior*, or the stories of Bharati Mukherjee.

In terms of method, this reeducation sharpens our ability to discern the various ways a text can participate in (or even produce) its context; in terms of pedagogy, it makes the literature classroom part of a general project of historical recollection, analysis, and criticism; in terms of politics, it confronts the institution, the teacher, and the student with the imperative to appreciate the achievements of distinct cultural groups, which cannot be whitewashed with humanistic clichés about the universality of art, the eternal truths of the soul, or the human condition. In sum, a multicultural pedagogy initiates a cultural re-vision, so that everyone involved comes not only to understand another person's point of view, but to see her or his own culture from the outsider's perspective. This decentering of cultural chauvinism can only be healthy in the long run, especially if it leads each of us to stop thinking of ourselves as subjects of only one position or culture.

From the standpoint of literary theory, this approach treats written works as active agents in the socio-political process. This need not mean, as numerous critics have shown, abandoning attention to the formal properties of writing. On the contrary, it strengthens that focus by locating the historical and material specificity of those forms and by charting how they take effect, are appropriated or transformed in concrete contexts. This *does* mean that purely formalist generic categories such as "the novel" or "the elegy" or "tragedy" be called back from the hazy pedagogy of a naïve aestheticism. Theorists from Virginia Woolf and Kenneth Burke to Jameson and Baker and beyond have shown that forms of writing are socially symbolic actions. Styles are linguistic and material practices that negotiate between the binary illusions of documentation and fabrication, or history and fiction. In other words, a renovated rhetorical criticism can frame the written work as an historical utterance, as addressed both to the cultural traditions it draws upon and to the audiences it assumes or even transforms (see Mailloux). Such forms as the slave narrative (produced for abolitionists) or the Native-American autobiography (as told to an ethnographer) provide rich opportunities for deconstructing our categories and concepts of literary authorship and production.

Clearly a multicultural reconception of "Writing in the United States" will lead us to change drastically or eventually abandon the conventional historical narratives, period designations, and major themes and authors previously dominating "American literature." "Colonial" American writing, as I have already suggested, looks quite different from the standpoint of postcolonial politics and theory today, and that period will be utterly recast when Hispanic and Native-American and non-Puritan texts are allowed their just representation. What would be the effect of designating Columbus's *Journal*, the *Narrative of Alvar Nuñez Cabeza de Vaca*, or the creation myths of Native peoples as the origins of US literature, rather than Bradford's *Of Plymouth Plantation*? To take another example, the already shopworn idea of the "American Renaissance," probably the most famous and persistent of our period myths, ought to be replaced by one that does not reinforce the idea that all culture—even all Western culture—has its authorized origins in Greco-Roman civilization. The period of 1812–1865 would better be called that of "America during the Wars," since the final colonial war and the wars to take the property of the Native Americans and Mexican-Americans and to keep enslaved the bodies of African-Americans dominated the socio-political scene and heavily determined its literary output, including that of such canonical figures as Cooper, Hawthorne, Melville, Emerson, and Thoreau. This designation would bring back the historical context and along with it the verbal productions of those marginalized groups or cultures which were busy representing themselves in a rich array of spoken and written discourses. The transformation of this period has already begun through emphasis on Native- and African-American texts and on the writing of women in this period, many of whom were actively engaged in these political struggles. Likewise the era of "Modernism" as the period of Eliot, Pound, Stevens, Williams, Hemingway, and Faulkner has been shattered by questions about the gender and race limitations of this historical construct, prompting renewed attention to Stein, H. D., Moore, and Barnes and a reconsideration of the Harlem Renaissance.

Take finally the currently fashionable tag "postmodern," originally used in literary studies to categorize the self-reflexive fiction of white men (Barth, Coover, Barthelme, Vonnegut, Pynchon) who struggled with the legacy of their modernist fathers. In the popular formulation of Jean-Francois Lyotard, postmodernism names a period without "metanarratives," a sort of extended epistemological and semiotic version of what we used to call the death of God. From his locations in

Paris and Irvine, however, Lyotard sees this as the crisis of peculiarly disembodied, abstract, and metaphysical concepts, whereas these meta-narratives belong to the ideological apparatus of identifiable institutional and historical groups. As Edward Said points out in his critique of Lyotard, the (supposed) breakdown of the metanarratives of "emancipation" and "enlightenment" cannot be comprehended as solely an internal event of Western civilization. The collapse of Western metaphysical metanarratives, especially those of what is called "the Subject," is (and it's no coincidence) contemporary with the struggle of non-European populations and countries for historical self-determination — for the freedom to be agents rather than subjects.

According to Said, Lyotard "*separates* Western postmodernism from the non-European world, and from the consequences of European modernism — and modernization — in the colonized world." Moreover, the crisis of legitimacy characterizing Western modernism involved

> the disturbing appearance in Europe of various Others, whose provenance was the imperial domain. In the works of Eliot, Conrad, Mann, Proust, Woolf, Pound, Lawrence, Joyce, Forster, alterity and difference are systematically associated with strangers, who, whether women, natives, or sexual eccentrics, erupt into vision, there to challenge and resist settled metropolitan histories, forms, modes of thought. (222–23)

Once one puts the color back into postmodernism, if you will, then the period's inseparability from postcolonialism appears crucial. And this is not simply a matter of discerning the origins of modernism's traumatized consciousness in the West's confrontation with its Others or even of deconstructing the representations of those Others passed off by dominant discourses. Postcolonialism means recognizing, or at least trying to find a way to read, the texts produced by dominated peoples, and acknowledging their participation in narratives of resistance. The literary and cultural works of the marginalized during the nineteenth and twentieth centuries, then, suddenly appear as part of the ongoing development of a postmodern literature, insofar as they contradict the metanarratives of Western modernism. One could argue that, among "Americans" writing in English, a different canon of post-moderns could be compiled from the explosion of texts by contemporary African-, Asian-, and Native-American writers (see Vizenor).

Themes, like periods, derive from and are determined by a previously canonized set of texts and authors. The classic themes of American literature — the Virgin Land, the Frontier West, the Individual's conflict with Society, the City versus the Country, Innocence versus Experience, Europe versus America, Dream versus Reality, and so on — simply make no sense when applied to marginalized texts and traditions, including those produced by women. Thematic criticism can be especially discriminatory since these are by definition repeated elements of a totality or metanarrative centered in an historically limited point of view, though thematic criticism regularly universalizes that perspective and so transforms an angle of insight into an oppressive ideological fabrication. The cartoon simplicity of these themes serves as a mask for this ideological pretension: It presents a partial experience in the form of an eternal verity, thus at once obstructing any analysis of the historical construction of that perception or any analysis of viewpoints that don't conform to the theme or which lose their difference and cultural truth when they are made to conform to the theme.

To supplement or replace periods and themes as points for organizing classes and critical studies, I would offer rather a list of problematics whose analysis would put texts from different cultures within the US into dialogue with one another. Unlike a theme, a problematic does not designate a moment in the history of the consciousness of a privileged subject. A problematic rather indicates an event in culture made up simultaneously of material conditions and conceptual forms that direct the possibilities of representation. A problematic acts as one of the determinants of a representation, though it does not operate as an origin. A problematic indicates how and where the struggle for meaning *takes place*. Each of us could construct a list of problematics conditioning US writing, but for illustrative purposes I would argue for the following: (1) origins, (2) power, (3) civilization, (4) tradition, (5) assimilation, (6) translation, (7) bodies, (8) literacy, and (9) borders. While these problematics have indeed been addressed by some writers, and thus may appear to be themes, I want to resist reducing them to intentionalities or structures of consciousness. Having touched on most already, I want to end by saying something more about origins and power.

The deconstruction of metaphysical ideas about origins played a key role in the development of poststructuralist criticism and initially was resisted by advocates of marginalized groups, who rightly insisted on the need to affirm and recollect the difference of their beginnings (Gates, "The Master's Pieces"). I think we have a consensus today that no choice exists between essentialism and nihilism, as they are two sides of the same metaphysical coin. Because of the historic destruction of dominated (sub)cultures by privileged classes, much writing by women and persons of color tries to recover traditions rather than rebel against them. But as Michael Fischer argues, ethnicity is less an essence than a constantly traversed borderland of differences, "something reinvented and reinterpreted in each generation by each individual. . . . Ethnicity is not something that is simply passed on from generation to generation, taught and learned; it is something dynamic, often unsuccessfully repressed or avoided" (195). This process of recollection does not entail a simple nostalgia or the dream of recreating a lost world: more painfully and complexly it involves a risky translation of recovered fragments into imagined futures by way of often hostile presents.

"The constituency of 'the ethnic,'" writes R. Radhakrishnan, "occupies quite literally a 'pre-post'-erous space where it has to actualize, enfranchise, and empower its own 'identity' and coextensively engage in the deconstruction of the very logic of 'identity' and its binary and exclusionary politics" (199). What should be resisted are myths of origin that function in totalitarian fashion; what should be solicited are myths of beginning that delineate the historical and cultural specifics of a group's experiences and interactions (see Said's *Beginnings*). In multicultural studies we examine multiple sites of origin and multiple claims to foundational perspectives. Rather than adjudicate between these claims in a timeless philosophical tribunal, the student of culture ought to analyze the historical development of the conditions for these narratives and the consequences of their interactions. This would mean, for example, contrasting the disparate creation myths of Native and Puritan Americans and speculating upon how the values embodied in these myths shaped the outcome of the conflict between these groups.

Thus a deconstructive thinking about origins can work along with a politically charged criticism that affirms a dialogue with the Other, so that multicultural study need not lead to the metaphysical dead end of "identity politics." This point is made with exemplary tact by Meese in her chapter on Silko's *Ceremony* (29–49). The novel's choice of a "half-breed" protagonist and multiracial cast of characters and the plot turns that entangle them make it impossible, she argues, to interpret it as calling for a return to a fabled purity of Indian identity. Instead a more intricate process of "crossing cultures" gets represented and played out, one that analyzes the changing economy of values between acculturated subjects—and between that economy and the values of the reader.

Michel Foucault stressed the inseparability of knowledge and power, a problematic he revolutionized by using his experience as a gay man to rethink its traditional scenario. Multicultural studies cannot evade the question of power, since power is both a prime subject for analysis and a constitutive element of the situation of the analysis: the student and the professor are empowered in relation to the object of study, and this disciplinary power usually has its affiliations with distributions of power along lines of gender, region, class, age, ethnicity, and so on. While texts may be studied as expressions of struggles for power, and while we may reflect self-consciously on how scholarship participates in the institutions of power, we should not forget the cautions offered by poststructuralism regarding the fallacies of reference and mimesis. We cannot assume the veracity of a text's representations, and the powers of a text are certainly not confined to its correspondence to an objectively verifiable reality. We must discern how texts take power—how they gain power through the modes of their composition as well as through the modes of their (re)production.

The canonical status of a text is often justified by reference to its superior "power" and its endurance ascribed to the timeless claim it makes on readers. In response we need to question the aesthetics of power and the power of aesthetics. Once one demonstrates that the power of a text to move a reader is a culturally produced effect—that literary "taste" is not natural but taught, and taught in a way that reproduces values that go beyond aesthetics—then the issue of power becomes of vital pedagogical concern. Yet no teacher or text can ensure that the student will receive the letter as it is prescribed. No pedagogy or text, no matter the care of its address, can predetermine exactly the effect it has on everyone, for everyone's subjectivity is plural. Moreover texts are not clear messages or simple unities but occasions when a mediation of conflicts is symbolically enacted. Teachers have the responsibility to empower previously marginalized texts and readers, and to teach in a way that we risk surprising and painful changes in the interpretive habits, expectations, and values of our students—and of ourselves. If we acknowledge that the aesthetic power of a text is a function of the distribution of material and cultural power in society, our pedagogy cannot help but become politically embroiled. In teaching students to value other cultures and other worldviews we necessarily draw them with us into conflicts with the dominant culture that has produced and sustained our identities and which has the power to enforce its opinions as law. At the same time, we as readers and writers may become agents of change, not just subjects of discourse; we may draw or take power from the canon, from history, from the institution, and turn it in unexpected directions. "We" can fight the power.

Works Cited

Baker, Houston A., Jr. *The Journey Back: Issues in Black Literature and Criticism.* Chicago: U of Chicago P, 1980.

———, ed. *Three American Literatures.* NY: MLA, 1982.

Baym, Nina. "Early Histories of American Literature: A Chapter in the History of New England." *American Literary History* 1 (1989): 459–88.

Bercovitch, Sacvan. "America as Canon and Context: Literary History in a Time of Dissensus." *American Literature* 58 (1986): 99–108.

Bourne, Randolph. "Trans-National America." *Atlantic Monthly*, July 1916: 86–97.

Clifford, James. Introduction. "Partial Truths." Clifford and Marcus 1–26.

Clifford, James, and George E. Marcus, eds. *Writing Culture: The Poetics and Politics of Ethnography.* Berkeley: U of California P, 1986.

de Lauretis, Teresa. *Alice Doesn't: Feminism, Semiotics, Cinema.* Bloomington: Indiana UP, 1984.

Elliot, Emory. "New Literary History: Past and Present." *American Literature* 57 (1985): 611–25.

———. "The Politics of Literary History." *American Literature* 59 (1987): 268–76.

Fischer, Michael M. J. "Ethnicity and the Post-Modern Arts of Memory." Clifford and Marcus 194–233.

Foucault, Michel. Afterword. "The Subject and Power." *Michel Foucault: Beyond Structuralism and Hermeneutics.* Ed. Herbert L. Dreyfuss and Paul Rabinow. 2nd ed. Chicago: U of Chicago P, 1983.

Gates, Henry Louis, Jr. *Figures in Black: Words, Signs, and the "Racial" Self.* NY: Oxford UP, 1987.

———. "The Master's Pieces: On Canon Formation and the African American Tradition." *South Atlantic Quarterly* 89 (1990): 89–112.

Giroux, Henry A. "Liberal Arts Education and the Struggle for Public Life: Dreaming about Democracy." *South Atlantic Quarterly* 89 (1990): 113–38.

Gómez-Peña, Guillermo. "Documented/Undocumented." *The Graywolf Annual Five: Multicultural Literacy.* Ed. Rick Simonson and Scott Walker. Saint Paul: Graywolf, 1988.

Graff, Gerald. *Professing Literature: An Institutional History.* Chicago: U of Chicago P, 1987.

———. "Teach the Conflicts." *South Atlantic Quarterly* 89 (1990): 51–68.

JanMohamed, Abdul R., and David Lloyd. Introduction. Special issue on "The Nature and Context of Minority Discourse." Vol. 1. *Cultural Critique* 6 (1987): 5–12.

Kolodny, Annette. "The Integrity of Memory: Creating a New Literary History of the United States." *American Literature* 57 (1985): 291–307.

Lauter, Paul, ed. *The Heath Anthology of American Literature.* 2 vols. Boston: Heath, 1989.

———, ed. *Reconstructing American Literature: Courses, Syllabi, Issues.* Old Westbury, NY: Feminist P, 1983.

Lyotard, Jean-Francois. *The Postmodern Condition: A Report on Knowledge.* Trans. Geoff Bennington and Brian Massumi. Minneapolis: U of Minnesota P, 1984.

Mailloux, Steven. *Rhetorical Power.* Ithaca: Cornell UP, 1989.

Meese, Elizabeth. *(Ex)Tensions: Refiguring Feminist Criticism.* Urbana: U of Illinois P, 1990.

Moraga, Cherríe. "La Guera." *This Bridge Called My Back: Writings by Radical Women of Color.* Ed. Cherríe Moraga and Gloria Anzaldúa. NY: Kitchen Table P, 1983.

Radhakrishnan, R. "Ethnic Identity and Post-Structuralist Difference." *Cultural Critique* 6 (1987): 199–220.

Ravitch, Diane. "Multiculturalism: E Pluribus Plures." *American Scholar* (Summer 1990): 337–54.

Reising, Russell. *The Unusable Past: Theory and the Study of American Literature.* NY: Methuen, 1986.

Rich, Adrienne. *Blood, Bread, and Poetry: Selected Prose 1979–1985.* NY: Norton, 1986.

Rosaldo, Renato. "Politics, Patriarchs, and Laughter." *Cultural Critique* 6 (1987): 65–86.

Said, Edward W. *Beginnings: Intention and Method.* NY: Basic, 1975.

———. "Representing the Colonized: Anthropology's Interlocutors." *Critical Inquiry* 15 (1989): 205–25.

Saldívar, José David. "The Limits of Cultural Studies." *American Literary History* 2 (1990): 251–66.

Sedgwick, Eve Kosofsky. "Pedagogy in the Context of an Antihomophobic Project." *South Atlantic Quarterly* 89 (1990): 139–56.

Smith, Barbara Herrnstein. *Contingencies of Value: Alternative Perspectives for Critical Theory.* Cambridge: Harvard UP, 1988.

Spengemann, William. "American Things/Literary Things: The Problem of American Literary History." *American Literature* 57 (1985): 456–81.

Vizenor, Gerald. "A Postmodern Introduction." *Narrative Chance: Postmodern Discourse on Native American Indian Literatures.* Albuquerque: U of New Mexico P, 1989: 3–16.

Whitman, Walt. *Leaves of Grass and Selected Prose.* Ed. Lawrence Buell. NY: Random, 1981.

Considering Literary
and Social Movements

Many instructors struggle with how to make literature accessible to their students, particularly when the material seems so removed from students' lives. While I often begin class discussions with student responses to the literature, I want to make sure that we not only consider the text from our current vantage point but also attempt to approach the work from its own sociohistorical context. The further back in time we go, the harder this gets. When I teach the literature of the Harlem Renaissance, it can be a stretch to get students to see the significance of race since so many of them think we are beyond racism, but it is even more of a stretch to provide the context for Thoreau's *Walden* or Jonathan Edwards's *Sinners in the Hands of an Angry God*. The nature of American culture and society continues to change, but an understanding of past literary and social movements helps contextualize these changes.

This collection of essays on Puritanism, modernism, the New Negro Movement, and postmodernism, while not an exhaustive discussion of literary and social movements, highlights earlier periods and complements the works frequently taught in American literature survey courses. For instance, Puritanism is often seen as a difficult topic to address; however, with the rise of the evangelical movement and students' increased investment in their religious views, the topic begins to seem less remote. Emory Elliott's "1670: The American Jeremiad" shows Puritanism's continued influence despite its passing by tracing the development and persistence of the jeremiad. Puritan minister Reverend Samuel Danforth established a model followed by New England clergy of the 1670s and 1680s, taking sermons "from the Book of Jeremiah, in which the Old Testament prophet chastised the Hebrews for their loss of religious zeal and their fall from God's favor" (pp. 72–73). Elliot argues that these sermons, known as jeremiads, are evident in the twentieth and twenty-first centuries, such as when F. Scott Fitzgerald employed the jeremiad to examine the nation's failures in *The Great Gatsby*.

Daniel Joseph Singal notes the difficulty of characterizing modernism in his essay, "Towards a Definition of American Modernism." According to Singal, the modernist worldview conceives of the universe as unpredictable and moral absolutes thus impossible to sustain; one of the fundamental aspects of modernism is the idea that morality must fluctuate and adapt to changing circumstances. Singal's essay concludes by pointing toward the beginning of postmodernism.

The New Negro Movement, also known as the Harlem Renaissance, is clearly both a social and literary movement. According to Venetria K. Patton and Maureen Honey's "Revisioning the Harlem Renaissance," the literature of the period reflects the self-assertive character of the "New Negro," who would no longer be satisfied with second-class citizenship. The literary movement was an outgrowth of civil rights organizations, which sought to prove the humanity of African Americans by showcasing their creative abilities. *The Crisis* and *Opportunity* (publications of the National Association for the Advancement of Colored People and the National Urban League, respectively), sponsored literary contests and award programs to showcase the best and brightest and to forge connections between black writers and white publishers. These same publications—as well as *The Messenger* and *The Nation*—can be excellent sources for contextual material that paints the scene of the period's race relations. For example, students might read W. E. B. Du Bois's "Returning Soldiers," Marcus Garvey's "The Future as I See It," Langston Hughes's "The Negro Artist and the Racial Mountain," excerpts from Zora Neale Hurston's "Characteristics of Negro Expression," and Richard Wright's "Blueprint for Negro Writing" to get a sense of black and white relations in general as well as an understanding of the concerns of African American writers specifically.

While many of the essays in this chapter seek to define a particular literary or social movement, Jason Gladstone and Daniel Worden's essay, "Introduction: Postmodernism, Then," is inspired by the declaration of postmodernism's demise. The authors note the recent trend to dismiss postmodernism in favor of finding continuity between post-1945 literature and modernism. They seek to find common ground between those who have abandoned postmodernism and those who continue to see its value as an organizing principle.

Although the essays included here discuss very different movements, they all point toward the difficulty of definition. The contours of these movements tend to be blurred and participants may have ideological differences; however, there is enough of a connection to allow these diverse individuals to coalesce and form a social movement. They form a collective identity in relation to their particular movement, an identity that can only be fully appreciated by addressing their particular socio-historic context.

1670: The American Jeremiad

Emory Elliott

In this essay taken from Greil Marcus and Werner Sollors's 2009 collection A New Literary History of America, *Elliott demonstrates the continued relevance of the American Jeremiad beyond the Puritans. He begins by providing the history of the jeremiad, which can be traced back to Reverend Samuel Danforth, and comes to the established formula: "recollection of the community's original joy and fervor; castigation for recent and current sins and backsliding; pleas for the congregation to repent and pray for forgiveness; and assurances that God will forgive his Chosen People and restore harmony" (p. 73). According to Sacvan Bercovitch, the jeremiad transformed from a rhetorical tool to frighten congregations to a ritual to assure triumph over their enemies. Because of the effectiveness of this ritual, the jeremiad remained after the passing of the Puritans. Elliott asserts that the jeremiad persists because of its effectiveness in inspiring ideals and motivating action. As examples, Elliott points to such diverse writers as Reverend Martin Luther King Jr., F. Scott Fitzgerald, Herman Melville, and Toni Morrison.*

I n 1670, during a very turbulent period for the Massachusetts Bay Colony's American Puritans, the Reverend Samuel Danforth preached his Election Day Sermon, "A Brief Recognition of New England's Errand into the Wilderness." Danforth took his text from Matthew II:7–9, where Jesus asks the people who sought out John the Baptist in the desert, "What went ye out into the wilderness to see?" As John's supporter, Jesus tells them that they went expecting to see a spectacle but they should have gone to listen to John preach the truth. As they, too, seemed to have forgotten their purpose, Danforth asked his listeners what their reasons were for going into the wilderness. He reminded them that for decades they had embraced their spiritual errand—but now they were succumbing to a "radical disease too tremendously growing upon us." He observed that the community was in the grip of a deadly "declension justly calling for so meet an antidote" as he had to offer. In his conclusion Danforth recalled that the first settlers had journeyed "over a vast ocean

---

From *A New Literary History of America*, eds. Greil Marcus and Werner Sollors (Cambridge: Harvard UP: 2009): 40–44.

into this waste and howling wilderness," which they had transformed into God's garden. But now, he said, "the vineyard is all overgrown with thorns, and nettles cover the face thereof, and the stone wall is broken down," and there was a "certain sign of calamity." In the final pages of his sermon, Danforth implored the people to acknowledge the falling away of their faith, confess their sins, and beg for forgiveness. He warned the newly elected leaders that if they did not take religion into consideration in all of their decisions, the people would know whom to blame if the dark days were to continue. If the leaders were to heed his guidance and the people to pray for grace and salvation, Danforth assured them that God would show his favor toward them again.

Fifty years before, in 1620, William Bradford and his small colony of Protestant religious separatists, later known as the Pilgrims, had arrived in New England to found Plymouth Plantation. After facing severe hardships during their first few years, the community of survivors became so successful that, starting in 1630, thirty thousand nonseparating English Congregationalists followed to establish the Massachusetts Bay Colony in Boston. In spite of a brutal war with the Pequot people in 1636 and many internal conflicts over theology and property, the Congregationalists—who were called Puritans by their enemies—built a thriving colony that, in the face of decades of persecution and war in England, attracted thousands more to Massachusetts between 1635 and 1660.

In 1649, the Puritan dissenters in England overthrew the monarchy and executed King Charles I. Oliver Cromwell and the English Presbyterians ruled England until their government collapsed, allowing King Charles II to return from France and restore the monarchy in 1660. Immigration to New England accelerated again after the Puritans lost power in England, but tensions arose when the newcomers could not meet the New England church's strict standards for conversion and church membership and were denied land and voting rights, which were reserved for the converted. Such privileges were also withheld from those adult children and grandchildren of the original settlers who had not had a conversion experience. While the clergy tried to sustain the original Calvinist doctrines and principles, bitter divisions occurred and many of the older members began to demand that their offspring be granted church membership so that they, rather than outsiders, would benefit from the wealth of the colony. A rancorous synod was held in 1662, and the Half-Way Covenant doctrine was devised to allow grandchildren of the founders to be baptized even if their parents were not converted. The 1660s marked a significant transition in New England from corporate assurance and religious fervor to a decline of confidence in the churches and communities.

Throughout the 1670s and 1680s, the New England clergy followed Danforth's model by taking many of their sermon texts from the Book of Jeremiah, in which the Old Testament prophet chastised the

Hebrews for their loss of religious zeal and their fall from God's favor. Twentieth-century scholars, such as Perry Miller, have called these sermons "jeremiads." Texts in this genre follow a standard formula: recollection of the community's original joy and fervor; castigation for recent and current sins and backsliding; pleas for the congregation to repent and pray for forgiveness; and assurances that God will forgive his Chosen People and restore harmony. Because the Puritans believed that the Bible and nature should both be closely studied for signs of God's intentions, they were acutely alarmed by a series of terrible events that occurred in these years: earthquakes, plagues, violent storms, explosions and fires in towns and aboard ships, murders and suicides—all providing evidence of God's anger. A few sermon titles from those decades indicate the prevailing themes and tone: "Righteousness Rained from Heaven"; "Days of Humiliation, Times of Affliction"; "The Day of Trouble Is Near"; "Nehemiah on the Wall in Troublesome Times." The most devastating event in these decades was the conflict known as King Philip's War (1674–1676). This war with the Wampanoag people, whose leader, Metacom, was known as Philip to the English, resulted in the loss of 10 percent of the population on each side, making it one of the bloodiest wars ever fought in North America.

While the jeremiads are especially valuable as indicators of the mood and direction of individual churches and communities, many other sermons were devoted to domestic themes—including marriage, the family, the rearing and instruction of children, fairness in business—as well as to a range of theological subjects. Sermons were high points in the week of the congregation. While most church members valued education and were literate, the Puritans were suspicious of all forms of human verbal expression except that found in the Bible, and they considered entertainment sinful (which led them to close the theaters in London during their reign). Thus, sermons and the discussions of them provided the only challenging intellectual stimulation in the society, and it is not surprising that the community was centered around the weekly three-hour sermons preached on Thursdays and Sundays. Members of the congregation took notes, formed study groups for discussions, and debated their minister's interpretations of the scriptures. As scholars and teachers, most ministers possessed the education and rhetorical skills to inspire congregations through their own piety, faith, and learning. Indeed, the Puritans founded Harvard College in 1636 to ensure they would have a well-educated clergy. Because the Puritans believed that people should never presume to compete with the beauty of the Bible, the Puritan clergy practiced a "plain style" designed to convey ideas clearly and without embellishment. They did, however, employ figurative language powerfully and extensively to dramatize their message.

While many Puritan sermons were published in the seventeenth century, few scholars had much interest in those printed texts until the

1930s, when Perry Miller brought his considerable analytical talents to the subject and proposed that Puritan sermons should be studied as literary art, as they offer a "way of conceiving the inconceivable, of making intelligible order out of the transition from European to American experience." For Miller, the sermons were not pedagogical tools; rather, they were dramatic narratives that enabled their audiences to form images and allegories in which they imagined themselves to be part of the unfolding of a sacred history. Miller demonstrated that, through Puritan typology, the clergy and colonial magistrates had produced a myth of America. Through their New Covenant with God, the colonists in the New World became the new Chosen People, members of a new Zion, a new Israel. The center of the Christian world no longer resided in Europe but was now in New England, where it would remain a beacon for those predestined to be converted and saved. For the Puritans, the American continent had been held in reserve by God until this evil time of corruption and persecution had emerged in Europe. God had revealed the New World to enable the exodus of his Chosen People, who would found a Christian utopia there and prepare the way for the new millennium and the return of Christ on the Last Day. The jeremiad always moves from God's wrath to reassurance because, having established a covenant with His Chosen, God would never abandon them.

In his extension and revision of Miller's research on the jeremiad, Sacvan Bercovitch has argued that in time the jeremiad ceased to be a rhetorical tool for frightening congregations into reform and became instead a ritual. From the opening of a jeremiad, listeners knew that the ending would depict a repentant congregation, reassurance of God's love, and the promise of a more zealous and more prosperous future. In Bercovitch's view, the jeremiad ritual was mainly intended to assure them that they would always triumph over sin, Satan, and their enemies. This ritual proved so effective that it did not fade away when the Puritans passed into history.

For many years, in State of the Union addresses and Fourth of July orations, American presidents have offered similar jeremiads. They follow Danforth's familiar formula: we must beware of enemies who plot to destroy us; we must acknowledge the gap between our ideals and current realities; we must reject corruption, greed, selfishness, and other sins; and finally, we must work together to restore our superiority among the world's nations. With God on our side, we shall continue the American mission and fulfill our sacred Manifest Destiny. Bercovitch points out that, as Max Weber argued early in the twentieth century, the Puritan emphasis on working hard in one's earthly calling while seeking spiritual salvation functions well with the spirit of capitalism. From early on, the Puritans had difficulty keeping God's grace and business profits separated. Those who appeared to be genuinely pious seemed to be the same people who grew wealthy. One of the Reverend Samuel Willard's sermons, "Heavenly Merchandize; or the Purchasing of TRUTH Recommended and the Selling of it Diswaded," was written to appeal to the religious pragmatism of his parishioners, who were members of what was known as the merchants' church. The Puritans might have difficulty understanding Weber's or Bercovitch's arguments; their behavior unconsciously reflected a recognition of the ways that the spiritual calling and the material calling, as they understood them, could yield heavenly and earthly rewards at the same time.

The tragic events of the Salem witchcraft trials in the summer of 1692 brought Puritan standards of judgment into question. Community leaders like Samuel Sewall were humbled by their fatal errors and the shattering results, and they began to change their religious and political thinking. By the late 1690s, there were few remnants of the fusion of religion and politics that Perry Miller described as "Federal Theology." Many elements of Puritan thought and practice would endure in American culture in more subtle forms, however — appearing, for example, in Benjamin Franklin's *Autobiography* and other works as a secular version of Puritanism.

In the two years leading up to the American Revolution, the Protestant clergy played a key role in arousing a rather indifferent populace to embrace the spirit of revolt. When the British Parliament passed the Port Bill, several clergymen held a traditional Puritan fast day and preached jeremiads invoking biblical images of the British as tools of "Satan," who had unleashed "the great Whore of Babylon" to ride her "great red dragon" upon America. Of this event, Thomas Jefferson declared: "This day of fasting and humiliation was like a shock of electricity throughout the colonies, placing every man erect." John Adams asked Abigail to urge their local ministers to preach similar jeremiads, and after the war Tories like Peter Oliver and Thomas Hutchinson attributed the success of the Revolution to the "black regiment," the dark-clothed ministers who had encouraged their congregations. During the Civil War, clergymen on both sides again employed the jeremiad to inspire support for their cause.

In the twentieth and twenty-first centuries, the jeremiad has persisted because of its effectiveness in creating mythic imagery that inspires ideals and motivates action. In 1963, in his "Address to the March on Washington for Jobs and Freedom," Reverend Martin Luther King, Jr., depicted the United States as a great country with strong religious traditions that had gone astray. He called for a return to the original ideals of social equality expressed in the Declaration of Independence, and he urged a reassertion of the American dream of freedom and equality for all men and women. Many American writers of the past hundred years adopted the jeremiad pattern to compose their stories; in *The Great Gatsby*, F. Scott Fitzgerald used it to examine the failures of the nation, as symbolized in *Gatsby* by the 1919 Chicago Black Sox scandal. From Melville to Morrison, the list of American novels and plays that follow the jeremiad form would be very long. Since the destruction of the World Trade Center at the start of this century, a host of nonfiction books have appeared that critique the failures in American society that led to that disaster and seek answers for restoring the country to an earlier stability and security. Books on the environment today also follow the formula of failure, blame, reform, and projections of a future that will fulfill original goals and ideals. Every year at Independence Day celebrations, the president and other military and political figures around the country invoke the formula of the jeremiad in remembering the courage and persistence of the Puritans and the revolutionary founders of this nation, lamenting the decline of patriotism and self-sacrifice, and holding up the promise that soon the country will recall the proper direction of its errand into the wilderness.

Bibliography

Bercovitch, Sacvan. *The American Jeremiad* (Madison, WI, 1978).

Danforth, Samuel. "A Brief Recognition of New-Englands Errand into the Wilderness. Made in the Audience of the General Assembly of the Massachusetts Colony, at Boston in N. E. on the 11th of the third Moenth, 1670. Being the Day of Election there," in *American Sermons*, ed. Michael Warner (New York, 1999).

Hall, David. *The Faithful Servant: A History of New England Ministry in the Seventeenth Century* (Chapel Hill, NC, 1972).

Looby, Christopher. *Voicing America: Language, Literary Form, and the Origins of the United States* (Chicago, 1995).

Miller, Perry. *The New England Mind: From Colony to Province* (Cambridge, MA, 1939).

Wald, Priscilla. *Constituting America: Cultural Anxiety and Narrative Form* (Durham, NC, 1995).

Winship, Michael P. *Seers of God: Puritan Providentialism in the Restoration and Early Enlightenment* (Baltimore, 1996).

Towards a Definition of American Modernism

Daniel Joseph Singal

In "Towards a Definition of American Modernism," Singal notes that although there is no consensus regarding what constitutes modernist culture, there is a growing agreement about what it is not. Singal distinguishes between modernization *and* modernism, *two related but distinct terms. According to Singal, modernization, a process of social and economic development, is characterized by the rise of industry, technology, and urbanization, while modernism is a culture with a set of related beliefs, ideas, and values. Singal associates modernism with efforts to order the human*

From *American Quarterly* 39.1 (1987): 7–26.

*experience despite the chaos of the twentieth century, and puts it on par
with such historical moments as Victorianism and the Enlightenment.*

*Singal describes the development of American modernism by consider-
ing Victorianism, European Modernism, and cubism. According to Singal,
the modernist worldview "begins with the premise of an unpredictable
universe where nothing is ever stable, and where accordingly human beings must be satisfied with knowledge that is partial and transient at
best" (p. 86). He concludes by addressing the beginning of the end of
modernism in the 1960s and the move toward postmodernism. Singal's
essay originally appeared in* American Quarterly *in 1987.*

"On or about December 1910, human character changed." So declared Virginia Woolf in a statement that virtually all subsequent writers on Modernism have felt obliged to quote. Though historians
tracing the origins of Modernist culture have quarreled with Woolf's
exact choice of date, they have increasingly come to agree that sometime
around the turn of the century the intelligentsia in Europe and America
began to experience a profound shift in sensibility that would lead to
an explosion of creativity in the arts, transform moral values, and in
time reshape the conduct of life throughout Western society. Modernism, Peter Gay reports, "utterly changed painting, sculpture, and music;
the dance, the novel, and the drama; architecture, poetry, and thought.
And its ventures into unknown territory percolated from the rarefied
regions of high culture to general ways of thinking, feeling, and seeing."
Indeed, notwithstanding the growing evidence that a new sensibility
of "postmodernism" has recently made its appearance, many writers
would contend that Modernism itself has served as the dominant culture of twentieth-century America from the period just after the First
World War up to the present.[1]

Although there is assuredly no consensus on exactly what Modernist culture is, there does seem to be a growing accord on what it is not.
Perhaps the commonest misconception is the practice of equating it
with "modernization," a concept emanating from Max Weber and still
fashionable among many social scientists. Put simply, Modernism
should properly be seen as a *culture*—a constellation of related ideas,
beliefs, values, and modes of perception—that came into existence during the mid to late nineteenth century, and that has had a powerful
influence on art and thought on both sides of the Atlantic since roughly
1900. *Modernization*, by contrast, denotes a *process* of social and economic development, involving the rise of industry, technology, urbanization, and bureaucratic institutions, that can be traced back as far as the
seventeenth century. The relationship between these two important
historical phenomena is exceedingly complex, with Modernism arising
in part as a counterresponse to the triumph of modernization, especially
its norms of rationality and efficiency, in nineteenth-century Europe

and America. Despite that initial hostility, however, the Modernist stance toward modernization has typically been marked by ambivalence, with Modernists simultaneously admiring the vitality and inventiveness of technological progress while decrying the dehumanization it appears to bring in its wake. Thus, despite the etymological similarity, Modernism and modernization must be sharply differentiated; nor should "modern" and "Modernist" ever be treated as synonyms.[2]

Another problematic view of Modernism equates it exclusively with the philosophy and style of life of the artistic avant-garde at the turn of the twentieth century. "Modernism" in this sense usually connotes radical experimentation in artistic style, a deliberate cultivation of the perverse and decadent, and the flaunting of outrageous behavior designed to shock the bourgeoisie. The entire movement, according to this definition, was comprised essentially of a small number of highly talented poets and painters based on the bohemian quarters of certain large cities, such as Paris, New York, Vienna, and Berlin, culminating around the time of the First World War in the work of such "canonical" masters as Picasso, Pound, and Joyce. A variation on this definition, put forth by literary critics like Irving Howe and Lionel Trilling, allows Modernism slightly more range by viewing it as an "adversary culture" originating in bohemia but later adopted by twentieth-century intellectuals in their growing estrangement from mass society, and ultimately reappearing as a virtual parody of its earlier self in the form of the 1960s counterculture. In either case, this perspective sees Modernist thought as essentially negative and rebellious in character, and far too amorphous ever to be susceptible to definition.[3]

As the present essay will attempt to show, however, there is a more recent and far more satisfactory approach to Modernism that takes issue with the "bohemian" interpretation, contending that those writing in the Trilling tradition confuse the tip for the whole iceberg by focusing on the more visible and spectacular manifestations of the culture during its period of ascendancy while missing its underlying structure. Far from being anarchic, Modernist thought in this view represents an attempt to restore a sense of order to human experience under the often chaotic conditions of twentieth-century existence, and it most assuredly does contain a unifying principle if one knows where to look. Not just the plaything of the avant-garde, it has assumed a commanding position in literature, music, painting, architecture, philosophy, and virtually every other realm of artistic or intellectual endeavor. Moreover, Modernism in this formulation has cast its influence well beyond the intellectual elite to encompass much of contemporary middle-class Western society. Its values, though somewhat diluted, are held by a majority of present-day Americans, and its style is manifested in such diverse contexts as suburban architecture, television advertising, and popular music. In short, the definition being proposed here suggests that Modernism deserves to be treated as a full-fledged historical culture much like Victorianism or the Enlightenment, and that it supplies nothing less than the basic contours of our current mode of thought.

To locate the inner dynamics of Modernism and to see how it came into being, it is necessary to return briefly to the culture against which the early Modernists rebelled. Victorianism, whose reign in America ran roughly from the 1830s to the early twentieth century, was closely associated with the rapidly expanding urban bourgeois class of that era. Its guiding ethos was centered upon the classic bourgeois values of thrift, diligence, and persistence, so important for success in a burgeoning capitalist economy, along with an immense optimism about the progress that industrialization seemed sure to bring. At the same time, Victorian culture, with its ideal vision of a stable, peaceful society free from sin and discord, proved immensely helpful in enabling the members of this new middle class to keep their balance in a world that was changing very fast, in ways they did not always expect or understand.[4]

At the core of this new culture stood a distinctive set of bedrock assumptions. These included a belief in a predictable universe presided over by a benevolent God and governed by immutable natural laws, a corresponding conviction that humankind was capable of arriving at a unified and fixed set of truths about all aspects of life, and an insistence on preserving absolute standards based on a radical dichotomy between that which was deemed "human" and that regarded as "animal." It was this moral dichotomy above all that constituted the deepest guiding principle of the Victorian outlook. On the "human" or "civilized" side of the dividing line fell everything that served to lift man above the beasts — education, refinement, manners, the arts, religion, and such domesticated emotions as loyalty and family love. The "animal" or "savage" realm, by contrast, contained those instincts and passions that constantly threatened self-control, and which therefore had to be repressed at all cost. Foremost among those threats was of course sexuality, which proper Victorians conceived of as a hidden geyser of animality existing within everyone and capable of erupting with little or no warning at the slightest stimulus. All erotic temptations were accordingly supposed to be rooted out, sexual pleasure even within marriage was to be kept to a minimum, and, as Nancy F. Cott has shown, the standard of respectable conduct, especially for women, shifted decisively "from modesty to passionlessness." A glorious future of material abundance and technological advance was possible, Victorians were convinced, but only if the animal component in human nature was effectively suppressed.[5]

Equally important was the way this moral dichotomy fostered a tendency to view the world in polar terms. "There is a value in possibilities," Masao Miyoshi observes, ". . . but the Victorians too often saw them in rigid pairs — all or nothing, white or black." Sharp distinctions were made in every aspect of existence: Victorians characterized societies as either civilized or savage, drew a firm line between what they considered superior and inferior classes, and divided races unambiguously into black and white. They likewise insisted on placing the sexes in "separate spheres," based on what Rosalind Rosenberg describes as "the Victorian faith in sexual polarity," which deemed women as "by nature emotional and passive," while men were "rational and assertive." Such dichotomies, it was believed, were permanently rooted in biology and in the general laws of nature. The "right" way, the moral way, was to keep these various categories distinct and segregated.[6]

Put in slightly different terms, what the Victorians aspired to was a radical standard of innocence. They were engaged in an attempt to wall themselves off as completely as possible from what they regarded as evil and corruption, and to create on their side of the barrier a brave new world suffused, in Matthew Arnold's words, with "harmonious perfection." Nineteenth-century thinkers, writes Donald H. Meyer, "longed for a universe that was not just intelligible, reassuring, and morally challenging, but symphonic as well." To be sure, actual behavior at times seemed to undercut this pursuit of innocence, but the point is that for the Victorian middle class innocence still remained a powerful and almost universal cultural ideal. Even when behavior diverged from it, as doubtless happened quite often, the ideal continued to be venerated. Nor was the Victorian ethos regarded as especially oppressive by the great majority of its nineteenth-century middle-class adherents. Rather, in the context of their experience it was both comforting and distinctly uplifting—a set of values that offered moral certainty, spiritual balm, and the hope that civilization might at last rid itself of the barbaric baggage remaining from humankind's dark, preindustrial past.[7]

Nevertheless, by the end of the century various individuals in Europe and the United States were beginning to chafe under the burden of Victorian repression and to challenge their inherited culture in different ways. A belief developed that modern bourgeois existence had become perilously artificial and "over-civilized," and that the degree of self-control that Victorian morality required of each individual was stultifying the personality. "Many yearned to smash the glass and breathe freely," writes T. J. Jackson Lears, "to experience 'real life' in all its intensity." In most instances, though, these early rebels should be seen as post-Victorians rather than incipient Modernists, for they did not at bottom desire to overthrow nineteenth-century moralism, but rather to temper or amend it in ways that would make it more bearable. Lears skillfully documents the various exotic devices they resorted to in their futile attempts to break with their conventional existence and regain contact with "reality." But, as he also shows, identifying with medieval knights or taking up Oriental religion were no more than safe substitutes for actual liberation and could not resolve the cultural crisis these people were caught up in. The overwhelming majority of post-Victorians were accordingly fated to dwell in a kind of no-man's land. "Wandering between two worlds," Lears reports, these victims of cultural transition typically "remained outsiders in both."[8]

The first true signs of Modernism appeared in Europe during the latter half of the nineteenth century in the form of a succession of small movements, each making its unique contribution to the new culture that was gradually coming into being. Most conspicuous at the outset were the French symbolist poets, beginning with Charles Baudelaire in the 1850s, who overturned the traditional mimetic conventions of art by writing as much about what was transpiring within their own minds as about events or objects in the "real" world. "Paint not the thing, but the effect it produces," ran Stephane Mallarmé's dictum. To that end, Symbolist verse employed highly allusive language and imagery that described the subject of the poem only indirectly, but conveyed as fully as possible the poet's emotional response to that subject. The Symbolists were soon joined by the Impressionist painters, who in similar fashion devalued the ostensible subject matter and resolved to capture on canvas their own subjective reactions. Both movements, in other words, moved beyond the stable, rational, and seemingly objective world decreed by nineteenth-century positivism in order to explore the far murkier and less predictable operations of human perception and consciousness. In Symbolism, Impressionism, and other allied movements, then, one sees emerging one of the foremost tendencies of Modernism—the desire to heighten, savor, and share all varieties of experience.[9]

At the same time developments taking place in more organized fields of thought were providing a philosophical underpinning for this urge to seek out experience. Writers as diverse as Henri Bergson, Friedrich Nietzsche, and William James agreed in rejecting the prevailing theory that divided the mind into separate compartments or "faculties," and in depicting experience as a continuous flux of sensations and recollections—what James would term "the stream of consciousness." That raw sensory flux, they concurred, was as close as human beings could come to knowing reality. Abstract concepts, along with all the other products of rationality that the Victorians had gloried in as the highest achievements of civilization, were seen as inherently faulty and misleading precisely because they represented an attempt to stop the experiential flow and remove knowledge from its proper dynamic context. A perception imprisoned in an abstraction was as lifeless and imperfect a model of reality as a butterfly impaled in a specimen box. As James insisted: "When we conceptualize we cut and fix, and exclude anything but what we have fixed, whereas in the real concrete sensible flux of life experiences compenetrate each other." To be sure, most of these early Modernist thinkers regarded rational concepts, especially the truths of science, as useful fictions that helped to get the world's work done, so long as those concepts were not confused with permanent truths. Yet the main thrust of their writings involved the obligation to loosen formal and rational restraints, expand one's consciousness, open oneself to the world, and perfect one's ability to experience experience—exactly what the Victorians had most feared.[10]

Further momentum for this cultural sea-change came from new findings in the physical sciences. "In the twenty years between 1895 and 1915," notes Alan Bullock, "the whole picture of the physical universe, which had appeared not only the most impressive but also the most secure achievement of scientific thought, was brought into question." The certainties of Newtonian mechanics, and the Euclidian geometry on which it was based, gave way to a new physics in which everything depended on the relative position and motion of the observer and the object being observed. Non-Euclidian versions of geometry abounded, all equally verifiable, until Henri Poincaré was led to suggest in 1902 that "one geometry cannot be more true than another; it can only be more convenient." Radical theoretical shifts that served to demolish a host of familiar and distinct concepts were taking place at both the cosmic and microscopic levels: Space, far from being a void, was now seen as filled by fields of energy, while the atom, far from being solid, was itself made up of tiny particles that orbited each other at a distance. The discovery of radium, demonstrating that seemingly solid matter could turn into energy, was shocking enough, but it was soon followed by Albert Einstein's proof early in the century that space and time could no longer be construed as separate and distinct entities, but must be placed on a continuum. Clearly, the new science had little use for the rigid, dichotomous categories that the Victorians had relied upon to organize their world; it was as enamored of dynamic process and relativism as the new philosophy and art.[11]

By the early twentieth century the profusion of artistic and intellectual movements was striking, especially in Paris, which was fast becoming the international center of Modernist activity. Most important during the first two decades of the century were Post-Impressionism, Cubism, Imagism, Vorticism, and the Italian variant, Futurism, to be followed after the war by Expressionism (mainly based in the Germanic countries), Dadaism, Surrealism, and Russian Constructivism—and eventually by Existentialism and Structuralism. Modernist masters came to dominate in all the arts, from Picasso, Cézanne, Braque, and Klee in painting, to Joyce, Pound, Eliot, and Malraux in literature, Stravinsky and Webern in music, along with Mies van der Rohe and Frank Lloyd Wright in architecture. Moreover, the new theories and values being fashioned by the intellectual elite were increasingly paralleled by similar developments at the level of popular attitudes and behavior, becoming unmistakable in the rampant consumerism and youth culture of the 1920s. In both cases the motor source was the same: a response to the cultural malaise brought about by late Victorian repression.

What all these various manifestations of Modernism had in common was a passion not only for opening the self to new levels of experience, but also fusing together disparate elements of that experience into new and original "wholes," to the point where one can speak of an "integrative mode" as the basis of the new culture. Put simply, the quintessential aim of Modernists has been to reconnect all that the Victorian moral dichotomy tore asunder — to integrate once more the human and the animal, the civilized and savage, and to heal the sharp divisions that the nineteenth century had established in areas such as class, race, and gender. Only in this way, they have believed, would it be possible to combat the fundamentally dishonest conception of existence that the Victorians had propagated, free the natural human instincts and emotions that the nineteenth century had bottled up, and so restore vitality to modern life. In the blunt words of William Carlos Williams: "Man is an animal, and if he forgets that, denies that, he is living a big lie, and soon enough other lies get going." In short, Modernists were intent on nothing less than recovering an entire aspect of being that their predecessors had tried to banish.[12]

Again and again, from art to social policy, Modernists have attempted to bring together that which the previous culture tried to keep separate. Far from being "the mere rehabilitation of the irrational," Malcolm Bradbury and James McFarlane write, Modernism involves "the interpretation, the reconciliation, the coalescence, the fusion — of reason and unreason, intellect and emotion, subjective and objective." McFarlane in fact identifies three stages in the development of the culture: a first stage of early rebellion (in other words, the bohemian stage that is often mistaken for the culture as a whole) during which "the emphasis is on fragmentation, on the breaking up and the progressive disintegration of those meticulously constructed 'systems' and 'types' and 'absolutes'" that the Victorians had assiduously created; a second stage marked by "a re-structuring of parts, a re-relating of the fragmented concepts"; and a final, mature stage characterized by "a dissolving, a blending, a merging of things previously held to be forever mutually exclusive." Thus, he concludes, "the defining thing in the Modernist mode is not so much that things fall *apart* but that they fall *together*"; the true end result of Modernism "is not disintegration but (as it were) superintegration."[13]

The most graphic manifestation of this integrative mode was certainly Cubism, a movement that deliberately sought to revitalize the experience of perception by challenging artistic conventions that had stood since the Renaissance. Since there was no such thing as fixed reality or truth, Picasso and his colleagues maintained, all objects would have to be seen in shifting relation to each other. The painter's task was thus to break up forms into component parts and have those parts continuously overlap, conveying not so much a sense of fragmentation as of wholeness. Sharp outlines were always to be avoided; rather, colors and textures were to bleed from one object into another, with subdued colors usually employed to enhance the sense of unity. Whenever possible, both the interior and exterior of a form were to be rendered alongside each other; likewise, the background was to have the same value and prominence as the main subject of the painting, and the two were to interpenetrate. Finally, in Cubist collage "found" objects from the "real" world, such as scraps of metal or pieces of newspaper, were to be incorporated into the work to juxtapose the spheres of aesthetic creation and everyday life, emphasizing how the painting was both a collection of pleasing shapes and colors on a flat surface *and* simultaneously a statement about perceived reality. In this manner, as Eugene Lunn tells us, the Cubists mounted their "revolutionary assault on the seeming stability of objects, which are taken apart, brought into collision, and reassembled on the picture surface" into a series of "contingent syntheses by which human activity and perception remake the world."[14]

This ever-present drive for integration explains so much about the history of Modernism. It allows one to make sense, for example, of the predilection of twentieth-century thinkers and writers for such devices as paradox (which joins seeming opposites) and ambivalence (the fusing of contradictory emotions, such as love and hate), and for their tendency to place concepts and empirical observations along a continuum or spectrum rather than in tightly demarcated categories. It also helps account for the practice of cinematic montage, with its juxtaposition of events and experiences; the attempt to break down boundaries between stage and audience in twentieth-century theater; the resort to multiple overlapping harmonies and rhythms in contemporary music, especially jazz (which also blends the primitivism of its African origins with modern sophistication); and the concern for maximizing the simultaneity of experience in literature—perhaps most fully achieved in Joyce's *Ulysses*, a novel structured, as Stephen Kern points out, so that "traditional dividers of sequence and distance collapse into a unified whole which the reader must envision after several readings." In the realm of social action, it was this stress on breaking down barriers that created the necessary cultural preconditions for the twentieth century's concerted campaigns to eliminate a "separate sphere" for women, and to overthrow that most noxious by-product of Victorian dichotomizing, racial segregation.[15]

Underlying all these efforts at integration has been the Modernist reconstruction of human nature. If the Victorians sought to place a firm barrier between the "higher" mental functions, such as rational thought and spirituality, and those "lower" instincts and passions that Freud would in time ascribe to the "id," Modernists strove to unite these two levels of the psyche. Thus where the Victorians held "sincerity" to be their most prized character trait, with its injunction that a person's conscious self remain honest and consistent, Modernists have demanded nothing less than "authenticity," which requires a blending of the conscious and unconscious strata of the mind so that the self presented to the world is the "true" self in every respect. This, as Trilling observes, represents a far "more strenuous" standard than did the code of sincerity, and necessitates precisely the sort of intense self-knowledge that the Victorians sought to avoid. Hence the resort to stream-of-consciousness technique in Modernist novels in order to capture what D. H. Lawrence called the "real, vital, potential self" as opposed to "the old stable ego" of nineteenth-century character.[16]

Yet it is just at this point that a massive paradox arises within the culture, for with the universe characterized by incessant flux, and human beings unable to know its workings with anything approaching certainty, the goal of perfect integration must always remain unattainable, at least within the natural world. Thus, although the Modernist seeks integration and authenticity, he or she must also be aware that they will never fully arrive. Nor would complete integration really be desirable, for that would mean stasis. The coalescing of the varied fragments of our contemporary existence can never be consummated, but must constantly be sought. The sole exceptions to this rule are found in self-contained intellectual systems such as mathematics, language or logic, as the logical positivists affirmed, or in imaginary settings conjured up for the purposes of art (though Modernist practice typically demands that artifice of this sort be clearly identified as such). Otherwise, all that pertains to nature and life must be construed dynamically, as a continuous process; the only lasting closure, in Modernist terms, come with death.

Here lies the reason why personal identity has often become problematic and tension-ridden for those living in the twentieth century. The Victorian expectation that a person be consistent and sincere rested on the assumption that character was defined largely by social role, which in turn was normally fixed by heredity, upbringing, and vocation. Accordingly, once an individual matured, any shift in his or her character was viewed with suspicion. By contrast, the Modernists, as Ronald Bush puts it, view human nature "in a state of continuous becoming." Neither the self, nor any work of art designed to portray the self, Bush explains, can achieve "completeness or closure"; such closure would automatically violate the criterion of authenticity. As a result, one must constantly create and re-create an identity based upon one's ongoing experience in the world. Difficult though this effort may be at times, nothing less will meet the Modernist standard.[17]

Finally, this paradoxical quest for and avoidance of integration accounts for the special role of the arts within Modernist culture. Precisely because they represent a realm where that quest can be pursued with relative safety through surrogate experience, the arts have become a medium for radical experimentation in new ways of amplifying perception, organizing the psyche, and extending culture. As Susan Sontag points out, art in this century "has come to be invested with an unprecedented stature" because of its mission of "making forays into and taking up positions on the frontiers of consciousness (often very dangerous to the artist as a person) and reporting back what's there." Art is aided in this task by its ready access to the devices of symbolism, metaphor, and myth, all of which, in Jerome Bruner's words, serve to connect "things that were previously separate in experience" and that cannot be joined through logic. Art in this way "bridges rationality and impulse" by fusing together metaphorically the objective and subjective, the empirical and the introspective—breaking apart conventional beliefs and rejoining the resulting fragments in a manner that creates relationships and meanings not suspected before. In short, where the Victorians saw art as didactic in purpose—as a vehicle for communicating and illustrating preordained moral truths—to Modernists it has become the principal means of creating whatever provisional order human beings can attain.[18]

Thus the Modernist worldview has taken shape. It begins with the premise of an unpredictable universe where nothing is ever stable, and where accordingly human beings must be satisfied with knowledge that is partial and transient at best. Nor is it possible in this situation to devise a fixed and absolute system of morality; moral values must remain in flux, adapting continuously to changing historical circumstances. To create those values and garner whatever knowledge is available, individuals must repeatedly subject themselves—both directly, and vicariously through art—to the trials of experience. Above all they must not attempt to shield themselves behind illusions or gentility, as so many did during the nineteenth century. To be sure, with passing time the Modernist worldview has, especially at the hands of the mass media, undergone the same tendencies toward corruption and routinization that have beset other major historical cultures. But in its ideal form at least, Modernism—in stark contrast to Victorianism—eschews innocence and demands instead to know "reality" in all its depth and complexity, no matter how incomplete and paradoxical that knowledge might be, and no matter how painful. It offers a demanding, and at times even heroic, vision of life that most of its adherents may in fact have fallen short of, but which they have used to guide themselves by nonetheless.

Although it has become common practice to identify the New York Armory Show of 1913, with its exhibition of Cubist and Post-Impressionist painting, as the first shot fired in the battle to establish Modernism on this side of the Atlantic, significant skirmishes had in fact been underway for several decades. By the time the show opened, Gertrude Stein and Ezra Pound, the two principal intermediaries between the United States and European Modernism, were already firmly entrenched at their posts overseas, Greenwich Village was filling up with cultural and artistic rebels, and proponents of the major intellectual breakthroughs in fields such as physics, biology, philosophy, psychology, and the social sciences had long since established beachheads at American universities. Both the Armory Show and the opening of Alfred Stieglitz's famous gallery were important vehicles for communication with headquarters overseas, but in America the war had long since been started, and by the period just before the First World War its effects could be seen everywhere, from muckraking journalism to the irreverent history of Charles A. Beard to the calls for personal and political liberation in *The Masses*. There were of course some differences from Europe—in John Higham's neat formulation, "Americans rebelled by extending the breadth of experience, Europeans by plumbing its depths"—but the essential values and dynamics of the culture were the same. "What was happening," Richard Hofstadter sums up, ". . . was that a modern critical intelligentsia was emerging in the United States. Modernism, in thought as in art, was dawning upon the American mind."[19]

Surely the two key figures in the process of importing the new culture to this country and giving it American roots were William James and John Dewey. James, as conversant with the latest European thought as any American of his day, was won over early in his career to the Darwinian premise that human beings existed on a continuum with other animals, and that the human brain was no more or less than a biological organ designed to select from the environment those perceptions useful for survival. For James that meant that the Victorian practice of radically separating the "higher" rational faculties from the "lower" instinctual ones made no sense. Rather, the mind must be conceived of as functionally integrated: "Pretend what we may, the whole man within us is at work when we form our philosophical opinions. Intellect, will, taste, and passion co-operate just as they do in practical affairs. . . ." Once the mind, guided by its passions, had chosen which perceptions to bring to consciousness, it might proceed to formulate abstract concepts based on them, but in doing so, James insisted, it necessarily introduced further distortions. The initial raw sensory experience, he believed, was the closest we could come to knowing reality; each application of the intellect, however valuable it might be for practical purposes, took us further from the "truth."[20]

For this reason, James concluded, human beings were doomed forever to epistemological uncertainty. To the great majority of his contemporaries this was a horrible revelation, but to James it was infinitely exciting, precisely because it banished the closed, deterministic universe of nineteenth-century positivism in favor of an "open" universe governed by change and chance where the process of discovery would be continuous. Embracing pluralism as a positive good, and grounding his own system of thought on the experiential basis of "radical empiricism," James became the first important American Modernist intellectual.[21]

Dewey, although heavily influenced by James, was a more systematic thinker inclined to give greater recognition to the virtues of rationality and science. More explicitly, the central purpose of all of Dewey's thought was eradicating the dichotomy between intellect and experience, thought and action, that he and James had inherited. Sensory perceptions, he contended, must be filtered through intelligence to become meaningful, while at the same time scientific theorizing must always be controlled by testing in the real world. One might even say that Dewey, in keeping with the "integrative mode" of Modernist culture, devoted his career to combating dualisms of all kinds—including those dividing mind from body, science from art, the city from the countryside, and the elite from the common people—all the while, of course, resisting final closure. Everywhere one looks in his writings one finds this sensibility at work, as in his discussion of how the basic task of both art and science is to blend elements of perception into integrated "relationships" in such a way that the process can "recur" indefinitely:

> A well-conducted scientific inquiry discovers as it tests, and proves as it explores; it does so in virtue of a method which combines both functions. And conversation, drama, [the] novel, and architectural construction, if there is an ordered experience, reach a stage that at once records and sums up the value of what precedes, and evokes and prophesies what is to come. Every closure is an awakening, and every awakening settles something.

One can likewise see the Modernist ethos at work in Dewey's plan for "progressive education," with its effort to connect the classroom with "real life" experience, its pluralistic stress on breaking down social barriers by encouraging interaction among students from diverse class and ethnic backgrounds, and its imperative that teachers not deliver fixed truths, but rather impress upon children at the earliest age the tentative, pragmatic character of knowledge.[22]

Indeed, one might rightfully speak of two predominant "streams" of American Modernist culture, proceeding respectively from James and Dewey. The Jamesian stream centers its interest on the individual consciousness, celebrates spontaneity, authenticity, and the probing of new realms of personal experience, and flows mainly through the arts and humanities. The Deweyan stream, by contrast, tends to focus on society as a whole, emphasizes the elimination of social barriers (geographic, economic, ethnic, racial, and gender), and tries to weld together reason and emotion in the service of programmatic social aims. With each passing decade of the twentieth century these two streams have increasingly diverged, ultimately creating an important internal tension within American Modernism, but that fact should not be allowed to obscure their many close resemblances, particularly at the beginning. James, after all, considered himself a professional scientist, while

Dewey's educational program was always centered on the individual and designed to tap the child's natural spontaneity. Both strains, moreover, have reflected the frequent preoccupation of American Modernists with pragmatic empiricism and democratic pluralism, as opposed to the tendency of Modernists in war-ravaged Europe to focus on apocalyptic experience and a concomitant cult of the irrational.

By the latter part of the Progressive Era, as Henry May has shown, the cultural revolution that James and Dewey had helped to initiate in America was spreading everywhere. Muckraking journalists were setting aside Victorian codes of gentility and exposing corruption at the highest levels of American life, naming specific names when necessary. Scholars like Charles Beard and Thorstein Veblen were taking a new critical look at their society and its history, determined to shed their nineteenth-century innocence and ferret out "reality" no matter how sordid it might be. Social workers like Jane Addams were praising the earthy vitality of immigrant cultures and insisting that such Old World heritages be blended with rather than overwhelmed by the dominant national culture. In New York, the Young Intellectuals, including Max Eastman, John Reed, Floyd Dell, Margaret Sanger, Eugene O'Neill, Randolph Bourne, and Walter Lippmann, were meeting at Mabel Dodge Luhan's salon, discussing the latest European Modernist authors and calling noisily for sexual, artistic, and political liberation in their own country. At the same time Frank Lloyd Wright was busy reshaping American architecture along Modernist lines, stripping away "false" ornamentation and facades, employing "authentic" materials such as untreated wood, glass, and stone, and using an abundance of windows and doors to erase the demarcation between interior and exterior. "Wright's first objective," one historian notes, "was to reduce the number of . . . separate parts and make a unified space so that light, air, and vistas permeated the whole." His designs, though attenuated in quality as they were popularized, supplied the basic patterns for the mass suburban housing boom following World War II, ensuring that a majority of middle-class Americans in the second half of the century would live in Modernist-styled homes.[23]

Yet perhaps the most influential stirrings of the new culture in America could be found in the work of the anthropologist Franz Boas and the extraordinary group of disciples he trained at Columbia University. In *The Mind of Primitive Man*, published in 1911, Boas took direct aim at the bedrock Victorian dichotomy between civilization and savagery, contending that so-called savage peoples were fully capable of logic, abstraction, aesthetic discrimination, and the inhibition of biological impulses, while Europeans practiced any number of customs, taboos, and rituals that could only be construed as irrational. For Boas such attributes as "human" or "animalistic" were all a matter of cultural perspective, and there was no scientific reason for granting the European perspective superiority over another—the only permissible criterion for normative judgment was the Darwinian one of how successfully a culture allowed a particular society to adapt to its environment. These insights, spreading first within the ranks of social scientists and then through the general population, would in time transform American attitudes concerning race by undermining the reigning stereotype of black people, whom the old moral dichotomy had consigned to "savagery." Indeed, by knocking away the cultural and scientific props of racism and replacing them with a new cultural modality that favored pluralistic integration, this attitudinal change in turn provided the essential foundation upon which the various movements to secure black rights were able to build. As Marshall Hyatt concludes, "Boas's critical contribution . . . lay in providing a new way of thinking, without which America could not have traveled the long road from *Plessy v. Ferguson* to *Brown v. Board of Education.*"[24]

Finally, one should take note of how the Modernist sensibility invaded popular culture during the Progressive Era. That process is clearly visible in Lewis Erenberg's study of New York City nightlife, which charts the way members of the more prosperous classes overcame post-Victorian malaise by gradually throwing aside the restraints of gentility and seeking out more sensuous forms of entertainment. In the nineteenth century, he observes, each "sex, class, and race . . . was expected to occupy its exclusive sphere. Public life was increasingly divided, and the private realm of the home diverged from the values of public life." But the cabaret, the focal institution of the new nightlife, was notable precisely because it "relaxed boundaries between the sexes, between audiences and performers, between ethnic groups and Protestants, between black culture and whites." For example, traditional "barriers between the entertainer and his audience" fell with the elimination of the raised stage, curtain, and footlights; performers even went out into the audience during their acts. Moreover, the majority of the leading entertainers and songwriters came from immigrant backgrounds that fell outside the orbit of Victorian respectability and hence were valued in large measure for their ability to put well-to-do patrons in touch with the vitality and experiences of lower-class life — an attribute that became even more prized during the 1920s when cabaret-goers went "slumming" in Harlem in search of black performers thought to be especially "natural, uncivilized, [and] uninhibited." To be sure, patrons demanded an atmosphere of sumptuous elegance to provide a sense of order and guarantee that they would not be declassed themselves. But the basic thrust of this newly created and rapidly expanding popular culture remained the effort to erase the Victorian dividing line between human and animal and thus "to liberate some of the repressed wilder elements, the more natural elements, that had been contained by gentility."[25]

The most unmistakable evidence of this transformation in public sensibility was surely the dancing craze that swept the nation between

1912 and 1916, foreshadowing the youth rebellion of the 1920s. Victorian-era dances such as the waltz, Erenberg observes, had emphasized "control, regularity, and patterned movement," along with "a look but do not touch approach to one's partner." The scores of dances introduced after 1912, most of which had originated in black culture, featured "heightened bodily expression" and far more "intimacy" between partners. The very names of the dances—bunny hug, monkey glide, grizzly bear, and lame duck—suggested a delectable surrender to animality and "rebellion against the older sexual mores." Most notorious was the shimmy, "a black torso-shaking dance" that became the rage just after the war. It was accompanied by a new form of music called jazz, also of black origins, which featured still wilder rhythms, frequent improvisation, and recurrent attempts by early bands to make their instruments "duplicate animal sounds." Moral reformers, ministers, and members of the older generation were predictably aghast at this outbreak of impulse. "Jazz and modern dancing" in their eyes, writes Paula Fass, seemed to herald "the collapse of civilized life." It is clear in retrospect that, viewed from a Victorian perspective, such forebodings were not without justification, for the behavior of middle-class youth during the 1920s demonstrated just how widely Modernist values had spread within the nation and how quickly they were approaching dominance.[26]

To trace the course of Modernist culture in America in full detail would require far more space than is available here. Such a narrative would necessarily include 1920s novelists like Fitzgerald, Hemingway, Dos Passos, and Faulkner, who chronicled the disintegration of modern society and culture, but whose primary concern, Bradbury rightly observes, was somehow "to make the world re-cohere." It would also encompass the documentary-style writers of the 1930s who sought to immerse themselves in the consciousness of socially marginal groups like southern sharecroppers—most notably James Agee and Walker Evans, in their *Let Us Now Praise Famous Men*, with its impassioned effort to pare away the separation between the authors' consciousness and that of their impoverished, illiterate subjects (along with Agee's pained realization of the impossibility of breaking down those barriers). Other illustrations of the mature American Modernist sensibility would run the gamut of cultural and intellectual activity from the interwar period onward, including the "humanist existentialism" of postwar literature, the neo-orthodox theology of Reinhold Niebuhr and Paul Tillich, the pluralism of social science-oriented writers such as Richard Hofstadter and Daniel Bell, the pragmatic social reform initiatives of the New Deal and Great Society, the "International Style" in urban architecture, and the rise of modern advertising, where, as Bruce Robbins puts it, the "techniques of the modernist classics have been incorporated into modernist commercials." Finally, a complete account of the new culture's fortunes in America could not leave out the various countervailing movements that arose to challenge Modernist values, either seeking, like the Fundamentalists, Ku Klux Klan, and "New Right," to restore nineteenth-century certainties, or to proffer some new form of absolutism in the manner of scientism, orthodox Marxism, and the behaviorism of B. F. Skinner, or to provide refuge from the tensions accompanying Modernism through an emphasis on bureaucratic process, as have some varieties of corporate culture.[27]

It would appear that the culminating moment for American Modernism — and perhaps also the beginning of its end — came in the 1960s. The celebration of the animal component of human nature, the quest for spontaneity and authenticity, the desire to raze all dualisms and distinctions, the breaking down of social and cultural barriers, the quest for "wholeness," and the effort to expand consciousness and discover new modes of experience — all were given heightened realization. A new generation of rebels, ironically spoken of as a "counterculture" when they were in fact riding the crest of a cultural tidal wave, carried the Modernist embrace of natural instinct and primitivism to its seemingly inevitable conclusion by letting hair grow wild, experimenting with mind-altering drugs, overthrowing the last vestiges of conventional sexual mores, and creating in acid rock a music of pounding sensuality. The same forces could be found at work among the intellectual elite, where writers like Susan Sontag condemned a supposed "hypertrophy of the intellect at the expense of energy and sensual capability" in contemporary life and demanded that critics forego all attempts at describing or interpreting art. Contending that "our world" is "impoverished enough," she insisted that we abandon "all duplicates of it, until we again experience more immediately what we have." Numerous performing groups took this philosophy to heart, endeavoring to achieve authenticity by bridging life and art — most notably the Living Theater, whose *Paradise Now* invited members of the audience to disrobe on stage and join the troupe in sexual high jinks. Viewed in retrospect, what seems most striking about such excesses is the way matters once vested with deep emotion and commitment by those engaged in the initial battle against Victorianism were now often reduced to a pointless game. One senses that the pendulum was again starting to swing, that Modernism, much like late Victorian culture in the 1890s, was at last becoming overripe and starting to caricature itself. If so, then the 1960s, instead of marking the dawn of an Aquarian age, might be more accurately viewed as the death-rattle of a fast aging culture.[28]

Since that decade, and partly in reaction to it, there has been increasing discussion of the possible arrival of "postmodernism." As one might expect, those attempting to describe this new sensibility have often disagreed with each other, but they do seem to concur that its presence first became unmistakable during the 1960s. It has manifested itself, according to most accounts, in the form of Pop and minimalist art, in an architecture that intentionally draws on cliches from popular culture ("learning from Las Vegas," as Robert Venturi puts it), and in the literary productions of Tom Wolfe, Donald Barthelme, and Joseph Heller, among others. What these various tendencies appear to have in common is what Richard Wolin calls "the valorization of mass culture" by the intellectual elite, "a pseudo-populist ethos which suggests that the gap between (high) art and life has been definitely bridged." To put this in slightly different terms, one might say that the democratic urge within Modernism to break down all division between the elite and the popular has at last overcome the long-standing practice of Modernist thinkers to dismiss mass culture on the grounds of inauthenticity. The result, Wolin argues, is a sensibility that is impatient with "complexity" and "wants instead works of literature . . . as absolute as the sun, as unarguable as orgasm, as delicious as a lollipop."[29]

Fredric Jameson likewise speaks of an "aesthetic populism" as the essence of postmodernism, and complains of a new superficiality, a "waning of content," in which "depth is replaced by surface, or multiple surfaces." "The postmoderns," he claims, "have in fact been fascinated precisely by this whole 'degraded' landscape of schlock and kitsch, of TV series and *Readers' Digest* culture, of advertising and motels . . . materials they no longer simply 'quote,' as a Joyce or Mahler might have done, but incorporate into their very substance." As he sees it, this new "cultural dominant" has resolved the Modernist crisis of personal identity by the simple expedient of eliminating the self as a subject of art or intellectual speculation. With no ego, there is conveniently no emotion, no troublesome conflict—just problems of "style," to the point where art becomes little more than a matter of "codes" and "pastiche," a "virtual grab-bag" of "random raw materials and impulses" reflecting the peculiar commodity fetishism of "late capitalism." What postmodernism seems to lack, in short, is the creative tension—the refusal to achieve closure—that had characterized Modernist art and thought at their best and provided their special resonance.[30]

If Jameson and Wolin are correct in their descriptions of post-modernism, what its advent may signal is a growing inability to tolerate the formidable demands made by Modernist culture, especially its abiding lack of resolution and certainty—just as post-Victorianism in the 1890s represented an effort to escape nineteenth-century moral constraints. Where Americans once sought an antidote to excessive repression, they may now be searching out a remedy for excessive liberation. The real underlying force beneath our present cultural activity may thus be the desire to find a stable point of reference, some firm rock upon which to rest our perceptions and values—though preferably without giving up the lessons about the relative nature of truth that Modernism itself provided. Thus we even find Jameson himself at the end of his critique calling almost plaintively for a new kind of cultural sextant and compass to fashion what he calls an "aesthetic of *cognitive mapping*."[31]

Some, including Jameson, seem to believe that the surest path to such regenerative intellectual cartography can be found in French poststructuralist theory, including the work of Derrida, Lacan, Foucault, and Althusser. One suspects, however, that, useful as some of its specific insights and techniques may be, poststructuralism in the long run will be viewed more as part of the postmodernist malady than as a cure. The prime characteristic of its grand systems, as Frederick Crews recently pointed out, has been "a growing apriorism—a willingness to settle issues by theoretical decree, without even a pretense of evidential appeal." In eschewing empiricism this way, he continues, the poststructuralists and their disciples have been proceeding from "an unarticulated feeling that one at least deserves the haven of an all-explanatory theory, a way of making the crazy world cohere." But in the midst of the cultural dilemma posed by late Modernism it does not seem likely that the world will agree to cohere that easily; the expedient of intellectual game-playing, for all its temptations, will not solve the problem.[32]

Moreover, it seems clear that the postmodernist initiative to date has taken place within an essentially Modernist framework. The democratic urge to close the gap between the intellectuals and the "people," the stipulation (in Pop art and architecture, for example) that all artifacts be clearly identified as artificial and inauthentic while at the same time being seen paradoxically as authentic artifacts, the poststructuralist resort to semiotic analysis—these and other postmodernist traits surely represent extrapolations from the basic Modernist methods. "Postmodernist anti-art was inherent in the logic of the modernist aesthetic," Gerald Graff observes astutely in support of his contention that a major cultural "breakthrough" has yet to occur in our time. Robert Martin Adams similarly finds that "where modernism has simply pushed ahead, it has exaggerated tendencies which were in it from the very beginning, by making symptomatic jokes out of them." In short, as was the case earlier with post-Victorianism, it would appear that those attempting to free themselves from inherited beliefs and values have thus far been unable to do so. Long-standing internal contradictions have surfaced, the old culture is wobbling, but its successor is still not here.[33]

Where then are we headed? If there is a lesson to be gleaned from the study of history, it is the necessity of expecting the unexpected. Few people at the turn of the twentieth century were able to discern the shape of the cultural era they were entering, and those few saw that shape only in its vaguest outline. There is no reason to think that prognostication will fare better this time. In the meanwhile, now that we are gaining a modicum of critical distance from it, perhaps the wisest course of action would be to occupy ourselves with improving our understanding of Modernism, as well as the more general process of cultural change in America, in order to gain as much perspective as possible on our recent historical experience. That seems the best answer available, though doubtless some will object that, with its relativism and contingency, it is indelibly a Modernist one.

Notes

1. Virginia Woolf, *Mr. Bennett and Mrs. Brown* (London, 1924), 4; Malcolm Bradbury and James McFarlane, "The Name and Nature of Modernism," in Bradbury and McFarlane, eds., *Modernism, 1890–1930* (New York, 1976), 20, 28, 34–35; Peter Gay, *Freud, Jews and Other Germans: Masters and Victims in Modernist Culture* (New York, 1978), 21–22; Bruce Robbins, "Modernism in History, Modernism in Power," in Robert Kiely, ed., *Modernism Reconsidered* (Cambridge, Mass., 1983), 231–32, 234–39; Daniel Joseph Singal, *The War Within: From Victorian to Modernist Thought in the South, 1919–1945* (Chapel Hill, 1982), 3–4.

2. On modernization theory, see especially Cyril E. Black, *The Dynamics of Modernization: A Study in Comparative History* (New York, 1966), 7, 9–26, 46–49; and Alex Inkeles and David H. Smith, *Becoming Modern: Individual Change in Six Developing Countries* (Cambridge, Mass., 1974), 15–25; for its applicability within the context of American history, see Richard D. Brown, *Modernization: The Transformation of American Life, 1600–1865* (New York, 1976), especially 3–22. The dialectical linkage between Modernism and modernization is explored in Peter Berger et al., *The Homeless Mind: Modernization and Consciousness* (New York, 1973), though the authors use the term "demodernizing consciousness" in place of "Modernism." See also Eugene Lunn, *Marxism and Modernism: An Historical Study of Lukacs, Brecht, Benjamin and Adorno* (Berkeley, 1982), 40–42. For one among many examples of works that badly confuse Modernism and modernization, see Richard Wolin, "Modernism vs. Postmodernism," *Telos* 62 (Winter 1984–85): 9–11.

3. Gay, *Freud, Jews and Other Germans*, 22–26; Lionel Trilling, *Beyond Culture: Essays on Literature and Learning* (New York, 1968), xiii, 3, 30; Irving Howe, *The Decline of the New* (New York, 1968), 3–5, 9–10, 21–25; Mark Krupnick, *Lionel Trilling and the Fate of Cultural Criticism* (Evanston, 1986), 135–36, 143–45; Daniel Bell, *The Cultural Contradictions of Capitalism* (New York, 1976), 46–48.

4. Daniel Walker Howe, "American Victorianism as a Culture," *American Quarterly* 27 (December 1975); 508, 511–14, 521.

5. Walter E. Houghton, *The Victorian Frame of Mind, 1830–1870* (New Haven, 1957), 14, 144–45, 420; John S. Haller and Robin M. Haller, *The Physician and Sexuality in Victorian America* (New York, 1977), 126–28, 109; Nancy F. Cott, "Passionlessness: An Interpretation of Victorian Sexual Ideology, 1790–1850," in Nancy F. Cott and Elizabeth H. Pleck, eds., *A Heritage of Her Own: Toward a New Social History of American Women* (New York, 1979), 166–68.

6. Houghton, *Victorian Frame of Mind*, 162, 171, 144–45; Masao Miyoshi, *The Divided Self: A Perspective on the Literature of the Victorians* (New York, 1969), xv; Rosalind Rosenberg, *Beyond Separate Spheres: Intellectual Roots of Modern Feminism* (New York, 1982), xiv.

7. Houghton, *Victorian Frame of Mind*, 266, 297–300, 356; Matthew Arnold, *Culture and Anarchy*, ed. J. Dover Wilson (Cambridge, Eng., 1971), 11; Donald H. Meyer, "American Intellectuals and the Crisis of Faith," *American Quarterly* 27 (December 1975): 601; W. L. Burn, *The Age of Equipoise: A Study of the Mid-Victorian Generation* (New York, 1964), 41, 106.

8. T. J. Jackson Lears, *No Place of Grace: Antimodernism and the Transformation of American Culture, 1880–1920* (New York, 1981), 5–6, 13, 37, 48, 53, 57, 105–06, 166, 174; John Higham, "The Reorientation of American Culture in the 1890's," in Higham, *Writing American History: Essays on Modern Scholarship* (Bloomington, Ind.: 1970), 78–79, 99.

9. Bradbury and McFarlane, "Name and Nature of Modernism," 31; Lunn, *Marxism and Modernism*, 42–43, 45; Stephane Mallarmé, quoted in Stephen Kern, *The Culture of Time and Space, 1880–1918* (Cambridge, Mass., 1983), 172; Clive Scott, "Symbolism, Decadence and Impressionism" in Bradbury and McFarlane, *Modernism*, 219; Gay, *Freud, Jews, and Other Germans*, 275. For a detailed account of the transition to Modernism in an American setting, see Singal, *The War Within*.

10. Kern, *Culture of Time and Space*, 204; James, quoted in ibid., 204; Sanford Schwartz, *The Matrix of Modernism: Pound, Eliot, and Early Twentieth-Century Thought* (Princeton, 1985), 5–6, 12, 17–19.

11. Alan Bullock, "The Double Image," in Bradbury and McFarlane, *Modernism*, 66–67; Robert W. Wald, *Space, Time, and Gravity: The Theory of the Big Bang and Black Holes* (Chicago, 1977), 10–11; Schwartz, *Matrix of Modernism*, 15–17; Henri Poincaré, quoted in ibid., 16; Kern, *Culture of Time and Space* 18–19, 132–36, 183–85; 153, 206; Albert Einstein, *Relativity: The Special and General Theory* (New York, 1961), 56–57, 94–96, 141–44; George Gamow, "The Declassification of Physics," in John Weiss, ed., *The Origins of Modern Consciousness* (Detroit, 1965), 167, 176–77, 188.

12. Singal, *The War Within*, 7–8; Peter Faulkner, *Modernism* (London, 1977), 19; Richard Hofstadter, *The Progressive Historians: Turner, Beard, Parrington* (New York, 1968), 185; William Carlos Williams, quoted in Robert Coles, "Instances of Modernist Anti-Intellectualism," in Kiely, *Modernism Reconsidered*, 217.

13. Bradbury and McFarlane, "Name and Nature of Modernism," 46, 48–49; James McFarlane, "The Mind of Modernism," in Bradbury and McFarlane, *Modernism*, 80–81, 83–84, 92.

14. Panthea Reid Broughton, "The Cubist Novel: Toward Defining a Genre," in Ann J. Abadie and Doreen Fowler, eds., *A Cosmos of My Own: Faulkner and Yoknapatawpha, 1980* (Jackson, Miss., 1981), 48–52; Eric Cahm, "Revolt, Conservatism and Reaction in Paris, 1905–25," in Bradbury and McFarlane, *Modernism*, 169; Kern, *Culture of Time and Space*, 143–45, 195, 7, 161–62; Lunn, *Marxism and Modernism*, 48–51.

15. McFarlane, "Mind of Modernism," 84–85; Kern, *Culture of Time and Space*, 219–20, 199–201, 75–79; Lunn, *Marxism and Modernism*, 35.

16. Singal, *The War Within*, 7–8; Lionel Trilling, *Sincerity and Authenticity* (Cambridge, Mass., 1972), 6, 11, 143–47; Gay, *Freud, Jews and Other Germans*, 72; Karen Halttunen, *Confidence Men and Painted Women: A Study of Middle Class Culture in America, 1830–1870* (New Haven, 1982), xvi–xvii, 51–54; D. H. Lawrence, quoted in Ronald Bush, "Modern/Postmodern: Eliot, Perse, Mallarme, and the Future of the Barbarians," in Kiely, *Modernism Reconsidered*, 197.

17. Jerome H. Buckley, "Towards Early-Modern Autobiography: The Role of Oscar Wilde, George Moore, Edmund Gosse, and Henry Adams," in Kiely, *Modernism Reconsidered*, 1–3; Bush, "Modern/Postmodern," 214, 196–201; McFarlane, "Mind of Modernism," 81; Singal, *The War Within*, 370;

Trilling, *Sincerity and Authenticity*, 11; Erik H. Erikson, "The Problem of Ego Identity," in Erikson, *Identity and the Life Cycle* (New York, 1959), 118.

18. Bradbury and McFarlane, "Name and Nature of Modernism," 50; McFarlane, "Mind of Modernism," 82–89; Susan Sontag, "The Pornographic Imagination," in *The Susan Sontag Reader* (New York, 1982), 212; Jerome S. Bruner, *On Knowing: Essays for the Left Hand* (Cambridge, Mass., 1962), 62–63. McFarlane, in his otherwise excellent essay, makes the error of describing the "logic" of the dream as the guiding sensibility of Modernism. He notes, for example, how "a great many of the artists and writers of the first two decades of the twentieth century" found in the dream a "paradigm of the whole *Weltbild* in which reality and unreality, logic and fantasy, the banal and the sublime form an indissoluble and inexplicable unity." But surely this is an early and more extreme version of Modernism, and not necessarily a characteristic of the more mature culture. The latter involved not simply an attempt to assimilate the fiery processes of the unconscious, but also an effort to integrate them with those of rational thought. That is why metaphor provides a more accurate representation of the "logic" of Modernism than does dreamwork. See McFarlane, "Mind of Modernism," 86.

19. Higham, "Reorientation of American Culture," 101; Hofstadter, *Progressive Historians*, 184–85.

20. William James, "The Sentiment of Rationality," in James, *The Will to Believe and Other Essays* (New York, 1956), 92, 65–70; Elizabeth Flower and Murray G. Murphey, *A History of Philosophy in America*, 2 vols. (New York, 1977), 2: 643–44, 649–50, 669.

21. William James, *A Pluralistic Universe* (New York, 1909), 318–19; Flowers and Murphey, *History of Philosophy*, 2: 683.

22. John Dewey, *Art as Experience* (1934; New York, 1958), 169; idem, *The School and Society* (1900; Chicago, 1943), 11–14, 26–27. Dewey, with his Modernist animus against dichotomies of any sort, could even wax eloquent about integrating the various levels of education: "We want to bring all things educational together; to break down the barriers that divide the education of the little child from the instruction of the maturing youth; to identify the lower and the higher education, so that it shall be demonstrated to the eye that there is no lower and higher, but simply education." Ibid., 92.

23. Henry F. May, *The End of American Innocence: A Study of the First Years of Our Own Time* (New York, 1959), 220, 280–84; Hofstadter, *Progressive Historians*, 184; John Higham, *Strangers in the Land: Patterns of American Nativism, 1860–1925* (New York, 1963), 251, 121; Kern, *Culture of Time and Space*, 186–87, 179; Frank Lloyd Wright, *The Natural House* (New York, 1954), 14–20, 38–40, 51–54, 62–65. The best treatment of the Greenwich Village movement is Leslie Fishbein, *Rebels in Bohemia: The Radicals of The Masses, 1911–1917* (Chapel Hill, 1982).

24. Franz Boas, *The Mind of Primitive Man* (1911; New York, 1965), 17, 29, 160–61, 154, 201, 205–10; Lewis Perry, *Intellectual Life in America: A History* (New York, 1984), 320–23; George W. Stocking, Jr., *Race, Culture, and Evolution: Essays in the History of Anthropology* (New York, 1968), 217–22, 226, 190–91; Marshall Hyatt, "Franz Boas and the Struggle for Black Equality: The Dynamics of Ethnicity," *Perspectives in American History* 2 (1985): 295, 269.

25. Lewis A. Erenberg, *Steppin' Out: New York Nightlife and the Transformation of American Culture, 1890–1930* (Westport, Conn., 1981), 5, 23, xii–xiv, 113, 125–26, 131, 187, 195, 255–56, 240–41, 154.

26. Ibid., 148, 150–51, 153–54, 249–51; Paula S. Fass, *The Damned and the Beautiful: American Youth in the 1920's* (New York, 1977), 301–03, 22.

27. Malcolm Bradbury, *The Modern American Novel* (New York, 1983), 61–62; James Agee and Walker Evans, *Let Us Now Praise Famous Men* (1941; New York, 1966), esp. 121, 129, 376–77; William Stott, *Documentary Expression and Thirties America* (New York, 1973), 302, 305–07, 310–11; Daniel Joseph Singal, "Beyond Consensus: Richard Hofstadter and American Historiography," *American Historical Review* 89 (October 1984): 978, 996; Howard Brick, *Daniel Bell and the Decline of Intellectual Radicalism: Social Theory and Political Reconciliation in the 1940s* (Madison, 1986), 20–21, 38–39, 165, 191–92, 208; Robbins, "Modernism in History," 234–35.

28. William L. O'Neill, *Coming Apart: An Informal History of America in the 1960s* (New York, 1971), 200–02, 204–08; Susan Sontag, "Against Interpretation," in *Sontag Reader*, 98–99, 104.

29. Fredric Jameson, "Postmodernism, or the Cultural Logic of Late Capitalism," *New Left Review* 146 (July–August 1984), 53–54; Wolin, "Modernism vs. Postmodernism," 18–20, 25, 26; Gerald Graff, "The Myth of the Postmodernist Breakthrough," *Triquarterly* 26 (Winter 1973): 392; Bradbury, *Modern American Novel*, 160–64; Robert Venturi et al., *Learning From Las Vegas: The Forgotten Symbolism of Architectural Form* (Cambridge, Mass., 1977), 6–9 and passim; Dell Upton and John Michael Vlach, eds., *Common Places: Readings in American Vernacular Architecture* (Athens, Ga., 1986). For an early view of literary postmodernism that now seems somewhat dated, see Ihab Hassan, "POSTmodernISM," *New Literary History* 3 (Autumn 1971): 5–30.

30. Jameson, "Postmodernism," 54–55, 59–62, 65, 72–73, 75.

31. Ibid., 87, 89–90.

32. Ibid., 71–72, 91–92; Frederick Crews, "In the Big House of Theory," *New York Review of Books*, 33 (May 29, 1986), 37, 39–42. On this debate, see also Jean Lyotard, *The Postmodern Condition*, trans. Geoff Bennington and Brian Masumi (Minneapolis, 1984).

33. Graff, "Myth of the Postmodernist Breakthrough," 387; Robert Martin Adams, "What Was Modernism?" *Hudson Review* 31 (Spring 1978): 29–30.

Revisioning the Harlem Renaissance

Venetria K. Patton and Maureen Honey

This excerpt from Patton and Honey's introduction to Double Take: A Revisionist Harlem Renaissance Anthology *(2001) provides an overview of the Harlem Renaissance or New Negro Movement. The editors argue that*

From *Double Take: A Revisionist Harlem Renaissance Anthology* (New Brunswick: Rutgers UP, 2001): xix–xxxix.

*a broader approach to the New Negro Movement allows a better under-
standing of its recurring themes. Thus while a black folk-tradition is celebrated and Africa is shown to be a source of pride, the works of the
Harlem Renaissance also validate mothers and motherhood. The writers
of the period also consider the effect of migration and the role of nature
as well as address issues of identity.*

*In addition to discussing the various themes associated with the
movement, Patton and Honey address the contested periodization of the
Harlem Renaissance, arguing that 1916 and 1937 mark the beginning
and end of the period. These dates are significant for the production of
Angelina Weld Grimké's play* Rachel *and the publication of Zora Neale
Hurston's* Their Eyes Were Watching God. *The essay closes by discussing
the relationship of literary works to developing civil rights organizations:
the National Association for the Advancement of Colored People, the National Urban League, and the Universal Negro Improvement Association.*

On March 21, 1924, almost all of the future stars of the Harlem
Renaissance gathered at Manhattan's Civic Club to inaugurate
what would become known as the New Negro Movement of the 1920s
and 1930s. This event was a dinner arranged to honor Jessie Fauset for
the publication of her first novel, *There Is Confusion*, just published by
Boni and Liveright. Poet Gwendolyn Bennett wrote her poem "To Us-
ward" especially for the occasion and recited it that evening. In the audience receiving a round of applause was the most famous black woman
poet of her day, Georgia Douglas Johnson, author of two recent books of
poetry: *The Heart of a Woman* (1918) and *Bronze* (1922).

Despite the reason for this gathering, Fauset's prominent role as
literary editor of *The Crisis*, the leading African American periodical in
the nation, and the spotlighted presence of Bennett and Johnson, the
evening was dominated by men. Most notably, the absent Jean Toomer,
whose astonishing experimental novel *Cane* (1923) had also recently
been published by Boni and Liveright, and Walter White, whose first
novel, *The Fire in the Flint* (1924), would soon appear from Alfred A.
Knopf, were praised effusively by the stream of male speakers who
made up the program. Bennett's single poem was eclipsed by the evening's literary centerpiece, a poetry reading by rising star Countee
Cullen. The most influential black power broker of the era, Alain Locke,
was master of ceremonies—and known for his cultivation of male
writers. . . .

Recurring Themes

Placing the texts of men and women, minor and major writers, lesser
known and canonized selections, multiple genres, and homoerotic texts
side by side, this anthology opens opportunities for new understandings of the Harlem Renaissance. The movement is traditionally viewed

as one characterized by generational splits (rear guard vs. vanguard) or divides based on the debate over art versus propaganda; on the contrary, we have made selections that point to the connections shared by this diverse set of writers. Although women poets are associated with nature poetry, Langston Hughes wrote about nature too, for instance, and Georgia Douglas Johnson, like many male writers, used folk vernacular in her prose. A poem ignored by anthologies, such as Hughes's "Lullaby" (*The Crisis*, 1926), can suggest linkages to women who wrote about babies or motherhood. Similarly, Claude McKay's "Like a Strong Tree" (*Survey Graphic* and *The New Negro*, 1925) echoes Angelina Weld Grimké's often anthologized "The Black Finger" (*Opportunity*, 1923). An aesthetically flawed poem by gifted writer Zora Neale Hurston, "Passion" (*Negro World*, 1922), can illustrate the period's early focus on traditional love lyrics. By including the poetry, prose, or drama not often anthologized or associated with particular writers, we hope to illustrate the multidimensional commonalities that characterize the Harlem Renaissance.

Sterling Brown and others have identified certain themes that reappear despite the gender and generational differences so often commented upon: Africa is a source of race pride, black American heroes or heroines are apotheosized, racial political propaganda is considered essential, the black folk tradition is affirmed, and candid self-revelation is on display.[1] Nathan Huggins adds to this list an emphasis on the urbanity of the New Negro and joy of discovering both the variety and unity of black people. Much of the literature sought to define this "New Negro" or in some way addressed the issue of identity, according to Huggins: "What did Africa mean? What did the slave and peasant past mean? What could a folk tradition mean to the 'New Negro'? What was color, itself? Blackness, clearly, was not only a color, it was a state of mind. So, what of the mulatto, and what of 'passing'?"[2] Huggins and David Levering Lewis point to questions about the important role of art in the Renaissance. These questions are reflected in the debate about art and propaganda, but are also related to the issue of artistic integrity—could black artists avoid mimicking European forms and still produce great art? Other themes that critics have noted in relation to the movement are the prominent role of the Christian church in this very secular artistic movement, anger at racism, and an indictment of Western culture.

In addition to these themes, we have noticed recurring discussions across both genders of migration, domestic servitude, motherhood, children, nature, and passionate love. Because of the new urban identity of the New Negro, discussions of migration from the South or other rural areas are quite frequent. Washerwomen are another frequent subject for both genders, perhaps because they symbolized the exploitation of black labor as a whole and because white soap suds were an apt metaphor for white supremacy. Motherhood was a site of artistic production because it encompassed the past rape of black women by white masters during slavery and because black mothers represented the anticipated better future of the race. The validation of mothers present in the dominant culture had been denied African American women, whose representation as mammies caring for white people was a familiar stereotype. Writers of the Harlem Renaissance addressed this erasure by creating images of black women as maternal figures and centered their concept of artistic awakening on birth. Nature was a central source of imagery for both genders as well. Images of night, shadow, trees, dawn, dusk, earth stood for black pride, resilience, awakening, or protection. Finally, love and sensuality were important subjects for all of these writers. As Bernard Bell has noted, African Americans were dehumanized by a racist culture as incapable of romantic love, denied positive identities as sensual beings.[3] Participating in a larger cultural rebellion against Victorian prudery, writers of the Renaissance proclaimed themselves fully human followers of the heart, celebrants of the flesh.

There are key differences between male and female writers, however. As Cheryl Wall, Gloria Hull, Deborah McDowell, Claudia Tate, and others have pointed out, the system of patronage operating during the Harlem Renaissance privileged men.[4] As a result, it was harder for most women to get the financial and professional support they needed to get into print. While many of them had work published in the period's journals and anthologies, relatively few collections of poetry or short stories were published by women, and not as many of their plays were produced.

Critics also point to women's avoidance of the urban vernacular and "primitivism," particularly in their poetry (with the important exception of the blues singers). This vernacular and associations with "the primitive" of Africa resonated with sexuality, problematic terrain for black women at the time, who were burdened with a stereotype of themselves as prostitutes in the larger culture. To claim their humanity, intelligence, and artistic creativity, therefore, they tended to turn to middle-class subjects and traditional poetic forms even when celebrating their African roots. This tendency was fostered by the fact that most of them came from middle-class backgrounds, even though they were financially strapped. When women did dip into the vernacular, they tended to recuperate the folk dialect of the generation preceding them, a safer discourse in terms of its association with rural family life.

Women addressed gender oppression in their writing as well as racism. Essays by women frequently emphasized gender issues and the double burden of being female and black. Cheryl Wall notes that images of rooms, a symbol of confinement, reappear in women's texts, and allusions to journeys abound. Restricted in their ability to travel, they took imaginative flights instead. Women, like men, wrote about nature, but they infused these natural images with a feminist subtext. Pastoral settings dominated by female allusions are often contrasted with alien manmade urban spaces, for example, or nature is portrayed as a liberating force for women's spirits. Birds and flowers appear as representations of women's imprisonment or freedom. In these ways, women of the Harlem Renaissance responded to the feminist stirrings that resulted in gaining female suffrage in 1920, but they grappled uneasily with the sometimes conflicting imperatives of racial solidarity and feminist revolt.

Contested Periodization

Another issue highlighted by gender awareness, as we will explicate later, is the contested nature of periodization. While there is general agreement about the significance of the Harlem Renaissance, there is less accord on when the movement begins and ends, since it is not marked by a consistent set of aesthetics or recognizable style. Literature from the period covered a wide range of forms from classic sonnets to modernist verse to blues and jazz aesthetics to folklore. The movement is associated with the 1920s, the Jazz Age, but just when it emerged and disappeared is a source of debate. In fact, Nathan Huggins refers to the Harlem Renaissance as a "convenient fiction,"[5] because there is no clear demarcation separating the old from the "New Negro." Despite this lack of clarity, writers and scholars have sought to impose order and meaning on this rather organic surge in artistic creativity; a brief review of this debate helps define this anthology's contribution.

In *The Harlem Renaissance Remembered*, Arna Bontemps divides the period into two phases: black propaganda (1921–1924) and connection of black writers to the white intelligentsia and publishing establishment (1924–1931), ending with the Depression of the 1930s. Nathan Huggins, in *Voices from the Harlem Renaissance*, follows Bontemps's lead by dating the era's beginnings to the end of World War I and its demise to the Depression. The editors of the more recent *Call and Response* echo these assessments in their preference for two distinct terms: *Harlem Renaissance* and the *Reformation*, the latter referring to the post-Renaissance aftermath of the thirties and forties.

However, for others, including ourselves, the 1930s are merely an extension of the Harlem Renaissance. For example, Alain Locke describes the thirties as the "second and truly sound phase of the cultural development of the Negro in American literature and art."[6] This extension of the movement into the 1930s is embraced by *The Norton Anthology of African American Literature*, edited by Henry Louis Gates Jr. and Nellie Y. McKay. According to its time line, 1919–1940, the years of the Harlem Renaissance traverse two full decades. David Levering Lewis also uses a more comprehensive time frame. In *The Portable Harlem Renaissance Reader*, he ascribes the years 1917–1935 to the movement, from the opening of American theater to black actors with the Broadway productions of Ridgely Torrence in 1917 to the Harlem Riot of 1935, and he places a great deal of importance on World War I and the race riots of 1919 as watershed events ushering in the concept of the New Negro.

Despite general agreement that the 1920s represent its zenith, then, periodization of the Harlem Renaissance is clearly an issue of some debate. Our anthology contributes to that conversation by heeding the observation of Cheryl Wall and Gloria Hull that narrower time and geographical parameters for the Harlem Renaissance work against women, most of whom published in a scattered way across a continuum of time and from regions outside Harlem. In that spirit, we are attaching the movement's parameters to two landmark works, neither of which was written in Harlem nor in the 1920s: the production of Angelina Weld Grimké's play *Rachel* (1916) and the publication of Zora Neale Hurston's novel *Their Eyes Were Watching God* (1937). Bracketing the Renaissance with these two texts not only opens up debates about gender and the movement's vast literary range, it pins the period to African American–authored creative literature rather than to political events, economic events, expository prose, or texts generated by whites: all areas dominated by men. Our parameters also underscore the importance of women to the movement, despite the handicaps of gender that limited their ability to get into print.

Although flawed aesthetically and outside the militant and vernacular discourse that has come to be identified with the Harlem Renaissance, there are sound reasons for tracing the period's beginnings to *Rachel* and for scrutinizing Grimké's play more carefully than we have done in the past. The play's groundbreaking nature is rooted in the fact that it was the first serious drama by an African American playwright to be performed on stage with an African American cast. It was performed in both Washington, D.C., and in New York. Subtitled "A Play of Protest," *Rachel* anticipated Du Bois's call to combine art with propaganda since the play centers on the evils of racism and lynching. It was seeing *Rachel* that persuaded the Renaissance's premier playwright, Willis Richardson, to devote his creative life to drama and directly led to his first play, *The Chip Woman's Fortune* (1923), the first serious African American–authored play to be produced on Broadway. We can see in *Rachel*'s foregrounding of racism's devastating impact on mothers and children glimpses of a major theme of women in the Harlem Renaissance: the equation of motherlessness with protest against racism. Finally, we see in this play some of the seeds about racism and family life sown for contemporary women writers, particularly Toni Morrison in her novels *The Bluest Eye* (1970) and *Beloved* (1991).

Hailed in its own day as the first drama to portray black people positively, a corrective to ubiquitous plantation stereotypes, *Rachel* was produced by the NAACP as a counter-narrative to D. W. Griffith's blockbuster film *The Birth of a Nation* (1915). Griffith's racist narrative glorified the Ku Klux Klan at a time when record numbers of black people were being lynched (by some estimates nearly two thousand in the century's first three decades alone). The propaganda function of *Rachel* was overtly theorized by Grimké, who aimed it at a white audience to gain support for anti-lynching legislation, although it was actually seen by mainly African American audiences. This was in part why it eschewed the folk vernacular that would become a hallmark of much Renaissance writing.

More importantly, *Rachel*'s urban and middle-class characters constituted a dramatic change from the minstrel stereotypes to which American audiences were accustomed, and its language was a departure from the dialect art forms of Paul Laurence Dunbar, Joseph Cotter Sr., and Charles Chesnutt, who had dominated the first decades of the twentieth century. In this way Grimké's play was an important step toward expanding the limited forms in which black artists were trapped. It inaugurated the literature from Georgia Douglas Johnson, Countee Cullen, Jessie Fauset, Claude McKay, and others that would illustrate Du Bois's contention that African Americans should lay claim to the high art forms of the dominant culture in order to advance their acceptance as first-class American citizens and end segregation.

Ending the Harlem Renaissance with Hurston's *Their Eyes Were Watching God* (1937) conforms to critical consensus about the death of the movement, which is anywhere from 1935 to 1940. It also signals the devastating impact of the Depression on publishing opportunities for black writers and points to the coming ascendancy of urban realism and naturalism in African American letters with the publication of Richard Wright's *Black Boy* (1939) and *Native Son* (1940). Indeed, it was Wright's highly critical review of Hurston's novel in *New Masses* that helped bury the Renaissance. Wright's perspective sounded the death knell for rural folk vernacular as the basis of an authentic African American aesthetic and for women writers of the Harlem Renaissance—even the gifted Hurston, whose now-acclaimed novel went out of print for thirty years after its first run. . . .

The Arts as Civil Rights

Because of the large and growing black population and the city's history of African American excellence in the arts, New York was a natural center for the Harlem Renaissance. New York was America's cultural capital, and it was the center of publishing, drama, music, and painting. It was also the headquarters of the three biggest civil rights organizations: the NAACP (National Association for the Advancement of Colored People) founded by W. E. B. Du Bois (publisher of *The Crisis*) in 1909; the NUL (National Urban League) founded by Charles S. Johnson (publisher of *Opportunity*) in 1910; and the UNIA (Universal Negro Improvement Association) founded by Marcus Garvey (publisher of *Negro World*) in 1914.

These periodicals played a significant role in the development of the Harlem Renaissance because the organizations to which they were attached viewed support of the arts as the primary means to access civil rights. As David Levering Lewis notes: "The Harlem Renaissance was a somewhat forced phenomenon, a cultural nationalism of the parlor, institutionally encouraged and directed by leaders of the national Civil Rights Establishment for the paramount purpose of improving race relations."[7] Leaders of the movement believed that whites would be persuaded to accept the humanity of African Americans if blacks could achieve artistic equality and that such equality would lead to the achievement of civil rights. The NAACP and the NUL sought to encourage interracial collaboration between liberal whites and Du Bois's "Talented Tenth," the best and brightest of African American artists and intellectuals. They worked actively to connect black writers with white publishers.

The relative paucity of African American literature produced before the launching of the Harlem Renaissance pointed to the lack of a cultural agenda for African Americans, in the view of civil rights leaders. According to David Levering Lewis, between 1908 and 1923 only a handful of significant literary works by black writers appeared: Sutton Griggs's *Pointing the Way* (1908), W. E. B. Du Bois's *The Quest of the Silver Fleece* (1911), James Weldon Johnson's *The Autobiography of an Ex-Colored Man* (1912), Du Bois's *Darkwater* (1920), McKay's *Harlem Shadows* (1922), and Jean Toomer's *Cane* (1923). We would add to that list Angelina Weld Grimké's *Rachel* (1916), Willis Richardson's *The Chip Woman's Fortune* (1923), Georgia Douglas Johnson's two books of poetry published in 1918 and 1922, and Joseph Cotter Jr.'s poetry collection, *The Band of Gideon* (1918). Leaders like Du Bois and Locke felt there was an opportunity to convince white America that African American writing was worthy of publication and that the race had the intellectual fortitude necessary to create such work. According to Du Bois, "until the art of black folk compels recognition they will not be regarded as human."[8] James Weldon Johnson also argued that the arts were a useful means for asserting the cultural dignity of African Americans: "No people that has produced great literature and art has ever been looked upon by the world as distinctly inferior. . . . And nothing will do more to change the mental attitude and raise his status than a demonstration of intellectual parity by the Negro through the production of literature and art."[9] These were the core beliefs that fueled the Harlem Renaissance.

The NAACP membership rolls included a number of scholarly writers who contributed frequently to *The Crisis*. Foremost among these were James Weldon Johnson, whose landmark anthology, *The Book of American Negro Poetry* (1922), brought many new writers to the fore; editor Du Bois; field organizer and novelist Walter White; and Jessie

Redmon Fauset. In 1919 Du Bois appointed Fauset as literary editor because he wanted to nurture the best African American talent in the nation. Fauset was not only an excellent editor, but a talented writer in her own right, whose exceptional literary career flourished during the 1920s. Fauset has been frequently described as midwife to the Harlem Renaissance because she discovered and encouraged so many new writers: Gwendolyn Bennett, Countee Cullen, Langston Hughes, Georgia Douglas Johnson, Claude McKay, and Jean Toomer. Fauset mined this talent in such a way as to make *The Crisis* the premier African American magazine of the era. As early as 1919, its circulation had reach 104,000, whereas the circulation of *Opportunity*, the closest competitor, reached only 11,000 by 1928.

Although *Opportunity* did not enjoy the same level of success as *The Crisis*, its editor, Charles S. Johnson, was another key figure of the Harlem Renaissance. According to Langston Hughes, Johnson "did more to encourage and develop Negro writers during the 1920s than anyone else."[10] This point is affirmed by Zora Neale Hurston, who believed that the Renaissance was Johnson's doing, but "his hush-mouth nature has caused it to be attributed to many others."[11] Johnson was particularly frustrated by the lack of respect and visibility accorded to black writers who did not write in dialect, and he used *Opportunity* to break down the stereotypes that confined African American writers to that form. According to Robert Hemenway, Johnson "single-handedly made *Opportunity* an expression of 'New Negro' thought, and 'New Negroes' made it clear that they would not accept a subordinate role in American society."[12] However, Johnson needed the proper means of getting this point across; it was not sufficient merely to bring these great artists to a black audience.

This was the motivation behind Johnson's organization of the March 21, 1924, Civic Club dinner to celebrate Jessie Fauset's new novel, although it was Regina Anderson of the 134th Street Branch of the New York Public Library in Harlem and Georgia Douglas Johnson who had urged him to honor her. He wanted to bring white literary giants shoulder to shoulder with black writers. The dinner proved to be a tremendous success, with black artists securing financial support or the promise of future support. Among the carefully selected white editors, writers, and publishers whom Johnson invited was Paul Kellogg, editor of *Survey Graphic*. Kellogg was so impressed with what he saw that he decided to commission a special issue devoted to Harlem and selected as editor Alain Locke, whom Johnson hailed as "dean" of the New Negro movement. This special issue was later revised and expanded into Locke's landmark anthology, *The New Negro* (1925).

Shortly after this momentous dinner, *The Crisis* and *Opportunity* instituted award ceremonies to recognize black artists, which also helped solidify collaboration between them and the white publishing industry. In 1924 *The Crisis* announced the Amy Einstein Spingarn

Prizes in Literature and Art. Amy Spingarn, wife of NAACP board member Joel Elias Spingarn, funded the program. She also served as a judge along with a racially integrated group of popular writers: Edward Bok, Witter Bynner, Charles Waddell Chesnutt, Sinclair Lewis, Robert Morss Lovett, Van Wyck Brooks, Carl Van Doren, Zona Gale, James Weldon Johnson, and Eugene O'Neill. The first *Opportunity* prizes were dispersed in May 1925 at an elaborate ceremony with approximately three hundred participants. The prizes were funded by the wife of National Urban League board chairman and Fisk University trustee L. Hollingsworth Wood. A week after the ceremony *The New York Herald Tribune* predicted that the country was "on the edge, if not already in the midst of, what might not improperly be called a Negro renaissance."[13] A second *Opportunity* awards banquet was followed by donations for future prizes and the establishment of other prizes related to African American arts and letters.

It is this interracial cooperation that sparked the influential anthology *The New Negro* in 1925 which grew out of the special issue of *Survey Graphic*, "Harlem: Mecca of the New Negro." Reaching a record number of 42,000 readers, the issue's sales persuaded Albert and Charles Boni to publish a revised and expanded collection of its poetry and prose, along with winners of the first *Opportunity* contest. In his foreword to the anthology, Locke set the terms that have come to be identified with the Harlem Renaissance: "There is a renewed race-spirit that consciously and proudly sets itself apart. Justifiably then, we speak of the offerings of this book embodying these ripening forces as culled from the first fruits of the Negro Renaissance." In the collection's first essay, his own "The New Negro," he sought to define this spirit: "[T]he younger generation is vibrant with a new psychology; the new spirit is awake in the masses."

Despite its limitations, *The New Negro* continues to hold a place of significance because it both alerted the world to the emergence of an international cultural revolution and attempted to define it. Although the text was held in high regard by its original audience, it is important to note the controversy surrounding it, strains of which run through the material here. Hailed as a definitive anthology, it was at the same time immediately critiqued by some contributors and even repudiated by others. These different responses appear to be rooted in Locke's attempts to smooth over important differences between the writers brought together in the collection, who differed in terms of ideology and aesthetics. For example, Jean Toomer would later write that Locke "tricked and misused" him because he did not consider himself a black writer despite his African American ancestry,[14] while Bruce Nugent was at least as concerned with his sexual identity as with his racial one. Langston Hughes and Countee Cullen were at opposite ends of the aesthetic spectrum, with Hughes preferring jazz- and blues-inspired poems over Cullen's lyrical verse. In fact, Cullen would later be the object of a veiled attack in Hughes's "The Negro Artist and the Racial Mountain" (1926) in which Hughes disparaged him for wishing to be known as a poet who "happened to be Negro," not as a "Negro poet" (see the essay section).

The New Negro did not address these important differences regarding aesthetics, politics, sexuality, and other pertinent issues dividing the younger and older generations of the movement. Indeed, Locke sought to gloss over these tensions. He omitted some of socialist Claude McKay's most militant poems, such as "If We Must Die" (see the creative writing section) and "Mulatto," and toned down a McKay poem he did include, "The White House," by changing the title to "White Houses," something McKay bitterly denounced. Despite A. Philip Randolph and Chandler Owen's important contribution to the movement through their editing of *The Messenger*, they were not included. Locke also ignored Garveyism, which has been characterized as the most important mass movement in black America of the 1920s. Garvey's *Negro World*, with a circulation of 200,000 at its peak, made literature readily available to the black masses. However, Locke's exclusion of Garveyism was probably in deference to Du Bois, whose integrationist philosophy clashed with Garvey's more radical separatism. Locke's rather conservative and elitist view of culture seems to stem from what Lewis describes as his Eurocentric definition of culture, a limitation that has since come to be blamed for many of the Renaissance's failures.[15]

The ideological and artistic differences that Locke attempted to minimize in his anthology could not be contained. This is particularly true of the very public ongoing debate between Locke and Du Bois regarding the role of literature and whether black writing should be art or propaganda, a debate worth summarizing here. Locke had spent his career developing a particular theory of African American art, which he articulated and defended through the duration of the Harlem Renaissance. As literary critic for *Opportunity*, he urged black writers to make their work "universally" relevant. In an early essay, "The Colonial Literature of France" (1923), he argued that the black artist should embrace "art for its own sake, combined with that stark cult of veracity—the truth whether it hurts or not."[16] Thus, in editing *The New Negro*, he sought to show that the new Renaissance writers should create "art for art's sake," which distinguished them from the previous wave of African American writers, like Grimké and Fauset, who addressed social issues in their creative work, explicitly using it as a propaganda tool.

This distinction did not sit well with many members of the civil rights establishment, particularly Du Bois, who was not only a writer, but a sociologist and political leader. Although he and Locke both looked at literature as a way to advance the race, they differed sharply over what constituted propaganda: "Mr. Locke has newly been seized with the idea that Beauty rather than propaganda should be the object of

Negro literature and art. His book proves the falseness of this thesis. . . . If Mr. Locke's thesis is insisted upon too much, it is going to turn the Negro Renaissance into decadence. It is the fight for Life and Liberty that is giving birth to Negro literature and art today and when turning from the fight or ignoring it, the young Negro tries to do pretty things or things that catch the passing fancy of the really unimportant critics and publishers about him, he will find that he has killed the soul of Beauty in art."[17] Locke responded by arguing that art as propaganda perpetuated notions of black inferiority.[18]

Although Du Bois and Locke were the primary figures in this debate, they were outdone by a group of young writers who took Locke's position much further than he had intended. Langston Hughes spoke for them in his 1926 essay, "The Negro Artist and the Racial Mountain" (see the essay section), which appeared in *The Nation*: "We younger Negro artists who create now intend to express our individual dark-skinned selves without fear or shame. If white people are pleased we are glad. If they are not, it doesn't matter. We know we are beautiful. And ugly too. The tom-tom cries and the tom-tom laughs. If colored people are pleased we are glad. If they are not, their displeasure doesn't matter either. We build our temples for tomorrow, strong as we know how, and we stand on top of the mountain, free within ourselves."

Following this manifesto of artistic freedom, Hughes and Richard Bruce Nugent envisioned a new magazine, which they named *Fire!!* They, along with Zora Neale Hurston, Gwendolyn Bennett, Aaron Douglas, and John Davis, selected the multitalented writer Wallace Thurman as editor. The editorial board members were determined to express their own sensibilities and to break free of the notion of art as politics to express instead the multiple dimensions of being African American. *Fire!!* promised "to burn up a lot of old, dead conventional Negro-white ideas of the past." The foreword to the first and only issue of November 1926 proclaimed to weave "vivid, hot designs upon an ebon bordered loom and . . . satisfy pagan thirst for beauty unadorned." In other words, this would be a daring and controversial journal. In fact, in order to underline its radical nature, Thurman decided that they needed to include at least one piece on homosexuality and another on prostitution. He and Nugent flipped a coin to determine who would write which story. Nugent's "Smoke, Lilies, and Jade!" about homoerotic attraction, and Thurman's "Cordelia the Crude," about a young prostitute, were the result (see the creative writing section).

Both pieces outraged middle-class African American sensibilities. Rean Graves of the *Baltimore Afro-American* was incensed by the magazine and wrote in his review, "I have just tossed the first issue of *Fire!!* into the fire." Benjamin Brawley went so far as to say that if the U.S. Post Office found out about Thurman's "Cordelia the Crude," the magazine might be barred from the mail.[19] Locke, although more balanced in his review, disapproved of the "effete echoes of contemporary decadence" he found throughout the issue.[20] For a time the writers associated with the project were ostracized by the black community. However, the real source of the magazine's demise was financial. The magazine was expensive to buy (one dollar), expensive to produce (one thousand dollars), lacked institutional support, and was poorly distributed. Ironically, hundreds of unsold copies burned in an actual apartment fire.

In many ways *Fire!!* was the antithesis of *The New Negro*, and it is telling that Alain Locke was not among its nine editors. Less than a year after appearing in his anthology, the younger writers had moved on without Locke. Symbolizing their upstart independence from the NAACP and NUL was Zora Neale Hurston's impudent dubbing of the influential whites that supported their contests and attended their parties as "Negrotarians," and her referral to prominent Harlem writers as the "Niggerati." In hopes of ironing out the differences between the younger and older generations, in late 1926 Du Bois organized a symposium entitled, "The Criteria of Negro Art" (see essay of the same name in the essay section). He feared that politics were disappearing from the Renaissance and that whites would point to the success of a handful of writers as evidence that there was no color line. However, the fissure remained, and the rebelling younger artists gained momentum, particularly with the publication of Claude McKay's *Home to Harlem* in 1928. This first bestseller of the Renaissance embodied the values of the younger generation.

Whether major or minor, female- or male-authored, texts of the Harlem Renaissance enrich our understanding of African American history and culture. These texts served as inspiring, pathbreaking trails—away from silence, against all odds, toward futures their creators only dimly perceived.

Notes

1. Steven Watson, *The Harlem Renaissance: Hub of African-American Culture, 1920–1930* (New York: Pantheon Books, 1995).
2. Nathan Huggins, *Voices from the Harlem Renaissance* (New York: Oxford University Press, 1976), 9. See also David Levering Lewis, ed., *The Portable Harlem Renaissance Reader* (New York: Viking, 1994).
3. Bernard Bell, *The Afro-American Novel and Its Tradition* (Amherst: University of Massachusetts Press, 1987).
4. Cheryl Wall, *Women of the Harlem Renaissance* (Bloomington: Indiana University Press, 1995); McDowell, *Changing Same*; and Claudia Tate, ed., *Georgia Douglas Johnson: The Selected Works* (New York: G.K. Hall, 1997).
5. Huggins, *Voices from the Harlem Renaissance*, 9.
6. Quoted in Patricia Liggins Hill, et al., *Call and Response: The Riverside Anthology of the African American Literary Tradition* (Boston: Houghton Mifflin, 1998), 791.
7. Lewis, *Portable Harlem Renaissance Reader*, xv.

8. Quoted in Lewis, *Portable Harlem Renaissance Reader*, xvi.
9. James Weldon Johnson, ed., *The Book of American Negro Poetry* (New York: Harcourt, Brace & Company, 1922), vii.
10. Quoted in Arna Bontemps, ed., *The Harlem Renaissance Remembered* (New York: Dodd, Mead, 1972), 215.
11. Quoted in Bontemps, *Harlem Renaissance Remembered*, 215.
12. Robert E. Hemenway, *Zora Neale Hurston: A Literary Biography* (Champaign-Urbana: University of Illinois Press, 1977), 9.
13. Quoted in Lewis, *Portable Harlem Renaissance Reader*, xxviii. According to Lewis, this statement gave the movement its name.
14. Quoted in Arnold Rampersad, Introduction to *The New Negro: Voices of the Harlem Renaissance*, ed. Alain Locke (New York: Athenaeum, 1992), xxii.
15. See Lewis, *When Harlem Was in Vogue*.
16. Quoted in Hill et al., *Call and Response*, 788.
17. Quoted in Hill et al., *Call and Response*, 789.
18. See Hill et al., *Call and Response*, 790.
19. Quoted in Trudier Harris and Thadious M. Davis, eds. *Afro-American Writers from the Harlem Renaissance to 1940*, vol. 51 of *Dictionary of Literary Biography* (Detroit: Gale, 1987), 263.
20. Quoted in Harris and Davis, *Afro-American Writers*, 220.

Introduction: Postmodernism, Then

Jason Gladstone and Daniel Worden

Gladstone and Worden's essay is an introduction to a special issue of Twentieth-Century Literature, *"Postmodernism, Then" (2011), which was inspired by declarations of postmodernism's demise, including a 2007* Twentieth-Century Literature *special issue, "After Postmodernism." In addition to the tendency to announce the end of postmodernism, Gladstone and Worden note the recent trend to dismiss postmodernism as an organizing principle. These authors, however, contend that recent studies of post-1945 literature instead tend to find continuity with modernism, and their essay traces the movement from postmodernism's dominance in the 1990s to Modernism's resurgence in the 2000s. Although Gladstone and Worden identify two discrete literary camps, they seek continuities between those who have abandoned postmodernism and those who continue to see its value. The essay is a good starting point for considering what postmodernism means now.*

From our contemporary vantage point, a case can certainly be made for the predictive or, perhaps, programmatic power of David Foster Wallace's 1993 essay "E Unibus Pluram: Television and U.S. Fiction." In this essay, Wallace posits a shift away from the postmodern irony of authors such as Don DeLillo, Mark Leyner, and Thomas Pynchon and towards a literature of sincerity that would be pioneered by a younger generation of writers raised with television.[1] And, indeed, in contemporary US literary culture, one can locate a shift away from "ironic watching" and towards the embrace of "single-entendre principles" almost everywhere: *McSweeney's Quarterly Concern*'s emo-sincerity, the ethnic bildungsroman's emphasis on multicultural identity as upward mobility, Jonathan Franzen's social realism, *n+1*'s enthusiastic recuperation of "high" cultural critique, novelists such as Michael Chabon's heartfelt embrace of genre fiction, and the memoir's ascension of best-seller lists, to name a few (Wallace 81). At the same time, alongside this concerted, professional abandonment of postmodernism's signature affective stance in recent North American literary enterprises, postmodernism has begun to drop out of academic discourse as well. While at least since 9/11 critics have been routinely declaring that postmodernism is, now, over, in the last five years an increasing number of critics have also begun to question whether postmodernism was ever a significant aspect of postwar American literary culture. It is these contemporary abandonments of postmodernism that provide the occasion for this special issue of *Twentieth-Century Literature*: the position papers and essays that compose *Postmodernism, Then* take the partial if not total eclipse of postmodernism in both contemporary American literature and literary criticism as the condition of possibility for returning to the category of the postmodern. In so doing, this special issue explores how postmodernism means, when it can be thought of as not only the present but also the recent past, not only a synonym for the postwar condition but also an instituted critical fiction, not only what comes after the close of high modernism but also as a strain of modernism, not only a unifying category that contains all late twentieth-century literature but also one aesthetic among many.

As Andrew Hoberek notes in his introduction to the *After Postmodernism* special issue of *Twentieth-Century Literature*, declarations of the decline of postmodernism have become enough of a critical commonplace that it has now become something of a critical commonplace to even cite this fact (233–34). And, as Brian McHale elucidates in "1966 Nervous Breakdown; or, When did Postmodernism Begin?," declarations and interrogations of the actual start-date of postmodernism have become equally commonplace (391–93). Of course, the expression of uncertainty about the beginning or end of postmodernity has been a standard feature of periodizing accounts of postmodernism at least since David Harvey prefaced his foundational *The Condition of Postmodernity* by asserting that "it does not matter whether postmodernism is or is not on the way out" (ix). Indeed, as Bill Brown suggests in "The Dark Wood of Postmodernity (Space, Faith, Allegory)," this recursive process of relocating the periodizing breaks that define postmodernity can, itself, be understood as part of the logic of postmodernism

(734–35).[2] And, accordingly, the infinite revisability of postmodernism as a periodizing concept can then be understood as an iteration of the malleability of a postmodernist aesthetic—an aesthetic that underwrites those studies that Ursula Heise describes as ones in which "certain sets of postmodern theories and philosophical perspectives (usually, but not always, influenced by one of several strains of French poststructuralism) . . . [are] brought to bear on texts and artworks not necessarily associated with [the post-1960] period" (966). From this perspective, the contemporary eclipse of postmodernism might, then, register as its ultimate triumph, as methods of reading or aesthetics once thought to be specifically tied to the postmodern era are now disseminated as reading practices in many, even all, historical periods, and as standard reference points for contemporary art and literature.[3]

More recently, the declarations and redeclarations of the ends of postmodernism have begun to be eclipsed by accounts of modernism, American literary history, and, most notably, postwar US literature and culture that not only abjure the employment of postmodern critical modes, but also either mount critiques of postmodernism or abandon it altogether as a periodizing concept or theoretical coordinate. This set of developments is made most apparent by the absence of an entry for either "postmodernism" or "postmodernity" in two recent reference volumes of American cultural and literary studies: Bruce Burgett and Glenn Hendler's *Keywords for American Cultural Studies* and Greil Marcus and Werner Sollors's *A New Literary History of America*. In *Keywords for American Cultural Studies* terms such as "globalization" and "postcolonialism" seem to demarcate the late twentieth- and early twenty-first centuries, yet in this volume these terms also refer back to earlier national and transnational moments, thus side-stepping the issue of postmodernism. In *A New Literary History of America*, late twentieth- and early twenty-first-century culture is atomized, and larger periodizing categories are rarely invoked. Instead, the volume focuses on individual writers, artists, and works. To be sure, these volumes' approaches differ. Burgett and Hendler's *Keywords for American Cultural Studies* dislocates the contemporary through the use of terms such as "globalization"—in her entry on that keyword, Lisa Lowe critiques globalization's common usage, to describe the late-twentieth and twenty-first centuries, because "it obscures a much longer history of global contacts and connections" (120). Marcus and Sollors, by contrast, break the contemporary into individual figures and discrete movements, seemingly disconnected from larger periodizing categories. For example, Hal Foster's entry on artist Robert Smithson's 1968 essay "A Museum of Language in the Vicinity of Art" discusses the "textual turn in art of the 1960s that parallels the more celebrated version of this turn in theory and philosophy" (947). But whereas in his 1979 essay "Earthwords," Craig Owens famously identifies Smithson's essays as a marker of the "transform[ation of] the visual field into a textual one" that "is coincident with, if not the definitive index of, the emergence of postmodernism," in *The New Literary History of America*, the "textual turn" described by Foster registers as less of an aesthetic shift than a stylistic choice made by Smithson and some other individual artists and writers (45–47).

The abandonment of postmodernism that is exemplified by reference volumes such as *Keywords for American Cultural Studies* and *A New Literary History of America* is in no way limited to such general approaches to US literary history. Rather, more direct versions of this abandonment characterize an increasing number of studies of twentieth-century and post-1945 literature. Driven by the "New Modernist Studies," the category of modernism has become quite elastic in recent scholarship. Modernist critics have convincingly dismantled the high/low divide, pushed modernism back into the nineteenth century and forward into the late twentieth century and demonstrated the value of turning to periodicals rather than discrete texts to map modernism as a more complex, varied aesthetic and historical period.[4] Often in support of this expansion of modernism, studies of contemporary literature have also increasingly set aside "postmodernism" as an organizing category. Concretized in the *After Postmodernism* special issue of *Twentieth-Century Literature*, and present in a number of other works that preceded and followed it, critics have begun to think of the contemporary moment as no longer postmodern.[5] In fact, recent studies have positioned the decade of the 1990s as the end or exhaustion of postmodern aesthetics, as well as the site for the emergence of contemporary literary styles that seem to critique and posit alternatives to postmodern aesthetics.[6] Along with this revaluation of the contemporary against the postmodern, another set of recent studies of postwar literature and culture has emphasized the ways in which postmodernism was never, in fact, the dominant cultural logic or literary rubric of the late twentieth century. For example, works by Michael Clune, François Cusset, James English, Amy Hungerford, Caren Irr, Alan Liu, Sean McCann, Mark McGurl, and Ted Striphas have focused on institutions such as creative writing programs, literary prizes, religion, the presidency, copyright law, the free market, the publishing industry, the information economy, and the English Department's ties to a specific form of reading as determining forces in post-1945 literature and literary studies.

One of the effects of these approaches to post-1945 literature has been to displace postmodernism as an explanatory category in the name of more pragmatic institutional histories, circulation studies, sociological inquires, and reception models. For Sean McCann and Michael Szalay, this shift marks a rejection of New Left politics and, by extension, postmodernism, for it entails a recognition that many of the concepts and theories central to postmodernism—the poststructuralist theory of language, Foucauldian understandings of discipline and the subject, Althusserian accounts of compromised agency, and gender/

queer theory's emphasis on the power of the "unspeakable"—are, in fact, not radical ideas but rather "cherished and ultimately comforting folklore of the late capitalist economy" (460). At the same time critics like Sianne Ngai and Ursula Heise have produced accounts of the postwar period that dispense with postmodernism as an explanatory category while retaining it as an aspect of their analyses of the contemporary condition. In essays such as "Merely Interesting" and "Our Aesthetic Categories," Ngai extends David Harvey's claim that modernism and postmodernism are "diverging responses to a single process of modernization" by describing our ongoing modernity as one characterized by "aesthetic categories" that "cut across modernism and postmodernism" and which cannot, therefore, be usefully or accurately described as either modern or postmodern (951–53). And whereas the "ecocritical insurgency" that was consolidated by the 1995 publication of Lawrence Buell's *The Environmental Imagination* was largely organized against postmodernism's instituted eradications of nature, in *Sense of Place and Sense of Planet* Heise identifies a set of characteristically postmodernist features of post-1960 novels as literary modes of engaging with the scenarios of ecological risk and global connectedness that, on her account, characterize the postwar period (17–67).

In terms of periodization, these new approaches to post-1945 literature often find continuity where advocates of postmodernism find rupture. Citing Wendy Steiner's "Postmodern Fictions, 1970–1990" as a foundational text in her essay "On the Period Formerly Known as Contemporary," Amy Hungerford argues that the last decade of postwar literary criticism is characterized by works that identify the postwar period not as the supercession of modernism, but as the "triumph" of "modernism's aesthetics" (418). Indeed, the two most important periodizing studies of the last decade, Walter Benn Michaels's *The Shape of the Signifier* and Mark McGurl's *The Program Era*, both identify the post-1945 period as a continuation or extension of modernism. In *The Shape of the Signifier*, Michaels argues that the theoretical framework of postmodernism—the dual commitment to the materiality of the text and the primacy of the subject position—is, in fact, a postwar iteration of a modernist problematic: the imbrication of concerns about the ontology of the artwork with a distinctly modern notion of identity. Both here and in subsequent essays, such as "Going Boom" and "The Un-usable Past," Michaels then also identifies postmodernism as the still active cultural style of a neoliberalism that works to project the world postwar America wants neoliberalism to have produced (a world organized by subject positions and divided into identities) rather than the world it has actually produced (a world structured by economic inequality). In *The Program Era* McGurl redistributes a number of more and less agreed upon descriptions of the characteristic formal and thematic features of postwar American fiction—including those that are regularly identified as being definitive of postmodernist fiction—in order to document how the postwar literary field is structured not by the emergence of postmodernism but by the fact that modernist principles of writing were "institutionalized as another form of original research sponsored by the booming science-oriented universities of the Cold War era" (4). McGurl then identifies the aesthetics usually identified as postmodernism as one of the three "relatively discrete but in practice overlapping aesthetic formations" (32) that compose "the totality of postwar American fiction," and he suggests that this particular formation is best described as "technomodernist" (42) (rather than postmodernist) in order to both register its engagement with information technology and to reassert its "obvious continuity" with interwar literary modernism. In his recent essay "Ordinary Doom: Literary Studies in the Waste Land of the Present," McGurl further argues that "the return of the rhetoric of 'modernity' and the partial eclipse of 'postmodernism'" (337) in recent criticism is an aspect of the emergent recognition that "the contemporary" is best described as the current stage of an ongoing modernity (342–43).

As Hungerford also notes, whereas the field of postwar American literature is, for the most part, still structured by the "reigning bifurcation of contemporary fiction into the 'postmodern' avant-garde" and "realist" writing of "women and people of color," studies such as Michaels's and McGurl's follow on Steiner's to the extent that they demonstrate how "a reading of experimentalist novels . . . must be . . . integrated with a discussion of realist writing" (411).[7] To the extent that this is the case, a parallel development can be traced in the field of African-American literary studies. Following on Phillip Brian Harper's 1994 study *Framing the Margins: The Social Logic of Postmodern Culture*, in which he argues that "the fractured subject" that many critics identify as a hallmark of postmodern culture "has long formed a staple element of minority literatures" (Dubey 21), Madhu Dubey's 2003 study *Signs and Cities: Black Literary Postmodernism* demonstrates how anti-realist postwar African-American fiction performs a version of the cultural and historical labor that critics continue to arrogate to realist modes of minority literature. Moreover, in making her argument for the utility of postmodernism as a periodizing concept in regards to African-American literary and cultural studies, Dubey develops Harper's argument that the social marginalization that underwrites the modes of postwar minority literature is, itself, a "condition of possibility for postmodern culture" (Dubey 21). These locations of the postmodern as an amplification of, rather than a departure from earlier moments in literary history are, then, continuous with Kenneth W. Warren's *What Was African-American Literature?* which argues that "African-American literature" — a field concretized under the sign of postmodern and poststructuralist theory in works such as Houston A. Baker's *Blues, Ideology, and Afro-American Literature* and Henry Louis Gates's *The Signifying Monkey* — is itself a construct of an aesthetically and politically modernist notion of literature's relationship to the social world (1–43).

These recent shifts in how critics understand postmodernism also register in the work of one of the major theorists of postmodernism, Fredric Jameson. Charting his work from *Postmodernism, or, the Cultural Logic of Late Capitalism* to the present, one notices a movement away from thinking of postmodernism as an unreadable and vertiginous system to the positing of a "singular modernity" and, most recently, a renewed interest in the dialectic—something that Jameson's earlier work suggested had stalled out in postmodernism but, it seems, is now moving again. In *Postmodernism*, Jameson critiques the historical amnesia and cognitive vertigo dominant in late capitalism, famously positing that postmodernism signals an impasse, a cultural logic that annihilates both history and utopia with its celebratory consumerist and technological ideologies. Unable to map the present, we must await a "new political art" that can achieve

> a breakthrough to some as yet unimaginable new mode of representing [the world space of multinational capitalism], in which we may again begin to grasp our positioning as individual and collective subjects and regain a capacity to act and struggle which is neutralized by our spatial as well as our social confusion. (54)

In *A Singular Modernity*, Jameson adjusts this construction of postmodernism by setting it into relation with modernism. In that book, Jameson supplements his account of postmodernism by characterizing "interwar modernism" as a largely "American invention" of the "years *following* World War II" (164–65, emphasis added). He then characterizes both this "late modernism" and the recent critical investments in it—the same investments that Hungerford, McGurl, and others identify with the eclipse of postmodernism—as expressions of a regressive "ideology of modernism" (210) which is, itself, an aspect of a continuing postmodernity. Following that invocation of singularity (itself a concept seemingly inaccessible from within the postmodern landscape Jameson outlines in the 1990s), Jameson turns to utopia in *Archaeologies of the Future*, arguing that a "post-globalization Left" can now engage in utopian thought as a negation of the world market's "invincible universality" (xii) under the "slogan of anti-anti-Utopianism" (xvi). These movements away from a totalizing, rigid construction of late capitalism and toward a sense of the political possibilities that allow for the construction of alternatives to late capitalism have, in recent years, been followed by *Valences of the Dialectic* and *The Hegel Variations*, both of which aim to recuperate the dialectic for the contemporary moment. Indeed, Jameson concludes a recent essay on Marx's *Capital* with nothing less than a slogan of his own—"Cynicism of the Intellect, Utopianism of the Will!"—that makes clear his increasing emphasis on action as a necessary complement to thought in our contemporary moment ("A New Reading of *Capital*" 13).

While Jameson's method differs greatly from that practiced by most of the critics mentioned thus far, the shifts in his thinking over the past two decades also reflect the same story of postmodernism's role in literary studies that we have been tracing elsewhere. In the 1990s, postmodernism is unquestionably dominant, only to be offset by a stronger notion of modernism in the 2000s. In recent years, Jameson's work signals a further shift into the contemporary, as he returns to some of Marxist critique's first principles — the dialectic and utopia, and to foundational texts — Hegel's *Phenomenology of Spirit* and Marx's *Capital*. Here and elsewhere the contemporary now signals renewed possibility. At the same time, both Jameson's 1984 essay and 1991 book on postmodernism are now generally regarded as *loci classici* of American accounts of the postwar period. As critics like Phillip Wegner continue to extend the specific account of the postwar period that these works initiated, the "postmodernism" that these works consolidated also continues to serve as the basis for a range of critical studies of postwar American literature and culture. In their introduction to *The Way We Read Now* special issue of *Representations*, Stephen Best and Sharon Marcus identify the publication of Jameson's 1981 book *The Political Unconscious* as the key episode in the institutionalization of the mode of interpretation — "symptomatic reading" — that, in their account, continues to characterize postwar American literary and cultural criticism. Of course, many other contemporary movements in literary criticism and theory similarly draw from the theoretical tradition established under the category of the postmodern. These include the influential posthumanist accounts of the postwar period advanced by critics such as Donna Haraway and N. Katherine Hayles, who assume the basic features of Jameson's account of postmodernism while inverting his critique of late capitalist technology by prioritizing the development of technology over that of capital. Extending this mode, Cary Wolfe's advocacy of a particularly Derridean construction of posthumanism and scholars, such as Brian Massumi, who draw on the works of Gilles Deleuze and other theorists to posit virtuality and affect as central terms in contemporary culture, retain much of the theoretical and aesthetic discourse first introduced under the name of the postmodern.

Moreover, the influence of French philosophers Alain Badiou and Jacques Rancière, along with other European thinkers like Giorgio Agamben, Zygmunt Bauman, Antonio Negri, and Paolo Virno, in the past decade point to the continuing relevance of postmodern theory to contemporary literary studies. In his introduction to the *PMLA* special section on "Literary Criticism for the Twenty-First Century," Jonathan Culler makes the argument that the future of literary criticism will be, if not necessarily Derridean, then one that was at least made available by "the theory revolution" (914). In the same special section of *PMLA*, Richard Klein argues for a specifically Derridean future for literary criticism—a future which seems to be taking shape in works such as Rei Terada's *Looking Away* and Anne-Lise François's *Open Secrets*—and in their *Theory Now* special issue of *South Atlantic Quarterly*, Grant Farred and Michael Hardt present a collection of essays on the states of theory in contemporary literary studies that, at the very least, demonstrates the resilience of the link between theory and emancipatory politics for many critics. There are then also recent studies such as Rey Chow's *The Age of the World Target* and Lydia H. Liu's *The Freudian Robot* which employ renovated versions of poststructuralism in order to recalibrate the relationship between poststructuralism and modernity: Chow through an account of the interdependent institutionalizations of comparative literature, area studies, and poststructuralism in the postwar US academy; Liu through an account of interwar literary modernism, deconstruction, and cybernetics. In these theory-inflected strains of contemporary literary and cultural criticism, postmodernism, then, is alive and well, even if it is not always invoked by name.

At the same time, there are a number of critics who have proposed new programs for doing literary critical work that are explicitly pitched as alternatives to the now instituted modes of criticism associated with postmodernism and backed (most often) by poststructuralism. In the introduction to *The Way We Read Now*, Best and Marcus propose that the mode of "surface reading" they delineate in their essay "broadens the scope of critique to include the kinds of interpretive activity that seek to understand the complexity of literary surfaces—surfaces that have been rendered invisible by symptomatic reading" (1). In *Graphs, Maps, Trees*, Franco Moretti heralds the "disappearance of the text" and proposes a mode of "distant reading" backed by "*a materialist conception of form*" which attends to units both far smaller and far larger than the individual work (92). Wai Chee Dimock's *Through Other Continents* abandons both poststructuralist and historical-materialist modes of reading while renovating the protocols of close reading in order to read American literature across deep time and, hence, outside of the temporal and spatial constraints imposed by the nation state (1–6). While these programs differ significantly from one another, what they have in common—and what they also have in common with the periodizing or period-specific projects of critics such as Hungerford, McCann and Szalay, McGurl, and Michaels—is that they are backed by diverse invocations of "form," invocations that are conceived of as rejections or departures from postmodernism. In recent essays such as "The Politics of a Good Picture" and "Neoliberal Aesthetics: Fried, Rancière and the Form of the Photograph," Michaels has made an explicit, programmatic, version of this argument for form and against postmodernism. In these essays Michaels has positioned form against multiculturalist, identity-focused approaches to literature dominant in the past two decades: here, the return to form promises actual engagements with both history and the contemporary moment that bypasses what are, by now, quite familiar and, for Michaels, quite obviously ineffective claims about literature's role in troubling social hierarchies.[8]

From the perspective of this special issue of *Twentieth-Century Literature*, what needs to be noted here is that a shift away from tired liberal politics and towards a reinvigorated notion of form also motivated early critics and theorists of postmodernism in the 1960s and 1970s. For example, in an account of what she called the "new sensibility" in a 1965 essay in *Mademoiselle*, Susan Sontag claims that contemporary art, ranging from Samuel Beckett, William S. Burroughs, and Robert Rauschenberg to the Supremes, Budd Boetticher, and Jean-Luc Godard, "demands less 'content' in art, and is more open to the pleasures of 'form' and style . . . is also less snobbish, less moralistic—in that it does not demand that pleasure in art necessarily be associated with edification" (303). This argument against content is also key to John Barth's well-known 1967 essay, "The Literature of Exhaustion." Central to any account of metafiction, Barth's advocacy of "virtuosity" and exuberance at the possibilities offered by exhaustion rests on the novel's obsolescence and the ways in which this frees the writer to focus on form rather than content. In Barth's essay, metafiction signals a revitalization of the novel as the novelist is able to examine the text's own status as an object in the world: "A novel is as much a piece of the real world as a letter" (145). Accordingly, for Barth and Sontag, postmodernism inaugurates a renewed attention to form, one that is, perhaps, instructive for our contemporary moment, when critics are similarly troubled by literature's, and the English Department's, changing, even receding, role in the twenty-first century.[9] Indeed, the argument could be made that returning to form is, in a way, returning to postmodernism, but a postmodernism that looks quite different than the version ultimately dominant in English Departments in the 1990s. At the same time, in the optic introduced by the recent work we have been discussing in this essay, it could also be claimed that this return to form recasts the turn to form that characterized the advent of postmodernism as something other than the advent of postmodernism: as an extension of modernism, as an aspect of the postwar system of American fiction, as a component of emergent neoliberalism, or as an aspect of a contemporary aesthetic that has yet to be adequately described.

By briefly sketching the question of form at postmodernism's emergence in the US, we hope to gesture to some continuities between what we see as two camps in recent scholarship on late twentieth- and early twenty-first-century literature and culture. On the one hand, postmodernism still retains the explanatory force that it once did for scholars who draw heavily on theory and who look to literature for moments of disruption, resistance, and utopian imagining. On the other hand, postmodernism is reduced or abandoned by critics who turn to institutional histories of post-1945 literature and who see in that literature continuity with, and the institutionalization of, modernism. Both of these approaches hinge upon competing accounts of literary form and its connection to the social world. Accordingly, we believe that a reevaluation of postmodernism might be useful for thinking of form today, especially since early critics of postmodernism found themselves to be equally uncertain and divided about what forms and functions literature might take in the late twentieth century. We can look back now to that speculation and uncertainty with a degree of familiarity, as postmodernism itself becomes a question, again, rather than a dominant category.

At the very least, what these divergent approaches to post-1945 literature make apparent is that, at present, the question of the postmodern is a peculiarly pressing one. Did postmodernity ever begin? Is it now over? Has it been replaced by the contemporary or superseded by the global? Does the postmodern provide a rubric for conceiving of new aesthetic and political practices? Is it a term that remains necessary for the current discourse in postwar US literary studies? Was postmodernism an instituted critical fiction? Was it a major or minor aspect of postwar American literature and culture? Is the postmodern just modernism, after all? Does the postmodern now mark out the basic condition of life in the early twenty-first century, rather than an aesthetic vanguard? However the question of the postmodern is posed, it is clear that it remains central to any adequate conception of both the present moment and its immediate past. . . .

Notes

1. David Foster Wallace's "E Unibus Pluram: Television and U.S. Fiction" was originally published in *Review of Contemporary Fiction* 13.2 (1993): 151–94.

2. Other influential periodizing accounts of postmodernism include Anderson's genealogy of the term from the early twentieth century to the 1990s, DeKoven's case for the 1960s as the site for postmodernism's emergence, and Huyssen's account of postmodernism's critiques of and departures from modernism.

3. For instance, Jean-François Lyotard's foundational postmodern critique of "metanarratives" has been absorbed into literary studies under the heading of the New Historicism, and postmodern art's frequent critique of the museum—as theorized by Douglas Crimp—has itself become a mainstay of the contemporary art museum, with its emphasis on interactivity, site-specific installations, and critique of the high/low divide.

4. For a gloss on the "New Modernist Studies," see Mao and Walkowitz's definitional essay. Notable anthologies of scholarship in the New Modernist Studies that exhibit the above-mentioned critical impulses include those edited by Ardis and Collier, Caughie, Doyle and Winkiel, and Mao and Walkowitz.

5. While Hoberek's *After Postmodernism* special issue solidified postmodernism's waning influence in literary criticism, this shift can also be seen earlier, in many of the short essays in Hoberek's 2001 "Twentieth-Century

Literature in the New Century: A Symposium." Hoberek prefaces the symposium essays with an account of the new choice that scholars of twentieth-century literature have in the twenty-first century:

> [W]e can now construe ourselves as either historicists or contemporarists, depending on our taste. That is, we can either continue to study new literature, or else we can devote ourselves to the twentieth century as a completed historical period (ceding new work by Rushdie or Morrison, Ai or Stoppard, to our colleagues in twenty-first century lit, or else treating it as an embarrassing coda, somewhat like Faulkner's post-World War II novels). (9)

Hoberek's reference to Faulkner points to the periodizing function of the category "modernism," and, by implication, the question of postmodernism's usefulness as a period marker for the late twentieth and early twenty-first centuries. At this moment, one cannot imagine the successful formation, or even the desirability, of a "Postmodernist Studies Association" that would mirror the Modernist Studies Association. Instead, groups implicitly organized against the periodizing claims of postmodernism, Post45 and ASAP (The Association for the Study of the Arts of the Present), have begun to serve that function.

6. Recent scholarship that locates the 1990s as a hinge point between postmodernism and the contemporary moment includes Adams, Cohen, Green, Heise, Steiner, and Wegner.

7. Of note in this regard is the way in which a number of recent accounts of postwar, contemporary, and even postmodern literature seek to replace characteristically postmodernist features with features that are routinely associated with ethnic literature. Rachel Adams does this sequentially in her essay "The Ends of America, The Ends of Postmodernism," insofar as the "American literary globalism" she describes as following postmodernism is, essentially, an expanded version of ethnic American literature. Ursula Heise does this synchronically in her essay "Postmodern Novels," insofar as her argument is that postmodernism needs to be understood as a response to mass media that consists of an effort to capture or preserve "oral culture"—which is, itself, a long-standing description of the central project of ethnic American literatures. We are indebted to Maria A. Windell for this insight.

8. For example, in "The Politics of a Good Picture," an essay on Jeff Wall's 1982 photograph *Mimic*, Michaels reads the photograph as "[asserting] the irreducibility of form to affect," which, in the photograph, is split between class inequality, a formal relation, and racial discrimination, an affective relation (183). That is, for Michaels, this irreducibility is something that is often present in aesthetic objects, but it is often neglected, ignored, or conflated with affective content by critics who read texts through a multiculturalist methodology.

9. While this brief gloss deals with literary—and, novelistic—form, the same tracing could be accomplished for the question of modernism's relation to postmodernism, a connection that is central to Ihab Hassan's 1971 "paracritical bibliography" of postmodernism. Hassan claims that postmodernism is "the change in Modernism" (190), but also that postmodernism operates through "Anarchy," a radical departure from modernist

"Authority" (205). In Hassan's early accounts of postmodernism, we see the history to contemporary debates about the efficacy of postmodern politics as well as postmodernism's connection to or rupture with modernism. Removed from the critical imperative to advocate for (or, against) postmodernism that motivated Hassan and other critics, our contemporary moment offers a unique vantage point by which to reevaluate the stakes of postmodernism.

Works cited

Adams, Rachel. "The Ends of America, The Ends of Postmodernism." Hoberek, *After Postmodernism* 248–72.

Anderson, Perry. *The Origins of Postmodernity*. New York: Verso, 1998.

Ardis, Ann L., and Patrick Collier, eds. *Transatlantic Print Culture, 1880–1940: Emerging Media, Emerging Modernisms*. New York: Palgrave, 2008.

Baker, Jr., Houston A. *Blues, Ideology, and Afro-American Literature: A Vernacular Theory*. Chicago: U of Chicago P, 1984.

Barth, John. "The Literature of Exhaustion." *Postmodernism and the Contemporary Novel: A Reader*. Ed. Bran Nicol. Edinburgh: Edinburgh UP, 2002. 138–47.

Best, Stephen, and Sharon Marcus. "Surface Reading: An Introduction." *The Way We Read Now*. Spec. issue of *Representations* 108.1 (2009): 1–21.

Brown, Bill. "The Dark Wood of Postmodernity (Space, Faith, Allegory)." *PMLA* 120.3 (2005): 734–50.

Buell, Lawrence. "The Ecocritical Insurgency." *New Literary History* 30.3 (1999): 699–712.

———. *The Environmental Imagination: Thoreau, Nature Writing, and the Formation of American Culture*. Cambridge: Harvard UP, 1995.

Burgett, Bruce, and Glenn Hendler, eds. *Keywords for American Cultural Studies*. New York: New York UP, 2007.

Caughie, Pamela L., ed. *Disciplining Modernism*. New York: Palgrave, 2009.

Chow, Rey. *The Age of the World Target: Self-Referentiality in War, Theory, and Comparative Work*. Durham: Duke UP, 2006.

Clune, Michael. *American Literature and the Free Market, 1945–2000*. Cambridge: U of Cambridge P, 2010.

Cohen, Samuel. *After the End of History: American Fiction in the 1990s*. Iowa City: U of Iowa P, 2009.

Crimp, Douglas. *On the Museum's Ruins*. Cambridge: MIT Press, 1993.

Culler, Jonathan. "Critical Paradigms." *PMLA* 125.4 (2010): 905–15.

Cusset, François. *French Theory: How Foucault, Derrida, Deleuze, & Co. Transformed the Intellectual Life of the United States*. Trans. Jeff Fort, Josephine Berganza, and Marlon Jones. Minneapolis: U of Minnesota P, 2008.

DeKoven, Marianne. *Utopia Limited: The Sixties and the Emergence of the Postmodern*. Durham: Duke UP, 2004.

Dimock, Wai Chee. *Through Other Continents: American Literature Across Deep Time*. Princeton: Princeton UP, 2006.

Doyle, Laura, and Laura Winkiel, eds. *Geomodernisms: Race, Modernism, Modernity*. Bloomington: Indiana UP, 2005.

Dubey, Madhu. *Signs and Cities: Black Literary Postmodernism*. Chicago: U of Chicago P, 2003.

English, James F. *The Economy of Prestige: Prizes, Awards, and the Circulation of Culural Value*. Cambridge: Harvard UP, 2005.

Farred, Grant, and Michael Hardt, eds. *Theory Now*. Spec. issue of *South Atlantic Quarterly* 110.1 (2011): 1–230.

Foster, Hal. "The Illusory Babels of Art." Marcus 943–48.

François, Anne-Lise. *Open Secrets: The Literature of Uncounted Experience*. Stanford: Stanford UP, 2008.

Gates, Jr., Henry Louis. *The Signifying Monkey: A Theory of African-American Literary Criticism*. New York: Oxford UP, 1988.

Green, Jeremy. *Late Postmodernism: American Fiction at the Millennium*. New York: Palgrave, 2005.

Haraway, Donna. *Modest Witness@Second Millenium. FemaleMan Meets Onco-Mouse™: Feminism and Technoscience*. New York: Routledge, 1997.

———. *Simiams, Cyborgs and Women: The Reinvention of Nature*. New York: Routledge, 1991.

Harper, Phillip Brian. *Framing the Margins: The Social Logic of Postmodern Culture*. New York: Oxford UP, 1994.

Harvey, David. *The Condition of Postmodernity: An Enquiry into the Origins of Cultural Change*. Malden, MA: Blackwell, 1990.

Hassan, Ihab. "POSTmodernISM: A Paracritical Bibliography." *Postmodernism and the Contemporary Novel: A Reader*. Ed. Bran Nicol. Edinburgh: Edinburgh UP, 2002. 186–206.

Hayles, N. Katherine. *How We Became Posthuman: Virtual Bodies in Cybernetics, Literature, and Informatics*. Chicago: U of Chicago P, 1999.

———. *My Mother Was a Computer: Digital Subjects and Literary Texts*. Chicago: U of Chicago P, 2005.

Heise, Ursula. "Postmodern Novels." *The Cambridge History of the American Novel*. Ed. Leonard Cassuto. Cambridge: U of Cambridge P, 2011. 964–86.

———. *Sense of Place and Sense of Planet: The Environmental Imagination of the Global*. New York: Oxford UP, 2008.

Hoberek, Andrew. "Introduction: After Postmodernism." *After Postmodernism: Form and History in Contemporary American Fiction*. Spec. issue of *Twentieth-Century Literature* 53.3 (2007): 233–47.

Hoberek, Andrew, ed. *After Postmodernism: Form and History in Contemporary American Fiction*. Spec. issue of *Twentieth-Century Literature* 53.3 (2007): 233–393.

———. "Twentieth-Century Literature in the New Century: A Symposium." *College English* 64.1 (2001): 9–33.

Hungerford, Amy. "On the Period Formerly Known as the Contemporary." *American Literary History* 20.1–2 (2008): 410–19.

———. *Postmodern Belief: American Literature and Religion since 1960*. Princeton: Princeton UP, 2010.

Huyssen, Andreas. *After the Great Divide: Modernism, Mass Culture, Postmodernism*. Bloomington: Indiana UP, 1986.

Irr, Caren. *Pink Pirates: Contemporary American Women Writers and Copyright*. Iowa City: U of Iowa P, 2010.

Jameson, Fredric. *Archaeologies of the Future: The Desire Called Utopia and Other Science Fictions*. New York: Verso, 2005.

———. *The Hegel Variations: On the Phenomenology of Spirit*. New York: Verso, 2010.

———. "A New Reading of *Capital*." *Mediations* 25.1 (2010): 5–14.

———. *Postmodernism, or, the Cultural Logic of Late Capitalism*. Durham: Duke UP, 1991.

———. *A Singular Modernity: Essay on the Ontology of the Present*. New York: Verso, 2002.

———. *Valences of the Dialectic*. New York: Verso, 2009.

Klein, Richard. "The Future of Literary Criticism." *PMLA* 125.4 (2010): 920–23.

Liu, Alan. *The Laws of Cool: Knowledge Work and the Culture of Information*. Chicago: U of Chicago P, 2004.

Liu, Lydia H. *The Freudian Robot: Digital Media and the Future of the Unconscious*. Chicago: U of Chicago P, 2010.

Lowe, Lisa. "Globalization." Burgett 120–23.

Lyotard, Jean-François. *The Postmodern Condition: A Report on Knowledge*. Trans. Geoff Bennington and Brian Massumi. Minneapolis: U of Minnesota P, 1984.

Mao, Douglas, and Rebecca Walkowitz. "The New Modernist Studies." *PMLA* 123.3 (2008): 737–48.

Mao, Douglas, and Rebecca Walkowitz, eds. *Bad Modernisms*. Durham: Duke UP, 2006.

Marcus, Greil, and Werner Sollors, eds. *A New Literary History of America*. Cambridge: Harvard UP, 2009.

Massumi, Brian. *Parables for the Virtual: Movement, Affect, Sensation*. Durham: Duke UP, 2002.

McCann, Sean. *A Pinnacle of Feeling: American Literature and Presidential Government*. Princeton: Princeton UP, 2008.

McCann, Sean, and Michael Szalay. "Do You Believe in Magic? Literary Thinking after the New Left." *Countercultural Capital: Essays on the Sixties from Some Who Weren't There*. Ed. Sean McCann and Michael Szalay. Spec. issue of *Yale Journal of Criticism* 18.2 (2005): 435–68.

McGurl, Mark. "Ordinary Doom: Literary Studies in the Wasteland of the Present." *New Literary History* 41.2 (2010): 329–49.

———. *The Program Era: Postwar Fiction and the Rise of Creative Writing*. Cambridge: Harvard UP, 2009.

McHale, Brian. "1966 Nervous Breakdown; or, When Did Postmodernism Begin?" *Modern Language Quarterly* 69.3 (2008): 391–413.

Michaels, Walter Benn. "Going Boom." *Bookforum* 15.5 (2009).

———. "Neoliberal Aesthetics: Fried, Rancière and the Form of the Photograph." *nonsite.org*. January 25, 2011.

———. "The Politics of a Good Picture: Race, Class, and Form in Jeff Wall's *Mimic*." *PMLA* 125.1 (2010): 177–84.

———. *The Shape of the Signifier: 1967 to the End of History*. Princeton: Princeton UP, 2004.

———. "The Un-usable Past." *The Baffler: Civilization With a Krag*. 16 December 2009.

Moretti, Franco. *Graphs, Maps, Trees: Abstract Models for a Literary History*. New York: Verso, 2005.

Ngai, Sianne. "Merely Interesting." *Critical Inquiry* 34 (2004): 777–817.

———. "Our Aesthetic Categories." *PMLA* 125.4 (2010): 948–58.

Owens, Craig. *Beyond Recognition: Representation, Power, and Culture*. Ed. Scott Bryson. Berkeley: U of California P, 1992.

Sontag, Susan. "One Culture and the New Sensibility." *Against Interpretation and Other Essays*. New York: Farrar, Straus and Giroux, 1966. 293–304.

Steiner, Wendy. "Postmodern Fictions, 1970–1990." *The Cambridge History of American Literature*. Ed. Sacvan Bercovitch. Vol. 7. New York: Cambridge UP, 1999. 425–538.

Striphas, Ted. *The Late Age of Print: Everyday Book Culture from Consumerism to Control*. New York: Columbia UP, 2009.

Terada, Rei. *Looking Away: Phenomenality and Dissatisfaction, Kant to Adorno*. Cambridge: Harvard UP, 2009.

Wallace, David Foster. "E Unibus Pluram: Television and U.S. Fiction." *A Supposedly Fun Thing I'll Never Do Again: Essays and Arguments*. Boston: Back Bay, 1997. 21–82.

Warren, Kenneth W. *What Was African-American Literature?* Cambridge: Harvard UP, 2011.

Wegner, Phillip E. *Life Between Two Deaths, 1989–2001: U.S. Culture in the Long Nineties*. Durham: Duke UP, 2009.

Wolfe, Cary. *What is Posthumanism?* Minneapolis: U of Minnesota P, 2010.

3

Considering Identities

W hat difference does identity play in our reading or teaching of literature? Does knowing that Paul Laurence Dunbar was African American impact our reading of the "we" in "We Wear the Mask"? Must this image of a two-faced existence be an African American existence? What effect does Amy Lowell's sexuality have on our reading of her poetry? Does it matter whether the beloved in "The Letter" is a man or a woman? What about the instructor's identity? Would an atheist be just as effective as a Methodist teaching Edward Taylor's "Upon a Spider Catching a Fly"? I think we have come to a point at which we recognize our ability to teach across identities while also realizing the continued significance of these social constructions.

The essays collected in this section explore some of the considerations related to identity that affect our reading and teaching of American literature, including identity construction, whiteness, ethnic literature, gender, class, and sexuality. Of course, this is not an exhaustive list of identities, but it does highlight some of the prevalent concerns of American literary studies. The opening essay, "Assumed Identities" by David Palumbo-Liu, addresses some social critics' belief that we should move "beyond identity" (p. 130). He argues that we need to move beyond racial typing in order to actually reach individual identities. According to Palumbo-Liu, assumed identities do not rely on mutual recognition, but instead are based on indirect experience that shapes individual encounters. This indirect experience is related to dominant assumptions about racially marked people that are embedded within institutional practices. Thus, Palumbo-Liu makes an effective argument for the continued importance of considering identities.

AnaLouise Keating's "Interrogating 'Whiteness,' (De)Constructing 'Race'" addresses the importance of examining whiteness while avoiding the reinforcement of permanent racial categories. Keating explores the tricky balancing act of deconstructing race without losing sight of the fluidity of racial identities. To illustrate her own struggles with this balancing act, Keating provides several examples from her classes. She notes her successful practice of providing important contextual information to aid her students in identifying the influence of race in the writing of a Native American author, Scott Momaday, and an African American writer, Nella Larsen. But when she asked students to discuss the impact of Ralph Waldo Emerson's whiteness, they could not respond. It was much easier for students to recognize racial subtexts in literature by nonwhites. Keating asserts that the invisible omnipresence of whiteness allows it to operate as an unacknowledged norm and thus makes it much more difficult to analyze. She also notes the temptation in class discussions to slip from discussions of whiteness to discussions of white people and thus to reinforce the notion of permanent racial categories. In order to highlight the fluidity of race, Keating argues for an approach that addresses the artificial and fluctuating nature of race while also recognizing the material effects of racism. Her essay includes extended discussions of such writers as Zitkala-Sä (Gertrude Simmons Bonnin), Emerson, Frederick Douglass, and Henry Thoreau.

The essays by Keating and Palumbo-Liu address broader issues regarding racial identity; the next four essays are each devoted to a particular ethnic literature. A. LaVonne Brown Ruoff's "Introduction to American Indian Literatures" focuses on worldviews and values shared by a diverse Native American population. Ruoff provides a brief history of Native–Anglo American relations, including major events and key government policies. She also discusses Native American oral and written literature in relation to Indian worldviews and within the context of Indian–white relations. Marta Caminero-Santangelo's "Introduction: Who Are We?" problematizes umbrella terms such as *Latino/a literature* by noting the significant differences between Mexican Americans, Cubans, Dominicans, and Puerto Ricans who have different histories and experiences. Trudier Harris's "African American Literature: A Survey" provides a brief overview of African American literature, while paying particular attention to the continued influence of the oral tradition and the slave narrative. Elaine H. Kim's "Asian American Literature" briefly defines Asian American literature and discusses major trends within the field. Because each of these essays takes a broad approach, they provide useful contextual information for instructors who are not trained in these literatures but would like to include ethnic literature in their American literature courses and provide a more representative slice of American literature.

The authors of the final set of essays all address gender, but from different perspectives. Shari Benstock, Suzanne Ferriss, and Susanne

Wood define feminist literary criticism and trace its history in "Feminist Literary Criticism and Theory." David Leverenz's "Manhood, Class, and the American Renaissance" is particularly useful in illustrating that discussions of gender should not be limited to discussions of women as he addresses the interconnection between manhood and middle-class consciousness in the literature of the American Renaissance. Michael Ryan's "Gender Studies" addresses the linkages between gender studies and gay/lesbian studies and provides examples of literary readings that are attuned to sexuality.

Although the texts gathered here only scratch the surface of identity concerns, they provide a good starting point for instructors delving into less familiar areas. An instructor armed with this material might create an American literature survey course organized by or informed by identity concerns. Students would address the implication of race not only in Phillis Wheatley's poetry, but also in Benjamin Franklin's autobiography. Discussions of gender would include Herman Melville as well as Harriet Jacobs. Conversations about sexuality might include commentary about Amy Lowell, Walt Whitman, and Richard Wright. These types of classroom discussions would break down notions that race equals nonwhite, gender means feminine, and sexuality refers to homosexuality.

Assumed Identities

David Palumbo-Liu

Palumbo-Liu begins by noting that many think the topic of identity has been fully addressed and that we have moved beyond those concerns. This line of thought asserts that people should see themselves as part of "the Nation" rather than as members of particular groups. However, Palumbo-Liu suggests that the real need is to get at individual identity by moving beyond racial typing, the assumption that racially marked people are predisposed to actions that reveal their racial character. This assumption of identity is marked by a power differential in which dominant assumptions are reinforced by institutional practices, maintaining inequitable power distributions.

Palumbo-Liu suggests that sociological discourse on identity tends to overlook "extrasituational experiences" (p. 135) in favor of the individual encounter. Yet indirect experience feeds into notions of social roles. Palumbo-Liu questions whether, when discussing ethnicity, gender, sexual orientation, etc., we are speaking of identity that relies on mutual recognition or on assumed identities. He concludes that the problem with the notion of postethnicity is that it supposes "extrasituational experiences" can

From *New Literary History* 31 (2000): 765–801.

*be erased from memory and that identity is determined. This essay ap-
peared in a special issue of* New Literary History *(2000), "Is There Life
After Identity Politics?," which grew out of a two-day symposium of the
same title, held at the University of Virginia in the spring of 1999.*

> We know of no people without names, no languages or cultures in which
> some manner of distinctions between self and other, we and they, are not
> made. . . . Self-knowledge—always a construction no matter how much it
> feels like a discovery—is never altogether separable from claims to be
> known in specific ways by others.
> —Craig Calhoun, *Social Theory and the Politics of Identity*[1]

One would think that the topic of identity (post-, or otherwise)
would have been exhausted by now. When the word is mentioned
these days, it tends not to meet with a straightening of the back and a
defiant stare, nor even a wince and an evasive move, but rather a re-
signed sigh—"Oh, *that* again?" The constant probing, critiquing, stretch-
ing, shrinking of the term over the past two decades seems not to have
resolved anything. At best it has marked off a set of common problems
and positions to which one refers from time to time when the occasion
calls for it. I shall not rehearse all those moves and arguments—they
are well enough known. Suffice it to say that identity politics has acquired its own identity, which has made any inquiry into identity a
suspect act that stands outside the decorum of polite academic talk.
Identity politics has been reserved now to name a particular *bad* politics that intrudes upon what is taken to have been a polite consensus
on how to seem not to do identity politics while all the while doing
them.[2] It is minorities (sexual, racial, ethnic, class, and so on) whose
articulation of identity is seen to be not only annoying, but impolite, for
their voicing of these concerns forces others to engage in something
they thought they had settled, and settled in their favor.

Besides this general aversion to speak any longer about identity,
there is the specifically political move proposed by several social critics
to move "beyond identity" and, in particular, into a "postethnic" era.
These proposals do not necessarily come from the right; indeed, some of
the more eloquent and persuasive advocates for this position identify
themselves within a tradition of leftist (if not radical) thought. For
these critics of "identity politics," the real issue of bettering the lives of
people can only take place if we set aside the distinctions identity politics seems to fix upon, and work together on a common platform of
economic rights. Those associated with this position include Todd Gitlin,
Richard Rorty, David Hollinger, Michael Tomasky, and others. Each in
his own way has argued that the progressive movement of the New Left
was compromised by the emergence of identity politics. These critics
argue that, whatever salutary value feminist, queer, or critical race and
ethnic studies have had, they have caused the left to veer off track and

into the minutiae of finer and finer distinctions of special interest groups, each claiming priority over the others. This blocks any effective coalition building.

I have elsewhere gone into some detail to outline the historical context for and rebut the basic assumptions of such arguments; here, suffice it to say that this argument has a stake in both downplaying the pervasive significance of racism, sexism, homophobia, and other violent manifestations of prejudice against those who are particularly *identified* (that is, those not just "claiming" identity, but having identities foisted on them), and overplaying the economic as an isolatable space outside the racial, gendered, and otherwise identified social and political spheres.[3] "The economic" is taken as the firm foundation on which all else rests—if economic life is improved for all, is that not all we can hope for? Others, such as myself, while certainly not disavowing the genuine virtue of coalition building around issues of economic justice, are less willing to accept at face value the subordinated position into which issues of race, ethnicity, gender, and sexual orientation are relegated.

In this essay I will argue that "postethnic" thinking subordinates group or collective rights to advocate as primary individual rights to economic justice. A corollary to this is the argument that individuals should set aside particular group identifications and see themselves as part of a larger, more encompassing whole, that is, the Nation. Nevertheless, I assert that foundational notions about identity production in sociological literature make a key and useful distinction between "identity" and "type" (that is, between individual and group identities) that alerts us to the way racial typing comes to stand in for individual identity. The real question thus is not how to get beyond identity, but rather how to *get to it* in the first place—how to make the transition from typecasting to a recognizing of, precisely, individual identity? The real difficulty in making this move is that "identity" is predicated upon a set of behaviors that, for racial and other minorities and women, is geared to a set of historical narratives about "them" precisely as groups, rather than as individuals, and these narratives form the perceptual grid that precedes them in the social discourse of identity.

Wahneema Lubiano provides a concise and astute way of opening this topic of what I will call "assumed identities":

> "Like being mugged by a metaphor" is a way to describe what it means to be at the mercy of racist, sexist, heterosexist, and global capitalist constructions of meaning of skin color on a daily basis. Like a mugging, this attack involves an exchange of assets: some aspect of the social order is enriched domestically and internationally by virtue of material inequities stabilized and narrativized by race oppression and I lose symbolically and monetarily. Further, I am physically traumatized and psychologically assaulted by an operation that is mystified. It goes on in the dark, so to speak—in the dark of a power that never admits its own existence.[4]

Lubiano's treatment nicely opens up this idea of stepping into a narrative-in-progress, of being cast in a role that has been worked out and placed into the realm of a naturalized assumption. In such cases, identity has been produced well in advance of the interpersonal encounter itself, and indeed this mystified operation counts on such preparation in advance, in the dark, in a set of assumptions which all have deep material origins and consequences.

Now what, exactly, do we mean by "identity"? The OED gives a partial answer. "Identity": "the sameness of a person or thing at all times or in all circumstances; the condition or fact that a person or thing is itself and not something else." In this definition, there is an overwhelming sense of determinateness and solidity attached to identity, which is transferable into all times and all circumstances—identity yields the same results no matter where or when it is called upon. But how do we know that this identity is identical to what was before, or elsewhere? Identity posits a certain set of actions and behaviors, a presumed set of characteristics and dispositions that are to be reiterated. Identity is manifest in its constancy, in the fact that the person or thing in itself always expresses the contents of its identity by acting in certain ways. My particular focus here is on the moment of intersubjective encounter, when identity is still virtual, comprised of a set of actions and behaviors assumed to inhere in a particular identity. The result of that encounter will reinforce identity, perhaps *not* because of any action taken by the object of identification, but rather by the sustaining of an assumed, *virtual* act. To put this more plainly, we expect certain types of behavior from certain people, and these expectations may well persist despite any evidence to the contrary. Indeed, evidence to the contrary may be dismissed as aberrational and kept from view by the predominance of those assumptions.

I am concerned here with the assumption that certain people marked by race are predisposed toward certain actions that in turn disclose their racial character. My contention is that in this case we are speaking not of identity, but of social roles, or types, which *pass* for identities (the collective passes for the individual), and that this confusion sometimes brings with it profoundly destructive outcomes. Most specifically, I want to address the situation wherein the interpretive act that assumes that certain behaviors accrue to certain identities moves along a set of put-in-place narratives that proleptically inscribe the outcome of acts which are themselves presupposed to be in the making. In these cases, there is a clear sense that it is the interpreter who has taken upon him- or herself the power to assign an identity to another. This assumption of power could not have been made without assuming as well the projectability of identity upon that Other.[5]

The definition of "assume" contains within it a powerful articulation of this complex phenomenon of taking on the mastery of positing identity on something or someone else. I will not run through the entire

gamut of the definitions of "assume," but it is useful to trace a particular trajectory that will lead us directly into the issue at hand with
my discussion of assumed identity. First, "to assume" is: "To take to be
with one, to receive into association, to adopt into partnership, employment service, use; to adopt, take." That is, to assume is to enter into a
particular relationship with the object of assumption. That relationship, I will argue, takes place against and within the backdrop of a
history of narratives of similar encounters, real and imagined; the
racial encounter—or, more broadly, the encounter with difference—
manifests a story that has been told and silenced, repressed, left for
dead even, and that story is the history of the production of racism. The
encounter, and the assumptive act, at once requires and produces the
articulation of both the raced and the racist, as an assumed identity is
placed upon the other, an identity that has preceded that object already
in a preexisting narration of race.

But even as this act of assuming is appropriative—in the sense
that the racist has laid claim to the truth of the person he or she encounters, laid claim to the scene and made it, in short, a *pre-text* for
the narrativizing of its own identity ("To take as being one's own, to
arrogate, pretend to, claim, take for granted")—it may also be *in*appropriate: "To take to oneself as a right or possession; to lay claim to
appropriate, arrogate, usurp." In my use of this definition, I argue that
in the scene of identity production—in which the racist assumes
the right to name the other as particularly raced, to invent the story
which conveys the other—there is an area of indecidability, a gap that
must be elided. For to name the scene, to create the other in the image
of a character in one's own story, the racist must assume the consequence of a chain of events that he or she can *only* assume: "To take for
granted as the basis of argument or action; to suppose: that a thing is,
a thing to be."

The seemingly smooth transfer of narrative power from the extrasituational sphere to the encounter itself, from the historical narration
of race to the specific moment of the discrete encounter, assumes that
the movement from the universal to the particular is justified. How
can we tell that racial identity is the same time and again, everywhere? In logic, the assumption is hidden: "The antecedent is assumed
when the words of it are barely repeated in the second proposition, or
assumption." It is here that we can draw together all these elements
into an imputation not only of being, but of action, and identity.
The action, in the case I am outlining, is *assumed* to be *going* to take
place, about to reveal the name/identity of the actor in its acting out.
The force of the assumption is in its ability to drive the narrative
forward to its identificatory conclusion in the absence of any explicit voicing. It does not *need* to be said, its story does not need to
be recalled, because it is so ingrained in the minds of the participants
and reinforced by the historical persistence of institutionalized racism

which repeats the story over and over again in its public policy, juridical decisions, and so on.

The elided term is exactly the composite of the narratives of the racial unconscious, the repertoire of stories about "those people" that are assumed to hold true. Crucially, these elided (yet functional) terms preclude the potential narrative for that person *not* to be *as such*. The thing that fortifies this elision, that erases evidence to the contrary and sets to work against the utopian hope of liberation, is precisely the material-historical reiteration of racism—its structural and institutional function: "The construction of identities uses building materials from history, from geography, from biology, from productive and reproductive institutions, from collective memory and from personal fantasies, from power apparatuses and religious revelations. . . . [T]he social construction of identity always takes place in a context marked by power relationships."[6] Here I will emphasize this issue of power, arguing that, as much as we might believe that assumptions of identity work both ways, to and fro between the dominant and the minority identity, we cannot ignore the way that one set of assumptions is embedded within a firm set of institutional practices that maintain an uneven distribution of power.

My essay follows a line of reasoning developed by sociological discourses on identity, namely the interactive model of identity production, and tries to show how the limitations of this model may produce important insights into not only the nature of social identities, but also into the way the imputation of identity through an assumed narrative of being and acting has important connections with both public actions and policy making, and the study of literature and society.

Since the 1930s, and especially in the 1970s, we find a vast sociological literature devoted to the study of identity that is focused on interactive encounters between the subject identified and other social agents. These studies build on early philosophical, and, later, psychological notions of the social production of the self. For instance, Locke has been noted for offering an early dialectical theory of socialization.[7] In 1890 we find William James giving a striking account of the production of "social selves" in relation to the interaction of self and other: "Properly speaking, *a man has as many social selves as there are individuals who recognize him* and carry an image of him in their mind. To wound any of these his images is to wound him. But as the individuals who carry the images fall naturally into classes, we may practically say that he has many different social selves as there are distinct *groups* of persons about whose opinion he cares."[8] Here we find a set of interests that will be central to later sociological treatments of identity: the notion of "recognition" as such, the *image* of that identity as something internalized by the viewer and mobilized situationally, and the shift from individual-to-individual encounters to individual-to-group judgments.

The conception of identity as founded upon social contingency and conventions that may be ascertained through evidence, measured, and quantified, takes us squarely into the realm of sociology.

It was Erik Erikson who first took the study of social selves into the realm of identity and coined the term "identity crisis," describing identity as a product of interaction between an essential self and society. For him, the process of identity formation was "a process 'located' *in the core of the individual* and yet also *in the core of his communal culture*, a process which establishes, in fact, the identity of those two identities."[9] However, while Erikson retains some sense of an inner biological identity that withstands, ultimately, the forces of social interaction, sociologists place more emphasis on the latter.[10] It is this attitude that forms the core of sociological theories of identity formation. We find it encapsulated in Peter L. Berger's statement: "Looked at sociologically, the self is no longer a solid, given entity. . . . It is rather a process, continuously created and re-created in each social situation that one enters, held together by the slender thread of memory."[11] It is worth pausing here over this "slender thread." This thread, however slender, is seen as the very thing that ties together a history of precedents—each one contributes to the reformulation of identity, as new elements are added in.

Yet the primacy placed on the individual encounter downplays the considerable extrasituational experiences that also feed into that encounter. The prejudices formed from indirect experience may play just as much, or, indeed, *more* of a role in shaping the encounter itself, and we can include in this group narrative texts. That is to say, the running narrative of identity formation brings together a diverse set of narratives both of past encounters (and the reinterpretation of those encounters), and of other information-bearing stories that may have either a close or quite distant and indirect bearing on actual encounters. And their weight may be so strong as to lead the interpreter to distrust his or her own experience in favor of that evidence. For example, consider an anecdote from Korean-American cultural critic and filmmaker, Elaine Kim: a friend of Kim's was presented with a copy of *The Woman Warrior*. The presenter exclaimed that, having read the novel, she finally understood Kim's friend. Somehow Kingston's novel had the power to explain human beings in a way that direct personal contact could not. In its particular discourse the novel provided a mode of understanding that surpassed and even stood in for human relations.[12] What about that text allowed it to achieve such a potent reality effect? I would argue that it was the existence of a powerful discursive network of threads woven together from divergent sources that then rendered Kim's friend suddenly legible, believable, complete, in that she now was seen to fill in a role carved out of the novel, a legitimizing narrative.

The hermeneutic weight of extrasituational texts goes a long way to account for the interpretation of identity-forming encounters, which, as Thomas Scheff tells us, are predicated on sequences of actions that are expected from the individual, that is, what I have called assumed identities. Scheff sets up this idea of sequences and identity formation: "We have treated social relations and identity as merely different terms for referring to the same phenomena: the establishment of mutually recognized, expected sequences of behavior in a transaction. Identity refers to the individual's sequence of acts; relationship refers to the ensemble of acts made up by the sequences of all the parties involved."[13] That is, the very formation of identity is identical with social interaction, which is interactive to the degree that a sequence of actions emanating within and out of that encounter are assumed in advance. But we must note here the second crucial component of this transaction: the insistence on the ideas of reciprocity and symmetry, in other words, the emphasis placed on a *democratic transaction*. For identity to be formed according to this model, for a social relation to happen, there must be a *mutually* recognized sequence of actions that, implicitly, yields the same hermeneutic outcome for all parties involved. Scheff's theory of communicative action requires a social act that is assumed to be able to take place (indicating the parameters of reasonable behavior), emanating from social actors whose identities have given us those expectations about them.

The crucial importance of this mutual recognition is that it differentiates "identity" from "social role":

> We have taken social role to be a structural concept which differs in two ways from its complementary processual concept, identity. First, role is at a lesser level of complexity, since it is made up of a component part of the definition of identity; i.e., the expected sequence of acts in a transaction. Role, therefore, does *not* contain the added requirement of mutual recognition by the parties to the transaction. Secondly, role is treated to be part of a generalized pattern of expectations in the community, in contrast to a situational identity, which is the sequence of acts expected of a given participant in a transaction by all the parties to that specific transaction. (206)

The crucial issue here is whether, when discussing race, ethnicity, gender, class, sexual orientation, and so forth, we can speak of identity, which hinges upon *mutual* recognition, a *consensual* sense of the identities produced, and the sequence of actions and behaviors to be "expected," or whether we are not indeed speaking of social roles, posited not on individuals but upon "such people" without their consent. Furthermore, the question in Scheff is muted as to the likelihood that the "expectation" is, indeed, well founded (consensual or no). What kind of "assumptions" go into this encounter? It is here that Erving Goffmann productively revises Scheff's model by introducing both a more complicated temporal schematization and a real questioning of the agent of assumption:

> Typically, we do not become aware that we have made these demands or aware of what they are until an active question arises as to whether or not they will be fulfilled. It is then that we are likely to realize that all along we have been making certain assumptions as to what the individual before us ought to be. Thus, the demands we make might better be called demands made "in effect," and the character we impute to the individual might better be seen as an imputation made in potential retrospect — a characterization "in effect," a *virtual social identity*.[14]

In his study of social "stigma," Goffmann speaks of the ways stigmatized groups (cripples, disfigured people, people from the working class, racial and ethnic minorities, and so on) attempt to manage their stigmatization. Yet, importantly, once a stigma theory has been invented to account for both the justness of stigmatization and the behaviors and characteristics inherent in stigmatized groups, it is tremendously difficult for the stigmatized to respond without *confirming* his or her stigmatized identity: "We may perceive his defensive response to his situation as a direct expression of his defect, and then see both defect and response as just retribution for something he or his parents or his tribe did, and hence a justification of the way we treat him" (*S* 6). This produces an unsettling effect: "We normals will find these situations shaky too. We will feel that the stigmatized individual is either too aggressive or too shamefaced, and in either case too ready to read unintended meanings into our actions" (*S* 18). Isn't this precisely a description of what is called "political correctness"? Here we can come back to the notion that identity politics is an identity in itself, that calling attention to the undemocratic transactivity which undergirds the production of minoritarian identities reflects back on the protester to solidify his or her "difference," and that the narratives that serve to set up in advance "expected behaviors" of such individuals and groups are written under certain ideological and historical conditions. Thus, what Goffmann calls "cognitive recognition," "the perceptual act of 'placing' an individual," assumes a particular *mis*recognition because it assumes outcomes, behaviors, and so forth, that are based not on individuals, but on types that are fabricated in extrasituational texts (*S* 18).

The assumption of outcomes, the link between virtual identity and an assumed behavior that both manifests and confirms that identity, is deeply linked to social behavior and political and legal policy. It is precisely here that the slippage between social roles and individual identities is most pernicious: individual identities are subordinated to and confused with social types. One is not left wanting for examples of this issue. One has only to think of the 1986 Howard Beach incident commented upon forcefully by Patricia Williams, in which a group of young black men were beaten (and one died) on a public street because they were thought to be up to no good—what would blacks be doing in a white neighborhood in the middle of the night?[15] Or a 1997 case in Rohnert Park, California, an upscale bedroom community in which a young Asian man, Kuan Chung Kao, was shot to death by police in front of his house after neighbors called about a disturbance early in the morning. They claimed that he had posed a "martial arts threat" to the police officer who shot him. He had been playing with a broomstick over his head. He was very drunk and very doubtfully a real threat to life, yet the police officer felt that this Asian male could likely be a real threat because all Asians naturally know martial arts.[16]

Or the recent and deeply disturbing case of Amadou Diallo, a twenty-two-year-old West African immigrant who was shot forty-one times in February 1999, after being mistaken for a suspected serial rapist. The police officers were acquitted of all charges in March 2000. Reading the new accounts of the event, and the manner in which the body of Diallo is offered up to representation via an elaborate circuit of bureaucratic formulations and denials, Ebony Chatman brilliantly notes, "The corporeal body is subordinate to the textual circuit, if not locked out entirely. The text is entrusted with the two-dimensional task of representing a body that is *unacceptable* outside of the autobiographical fragments that are solicited. Under these terms and conditions, bureaucratic correspondence enacts its authority through a process of acceptance and denial that refuses to touch the actual body, but acts as if the document were that body—or the only body worth addressing."[17] Here again we find the mechanism whereby identity is recast as a statistical confirmation of a preexisting type, the narrative which conveys this identity at once presents identity and eclipses all other narratives. It is in this sense that Homi Bhabha's notion of forbearance comes into play.[18] And we can note that in all these examples, the state intervenes to be the ultimate arbiter, the final interpreter of the action and the reaction. I mention each of these cases to make the argument that none of them can be understood in isolation, although each has its own particular set of issues. Rather, I want to outline a pervasive history of institutional action that confirms and reconfirms, time and again, the logic of assumption and its deadly effect—there is no identity, only type.

Janet E. Halley's recent study of the "Don't Ask, Don't Tell" policy on gays in the military captures all these issues well and allows us a deeper insight into the production of legal discourses of identity, type, and behavior. She argues that the 1993 revision of the military's anti-gay policy by the Department of Justice produced: "a new set of rules that allows homosexual conduct to be inferred from supposed homosexual status": "What actually emerged from the legislative process was a complex new set of regulations that discharge people on grounds that tie status to conduct and conduct to status in surprising, devious, ingenious, perverse, and frightening ways. . . . The most important innovation is a provision that all discharges for homosexuality will be grounded on the servicemember's commission of conduct that would manifest, to a reasonable person, a propensity to engage in homosexual acts. 'Telling' isn't speech in this formulation: it is an act that manifests a propensity."[19] This propensity is conveyed in what we may call the assumptive narrative of identity—it puts into place (as much as it may rehearse and reiterate) extrasituational narratives that are assumed to be the inherent dispositions and likely behaviors of those identified. In so doing, it erases the distinction between individual and group, between identity and social role. Once again, individual "essence" is made indistinguishable from social type; the behavior of the individual is assumed to be commensurate with the behavior of the group. For stigmatized people (to harken back to Goffmann's term), this institutes a "psychometric model of propensity. It attributes a pathological personal trait to each individual homosexual": "Presumptions are possibly the single easiest way to make sure that one party to a dispute steps up to the starting line with a heavy handicap. They are a classic way to achieve substantive outcomes under the guise of a merely technical change in procedure. . . . Most decisively, proponents of the 1993 revisions claim that giving the servicemember an 'opportunity' to rebut a presumption that he or she has a propensity to engage in homosexual conduct transforms a legal and actuarial prediction about a group into a *fact* about that *servicemember*" (*D* 64, 86). The construct used to measure both the normativeness of behavior and the reasonableness of the attribution of propensity is, precisely, that of a "reasonable person," which "makes the interpretive standpoint of heterosexual personhood an indispensable reference point for enforcement" (*D* 117). We should note that appeals to such a construct again make reference to the act of assumption—in this case, societies posit an ideal mental type to house and ventriloquize their own prejudgments; any fallabilities of a reasonable person will reflect "normal" errors, and are thus excused. And the very credentials of a reasonable person can only be ascertained to the degree that this person confirms or departs from expected behavior. Recourse to constructs like "reasonable person" or "common man" are last-ditch efforts to name an ideal type toward which we must all aspire, without interrogating the assumptions that undergird that construction. Indeed, the validity, or reasonableness of that attribution is often only gained in retrospect, after its judgment is rendered. Nevertheless, like all these cases of assumption, the conclusion to the narrative sequence that expresses and confirms the assumption of identity is often a foregone conclusion.

What better example than the 1922 case of *United States v. Thind*, in which a South Asian man petitioned for naturalization based on the fact that as a South Asian, he satisfied the "scientific" "Caucasian" criterion imposed by the court? When that was disputed, he argued that he also satisfied the "Aryan" criterion argued by the court. Finally, having used up its arsenal of weapons based on geography and biology to label the petitioner as ineligible, the court put forward the argument of the "common man": "We venture to think that the average well informed white American would learn with some degree of astonishment that the race to which he belongs is made up of such heterogeneous elements."[20] We may note how "common man" is itself a construct based on supposed behavior and judgment *that confirms and affirms his own race* at an encounter (need I point out that the "common man" designates maleness and whiteness, that this seemingly modest commonality does not hide the power that is there?). "He" is produced precisely as a narrated subject—what "he would do" were he confronted with the idea that "white" could include South Asians, who are assumed to be variously "oriental" or "mongoloid," or "Asiatic," and therefore prohibited from being considered "white." But note too that this construct serves to ventriloquize power, that "common man" is a dubious and self-fulfilling identity, but this encounter and judgment is not mutually agreed upon, but the narrative construction of the "common man" gives it that illusion. The court chose to *narrate* an imaginary scene of social intercourse that replicates the model of interaction: the common man is presented with a figure that astounds him, it breaches the assumptions he naturally held as to the notion of "white," that is, his notions of *himself*, the "race to which he belongs." In Halley's case, the "common man" is simply updated to be a "reasonable person," for whom the logic of "reason" confirms the heterosexual norms of interpreting its own centeredness by rejecting the other. It is here that we can question Goffmann's claim that: "The stigmatized and the normal are part of each other; if one can prove vulnerable, it must be expected that the other can, too" (*S* 135). For Goffmann seems to suggest the democratic, evenly balanced model of identity formation in which the subject and object of identifying agree on the appropriateness of the identity created in their encounter. I, on the contrary, have tried to draw attention to the unequal relations that obtain and that cancel out evidence to the contrary in favor of a preinscribed narrative of being. Yet Goffmann's democratic rendering offers a utopian moment: When will it be the case that identity is produced democratically?

Let me come back to the argument that we should move beyond identity (which certainly does not mean what it says—it is rather *particular* identities that are to be laid to rest). The urge to move beyond identity is first supported by the hypothesis that ethnic identification is already past us. As early as 1979, Herbert Gans argues that "ethnicity may be turning into symbolic ethnicity, an ethnicity of last resort."[21] Gans contends that, as more and more generations are born in the United States, ethnicity will be gradually loosened from formal organizations and even collective rituals—it will become more a matter of individual performance at discrete moments: "They may retain American forms of the religions their ancestors brought to America, but their secular cultures will be only a dim memory, and their identity

will bear only the minutest trace, if that, of their national origins"
(449). This sort of wishfulness indeed informs most of the social-science
literature on race and ethnicity in the United States since at least the
1920s—sheer exposure to American life will gradually but inevitably
wear away ethnic identity, and with that will come acceptance.[22]
Yet, even as this view has persisted, there has also emerged a sense
that the pace of change is much too gradual, and that Americans must
take a more proactive role in erasing any facet of ethnic identity
that might impede the full particulation of the ethnic subject in national life.

The most respected contemporary liberal view on the need to move
beyond ethnicity comes in David Hollinger's *Postethnic America*.
Hollinger pleads for us to set aside the insistence on ethnicity, and to
focus rather on a common ground: "I have taken for granted that the
economic, political, and cultural obstacles to a postethnic America are
truly formidable, but I also take for granted that revulsion against
ethno-racial prejudice is strong enough in the United States today to
render the ideal of postethnicity worth developing."[23] It is interesting
to note that Hollinger's argument here is nothing if not a pair of assumptions ("taking for granted"). The huge difference between the two
assumptions is, of course, that while the "economic, political, and cultural obstacles to a postethnic America" are well documented historically and evinced in everyday life, as my examples above show, the faith
Hollinger places in "revulsion against ethno-racial prejudice" is evinced
only locally and discretely. While legislation against hate crimes can be
pointed to as evidence to support Hollinger's faith, one can also point to
an overwhelming body of evidence showing that prejudice is not only
well and alive, but thriving (besides the widely documented cases of
court-sanctioned violence against minorities and women, we can point
to socioeconomic policies such as Clinton's "welfare reform," and so on).
As worthy as Hollinger's plea for a "postethnic America" may be, it is
important to note whom he is addressing—for he has in mind precisely
those who argue in favor of multiculturalism. Hollinger asks us to drop
our weapons and shake hands with a historical institutional situation
that is armed to the teeth.[24]

Rather than to place the responsibility for moving beyond ethnicity
on ethnic and racial minorities, it would be better to respect the dialectical engagement of race and ethnicity across multiple tableaux. Rather
than to place faith in an assumption of psychological revulsion against
racism and the historical efficacy of that revulsion, it would be better
to see the production of inequality as taking place in specific institutional practices that are often as not shielded from sight, bureaucrati-
cally rationalized on the basis of assumed identities. Such cases require
the *identification* of racism to bring them out from their assumed neu-
trality to their actual everyday historical life: "We can speak of identity
only in terms of what Marx calls the 'ensemble' of social relations, a set

of relations whose historicity is a fundamental aspect of identity's existence" (RI 115).

But the real problems with the argument for postethnicity, at least in terms of the sociological tradition that still deeply informs our sense of how identity is formed in the first place, are that, first, it imagines that the narratives which precede the social encounter can be erased from memory and made inactive. Rather, it is the case that the historical narratives of prejudice are carried forward in handed-down stories, and realized in present-day violence, as my several examples illustrate. Second, it assumes that the determination of identity is equally decided (that is, that we are dealing with a case of identity and not type). The pervasiveness of racism comes from the refusal to grant identity and the assumption that, for minorities, women, and other groups, behavior is that of the group identity, particularly arrived at. The question, again, is not how to get beyond identity in the classic sociological sense of "identity," but how to get to identity in the first place, that is, how to move beyond type to individuals whose identity formation is arrived at in democratic interaction. This move is necessary before we can go beyond ethnicity and see our way clear to a postethnic coalition (one which I would then heartily endorse). Yet this move will be far from easy, not because minorities and women obstinately cling to identity, but precisely because the narratives that have been put into place to deny them identity are deeply rooted, and the psychic form of racism is thoroughly entangled in institutional forms.

Cornelius Castoriadis's notion of the "imaginary" reveals a more precise and profound view into the murky terrain between institutional forms and psychic ones. For him, the imaginary is:

> the operative condition for every subsequent representation: the fundamental phantasy of the subject, his or her nuclear (and not "primitive") scene, where that which constitutes the subject in his or her singularity exists; the organizing-organized schema that provides its own image and exists not in symbolization but in the imaginary presentification that is already for the subject an embodied and operative signification, the initial grasp and the first, overall constitution of an articulated, relational system positing, separating and uniting the "inside" and the "outside," the sketch of gesture and the sketch of perception, the division into archtypal roles and the originary ascription of a role to the subject as such.[25]

More precisely, his comments on the particular gap between the social and the functional may be taken as approximating the area wherein what I have denoted as "assumption" takes place:

> [S]ocial significations do not exist strictly speaking in the mode of representation. . . . They can be grasped only indirectly and obliquely: as the

gap, at once obvious and impossible to delimit precisely, between a first term—the life and actual organization of a society—and a second term, likewise impossible to define—this same life and organization conceived of in a strictly "functional-rational" manner; as a "coherent deformation" of the system of subjects, objects and their relations; as the curvature specific to every social space; as the invisible cement holding together this endless collection of real, rational and symbolic odds and ends that constitute every society. . . . (142–43)

It is in shifting between these spheres that we witness the performance of assumptions, the playing-out of elided terms, the surpassing of evidence to the contrary, the insistence on a particular way of rationalizing racism. It is here, too, that we find the possibility of intervention, but not, I would argue, solely in the private psychological adjustments of antiracism, but more importantly and significantly in the reformulation of institutional structures that underwrite the repetition of racism. For without this structural-functional change, the material histories that perpetuate these assumed identities will continue to populate in their specific phantasmatic manners the narration of identity.

Notes

1. Craig Calhoun, *Social Theory and the Politics of Identity* (Oxford, 1994) pp. 9–10.
2. See, among others, George Lipsitz, *The Possessive Investment in Whiteness: How White People Profit from Identity Politics* (Philadelphia, 1998).
3. See my essay, "Awful Patriotism: Richard Rorty and the Politics of Knowing," *Diacritics*, 29.1 (1999), 37–56.
4. Wahneema Lubiano, "Like Being Mugged by a Metaphor: Multiculturalism and State Narratives," in *Mapping Multiculturalism*, ed. Avery F. Gordon and Christopher Newfield (Minneapolis, 1994), p. 64.
5. Here I should also say that I do not have in mind the notion of performance and assumption outlined by Judith Butler in *Bodies That Matter: On the Discursive Limits of "Sex"* (New York, 1993), especially pp. 93–120. It is not that I disagree with Butler, but rather that my interest will lie in a different dynamic.
6. Manuel Castells, *The Power of Identity* (Oxford, 1997), p. 7.
7. See, for instance, Aronowitz, Stanley. "Reflections on Identity," in *The Identity in Question*, ed. John Rajchman (New York and London, 1995), pp. 111–46; hereafter cited in text as RI.
8. William James, *The Principles of Psychology*, Vol. 1 (New York, 1890), p. 294.
9. Erik Erikson, *Identity and the Life Cycle, Selected Papers* (New York, 1959), p. 22.
10. Philip Gleason, "Identifying Identity: A Semantic History," *The Journal of American History*, 69.4 (1983), 910–31.

11. Peter L. Berger, *Invitation to Sociology: A Humanistic Perspective* (New York, 1963), p. 106.
12. Elaine Kim, *Asian American Literature: An Introduction to the Writings and Their Social Context* (Philadelphia, 1982), p. xix.
13. Thomas J. Scheff, "On the Concepts of Identity and Social Relationship," in *Human Nature and Collective Behavior: Papers in Honor of Herbert Blumer*, ed. Tamotsu Shibutani (Englewood Cliffs, N.J., 1970), p. 206; hereafter cited in text.
14. Erving Goffmann, *Stigma: Notes on the Management of Spoiled Identity* (New York, 1963), p. 2; hereafter cited in text as *S*.
15. Patricia Williams, *The Alchemy of Race and Rights: Diary of a Law Professor* (Cambridge, Mass., 1991), p. 58.
16. Michael Chang, "Asian American Public Interest Organizations in the Pursuit of Legal and Social Remedies to Anti-Asian Hate Crimes," *Asian Law Journal*, 7 (2000). I thank him for providing the details on this case.
17. Ebony Chatman, "Deciding Mistakes: Rethinking the Death of Amadou Diallo" (Department of Modern Thought and Literature, Stanford University, 1999), 3.
18. Homi Bhabha, "The Art of Forbearance," Presidential Lecture in the Humanities presented at Stanford University, 6 March 2000.
19. Janet E. Halley, *Don't: A Reader's Guide to the Military's Anti-Gay Policy* (Durham, N.C., 1999), pp. 1–4; hereafter cited in text as *D*.
20. *United States v. Thind*, 261 US 204, 211 (1922), cited in Ian Haney Lopez, *White By Law: The Legal Construction of Race* (New York, 1996), p. 8. See also my *Asian/American: Historical Crossings of a Racial Frontier* (Stanford, 1999), p. 39, and Stanford M. Lyman's excellent study, "Marginalizing the Self: A Study of Citizenship, Color, and Ethnoracial Identity in American Society," *Symbolic Interaction*, 16.4 (1968), 16–22.
21. Herbert J. Gans, "Symbolic Ethnicity: The Future of Ethnic Groups and Cultures in America" in *On the Making of Americans: Essays in Honor of David Riesman*, ed. Herbert J. Gans, Nathan Glazer, Joseph R. Gusfield, Christopher Jenks (Philadelphia, 1979), p. 425.
22. This was of course the hope of the Dillingham Commission, which was established by Congress in 1907 to investigate increased immigration from new and much more foreign shores.
23. Hollinger, David. *Postethnic America: Beyond Multiculturalism* (New York, 1995), p. 170.
24. For a sharp critique of the discourse of postethnicity, see Tim Libretti, "Leaping Over the Color Line: Postethnic Ideology and the Evasion of Racial Oppression," *Working Papers Series* (Washington State University, 1999).
25. Cornelius Castoriadis, *The Imaginary Institution of Society* (Cambridge, Mass., 1987), pp. 142–43.

Interrogating "Whiteness," (De)Constructing "Race"

AnaLouise Keating

Keating's essay originally appeared in a 1995 issue of College English, *and was later reprinted in the collection* Teaching African American Literature *(1998), edited by Maryemma Graham, Sharon Pineault-Burke, and Marianna White Davis. Keating begins by acknowledging the importance of examining whiteness, but also expresses concern that "theorists who attempt to deconstruct 'race' often inadvertently reconstruct it by reinforcing the belief in permanent, separate racial categories" (p. 147). Keating worries that an emphasis on racialized identities may ignore the fluidity of racial designations. She argues that scholars should discuss the artificial and changing nature of race while also acknowledging the material effects of racism. One way that Keating approaches this is by looking at "passing" texts, which destabilize her students' notions of ahistorical, fixed races. She also uses the idea of cultural* mestizaje *to highlight the constant interaction and exchange of cultural identities. Thus she is able to emphasize the "mutually constituted and constantly changing nature of all racialized identities" (p. 161) and the importance of educating students about the sociohistorical forces that inform these changes.*

> Race is a text (an array of discursive practices), not an essence. It must be read with painstaking care and suspicion, not imbibed.
>
> —Henry Louis Gates Jr., *Loose Canons*

> Race has become metaphorical—a way of referring to and disguising forces, events, classes, and expressions of social decay and economic division far more threatening to the body politic than biological "race" ever was.
>
> —Toni Morrison, *Playing in the Dark*

> Sticks and stones may break our bones, but words—words that evoke structures of oppression, exploitation, and brute physical threat—can break souls.
>
> —Kwame Anthony Appiah, "The Conservation of 'Race'"

My title reflects several trends in contemporary cultural and literary studies. Because these trends involve exposing the hidden assumptions we make concerning racialized identities, they have far-reaching theoretical and pedagogical implications. The first phrase, "Interrogating 'Whiteness,'" refers to the recent demand for an analysis of "white" as a racialized category. Toni Morrison, for example, calls for an examination of "whiteness" in canonical U.S. literature. What,

---

From *Teaching African American Literature: Theory and Practice*, ed. Maryemma Graham, Sharon Pineault-Burke, and Marianna White Davis (New York: Routledge, 1998): 186–209.

she asks, are the implications of "literary whiteness"? How does it function in the construction of an "American" identity? Arguing that a "criticism that needs to insist that literature is not only 'universal' but also 'race-free' risks lobotomizing that literature, and diminishes both the art and the artist," she urges scholars to examine the hidden racial discourse in U.S. literature.[1] Similarly, some educators have begun emphasizing the importance of developing critical pedagogies that examine how "whiteness" has (mis)shaped knowledge production in U.S. culture. According to Henry Giroux and Peter L. McLaren, the traditional Western view "of learning as a neutral or transparent process" is inaccurate and prevents us from recognizing the highly political, racialized nature of all pedagogical methods. They maintain that

> Teachers need critical categories that probe the factual status of white, Western, androcentric epistemologies that will enable schools to be interrogated as sites engaged in producing and transmitting social practices that produce the linear, profit-motivated imperatives of the dominant culture, with its attendant institutional dehumanization.[2]

bell hooks takes this demand for an interrogation of the relationship between "whiteness" and cultural dominance even further in her discussion of "white" theorists' exclusive analysis of the racial *Other.* According to hooks, "Many scholars, critics, and writers preface their work by stating that they are 'white,' as though mere acknowledgment of this fact were sufficient, as though it conveyed all we need to know of standpoint, motivation, [and] direction." Because she believes that this unquestioned acceptance of "whiteness" distorts contemporary cultural studies, she challenges "white" theorists to incorporate an analysis of their own racialized identities into their work:

> One change in direction that would be real cool would be the production of a discourse on race that interrogates whiteness. It would be just so interesting for all those white folks who are giving blacks their take on blackness to let them know what's going on with whiteness.[3]

These calls for an interrogation of "whiteness" cannot be dismissed as the latest scholarly fad in academia's publish-or-perish game. As Kobena Mercer and other contemporary theorists have argued, "whiteness" and its "violent denial of difference" serve a vital function in masking social and economic inequalities in contemporary Western cultures.[4] By negating these people—whatever the color of their skin—who do not measure up to "white" standards, "whiteness" has played a central role in maintaining and naturalizing a hierarchical social system and a dominant/subordinate worldview.

However, as I began exploring recent definitions of "whiteness" and incorporating this analysis into my literature courses I encountered a number of unexpected difficulties, and this is where the second part of my title, "(De)Constructing 'Race,'" comes in. The word "(De)Constructing"—with the prefix in parentheses—reflects my assessment of the dangers in recent interrogations of "whiteness" and other racialized identities. More specifically, it refers to the way theorists who attempt to deconstruct "race" often inadvertently reconstruct it by reinforcing the belief in permanent, separate racial categories. Although they emphasize the artificial, politically and economically motivated nature of all racial classifications, their continual analysis of racialized identities undercuts their belief that "race" is a constantly changing sociohistorical concept, not a biological fact.

In what follows, I first summarize recent theorists' explorations of "whiteness" and discuss what I see as the difficulties that can occur when we attempt to incorporate these analyses into classroom lectures and discussions. I then offer tentative suggestions for alternative approaches that investigate "whiteness" while deconstructing "race." Before I begin, however, I want briefly to describe my own pedagogy. Whenever possible, I try to integrate my scholarship with my classroom instruction. I believe that both areas can be enriched by this interchange. The classroom functions as a laboratory where the theory I read and write takes on concrete form as I attempt to translate theoretical perspectives into accessible, practical terms. Students benefit from this process; they are introduced to a variety of theoretical perspectives and become critical readers, capable of recognizing how literary canons are shaped by personal and cultural issues.

This twofold approach has played an important role in shaping the ways I began incorporating analyses of "whiteness" into my U.S. literature and composition courses. For the past several years both my scholarship and my teaching had been informed by a critical analysis of how "race," gender, and sexuality are socially constructed, but until reading Morrison's call for an interrogation of "whiteness" I had never considered including an analysis of "white" in my explorations of racialized meanings in literary texts. Yet it only made sense to do so; after all, we examine "black," Chicano/a, Native American, and Asian American literary traditions. Should we not also look at "white" literary traditions? And so, shortly after reading Morrison and several other theorists, I began to include explorations of "whiteness" in the courses I teach, which have ranged from surveys of U.S. literature to introductory composition to an upper-level/graduate elective course on "Race," Gender, and Literature. While approximately three-fourths of the students in my classes identify as "white," the remaining fourth—some of whom can easily pass for "white"—identify as "Hispanic," "Native American," and "black." But however they identify, the majority are first-generation college students from working-class backgrounds. They are motivated by their own versions of the American Dream, the belief that hard work and education will enable *anyone*—regardless of "race," gender, or economic status—to succeed. My comments in the following pages are based on these students' reactions.

Although students are often startled by the notion that language is racialized and literature can be examined for its hidden and overt racial meanings, they find it much easier to explore the racialized subtexts in works by non-"white" writers than to explore the racialized meanings in writings by "whites." When I taught Leslie Marmom Silko, Scott Momaday, or Paula Gunn Allen, for example, I described their perspectives on contemporary Native American literary and cultural conventions and asked students to consider the ways in which their poetry and prose simultaneously reflected and shaped these conventions. After an initial period of questioning, they arrived at important observations. Similarly, when I taught Nella Larsen and Paul Dunbar, I discussed W. E. B. Du Bois's theory of the "color line," described the status of African Americans in the early 1900s, and asked students to consider how their "race" might have influenced their work. Again, they arrived at insightful comments.

However, when I suggested that "white"—like "Native American" or "African American"—is a *racialized* identity, continually reinforced and reinvented in literature, students were startled. People with pale skin are often referred to as "whites," and of course there are ethnic groups whose members have "white" skin—Italian Americans, Polish Americans, many U.S. Jews, and so on—but a white "*race*"? Although I discussed Morrison's call for and interrogation of literary "whiteness" at length, when I asked students to speculate on the contributions that Joanna Russ, John Updike, and other contemporary "white" writers have made to "white" literary tradition, they were troubled and unable to reply. Nor could they discuss Ralph Waldo Emerson's "whiteness," or analyze how Henry David Thoreau's "race" shaped *Walden*. Clearly, they had no idea what this "whiteness" entailed.

My students are not alone in their inability to comprehend "whiteness"; as Kobena Mercer states, "One of the signs of the times is that we really don't know what 'white' is." Thus he asserts that "the real challenge in the new cultural politics of difference is to make 'whiteness' visible for the first time, as a culturally constructed ethnic identity historically contingent upon the disavowal and violent denial of difference."[5] In short, "whiteness" has functioned as a pseudo-universal category that hides its specific values, epistemology, and other attributes under the guise of a nonracialized, supposedly colorless, "human nature."

Yet the hidden dimensions of this unmarked "white" culture are slowly becoming more visible as theorists in literature, cultural studies, and pedagogy embark on the first stages of an interrogation of "whiteness." Not surprisingly, though, the most commonly mentioned attribute of "whiteness" seems to be its nonpresence, its invisibility. A number of scholars associate this ubiquitous hidden "whiteness" with an unmarked superiority. As Richard Dyer suggests in his ground-breaking analysis of representations of "whiteness" in mainstream U.S. and British film, "white power secures its dominance by seeming not to be anything in particular."[6] Drawing on scientific studies of chromatics, he explains that whereas black—because it is always marked as a color—refers to particular objects and qualities, white does not: It "is not anything really, not an identity, not a particularizing quality, because it is everything—white is no color because it is all colors."[7] In literary and cultural studies this "colorless multicoloredness" gives "whiteness" an omnipresence quite difficult to analyze:

> It is the way that black people are marked as black (are not just "people") in representation that has made it relatively easy to analyze their representation, whereas white people—not there as a category and everywhere everything as a fact—are difficult, if not impossible, to analyze *qua* white.[8]

This invisible omnipresence gives "whiteness" a rarely acknowledged position of dominance and power. As Henry Giroux suggests, "whiteness," domination, and invisibility are intimately related. He asserts that although "'whiteness' functions as a historical and social construction," the dominant culture's inability or reluctance to see it as such is the source of its hidden authority; "whiteness" is an unrecognized and unacknowledged racial category "that secures its power by refusing to identify" itself.[9] Morrison makes a similar point in her analysis of canonical U.S. literature when she maintains that this unacknowledged "whiteness" has created a literary "language that can powerfully evoke and enforce hidden signs of racial superiority, cultural hegemony, and dismissive 'othering.'"[10]

By thus erasing its presence, "whiteness" operates as the unacknowledged standard or norm against which all so-called "minorities" are measured. Consider, for example, the implications of "minority and ethnic studies" in U.S. literature. Although scholars generally conceptualize the Harlem Renaissance as a *"black"* literary movement (I suppose because those identified as Harlem Renaissance writers were people of African descent), they do not conceptualize Transcendentalism as a *"white"* movement, even though—to the best of my knowledge—the transcendentalists were all people of European descent. In our "multicultural" era, we have studies of *"Chicano"* narrative, *"Asian American"* novels, *"Native American"* poetry, and so on. But imagine a course or a book devoted exclusively to white-skinned writers (as so many courses and books still are) that acknowledge this fact in its title: say, "Classics of the *White* Western World," "The *White* American Experience," or *"White* Regional Writers." In this schema, "minority" writings become deviations from the unmarked ("white") norm. As Dyer explains,

> Looking, with such passion and single-mindedness, at non-dominant groups has had the effect of reproducing the sense of oddness, different-ness, exceptionality of these groups, the feeling that they are departures from the norm. Meanwhile the norm has carried on as if it is the natural, inevitable, ordinary way of being human.[11]

This invisible, omnipresent, naturalized "white" norm has lead to a highly paradoxical situation in literary and cultural studies: On the one hand, it is vital that we begin exploring the roles "whiteness" has played in shaping U.S. culture; on the other hand, its pervasive nonpresence makes it difficult—if not impossible—to analyze "whiteness" as "white-ness." As Dyer asserts, "if the invisibility of whiteness colonizes the definition of other norms—class, gender, heterosexuality, nationality, and so on—it also masks whiteness as itself a category."[12] Conse-quently, theorists of all colors have been compelled to adopt a relational approach, where "whiteness" is examined in the context of "blackness" or other non-"white" racialized categories. In "White Woman Feminist," for example, Marilyn Frye draws on African Americans' discussions of "white" people to explore what she calls "whiteliness"—or "white" ways of thinking and acting.[13] Dyer centers his analysis of "whiteness" in mainstream cinema on instances where the narratives "are marked by the fact of ethnic difference."[14] Morrison takes a similar approach in *Playing in the Dark*, where she maintains that "blackness"—or what she terms "Africanisms"—are central to any investigation of literary "whiteness." She begins with the hypothesis that "it may be possible to discover, through a close look at literary 'blackness,' the nature—even the cause—of literary 'whiteness.'"[15] Like Dyer, she restricts her analy-sis to textual moments where "black" and "white" people interact, and throughout *Playing in the Dark* she explores literary "whiteness" by examining how "notions of racial hierarchy, racial exclusion, and racial vulnerability" influenced "white" writers "who held, resisted, explored, or altered these notions."[16] For instance, in her discussion of Willa Cather's *Sapphira and the Slave Girl*—which depicts the interactions between Sapphira, a "white" slave mistress, and her female slaves—Morrison examines the ways "white" womanhood acquires its identity, as well as its power, privilege, and prestige, at the expense of "black" womanhood. And in her examination of *Huckleberry Finn* she demon-strates that the notions of independence and freedom in this novel rely on the presence of the unfree Jim.

Similarly, Aldon Lynn Nielsen focuses his analysis of literary "whiteness" on the ways "white" writers depict "blackness." In *Reading Race: White American Poets and the Racial Discourse in the Twentieth Century*, he associates "whiteness" with a racist symbolic system deeply embedded in U.S. thinking and explores how "white" identity has been constructed through racist stereotyping of the "black" other. More spe-cifically, he examines what he terms "frozen metaphors" or stereotypes of "blacks" that reinforce "an essentially racist mode of thought," privileging people of European descent while relegating people of African descent to an inferior position.[17] In the numerous racist stereotypes he describes, representations of "blackness" take a variety of sometimes contradictory forms yet have one thing in common: in each instance, they exist to affirm the validity of the power of "whiteness." By depicting people of African descent as lazy, carefree, unsophisticated, and primitive, he argues, Hart Crane, e. e. cummings, T. S. Eliot, and many other twentieth-century "white" writers locate "blackness" outside Western cultural traditions. He emphasizes that this racist stereotyping serves an important role by reinforcing already existing beliefs in the superiority of "white" aesthetics.

As Nielsen's investigation implies, this invisible, naturalized "white" norm also seems to encompass an authoritative, hierarchical, restrictive mode of thought. Frye, for example, associates "whiteliness" with the desire for personal and collective power by asserting that "Authority seems to be central to whiteliness, as you might expect from people who are raised to run things."[18] She describes "whitely" people as "judges" and "preachers" who—because they assume that their "ethics of forms, procedures, and due process" represent the only correct standard of conduct—attempt to impose their beliefs on all others.[19] Dyer makes a related point in his discussion of *Simba*, a colonial adventure film depicting the conflict between British colonizers and the Mau Mau in Kenya, in which "white" is coded as orderliness, rationality, and control, while "black" is coded as chaos, irrational violence, and total loss of control.[20] Morrison notes a similar pattern of restrictive "white" thinking which she associates with an insistence on purity, self-containment, and impenetrable borders. According to Morrison, "white" literary representations establish "fixed and major differences where the difference does not exist or is minimal." For instance, metaphoric references to "the purity of blood" have enabled writers to construct a rigid, inflexible division between "white" civilization and "black" savagery.[21] This division plays itself out in many works of U.S. literature, where false differences based on blood are used to empower "white" characters.

A number of theorists have associated "whiteness" with mystery, absence, and death. Morrison, for example, claims that although representations of "blackness" serve a variety of symbolic functions in U.S. literature, "Whiteness, alone, is mute, meaningless, unfathomable, pointless, frozen, veiled, curtained, dreaded, senseless, implacable."[22] Dyer, in his exploration of mainstream cinema, finds that on the infrequent occasions "when whiteness *qua* whiteness does come into focus, it is often revealed in emptiness, absence, denial, or even a kind of death."[23] In *Night of the Living Dead*, for instance, all "white" people are closely associated with death: "Living and dead are indistinguishable, and the zombies' sole *raison d'être*, to attack and eat the living, has resonance with the behavior of the living whites."[24] According to hooks, these literary and filmic representations of "whiteness" as mystery and death reflect a common belief in African American communities; during her own upbringing, she explains, "black folks associated whiteness with the terrible, the terrifying, the terrorizing. White people were regarded as terrorists."[25]

This shift from "whiteness" to "white *people*" concerns me, for it draws on false generalizations and implies that all human beings classified as "white" *automatically* exhibit the traits associated with "whiteness": They are, by *nature*, insidious, superior, empty, terrible, terrifying, and so on. Now, I know white folk who aren't like this, and while I would definitely agree that "white" skin and at least some of these "white" traits are often found together, I would argue that the relation between them is conditional. As Marilyn Frye suggests, "the connection between whiteliness and light-colored skin is a *contingent* connection: This character could be manifested by persons who are *not* white; it can be absent in persons who are."[26] In other words, the fact that the person is born with "white" skin does not necessarily mean that she will *not* think, act, and write in "white" ways. Leslie Marmon Silko beautifully illustrates this contingent nature of "whiteness" and skin color in *Ceremony*, where full-blood Native characters such as Emo, Harley, and Rocky think and act in "white" ways. Although she too demonizes "whiteness"—in *Ceremony* "whiteness" is associated with greed, restrictive boundaries, destruction, emptiness, absence, and death—Silko does not automatically associate "whiteness" with all "white" people. Indeed, it is the light-skinned mixed-blood protagonist, Tayo, who learns to recognize and resist this evil "whiteness."[27]

However, it's difficult not to equate the word "whiteness"—and, by extension, the negative qualities it seems to imply—with "white" people. In fact, when I first began reading about "whiteness," it became difficult for me not to make automatic assumptions about everyone who looked "white." I felt uncomfortable and distrustful around people I classified as "white"; and at this early stage in my own interrogation of "whiteness" I was tempted to draw on my African ancestry, disavow my "white" education, and entirely separate myself (intellectually, if not physically) from the so-called "white race." Interrogations of "whiteness" have had similar but far more extreme impact on my students. Despite my repeated attempts to distinguish between literary representations of "whiteness" and real-life people classified as "white," students of all colors found it extremely difficult (and at times impossible) not to blur the boundaries between them. Some became obsessed with highly negative explorations of "white" people.

Class discussion of "The School Days of an Indian Girl," an autobiographical narrative by early-twentieth-century mixed-blood writer Zitkala-Sä, illustrates this transition from "whiteness" to "white" people.[28] Although they could analyze the ways Zitkala-Sä depicted her early life in Sioux culture and her entrance into the "white" world of missionary school, students seem reluctant to take this analysis further by speculating on what these might tell us about representations of literary and cultural "whiteness." Instead, they focused their attention on the representations of "white" human beings, who, they believed, were portrayed in a highly negative light: "Whites" were emotionally and spiritually cold, overly concerned with rules and order, rude, and entirely dismissive of indigenous American cultures, peoples, and beliefs. Given the historical content of Zitkala-Sä's narrative—the U.S. government's repeated attempts to forcibly remove, assimilate, reeducate, sterilize, and Christianize Native peoples—my students' desire to demonize Zitkala-Sä's textual representations of "whiteness" is not surprising. Yet they made almost no distinction between literary "whiteness" and "white" people. Instead, they created a simplistic binary opposition between "good Indians" and "bad whites."

Classroom interrogations of "whiteness" can become even more confusing when analyzing texts by "white" writers, especially when these texts include no explicit reference to "race." Take, for example, an analysis of "whiteness" in Emerson's "Self-Reliance." Do we assume that, because Emerson was "white" his writings give insight into literary "whiteness" and should be placed in a canon of "white" U.S. literature? After all, this practice of categorizing literature according to the author's "race" has played a pivotal role in constructing African American, Native American, and other ethnic-specific canons. But this approach has problematic consequences. Should we code key themes in "Self-Reliance"—such as the desire for independence, a sense of self-confidence, a feeling of spiritual connection with nature and the divine, or a belief in the importance of creating one's own community—as "white"? To do so leads to additional problems when we encounter these "white" themes in texts by writers of color. If, for example, the quest for independence and self-trust is coded as "white," should we suggest that in his *Narrative* Frederick Douglass becomes or acts "white" when he asserts his intellectual independence from Covey, or when he resolves to "trust no one"? To my mind, such assumptions do not facilitate understanding of the literature we read.

These attempts to interrogate "whiteness" lead to other problems as well. How, for example, do we separate "whiteness" from masculinity and other forms of privilege? Is it "whiteness," masculinity, "white" masculinity, or some other combination that allows Emerson, Douglass, and Thoreau to attain remarkable levels of confidence and self-assertiveness in their prose? In class discussions of Emerson and Thoreau, several students assumed that both writers came from wealthy backgrounds and suggested that it was class privilege, rather than "whiteness," which enabled them to achieve self-reliance. Given the financial hardships both writers experienced at various points in their lives, this suggestion, while plausible, seems too simplistic.

My brief discussion of Zitkala-Sä, Emerson, Douglass, and Thoreau illustrates a few of the difficulties that can occur in classroom interrogation of "whiteness." To begin with, "whiteness" often becomes demonized and viewed as almost entirely evil and morally bankrupt, thus creating another binary between the good non-"whites" and the bad "whites." However, like all binary oppositions this dualism oversimplifies and conflates literary representations of "whiteness" and "white" people with real-life human beings classified as "white." Perhaps most importantly for my argument in the following pages, interrogations of "whiteness" and other racialized categories seem to confirm static concepts of identity which reinforce the already existing belief in entirely separate "races."

What I discovered from these classroom investigations of "whiteness" is that students' comments are generally based on the assumption that "race" is a permanent characteristic of U.S. life. In many ways, this perspective on "race" seems like common sense. After all, in the United States categorizing people by "race" has become an accepted way of comprehending and explaining ourselves and our world. Surveys, census forms, birth certificates, and job applications often ask us to identify ourselves according to our "race." Generally, we assume that physiological differences (in skin color, hair texture, and facial features, for instance) between the various so-called "races" indicate distinct underlying biological-genetic differences, differences implying permanent, "natural" divisions between disparate groups of people.

But, this commonly accepted view of "race" is far less accurate than most people realize. To begin with, the belief that each person belongs to only one "race" ignores many "biracial" and "multiracial" people living in this country. Indeed, the implicit belief in discrete, entirely separate "races" implies a false sense of racial purity, for we could all be described as multiracial. As Michael Thornton points out, "there are no such things as pure races."[29] Spaniards, for example, are a mixture of "Black Africans, Gypsies (from India), and Semites (Jews, Arabs, and Phoenicians), as well as Romans, Celts, Germans, Greeks, Berbers, Basques, and probably more."[30] Furthermore, the suggestion that we can automatically identify ourselves with others according to "race" assumes that we are fully cognizant of our ancestry. However, as one of the characters in Pauline Hopkins's *Contending Forces* asserts,

> It is an incontrovertible truth that there is no such thing as an unmixed black on the American continent. Just bear in mind that we cannot tell by a person's complexion whether he be dark or light in blood. . . . I will venture to say that out of a hundred apparently pure black men not one of them will be able to trace an unmixed flow of African blood since landing on these shores![31]

Similar comments can be made about people identified as "Latina," "Native American," or as members of any other so-called "race."

Appearances can be extremely deceptive, and not one of us is "unmixed." Perhaps most importantly, this mythical perspective on discrete, biologically separate "races" relies on nineteenth-century pseudoscientific theories. As Kwame Anthony Appiah notes, "What most people in most cultures ordinarily believe about the significance of 'racial' difference" is not supported by scientific evidence. While biologists can interpret the data in various ways, they cannot demonstrate the existence of genetically distinct "races," for "human genetic variability between the populations of Africa or Europe or Asia is not that much greater than that within those populations."[32]

"Race" is an ambiguous, constantly changing concept that has little—if anything—to do with scientific descriptions; as Michael Omi and Howard Winant persuasively demonstrate, "The meaning of race is defined and contested throughout society, in both collective action and personal practice. In the process, racial categories themselves are formed, transformed, destroyed, and re-formed."[33] Yet we often proceed in our interrogations of "whiteness" and other racialized categories as if these "races" were permanent, unchanging categories of meaning. To return to the second half of my title, although the theorists of "whiteness" attempt to deconstruct "race," all too often they inadvertently reconstruct it by reinforcing fixed categories of racialized meanings. Theorists find it difficult not to conflate literary or cultural representations of "whiteness" with "white" people, and this perpetual reconstruction of separate "races" can be even more difficult to avoid in the classroom, where "whiteness"—generally played out in the context of racialized "black," "Indian," and other "colored" bodies—is associated only with "white" people.

Yet even a brief look at a few of the many ways racial groups have been redefined in this country illustrates how *unstable* and *artificial* racialized identities are. For instance, throughout the nineteenth century many U.S. state and federal agencies recognized only three "races," which they labeled "White," "Negro," and "Indian." Given the extremely diverse mixture of people living in the United States, this three-part classification was, to say the least, confusing. How were U.S. Americans of Mexican or Chinese descent to be described? Were they "White"? "Negro"? or "Indian"? The state of California handled this dilemma in a curious way: Rather than expand the number of "races," the government retained the existing categories and classified Mexican Americans as a "white" population and Chinese Americans as "Indian." According to Omi and Winant, this decision had little to do with outward appearance; it was motivated by socioeconomic and political concerns, for it allowed the state to deny the latter group the rights accorded to people classified as "white."[34]

Since then, both groups have been redefined numerous times. U.S Americans of Chinese descent have been classified as "Orientals," "Asians," "Asian Americans," "Pan Asians," and "Asian Pacific Americans." Yet these terms are inadequate and erroneously imply a homogeneity un-warranted by the many nationalities, geographical origins, languages, dialects, and cultural traditions supposedly contained within these po-litically motivated categories. As Yehudi Webster notes, these monolithic labels indicate the U.S. government's attempt to group "heterogeneous populations into one category on the basis of apparent similarities in skin color, hair type, and eye shape."[35] Efforts to classify U.S. Americans of Mexican ancestry have been equally unsuccessful. Even in the last forty years, they have been redefined several times: In the 1950s and 1960s the government included them in an ethnic category labeled "Per-sons of Spanish Mother Tongue"; in the 1970s, they were redefined as "Persons of Both Spanish Surname and Spanish Mother Tongue"; and in the 1980s, the "Hispanic" category was created. This most recent government invention is especially confusing, for so many so-called "Hispanics" reject the term's association with Spanish ancestry and thus its "white" Eurocentric implications, as well as its erasure of their cultural specificity, and name themselves "Chicano/a," "Latino/a," "Cuban American," and so on. Indeed, in the 1990 census over 96 percent of the 9.8 million people who refused to identify themselves according to a particular race would have been classified by the government as "Hispanic."[36] As Omi and Winant observe, such changes "suggest the state's inability to 'racialize' a particular group—to institutionalize it in a politically organized racial system."[37]

The status of so-called "blacks" and "whites" is, perhaps, even more problematic. To begin with, the terms themselves are almost entirely inaccurate. "White" is the color of this paper, not the color of anyone's skin. And people referred to as "black" would be more accurately de-scribed as they are in Nella Larsen's *Quicksand*: as "taupe, mahog-any, bronze, copper, gold, orange, yellow, peach, ivory, pinky white" or even "pastry white."[38] Furthermore, although many "Hispanics," "Native Americans," and "Asian Americans" have lighter skin than some so-called "whites," they are not classified as such unless they are passing.

Though we generally think of "white" and "black" as permanent, trans-historical racial markers indicating distinct groups of people, they are not. In fact, Puritans and other early European colonizers didn't consider themselves "white"; they identified as "Christian," "En-glish," or "free," for at that time the word "white" didn't represent a racial category. Again, racialization was economically and politically motivated. It was not until around 1680, with the racialization of slav-ery, that the term was used to describe a specific group of people. As Yehudi Webster explains, "The idea of a homogeneous white race was adopted as a means of generating cohesion among explorers, migrants, and settlers in the eighteenth-century America. Its opposite was the black race, whose nature was said to be radically different from that of the white race."[39]

Significantly, then, the "white race" evolved in opposition to but simultaneously with the "black race." As peoples whose specific ethnic identities were Yoruban, Ashanti, Fon, and Dahomean were forcibly removed from their homes in Africa and taken to the North American colonies, the English adopted the terms "white" and "black"—with their already existing implications of purity and evil—and developed the concept of a superior "white race" and an inferior "black race" to justify slavery. It's important to note that the Europeans did not originally label the people who lived in Africa "black"; nor did they see them as evil savages. As Abdul JanMohamed explains, "Africans were perceived in a more or less neutral and benign manner before the slave trade developed; however, once the triangular trade became established, Africans were newly characterized as the epitome of evil and barbarity."[40]

The meanings of "black" and "white" are no more stable in the twentieth century than they were in the past. "Colored," "Negro," "black," "Afro-American," "African-American" (hyphenated), and "African American" (unhyphenated) all describe U.S. Americans of African descent. But these terms are not synonymous; each indicates a different racial identity with specific sociopolitical and cultural implications.[41] Although the term "white"—which has been used since the late seventeenth century to designate an elite group of people—seems more stable, its meaning has undergone equally significant changes. Many people today considered "white"—southern Europeans, light-skinned Jews, the Irish, and Catholics of European descent, for example—were most definitely *not* "white" in the eighteenth and nineteenth centuries. Since the late 1960s, with the rise of what Steven Steinberg calls "ethnic fever,"[42] the "white race" has undergone additional changes. Once again, the redefinition of "white" corresponded to shifts in the meaning of "black." As the Black Power movement developed an oppositional ideology to challenge existing definitions of "Negro," "white" ethnics began (re)claiming their European cultural "roots." Recently, conservative self-identified "whites" have attempted to redefine themselves as the new oppressed group. As Omi and Winant explain, the Far Right attempts "to develop a new white identity, to reassert the very meaning of *whiteness* which has been rendered unstable and unclear by the minority challenges of the 1960s."[43] This rearticulation of racialized identities continues today, in essays like hooks's "Loving Blackness as Political Resistance" (in her *Black Looks*) and in recent demands for an interrogation of "whiteness."

I have misgivings about this increased emphasis on "whiteness" and other racialized identities. Literary theorists who discuss representations of "race" rarely acknowledge the fluidity and the historical changes in the U.S. discourse on "race." Instead, they refer to "white," "black," "Indian," and other supposedly separate "races" as though these categories are permanent, unchanging facts. What are the effects of continually reinforcing these fictionalized identities? Whose interests does this uphold? Whose does it harm? To be sure, increased racial discourse has served an extremely important purpose by enabling people of color to gain a sense of historical and sociopolitical agency. Thus Houston Baker describes a "race" as "a recently emergent, unifying, and forceful sign of difference *in the service* of the 'Other.'" He explains that for people of color, racial identities function as "an inverse discourse—talk designed to take a bad joke of 'race' . . . and turn it into a unifying discourse."[44] Although Baker acknowledges the destructive, fictionalized aspects of "race" (it is, after all, a "bad joke"), he maintains that African Americans and other so-called "minority" groups can reverse its negative implications and use racial discourse in affirmative ways. For example, by aligning themselves with other people of African descent, self-identified African Americans attempt to challenge oppressive definitions of the so-called "black race."

Yet such oppositional tactics are problematic, for they cannot challenge the assumptions underlying *all* references to "race." Even the highly affirmative talk of a black, or Chicano/a, or Native American racial identity reinforces already existing conceptions of "race," conceptions that have functioned historically to create hierarchical divisions based on false generalizations concerning physical appearance and other arbitrary characteristics. By thus reinforcing fictionalized identities, contemporary racialized discourse creates further divisions between people. As Henry Louis Gates Jr. points out,

> The sense of difference defined in popular usage of the term "race" has both described and *inscribed* difference of language, belief system, artistic tradition, and gene pool, as well as all sorts of supposedly natural attributes such as rhythm, athletic ability, cerebration, usury, fidelity, and so forth. The relation between "racial character" and these sorts of characteristics has been inscribed through tropes of race, lending the sanction of God, biology, or the natural order to even presumably biased descriptions of cultural tendencies and differences.[45]

This naturalized use of "race" is especially insidious, for it reifies the destructive stereotypes already circulating in U.S. culture. Despite the many historic and contemporary changes in racial categories, people generally treat "race" as an unchanging biological fact. Often, they make simplistic judgments and gross overgeneralizations based primarily on appearance. You know the stereotypes: "Blacks are more athletic, and boy can they dance"; "All whites are bigots"; "All Hispanics are hot-blooded." Indeed, even social scientists (who should know better) acknowledge the politically, economically motivated nature of racial formation yet discuss the "black race," "the Hispanic race," "the white race," and so on as if these supposed "races" were God-given facts. In so doing, they reinforce oppressive social systems and erect permanent barriers between supposedly separate groups of people. One of the most striking examples I've encountered can be found in the 1992 best-seller *Two Nations: Black and White, Separate, Hostile, and Unequal*. In his introduction Andrew Hacker describes "race" as a "human creation," not a fixed biological fact, and acknowledges that because people use the word in numerous ways, clear-cut definitions are impossible.[46] Yet throughout the book he continuously refers to the "black race" and the "white race" without complicating the terms. Indeed, I would argue that by downplaying the economic, cultural, and ethnic diversity found within each of these two "races," Hacker heightens and reifies the tension between them. Moreover, by focusing almost entirely on the "black/white" binary, Hacker reinforces the myth of racial purity and ignores the incredible diversity found in this country.

This simplistic binary between fixed definitions of "blackness" and "whiteness" occurs in literary interrogations of "whiteness" as well. Take, for example, Nielsen's exploration of "whiteness" in *Reading Race*. Unlike Morrison—who begins blurring the artificial boundaries between "blackness" and "whiteness" by exploring what "white" representations of "blackness" tell us about literary "whiteness"—Nielsen focuses almost entirely on "white" poets' racist stereotypes of "blacks." Although he acknowledges the fictional, contradictory nature of these "white" representations of "blackness," his constant focus on the stereotypes themselves inadvertently reifies the racist imagery he tries to undercut. This approach seems especially dangerous in the classroom where, as Sharon Stockton points out, "students tend to think in terms of stereotyped binary oppositions."[47] In classroom interrogations of "whiteness," Nielsen's method leads to overly generalized discussions of racist, bigoted "whites" and lazy, ignorant, inferior blacks. Moreover, by continually emphasizing racism, we risk giving students the pessimistic belief that racism is inevitable and racialized barriers will never be overcome. As Omi and Winant argue in their discussion of 1960s theories of institutionalized racism, "An overly comprehensive view of racism . . . potentially served as a self-fulfilling prophecy."[48]

Let me emphasize: I am not saying that we should adopt a "color-blind" approach and ignore the roles racist thinking has played in constructing "whiteness." To do so simply reinforces the increasingly popular but very false belief that "race" no longer matters in twentieth-century U.S. culture. Racism is deeply embedded in U.S. society, and students of all colors must be aware of its systemic nature. Nor can we analyze racialized dimensions of texts by writers of color without also explaining "whiteness," for this partial analysis reinforces the long-standing belief in "white" invisibility. However, instructors must be aware of the impact interrogations of "whiteness" can have on our students. Although self-identified students of color find it satisfying to see the "white" gaze which has marked them as "Other" turned back on itself, I question the long-term effectiveness of this reversal. As I have argued, such reversals inadvertently support existing stereotypes. Moreover, these reversals trigger a variety of unwelcome reactions in self-identified "white" students, reactions ranging from guilt to anger to withdrawal and despair. Instructors must be prepared to deal with these responses. The point is not to encourage feelings of personal responsibility for the slavery, decimation of indigenous peoples, land theft, and so on that occurred in the past. It is, rather, to enable students of all colors more fully to comprehend how these oppressive systems that began in the historical past continue misshaping contemporary conditions. Guilt-tripping plays no role in this process. Indeed, guilt functions as a useless, debilitating state of consciousness that reinforces the boundaries between apparently separate "races." When self-identified "white" students feel guilty, they become paralyzed, deny any sense of agency, and assume that their privileged positions in contemporary U.S. culture automatically compel them to act as "the oppressor."

The compromise I've arrived at—admittedly temporary and always open to further revision—entails a twofold approach where we explore the artificial, constantly changing nature of "black," "white," and other racialized identities without ignoring their concrete material effects. I select texts by Nella Larsen, Zora Neale Hurston, and Langston Hughes, where students can clearly see these racialized identities as transitional states. In the stories collected in Hughes's *The Ways of White Folks*, for instance, we see "black" people reconstructing themselves as "white," self-identified "blacks" who act exactly like "whites," and "white" people who act just like "blacks."[49] These stories, as well as other textual representations of passing, destabilize students' "commonsense" beliefs in racial purity and ahistorical, fixed "races." Another topic I've employed is the concept of cultural *mestizaje*. I borrow this term from Cuban literary and political movements where its usage indicates a profound challenge to existing racial categories. As Nancy Morejón explains, *mestizaje* transculturation defies static notions of cultural purity by emphasizing

> the constant interaction, the transmutation between two or more cultural components with the unconscious goal of creating a third cultural identity . . . that is new and independent even though rooted in the preceding elements. Reciprocal influence is the determining factor here, for no single element superimposes itself on another; on the contrary, each one changes into the other so that both can be transformed into a third. Nothing seems immutable. [qtd. Lionnett 15–16][50]

This idea of constant transformation and change provides an important alternative to the well-known stereotype of the "American" melting pot. Unlike the melting pot, which works to assimilate culturally specific groups with distinct traditions into indistinguishable "whites," *mestizaje* emphasizes the mutually constituted and constantly changing nature of all racialized identities.

Yet these tactics are only temporary measures. I'm still searching for more effective ways of incorporating interrogations of "whiteness" into classroom discussions. Ironically, what began as an interrogation of "whiteness" has turned into an interrogation of "race," and I have even *more* questions than I had when I began. On the one hand, I agree with Mercer and others who call for an examination of the ways "whiteness" has been socially constructed. Because "whiteness"—*whatever* it is, and I would argue that at this point no one really knows—has functioned as an oppressive, mythical norm that negates people (whatever their skin color) who do not conform to its standard—we need to understand and deconstruct it. On the other hand, I worry that this analysis simply reifies already existing hegemonic conceptions of "race." As Gates explains, "we carelessly use language in such a way as to *will* this sense of *natural* difference into our formulations. To do so is to engage in a pernicious act of language, one which exacerbates the complex problem of cultural or ethnic difference, rather than to assuage or redress it."[51]

As I see it, the problems with discussing "whiteness" and other racial categories without historicizing the terms and demonstrating the relational nature of all racialized identities include (but aren't limited to) the following. First, our conceptions of "race" are scientifically and historically inaccurate; they transform arbitrary distinctions between people into immutable, "natural," God-given facts. Second, constant references to "race" perpetuate the belief in separate peoples, monolithic identities, and stereotypes. Third, in this country racial discourse quickly degenerates into a "black"/"white" polarization that overlooks other so-called "races" and ignores the incredible diversity among people. And fourth, racial categories are not—and never have been—benign. Racial divisions were developed to create a hierarchy that grants privilege and power to specific groups of people while simultaneously oppressing and excluding others. If, as Gates implies in the first epigraph to my paper, "race" is a text that everyone in this country unthinkingly "reads," I want to suggest that we need to begin reading—and rewriting—this text in new ways. At the very least, we should complicate existing conceptions of "race"—both by exploring the many changes that have occurred in all apparently fixed racial categories and by informing students of the political, economic, and historical facts shaping the continual reinvention of "race."

Notes

1. Toni Morrison, *Playing in the Dark: Whiteness and the American Literary Imagination* (Cambridge: Harvard University Press, 1992), p. 12.
2. Henry Giroux and Peter McLaren, "Radical Pedagogy as Cultural Politica: Beyond the Discourse of Critique and Anti-Utopianism," in *Texts for Change*

Theory/Pedagogy/Politics, ed. Donald Morton and Mas'ud Zavarzadeh (Urbana: University of Illinois Press, 1991), p. 160.

3. bell hooks, *Yearning: Race, Gender, and Cultural Politics* (Boston: South End Press, 1990), p. 54.

4. Kobena Mercer, "Skin Head Sex Thing: Racial Difference and the Homo-erotic Imaginary," in *How Do I Look? Queer Film and Video*, ed. Bad Object-Choices (Seattle: Bay Press, 1991), p. 206.

5. Ibid., pp. 205–06.

6. Richard Dyer, "White," in *The Matter of Images: Essays on Representations* (New York: Routledge, 1993), p. 44.

7. Ibid., p. 142.

8. Ibid., p. 143.

9. Henry Giroux, "Post-Colonial Ruptures and Democratic Possibilities: Multiculturalism as Anti-Racist Pedagogy," *Cultural Critique* 21 (1992): 15.

10. Morrison, *Playing in the Dark*, pp. x–xi.

11. Dyer, "White," p. 141.

12. Ibid., p. 143.

13. Marilyn Frye, "White Woman Feminist," in *Willful Virgin: Essays in Feminism, 1976–1992* (Freedom, CA: Crossing, 1992), pp. 147–69.

14. Dyer, "White," p. 144.

15. Morrison, *Playing in the Dark*, p. 9.

16. Ibid., p. 11.

17. Aldon Lynn Nielsen, *Reading Race: White American Poets and the Racial Discourse in the Twentieth Century* (Athens: University of Georgia Press, 1988), p. 3.

18. Frye, "White Woman Feminist," p. 156.

19. Ibid., p. 155.

20. Dyer, "White," pp. 146–48.

21. Morrison, *Playing in the Dark*, p. 68.

22. Ibid., p. 59.

23. Dyer, "White," p. 141.

24. Ibid., p. 157.

25. bell hooks, *Black Looks: Race and Representation* (Boston: South End Press, 1992), p. 170.

26. Frye, "White Woman Feminist," pp. 151–52, her emphasis.

27. Leslie Marmon Silko, *Ceremony* (New York: Penguin, 1977).

28. Zitkala-Sä [Gertrude Simmons Bonnin]. "The School Days of an Indian Girl," *Atlantic Monthly* 85 (1900): 37–45.

29. Michael C. Thornton, "Is Multiracial Status Unique? The Personal and Social Experience," in *Racially Mixed People in America*, ed. Maria P. Root (Newbury Park, CA: Sage, 1992), p. 322.

30. Carlos A. Fernandez, "La Raza and the Melting Pot: A Comparative Look at Multiethnicity," in *Racially Mixed People*, ed. Maria P. Root (Newbury Park, CA: Sage, 1992), p. 143.

31. Pauline E. Hopkins, *Contending Forces: A Romance Illustrative of Negro Life North and South* (1900; reprint, New York: Oxford University Press, 1988), p. 151.

32. Kwame Anthony Appiah, "The Uncompleted Argument: Du Bois and the Illusion of Race," in *"Race," Writing, and Difference*, ed. Henry Louis Gates Jr. (Chicago: University of Chicago Press, 1986), p. 21.

33. Michael Omi and Howard Winant, *Racial Formation in the United States from the 1960s to the 1980s* (Rev. ed., New York: Routledge, 1993), p. 61.
34. Ibid., p. 82.
35. Yehudi O. Webster, *The Racialization of America* (New York: St. Martin's Press, 1992), pp. 132–33.
36. Ibid., p. 143.
37. Omi and Winant, *Racial Formation*, p. 82.
38. Nella Larsen, *Quicksand and Passing* (1928; edited with an introduction by Deborah McDowell; reprint, New Brunswick: Rutgers University Press, 1986), p. 59.
39. Webster, *The Racialization of America*, p. 9.
40. Abdul R. JanMohamed, "The Economy of Manichean Allegory: The Function of Racial Difference in Colonialist Literature," in Gates, *"Race," Writing, and Difference*, pp. 78–106, 80.
41. Henry Louis Gates Jr., *Loose Canons: Notes on the Culture Wars* (New York: Oxford University Press, 1982), pp. 131–51.
42. Stephen Steinberg, *The Ethnic Myth: Race, Ethnicity, and Class in America* (1982; reprint with epilogue, Boston: Beacon, 1989), p. 3.
43. Omi and Winant, *Racial Formation*, p. 120.
44. Houston Baker, "Caliban's Triple Play," in Gates, *"Race," Writing, and Difference*, pp. 381–95, 386; his emphasis.
45. Gates, *"Race," Writing, and Difference*, p. 5.
46. Andrew Hacker, *Two Nations: Black and White, Separate, Hostile, and Unequal* (New York: Ballantine, 1992), p. 4.
47. Sharon Stockton, "'Blacks vs. Browns': Questioning the White Ground," *College English* 57 (1995): 70.
48. Omi and Winant, *Racial Formation*, p. 70.
49. Langston Hughes, *The Ways of White Folks* (1933; reprint, New York: Vintage, 1971).
50. Francoise Lionnett, *Autobiographical Voices: Race, Gender, Self-Portraiture* (Ithaca, NY: Cornell University Press, 1989), pp. 15–16.
51. Gates, op. cit., his emphasis.

Introduction to American Indian Literatures

A. LaVonne Brown Ruoff

Ruoff begins this essay by noting that the literature of the United States originated with American Indians, not Western Europeans. She presents basic background information regarding the American Indian population and languages. While noting the diversity among individual Indians, Ruoff maintains that they share certain worldviews and values, such as "an emphasis on the importance of living in harmony with the physical and spiritual universe, the power of thought and word to maintain this

From *American Indian Literatures: An Introduction, Bibliographic Review, and Selected Bibliography* (New York: MLA, 1990): 1–19.

balance, a deep reverence for the land, and a strong sense of community"
(p. 165). Ruoff observes that American Indian literature also reflects
Indian–white relations, and she provides a brief overview of major events
and government policies. Ruoff then moves into a discussion of Indian
oral literatures, noting that due to the diversity of lifestyles and languages,
these materials should be analyzed within their social and historical con-
texts. Using specific examples, she illustrates how Indian worldviews and
values are represented in their literature, pointing to a Yokuts prayer to
illustrate the power of the word and a Keres song to exemplify oneness
with the community. Other examples are drawn from contemporary In-
dian writers such as Leslie Marmon Silko and N. Scott Momaday. Ruoff
concludes with a discussion of the transmission of oral literature and the
effect of translation and transcription. This selection is taken from the intro-
duction to Ruoff's American Indian Literatures *(1990).*

> They carried dreams in their voices;
> They were the elders, the old ones.
> They told us the old stories,
> And they sang the spirit songs.
>
> —Big Tree (Kiowa)

> American literature begins with the first human perception of the Ameri-
> can landscape expressed and preserved in language.
>
> —N. Scott Momaday (Kiowa)

Backgrounds

The literature of this nation originated with the native peoples who migrated to North America over twenty-eight thousand years ago, not with the Western Europeans who began to immigrate in the late sixteenth and early seventeenth centuries. When Western Europeans arrived, 18 million people inhabited North America and 5 million lived in what is now the United States. After contact, the population of the native peoples of North America greatly diminished—primarily as a result of diseases brought by whites. According to the United States Census Bureau, there were only 210,000 left in this country by 1910. In the twentieth century, however, the Indian population in the United States has greatly increased. The 1980 census, which Indians feel gives a very low count, indicated that the native population of the United States (including Alaska) was 1,418,195. Of these, 681,213 lived on reservations and 736,982 lived off reservations. Thus over half of the Indian population now lives in towns or cities rather than on reservations.

At the time of contact, the native peoples of North America were divided into more than three hundred cultural groups and spoke two hundred different languages, plus many dialects, derived from seven basic language families. By 1940, 149 of these languages were still in use (Spencer, Jennings, et al. 38–39). Divided into numerous cultural and language groups, native North Americans practiced many different religions and customs. However, there are some perspectives on their place in the universe that many native American groups shared and continue to share. Among these are an emphasis on the importance of living in harmony with the physical and spiritual universe, the power of thought and word to maintain this balance, a deep reverence for the land, and a strong sense of community. Although individual Indians today vary in the extent to which they follow tribal traditions, their worldviews and values continue to reflect those of their ancestors.

The history of American Indian literature reflects not only tribal cultures and the experience and imagination of its authors but Indian–white relations as well. Although a detailed discussion of Indian–white relations is beyond the scope of this volume, a brief overview of some of the major events is important to understanding the interrelationship between Indian history and literature. Whites' settlement in Indian territory was inevitably followed by attempts to expand their land holdings and Indians' determined efforts to retain their ancestral land. During the seventeenth century, Indians rose up against white domination in the Pequot War in New England (1637), King Philip's War (1672–76) against the British, and the Pueblo Revolt of 1680 against the Spanish. As the fur trade expanded into Indian territories, Indians became increasingly dependent on whites for firearms, metal traps, and other trade goods. So important did trade become to Indians that from the late seventeenth century through the War of 1812, tribal relations were frequently dictated by trapping and trade opportunities. For example, between 1644 and 1680, the Iroquois, whose lands were depleted of fur-bearing game, defeated Indian tribes from the Hudson to Illinois in their westward invasion to gain new trapping territory in order to meet whites' demands for fur. Before the end of the War of 1812, the British, Americans, and French enlisted Indian tribes to help secure their claims to various territories or to defeat their enemies, Indian and non-Indian. Controversies over trade and Indian land helped precipitate the American Revolution. After the conclusion of the Revolutionary War, there was considerable racial animosity against Indians because of accusations about their wartime atrocities, the allegiance of most of the Iroquois to the British, and the demand by whites for Indian land. Settlers' westward migration into the Ohio Valley brought new conflicts. After the defeat of England in the War of 1812 essentially ended that nation's threat to American interests on the continent, the United States no longer felt it necessary to placate Indians to ensure that they would fight the British. Increasingly, legislators and settlers advocated the relocation of the Indians. During the debate on removal, the federal government negotiated numerous treaties between 1815 and 1830 arranging for immediate or ultimate resettlement. The death knell of Indian hopes for retaining tribal lands east of the Mississippi free from white encroachment was sounded in 1830, when Congress passed the

Indian Removal Bill, which authorized the federal government to move Indians from these areas to Indian Territory, now Oklahoma, and other locations deemed suitable. Some tribes were forced to move several times. No sooner had the Removal Bill been implemented than whites violated it by migrating westward into Indian territories.

In 1848, the Treaty of Guadalupe Hidalgo with Mexico brought new territory and numerous tribes under the jurisdiction of the United States. The discovery of gold in California in 1849 stimulated new encroachments on Indian land as hordes of emigrants passed through Indian land on their way to the California gold fields, Idaho ore deposits, or Oregon timber. What began as a stream of settlers in the 1830s became a flood by the 1850s.

The 1862 rebellion of the Santee Sioux in Minnesota and the allegiance of the Five Civilized Tribes in Oklahoma (Cherokee, Chickasaw, Creek, Choctaw, Seminole) to the Confederacy during the Civil War provided new excuses for removal of the Santee and drastic reductions in land holdings of the Five Civilized Tribes after the Civil War. In the Southwest, the withdrawal of federal troops led to attacks by Navajos and Apaches, who were then rounded up onto reservations by Kit Carson and others. Conflicts between Colorado Indians and whites resulted in the Sand Creek Massacre of 1864, in which Colonel J. M. Chivington and his men brutally murdered Cheyennes, primarily old men, women, and children. The opening of the Bozeman Trail through Indian land during the Civil War resulted in fierce retaliations by the Teton Sioux. Western migration, slowed during the Civil War, greatly increased when the end of the war brought renewed demand for land. As a result, the government was determined to pacify the Indians once and for all. To do so, they forced Indians onto reservations by destroying their food supplies—the buffalo and stored winter food. Public outrage over the Indians' victory over General George A. Custer and his men in 1876 brought swift retribution to defiant tribes. By the end of the 1880s, the buffalo had been exterminated from the Plains and the last of the tribes had been forced onto reservations.

As part of its policy of assimilationism, the government passed the General Allotment Act of 1887, which had been sponsored by Senator Henry L. Dawes. Popularly called the Dawes Act, it allotted in severalty land previously owned by tribes. This bill was supported by liberals, who felt the Indians could survive only by becoming independent farmers, and by land grabbers, who plotted to gain Indian territory by legal and illegal means. It was also supported by Indians like Sarah Winnemucca (Paiute) and Charles A. Eastman (Sioux), who felt it offered Indians independence and citizenship. The Allotment Act resulted in enormous losses of Indian land, however. Wilcomb E. Washburn estimates that by 1934, Indians had lost over sixty percent of the land they owned in 1887 (*The Indian in America* 242–43).

The last gasp of Indian resistance was the Ghost Dance religion, a messianic movement that swept across the Plains in the late 1880s and 1890. Its leader was Wovoka, or Jack Wilson (Paiute), who predicted that the Plains would again support millions of buffalo and that whites would disappear. By 1890, his words roused the Plains tribes and frightened whites before it died out. One tragic result was the massacre at Wounded Knee, South Dakota, in 1890, when Big Foot's band of Sioux Ghost Dancers was slaughtered after a dispute about turning in their weapons. This incident ended the Indian wars.

One dimension of the government's assimilationist policy was the education of Indian children in English and in Western European traditions. Many Indian children were shipped off to boarding schools in such faraway places as Carlisle, Pennsylvania, and Riverside, California, where they were separated for years from their families and forbidden to speak their native languages or practice their tribal customs and religions. The isolation of Indian children eroded strong family bonds and ancient tribal traditions.

Although official policy was to assimilate Indians into the dominant society, the government did not grant Indians citizenship until 1924. Because Indians volunteered, were wounded, and died in World War I far out of proportion to their numbers in the society, Congress awarded them citizenship out of gratitude for their service. Another major gain for Indians in the first half of the twentieth century was the passage of the Wheeler-Howard Indian Reorganization Act in 1934, which its advocates called the Indian Magna Carta. The act ended allotment in severalty, continued the trust period indefinitely, confirmed cultural pluralism, and reestablished tribal government. After World War II such policies came under increasing criticism, as politicians sought ways to end the "Indian problem." In 1953, House Concurrent Resolution 108 was passed, which began the campaign to terminate the federal government's role in Indian affairs. Under this policy, tribes such as the Klamath and Menominee lost their reservation status and the government actively encouraged Indians to move to cities. As a result, urban Indian populations greatly increased during this period, but termination was disastrous for the tribes. After fighting for years to regain reservation status for their land, the Menominee finally won their battle in 1973, when they again became wards of the government.

The battle for justice for Indians has increasingly been fought in Congress, state legislatures, and courts. Many Indian organizations — such as the Indian Rights Association, National Association of Indian Affairs, National Indian Education Association, and National Congress of American Indians — emerged to serve as effective advocates for Indian causes. Indian activism was stimulated by the American Indian Chicago Conference of 1961, after which many young Indian activists formed the National Indian Youth Council to mobilize "Red Power."

Other groups that developed during the 1960s include the American Indian Civil Rights Council, National Tribal Chairmen's Association, the American Indian Movement, and the National Council of Indian Opportunity. The revitalism of Indian identity during the 1960s led to renewed interest in tribal languages, customs, and religions. Increased Indian militancy resulted in the occupation of Alcatraz Island (1969); the Bureau of Indian Affairs office in Washington, D.C. (1972); and Wounded Knee, South Dakota (1973).

Strong Indian advocacy resulted in the passage of several bills that ensured Indian rights. The Indian Civil Rights Act (1968) provides for free exercise of religion, speech, press, and right of assembly; protection against the taking of property without just compensation; and tribal consent before the state can assume civil and criminal jurisdiction over Indian reservations within its borders. In 1971 the Alaska Native Claims Settlement Act was passed. The Indian Self-Determination and Education Assistance Act, which became law in 1974, allows tribes to contract with the government to provide educational and other services to tribal members. Two measures passed in 1978 were the American Indian Religious Freedom Act and Indian Child Welfare Act, which guarantee the exercise of native religion and ensure a tribal role in the adoption of Indian children.

Indian tribes continue to fight many crucial battles over such issues as control over their water, mineral, and wildlife resources; retention of rights guaranteed by treaties; just compensation for land; self-determination; and tribal legal jurisdiction over crimes committed on Indian land. The history of the native peoples of America is one of endurance despite adversity. Through the diversity of their cultures, significant achievements as tribes and individuals, and the richness of their literatures, American Indians remind us of their important contributions to the mosaic of American culture.

Oral Literatures

Indian oral literatures are a vibrant force that tribal peoples continue to create and perform and that strongly influence the written works of Indian authors, as Simon Ortiz (Acoma) makes clear:

> The oral tradition is not just speaking and listening, because what it means to me and other people who have grown up in that tradition is that whole process, . . . of that society in terms of its history, its culture, its language, its values, and subsequently, its literature. So it's not merely a simple matter of speaking and listening, but living that process. ("Interview" 104)

Because the oral literatures of Native Americans reflect the diversity of their religious beliefs, social structures, customs, languages, and lifestyles, these literatures should be studied within the contexts of both the cultural groups that produced them and the influences on these groups resulting from their interactions with other tribes and with non-Indians.

Central to American Indians' traditional way of life is the belief that human beings must live in harmony with the physical and spiritual universe, a state of balance vital to an individual and communal sense of wholeness or beauty; this theme pervades American Indian oral and written literatures as well. In traditional Indian societies, all aspects of life are conducted according to the religious beliefs and rituals deemed essential to the survival and well-being of the group. Breath, speech, and verbal art are so closely linked to each other that in many oral cultures they are often signified by the same word. The reverence for the power of thought and the word that is an integral part of American Indian religions is exemplified in Navajo culture. In *Language and Art in the Navajo Universe*, Gary Witherspoon points out that the Navajo world was brought into being by the gods, who entered the sweathouse and thought the world into existence. The thoughts of the gods were realized through human speech, song, and prayer (16). The following excerpt from Witherspoon's translation of the "Beginning of the World Song" illustrates the interrelation among knowledge, thought, and speech in Navajo culture:

> The earth will be, from ancient
> times with me there is knowledge of it.
> The mountains will be, from ancient
> times with me there is knowledge of it.
> [and so on, mentioning other things to be]
>
> The earth will be, from the very
> beginning I have thought it.
> The mountains will be, from the very
> beginning I have thought it.
> [and so on]
>
> The earth will be, from ancient times
> I speak it.
> The mountains will be, from ancient times
> I speak it.
> [And so on] (16)

According to Witherspoon, the language of the Navajo emergence myth indicates "that in the beginning were the word and the thing, the symbol, and the object." For the Navajos, the awareness of symbol is knowledge. "Symbol is word, and word is the means by which substance is organized and transformed" (46).

Such emphasis on word as symbol and the power of symbols to structure the universe is common among American Indian societies.

Jack Frederick Kilpatrick and Anna Gritts Kilpatrick (Cherokee) stress in *Run toward the Nightland* that in "any magical ritual all generative power resides in thought" and that the songs which focus and direct the thought are alone inviolate. The singer or medicine man merely augments the authority of thoughts, applies or disseminates it more effectively (6). Lame Deer emphasizes that the Sioux live "in a world of symbols and images where the spiritual and the commonplace are one":

> To us they are part of nature, part of ourselves—the earth, the sun, the wind and the rain, stones, trees, animals, even little insects like ants and grasshoppers. We try to understand them not with the head but with the heart, and we need no more than a hint to give us the meaning. (*Lame Deer: Seeker of Visions* 109)

The power of thought and word to create and the continuum of the oral tradition from the mythic past of the Lagunas to the present are beautifully demonstrated by Leslie Marmon Silko (Laguna) in her introduction to her novel *Ceremony*. In the following passage, Silko describes how the Laguna creator thought the universe into existence:

> Ts'its'tsi'nako, Thought-Woman
>   is sitting in her room
> and whatever she thinks about
>   appears.

> ———

> Thought-Woman, the spider,
>   named things and
>   as she named them
>   they appeared.

> She is sitting in her room
>   thinking of a story now
> I am telling you the story
>   she is thinking. (1)

American Indians hold thought and word in great reverence because of their symbolic power to alter the universe for good and evil. The power of thought and word enables native people to achieve harmony with the physical and spiritual universe: to bring rain, enrich the harvest, provide good hunting, heal physical and mental sickness, maintain good relations within the group, bring victory against an enemy, win a loved one, or ward off evil spirits. Thought and word can also be used for evil against one's enemies. Because of their power and because words spoken can turn back on the speaker, for good or evil, thought and word should be used with great care. The power of the word to help the individual fit into the universe is exemplified in the Yokuts prayer below:

My words are tied in one
With the great mountains,
With the great rocks,
With the great trees,
In one with my body
And my heart.
Do you all help me
With supernatural power,
And you, Day
And you, Night!
All of you see me
One with this world!

—Kroeber, *Handbook of Indians of California* 511

Coupled with the power of the word is the power of silence. Momaday, in "The Native Voice," calls silence "the dimension in which ordinary and extraordinary events take their proper places." In the American Indian oral tradition, "silence is the sanctuary of sound. Words are wholly alive in the hold of silence; there they are sacred" (7). The Mescalero Apache express this reverence for the power of silence. In "Singing for Life," Clare R. Farrer indicates that the Apache believe that the Creator God communicates through the power of thought in dream. People can utilize this channel through "communicating without words." To think a thought during this state is often all that is necessary for action to occur (151). Keith H. Basso concludes in "'To Give Up on Words'" that the critical factor in a Western Apache's decision to speak or keep silent was the nature of his or her relationships to other people. Apaches "give up on words" in such diverse situations as a meeting with strangers, the initial stages of courting, verbal attack, and the presence of someone for whom they sing a ceremony (153–58). Although attitudes toward silence vary from tribe to tribe, those outlined by Basso emphasize the importance of understanding the social customs governing the use of silence in individual Indian communities.

American Indians' desire for harmony is also reflected in their deep reverence for the land, another recurrent theme in their oral and written literatures. Because the earth nurtured them and because their tribal origins and histories are associated with specific places, Native North Americans have a strong sense of the sacredness of these places. In "Native Oral Traditions," Larry Evers and Paul Pavich say this sense of place is made possible by the "cultural landscape," which is created "whenever communities of people join words to place" (11). The words of a Havasupai Medicine Song, sung by Dan Hanna, illustrate tribal identification with the land:

The land we were given
The land we were given

It is right here
It is right here

Red rock
Red rock

Streaked with brown
Streaked with brown

Shooting up high
Shooting up high

All around our home
All around our home

—Hinton and Watahomigie, *Spirit Mountain* 108–09

American Indian authors continue to emphasize in their writings the importance of place, as Momaday movingly does in *The Way to Rainy Mountain*:

> Once in his life a man ought to concentrate his mind upon the remembered earth, I believe. He ought to give himself up to a particular landscape in his experience, to look at it from as many angles as he can, to wonder about it, to dwell upon it. He ought to imagine that he touches it with his hands at every season and listens to the sounds that are made upon it. He ought to imagine the creatures that are there and all the faintest motions of the wind. He ought to recollect the glare of noon and all the colors of the dawn and dusk. (83)

In an interview, Silko reveals the importance of cultural landscape when she describes how the river that runs through Laguna pueblo influenced tribal stories and her own work. Though muddy and shallow, the river was "the one place where things can happen that can't in the middle of the village." It was a special place where all sorts of things could go on. As an adolescent, Silko realized that the river was a place to meet boyfriends and lovers: "I used to wander around down there and try to imagine walking around the bend and just happening to stumble upon some beautiful man." Later she understood that these fantasies were exactly the kind of thing that happened in the Laguna Yellow Woman stories, a series of abduction/seduction myths, as well as in the pueblo's stories about those who used the river as a meeting place:

> These stories about goings-on, about what people are up to, give identity to a place. There's things about the river you can see with your own eyes,

of course, but the feeling of the place, the whole identity of it was established for me by the stories I'd hear, all the stories. . . . (Evers and Carr, "A Conversation with Silko" 29)

Linked to reverence for the land is the emphasis on directionality and circularity that occurs frequently in American Indian oral and written literatures. Following the natural order of the universe, humankind moves in a circle from east to south to west to north to east. For many tribes, the numeral four, representing the cardinal directions, seasons, and stages of human life, is a sacred number often incorporated into the content and form of their literatures. Multiples of four and the number six, representing the cardinal directions plus the directions above and below the earth, are also common.

The circle symbolizes the sun and its circuit. It also represents the cycle and continuum of human life as it passes through infancy, childhood, adulthood, old age. Black Elk explains the significance of the circle to the Sioux:

You have noticed that everything an Indian does is in a circle, and that is because the Power of the World always works in circles, and everything tries to be round. In the old days when we were a strong and happy people, all our power came to us from the sacred hoop of the nation, and so long as the hoop was unbroken, the people flourished. The flowering tree was the living center of the hoop, and the circle of the four quarters nourished it. The east gave peace and light, the south gave warmth, the west gave rain, and the north with its cold and mighty wind gave strength and endurance. This knowledge came to us from the outer world with our religion. Everything the Power of the World does is done in a circle. The sky is round, and I have heard that the earth is round like a ball, and so are the stars. The wind, in its greatest power, whirls. Birds make their nests in circles, for theirs is the same religion as ours. The sun comes forth and goes down again in a circle. The moon does the same, and both are round. Even the seasons form a great circle in their changing, and always come back again to where they were. The life of a man is a circle from childhood to childhood, and so it is in everything where power moves. Our tepees were round like the nests of birds, and these were always set in a circle, the nation's hoop, a nest of many nests, where the Great Spirit meant for us to hatch our children. (*Black Elk Speaks* 198–200)

The circle is also reflected in many American Indian ceremonies and dances. Among the Mescalero Apache, for example, the girls performing the puberty ceremony provide a visual reminder of the circularity of time and the cycles of life by running around a basket four times (Farrer 150). In addition, circularity and cycles are often incorporated into the structure of narratives. For instance, mythic culture heroes or heroines may leave the community only to return after many trials and adventures.

A strong sense of communality and cooperativeness, reflecting Native Americans' belief in the importance of harmony, is another recurrent theme in American Indian literatures. Tribes often stress cooperation and good relations within the group, demonstrated in communal rituals, work and play, and decision making. Among many tribes, generosity, helpfulness to others, and respect for age and experience are highly valued virtues that enabled them to survive. Ella C. Deloria comments in *Speaking of Indians* (1944) that her people, "the Dakotas, understand the meaning of self-sacrifice, perhaps because their legends taught them that the buffalo, on which their very life depended, gave itself voluntarily that they might live" (14). In *The Life, Letters and Speeches of Kah-ge-ga-gah-bowh* (1850), George Copway describes how his Ojibwa father taught him the importance of generosity to the aged:

> *If you reverence the aged, many will be glad to hear of your name.* . . . The poor man will say to his children, "my children, let us go to him, for he is a great hunter, and is kind to the poor, he will not turn us away empty." The Great Spirit, who has given the aged a long life, will bless you. (24)

The following Keres song, which Paula Gunn Allen learned from her cousin, exemplifies this sense of oneness with the community and with the land:

> I add my breath to your breath
> That our days may be long on the Earth
> That the days of our people may be long
> That we may be one person
> That we may finish our roads together
> May our mother bless you with life
> May our Life Paths be fulfilled.
>
> —Qtd. in *The Sacred Hoop* 56

Some themes are more culturally specific. For example, the narratives of the pueblo-dwelling Hopis tend to stress hard work, while those of the nomadic Navajos tend to emphasize movement (Courlander, *Hopi Voices* xxvii–xxix; Astrov, "Concept of Motion as the Psychological Leitmotif of Navaho Life and Literature").

American Indian oral literatures were most often transmitted aurally. However, some groups did record portions of their literatures. The Ojibwa, for example, used pictographic symbols to preserve their Midé (Grand Medicine) rituals on birchbark scrolls and other materials; other tribes, such as those on the Plains and Northwest Coast, also kept pictographic accounts. One of the few tribes to record their literature in books was the Quiche Maya of the Guatemala highlands, who preserved the stories of the origin of their culture in a work called the *Popol Vuh*, or *Council Book*. Their scribes continued to create books before the arrival of Western Europeans, who subsequently burned hundreds of hieroglyphic volumes. According to Dennis Tedlock, only four have survived, three in Europe and one recently discovered in Guatemala (*Popol Vuh* 23–27).

Native American oral literatures include both the works performed by American Indians within the communities that produced them and performances preserved in written transcriptions. These literatures reflect the mythology and history of the past as well as the experiences of the present. Although traditional ceremonies, myths, and songs follow general patterns established within the group over time, ceremonialists, storytellers, and singers create their own performances within those patterns. So long as the interpretations are accepted by the group as true to the spirit and content of the original, are performed appropriately, and achieve the desired result, many tribes may consider each performer's version as valid. The Iroquois follow this approach in their ceremonies, according to Michael K. Foster. After studying four Iroquois Longhouse speech events performed by seven speakers, Foster concludes in *From the Earth to beyond the Sky* that their rituals are not memorized verbatim but are composed, or "literally built anew," each time a performer rises to speak:

> What speakers share, and what gives continuity to the tradition across longhouse and reserve lines, is a set of composition rules for each ritual type (rules governing the statement, development and resolution of themes) and a common repertoire of conventionalized formulas. (vi)

Foster emphasizes that flexibility is the key resource for the speaker, who uses what works at the moment.

However, the degree to which improvisation is permissible may vary from one form of literature to another within the tribe. Discussing the magical rituals of the Cherokee in *Run toward the Nightland*, Kilpatrick and Kilpatrick state that master singers of rituals are "at perfect liberty to improvise a text if the spirit moves" them to do so. While the singers will not knowingly alter a text that has descended to them through tradition, they may occasionally elect to use only part of it (7). In *Singing for Power*, Ruth Murray Underhill comments that among the Papago, the storytellers work years to memorize the complicated mass of prose and verse that constitutes that tribe's bible. When the sun stands still, the storytellers recite this bible over four winter nights to those gathered in the ceremonial house. Although the storytellers may elaborate the prose with their own illustrations and explanations, they cannot do so with the verse. The words and tune of every song and the point at which they enter the story were given by Elder Brother, their culture hero. Nevertheless, as Underhill notes, some variations have crept in (12).

In *Kinaaldá*, Charlotte Johnson Frisbie indicates that improvisation is restricted in this Navajo girl's puberty rite and that an essential core exists in both myth and ceremony. Songs can be lengthened or shortened and verses within them ordered differently or even omitted, although the details of ceremonial songs per se may not be changed. Characters must retain their original names, costumes, and habitats; they must pursue their established journeys and perform determined acts. However, Frisbie also states that the timing and performances of the ceremony can vary not only for reasons inherent in Navajo customs and religion but also for more immediate, observable causes—available material, economic welfare, personal preference, environmental conditions, death of relatives, school restrictions, and regional customs and beliefs (82–84, 91–92). While tribal custom determines the degree to which improvisation is acceptable in communal rites as well as in traditional songs and narratives, American Indian artists also create oral literature that reflects their personal experience and imagination.

Even if verbatim memorization is not essential, the performance of oral literatures can sometimes demand great feats of recall. For example, the Navajo Night Chant, or Nightway, a healing ceremony, begins at sunset and ends eight and a half days later at sunrise. Because each ceremony, story, and song survived through time immemorial only in tribal memory, every generation faced the danger of losing its ancestral oral traditions if tribal members did not preserve them in their memories and encourage their performance. In *Indian Boyhood* Charles Eastman describes how his people, the Sioux, trained their young boys from an early age to assume the task of preserving and transmitting tribal and ancestral legends:

> Almost every evening a myth, or a true story of some deed done in the past, was narrated by one of the parents or grandparents, while the boy listened with parted lips and glistening eyes. On the following evening, he was usually required to repeat it. If he was not an apt scholar, he struggled long with his task; but, as a rule, the Indian boy was a good listener and has a good memory, so that the stories were tolerably well mastered. The household became his audience, by which he was alternately criticized and applauded. (42–43)

Many American Indians consider religious ceremonies, myths, and songs as too sacred to be discussed or collected for study by those outside the tribe. In an interview with Joseph Bruchac, Ray A. Young Bear (Mesquakie) describes his family's opposition to collecting the tribe's oral narratives:

> I have been consulting my Grandmother as well as other people, and I am afraid that it is simply impossible. The first and only stories we could have picked from Mesquakie people were published by William Jones, who was a protégé of Franz Boaz [sic], in the early 1900s. I tried to tell my relatives that there had been previously published material on Mesquakie people by our forefathers. I thought it would still be possible to, at least, try and

share some stories now before they are forgotten. But this idea of trying to keep a culture free of what would be called cultural contamination is still very prevalent among the Mesquakie. It would be easier just to forget the stories and not publish them at all. If one attempts to do that, they are risking their lives. As my grandmother [sic] told me, "I used to hear stories about William Jones being here on the Settlement when I was young. He must have gone around with a bag over his shoulder, collecting these stories. But what happened to him? He went overseas and was killed by the Philip[p]ines or some tribe in those islands in the Pacific." She uses that as a reference and I think it is reference that must be heeded. (*Survival This Way* 348)

Some Indians and non-Indians believe that printing oral literature dooms it as oral performance; others feel that because stories and songs are fast-vanishing relics, performed only for anthropologists and folklorists, they must be captured in books in order to survive. In *Yaqui Deer Songs*, Larry Evers and Felipe S. Molina emphasize that their experience suggests the contrary: "that Yaqui deer songs and the traditions which surround them are very much alive and that more than sixty years of recording and printing versions of them has complemented and reinforced more traditional oral modes of continuance, rather than contributing to their disappearance" (14).

Because the verbal arts are performed arts, the recordings and transcriptions of them should incorporate as much of the performance as possible. Elizabeth C. Fine comments in *The Folklore Text* that although the literary model of the text is the most widespread format for folklore publications, it ignores recording performance context and style. As Fine makes clear, the ethnolinguistic text, developed by early anthropologists and continued by modern linguistic anthropologists, is primarily an accurate verbatim transcript of "connected discourse to aid linguistic analysis and to preserve vanishing cultural traditions." Early ethnolinguistic texts preserved little, if any, information about "the informant, setting, or cultural significance of the tale." Many of the published folklore texts may be reports or summaries rather than records of authentic performances (55, 61).

In addition, many of those who recorded oral literatures sometimes abbreviated or revised the texts to suit the tastes of the time. Aspects of style and performance that are part of the total verbal art of a given work include choice of ritual or ordinary language, repetition, structure of the work, revisions of the text to incorporate relevant allusions to the present, appeals to the audience, and use of the voice and body to dramatize the content. As Andrew O. Wiget emphasizes in "Telling the Tale," performance theory sees stories as "storytelling events." Performance is simply one of many ways of providing a "frame" for communication, which Barbara Babcock-Abrahams defines in "The Story in the Story" as "an interpretative context or alternative point of view within which the content of the story is to be understood and judged"

(66). According to Wiget, "a frame signals to the receiver, through a variety of verbal and nonverbal markers, that a particular kind of message is being sent" that must be interpreted in a specific way to be intelligible (314).

In "The Poetics of Verisimilitude," Dennis Tedlock notes that Zuni narrators use a variety of the techniques of style and performance described above to create the appearance of reality. According to Tedlock, a few gestures seem to be standard usages in tale telling:

> A sweeping motion of a partially outstretched arm and hand may indicate the horizontal or vertical motion of a tale actor; a completely outstretched arm and hand, accompanied by the words, "It was at this time," may indicate the height of the sun at a particular point in the stories; the forefingers or palms may be held a certain distance apart to indicate the size of an object; and so forth. (166)

In keeping with the fact that tales take place "long ago," the Zuni narrators exclude modernisms from quotations and insert archaisms (167). Tedlock states that the narrators break the story out of its frame set in the "long ago" by alluding to the present, by such phrases as "It was about this time of year," centering the story action in the narrator's own house or alluding to members of the audience or their actions (168–69).

Whereas Tedlock bases his analysis of the storyteller's art on performances he attended and tape-recorded, Wiget bases his, in "Telling the Tale," on a videotaped performance by Helen Sekaquaptewa. Using photographs to illustrate his discussion, Wiget examines Sekaquaptewa's skill as a storyteller through her choice of words, the way she expresses the words, and the way she augments her tale with gestures and facial expressions. Discussing the kinesthetic features of her performance, Wiget notes, for example, that Sekaquaptewa basically sits in a neutral body position, erect and a bit forward on her sofa, hands in her lap and eyes slightly lowered. Though she varies this position, she always returns to it. Her most engrossing movements are those that reach into what is exclusively audience space, including actually touching the audience. Wiget concludes that gestures create suspense and climax (320–25).

The audience also plays a role in the performance of American Indian verbal arts. In *Verbal Art as Performance* Richard Bauman suggests that there is a "heightened intensity of communicative interaction which binds the audience to the performer in a way that is specific to performance as a mode of communication." The performers elicit the participative attention and energy of their audience. To the extent that audience members value the performance, "they will allow themselves to be caught up in it" (43).

Proper etiquette in many Indian cultures requires the audience to give the storyteller a gift, usually tobacco. Often the audience is expected to give a ritual response during the course of the story, to encourage the storyteller either to begin or to continue. If such encouragement is not forthcoming, the storyteller may stop. Audience participation becomes part of some ceremonies. Foster notes in *From the Earth to beyond the Sky* that in the Iroquois Longhouse, the speaker for the men of the leading side begins the day's events with the Thanksgiving Address. At the end of each section, the men of the opposite moiety utter a term of assent. The speaker for the nonleading side then takes the floor (28–29). In *Yaqui Deer Songs*, Evers and Molina point out that in the Yaqui ceremonies the old men serve as ceremonial hosts and clowns. They are always interacting with the audience, which is drawn to them. "During their joking and repartee, they constantly play to their audience and expect laughter and verbal response." Even when the eldest member delivers the opening and closing sermons, he expects the audience to respond with the formulaic affirmative *"heewi"* (78). Another example of audience participation in ritual is described by Joann W. Kealiinohomoku in "The Drama of the Hopi Ogres." Kealiinohomoku indicates that the "ogre" ritual is unique because it is one of the few Hopi ceremonies totally performed in public and because its dramatis personae include members of the audience — Hopi children and some of their adult relatives. Those depicting ogres interact with audience members by incorporating them into highly structured, improvised scenes (38).

Accurate and appropriate translation is crucial to the preservation in English of American Indian verbal arts. Unfortunately, all too often translations have not been true to the original texts. In the past, translations were rendered in the Victorian or pseudo-biblical styles considered by non-Indians to be appropriate for literature and incorporated elements common to Western European literature but not present in the literature of native North America. In "On the Translation of Style in Oral Narrative," Tedlock reveals how Frank Cushing, whose translations of Zuni literature were widely praised in the past, interjected such oaths as "Souls of my ancestors" and "By the bones of the dead" into his translations. According to Tedlock, the Zunis themselves have no such oaths and never make profane use of words denoting death, souls, ancestors, corpses, "Powers," and gods (35). He also points out that Cushing incorporated devices, lines, and whole passages of his own invention. At the opposite extreme were the highly literal and often graceless translations of Zuni literature made by the followers of the great anthropologist Franz Boas, whose work and disciples dominated the field of American Indian anthropology early in the twentieth century (36–37).

Other translations molded individual songs to fit the translators' or retranslators' interpretations of what the texts were about. Recently, poets and critics have reworked some of the early translations to produce their own versions. Evers and Molina illustrate in *Yaqui Deer*

Songs what can happen to the beauty of the original Yaqui text. Working in 1982 from Juan Ariware's original performance of a Yaqui song
recorded on phonographic cylinder by Frances Densmore in 1922,
Molina transcribed the following song:

> Sikili . . .
>> kaita va vemu weamakasu
>>> hakun kukupopoti hiusakai

> Sikili . . .
>> kaita va vemu weamakasu
>>> hakun kukupopoti hiusakai

> lyiminsu seyewailo
>> huya nainsasukuni
>>> kaita va vemu weamakasu
>>>> hakun kukupopoti hiusaka

> Sikili . . .
>> kaita va vemu weamakasu
>>> hakun kukupopoti hiusaki. (26)

Densmore, one of the earliest and most prolific recorders and translators of American Indian music, translates this simply as "The quail in
the bush is making his sound (whirring)" (song 84, *Yuman and Yaqui
Music* 157). Molina's translation demonstrates how much is lost in
Densmore's paraphrase.

> Little red [quail],
>> walking afar where there is no water,
>>> where do they make the kukupopoti sound?
> Little red [quail],
>> walking afar where there is no water,
>>> where do they make the kukupopoti sound?

> Over here, in the center
>> of the flower-covered wilderness,
>>> walking afar where there is no water,
>>>> where do they make the kukupopoti sound?
> Little red [quail],
>> walking afar where there is no water,
>>> where do they make the kukupopoti sound? (26)

As Evers and Molina make clear, Densmore's paraphrase omits the
line, stanza structure, rhetorical structure, action, onomatopoeic representation of the sound of the quail, and other features that contribute
to the song's aesthetic effect in Yaqui (26–27). They also demonstrate
the dangers of generalizing about American Indian songs on the basis

of faulty translations. This danger is exemplified by Kenneth Rexroth's comments in "American Indian Songs." Using Densmore's abbreviated translations, Rexroth erroneously concludes not only that "the texts of almost all these songs are . . . extremely simple, but that most of them are pure poems of sensibility resembling nothing so much as classical Japanese poetry or Mallarmé and certain other modern French and American poets" (282). Although Densmore may sometimes provide paraphrases rather than translations, she nevertheless made invaluable contributions to the history of American Indian song. Indefatigable, she moved from tribe to tribe recording, transcribing, and translating or paraphrasing a voluminous collection of songs.

The history of the collection of oral literatures of native America begins in Mesoamerica in the books of the Maya. After contact, some of the Spanish priests helped to preserve the literature. In his *General History of the Things of New Spain*, Fray Bernardino de Sahagun included considerable native literature, which he translated into Spanish. His example was followed by other priests, who encouraged their Indian converts to record their cultural heritage. Tedlock notes in *Popol Vuh* that although the priests' primary concern was to prepare grammars and dictionaries, their interest encouraged their pupils to preserve their Indian literary legacy (28). In North America, some myths were incorporated into the accounts of Jesuits and other early explorers of the continent. However, the systematic collection of the oral literature of what is now the United States was stimulated by the publication of Henry Rowe Schoolcraft's *Algic Researches* (1839), which focused on Ojibwa culture and literature. Presses responded to the public's subsequent interest in the culture of the supposedly vanished "noble savages" and in their literature by publishing a number of life histories and autobiographies, most of which included selected examples of oral literature.

The scholarly collection of oral literatures did not flourish until the development of the anthropological and linguistic study of American Indian cultures in the late nineteenth and early twentieth centuries. In *The Folklore Text*, Fine credits John Wesley Powell, founding director of the Bureau of American Ethnology from 1879–1902, and Boas with establishing the ethnolinguistic approach that dominated the collection of American Indian verbal arts during this period. One of Powell's main reasons for collecting oral literatures was to provide samples of connected discourse to aid in learning the structure of Indian languages. The verbal arts also provided insights into Indian culture. Boas had a deeper interest in the literature itself. Fine concludes that his rejection of cultural evolutionism, respect for American Indian culture, and appreciation of the aesthetic values and important cultural functions of Indian folklore strongly influenced other anthropologists and linguists (19–22).

Tribes and individual scholars vary considerably in their categorization of oral literatures. Native Americans have their own distinctive terms to identify particular genres, which often do not correspond to Euroamerican genres. Dan Ben-Amos's history of the attempts to categorize oral literatures, in the introduction to *Folklore Genres*, demonstrates the complexity of the task. Ben-Amos stresses that ethnic-particular and cross-cultural systems may use different concepts of genre. Forms of oral tradition are not merely analytical constructs but "distinct modes of communication which exist in the lore of peoples" (xxv, xxi).

Works Cited

Allen, Paula Gunn (Laguna/Sioux). *The Sacred Hoop: Recovering the Feminine in American Indian Traditions*. Boston: Beacon, 1986.

Astrov, Margot. "The Concept of Motion as the Psychological Leitmotif of Navaho Life and Literature." *JAF* 63 (1950): 45–56.

Babcock-Abrahams, Barbara. "The Story in the Story: Metanarration in Folk Narrative." Bauman, *Verbal Art* 61–79.

Basso, Keith H. "'To Give Up on Words': Silence in Western Apache Culture." *Southwestern Journal of Anthropology* 26 (1970): 312–30. Rpt. in *Apachean Culture History and Ethnology*. Ed. Basso and Morris E. Opler. Anthropological Papers of the Univ. of Arizona 21. Tucson: U of Arizona P, 1971. 151–61.

Bauman, Richard. *Verbal Art as Performance*. 1977. Prospect Heights: Waveland, 1984.

Ben-Amos, Dan, ed. *Folklore Genres*. Austin: U of Texas P, 1976.

*Black Elk (Sioux). John G. Neihardt. *Black Elk Speaks*. 1932. Introd. Vine Deloria Jr. Lincoln: U of Nebraska P, 1979. New York: Washington Square, 1972. Autobiography.

Bruchac, Joseph (Abenaki), ed. *Survival This Way: Interviews with American Indian Poets*. Sun Tracks 15. Tucson: U of Arizona P, 1987. Interviews with Paula Gunn Allen (Laguna/Sioux), Peter Blue Cloud (Mohawk), Diane Burns (Ojibwa/Chemehuevi), Elizabeth Cook-Lynn (Sioux), Louise Erdrich (Ojibwa), Joy Harjo (Creek), Lance Henson (Cheyenne), Linda Hogan (Chickasaw), Karoniaktatie (Mohawk), Maurice Kenny (Mohawk), Harold Littlebird (Laguna/Santo Domingo), N. Scott Momaday (Kiowa), Duane Niatum (Klallam), Simon Ortiz (Acoma), Carter Revard (Osage), Wendy Rose (Hopi/Miwok), Luci Tapahonso (Navajo), Gerald Vizenor (Ojibwa), James Welch (Blackfeet/Gros Ventre), Roberta Hill Whiteman (Oneida), and Ray A. Young Bear (Mesquakie).

Chapman, Abraham, ed. *Literature of the American Indians: Views and Interpretations*. New York: NAL, 1975.

Coltelli, Laura, ed. *Winged Words: American Indian Writers Speak*. American Indian Lives. Lincoln: U of Nebraska P, 1990. Interviews with Paula Gunn Allen (Laguna/Sioux), Michael Dorris (Modoc), Louise Erdrich (Ojibwa), Joy Harjo (Creek), Linda Hogan (Chickasaw), N. Scott Momaday (Kiowa), Simon Ortiz (Acoma), Wendy Rose (Hopi/Miwok), Gerald Vizenor (Ojibwa), and James Welch (Blackfeet/Gros Ventre).

Copway, George (Ojibwa). *The Life, History, and Travels of Kah-ge-ga-gah-bowh (George Copway)*. . . . Albany: Weed and Parsons, 1847. Rev. ed. *The*

Life, Letters and Speeches of Kah-ge-ga-gah-bowh, or G. Copway.... New York: Benedict, 1850. Autobiography.

Courlander, Harold, ed. *Hopi Voices: Recollections, Traditions, and Narratives of the Hopi Indians*. Albuquerque: U of New Mexico P, 1982.

Deloria, Ella C. (Sioux). *Speaking of Indians*. Ed. Agnes Picotte (Sioux) and Paul N. Pavich. 1944. Vermillion: Dakota P, 1979.

Densmore, Frances, ed. *Yuman and Yaqui Music*. BBAE 110 (1932). Music Reprint Ser. New York: Da Capo, 1972.

Eastman, Charles A. [Ohiyesa] (Sioux). *Indian Boyhood*. 1902. New York: Dover, 1971. Autobiography.

Evers, Larry, and Denny Carr. "A Conversation with Leslie Marmon Silko." *Sun Tracks* 3 (1976): 28–33.

——, and Felipe S. Molina (Yaqui). *Yaqui Deer Songs / Maso Bwikam: A Native American Poetry*. Sun Tracks 14. Tucson: U of Arizona P, 1987.

——, and Paul Pavich. "Native Oral Traditions." Lyon and Taylor, *A Literary History of the American West* 11–28.

Farrer, Clare R. "Singing for Life: The Mescalero Apache Girls' Puberty Ceremony." Frisbie, *Southwestern Indian Ritual Drama* 125–59.

Fine, Elizabeth C. *The Folklore Text: From Performance to Print*. Bloomington: Indiana UP, 1984.

Foster, Michael K. *From the Earth to beyond the Sky: An Ethnographic Approach to Four Longhouse Iroquois Speech Events*. National Museum of Man, Mercury Ser., Canadian Ethnology Service Paper 20. Ottawa: National Museums of Canada, 1974.

Frisbie, Charlotte Johnson. *Kinaaldá: A Study of the Navaho Girl's Puberty Ceremony*. Middletown: Wesleyan UP, 1967.

——, ed. *Southwestern Indian Ritual Drama*. Albuquerque: U of New Mexico P, 1980.

Hinton, Leanne, and Lucille J. Watahomigie (Hualapai), eds. *Spirit Mountain: An Anthology of Yuman Story and Song*. Sun Tracks 10. Tucson: U of Arizona P, 1984.

Kealiinohomoku, Joann W. "The Drama of the Hopi Ogres." Frisbie, *Southwestern Indian Ritual Drama* 37– 69.

Kilpatrick, Jack Frederick, and Anna Gritts Kilpatrick (Cherokee), eds. *Run toward the Nightland: Magic of the Oklahoma Cherokees*. Dallas: Southern Methodist UP, 1967.

Kroeber, A. L., comp. *The Handbook of Indians of California*. ARBAE 78 (1925). Berkeley: California Book Co., 1953.

*Lame Deer [John Fire] (Sioux). Richard Erdoes. *Lame Deer: Seeker of Visions*. New York: Simon, 1972. Autobiography.

Momaday, N. Scott (Kiowa). "The Native Voice." *The Columbia Literary History of the United States*. Ed. Emory Elliott. New York: Columbia UP, 1988. 5–15.

——. *The Way to Rainy Mountain*. Albuquerque: U of New Mexico P, 1969. Autobiography, myth, history.

Ortiz, Simon J. (Acoma). "Interview." Coltelli, *Winged Words* 103–19.

Rexroth, Kenneth. "American Indian Songs." Chapman, *Literature of the American Indians* 278–91.

Sahagun, Bernardino de. *General History of the Things of New Spain: Florentine Codex*. Monographs of the School of American Research 14. 13 vols. in 12. Salt Lake City: U of Utah P, 1950–82.

Schoolcraft, Henry Rowe. *Algic Researches, Comprising Inquiries Respecting the Mental Characteristics of the North American Indians.* 2 vols. 1839. New York: Garland, 1979.

Silko, Leslie Marmon (Laguna). *Ceremony.* New York: Viking, 1977. New York: Penguin, 1986. Fiction.

Spencer, Robert F., Jesse D. Jennings, et al. *The Native Americans: Ethnology and Backgrounds of the North American Indians.* 2nd ed. New York: Harper, 1977.

Tedlock, Dennis. "The Poetics of Verisimilitude." Orig. pub. as "Pueblo Literature: Style and Verisimilitude." *New Perspectives on the Pueblos.* Ed. Alfonso Ortiz. Albuquerque: U of New Mexico P, 1972. 219–42. Rev. *The Spoken Word* 159–77.

———. "On the Translation of Style in Oral Narrative." *JAF* 84 (1971): 114–33. Rev. *The Spoken Word* 31–61.

———, trans. *Popol Vuh: The Mayan Book of the Dawn of Life.* New York: Simon, 1985.

Underhill, Ruth Murray. *Singing for Power: The Song Magic of the Papago Indians of Southern Arizona.* 1938. Berkeley: U of California P, 1976.

Washburn, Wilcomb E. *The Indian in America.* The New American Nation. New York: Harper, 1975.

Wiget, Andrew O. "Telling the Tale: A Performance Analysis of a Hopi Coyote Story." Swann and Krupat, *Recovering the Word* 297–336.

Witherspoon, Gary. *Language and Art in the Navajo Universe.* Ann Arbor: U of Michigan P, 1977.

Introduction: Who Are We?

Marta Caminero-Santangelo

Caminero-Santangelo troubles the notion of "we" by noting that scholars increasingly question the idea of a singular Latino identity. She suggests that "Hispanic" ethnicity in the United States originated as much from outsider perception as from a sense of group identity. Caminero-Santangelo addresses the problem of umbrella terms—such as Latino *or* Hispanic—*masking significant differences between grouped peoples with different histories and experiences. This point is reflected in examples of Latino/a literature as she notes that "[i]nteractions between characters from the author's own ethnic group and other 'Latino' groups have been represented infrequently or not at all" (p. 193). Thus Sandra Cisneros writes about Mexican Americans, Cristina García about Cubans, Junot Díaz about Dominicans, and Piri Thomas about Puerto Ricans. Though Caminero-Santangelo notes some exceptions, writers have not appeared to accept* Latino *or* Hispanic *as a label despite the movement toward producing Latino/a literature anthologies. Caminero-Santangelo observes*

From *On Latinidad: U.S. Latino Literature and the Construction of Ethnicity* (Gainesville: UP of Florida, 2007): 1–35.

that only recently has literary scholarship begun to employ Latino *as an umbrella term, but scholarship that "directly addresses the panethnic implications of this label has made it much less easy to generalize about common culture, common political orientation, or even common experiences of marginalization within the United States" (p. 197). The author provides a thorough overview of recent studies of Latino/a literature and the approaches taken toward panethnic identity. The essay serves as the introduction to her book,* On Latinidad *(2007).*

Earl Shorris's hefty tome *Latinos: A Biography of the People* (1992) begins with a telling anecdote. Shorris, in his ethnographer persona, asks one of his subjects, Margarita Avila, "If you were writing this book, what would you want it to say?" Avila responds, "Just tell them who we are and that we are not all alike." Shorris interprets Avila's comments as a statement about the differences that divide Latinos, noting that he has heard the same sentiment expressed countless times by interviewees across the country.

But those differences are more profound, perhaps, than even Shorris perceives. In his prologue (entitled "The Name of the People"), Shorris expresses an interest in nomenclature, terminology—he wants to pin Avila down about how he should refer to the group: "Before I could begin, there was a word to be chosen, a name to be given to the noun represented by 'we.'" But when he asks Avila who "we" is, she responds, "Mejicanos." When he prods, "Yes, but there is a larger group"—still apparently assuming that it was this larger entity that Avila originally referred to when she said "we are not all alike"— Avila insists (and resists), "We are Mejicanos" (xv). Shorris then recounts a litany of resistance:

> "Hispanic?" I asked.
> "Mejicano," she said. [. . .]
> "Hispano, Latino, Latin, Spanish, Spanish-speaking."
> "Mejicano," she said. (xvi)

Of course, Shorris understands Avila's point; she is rejecting any umbrella term. And yet, he never lets go of the assumption that there *is* a "set of people" (xvi) named by such a term, or that this is the "we" Avila originally referred to when she said "we are not all alike." The idea that Avila might have been commenting on what Suzanne Oboler calls "the heterogeneity of the Mexican-American population" (68),[1] rather than on the diversity of "Latinos"—that is, that she might have been talking only about "Mejicanos" all along—does not seem to occur to him.

The story is a vivid enactment, in brief, of the ways in which the *category* "Latino" (or "Hispanic") has, at least at times, been applied from outside while adamantly rejected from within. Avila *refuses* to acknowledge any "we" outside of "Mejicanos"; anyone else, in her construction, is "them" (as in, "Tell them . . ."). Suzanne Oboler's interviews with people of Latin American origin, in her 1995 study *Ethnic Labels, Latino Lives*, confirms this sense of umbrella terms such as "Hispanic" or "Latino" being "imposed by Americans" (155). When respondents were asked about how they might identify Latin Americans in the United States who were of national origins different from their own, one Latin American immigrant replied, "If I introduce you to someone I would say 'This is my friend, she's from Peru.' Or else, I'd say, 'She's South American, or Peruvian.'" Another responded, "I always call people according to their country: a Salvadorean, an Uruguayan, an Argentinean" (153).[2] As happened with Shorris, this response prompted further questioning:

> *But not a Hispanic?*
> Soledad: No, I identify them according to their country.
> Why wouldn't you say they're Hispanic?
> Soledad: Well, it just doesn't sound right to me. [. . .] [W]e're not just a lump [. . .] — because even though we may use the same language, our cultures are different and we have to think about what we're going to say to each other. [. . .] Many of the things we might say in Spanish [are] offensive to one person, funny to another. Another thing is the food. . . . For example, we have to learn to eat what [Central Americans] eat. (153–54)

On the basis of *cultural difference* (not, as so many commentators seem to insist, a "common culture"), indicated by the differences in "ethnic markers" such as food and language usage, Oboler's interviewees repudiate the use among themselves of an umbrella term. Oboler notes that they are engaged "in the process of defining the group's internal boundaries" (153), but what is striking is that the sense of "group" as Oboler is using it is simply not present at all.

The question of whether a single, identifiable "Latino" identity exists has been asked, in various ways and under a multitude of rubrics, by an increasing number of scholars. And that is a welcome development, certainly, since the state of affairs prior to the deliberate asking of the question was generally simply to assume from the outside — along with U.S. popular culture and the census — that "Latinos" were, in fact, a group and proceed from there.[3]

The critical insight, by now a commonplace, that ethnicity is a "social construct" has gone a significant way toward modifying and complicating this assumption. As Nicholas De Genova and Ana Y. Ramos-Zayas put it, "there is no automatic or inevitable necessity to the emergence of a shared sense of Latino identity, as indeed there are never any natural or self-evident positive grounds for *any* identity. Identities must be *produced* through social relations and struggle" (21). Werner Sollors, one of the leading early theorists of ethnicity in relation to literature, has drawn (in *The Invention of Ethnicity*, 1989) on Benedict Anderson's writings to call attention to the premise that ethnicities, like nations, are "imagined communities" rather than peoples connected by any essential, natural, or unchanging relations. What connects these communities is a set of "collective fictions" that, far from being themselves stable, are "intensely debated" and "continually reinvented" (xi). This is where literature comes in, for, as Sollors argues elsewhere, literature and its study play a crucial role in generating a sense of ethnicity based on contrast ("X writes like an X, not like a Y") and also "help to create the illusion of a group's 'natural' existence from 'time immemorial'" ("Ethnicity" 290).

Stephen Cornell and Douglas Hartmann, grappling in *Ethnicity and Race* (1998) with the question of how to define ethnicity in a way that accounts for its power as an idea as well as its "constructed" nature, have invoked German sociologist Max Weber's contention that it is based on "a subjective belief in [. . .] common descent" (Weber 389, qtd. in Cornell and Hartmann 16), as well as Richard A. Schermerhorn's criteria that "[e]thnic groups are self-conscious populations; they see themselves as distinct" (19) and that, more than "actual cultural distinctiveness" (19), they share "a cultural focus on one or more symbolic elements defined as the epitome of their peoplehood" (12, qtd. in Cornell and Hartmann 19). Cornell and Hartmann go on to clarify that "[t]o say that ethnicity is subjective is not to say that it is unaffected by what others say or do. Indeed, outsiders' conceptions of us may be a major influence leading to our own self-consciousness as an ethnic population. Others may assign to us an ethnic identity, but what they establish by doing so is an ethnic category. It is our own claim to that identity that makes us an ethnic group" (20). It is arguable that the origins of "Hispanic" ethnicity in the United States lie at least as much in outsider perception of a singular group (e.g., "They all speak Spanish") as in the group's own perception of "groupness."

Much has been made of the fact that the U.S. Census Bureau introduced "Hispanic" as a classification in the 1980 census,[4] a possible example of Cornell and Hartmann's point that ethnic group identity can *originate* in "outsiders' conceptions of us," though it is only when the group itself takes on that identification as its own that it becomes an ethnic group. Rubén Rumbaut conveys precisely this dynamic when he writes that "Hispanic" is "a label developed and legitimized by the state, diffused in daily and institutional practice, and finally internalized" ("Making" 19). The force of outsider perception is also what Oboler suggests through the title of her book's first chapter: "Hispanics? That's What *They* Call Us." As one Puerto Rican mainland respondent interviewed by Oboler puts it, "White people have a name for everybody else. [. . .] I mean, Puerto Ricans never call each other Hispanic. [. . .] When they ["white people"] said Hispanics, that's just a group of people that they've just put together that speaks Spanish. . . . They just count all Latin people in one bunch" (155).

Most savvy commentators now disavow (at least explicitly) the notion of an essential Latino identity—after all, by now we know that even gender and national identities are not "essential" (there is no defining female "soul" or inherent American "spirit")—even though those same commentators often follow up by sneaking in suspiciously "essentialist"-sounding statements about Latino identity through the back door, in the guise of comments on "Latino culture."[5] But that does not mean that Latino identity "doesn't exist," for, as is frequently pointed out, social constructs still exist and can exert a strong force. Perhaps a better question would be, Is there such a thing as a collective, *panethnic* Latino identity—one that Latinos themselves generally recognize? For, as Felix Padilla has persuasively argued, there is a world of difference between exhibiting ethnic consciousness as a Mexican American or Puerto Rican and doing so as a Latino or Hispanic; the latter implies a sense of relations between and among Latino groups (2). Or is the category really little more than a label "assigned," in Cornell and Hartmann's terminology, by "outsiders" rather than a real way in which so-called Latinos understand themselves?

At first glance, the 2000 census gives some indication that perhaps Latinos are identifying panethnically in greater numbers. The census finds that the number of people writing in the word "Hispanic," as opposed to a specific national origin that had not been already named in the previous options, increased, from 6.4 percent of the total responding Hispanic population (in 1990) to 15.7 percent. Write-ins of the category "Latino" also increased from a mere 1,577 (or 0 percent) to 1.2 percent (Cresce et al., table 2). As Matt A. Barreto notes, some Latino organizations, such as the National Council of La Raza (NCLR) and the League of United Latin American Citizens (LULAC), have postulated that "the increase in the 'other' category may be primarily due to a growing pan-Hispanic identity" (46).

Elizabeth Martin cautions, however, that while "[i]t might be tempting to conclude that a decline in reporting of detailed groups [i.e., of specific national origin] was due to Hispanics' changing self-identifications over the past decade" (i.e., to an increasing identification with a general "Hispanic" or "Latino" category over a nation-specific category), "the change can be attributed [instead] to a change in the design of the mail questionnaire" (591). In 1990 the "write-in" option included examples of national origin such as "Argentinean, Colombian, Dominican, Nicaraguan, Salvadoran, Spaniard, and so on" (1990 census); in 2000 the examples were left out. The "other" option thus read simply "Yes, other Spanish/Hispanic/Latino—*Print group*." As Martin points out, this wording is "vague" and "may have been interpreted by some respondents as a request to indicate which of the three terms they preferred" (590).

The 2002 National Survey of Latinos conducted by the Pew Hispanic Center reveals that 85 percent of Latinos questioned believe that

"Hispanics from different countries [. . .] [a]ll have separate and distinct cultures," while only 14 percent believe they "[s]hare one Hispanic/ Latino culture" (chart 9); the 2004 National Survey finds 51 percent of registered Latinos believing that "Latinos from different countries" are "not working together politically," while only 43 percent say they are "working together to achieve common political goals" (chart 28). (While the findings from the 2002 Survey were similar on this question, the 2006 National Survey, by contrast, finds that 58 percent of Latinos, a new majority, feels that Latinos "are working together to achieve common political goals"—a result possibly attributable to Latinos' sense of discriminatory backlash from the immigration policy debates and to the pro-immigrant marches earlier in 2006 [Suro and Escobar i, 11].)

If a collective sense of self is constructed through "collective fictions" (Sollors's term) and "symbolic elements" which come to stand as "the epitome of their peoplehood" (Schermerhorn's), then it is quite telling that Puerto Ricans on the mainland and Chicano/as—the two groups most often connected to each other in scholarship on Latinos in the United States[6]—have historically derived their sense of peoplehood, and their political energy, from *different* myths and symbols. As Suzanne Oboler writes of the Chicano movement of the 1960s, "Chicanos grounded their version of Mexican Americans' 'colonized' history in the mythical space and time of 'Aztlán' [. . .] the name for the legendary northern Mexican lands to which all Chicanos would one day return" (66). The movement rallied around and was energized by this "nationalist narrative of [. . .] a legendary and heroic Aztec past" (66). Puerto Ricans who were becoming politically active during the same period were also adopting "a strong cultural nationalist rationale" (57), but were imagining a *different* "nation" and set of nationalist symbols. Instead of Aztlán, the Virgin of Guadalupe, and the Aztec eagle,[7] Puerto Ricans who were becoming "increasingly aware of the implications of their island's status [. . .] renamed the island Borinquen, and many began to self-identify as Boricuas in an effort to return to its pre-Columbian indigenous Taino roots" (57).

While the dynamics were quite similar, the *stories* were different. De Genova and Ramos-Zayas have written, in their fascinating study *Latino Crossings* (2003), about more recent symbolic struggles between Puerto Ricans and other Latino groups, especially Mexicans, in Chicago:

> In response to the perceived "threat" posed by an increasing Mexican and Central American influx into the Humboldt Park neighborhood— traditionally marked as "Puerto Rican," and indeed, symbolically central as "the" Puerto Rican barrio—grassroots activists launched strenuous campaigns during the 1990s to discourage Puerto Rican residents from moving out of the barrio. Local businesses and ambulatory vendors selling Puerto Rican–identified goods worked alongside of grassroots activists to enforce physical and symbolic "boundaries" that were intended to

> maintain the "Puerto Rican"-ness of the neighborhood, by deploying
> nationalist and even separatist Puerto Rican symbols (such as a cam-
> paigning to install a statue of renowned nationalist leader Pedro Albizu
> Campos) [. . .]. The simultaneous perceived onslaught of "encroachments"
> by gentrifying whites, displaced poor Blacks, and other poor Latinos, es-
> pecially Mexican migrants, produced a sense of alarm that Puerto Ricans
> were being "squeezed out." (53)

If a sense of peoplehood is deployed largely through symbols, it is striking that the most prominent symbols in the arsenal of U.S. Latino
history have so often been nationally specific, rather than panethnic,
in nature.

As a loud chorus of commentators have observed, it is difficult indeed to pinpoint what exactly might link people of Chicano/a, Puerto
Rican, Cuban, Dominican, and Central/South American descent into a
single, and singular, collective ethnicity labeled "Latino" or "Hispanic."
While, as Debra Castillo notes in *Redreaming America* (2005), the questions "Who is a Latino/a?" and "Who or what defines 'real' *latinidad*?"
have been asked (and answered) with sometimes increasing urgency
and stridency, often invoking "identitarian claims" (10–11), there is a
growing scholarly tendency to reject the category altogether, at least
insofar as it could be said to refer to an "identity." Earl Shorris simply
maintains that "there are no Latinos, only diverse peoples struggling to
remain who they are" (12) (yet his book is paradoxically entitled *Latinos: A Biography of the People*). Invoking the common association of
ethnicity with kinship and family (as Cornell and Hartmann have written, "Ethnicity is family writ very large indeed" [20])—Marcelo M.
Suárez-Orozco and Mariela M. Páez, in the introduction to their nuanced and sophisticated volume *Latinos: Remaking America* (2002),
note that "the tired and facile 'Latinos-are-a-big-family' glosses over the
contradictions, tensions, and fissures—around class, race, and color—
that often separate them. [. . .] Bluntly, what does an English-speaking
third-generation upper-status white Cuban American in Florida have
in common with a Maya-speaking recent immigrant from Guatemala?"
(3). (Debra Castillo adds, "[H]ow about a Jew from Argentina?" [11].)
Silvio Torres-Saillant agrees, deriding the popular construct of U.S. Hispanics as *"una sola familia"* (a single family; 445) and insisting that
"[t]he claim that Latinos constitute one big happy family conceals the
tensions, inequities, and injustices in our midst, contributing to a conceptual ambience that legitimizes the absence of black and Indian faces
and voices from Latino fora. The operating logic seems to be that, because everyone in our polychromatic community is really the same,
everyone is inherently represented even when only one color continues
to peer out at us from the tube" (444).

Commenting particularly on "Latino" cultural production,
Guillermo Gómez-Peña argues that "[t]erms like Hispanic, Latino [. . .]

are inaccurate and loaded with ideological implications. They create false categories [. . .]. There is no such thing as 'Latino art' or 'Hispanic art.' There are hundreds of types of Latino-American-derived art in the United States. Each is aesthetically, socially, and politically specific" (46, 48). Oboler, whose focus is precisely the meaning and impact of labels, insists that the term "Hispanic obscures rather than clarifies" issues of group identity with regard to a highly diverse population of peoples of Latin American origin (2).

One of the most eloquent and passionate critics of any umbrella term, Martha Gimenez, denies the validity of any "label" flat out. As early as 1989 Gimenez insisted that "the label [. . .] only creates an artificial population; i.e., a statistical construct formed by aggregates of people who differ greatly in terms of national origin, language, race, time of arrival in the United States, culture, minority status [. . .], social class, and socioeconomic status" ("Latino/'Hispanic'" 559).[8] Elaborating at length on the meaninglessness of the term for public policy, social scientists, health professionals, and so on, Gimenez reviews research about birth rates, fertility rates, and median ages for "Hispanics" (treated collectively) and points out that such statistics tell us absolutely nothing, because the figures for the various national-origin Hispanic groups differ widely.

Her observations still hold true. According to the National Campaign to Prevent Teen Pregnancy (NCPTP), "Since 1995, Latina teens have had the highest teen birth rate among the major racial/ethnic groups in the United States" ("Fact Sheet: Latinos" 2); it cites a statistic of 82.3 per 1,000 in 2003 ("Fact Sheet: Latinos" 2), compared to 63.8 per 1,000 for African Americans, the next highest group ("Fact Sheet: Black" 2). The report goes on to state, however, that the rate for Mexican Americans was 93.2 (in 2003); for Puerto Ricans, by contrast, it was 60.8, and for "other" national-origin Latino groups (again grouped together), it was 60.4 ("Fact Sheet: Latinos" 2–3).[9] It is important, then, to note that, if Puerto Ricans (for example) were taken separately, their rate would *not* be the highest of any ethnic group in 2003; this happens only when they are grouped in with Mexican Americans, whose rate is over 30 per 1,000 higher.[10] The report also cites that 76.2 percent of teenaged Latina mothers who gave birth in 2003 were unmarried. But this figure, too, conceals substantial differences: "Mexican-American teen mothers [. . .] were least likely to give birth out-of-wedlock [. . .] (69.4%), followed by Cuban-American teen mothers (72.5%) [while] [t]he highest percent nonmarital was among teens of Puerto Rican descent (87.7%)" ("Latinos" 3)[11]—in other words, a difference of almost 20 percent between the least- and most-likely groups.

Similarly, the results of the 2000 census tell us that only 56 percent of Latinos aged twenty-five or older are high school graduates, while a mere 11 percent are college graduates (compared to 83 percent high school graduates and 25 percent college graduates nationwide) (U.S.

Dept. of Health and Human Services, *Mental Health* 131). Yet again this figure masks significant disparities: for Cuban Americans over 25 the figure is 70 percent who have graduated from high school, compared to 64 percent of Puerto Ricans and 50 percent of Mexican Americans; the figures for college are roughly 25 percent for Cuban Americans, compared to 11 percent for Puerto Ricans and 7 percent for Mexican Americans (*Mental Health* 132). In another example, the Census Bureau reports that the median age of Hispanics in 2000 was 25.8, but this figure encompasses a range from 24.3 years for Mexican Americans to 40.1 years for those of Cuban origin (U.S. Census Bureau). Given such differences among national groups, what can lumping them together and taking an average possibly tell us that the breakout statistics do not? Does the aggregate statistic, rather, obscure pertinent information?[12]

With somewhat more ambivalence than Gimenez, Juan Flores, in his provocative *From Bomba to Hip-Hop* (2000), is highly critical of the use of the catchall categories when they are used to refer to a single homogeneous group, without adequate attention to "structural variations in the placement [within a U.S. context] of the different national groups relative to hierarchies of power and attendant histories of racialization" (203).[13] The experience of upper- and middle-class Cuban exiles, welcomed with open arms into the United States as immigrants (until the Clinton administration) and given substantial government aid, is quite different, for example, from that of poverty-stricken Puerto Rican "immigrants" in New York (not immigrants at all, since all Puerto Ricans are U.S. citizens), which is different in turn from that of Mexican Americans in the Southwest, who frequently recount fear of or problems with "la migra" even when they are citizens.[14] The INS, now renamed U.S. Citizenship and Immigration Services (USCIS), is repeatedly portrayed by Chicano/a authors as assuming that Mexican Americans who cannot immediately produce proof of identity are "illegal." In contrast, since all Puerto Ricans are U.S. citizens who can therefore enter the country freely, they do not face this particular threat; De Genova and Ramos-Zayas, as well as Michael Jones-Correa, have argued quite powerfully that such differences in citizenship status have created marked divisions between Puerto Ricans and other groups.[15] A dominant U.S. culture's racial perceptions of the different groups, and consequently their historical and even current treatment, also vary: Cuban exiles have generally been perceived as "white"; Mexican Americans are perceived as part of the (nonexistent) "Hispanic" race (i.e., they are "brown"); Puerto Ricans have frequently been perceived as (close to) "black," as countless social scientists comparing Puerto Ricans to African Americans demonstrate.[16]

Commenting on the interests and perceptions of "Latinos" themselves, Geoffrey Fox writes that U.S. Hispanics include "some 25 million people who don't know or care much about one [an]other, don't think or talk alike, and have not until recently thought of themselves as having any common interests" (22). As if to prove Fox's point, most prominent examples of Latino/a literature virtually do not address the differences—or even the relationships—between the various Latino/a groups at all. Sandra Cisneros, Rudolfo Anaya, and Ana Castillo write about Mexican Americans. Cristina García and Oscar Hijuelos write about Cubans.[17] Julia Alvarez and Junot Díaz write about Dominicans. Esmeralda Santiago, Judith Ortiz Cofer, and Piri Thomas write about Puerto Ricans. And so on. Interactions between characters from the author's own ethnic group and other "Latino" groups have been represented infrequently or not at all. (Literary critics have generally followed suit by dealing with the separate ethnicities separately, even in critical texts that wrap them together under the broader umbrella term "Hispanic" or "Latino" in the title.) And while some novels have, at the very least, raised the looming specter of cultural "authenticity" by writing about Latino groups other than their own (examples include *In Search of Bernabé* [1993], a novel about the civil war in El Salvador, written by Graciela Limón, a Chicana; *The Infinite Plan* [1993], which in part depicts a Mexican American community in Los Angeles, by Isabel Allende, a Chilean immigrant and prominent Latin American author; *Send My Roots Rain* [1991], again about Chicanos, by Ibis Gómez-Vega, a Cuban American; *The Love Queen of the Amazon* [1992], set in Peru, by Chicana Cecile Pineda), these texts have not foregrounded the groups' interrelations, connections, or differences among the groups—leading readers either to assume that the authors, being "Latino" themselves, are writing from a standpoint of cultural "authority" or, conversely, that they are simply doing what writers do all the time: inventing worlds of fiction unrelated to their own experience.[18] Prominent Chicana writer Gloria Anzaldúa, in her groundbreaking classic *Borderlands / La Frontera* (1987), seems to suggest that umbrella terms such as "Latino" or "Hispanic" undermine a specific, politicized Chicano/a community: "We call ourselves Hispanic or Spanish-American or Latin American or Latin when linking ourselves to other Spanish-speaking peoples of the Western hemisphere and when copping out" (62). Cuban American author Gustavo Pérez Firmat puts the case in its perhaps most extreme form: "Latino is a statistical fiction, a figment of the imagination of ethnic ideologues, ad executives and salsa singers. [. . .] [T]o me, Latino is an empty concept. Latino doesn't have a culture, a language, a place of origin" (qtd. in Alvarez Borland 150). In *Cincuenta lecciones de exilio y desexilio*, Pérez Firmat insists on being Cuban rather than Hispanic and adds, "Si me dicen *Latino*, respondo, la tuya" (If they say to me *Latino*, I respond, up yours; 108). Pérez Firmat suggests that "Latino" is not essence but invention and implies that—despite the occasional sellout "salsa singer"—it is not an invention participated in by the community itself (a "collective fiction") but one imposed from the outside and to which he takes offense.

Of course, it is more than just offensive "ad executives and salsa singers"—or even official government forms and mainstream media—that have participated in the construction of a group category now known as "Latino." The academic publishing industry, to name just one other example, has for years now been producing anthologies under the rubric of "Latino/a literature," and college courses under this title abound. Yet, as Karen Christian has noted in *Show and Tell* (1997), until quite recently most literary scholarship did not follow suit: "A survey of U.S. Latina/o literary criticism indicates that the prevailing tendency has been to regard Chicana/o, Nuyorican, and U.S. Cuban literatures as distinct cultural phenomena. The most recent comprehensive scholarly studies continue this trend" (4).[19] (George J. Sánchez has made the same argument about historical monographs and articles.)

Alternatively, even some studies employing the "panethnic" label pay scant attention to the implications of its use. Ellen McCracken's *New Latina Narrative* (1999), still one of only a few full-length literary treatments of Latino *or* Latina literature as a panethnic grouping, briefly raises the issue of the label's "homogenizing" effects (4-5) but quickly goes on to assert the "difficulty of placing writers into discrete national categories" (5), and then drops the subject. Another study, Paul Allatson's *Latino Dreams* (2002), justifies the "overarching" category of his title by noting that his "aim is to set up a cumulative dialogue between disparate experiences and understandings of 'America,' the locus for a range of myths and discourses of belonging"—a rationale which leaves open the question of what the internal coherency of the group might be. In yet a third, *Reading U.S. Latina Writers* (2003), Alvina E. Quintana defends the "'Latina' designation [. . .] as a strategic intervention aimed at highlighting some of the cultural and political similarities that emerge when individuals living in the United States are identified by the mainstream press under a 'Hispanic' label" (3). For Quintana the difference between "Latina" and "Hispanic" is, shall we say, essential: she argues that, "[a]lthough the terms 'Hispanic' and 'Latino' both make reference to categories of difference, it is only the latter that allows for a recognition of the cultural hybridization created by the European fusion with Indigenous, Asian, or African peoples" (3-4), a rather far-fetched claim—given that "Latino" certainly does not refer etymologically to any of these peoples any more than "Hispanic" does—which goes unelaborated. "Latinas," for Quintana, are implicitly connected by their hybrid cultural and racial backgrounds (an argument I will return to shortly) as well as by some "cultural and political similarities" that emerge (but were not originally present) as a result of their homogenization as "Hispanic" within U.S. culture. "Hispanic," as an imposed term, apparently erases differences, while "Latina" offers an intervention into this homogenizing dynamic, presumably by allowing for its scrutiny. Yet Quintana's subsequent comments on hybridization would seem to replicate the homogenizing tendency by

subsuming various cultural and racial hybridizations unproblemati-
cally (and without scrutiny) under the "Latino" category.

Fatima Mujčinović's *Postmodern Cross-Culturalism and Politicization in U.S. Latina Literature* (2004) explains her use of the umbrella
term for practical reasons: "it would be hard to use specific terms [. . .]
when referring to the entire range of the ethnic grouping"; she adds
that it "serves my argument for a more [. . .] unified conception of
Latino/a literary production" (169 n. 1). She justifies this argument on
the basis of a shared marginality that—once again—ignores some significant differences in the nature of the "experience of oppression"
among different groups (6). For Mujčinović, the collision between origi-
nary culture and Anglo-American culture "exposes the incompatibility
and contradictions of different cultural signifiers" (8); but the cultural
signifiers among different Latino-origin groups are assumed to be
roughly the same, or at least certainly compatible (7).

William Luis's monograph *Dance between Two Cultures* (1997)
presents a similar argument: Luis comments on "differences in development" and "varying political and economic conditions" among Caribbean Spanish-speaking nations, then goes on to say that, "[w]hen
Hispanics migrate to the United States, native differences are reinforced and others are created. They speak a 'foreign' language many do
not understand, and because of barriers in communication and widespread attitudes toward foreigners, stereotypes are created" (xiii).
Though Luis discusses differences among Caribbean countries, the
"native differences" exacerbated by migration to the United States can
apparently only be Anglo-Hispanic differences, while inter-Caribbean
differences are erased or forgotten. (As we will see in my discussion of
Achy Obejas's *Memory Mambo*, however, the U.S. context can in fact mag-
nify inter-Caribbean conflicts between Cubans and Puerto Ricans.)

For Luis, as for Mujčinović, Latinos are bound together by their
marginality within U.S. culture: "for many Anglo-Americans, [. . .] Hispanics, whether born in the United States or abroad, from privileged or
low socioeconomic classes, economic or political exiles, black or white,
are grouped into a single category and viewed as foreigners." But Luis
goes on to argue that, "[r]egardless of the differences among them, Latinos share *the same* marginal experience in the United States" (xiv;
emphasis added). Such glib generalizations overlook sometimes substantial differences in the ways that groups have been treated in the
United States. Consider again De Genova and Ramos-Zayas's arguments about how U.S. citizenship has created an experience of marginalization for Puerto Ricans that is qualitatively *different* (not "the
same") from that of Mexican immigrants; Cuban immigrants were, for
decades, offered a degree of federal aid unbeknownst to other groups.
Indeed, as María Cristina García documents in *Havana U.S.A.* (1996),
Cuban exiles in Florida in the early 1960s received more federal assistance than was available for Miami's non-Cuban U.S. citizens (28–29,

41). By contrast, Central American political refugees in the 1980s were often not only not provided aid, but denied asylum altogether.

Other scholars who have attempted to answer the questions "Who are Latinos?" and "What is Latino/a literature?" (or perhaps more simply, "Why consider these texts together?") have frequently generalized about "cultural resistance and/or protest" and a "Third world stance" (Rivero 187, 183), about a "timeless struggle for social justice" (Ray Gonzalez xiii–xiv), about "a working-class identity and aesthetic" (Kanellos 4), or about a "Latino imaginary" pitted against "ongoing oppression" and directed toward justice, civil rights, and sovereignty (Flores 199–200). The prevailing assumption in much of the history of Latino/a literary scholarship has seemed to be that Latino/a literature will generally—perhaps even essentially, by definition—advance a progressive ideology. When actual Latino/a literary texts turn out not to fit the mold, critics may decide not to "count" them as "real" Latino/a literature.[20] Or they might try to force them into the mold.[21] Or—perhaps more commonly—differences in the artistic production of the different Latino/a groups (including, sometimes, political and ideological differences) may simply be glossed over, ignored.

Ray Gonzalez, in his introduction to *Currents from the Dancing River* (1994), demonstrates the powerful impulse to construct a unified Latino/a identity that elides significant group distinctions by asserting, amazingly, that, "[a]lthough cultural differences remain between Mexican Americans, Puerto Ricans in the United States, and Cuban Americans, Latino writers *are coming together in a cohesive* [. . .] *whole*" (xiii–xiv; emphasis added).

At the opposite end, prominent performance artist and cultural critic Guillermo Gómez-Peña insists that there is no single, or even dominant, ideology discernable in "Latino art," distinguishing even between Latinos that most people would group together, at least in terms of their cultural production: "California Chicanos and Nuyorricans [*sic*] inhabit different cultural landscapes. [. . .] Right-wing Cubanos from Miami are unconditional adversaries of leftist South American exiles. The cultural expressions of Central American and Mexican migrant workers differ drastically from those of the Latino intelligentsia in the universities, ad infinitum" (48).

The Chronicles of Panchita Villa and Other Guerrilleras (2005), by Tey Diana Rebolledo, who could accurately be called a "foremother" of Chicana literary criticism (it was she and Eliana Rivero who edited the canon-shaping anthology *Infinite Divisions* in 1993, which Rebolledo followed with a critical book on Chicana writers, *Women Singing in the Snow*, in 1995), is remarkably refreshing in that it does not claim any fundamental, underlying similarity for her grouping of both Mexican American and other Latina writers, despite the fact that her selection thus admittedly "disrupts what might be a more coherent focus on just Chicana writers" (7). Rather, Rebolledo states quite simply, "[I]n this collection I wanted to include essays on writers who have influenced me, molded me, and impressed me over the years" (7). This principle of selection is related to two wonderful anecdotes Rebolledo tells about hearing stories told to her by others that were actually taken from her own life, eliciting from her the reaction, "Hey, that's MY story!" (9).

Rebolledo's reflections here get at an undeniable phenomenon: in teaching classes on U.S. Latino/a literature, I (and others) frequently hear Latino/a students describe feeling some sort of identification with the stories that they read, despite the authors' ethnic backgrounds not always being the students' own. It is intriguing to mull over why, and under what circumstances, this feeling of "Hey, that's MY story!" might be generated without necessarily jumping from there to claims of fundamentally similar cultures or experiences among all Latino groups. (I will return to this point near the end of this chapter and again in the Conclusion.)

Despite the continuing and often un-self-reflective use of the umbrella term "Latino" as a singular category, much scholarship that directly addresses the panethnic implications of this label has made it much less easy to generalize about common culture, common political orientation, or even common experiences of marginalization within the United States. At the very least, this scholarship openly acknowledges the differences (in culture of origin, in racial and class demographics, and even in "official" treatment by the U.S. government) among the various Latino groups that threaten to make the term all but meaningless. (Scholars such as Marcelo Suárez-Orozco and Mariela Páez, Suzanne Oboler, Juan Flores, and Earl Shorris, for example, all vehemently decry the "homogenizing" of the various groups through an unthinking assumption of a singular identity.) At best, this scholarship also searches for alternative means of understanding a "Latino" collective identity that is not based in reductive essentialisms about language or culture.

For instance, scholars have forcefully challenged a long intellectual tradition of constructing *latinidad* in terms of a racial and cultural hybridity, as Quintana does—and as José Martí did in his landmark essay "Nuestra América." Amaryll Chanady describes how "the hybrid nature of the newly developing societies in the New World and the heterogeneous influences they received [came to be] considered as constitutive of its [Latin American] identity. Terms such as Martí's 'mestizo America,' José María Arguedas's 'Indo-America,' Angel Rama's 'transculture,' and Ventura García Calderón's 'Indo-Afro-Sino-Ibero-America' [. . .] indicate an attempt to conceive of Latin American culture as hybrid" (xxxii–xxxiii; Ortega 86 qtd. in Chanady).[22] "To this day," José Piedra reminds us, "Hispanic unity is celebrated among Spanish-Americans as Día de la Raza ('Day of [the?] Race') on the date of Columbus's first landing" (285; brackets in original). As Cornell and Hartmann explain, "Ethnic ties are blood ties" (16); ethnicity presupposes a belief in common descent.[23]

Yet—even setting aside for a moment the understanding that race is always a social construct, with no scientific validity—the idea of a single Hispanic race makes no sense, given the presence of people of indigenous, European, and African origin in Latin America. (It would make as much sense to say that there is a U.S. "race.") As Shorris puts it, "there is no Hispanic or Latino race. The spectrum of races is the American [that is, U.S.] spectrum, although the proportions are different" (151). For one thing, of course, the Hispanic-race-as-melting-pot construction, in its most extreme form, ignores the *continuing* existence of indigenous or African-descent populations in Latin America. (Not *everyone* identifies as "mestizo" or "mulatto.") For another, not all historical manifestations of syncretism are the same; the mixture of peoples and cultures looks very different in the Caribbean, where the indigenous peoples were decimated and large numbers of African slaves imported to sugar plantations, from how it looks in Mexico, Guatemala, or El Salvador, where the influence of the indigenous presence is much more obvious. And, needless to say, the indigenous peoples in different geographical spaces were themselves different peoples.[24]

Another persistent line of argument now being more rigorously challenged is that Latinos are connected by their "mother tongue"; here Spanish itself is the bond that makes of the various groups a single "family."[25] "Speaking Spanish," John A. García writes in *Latino Politics in America* (2003), "is still a fairly universal experience for most Latinos" (40). Perhaps recognizing the problem of asserting that Spanish is "universal," but only for "most," García falls back on the metaphor of family: "While not totally analogous, variations in character, lifestyle, personality, and so on, [. . .] can be found within most families" (22). The implication is that, like diverging members of a family, Latinos need not all speak Spanish to be connected; but this only begs the question of what, then, initially connects them.

Yet the notion of Spanish as the basis for a common culture, too, is being increasingly and resoundingly repudiated by other scholars. Tackling the topic of panethnic (or at least interethnic) *latinidad* in a U.S. context as early as 1985, Felix Padilla avoided terminology that suggested a *preexisting* group identity by referring to the Mexican and Puerto Rican populations under discussion as "Spanish-speaking" rather than as "Latino" or "Hispanic" (see, e.g., 16ff). In the conclusion of his study, Padilla—gesturing briefly toward the possibility of English-dominant, second- or third-generation Latinos (151)—switches briefly to the term "Spanish-surname" (148). As De Genova and Ramos-Zayas have commented, "prior administrative/demographic categories [such] as 'Spanish-surname' and 'Spanish-speaking' [. . .] inevitably failed to adequately encompass the anomalies of U.S.-born English-speaking Latinos, or Latinos with non-Spanish surnames" (19)—"anomalies" that have only increased in number since the mid-eighties.[26] Oboler, likewise commenting on the use of a common language as a justification for the panethnic grouping "Latino," notes that an increasing number of Latinos do not fit this characterization (xvi). Most recently, a 2004 study by the Pew Hispanic Center revealed that 25 percent of U.S. Latinos—including both citizens and noncitizens—speak primarily English ("2004 National Survey" 13); and this statistic does not include the additional 29 percent who are bilingual.[27] If, as Shorris puts it, "third or fourth generation Latinos who live in suburbs of Minneapolis or Atlanta have no more reason to know Spanish than Polish-Americans need to know Polish" (181–82), then what makes them "Latinos" at all (rather than simply being, say, Mexican American, the accurate analogy to Polish American)? As Chanady has reminded us, furthermore, even in the context of Latin American studies the paradigm of the Spanish language as a unifying element has come under fire: "the restriction of the concept of 'Latin American literature' to cultural productions written in European languages [. . .] necessarily entails the marginalization of autochthonous and popular literary traditions" (xxxiii–xxxiv).[28]

Even among those who do speak Spanish, however, its deployment as a common denominator apparently runs up against problems. It is worth recalling here that a majority of Latinos do not see themselves as sharing a common culture, regardless of the potential commonality of Spanish (Suro and Escobar 10), as one person snipes, "[t]hat's like saying that White Americans and Black South Africans are the same people because they both speak English" (Alderete). In *Latino Crossings*, which revisits Felix Padilla's earlier theme of the possibility of panethnic *latinidad* among Mexicans and Puerto Ricans in Chicago, De Genova and Ramos-Zayas note that "Spanish language was not a natural or automatic source of mutual recognition or Latino unity [for their interview subjects] and frequently became a source of further division. [. . .] Thus, even language—the one element commonly presumed to supply a basis for Latino-identified unity between the two groups—often served instead as a forcefully divisive basis for racializing their divergent identities as 'Mexican' or 'Puerto Rican'" (29).

Suárez-Orozco and Páez also acknowledge this difficulty; even while pointing out that Latinos statistically retain Spanish language use for longer than any other ethnic group, they add that "the language of Latinos in the United States presents a complicated picture. [. . .] [S]pecific words, folk sayings, and accents often produce different meanings and values within the different Latino communities. Language varieties act as a way of signifying subethnic identifications and marking subgroup identities" (8). For example, as Ana Celia Zentella elaborates, "Colombians in New York City [. . .] think very highly of Colombian Spanish and very little of Caribbean Spanish [. . .]. Linguistic differences as simple as the presence or absence of an /s/ at the end of a syllable can become identified with superiority or inferiority" (324).

There is plenty of anecdotal evidence to suggest that the "Common" Spanish language can lead to a sense of cultural difference as often as of commonality. In an intriguing autobiographical essay, Berta Esperanza Hernández-Truyol—writing about her experience arriving in Albuquerque to teach at the University of New Mexico—represents herself as buying into the illusion of a common Hispanic culture: though she is Cuban, the Mexican-infused culture of Albuquerque "felt like home, the familiar Spanish influence, the rice and beans, the sunlight and the bright clothing" (28). In a subsequent hilarious vignette, Hernández-Truyol describes her search for food on her first night:

> I went into the only place I found open and ordered a tortilla, a plain tortilla. There, I was so happy, I could even order food in Spanish. The waitress looked at me kind of funny and asked, simply, "Are you sure all you want is a tortilla?" "Yes," I said. "Plain?" she asked. "Yes," I said, "it's late." So with a shrug of the shoulders she disappeared and promptly returned and put this plate in front of me. Sitting on the plate was this flat thing, white, warm, soft. My turn to ask, "And what is this?" "Your order, ma'am." And we stared at each other. I ate this thing, although I did not quite know how I was supposed to do that. I got funny looks when I went at it with fork and knife. (25)

Hernández-Truyol was, of course, thinking of what is now referred to in the United States as a "*Spanish* tortilla" (or "frittata")—that is, a sort of firm omelette with potatoes and onions baked into the egg mixture. She uses her anecdote to comment self-reflexively on the assumption of "home" and "common culture" ("Hey, that's MY story!") that even Latinos/as in the United States can participate in, and on the cultural gaps filled in by these assumptions. As she writes, "Here we were dealing with the same word: tortilla, and the same language: Spanish. Yet our different cultures give the word different meanings" (25). A common language, then, is in and of itself no guarantor of common culture for the various Latino ethnic groups.

As for religion—another cultural element frequently cited as part of Latino "common culture"[29]—while we can certainly acknowledge that the widespread influence of Catholicism has heavily impacted Latin American cultures, we should also keep in mind that the home-grown versions of Catholicism in Mexico and other Central American countries, heavily shaped by the indigenous spiritual beliefs and practices that preceded it, looks strikingly different from the home-grown versions in Caribbean nations, where the main syncretism was with beliefs imported from Africa and preserved by the slave populations. Juan Gonzalez, in his smart and comprehensive *Harvest of Empire* (2000), tells the story of getting a phone call from a Puerto Rican in East Harlem complaining about the Mexicans "taking over our church." The caller continued, "And the first thing they [the Mexicans] want to do [. . .] is put the statue of the Virgen de Guadalupe in the front of the church! [. . .] I told them, 'That's your Virgin, not ours'" (xvi–xvii). And if only about three-fourths of U.S. Latinos are Catholic at all (see Mosher et al. 376), do we still "count"?

Despite these substantial difficulties, nonetheless, several scholars are unwilling to do away entirely with the concept of a panethnic group identity. For one thing—and this is quite a persuasive argument—the category "Latino" allows scholarship at its best to be *more* nuanced about particular trajectories and dynamics by comparing and contrasting the various Latino groups. Suárez-Orozco and Páez, for example, make an excellent case that a fuller understanding of the phenomenon of transnationalism among immigrant Latino populations is achieved by comparing the trajectories of different Latino immigrant groups. Puerto Ricans and Dominicans, in particular, have been cited as having strong transnational ties, including periodic returns, a degree of political involvement in the homeland, and financial remittances to relatives and friends there. In contrast, Mexican immigration to the United States seems to be undergoing a trend away from transnational behaviors and toward a more "permanent" status within the United States (6–7). As Suárez-Orozco and Páez ask, "Will Dominicans, over time and across generations, follow the Mexican pattern? Or will they adopt the Puerto Rican version of transnationalism, which by some indicators has intensified rather than decreased over time?" (7). Only a panethnic framework of study allows scholars to ask such questions in this particular way. (Indeed, such an argument is the guiding principle of this book, which is precisely about how, and to what degree, writers of *differing* national origins have grappled with transnational and panethnic categories.)

Of course, such arguments assert less the "groupness" of Latinos than they do the usefulness of the category for other reasons. But scholars—Suárez-Orozco and Páez included—are also increasingly making use of more sophisticated arguments for asserting certain important commonalities that might go some way toward explaining a sense of Latino peoplehood. Historically, Flores asserts, "it is possible to find a common thread in the intricate 'Latino' weave, or at least a framework in which to interpret the [. . .] Latino presence in some more encompassing way" (145). Flores is adamant that any analysis of the panethnic category "Latino" must be undertaken within a broader view of the "larger international context, Latin America" (151). Latin Americans themselves have, for over a century, been engaged in the construction of a continental, panethnic identity: "The sense and practice of a 'Latino/Hispanic' unity across national lines [. . .] go way back, as does the recognized need for names to designate such tactical or enduring common ground" (148). Flores grounds this unity in the pan-national movement toward independence from Spain, making frequent references to José Martí's "Nuestra América" as a prominent historical example of the construction, in a Latin American continental context, of a panethnic identity. Further, Flores points out, these efforts took place on U.S. soil as well as within Latin America itself (148).

Agustín Laó-Montes, in his introduction to *Mambo Montage* (2001), concurs that Latinization—helpfully defined as an "overall process of production of *discourses* of latinidad" (4; emphasis added)—can be traced to national struggles for independence against Spain, as well as to resistance to U.S. domination in the region (6). As Chanady points out in a similar vein, the central contrast of Martí's "Nuestra América," "'Our [mestizo and Hispanic] America,' as opposed to the 'Other' America—the United States [. . .] must be situated within a strategy of resistance to U.S. hegemony, and related to the desire to constitute a specific Latin American identity as opposed to the United States, as well as to that of Spain" (Chanady xv; bracketed phrase in original). And as Oboler reminds us, the 1823 Monroe Doctrine, which declared that any European efforts to control the independent nations of the Western Hemisphere would be viewed by the United States as hostile, and which was largely aimed at preventing Spain from reasserting its power over its former colonies (as well as the 1904 Roosevelt Corollary, which asserted that the United States *did* have the right to intervene in Latin American nations), effectively constructed all of Latin America, from the point of view of the United States at least, as a single entity (4). Latin American unity, or a sense of continental peoplehood, has thus been instrumentally useful as a strategy of resistance: "Bolívar's dream [of a unified Latin America] has been continually (though selectively) invoked for over a hundred and fifty years to express solidarity in the face of outsiders. First as a revolutionary sentiment, then as an anti-imperialist slogan, the idea of an indivisible Latin America has been useful in Latin Americans' dealing with foreigners" (Jones-Correa, *Between Two Nations* 118).

This idea potentially gains even greater currency for U.S. Latinos when, as a multitude of scholars insist, current and past Latin American migration to the United States is understood to be a direct function of U.S. domination.[30] In this argument, it is the history of U.S. intervention in the various Latin American nations, as well as its current position within a global economy that (for example) exploits cheap labor abroad, which provides the "weave" of common experience (although within that weave differences inevitably emerge, such as the degree of direct intervention or of economic dependency). As Suárez-Orozco and Páez put it, "We are here because you were there" (18).

It may be noted, of course, that the specific nature of U.S. relations with any given nation determines that the character of immigration has taken substantially different forms. Poor Mexicans seeking better economic opportunities, especially in the wake of the North American Free Trade Agreement,[31] cannot be expected to share a "common" sensibility with the first wave of upper- and upper-middle-class Cuban exiles, many of whom were already used to having extensive business dealings with companies in the United States that controlled much of Cuba's economy.[32] But this divergence might, finally, be read through the lens of a general "common" history (U.S. economic domination) to which the various actors will respond differently. As Chanady glosses (and translates) Antonio Cornejo Polar's discussion of Latin American literatures, it is helpful to think in terms of a "paradigm of 'contradictory totality,' in which a 'single historical process' affects diverse [. . .] groups in different ways" (Cornejo Polar 128, qtd. in Chanady xxxiv). After all, analogously, any national history is shared by all of a country's citizens, although different constituencies among those citizens will respond to that history differently, based on their positioning within it. (This understanding allows us to conceive of the category "Latino" in a way which does not presuppose a particular ideological or political perspective.)

Oboler, however, diverges from the notion that the source of Latino identity can be found in the historical legacies of Spanish colonialism and U.S. domination, pointing out that the possibility of a transnational *latinidad* is "a debate that Latin American intellectuals have themselves waged since the nineteenth century" (17). Further, the question of a unified identity—which even Latin Americans have never agreed on—is still profoundly unresolved in the U.S. context (Oboler xiv). "Latino" is not the extension into the United States of a formerly stable "Latin American" identity. That identity has always been contested. (Here Laó-Montes's distinction between the multiplication of discourses [Latinization] and the category of identity [*latinidad*] is particularly helpful, because it allows us to conceive of the two things separately. The production of discourses may certainly be instrumental in constructing what eventually becomes internalized as an identity category, but their existence need not imply that the identity already exists in a stable form.)

Further, since collective identities are inevitably constructs, we cannot simply assume that a particular collective identity called into being in a given set of historical circumstances will then become fixed and remain unchanged over time. A common history is not enough for a collective identity. (The "common history" of European colonization—and miscegenation—followed by U.S. intervention has certainly not been enough to give Haiti and the Dominican Republic, which even share the same island, a common identity. Rather, historically they have seen themselves in opposition, calling on a history that emphasizes their differences.) Here we do well to remember—whatever the lingering power of Simón Bolívar's dream—that only a distinct minority of U.S. Latinos actually believe they share one culture (Suro and Escobar 10).

A study by Michael Jones-Correa and David Leal also presents some interesting findings in this regard; the authors found that the most significant predictor of whether someone Latino was likely to choose a panethnic label was whether she or he was a first-, second-, or third-generation immigrant.[33] That is, the further removed from the moment of immigration, the *more* likely the person was to use a term such as "Latino" or "Hispanic" to refer to himself/herself (224). The authors' conclusion is that "panethnic identification is, in fact, being constructed in the United States, not being brought fully formed by Latin American immigration" (229). Or, as Suárez-Orozco and Páez put it, "Latinos are made in the USA" (4).

One problem with the notion of a panethnic identity, from a Latin American perspective, is that national identity has always trumped continental identity in the home countries. Thus, as Jones-Correa explains, "Latin American immigrants' ethnic identities are shaped not just by the choices they make in the United States, but also by the weight of identity choices made in the past. Previous constructions of identity have a kind of inertia to them; they become the raw materials for ethnic choices and ethnic politics in the United States. The continuity of previous constructions of identity explains, in part, the difficulties in forming political coalitions among Hispanics of various national origins in the United States" (*Between Two Nations* 122). But the latent possibility of identifying as Latin American and of conceiving of a "common" continental history vis-à-vis both Spain and the United States—also a "previous construction of identity," even if not the primary one—can nonetheless be given new life under the right (or, perhaps, the wrong) set of circumstances within the United States. Chanady elaborates: "The *reactualization* of the past (as appropriation, invention, fictionalization, and institutionalization), [. . .] has always been an essential element of the constitution of cultural identity" (xxix; emphasis added). The past, that is to say, under certain circumstances is called into the service of the present. In Cornell and Hartmann's explanation of ethnicity (drawing on Schermerhorn), they suggest that "the common history a group claims" can be understood as one of several "symbolic elements that may be viewed as emblematic of peoplehood," but that "these claims need not be founded in fact" to be symbolically powerful (19). In explaining ethnic self-consciousness, the *invocation* of a common history (real or imagined) is more important than the factual existence of shared historical circumstances.[34] Ethnicity, like nation, is narration. If, as Flores puts it, a collective Latino identity is "always provisional and subject to reexamination" (164), then we must look at the particular "provisions" within the more recent context that would continue to call such an identity into being.[35]

The most common view among scholars who take this approach is that ethnicity, and in particular Latino panethnicity, is "instrumental," invoked to address pressing political, economic, and other disparities. The argument goes that the new U.S. context does, indeed, tend to homogenize the various groups and thus generates experiences that are similar across at least several of the various Latino groups. (In its most nuanced forms, this argument takes account of subgroup differences, especially when one group—most often Cubans—does not fit the general "profile" as well as the others. Thus the argument, at its best, focuses more on common "themes" that span several groups and are therefore properly panethnic than on giving the entire panethnic label coherence.) Felix Padilla was one of the earliest proponents of this view, insisting that "the expression of Latino ethnic-conscious behavior is *situationally* specific, crystallized under certain circumstances of inequality experience shared by more than one Spanish-speaking group at a point in time" (61). It is the experience of analogous inequalities—as well as U.S. policies and programs such as "civil rights laws, equal employment opportunities, and affirmative action" (Padilla 8)—that has spurred a strategic sense of "connectedness" among Latinos at certain times.

Elaborations on the particular types of structural inequalities experienced across national subgroups are many. John A. García cites educational attainment (25, 43), as well as "lower levels of family income, and corresponding higher rates of family poverty" (49), as "common ground" that places Latinos across various subgroups "at risk in terms of quality of life (e.g., housing conditions, educational isolation, limited employment opportunities, economic segregation, and vulnerability to violent crime)" (49). "Quite alarming," as Suárez-Orozco and Páez point out, "are the recent findings of the Harvard Civil Rights project, which established that Latino children are now facing the most intense segregation [. . .] of any ethnic and racial group in the United States" (28). Shorris is eloquent on the topic of poor education and its creation of diminished opportunities for working-class Latinos, particularly those who do not speak English as a first language: "a child who speaks only Spanish and is not allowed to develop his conceptual abilities in his own language while he learns to speak another will fall behind his peers. After the first failure, the next comes easily; the pattern develops so quickly that a child in the third or second or even the first grade may be lost to despair" (225). Shorris makes a compelling case that the educational problems for Latinos lie not with bilingual education—which others have claimed is responsible for holding Spanish speakers back—but with the poverty of many school systems in which bilingual programs are in place.

A related issue, as numerous scholars have pointed out, is the racialization of Latinos in the U.S. context (Suárez-Orozco and Páez 3). Noting that, officially, the "Hispanic" question on the U.S. Census is not about race but about ethnicity, De Genova and Ramos-Zayas argue that, "[n]evertheless, this hegemonic 'ethnic' distinction instituted by the U.S. state has been [. . .] widely treated as a racial condition all the same," since it designates Hispanics as a "'minority' population analogous to African Americans" and is used in determining "the allocation of affirmative action entitlements" (16). Quite strikingly, Clara E.

Rodríguez, in *Changing Race* (2000), discusses a 1993 proposal to amend the U.S. Census form for 2000 that "called for the elimination of the 'Hispanic' identifier and the addition of a 'Hispanic' race category to the race question" (159). Rodríguez notes that the proposal (notably *not* advanced by any Hispanic constituency) would, of course, have changed the "Hispanic" classification from an ethnic one, "in which Hispanics could be of any race," to a racial one, in which by implication "all Hispanics were one race" (159). The proposal did not pass, but Rodríguez records that this is not the first time such a proposal has been made (161). As Suárez-Orozco and Páez comment, "it is abundantly clear that in the context of the workings of the state apparatus, the subgroup labels are generally quite secondary to the panethnic construct" (6).

Here is an example of a label imposed from above that may well be influencing a people's own perception of itself, at least in part. Asked to identify *racially* in the 2000 census,[36] an amazing 47.4 percent of Latinos declined to identify themselves in the standard racial categories offered by the census form and instead volunteered some other term, usually a panethnic one such as "Latino" or "Hispanic"—that is, they constructed their own racial category (Logan 1, 3).[37] That is to say, our encounter with U.S. dominant culture, which sees us similarly, has made us one. This may well be partly the assumption of a strategic or instrumental identity; in the face of common treatment by dominant U.S. culture, crystallized by the assignation of an umbrella label such as "Hispanic," people of Latin American descent may well require the assumption of a group identity which provides strength in numbers. On the other hand, that group identity might more simply be an internalization of dominant racial ideology in the United States. Martha Gimenez, for one, argues that these labels can be seen as "forms of ideological interpellation which, under certain material conditions, are likely to produce 'Hispanic' or Latino subjects" ("Latino Politics" 178). As Jones-Correa and Leal have observed, "an identity may be constructed (by the state or by the individual within the parameters set by the state) without being instrumental" (239). Indeed, Silvio Torres-Saillant has argued powerfully that a notion of seamless and unified *hispanidad* is one constructed and sold by Spanish-language media such as Univisión and Telemundo; in this sense such an identity might be "instrumental" for the amassing of corporate profits rather than for political goals of the communities themselves (444–48). Nonetheless, needless to say, daily exposure to such messages must surely have some effect on the people whom they address. Considered in these contexts, panethnicity need not be understood only as a manifestation of "instrumental" resistance to hegemonic control; it might be precisely the opposite: "It is ironic [. . .] that in the United States the anti-imperial tradition of *el sueño de Bolívar* [Bolívar's dream] is invoked to reinforce a state-defined Hispanic identity" (Jones-Correa, *Between Two Nations* 119).

Further, shared experiences of educational disadvantage, poverty, and racialization are not, in and of themselves, enough to generate a sense of common peoplehood. For common experiences to be *experienced* as "in common," Latino groups—it has been frequently argued—need to be in close enough contact with one another, geographically speaking, that they can perceive the similarities. Juan Gonzalez makes a case for "the emergence during the last several decades of a rich new Latino identity on U.S. soil" precisely along these lines (187), observing that, "[f]rom what was at first largely a Mexican American population in the Southwest and a Puerto Rican enclave in New York City, the different Hispanic groups have undergone, and continue to undergo, cultural amalgamation among themselves—through intermarriage, through shared knowledge of one another's music, food, and traditions, through common language, through a common experience of combating anti-Hispanic prejudice and being shunted into the same de facto segregated neighborhoods" (187).

The "space" where this "momentous pan-Latinization" (Flores 142) has occurred is, needless to say, an urban one, since it is to urban centers such as New York, Los Angeles, Chicago, and Miami that the latest waves of Latino immigrants have flocked. This newest influx means that the Latino groups do interact in close proximity to one another and, often, build organizations around particular points of shared interest that span national-origin identities. As John A. García writes, "The co-existence of native-born and 'immigrant' living in the same or proximate neighborhoods, familial social networks, and common work environments and business interactions provide a regular basis for cultural exchanges and experiences. These interactions can reinforce cultural expressions and values" (41). The importance of close and regular contact over time cannot be underestimated as an important factor in community building, as Jean Wyatt argues in *Risking Difference* (188–90). At the level of the city, then, a notion of panethnic, Latin American–origin identities may indeed begin to make sense. In the view of Juan Flores, the realities of lived experience for Puerto Ricans in New York summon up, of necessity, some concept of *latinidad*—a useful category for referring to their enmeshed relationships with other Latino groups (142).

Approaching the notion of an emerging Latino community from another angle, some linguists—in a new take on the old notion of a "common language"—were engaged in a study that compared pronoun use (in Spanish) by various Latino groups in New York City; the study's goal, as reported in a December 2002 article in the *New York Times*, was to determine whether, in New York and other U.S. cities, the different linguistic traits of the various groups were coming together, thereby suggesting a new panethnic collectivity in formation (Scott). As Katherine Sugg comments, the immigrants being studied "demonstrate the persistence of national identifications in Latino communities. And yet the linguists' study and its guiding questions also suggest a perceived 'convergence' of these groups into a new Latino identity and community in the United States" (228). The linguists, that is, are engaged in a project of "tracing the linguistic origin point of a US-based *latinidad*" (228). Ana Celia Zentella, one of the linguists involved in the study, writes that Spanish usage in the United States changes to reflect its new context:

> Technology produces many *anglicismos* ("anglicisms"), such as *la compyuta/computadora* ("the computer"), *bipéame* ("beep me"), and *tu emilio* ("your e-mail") [. . .]. Other borrowings reflect the daily lives of most workers: *el bos/la bosa* ("the boss," male/female), *fultaim/partaim/overtaim* ("full-time/part-time/overtime"), *el cheque* ("the paycheck," "the restaurant bill"), *los biles* ("the bills"), and *trobol* ("trouble"). Most linguistic loans are shared across the country—for example, *chirona* ("cheater") is heard on the playgrounds of Los Angeles and New York City. (329)

These comments suggest the intriguing possibility that, existing side by side with linguistic habits that mark and distinguish separate national-origin communities, a new "made in the U.S.A." Spanish signals an emerging panethnic exchange.

This evolving sense of panethnic Latino communities—or at least panethnic contact—in U.S. cities is born out in some examples of literary production in the last two decades. In *The Forbidden Stories of Marta Veneranda* (1997; trans. 2001), a marvelous volume of short stories by Cuban exile Sonia Rivera-Valdés, Cubans and Puerto Ricans in New York are matter-of-factly married to each other. Working-class Puerto Ricans make brief appearances among the Cuban exiles in the New York of Cuban American writers Cristina García (*Dreaming in Cuban*, 1992) and Oscar Hijuelos (*The Mambo Kings Play Songs of Love*, 1989), as well as in the Chicago of Carlos Eire (*Waiting for Snow in Havana*, 2003). In the poem that opens Puerto Rican author Judith Ortiz Cofer's collection of autobiographical vignettes, stories, poems, and essays set largely in Paterson, New Jersey, *The Latin Deli* (1993)—whose title itself suggests a more collective sensibility, even though most of the stories feature primarily Puerto Rican "Latins"—the owner of the deli spends her days

> listening to the Puerto Ricans complain
> that it would be cheaper to fly to San Juan
> than to buy a pound of Bustelo coffee here,
> and to Cubans perfecting their speech
> of a "glorious return" to Havana—where no one
> has been allowed to die and nothing to change until then;
> to Mexicans who pass through, talking lyrically
> of *dólares* to be made in El Norte. (3)

In the Chicago of Achy Obejas's collection *We Came All The Way from Cuba So You Could Dress Like This?* (1994), a Mexican American and a Puerto Rican are friends in the story "Forever"; a Mexican American marries a Mexican immigrant to give him citizenship in "The Spouse"; and an unspecified Latino and his Anglo boyfriend banter about the "Latin fascination with baseball" and the "Latin inferiority complex" (60) in "Above All, a Family Man." In the title story, as well as in Obejas's subsequent two novels (*Memory Mambo* [1996] and *Days of Awe* [2001]), the Cuban narrators also find themselves in Chicago, much like Obejas herself.

In Héctor Tobar's *The Tattooed Soldier*, a mail service, El Pulgarcito Express ("The Little Thumb"), caters to Central American immigrants of varying national origins in Los Angeles, promising (but failing) to send their letters and packages safely home. A homeless Guatemalan immigrant wanders the streets of Los Angeles with his Mexican friend; when he has trouble speaking English, the narrator comments, "Los Angeles was the problem. In Los Angeles, Antonio could spend days and weeks speaking only his native tongue, breathing, cooking, laughing, and embarrassing himself with all sorts of people in Spanish" (3).

In a twist on the notion of urban center as Latino contact zone, in Guatemalan American writer Francisco Goldman's *The Ordinary Seaman* (1997), men of varying Central American origin (Honduran, Nicaraguan, Guatemalan) come to the United States to serve as crew for a ship under Panamanian registry docked at the Brooklyn waterfront (a strange, liminal contact zone floating in the margins of the urban center of New York), then find themselves stranded and abandoned aboard the ship. Eventually, one of the crewmen, Esteban, ventures off the ship into New York, where he encounters a Cuban beauty salon owner, a Mexican manicurist, a Dominican waitress, a Colombian factory owner, and several other Central Americans of diverse origin. As with Tobar's Los Angeles, we are told, "It's true, you can live in Nueva York [. . .] and never have to speak English to anyone but telephone operators and bill collectors" (246). (In Part Three, I discuss at greater length some works which pay sustained attention to the points of difference and tension among various national-origin Latino groups.) Perhaps it is fair to say that, as the conditions emerge in the United States for a collective Latino identity, we can begin to observe more "narration" of that identity in Latino literature. But it is nevertheless still striking how very tentative that particular form of narration seems to be.

Jean Wyatt has argued that any construction of multicultural community—and surely, at this point we can recognize that the "Latino community" at best must be conceived in this way—carries risks, for communities, by the very nature of their narratives of "community," strive for

> a collective form of identification. If cultural pluralism is an aim of multicultural community—and by pluralism I mean not just a principle of inclusiveness but an organizing principle that would give equal voice to all

and enable the full expression of diversity and dissension—then identification poses a threat to pluralism. For identification, at both individual and community levels, tends toward an assimilation of difference to the same. The desire for identification moves the subject toward an illusory unity of self and other that erases difference and threatens the perception of the other as other. ("Toward Cross-race Dialogue" 880)

Wyatt's comments add a cautionary note to the "Hey, that's MY story!" reaction. We can see her warning borne out in Michael Jones-Correa's discussion, in *Between Two Nations*, of tensions between Puerto Ricans and other Latino groups in New York City: "For the past several years, [. . .] there has been a *'Somos Uno'* ('We're All One') conference held in New York to set a statewide Latino political agenda. Every year there are complaints from non–Puerto Ricans. One Colombian complained to me that 'everything was about Puerto Ricans and Puerto Rican problems. Why do they call it *Somos Uno* if they are not going to include everyone?'" (116). Here we can see how efforts on the part of Latinos to imagine themselves as a single community come up against precisely the sort of problems that Wyatt predicts; identification as "one" occludes the equal expression of distinct voices, as Puerto Ricans "present themselves as the spokespersons for Latinos in the city" (116).

Even narratives of panethnicity offered by Latinos themselves do not necessarily reflect a true sense of consensus or collectivity, however instrumental they may be. De Genova and Ramos-Zayas add a further caveat to the notion of urban space as Latino contact zone, citing "robust evidence of significant divisions between" national-origin groups in Chicago and remarking that "this has tended to be especially so precisely in some of the predicaments where they found themselves in greatest proximity" (55). Close contact might result in a greater sense of panethnicity or at least of "instrumental" deployment of the category; but it can also result in confrontation, antagonism, and even alienation.

Indeed, as Jones-Correa and Leal's important 1996 study, "Becoming 'Hispanic,'" suggests, *neither* a view of "common culture" *nor* a view of instrumental, strategic ethnicity is enough to explain the use of the panethnic label among Latinos themselves. (As Jones-Correa has subsequently noted, a purely instrumental view of ethnicity cannot account for the persisting power within a U.S. context of national-origin identities, and the predominance of these over a panethnic identification, which would surely seem to have more instrumental value [*Between Two Nations* 116]). Jones-Correa and Leal's study revisits data first compiled in 1989–90 for the Latino National Political Survey. The original study would seem at first glance to suggest a relative absence of panethnic identity among respondents, most of whom preferred to identify by national origin (217). Jones-Correa and Leal found, however, that, when respondents "gave more than one answer to the question asking for their ethnic identification" (220), the number of respondents identifying either primarily or secondarily using a panethnic term went up. "Panethnic identification jumps from the 14% who used these identifiers as their primary identification to the 41.7% who used panethnic identifiers at some time" (220). While these figures are now of course dated, it is worth pointing out that a similar dynamic still seems to hold true, indeed, perhaps even more so today. For example, in the 2002 National Survey of Latinos by the Pew Hispanic Center, while only 24 percent of respondents chose "Latino" or "Hispanic" as their primary term of identification, this number went up to 81 percent when they were asked if they had *ever* described themselves using such a panethnic term (charts 4 and 5).

Jones-Correa and Leal argue that common culture cannot by itself account for panethnic identification, because "identifying panethnically does not have a *very pronounced* effect on how respondents perceive cultural commonalties" (230; emphasis added). They go on to explain: "The effect, when it occurs, is not among those who believe that these cultures are very similar"—these were notably a distinct minority, ranging from 14.65 percent to 18.45 percent, in *every* category of identification—

> but, rather, among those who believe that they are somewhat similar. For instance, [. . .] 65% of those who expressed a primary preference for panethnic identification (along with other identification choices) thought that all Hispanics in the United States shared a somewhat similar culture, versus 59% who expressed any preference at all for panethnic identification and 49% who expressed no such preference at all. The difference that panethnicity makes is at the margin; people are somewhat more likely to think that there is a shared Hispanic culture if they choose or prefer a panethnic label. (230)

I would revise this statement as follows: people are somewhat more likely to think that the different Hispanic cultures are *somewhat similar* (which is not the same thing as a single "shared culture")—if they identify panethnically.[38] For Jones-Correa and Leal, the difference in sense of cultural similarities between those who did *not* identify panethnically (49 percent) and those who did (up to 65 percent) is not enough to explain choosing to identify as "Latino" or "Hispanic"; almost half of those who *do not* identify panethnically still feel the cultures are somewhat similar, for one thing, and there is only a 16 percent increase for respondents with a much stronger panethnic identification.[39] Presumably, if the sense of "common culture" were the key to Latino identity, one would see a much smaller percentage of the nonpanethnics feeling this way, and a significantly greater proportion of the panethnics doing so.

Given the current state of scholarship, this is perhaps no great surprise; more intriguingly, however, Jones-Correa and Leal come up with similar findings with regard to political commonalities among the various groups: "The findings go in the right direction but are not significant" (230). For instance, a total of 35.48 percent of respondents who did not identify panethnically said that the political concerns of Mexicans and Cubans were "Somewhat Similar" or "Very Similar" compared to 47.69 percent of those who identified primarily with a panethnic label (but also identified with other labels). As we can see, use of a panethnic label such as "Latino" or "Hispanic" corresponded with a greater likelihood of seeing some political commonalities, but if common politics were the basis for panethnic identity, one would expect to see a lower number from those who *do not* identify as panethnic and a much higher one (surely a majority, at least) among those who do. When comparing Puerto Rican and Cuban concerns, the differences were even less notable: 48.44 percent of the nonpanethnics thought the concerns of these groups were somewhat or very similar, versus only 56.81 percent of those who identified primarily as panethnic (along with other secondary labels) (232).

As I have already discussed, by contrast, the most significant predictor of whether someone was likely to choose a panethnic label was whether she or he was a first-, second-, or third-generation immigrant. On the other hand, the authors reject the notion that panethnicity is instrumental or cultural in nature, since the results on each of these questions do not point to a definitive explanation of the panethnic label. The authors conclude that "[p]eople who choose a panethnic identifier seem to do so in general, regardless of the specific circumstances and apart from any strategic considerations. Nor is it [panethnicity] a feeling of solidarity with the political interests of other Latin American–origin groups" (239–41). In other words, we know that succeeding generations are more likely to identify as panethnic, but we do not know why.

The answer, perhaps, could be found in an earlier statement that is somewhat buried in the article—having to do with what the respondents themselves listed as their understandings of the panethnic label(s). As the authors note, the respondents listed *various* ways of understanding this label, including geographical, cultural, or political commonalities. What this suggests is the possibility that no *one* understanding of the term might be sufficient to explain people's *various* identifications with it. I would offer, then, that this study suggests the intriguing possibility that Latino identity may indeed be even more "elastic" than the authors themselves recognize (Jones-Correa and Leal 220). People may well have *varying* reasons for employing the term (when they do), ranging from a simple acceptance of the census categorization whereby individual national identities also "count" as Latino, to a belief in cultural similarities (that may have become more pronounced in a U.S. culture where the dominant language is English and Spanish-speakers are a minority who often face language-based discrimination), to an awareness of common historical dynamics (activated or energized for a variety of reasons by the U.S. context), to a growing sense that within U.S. society certain structural inequalities create similar political concerns for Latino groups under certain circumstances, to an "instrumental" conviction that such political concerns can be better addressed in larger numbers. As Debra Castillo puts it, "Strategic choices, internalized constraints, and historical and cultural factors *all* affect the degree to which individuals reinforce or resist identity claims made on their behalf" (8; emphasis added). None of these factors is enough to explain Latino identity in isolation; taken together, they provide a range of ways in which people can understand being "Latino." Put another way, these findings might confirm the plethora of explanations for *latinidad* that a multitude of scholars and commentators, from a wide variety of disciplinary fields, have offered. It perhaps goes without saying that *each* of these scholars is engaged in the construction of "Latino" ethnicity. The narratives that construct the boundaries of a collective group of people known as "Latino" continue to be told in competing and sometimes contradictory ways. Alternatively, as Castillo's comment implicitly suggests, certain counternarratives can continue to pose serious obstacles to a sense of *latinidad*, even when a belief in cultural, political, or historical convergences might be present.

As early as 1989 Werner Sollors was lamenting that, "by and large, [literary] studies tend less to set out to explore [ethnicity's] construction than to take it for granted as a relatively fixed or, at least, a known and self-evident category" (*Invention* xiii).[40] Elaborating on this complaint elsewhere, Sollors writes, "the notion has gained dominance that a 'people' is held together by a subliminal culture of fairy tales, songs, and folk beliefs [. . .]. As a result of this legacy 'ethnicity' as a term for literary study largely evokes the accumulation of cultural bits that demonstrate the original creativity, emotive cohesion, and temporal depth of a particular collectivity" ("Ethnicity" 290). (Largely, this approach to ethnic literature has treated signs of cultural difference in terms of their resistance to a dominant, mainstream U.S. culture bent on assimilation.) Sollors calls on literary criticism to ask, instead, "What is the active contribution literature makes, as a productive force, to the emergence and maintenance of communities [. . .] and of ethnic distinctions?" (*Invention* xiv). And he is less interested in the "cultural bits" than in the ways that ethnic literature might imagine the boundary lines of ethnic groupings. Sollors adopts "Fredrik Barth's thesis that ethnicity rests on the *boundary*, not on the 'cultural stuff that it encloses'" ("Ethnicity" 299), and points out that "Barth's theory can easily accommodate the observation that ethnic groups in the United States have relatively little cultural differentiation, that the cultural *content* of ethnicity is largely interchangeable [. . .]. From such a perspective, contrastive strategies—naming and name-calling among them—become the most important thing about ethnicity" (*Beyond Ethnicity* 28).[41]

Of course, Sollors's claim about the "largely interchangeable" nature of cultural content can surely be taken as exaggerated. A Cuban American who practices Santería *is* participating in a different culture from that of a Mexican American who prays to the Virgin of Guadalupe. Nevertheless, shifting attention from the content of ethnicity to the construction of its boundaries can highlight issues of inclusion and exclusion. What kinds of boundary-drawing maneuvers would allow the two people in my example above to get included in the same "ethnicity"? For that matter, what kind of boundary-drawing maneuvers would mean that the Mexican American in my example (let us assume now, for the sake of argument, that he is a light-skinned New Mexican) might not see a person of fully indigenous Mexican ancestry as part of his own "ethnicity" (despite the cultural "commonality" derived from centuries of syncretic Catholic/indigenous practices), or that the (again hypothetically, "white") Cuban American might not see a black Cuban as part of hers?

Karen Christian's *Show and Tell* is the first critical study of Latino/a literature, as a panethnic category, to give serious attention to the *construction* of Latino ethnicity, not only by those outside the ethnic "group" but by those within it. Her particular focus in literary analysis, however, is on the cultural content that gets marked as ethnic and its performance in particular literary texts. Christian is interested in the ways that individual characters "perform" *cubanidad* or *chicanismo*, in what texts do with "cultural markers" such as "the images of the Chicano migrant worker" and "the Latin Lover" as "symbols of Latina/o 'essence' in the American popular imagination" (16), and in the ways in which novels can undermine the illusion of authentic ethnicity that is generated by such performances.

In this project, however, I am more interested in looking at the *boundaries* of ethnicity: how they are narratively drawn; how they have fluctuated; who—in terms of race, national origin, citizenship (United States versus country of origin)—gets included and who gets excluded; and the like. My focus is on stories of collective identity (those "collective fictions" Sollors names), which are inevitably battle lines of sorts, designating an "us" and a "them," but which, as we will see in the texts that follow, can shift and be redrawn to suit particular sociohistorical contexts. Who gets to be "us" and who gets to be "them" are questions under constant debate and revision in literature.

I have chosen (after all my laborious dissection of it) to accept the category "Latino" and use it, without assuming any more fundamental connections between the various groups but in acknowledgment of the fact that a sense of a larger group identity has tentatively been constructed—often by popular culture—in the United States. Since the category "Latino" or "Hispanic" has acquired very real meaning and power in U.S. public discourse, inevitably, those named by the category must therefore engage with it somehow. Calling Cuban Americans, Mexican Americans, Puerto Rican mainlanders, and Dominican Americans (to name just a few groups) "Latino" allows me a certain easy (if dangerous) shorthand; but, more important, it also gives me the tools for discussing how the various groups engage with dominant-culture conceptions of themselves, as well as with each other. Sometimes—but not always, or even frequently—that engagement does indeed come to look something like a forged sense of peoplehood.

My main concerns in this book revolve around the question of how Latino/a narratives represent (or do not represent) various collectivities implicit in the social construction of "Latinoness," which forges an identity that makes of very different people a single group. This study asks how and when Latino/a literary texts imagine points of identity among specific ethnic "Latino" groups (e.g., Cubans, Mexicans), as well as between Latino/as and overlapping groups (e.g., indigenous peoples, African Americans), and when, indeed, such texts highlight the differences or fissures among groups that have come to constitute Latinoness. How do these texts respond to the homogenizing tendency on the part of mainstream U.S. culture to erase significant historical, cultural, and economic differences among Latino/a groups under the general heading of "Latino" or "Hispanic"? How do they respond to the equally pervasive assumptions that U.S. Latino/as are essentially connected to their countries and cultures of origin? And how do the works treat supposedly self-evident differences between Latino/as and other groups, such as African Americans or American Indians? How in general do these texts insert themselves into the politics of identity and difference that form such a central part of ethnic studies in academia today? Finally, what strains emerge when texts do, indeed, investigate the possibility of a panethnic "Latino" identity or solidarity?

This is a book about a particular set of issues and theoretical concerns rather than a comprehensive overview of Latino literature. Indeed, the latter becomes increasingly impossible; as the field of writers and texts expands exponentially every year, an overview of "Latino literature" in general becomes just as unimaginable as an overview of "American literature." This project, then, does not pretend to coverage. Rather, I am interested in texts which foreground, in particularly vivid and intriguing ways, the problematic nature of panethnic, transracial, transnational, and even transclass identities. For the sake of providing some coherence to the project I have chosen to limit myself to Latino/a narrative in the succeeding chapters—primarily fiction, although some fiction is, to a greater or lesser degree, autobiographically based, and one memoir, Piri Thomas's *Down These Mean Streets*, is inevitably to some degree fictionalized. Needless to say, addressing the issue of an imagined panethnic Latino/a identity requires that I examine texts from several national-origin groups; a focus on a single group would simply not permit an adequate exploration into the sorts of *cross*-group transactions and imaginings that intrigue me. Nonetheless, since many Latino/a writers have understood themselves primarily in terms of a more specific ethnicity of national origin, at times my discussion focuses on a collective identity imagined in those more specific terms; such texts nevertheless inevitably question and poke at group boundaries and present various cross-racial, cross-class, and transnational (i.e., U.S. *and* country-of-origin) notions of collective identity. In these texts I examine how the authors might recognize differences between themselves and "Others" (in terms of race, geography/citizenship, or class) and yet reach across those boundaries to pull the Others in. But I also turn, in Part Three, to how the authors deal more explicitly with the panethnic "Latino" category: how they question it, challenge it, appropriate it, and, at times, hope to reimagine it along more productive lines. . . .

Juan Flores has written that it is useful to distinguish between an "analytic" approach to Latinos, which always is predicated on "the need to break down, to identify not the sum total but the constituent parts" and which recognizes "the evident diversity of Latino groups and experiences" (195), and what he calls "the Latino imaginary," a "conceptual space of pan-group aggregation" in which the separate members imagine their relationship to the larger whole (199, 198). It is, of course, this imagining that I take as the subject of my book.

But the "Latino imaginary" is not one, but many. The various authors I explore understand their membership within a larger "ethnic" whole in different ways and sketch figurative lines to delineate the imagined membership of that whole. In almost all cases, those lines are tentatively drawn, with the understanding that group memberships overlap and fluctuate — that groups come together into (as Ray Gonzalez puts it) a "cohesive whole," and that groups also disassemble, dissipate. The relationship of literature to group formation is nothing so straightforward as a simple affirmation of an essentialist identity, as Sollors once seemed to suggest.[42] By engaging critically with the cultural production of Latino writers, we can begin to understand the multitude of ways in which people of Latin American heritage have answered the question, "Who Are We?"

Notes

1. Padilla notes, for instance, that in the first half of the twentieth century in Chicago, people of Mexican descent were themselves divided by time of immigration, class, and so on. It was not until the mid-1960s that an ethnic identity bridging these differences began to be self-consciously cultivated in earnest (34–35, 38). In other words, according to Padilla, even a strong sense of *Mexican* ethnic cohesiveness needed to be "constructed" in Chicago.

2. As Luis rightly comments, the presumption that Latin American immigrants begin to identify as "Latino" on entry to the United States is counter to common sense (283).

3. Both Flores (149) and Oboler (3) make this point.

4. The 1970 census, by contrast, asked the question, "Is this person's origin or descent" and then provided the following options: "Mexican"; "Central or South American"; "Puerto Rican"; "Cuban"; "Other Spanish"; or "No, none of these." It did not group these choices under a "Hispanic" category.

5. Stavans is perhaps one of the most problematic recent commentators on "Hispanic" peoples in the United States. Though, in *The Hispanic Condition* (1995), he nods toward the social-constructionist insight that "Latino" is not one culture but many (11), in practice he participates in the most egregious forms of essentializing, for example, "the entire Hispanic cultural experience in the United States" (8); "the Latino metabolism" (14); "a different collective spirit" (16). For an extended critique of Stavans, see Flores, esp. 172–76. Trueba, author of *Latinos Unidos* (1999), ostensibly, like Stavans, recognizes Latino diversity, yet also displays the pervasive impulse to claim a preexisting common culture and essential Latino identity, stating that Latinos "share culture, language, history, values, worldview, and ideals" (31)—surely an overly encompassing claim. Morales's *Living in Spanglish* (2002) is in many ways a direct descendant of Stavans's *The Hispanic Condition*. Again making the by-this-point prerequisite nod toward difference, Morales acknowledges, "It is a big mistake to lump Latinos together, but there are important ways we feel like one people. They have to do with physicality (dancing, body language, suspension of reserve) and spirituality (that strange syncretism between Catholicism and African and indigenous religions that allows us to be sacred and profane at the same time)" (28). Less egregiously, Shorris—who also insists at the outset that there are no "Latinos," only a diversity of cultures and peoples that have come collectively to be identified as such—also falls back at times on essentialist characterizations, such as the notion that the "traditional Latino family" has its origins in rural life, and that the patterns of rural life have pervasively structured all Latino culture (218). For a critique of this stereotype, see Gimenez, "Latino/'Hispanic'" 560–61; Gómez-Peña 48; Juan Gonzalez 200–201; and Oboler 64.

6. See, for example, Gimenez, "Latino/'Hispanic'"; Rivero; Padilla. Gimenez argues that public policy ought to distinguish between Mexican Americans and Puerto Ricans, on the one hand, and other so-called Latino groups. Padilla argues in his landmark 1985 study, *Latino Ethnic Consciousness*, that Puerto Ricans and Mexicans in Chicago were, at given crucial moments and under the right set of circumstances, forming panethnic coalitions. From a literary standpoint, Rivero bases the parameters of Hispanic literature on the "Third World stance of many Chicano and Nuyorican writers" (183) and, on this basis, excludes Cuban exile writing from her definition.

7. As Oboler notes, the latter two symbols were appropriated by César Chávez in organizing Mexican American farmworkers (61).

8. Gimenez also notes that, "[b]ecause the label is used in the context of affirmative action, it places professional and skilled [recent] immigrants in objective competition with members of the U.S. minority groups and forces

them to pass, statistically, as members of an oppressed group" ("Latino/
'Hispanic'" 557–58). Gimenez makes a compelling case for the idea that affirmative action should properly be reserved for groups that have *historically* been oppressed in the United States and that are still, as a group,
feeling the effects of that institutionalized oppression.

9. Data are drawn from Joyce A. Martin et al., "Births: Final Data for 2003."
10. Rumbaut notes that, since people of Mexican descent still account for by
far the largest percentage of U.S. Latinos (63.3 percent in the 2000 census),
"it should be underscored that aggregate statistics for the total Hispanic
population reflect the predominant weight of the characteristics of the
Mexican-origin population" ("Making" 33).
11. The specific national-origin figures provided here are from 2000 rather
than 2003, but the basic point remains valid. Data are drawn from U.S.
Department of Health and Human Services, "2000 Natality Data Set."
12. For that matter, Gimenez cautions, statistics based on national origin
alone can be equally misleading. Not only do we need to consider how and
why various populations come to reside in the United States, and the ways
in which those reasons might skew the representative sample in the
United States, but we must also note the different receptions the populations have faced once here ("Latino/'Hispanic'" 562).
13. Flores, however, insists on the need to retain a panethnic category and
concept, as I shall discuss shortly.
14. For statistics on income levels and poverty rates by national origin, see
U.S. Dept. of Health and Human Services, *Mental Health* 132; for statistics
on racial identification by national origin, see Pew Hispanic Center, "2002
National Survey" chart 8; Tafoya 7.
15. According to Jones-Correa, some Latinos in New York City report that
Puerto Ricans can be insensitive to the obstacles presented to other Latino
groups by lack of citizenship (*Between Two Nations* 115). Flores counters
by pointing out the "second-class nature of that supposedly privileged status," which, he argues, outweighs in the long run any advantages Puerto
Ricans may gain from it (162). See also DeGenova and Ramos-Zayas on
Puerto Rican citizenship versus presumptions of Mexican "illegality" (esp.
7–16, 58–62).
16. As Rodriguez-Morazzani writes, "much of the literature of the 1960s and
1970s in the social sciences concerning Puerto Ricans compares and contrasts their situation with that of African Americans. The propensity for
such linking could lead anyone unfamiliar with the existence of the two
different groups to view them as one" (145). For a discussion of the perceived link between Puerto Ricans and African Americans *on the part of
Mexican Americans*, see De Genova and Ramos-Zayas, 77–78.
17. In this book, I follow authors' own published usage of accent marks in their
Spanish names. Thus, although in Spanish the surname Rodríguez would
be accented, I do not use an accent mark for Richard Rodriguez; the same
goes for Julia Alvarez, although Álvarez is usually accented. Cristina García has published her most recent novels with an accent mark in her last
name; reissues of her first novel, *Dreaming in Cuban*, also show an accent
mark, although the original edition did not. In an interview, García told me
that she had intentionally reclaimed the accent mark; therefore, once
again, I follow her preferred usage.

18. Sollors observed (in 1986) that ethnic "literature is often read and e
    ated against an elusive concept of authenticity" (*Beyond Ethnicity* 1
    Thus, for example, the revelation that "Danny Santiago," the author of *Fa-
    mous All Over Town* (1983), a novel about Chicanos in East L.A., was actu-
    ally Daniel Lewis James, an Anglo-American, was greeted with critical
    outrage. (See Stavans 28–29, for a detailed discussion.) The same sort of
    "outrage," however, never accompanies the publication of a book on Chica-
    nos by a Chilean or Cuban American, or a book on Salvadorans or Peruvi-
    ans by a Chicana.

19. An intriguing case in point is TuSmith's critical study *All My Relatives*
    (1993), chapters of which are devoted to "Asian American Writers" and
    to "Native American Writers"; yet there is no equivalent, panethnic "La-
    tino" chapter, but, rather, a chapter specifically on "Chicano/a Writers"—
    suggesting the degree to which, in the early '90s, even scholarship which
    recognized other panethnic categories felt uncomfortable treating "Lati-
    nos" as a single ethnic "community."

20. Rivero, for example, wrote in 1985 that "the works by Cuban immigrants
    can never be considered" as ethnic minority U.S. literature (187) because
    they are not in line with the progressive ideology of Chicanos and Nuyori-
    cans.

21. Consider, for example, critical efforts to salvage María Amparo Ruiz de
    Burton's late-nineteenth-century novel *Who Would Have Thought It?* as
    somehow challenging racism (R. Sánchez and B. Pita, xvi–xxi). For a more
    sophisticated analysis of Ruiz de Burton's novel, including its racism, see
    Alemán.

22. Piedra locates the origins of the idea of Hispanic race even further back, in
    Spain's efforts at national and imperial consolidation (284–85).

23. Cornell and Hartmann do not claim that actual blood ties or common de-
    scent must exist in order for a people to understand itself as an ethnic
    group. Rather, following Max Weber, they are explaining the fundamental
    beliefs that bind ethnic groups: "The fact of common descent is less impor-
    tant than belief in common descent. What matters is not whether a blood
    relationship actually exists, but whether it is believed to exist" (16–17).

24. Sidestepping such problems, Ed Morales argues—explicitly invoking the
    "raza cósmica" of José Vasconcelos—that Latinos are united by a long his-
    tory of racial miscegenation and cultural hybridity, of various forms. The
    unifying factor is apparently the process of miscegenation, rather than its
    specific manifestation or results.

25. Critics who continue to assert Spanish as a fundamental connection in-
    clude John García; Shorris xvi; Stavans 32.

26. Cornell and Hartmann's conception of ethnicity as constructed around
    various symbols takes the burden of ethnic cohesiveness off of the actual
    speaking of Spanish and shifts it instead to the symbolic importance of
    Spanish to continued group cohesion, even among those who might not
    speak it. Thus, for example, second- or third-generation Latino children or
    grandchildren of immigrants (like me) might not be Spanish-dominant or
    even comfortably bilingual and yet might feel an "emotive aura" around
    Spanish—even being driven to learn the language as a manifestation of
    "symbolic identification" (Padilla 151). The Pew Hispanic Center report's
    findings would seem to support this emphasis on the symbolic importance

of Spanish; the report notes that "nearly nine in ten (88%) Latinos say that it is very (63%) or somewhat (25%) important for future generations of Latinos living in the United States to speak Spanish" ("2004 National Survey" 26). A decade-long study of children of immigrants in San Diego found that, "among the Mexican-origin respondents, [the] ability to speak and read in Spanish did not atrophy but rather improved appreciably from their teens to their twenties," suggesting a commitment to improving Spanish (Rumbaut, "Severed" 67). See also Demetria Martínez's essay, "Confessions of a Berlitz-tape Chicana," in her book of the same name.

27. The National Immigration Forum, however, cites predictions by the research firm Hispanic Trends that, by 2010, 70 percent of Latinos in the United States will be foreign-born. One can only expect that, given the large numbers of Latin American immigrants currently entering the country, the significance of Spanish dominance as a common denominator will increase.

28. Chanady here cites the work of Antonio Cornejo Polar.

29. See, for instance, John García 25.

30. See, for example, Flores 199; Juan Gonzalez xiii–xiv; Gracia, esp. 48–51; Oboler 9; Suárez-Orozco and Páez 16–20; Torres-Saillant 438.

31. For an excellent discussion of how free trade has affected Mexicans and increased immigration to the United States, see "Free Trade: The Final Conquest of Latin America," in Juan Gonzalez's *Harvest of Empire*, 228–45.

32. On U.S. capital in Cuba prior to 1959, see, for example, Louis Pérez, "Cuba" 87–88. See Oboler 9–10 on other comparisons of immigrant groups.

33. The authors found a "clear progression in the use of panethnic identification from the first to the third generation. Among those of Mexican origin, for example, 28.99% of the first generation chose some kind of panethnic identification, increasing to 45.83% in the second generation, [. . .] and to 60.46% in the third generation. The trends are similar for the other two national groups" (Jones-Correa and Leal 224).

34. Jorge Gracia, approaching the question of Hispanic identity from a philosophical perspective in *Hispanic/Latino Identity* (2000), takes precisely the opposite position, arguing that consciousness is irrelevant to identity: "It is not [. . .] necessary that the members of the group name themselves in any particular way or have a consciousness of their identity. Some of them may in fact consider themselves Hispanic and even have a consciousness of their identity as a group, but it is not necessary that all of them do. Knowledge does not determine being" (49). Most scholars interested in the question of panethnic identity, however, would reject the notion that it is irrelevant whether Hispanics see themselves as a group or not: *self-identification* is precisely the question at issue.

35. Fox makes a compelling argument that one of the pivotal factors in the construction of a sense of Latino peoplehood was the growth of media that attempted to appeal to *all* Hispanic groups at once in an effort to increase audiences. Prior to the 1970s, Fox argues, U.S. newspapers for Spanish-speaking audiences catered to specific Latino ethnic groups that "had little contact with one another, separated by geography, dialect, and radically different social and political concerns" (41).

36. Note that the race question is a *separate* question from the one which asks about Hispanic/Latino origin. In the 2000 census the Hispanic "ethnicity" question was asked *first*, so respondents identifying as "Hispanic" in the race question which followed were, in essence, identifying as Hispanic twice. Logan calls this group "Hispanic Hispanics" as opposed to white Hispanics, black Hispanics, and so on.

37. In the Pew Hispanic Center's 2002 National Survey of Latinos, this percentage of respondents rose to 56. This figure does not include the 20 percent who "[p]refer another option" (chart 7).

38. These findings serve as a corrective to those of Dutwin et al., who—noting that "[i]ndividuals who self-identify as Latino/Hispanic [...] associate themselves with the Democratic Party at higher rates than with the Republican Party" (154)—came to the conclusion that "Democratic affiliation [for Latinos] is situated upon the cherishing of an overarching Latino heritage" (156). Such a conclusion presupposes that using a panethnic identifier is in itself a sign of belief and investment in "an overarching Latino heritage," whereas Jones-Correa and Leal's study suggests that this link is relatively weak.

39. The widest range between respondent groups here tended to be between those who did not use a panethnic label at all and those who identified primarily using such a label but also employed other terms (such as national-origin terms). Oddly, the group of respondents that identified *only* using a panethnic term did not represent the furthest extreme in their responses from those who did not use such a term at all. Jones-Correa and Leal hypothesize that, for those who identify *solely* as "Latino" or "Hispanic," the term might signal merely an acceptance of a category imposed from "outside" rather than a strong sense of ethnic group identity (239).

40. Sollors observes that "[t]he ethnic approach to writing" jumps from the ethnicity of the author (e.g., "X writes like an X, not like a Y"). This approach, "circular and tautological [...] reveals first and foremost this very Xness, a quality which cumulatively achieves the status of a somewhat mystical, ahistorical, and even quasi-eternal essence" ("Ethnicity" 290).

41. Sollors gives the example of a "slur" which takes various forms, depending on its object: it labels certain "blacks as Oreos, Asians as bananas, Indians as apples, and Chicanos as coconuts—all with the structurally identical criticism 'they're white inside!' The warning had no specific cultural content but served as an interchangeable exhortation to maintain boundaries" (*Beyond Ethnicity* 28).

42. Sollors called on literary critics to ask, "How is the illusion of ethnic 'authenticity' stylistically created in a text?" (*Invention* xiv); but he did not seem to acknowledge the possibility that ethnic texts might, in fact, undermine this illusion.

Works Cited

"1990 Census: Instructions to Respondents." <http://www.ipums.umn.edu/usa/voliii/inst1990.html#7>. Accessed 17 Jan. 2006.

Alderete, Manuel. "Forced and Politically-correct Labeling" [on-line rev. of *Living in Spanglish* by Ed Morales]. 21 Nov. 2004. <www.amazon.com>. Accessed 13 Jan. 2006.

Alemán, Jesse. "'Thank God, Lolita Is Away from Those Horrid Savages': The Politics of Whiteness in *Who Would Have Thought It?*" In Amelia Maria de la Luz Montes and Anne Elizabeth Goldman, eds., *Maria Amparo Ruiz de Burton: Critical and Pedagogical Perspectives.* Lincoln: University of Nebraska Press, 2004. 95–111.

Allatson, Paul. *Latino Dreams: Transcultural Traffic and the U.S. National Imaginary.* New York: Rodopi, 2002.

Anderson, Benedict. *Imagined Communities: Reflections on the Origin and Spread of Nationalism.* Rev. ed. New York: Verso, 1991.

Anzaldúa, Gloria. *Borderlands/La Frontera: The New Mestiza.* San Francisco: Spinsters/Aunt Lute, 1987.

Barreto, Matt A. "National Origin (Mis)Identification among Latinos in the 2000 Census: The Growth of the 'Other Hispanic or Latino' Category." *Harvard Journal of Hispanic Policy* 15 (2002): 39–63.

Castillo, Debra A. *Redreaming America: Toward a Bilingual American Culture.* Albany: State University of New York Press, 2005.

Chanady, Amaryll, ed. *Latin American Identity and Constructions of Difference.* Minneapolis: University of Minnesota Press, 1994.

Christian, Karen. *Show and Tell: Identity as Performance in U.S. Latina/o Fiction.* Albuquerque: University of New Mexico Press, 1997.

Cornejo Polar, Antonio. "La literatura latinoamericana y sus literaturas regionales y nacionales como totalidades contradictorias." In Ana Pizarro, ed., *Hacia una historia de la literatura latinoamericana.* Mexico City: Colegio de México, 1987. 123–36.

Cornell, Stephen, and Douglas Hartmann. *Ethnicity and Race: Making Identities in a Changing World.* Thousand Oaks, Calif.: Pine Forge Press, 1998.

Cresce, Arthur R., Audrey Dianne Schmidley, and Roberto R. Ramirez. "Identification of Hispanic Ethnicity in Census 2000: Analysis of Data Quality for the Question on Hispanic Origin." U.S. Census Bureau. <http://www.census.gov/population/www/documentation/twps0075/twps0075.html#tabo2>. Accessed 17 Jan. 2006.

De Genova, Nicholas, and Ana Y. Ramos-Zayas. *Latino Crossings: Mexicans, Puerto Ricans, and the Politics of Race and Citizenship.* New York: Routledge, 2003.

Dutwin, David, Mollyann Brodie, Melissa Herrmann, and Rebecca Levin. "Latinos and Political Party Affiliation." *Hispanic Journal of Behavioral Sciences* 27.2 (May 2005): 135–60.

Flores, Juan. *From Bomba to Hip-Hop: Puerto Rican Culture and Latino Identity.* New York: Columbia University Press, 2000.

Fox, Geoffrey. *Hispanic Nation: Culture, Politics, and the Constructing of Identity.* Secaucus, N.J.: Carol Publishing Group, 1996.

García, John A. *Latino Politics in America: Community, Culture, and Interests.* New York: Rowman and Littlefield Publishers, 2003.

García, María Cristina. *Havana U.S.A.: Cuban Exiles and Cuban Americans in South Florida, 1959–1994.* Berkeley and Los Angeles: University of California Press, 1996.

Gimenez, Martha E. "Latino/'Hispanic'—Who Needs a Name? The Case against a Standardized Terminology." *International Journal of Health Services* 19.3 (1989): 557–71.

————. "Latino Politics—Class Struggles: Reflections on the Future of Latino Politics." In Rodolfo D. Torres and George Katsiaficas, eds., *Latino Social Movements: Historical and Theoretical Perspectives*. New York: Routledge, 1999. 165–80.

Goldman, Francisco. *The Ordinary Seaman*. New York: Grove, 1997.

Gómez-Peña, Guillermo. *Warrior for Gringostroika: Essays, Performance Texts, and Poetry*. St. Paul: Graywolf Press, 1993.

Gonzalez, Juan. *Harvest of Empire: A History of Latinos in America*. New York: Penguin, 2000.

Gonzalez, Ray, ed. *Currents from the Dancing River: Contemporary Latino Fiction, Nonfiction, and Poetry*. New York: Harcourt Brace, 1994.

Gracia, Jorge J. E. *Hispanic/Latino Identity: A Philosophical Perspective*. Malden, Mass.: Blackwell, 2000.

Hernández-Truyol, Berta Esperanza. "Building Bridges: Latinas and Latinos at the Crossroads." In Richard Delgado and Jean Stefancic, eds., *The Latino/a Condition: A Critical Reader*. New York: New York University Press, 1998. 24–31. Originally published in the *Columbia Human Rights Law Review* (1994).

Jones-Correa, Michael. "All Politics Is Local: Latinos and the 2000 Elections." *Harvard Journal of Hispanic Policy* 13 (2000/2001): 25–44.

————. *Between Two Nations: The Political Predicament of Latinos in New York City*. Ithaca, N.Y.: Cornell University Press, 1998.

Jones-Correa, Michael, and David L. Leal. "Becoming 'Hispanic': Secondary Panethnic Identification among Latin American–Origin Populations in the United States." *Hispanic Journal of Behavioral Sciences* 18.2 (May 1996): 214–54.

Kanellos, Nicolás. *Hispanic American Literature: A Brief Introduction and Anthology*. Berkeley, Calif.: HarperCollins, 1995.

Laó-Montes, Agustín. "Introduction: Mambo Montage: The Latinization of New York City." In Agustín Laó-Montes and Arlene Dávila, eds., *Mambo Montage: The Latinization of New York*. New York: Columbia University Press, 2001. 1–53.

Logan, John R. "How Race Counts for Hispanic Americans." Albany, N.Y.: Lewis Mumford Center for Comparative Urban and Regional Research at State University of New York, 14 July, 2003. <http://mumford.albany.edu/census/BlackLatinoReport/BlackLatin001.htm>. Accessed 17 Jan. 2006.

Luis, William. *Dance between Two Cultures: Latino Caribbean Literature Written in the United States*. Nashville: Vanderbilt University Press, 1997.

Martin, Elizabeth. "The Effects of Questionnaire Design on Reporting of Detailed Hispanic Origin in Census 2000 Mail Questionnaires." *Public Opinion Quarterly* 66 (2002): 582–93.

Martin, Joyce A., Brady E. Hamilton, Paul D. Sutton, Stephanie J. Ventura, Fay Menacker, and Martha L. Munson. "Births: Final Data for 2003." *National Vital Statistics Reports* 54.2 (8 Sept. 2005): 1–116.

Martínez, Demetria. *Confessions of a Berlitz-tape Chicana*. Norman: University of Oklahoma Press, 2005.

McCracken, Ellen. *New Latina Narrative: The Feminine Space of Postmodern Ethnicity*. Tucson: University of Arizona Press, 1999.

Morales, Ed. *Living in Spanglish: The Search for Latino Identity in America*. New York: St. Martin's, 2002.

Mosher, W. D., et al. "Religion and Fertility in the United States: The Importance of Marriage Patterns and Hispanic Origin." *Demography* 23 (1986): 367–79.

Mujčinović, Fatima. *Postmodern Cross-Culturalism and Politicization in U.S. Latina Literature: From Ana Castillo to Julia Alvarez*. New York: Peter Lang, 2004.

National Campaign to Prevent Teen Pregnancy. "Fact Sheet: Teen Sexual Activity, Pregnancy and Childbearing among Black Teens." Oct. 2005. <www.teenpregnancy.org/resources/reading/pdf/AfricanAmericanFactSheet.pdf>. Accessed 18 Jan. 2006. 1–5.

———. "Fact Sheet: Teen Sexual Activity, Pregnancy and Childbearing among Latinos in the United States." Nov. 2005. <www.teenpregnancy.org/resources/reading/pdf/latinofs.pdf>. Accessed 18 Jan. 2006. 1–5.

National Immigration Forum. "Civic Participation: Undecided Latinos Swing Democratic in Final Weeks of Campaign." 17 Nov. 2000. <www.immigrationforum.org/PrintFriendly.aspx?tabid=168>. Accessed 12 Jan. 2006.

Obejas, Achy. *We Came All the Way from Cuba So You Could Dress Like This?* San Francisco: Cleis Press, 1994.

Oboler, Suzanne. *Ethnic Labels, Latino Lives: Identity and the Politics of (Re)Presentation in the United States*. Minneapolis: University of Minnesota Press, 1995.

Ortiz Cofer, Judith. *The Latin Deli*. New York: W. W. Norton, 1993.

Padilla, Felix M. *Latino Ethnic Consciousness: The Case of Mexican Americans and Puerto Ricans in Chicago*. South Bend, Ind.: Notre Dame Press, 1985.

Pérez, Louis A., Jr. "Cuba, c.1930–1959." In Leslie Bethell, ed., *Cuba: A Short History*. Cambridge: Cambridge University Press, 1993. 57–93.

Pérez Firmat, Gustavo. *Cincuenta lecciones de exilio y desexilio*. Miami: Ediciones Universal, 2000.

Pew Hispanic Center/Kaiser Family Foundation. "2002 National Survey of Latinos." Chartpack. Dec. 2002. <http://pewhispanic.org/files/reports/15.4.pdf>. Accessed 24 Jan. 2006.

———. "The 2004 National Survey of Latinos: Politics and Civic Participation." Summary and chartpack. 22 July 2004. <http://www.immigrationforum.org/DesktopDefault.aspx?tabid=137>. Accessed 13 Jan. 2006.

———. "2006 National Survey of Latinos: The Immigration Debate." See Suro and Escobar.

Piedra, José. "Literary Whiteness and the Afro-Hispanic Difference." In Dominick LaCapra, ed., *The Bounds of Race: Perspectives on Hegemony and Resistance*. Ithaca, N.Y.: Cornell University Press, 1991. 278–310.

Quintana, Alvina E., ed. *Reading U.S. Latina Writers: Remapping American Literature*. New York: Palgrave Macmillan, 2003.

Rebolledo, Tey Diana. *Panchita Villa and Other Guerrilleras: Essays on Chicana/Latina Literature and Criticism*. Austin: University of Texas Press, 2005.

Rivero, Eliana. "Hispanic Literature in the United States: Self-Image and Conflict." *Revista Chicano-Riqueña* 13.3–4 (Fall–Winter 1985): 173–91.

Rodríguez, Clara E. *Changing Race: Latinos, the Census, and the History of Ethnicity in the United States*. New York: New York University Press, 2000.

Rodriguez-Morazzani, Roberto P. "Beyond the Rainbow: Mapping the Discourse on Puerto Ricans and 'Race.'" In Antonia Darder and Rodolfo D. Torres, eds.,

The Latino Studies Reader: Culture, Economy & Society. Malden, Mass.: Blackwell, 1998. 143–62.

Rumbaut, Rubén G. "The Making of a People." In Marta Tienda and Faith Mitchell, eds., *Hispanics and the Future of America*. Washington, D.C.: National Academies Press, 2006. 16–65.

———. "Severed or Sustained Attachments? Language, Identity, and Imagined Communities in the Post-Immigrant Generation." In Peggy Levitt and Mary C. Waters, eds., *The Changing Face of Home: The Transnational Lives of the Second Generation*. New York: Russell Sage Foundation, 2002. 43–95.

Sánchez, George J. "'Y tú, ¿qué?' Latino History in the New Millennium." In Marcelo M. Suárez-Orozco and Mariela M. Páez, eds., *Latinos: Remaking America*. Berkeley and Los Angeles: University of California Press, 2002. 41–58.

Sánchez, Rosaura, and Beatrice Pita. "Introduction." In María Amparo Ruiz de Burton, *Who Would Have Thought It?* Eds. Rosaura Sánchez and Beatrice Pita. Houston: Arte Público Press, 1995. vii–lxv.

Schermerhorn, Richard A. *Comparative Ethnic Relations: A Framework for Theory and Research.* Chicago: University of Chicago Press, 1978.

Scott, Janny. "In Simple Pronouns, Clues to Shifting Latino Identity." *New York Times*, 5 Dec. 2002: B1.

Shorris, Earl. *Latinos: A Biography of the People*. New York: W. W. Norton, 1992.

Sollors, Werner. *Beyond Ethnicity: Consent and Descent in American Culture*. New York: Oxford University Press, 1986.

———. "Ethnicity." In Frank Lentricchia and Thomas McLaughlin, eds., *Critical Terms for Literary Study*. Chicago: University of Chicago Press, 1995. 288–305.

———, ed. *The Invention of Ethnicity*. New York: Oxford University Press, 1989.

Stavans, Ilan. *The Hispanic Condition: Reflections on Culture and Identity in America*. New York: HarperCollins, 1995.

Suárez-Orozco, Marcelo M., and Mariela M. Páez, eds. *Latinos: Remaking America*. Berkeley and Los Angeles: University of California Press, 2002.

Sugg, Katherine. "Literatures of the Americas, *Latinidad*, and the Re-formation of Multi-Ethnic Literatures." *MELUS* 29. 3-4 (Fall-Winter 2004): 227–42.

Suro, Roberto, and Gabriel Escobar. "2006 National Survey of Latinos: The Immigration Debate." Washington, DC: Pew Hispanic Center, July 2006. <http://www.ime.gob.mx/investigaciones/pew/2006/debate_migratorio.pdf>. Accessed 21 Jan 2007.

Tafoya, Sonya. "Shades of Belonging." Pew Hispanic Center. 6 Dec. 2004. <http://pewhispanic.org/files/reports/35.pdf>. Accessed 19 Jan. 2006.

Tobar, Héctor. *The Tattooed Soldier*. New York: Penguin, 1998.

Torres-Saillant, Silvio. "Epilogue: Problematic Paradigms: Racial Diversity and Corporate Identity in the Latino Community." In Marcelo M. Suárez-Orozco and Mariela M. Páez, eds., *Latinos: Remaking America*. Berkeley and Los Angeles: University of California Press, 2002. 435–55.

Trueba, Enrique (Henry) T. *Latinos Unidos: From Cultural Diversity to the Politics of Solidarity*. New York: Rowman and Littlefield, 1999.

TuSmith, Bonnie. *All My Relatives: Community in Contemporary Ethnic American Literatures*. Ann Arbor: University of Michigan Press, 1993.

U.S. Census Bureau. "Hispanic Heritage Month 2002: Sept. 15–Oct. 15." <http://www.census.gov/Press-Release/www/2002/cb02ff15.html>. 3 Sept. 2002. Accessed 20 Jan. 2006.

U.S. Department of Health and Human Services. *Mental Health: Culture, Race, and Ethnicity—A Supplement to Mental Health: A Report of the Surgeon General*. Rockville, Md.: U.S. Department of Health and Human Services, 2001. <http://www.mentalhealth.samhsa.gov/media/ken/pdf/SMA-01-3613/sma-01-3613.pdf>. Accessed 25 Jan. 2006.

———. "2000 Natality Data Set" [CD-ROM]. CD-ROM Series 21.14 (2002).

Weber, Max. *Economy and Society*. Eds. Guenther Roth and Claus Wittich. Berkeley and Los Angeles: University of California Press, 1968.

Wyatt, Jean. *Risking Difference: Identification, Race, and Community in Contemporary Fiction and Feminism*. Albany: State University of New York Press, 2004.

———. "Toward Cross-race Dialogue: A Lacanian Approach to Identification, Misrecognition and Difference in Feminist Multicultural Community." *Signs* 29.3 (Spring 2004): 879–903.

Zentella, Ana Celia. "Latin@ Languages and Identities." In Marcelo M. Suárez-Orozco and Mariela M. Páez, eds., *Latinos: Remaking America*. Berkeley and Los Angeles: University of California Press, 2002. 321–38.

African American Literature: A Survey

Trudier Harris

Originally appearing in Africana Studies: A Survey of Africa and the African Diaspora *(1998), edited by Mario Azevedo, Harris's essay surveys the field of African American literature. She begins with a discussion of oral tradition and the slave narrative and connects these to the development of poetry, fiction, and drama. Her comments on poetry range from the eighteenth to twentieth centuries, with particular attention to Phillis Wheatley, Paul Laurence Dunbar, James Weldon Johnson, Langston Hughes, Robert Hayden, Gwendolyn Brooks, Michael Harper, and Rita Dove. Attention is also paid to the New Black Aesthetic or Black Arts movement and the role of jazz and blues. Harris's discussion of fiction and drama notes the influence of the slave narrative upon the novel form. She also comments on the less realistic novels of the Harlem Renaissance, which tended to stress positive images. According to Harris, African American fiction became more realistic in the 1930s with Zora Neale Hurston and Richard Wright, both of whom are discussed in greater detail. Finally, Harris provides a brief overview of drama, beginning with William Wells Brown and ending with August Wilson. She concludes by stressing the continued significance of oral tradition and the slave narrative in contemporary African American literature.*

From *Africana Studies: A Survey of Africa and the African Diaspora*, 2nd ed., ed. Mario Azevedo (Durham: Carolina Academic P, 1998): 329–40.

Introduction

I n order to understand African American literature, it is first necessary to understand the roles that the oral culture and the slave narrative had in its formation. This chapter examines those traditions in relation to the written literature and surveys the development of each genre (poetry, fiction, drama). Issues central to the literature begin with the role of the African American writer in relation to his or her community. Should a literate black individual devote a career to trying to improve the condition of the group, or should that person feel free to write out of individual desires and wishes?

This intersection of politics and art dominated discussions of African American literature well into the twentieth century. Issues include the representation of black characters: Should they always be complimentary or should they be realistic, even when they run the risk of damaging the group socially? In what language should literature be composed — black English or standard English? What of nationalism (the Black Aesthetic)? Who should teach the literature? African Americans? White Americans? Others? Where should it be taught? English Departments? Black Studies Departments? Others? To whom should black writers address their works? The problem of ghettoizing the African American creative effort was also raised in the twentieth century; black writers complained that critics discussed them only in connection with other black writers, not with the larger traditions of literary creativity. And today, the issue of the relevance of current critical theories to discussions of African American literature dominate the energies of many scholars.

MAJOR TERMS AND CONCEPTS: The role of writers in their communities, influences on literary creativity, racism, slavery, slave narratives, folklore, oral tradition, Harlem Renaissance, protest literature, Black Aesthetic, Black Arts Movement.

Oral Tradition and Slave Narrative

A study of African American literature naturally begins with the African American oral tradition and with the slave narrative. Africans brought to the United States and enslaved were obviously not brought here to produce poems, plays, short stories, and novels. Nor were they here with any consideration of perpetuating their own cultural traditions. Thus thrown into circumstances where their bodies were emphasized over their minds, and where the usual bonds of language were absent, enslaved Africans adapted the English language and used it to communicate as best they could. Through this hybrid, they passed on what they remembered of their own cultures, combined it with what they witnessed on new soil, or created something totally new. What

they communicated in the patterned forms known as folklore reflected
the best of the values they wished to pass on.

Their narratives, legends, jokes, songs, rhymes, and sayings recorded a world in which they reacted to their circumstances as an enslaved group and in which they passed on imaginative ways of interacting
within that world. Early tales reveal, for example, the discrepancies in
the economic conditions of slaves and masters. In 1853 in *Clotel; or, The
President's Daughter*, the first novel by an African American, William
Wells Brown recorded one of the earliest documented folk rhymes:

> The big bee flies high,
> The little bee make the honey;
> The black folks makes the cotton
> And the white folks gets the money.

It captures the thematic essence of the protest tradition that Richard
Wright and other writers of the twentieth century would advocate so
fervently. In a land so rich in resources and which professed to believe
so strongly in democracy, it was unconscionable, these folk artists and
literary writers would argue, for an entire group of people to be excluded from those resources, especially when those individuals had
played a key role in the building of the country.

The song tradition, whether in spirituals, blues, or Gospel, similarly
portrayed a people on the lower echelon of the social stratum who hoped
for resolution of their plight in the afterlife if not in this world. Spirituals frequently suggested being done with "de troubles of the world" and
going home to live with Jesus. While writers may not have advocated
a literal interpretation of that tradition, the general tenet of the need
for rectification of social conditions became a common theme in the literature. Music as an expression of the ability to deal with the troubles
of the world similarly informs the literature, whether it is a Richard
Wright character soothing her worries by singing in a short story like
"Bright and Morning Star" (1938) or a character in James Baldwin's
"Sonny's Blues" (1964) similarly singing to ease the burden of bearing
her troubles. Music captured the general *weltschmerz* (pessimism at
the state of the world; literally, "world pain") of being African and American in a country where simply being American was preferable.

Not only were the themes common to the written literature passed
on in the oral tradition, but the structures as well. In the 1920s, Langston
Hughes, in addition to adapting the themes of the blues, would adapt
the AAB rhyme scheme of the genre as one of his primary literary
structures. Thus compositions such as the following one from his "Miss
Blues'es Child" became common:

> If the blues would let me,
> Lord knows I would smile.

If the blues would let me,
I would smile, smile, smile.
Instead of that I'm cryin'—
I must be Miss Blues'es child.

In addition to the blues, folk narratives also provided the shaping force for literary creativity. The structure of Ralph Ellison's *Invisible Man* (1952) is based on an African American folktale.

Numerous writers drew upon the African American folk tradition for characters and concepts. "Badman" heroes, for example, pervade the literature from Charles W. Chesnutt's Josh Green in *The Marrow of Tradition* (1901) to Appalachee Red in Raymond Andrews's *Appalachee Red* (1978). Conjure women and other healers modeled on characters from the folk tradition make their debut in Brown's *Clotel*, continue through Chesnutt's *The Conjure Woman* (1899), get transformed in Alice Walker's "The Revenge of Hannah Kemhuff" (1970), and emerge with true supernatural powers in Toni Morrison's *Beloved* (1987) as well as in Gloria Naylor's *Mama Day* (1988). Other writers and works that draw upon this tradition of characterization include Charles R. Johnson, *Faith and the Good Thing* (1974); Toni Cade Bambara, *The Salt Eaters* (1980); and Tina McElroy Ansa, *Baby of the Family* (1989). Traveling bluesmen are the subject of Langston Hughes's *Not Without Laughter* (1930) and Albert Murray's *Train Whistle Guitar* (1974). The man-of-words tradition, as exemplified in Muhammad Ali's rhymes such as "Float like a butterfly/sting like a bee/That's why they call me/ Muhammad Ali," joins the preaching tradition as the focus of such works as Ellison's *Invisible Man* (1952), where mastery of language is the measure of reputation and effectiveness in the society. Other writers simply saturate their works with an aura of the folk tradition; these include Zora Neale Hurston, *Their Eyes Were Watching God* (1937); Ernest Gaines, *The Autobiography of Miss Jane Pittman* (1974); and Charles R. Johnson, *Middle Passage* (1990).

The slave narrative tradition, in which the protagonist documents (in the first person) his or her movement from slavery to freedom and from South to North, defines the autobiographical tradition that so informs the literature as well as the archetypal pattern of movement for literary characters, that is, from the South to the North. Perhaps the most exemplary of the slave narratives is Frederick Douglass's *Narrative of the Life of Frederick Douglass: An American Slave, Written by Himself* (1845), though Harriet Wilson's *Our Nig* (1859) and Harriet Jacobs's *Incidents in the Life of A Slave Girl* (1860) have gained prominence in recent years. Although it is technically classified as the first novel written by an African American woman, Wilson's *Our Nig* nonetheless documents the atrocities of enslavement; since the action is set in the Boston area, the book is especially interesting for providing a look at bondage on other than southern soil.

Douglass and Jacobs fit the tradition of documenting atrocities during slavery, the process by which they learned to read and write, how they became dissatisfied with their dehumanizing conditions, the aid they enlisted in planning and executing escapes, and the free existences that awaited them on northern soil. Douglass's work is as much literary as it is historical, for he is an effective storyteller who molds characters and circumstances to best advantage in making his points about slavery. He is also a master of figurative language usually identified with poetry and other consciously created imaginative works. Jacobs's narrative is particularly important for documenting the creation of a female self against the backdrop of sexual abuses during slavery. It, like Douglass's narrative, also recounts the process of literary creation, the assistance these early writers received in structuring their works and in getting them published.

The major theme of slave narratives, therefore, found a counterpart in the consciously created literary works. The progression from slavery or restriction (the South) to freedom and opportunity (the North) provides a prevailing pattern in the literature. The Great Migration that led to the tripling and quadrupling of African American populations in various northern cities between 1900 and 1930 illustrates the historical pattern as well. Writers who have their characters leave the South for presumed opportunities in the North include Wright in "Big Boy Leaves Home" (1938), Ellison in *Invisible Man* (1952), John Oliver Killens in *Youngblood* (1954), and a host of others.

Folklore and slave narratives, therefore, addressed the basic condition of black existence in the United States, of the discrepancy between a theoretical democracy and the reality of the failure of democratic principles. As the genres of the written tradition developed, they in turn were conceptualized, especially in the early years of development, with the larger issues of black life and culture in mind. Brown's *Clotel*, for example, is as much a treatise against slavery as it is a novel; it includes advertisements for runaways, accounts of dogs chasing slaves, abolitionist discussions, and characters who espouse one side of the slavery issue or the other. When Brown completed *The Escape; or, A Leap for Freedom* in 1858, that first drama by an African American also found its subject in slavery. Frances Ellen Watkins Harper, who published *Poems on Miscellaneous Subjects* in 1854, became a popular abolitionist lecturer, as did Brown. Her poems, such as "Bury Me in a Free Land" and "The Mother," depict the consequences of slavery on the family life of African Americans.

African American Poetry

Although the poetry in the latter part of the nineteenth century would be engaged with political issues, that was less true of the first verses composed by African Americans. Lucy Terry, who is credited with com-

posing the first poem by an African American in 1746, centered her composition upon an Indian raid in Deerfield, Massachusetts. As a slave
in a Deerfield home, she naturally identified more with the whites than
with the "savage" Indians; the poem, "Bars Fight," reflects her identification. It was not published, however, until 1895. The first African
American poet to publish a work in the United States was Jupiter
Hammon, whose broadside entitled *An Evening Thought: Salvation
by Christ, with Penitential Cries*, appeared on Christmas day in 1760.
Phillis Wheatley, perhaps the best known of the early poets, published
her *Poems on Various Subjects, Religious and Moral* in 1773. Brought
as a child to the United States, Phillis grew up learning English and
being encouraged to compose poetry in the Wheatley house in Boston. Her poems treat subjects as diverse as Africans being brought to
America, the antics of students at Harvard, the military successes of
George Washington, and the reception she received from the Countess
of Huntington when she traveled to England. George Moses Horton,
a slave poet in the country near Chapel Hill, North Carolina, put his
talents to use in the service of the students at the University of North
Carolina. He composed love poems and other sentiments at their re-
quests. His first volume, *The Hope of Liberty*, appeared in 1829; a second volume, *The Poetical Works of George M. Horton, The Colored Bard
of North Carolina*, appeared in 1845, the same year as Douglass's narrative.

It was Frances Harper, however, who retained the reputation
as America's best-known African American poet until Paul Laurence
Dunbar's reputation overshadowed hers in the last few years of the
nineteenth century. Dunbar, born in Dayton, Ohio, in 1872, began publishing poems in 1893, when his *Oak and Ivy* appeared. A combination
of standard English and dialect poems, the volume was well received
and was followed thereafter by *Majors and Minors* (1896), *Lyrics of
Lowly Life* (1896), and a host of others. He also wrote novels, the most
famous of which is *The Sport of the Gods* (1902), which appeared just
four years before his death in 1906.

African American poetry in the twentieth century has varied widely.
It began with the dialect tradition that Dunbar institutionalized, the
remnants of which were around well into the Harlem Renaissance of
the 1920s. James Weldon Johnson, whom Dunbar knew well, included
dialect poems such as "Sence You Went Away" in his first compositions
at the turn of the century, yet he recognized the limitations of the medium. James David Corrothers and James Whitfield Campbell also
wrote dialect poetry. The tradition finally led Johnson to complain in
the introduction to *The Book of American Negro Poetry* (1922), which he
edited, that dialect had "but two full stops, humor and pathos." He
longed for the day when African American poets would be able to represent the complexity of black life and experience without resorting to
"the mere mutilation of English spelling and pronunciation."

Certainly Langston Hughes's blues poetry in the 1920s was a move in a new direction, as was the folk poetry of Sterling Brown in the 1930s. Although Brown resorted to folk patterns of speech in *Southern Road* (1932), he did not rely on caricature and phonetic distortion. His characters, like those of Hughes in poems such as "Mother to Son," were able to retain a certain dignity and garner the respect of readers. Brown's successes in being more expansive in capturing the nuances of black language and life led Johnson to write a brief introduction to *Southern Road*. Another trend in poetry during the Harlem Renaissance was reflected in the works of Claude McKay, perhaps one of the most militant voices of the era. McKay's militancy derives not only from the sentiments he expresses but from his transformation of the traditional forms in which he writes. Using the Shakespearean sonnet, a form usually reserved for lofty sentiments of love, McKay documented the failures of democracy, painted the violence of societally sanctioned crimes such as lynching, and called upon African Americans to take up arms against all who would seek to destroy them. In his signature poem, "If We Must Die," he urges oppressed people to "meet the common foe" and to "deal one death-blow!" for the thousand blows of the enemy. He concludes the poem with this couplet: "Like men we'll face the murderous, cowardly pack,/Pressed to the wall, dying, but fighting back!" His poetry certainly did not distort African American experience in the way that Johnson believed dialect poetry did.

Perhaps Johnson's call for a different kind of poetry was more fully realized in the academic verses of Robert Hayden and Gwendolyn Brooks in the 1940s. These poets, steeped in the western traditions of verse, structure, composition, and density of language, were judged to be successful by the more literary poetic establishments in the country. Hayden published *Heart-Shape in the Dust* in 1940, which picks up some of the themes of the writers of the Harlem Renaissance, especially questions of identity. By 1948 and his publication of *The Lion and the Archer*, however, he had dramatically altered his style to reflect the influence of such poets as Gerald Manley Hopkins, Stephen Spender, C. Day Lewis, and Rainer Maria Rilke; the result was six poems generally judged to be "baroque" in structure and execution. These include "A Ballad of Remembrance" and "Homage to the Empress of the Blues" (Bessie Smith). A later poem, "Middle Passage," which describes the transportation of Africans to the West Indies and other parts of the New World for purposes of enslavement, is one of the most anthologized of Hayden's works. Like Hayden, Brooks preferred the density and structure of poetry that reflected white western influences upon her. Her subjects are certainly those of African American life and experience, but they are shrouded in styles that appear at times to be antithetical to the very experiences she records. Her first volume, *A Street in Bronzeville* (1945), focuses on black people on the South side of

Chicago and recounts occurrences in their everyday lives; narrative is the major technique she employs. She won the Pulitzer Prize for *Annie Allen* (1949), which is loosely based on the *Aeneid*; it follows a young girl growing up in a Chicago tenement. Although the volume was judged to be difficult and self-conscious, it nonetheless received more praise than not.

The New Black Aesthetic movement of the 1960s brought a poetic revolution in its wake. It introduced a group of poets who are still publishing today. Nikki Giovanni, Haki Madhubuti (formerly Don L. Lee), Amiri Baraka (formerly LeRoi Jones), Sonia Sanchez, and others fashioned the poets' response to social change during this period. Advocating a nationalistic approach to literature, they called upon black people to take an active role in freeing themselves from a racist, undemocratic society. They also provided the path by which blacks were to arrive at being a nation of African Americans. They were to change their hair and clothing styles, their patterns of behavior, and even their names; it became the age of dashikis and afros. The nationalistic bent was reflected in the language of the poetry itself; it attempted to imitate speech patterns and colloquialisms of common black folk, and it consciously sought to dissociate itself with the conventions of western poetry. New words were created ("blkpoets," "nationbuilding," "u," "bes"), and structures were designed to resemble African American cultural forms such as jazz, not traditional sonnets or free verse.

There were still poets during this period who continued in the more traditional veins, including Robert Hayden and Michael Harper. Like Madhubuti and others, however, Harper did give attention to African American themes and structures, including adapting stanzaic forms based on compositions by jazz great John Coltrane. The difference is that Harper did not alter his poetry as radically as did some of the younger poets; nor was he as consciously militant. Brooks joined the younger poets in reevaluating her role in relation to the black community as well as in modifying her stanzaic forms. She published several small volumes for children in the 1960s and 1970s and wrote a poem on the occasion of Harold Washington being elected mayor of Chicago, a first for a black politician.

Brooks's success in winning the Pulitzer Prize in 1950 for *Annie Allen* (1949) was matched in the mid-1980s when newcomer Rita Dove won the Pulitzer Prize for her volume, *Thomas and Beulah* (1986). Focusing on the relationship between a man and his wife over an extended period of time, the volume alternates voices between Thomas and Beulah, allowing them to recount and record their own perceptions. The collection illustrated that less self-conscious structures and themes in poetry could be equally appealing to a panel of judges for one of the most prestigious literary prizes currently available.

African American Fiction and Drama

Fiction moved from its dual function as slave narrative and literature in the mid-nineteenth century, to romance and imitation of white writers in the late nineteenth century, to the autobiographical mode and more consciously designed protest novels in the twentieth century. Chesnutt explored the color problem in *The House Behind the Cedars* (1900), a novel focusing on a light-skinned black woman whose brief attempt to pass for white ends in disaster. He also reflects social concerns in *The Marrow of Tradition* (1901), a novel about the Wilmington, North Carolina, riot of 1898. On that occasion, black people who tried to vote were attacked and many of them killed by the whites who were intent upon preserving white supremacy.

The influence of the slave narrative upon the novel form can be seen in the autobiographical mode of *The Autobiography of An Ex-Colored Man* (1912), which James Weldon Johnson published anonymously. Johnson executed the first-person narrative device so well that readers believed the novel was indeed the historical life story of its author. The novels follows the life of a talented mulatto musician who is caught between the opportunities his talent offers and the limitations his classification as a Negro ultimately brings. He finally opts to deny his black ancestry and "pass" for white. It was only when Johnson acknowledged authorship of the book in 1927 that tales of its authenticity abated. Indeed, Johnson recounted attending a party prior to 1927 in which one of the guests "confided" to the gathering that he was the author of *The Autobiography of An Ex-Colored Man.*

Fiction published by writers of the Harlem Renaissance ranged from Jean Toomer's *Cane* (1923), which (to a degree) romanticizes black life in Georgia, to Claude McKay's *Home to Harlem* (1929), an account of the adventures of a fun-loving world traveler. It also included the genteel tradition of fiction writing represented by Nella Larsen's *Quicksand* (1928) and *Passing* (1929), and Jessie Fauset's *Plum Bun* (1924). Fauset, who assisted W. E. B. Du Bois in editing the *Crisis* magazine in which many of the Renaissance writers were published, held *salons* at her Harlem apartment at which invited guests were expected to hold conversations in French about the latest developments in literature or world affairs.

One problem with these early novels was that very seldom were African Americans represented realistically in them. Indeed, there was a general movement in the first three decades of the twentieth century that might be referred to as "the best foot forward" tradition; writers were encouraged to portray complimentary images of African Americans. Characters should be engaged in pursuits that were in keeping with the objectives of the larger society. Therefore, general principles of democracy were to be upheld and education was a goal to be valued, as were habits of morality and cleanliness. "Bad niggers," whether male or female, were best left out of the literature. The belief that such positive images were important led in 1926 to a forum in *Crisis* magazine. It was entitled "The Negro in Art: How Shall He Be Portrayed? A Symposium." The forum received responses from Sherwood Anderson, Benjamin Brawley, Charles W. Chesnutt, Countee Cullen, W. E. B. Du Bois, Jessie Fauset, Langston Hughes, Georgia Douglas Johnson, Alfred A. Knopf, Sinclair Lewis, Vachel Lindsay, H. L. Mencken, Joel Spingarn, and Walter White.

Fictional portraits of African Americans began to be more realistic in the decade of the 1930s. Zora Neale Hurston depicted a black preacher in *Jonah's Gourd Vine* (1934) that any reader would recognize. Her portrait of Janie Crawford Logan Starks Killicks in *Their Eyes Were Watching God* (1937) brought a new dimension in realism to portraits of African American female characters. Janie is a working-class woman who prefers spiritual fulfillment to gentility. After two disastrous marriages, she finally finds happiness with an itinerant laborer who takes her to pick beans in the Florida muck. The novel does not raise large political issues, although the social issues of woman's place in the society and what sacrifices she must make to find personal happiness are certainly important ones.

Hurston's more individually focused issues gave way to the politics of Richard Wright, who dismissed her work because she did not write as consciously in the protest tradition as he would have expected. For Wright, any black author should use his or her pen to point out the hypocrisies in American democracy, how black people were ground under the heels of white privilege and prejudice. He began such depictions in his first collection of short stories, *Uncle Tom's Children*, which was published in 1938. Almost all the stories are violent, and at least two of them embrace the communist philosophy to which Wright was becoming attracted at this time; he believed that African Americans had a better chance of obtaining democracy in America through that philosophy. His stories document black people being lynched and shot, denied medical services or the sympathy that should attend them, beaten by mobs, and burned alive. The few who decide to fight back, such as Silas in "Long Black Song," only end up being killed more dramatically. However, in "Fire and Cloud," one of the stories that embraces communist philosophy, Reverend Taylor is able to gather white and black working-class people together to put pressure on a city government to provide food during the Depression. Before that possible hope, though, characters such as Big Boy in "Big Boy Leaves Home" and Mann in "Down by the Riverside" are simply buffeted by the misfortunes of the societies in which they live. They must either escape to the North or die in the attempt.

Wright's hard-hitting approach to fiction continued in 1940 with the publication of *Native Son*, his most famous work in the protest tradition. It posits that black men in America are so confined physically and psychologically that the fear they sometimes experience can drive them to kill almost instinctively. Bigger Thomas does just that when he is found in the bedroom of his white employer's daughter, whom he has helped there because she was in a drunken stupor. Smothering Mary Dalton to death gives him a feeling of horror, but also one of exhilaration, for it is the first time in his life that he has acted against the wishes of the white power structure.

Other novels from the forties that fit into the protest tradition include Chester Himes's *If He Hollers Let Him Go* (1945), about a black man forced to join the military or be sent to prison because he was accused of raping a white woman, and Ann Petry's *The Street* (1946), about a black woman who suffers the stings of poverty and sexual politics when she tries to rear her son alone in Harlem. Such literary voices did not portend a particularly inviting future for African Americans. It would be the next decade before writers could assert with authority that the promise of American democracy did indeed apply to African Americans.

That authoritative voice belonged to Ralph Ellison, who asserted in *Invisible Man* (1952) that blacks should "affirm the principles on which the country was founded"—even when the day-to-day execution of those principles seemed to leave them out of the great American experiment. His optimistic voice for the larger nationalist agenda led into the cultural nationalism that would inform the fiction of the 1960s, such as John A. Williams's *The Man Who Cried I Am* (1967), which asserts that blacks must fight as best they can against the forces of repression.

More focus on the black community tended to occupy fiction writers in the 1970s, which began with Toni Morrison's publication of *The Bluest Eye*. That novel indicts the entire society for judging little black girls by standards of beauty that are culturally antithetical to them, but it especially places the blame on unthinking, unfeeling members of the black middle class. The pattern of focusing on black communities continued in the 1980s with Toni Cade Bambara's *The Salt Eaters* (1980), Alice Walker's *The Color Purple* (1982), Terry McMillan's *Mama* (1987) and *Disappearing Acts* (1989), and Tina McElroy Ansa's *Baby of the Family* (1989).

The last couple of decades have also witnessed an outpouring of dramas by African Americans. The dramatic scene is a far cry from where it started in 1858 with Brown's *The Escape; or, A Leap for Freedom*. Brown's play was written to be read rather than produced; it was not until the musical comedy era of the 1880s and 1890s that black playwrights saw their works on the stage. One of the earliest such achievements was a collaboration between James Weldon Johnson and Paul Laurence Dunbar. They wrote music and lyrics for *Clorindy, or the Origin of the Cakewalk* (1898). In 1900 Dunbar collaborated with black composer Will Marion Cook in the production of *Uncle Eph's Christmas*.

The first three decades of the twentieth century did not see much development in traditional dramas by black Americans, although the musical comedy tradition was popular until well into the 1920s. The year 1920 saw the publication of Angelina Weld Grimké's *Rachel: A Play in Three Acts* (produced in 1916), but it would be well into the 1930s before a black writer completed a drama that would have a successful run on Broadway. That distinction belonged to Langston Hughes, whose *Mulatto*, a dramatic rewrite of his short story, "Father and Son," ran on Broadway from 1935 to 1936, as well as for an additional two years on tour.

In the 1930s and 1940s, several black theatre companies were formed; most of their productions, however, were reworkings of plays by continental and white American playwrights. Alice Childress, whose *Trouble in Mind* was optioned for Broadway in the mid-1950s, worked closely with one of these companies. Other plays by African Americans that were produced during this period include *St. Louis Woman* (1946), a collaboration by Arna Bontemps and Countee Cullen in which Bontemps's novel, *God Sends Sunday* (1931), was adapted for stage; Louis Peterson's *Take a Giant Step* (1953); and Hughes's *Simply Heavenly* (1957).

Perhaps the most dramatic event in the history of the production of plays by black Americans occurred in 1959, when Lorraine Hansberry's *A Raisin in the Sun* opened in Philadelphia. It was the first time, James Baldwin asserts, that black people truly recognized themselves on the American stage. Blacks flocked to see the play because they saw accurate reflections of themselves, and they recognized Hansberry as a witness to their blackness and their aspirations in American society. That event was followed in 1964 by LeRoi Jones's *Dutchman*, which, in its depiction of the sexual tempting of a black man by a white woman and her eventual killing of him, had an equally profound effect on the American theatre as well as on black viewing audiences. Playwrights such as Ossie Davis (*Purlie Victorius*, 1961), James Baldwin (*The Amen Corner*, 1965), Ed Bullins (*In the Wine Time*, 1968), and Charles Gordone all had plays produced in the very successful decade of the 1960s. Gordone became the first black playwright to win the Pulitzer Prize for drama, for his *No Place to Be Somebody* (1969).

The shocker for the next decade would be Ntozake Shange's *For Colored Girls Who Have Considered Suicide When the Rainbow Is Enuf* (1976), which focused critical attention on the problematic relationships between black males and black females. In 1981, Charles Fuller's *A Soldier's Play* opened on Broadway; the next year it followed the path of *No Place to Be Somebody* by winning the Pulitzer Prize for drama. The most publicized dramatic successes of the 1980s belonged to August Wilson, whose *Fences*, the story of an embittered player from the Negro Baseball League, won the Pulitzer Prize for drama in 1987. His other works include *Ma Rainey's Black Bottom* (1986), *The Piano Lesson* (1987), and *Joe Turner's Come and Gone* (1988).

Summary

In recent years, there has been a reevaluation of what southern territory means in African American literature, and writers have set their works on that soil and allowed their characters to define themselves and their world in that previously restricting territory. Such writers and works include Toni Morrison's *Song of Solomon* (1977), in which a spoiled middle-class black Michiganer returns to Virginia to uncover the meaning of personal history and ancestry; Alice Walker's *The Color Purple* (1982), in which a black woman who has been abused physically and psychologically overcomes these debilitations to become an entrepreneur in Memphis; and Gloria Naylor's *Mama Day* (1988), in which a descendant of slaves controls not only her family's destiny but the very elements of the universe. For these writers, the South is no longer forbidden territory, no longer a place of death, but a place where African Americans can choose reasonably well under what circumstances they will live in the world.

Its roots in the oral tradition and in the African American slave narrative have enabled African American literature to come of age in the twentieth century. From a literature that made obeisances to white reading audiences, as was the case with Charles W. Chesnutt, it has grown to insist, as Toni Morrison does, that readers come to meet it wherever it starts and agree to go wherever it takes them. Forms that were initially rooted in politics, such as Frances Harper's lyrics, gave way to the mythologically sophisticated verses of poets such as Jay Wright. And dramas that were initially intended for living room consumption serve as the origins of works that have won several Pulitzer Prizes.

The publishing industry has kept pace with audiences for African American literature, and today novels, poems, and plays by black writers are available for use in courses in American studies, African American studies, Religious studies, History, and Sociology, as well as in the traditional English Department classes. Readership has transcended languages and national boundaries; Morrison's works, for example, are available in German and Japanese, among other languages, and she won Italy's highest prize for a creative writer in 1990. Doctoral students in India, Spain, Germany, Japan, and the Netherlands routinely come to the United States to study with specialists in African American literature, and they regularly write dissertations on African American writers. From a creative effort with a purpose, African American literature has grown to be recognized internationally as a complex area of study that will sustain many generations of students, teachers, and scholars.

Study Questions and Activities

1. How has the portrayal of African American characters changed in literary works from the nineteenth to the twentieth centuries?

2. What are some of the influences of the African American oral tradition upon the literature?

3. What would have been the consequences for an African American writer who ignored the fact of his or her race during the nineteenth century?

4. What are the social, cultural, and political implications of writing in a language you grew up speaking as opposed to one you have been taught?

5. In what ways was the New Black Aesthetic movement purely literary? In what ways was it political?

References

Andrews, William L. *To Tell A Free Story: The First Century of Afro-American Autobiography, 1760–1865.* Urbana, IL: University of Illinois Press, 1986.

Baker, Houston A. Jr. *Blues, Ideology, and Afro-American Literature, A Vernacular Theory.* Chicago: University of Chicago Press, 1984.

Bell, Bernard. *The Afro-American Novel and Its Tradition.* Amherst, MA: University of Massachusetts Press, 1987.

Carby, Hazel V. *Reconstructing Womanhood: The Emergence of the Afro-American Woman Novelist.* New York: Oxford University Press, 1987.

Christian, Barbara. *Black Women Novelists: The Development of a Tradition, 1892–1976.* Westport, CT: Greenwood Press, 1980.

Gates, Henry Louis Jr. *The Signifying Monkey: A Theory of Afro-American Literary Criticism.* New York: Oxford University Press, 1988.

Henderson, Stephen. *Understanding the New Black Poetry: Black Speech and Black Music as Poetic References.* New York: William Morrow & Company, 1973.

Johnson, James Weldon, ed. *The Book of American Negro Poetry.* New York: Harcourt, Brace and World, 1922.

Levine, Lawrence. *Black Culture and Black Consciousness: Afro-American Folk Thought From Slavery to Freedom.* New York: Oxford University Press, 1977.

Mitchell, Loften. *Black Drama: The Story of the American Negro in the Theatre.* New York: Hawthorn Books, 1967.

Sherman, Joan R. *Invisible Poets: Afro-Americans of the Nineteenth Century.* Urbana, IL: University of Illinois Press, 1974.

Wagner, Jean. *Black Poets of the United States: From Paul Laurence Dunbar to Langston Hughes.* Urbana, IL: University of Illinois Press, 1973.

Asian American Literature

Elaine H. Kim

Kim defines Asian American literature as "published creative writings in English by Americans of Chinese, Filipino, Japanese, Korean, and Southeast Asian (for now, Burmese and Vietnamese) descent about their

From the *Columbia Literary History of the United States*, ed. Emory Elliott (New York: Columbia UP, 1988): 811–21.

American experiences" (p. 249n). While acknowledging the important role that autobiography has played in Asian American literature, particularly during earlier years, she notes that in more recent years Asian American literature has diversified in response to changes in immigration and naturalization laws, increased social integration, and greater ethnic awareness. Contemporary Asian American writers are finding a broader range of publishing opportunities and are more likely to experiment with genre and form. In this essay from Emory Elliott's Columbia Literary History of the United States *(1988), Kim traces the development of Asian American literature while commenting on recurring themes and highlighting major writers.*

As writers of all ethnic and racial minority groups in the United States have noted, it is difficult to publish from a perspective that is American but not white, English, and even Protestant. This difficulty has been especially intense for Asian American writers — in part because a great ocean separates the United States from Asia, and even more because a great cultural gap separates Asian American writers from readers who lack solid information about Asian cultures and their peoples. One of the big problems facing Asian American writers has been the tendency of readers to view their works as sociological or anthropological documents rather than as literary ones. Too often Asian American works are taken to be representations of entire groups rather than expressions of individual artists. Given the large role that political and military issues have played in relations between Asian peoples and the United States, most critical assessments of Asian American literature have been influenced by political concerns.[1]

Only in the last decade has criticism begun to place social and literary issues at the center of interpretations of Asian American literature, exposing its texture, topography, tensions, and beauty. What has been revealed is that, from a historical perspective, Asian American writing mirrors the evolving self-image and consciousness of an often misunderstood and increasingly significant racial minority group, not only by documenting the experiences of Asians in the United States, but also by giving powerful expression to individual experiences and perceptions through the particular voices of Asian American artists.

Autobiography has been a popular genre among Asian American writers, largely because it has been the most marketable. Given the popular image of Asian Americans as perpetual foreigners, some publishers preferred writings with anthropological appeal over fiction. Others encouraged Asian American writers to present their work as autobiographical even when it was not. Carlos Bulosan was persuaded to write *America Is in the Heart* (1946) as personal history because it seemed likely to sell best that way. Although Maxine Hong Kingston's *The Woman Warrior* (1975) is fiction, it has been classified and sold as autobiography, or more broadly as nonfiction.

During the latter part of the nineteenth century, scholars and diplomats, who had been exempted from exclusionary legislation, published a number of "life stories" intended to counter negative views of Asia and Asians. For the most part, these writers used charming superficialities of food and dress, or ceremonies and customs, to appeal to the benign curiosity of Western readers. The first published works of this kind were Lee Yan Phou's *When I Was a Boy in China* (1887) and New Il-Han's *When I Was a Boy in Korea* (1928), narratives about upper-class childhood in China and Korea respectively.

Perhaps the best-known interpreter of Asia to the West is Lin Yutang, a self-styled cultural envoy who during four decades published a score of books on subjects ranging from "the importance of living" to tracts against communism to the feel of American life from a "Chinese" point of view. Lin's best-known work, *My Country and My People* (1937), enjoyed enormous popularity in Europe and the United States, although Chinese critics have pointed out that Lin ignored the everyday life-and-death struggles of the Chinese people under foreign domination. In contrast, Younghill Kang's quasi-autobiographical *East Goes West* (1937) marks a transition from the viewpoint of a visitor acting as a "cultural bridge" to that of an immigrant searching for a permanent place in American life. *East Goes West* is a vivid portrait of the life of Korean exiles — their work, their aspirations, and their exclusion from American social and intellectual life.

These early autobiographical works disclose a marked dissociation between their authors and the common people of both Asia and the West. Even their tentative apologetic pleas for racial tolerance are made primarily for members of the authors' own privileged class. Publishers and readers accepted them as representing all Asian Americans, but with few exceptions these works ignored the large numbers of laborers recruited for agricultural and construction work in Hawaii and the American West between 1840 and 1924.

One exception is Carlos Bulosan's quasi-autobiographical *America Is in the Heart*. A self-educated Filipino migrant worker, Bulosan wrote in order "to give literate voice to the voiceless one hundred thousand Filipinos in the United States, Hawaii, and Alaska." Bulosan's work comes to us almost by accident: He was able to study and write while recuperating from tuberculosis in a California charity hospital. *America Is in the Heart* describes the lives of the Filipino migrant workers who followed the harvest, laboring in the fields and canneries from Alaska to the Mexican border during the 1920s and 1930s. The book, which emphasizes the promise of democracy against fascism, has been translated into several European languages and was hailed by *Look* magazine as one of the fifty most important American books ever published.

Among the first published works by American-born Asians are two Chinese American autobiographies, Pardee Lowe's *Father and Glorious Descendant* (1942) and Jade Snow Wong's *Fifth Chinese Daughter*

(1945). These appeared in print at a time when Chinese, like Filipinos, were viewed as American allies and enjoyed unprecedented popularity. Both Lowe and Wong attempt to claim America as their own country, Lowe because he is so very American and Wong because she is uniquely yet acceptably Chinese. In *Father and Glorious Descendant*, Lowe describes Chinese objects as "alien" and "strange," Chinese customs as "old junk," and Chinese people as "emotionless automatons." America, on the other hand, with its schools, libraries, bathtubs, toilets, and railroad trains, Lowe presents as "God's own country." In *Fifth Chinese Daughter*, Wong introduces the reader to exotic and harmlessly interesting aspects of Chinese American family and community life. Assuming the role of an anthropological guide, she takes the reader on a tour of San Francisco Chinatown, even offering recipes for tomato beef and egg foo yung, complete with exact measurements and instructions. Both books are presented as evidence of how America's racial minorities can "succeed" through accommodation, hard work, and perseverance; and both more or less blame Chinese Americans—their families, their communities, their race—for whatever difficulties they face or failures they suffer.

While publishers encouraged writers like Lowe and Wong, they discouraged or even suppressed writers who insisted on going in other directions. Toshio Mori's *Yokohama, California*, which indirectly challenged the views of writers like Lowe and Wong, was scheduled for publication in 1941 but did not appear until 1949, after World War II had ended. By 1953, when Monica Sone's *Nisei Daughter* was published, the Japanese had long since been released from wartime detention camps and were no longer concentrated in ethnic enclaves as they had been before the war. At first glance *Nisei Daughter* appears to be a cheerful Japanese version of *Fifth Chinese Daughter*—a reassuring picture of the appealing qualities of a recently maligned group. On closer reading, however, it becomes a story of the enormous price exacted from second-generation Japanese Americans by politics and racism. In *Nisei Daughter*, the warmth and harmony of Japanese American family and community life are totally disrupted by the relocation experience.

In spite of such protests, however, during the 1970s, when the effects of the civil rights movement were being felt all across America, Japanese American "success" stories were widely publicized as evidence that racial minorities should blame themselves rather than external factors, such as racial discrimination, for social inequality. In particular, Japanese American "success" stories came to be regarded as examples that blacks and other minorities should follow. In this climate, major American publishers welcomed Japanese American autobiographies, and among those published were Daniel Inouye and Lawrence Elliott's *Journey to Washington* (1967), Daniel Okimoto's *American in Disguise* (1971), Jim Yoshida and Bill Hosokawa's *The Two Worlds of*

Jim Yoshida (1972), and Jeanne Wakatsuki Houston and James D. Houston's *Farewell to Manzanar* (1973).

When it was first published, John Okada's *No-No Boy* (1957) was not favorably received. *Fifth Chinese Daughter* had been read by a quarter of a million people and was still being used in junior high and high school literature classes in 1975 as the best example of Chinese American literature. The first edition of *No-No Boy* had still not sold out when Okada died in 1971. Far from being another "success" story, *No-No Boy* explores the devastating effects of racism on the Japanese American community of Seattle just after the end of the war. Depicting a people incapacitated by uncertainty and self-hatred, Okada refuses to celebrate Japanese Americans as merely patient, hardworking, law-abiding, and long-suffering. To the contrary, he presents them as disfigured by the experience of relocation and racial hatred. In the *nisei* world of *No-No Boy*, no sacrifice is too great for the prize of social acceptance: The people in the community envy the war veteran who has lost his leg because his "patriotism" is evident at a glance. In Okada's confused and torn world, no one is complete: Brothers betray brothers, children turn against their parents, parents turn to alcohol or suicide, husbands desert their wives, and wives commit adultery with their husbands' friends.

In many stories that portray Asian American community life, there are no white characters at all simply because segregated existence excluded them. As a result, issues of racism and race relations are submerged. In *Yokohama, California* and *The Chauvinist and Other Stories* (1979), Toshio Mori presents Japanese American community life—featuring new immigrants and American-born characters of both sexes and all ages, farmers, laborers, small business owners, housewives, and students—in vignettes that bring out what he sees as deeply human joys and sorrows.

In half a dozen remarkable short stories published between 1949 and 1961, Hisaye Yamamoto offers a vivid picture of prewar family and community life among Japanese Americans on the West Coast, with a particular focus on women's perspectives. Yamamoto's stories concentrate on the relationships between immigrant husbands and wives and those between immigrant parents and their American-born children. Marked by subtle irony and understatement, Yamamoto's style juxtaposes two currents that reflect one of the quintessential qualities of Japanese American life. Beneath an apparently placid surface, often represented by a wholesome young *nisei* narrator, there are hints of hidden tragedy, usually tinged with death and violence. Sometimes, as in *Seventeen Syllables* (1949), Yamamoto accomplishes this by presenting fleeting glimpses into the mother's dark past and repressed desires through the half-uncomprehending eyes of the narrator daughter.

Milton Murayama's *All I Asking For Is My Body* (1975) is a powerful critique of authoritarianism and tyranny among Japanese Americans in Hawaii during the years immediately preceding World War II. Un-questioning acceptance of hierarchical authority thwarts the human freedom of dutiful sons who obey their fathers and of plantation work-ers who accept exploitation. The fictional company town of Pepelau is structured exactly like a pyramid: The plantation boss's house is built on top of the hill, followed by the houses of the Portuguese, Spanish, and *nisei* lunas (plantation foremen). Below these are the identical wood frame houses of the Japanese laborers, and at the bottom of the hill, where the toilet pipes and outhouse drainage ditches empty down-hill, are the run-down shacks of the Filipino workers.

Both Lin Yutang's *Chinatown Family* (1948) and Chin Yang Lee's *Flower Drum Song* (1957) present euphemistic portraits of Chinatown, and both quickly earned popular and financial success. By contrast, Louis Chu's *Eat a Bowl of Tea* (1961) offers a more realistic insider's view of the daily life, manners, attitudes, and problems of the Chinese American community—and it failed to gain readers or make money. Focusing on the hypocrisy and self-deception that governs Chinese American life, Chu, like Murayama, presents the picture "with love, with all the warts showing." The vital quality of Chu's portrayal results in part from his ability to appreciate the spoken language of a people who regarded verbal skill and witty exchanges as a social art.

In recent decades, the Asian population in the United States has grown and diversified primarily as a result of changes in immigration and naturalization laws. Contemporary Asian American literature re-flects this increasing diversity. Both greater social integration and new ethnic awareness have stimulated Asian American writing, in part by giving today's writers new confidence, and in part by creating markets that are less circumscribed by mainstream expectations. Some contem-porary Asian American works are privately published; others appear in Asian American or minority journals and anthologies; still others are published by small presses interested in ethnic literature. But major publishing houses have also begun to express interest in the literature emerging from the Asian American community. Having first been per-formed for Asian American audiences, David Henry Hwang's plays be-came successful in New York theaters. In 1983, four of Hwang's works appeared together under the title *Broken Promises*, making him one of the first Asian American playwrights to be published.

In a growing spirit of self-determination, contemporary Asian American writers are experimenting with genre, form, and language to express sensibilities that are uniquely their own. Poetry presentations and dramatic readings with music and dance are flourishing in com-munity forums. Recent writers blend drama with prose and poetry, fic-tion with nonfiction, and literature with history. Maxine Hong Kingston combines history, folk legends, and fictional interpretations, no one form dominating her work. Janice Mirikitani writes short stories that blend prose with poetry and poetry that is written to be accompanied by *koto* music and dance interpretations. Bienvenido N. Santos's *You Lovely People* (1965) combines the short-story and novel forms in a collection of self-contained short episodes that come together like a novel through the counterpointing of two narrative voices representing different aspects of Filipino American identity. The prose and poetry in the late Theresa Hak Kyung Cha's *Dictee* (1982) is presented in English and French and is illustrated with graphics derived from old photographs of Korea. Many writers, especially poets, are experimenting with Asian American colloquialisms. In *Yellow Light* (1982), Garrett Kaoru Hongo combines Japanese words with colloquialisms used in Japanese American communities in Hawaii and Gardena, California. The novelist Milton Murayama presents dialogue that combines direct translations of formal Japanese with both standard English and the pidgin spoken in Hawaii. *Sansei* poet Ronald Tanaka mixes traditional Japanese poetic forms with Japanese American expressions in the *Shino Suite* (1981).

Since the 1970s, Asian American writers have been concerned with filling in spaces, mending rifts, and building bridges across generations. Self-determination means telling the Asian American story from an Asian American perspective, "restoring the foundations" of a culture that has been damaged or denied by racism. Such efforts, especially the search for historical foundations, have involved not only searching for works by little-known Asian American writers but also locating and translating works written by immigrants in their native languages. *Island: Poetry and History of Chinese Immigrants on Angel Island* (1980) consists of poetry discovered on the walls of the Angel Island Detention Center barracks. The editors present this poetry as "a vivid fragment of Chinese American history and a mirror capturing the image of the past." In *Island* we hear the voices of thousands of immigrants that might otherwise have been forever lost.

Chinese American writer Laurence Yep helps repair the foundations of the Asian American heritage in *Dragonwings* (1975)—a historical novel based on a newspaper account of the Chinese Fung Joe Guey, who invented and flew a biplane in 1901. Lacking information about Guey, Yep fashions a complex character, filled with apprehensions and motivated by dreams and longing, who proves to be capable of intense love and loyalty.

Rewriting Asian American history in literature from an Asian American perspective has given life to new heroes and heroines. Playwright David Henry Hwang's *The Dance and the Railroad* (1982) is about the 1867 Chinese railroad workers' strike, and the two main characters are railroad laborers. A number of contemporary Japanese American writers have re-created the World War II era in their works to show the effects of internment on individual lives. Lawson Inada's poetry anthology is titled *Before the War* (1971), reminding us that many Japanese Americans were marked for life by the relocation experience. In *kibei* Edward Miyakawa's *Tule Lake* (1979) and Jeanne Wakatsuki Houston's *Farewell to Manzanar*, contemporary Japanese American writers probe the effects of the camp experience, as does the Japanese Canadian poet and novelist Joy Kogawa in *Obasan* (1981).

Attempts to reconstruct the lost past have also involved exploring the half-buried mysteries of parents' and grandparents' experiences. Today's Asian American writer is often forced to seek the meaning of the past in shreds of stories heard in childhood. In Wing Tek Lum's "A Picture of My Mother's Family" (1974), a poet searches for the significance of each detail in an old photograph of his family, hoping to piece together a relevant story about his half-forgotten ancestors. Similarly, Filipino poets Al Robles and Presco Tabios have devoted years to collecting the life stories and oral histories of the Filipino elderly of San Francisco—men who, like Carlos Bulosan, immigrated to America as youths and then spent their lives laboring in fields and canneries. Bienvenido N. Santos, a Filipino expatriate who has lived in the United States since 1982, says that he has tried to write about the recent immigrant community but that his attention returns continually to "old-timers among our countrymen who sat out the evening of their lives before television sets in condemned buildings." Santos continues to write about the old exiles (*You Lovely People* [1965]; *The Day the Dancers Came* [1967]; *Scent of Apples* [1979]) because "now I realize that perhaps I have also been writing about myself."

The paucity of female characters in early writings by Asian American men reflects the harsh realities of the bachelor life created by American exclusion and antimiscegenation laws. Aside from Toshio Mori, few Asian American male writers have attempted multidimensional portrayals of Asian American women, focusing instead on defining themselves as men and on exploring their status as members of a minority. With the exception of the mother in the Philippines, most of Carlos Bulosan's women are either non-Asian prostitutes or idealized white women who represent the America that the narrator seeks to enter. The Chinese woman named Mei Oi in Louis Chu's *Eat a Bowl of Tea* is part seductress and part child, which makes her intrusion into the confines of the male-dominated Chinatown ghetto of the late 1940s profoundly disruptive. But the novel is about the men. Although Mei Oi reminds us that the men have failed as husbands and fathers, she lacks their dimensions as a character: She fails to understand, let alone consciously influence, the forces that shape both her life and theirs. The female characters in John Okada's *No-No Boy* are also stick figures. In the early 1970s, Frank Chin and Jeffery Paul Chan argued that Asian American men in particular were victims of "racist love" in American society. Citing the popular image of Asian men as asexual and the popular image of Asian women as wholly sexual, imbued with an innate understanding of how to please and serve men, they noted that both images served to bolster the notion of the white man's virility. But even when female characters play significant roles, as they do in the works of Frank Chin and Jeffery Paul Chan, they usually emerge either as domineering wives or mothers or as empty-headed girl friends who provide little more than an ironic audience for the metaphysical angst of male protagonists.

Although men are sometimes portrayed compassionately and convincingly in the writings of Asian American women, they generally remain in the shadows. Hisaye Yamamoto's men are conventional and colorless compared with the spirited women who must be subdued by husbands and fathers who resemble jailers. Unable to protect, inspire, or even understand women, many male characters in Asian American women's writing tend to seek emotional or physical escape rather than confront the things that limit them. The would-be lover in Eleanor Wong Telamaque's *It's Crazy to Stay Chinese in Minnesota* (1978) departs for China, leaving the heroine to battle her problems alone. Sometimes there are striking contrasts between female characters who are triumphant boundry breakers and male characters who are too narrow and inflexible to flourish in American society. The brother in Wendy Law Yone's *The Coffin Tree* (1983) had been the strong one in Burma, but it is the sister who survives in America. The brother dies insane, leaving his sister in an alien world as the family's sole survivor.

Among both men and women writers today, intense longing for reconciliation persist. The narrator in Wakako Yamauchi's "That Was All" (1980) is haunted by her vision of the slim brown body and mocking eyes of the man whom she sees, as an aging woman, in a fleeting dream. In "The Boatmen on River Toneh" (1974), the female narrator is "swept against the smooth brown cheeks of a black-haired youth . . . and into his billowing shirt" only in death. Yet a mending of the rift may be at hand. The narrator in Shawn Hsu Wong's *Homebase* (1979) dreams of the woman he loves, while in David Henry Hwang's play *FOB* (1979), the gap between the immigrant and the American-born Chinese is bridged. During the play, the legendary woman warrior Fa Mu Lan teaches Gwan Kung, god of warriors and writers, how to survive in America; and at the end of the play Gwan Kung goes off with Steve, the immigrant. Perhaps Hwang, who says he was inspired by both Maxine Hong Kingston and Frank Chin, is consciously attempting to bridge the gap between Kingston and Chin, who have often been characterized respectively as writers for women or men.

In Asian American writing, gender has many dimensions. The "failure" of fathers is a favorite theme in Frank Chin's plays and short fiction and in Jeffery Paul Chan's short stories. Deprived of a masculine image and marked by their experience in a racist culture, male writers have struggled to destroy the myths that threaten their identities as men. The identity crises of the young stems in part from the complicity of older generations of Chinese Americans, who cling to "mildewed memories" of China or cater to tourists' exotic fantasies. Chinatown is a place of death, a "human zoo," an "elephant graveyard," and its people are like mechanical wind-up toys. Both the self and the family disintegrate, making flight the only possible means of surviving a suffocating environment. The young protagonists find establishing a new identity almost impossible, in part because the older men refuse to relinquish illusions that have limited their lives, preventing them from becoming real men. Both Chin's *Chickencoop Chinaman* (1974) and Chan's "Jackrabbit" (1974) focus on failed father-son relationships. One variation on this theme occurs in Shawn Hsu Wong's lyrical short novel, *Homebase*, where the narrator seeks and finds his true American identity through the reconciliation of a father and son who share American roots as well as a Chinese American heritage. By claiming America as his own while reaffirming the love that connects his life to the lives of his father and forefathers, the narrator affirms his American identity. Wong's Chinese American is like a wild plant commonly "condemned as a weed" that survives to bear flowers, creating beauty and shade in the most difficult conditions.

The quest for a place in American life is a recurrent theme in Asian American literature. Contemporary writers, however, focus not on accommodation or racial self-negation but on the ideal that Carlos Bulosan articulated in the 1940s, of an America of the heart, where it is possible to be both American and nonwhite. Indeed, several contemporary Asian American writers express kinship with other nonwhite Americans, especially blacks and Native Americans, who frequently appear in their works. It is a Native American who tells the narrator in *Homebase* that he must find out where his people have been and see the California town he is named for before he can claim his home, his history, and the legacy of his forefathers in America. "Soon the white snow will melt," writes poet Al Robles, and "the brown, black, yellow earth will come to life."

During the late 1960s and early 1970s, many Asian American writers began to reject assimilation into what they view as a sterile and spiritually bankrupt white American mainstream that demands nothing less than denial of one's ancestry and heritage. The war in Vietnam strengthened such attitudes, as we see in "Japs" (1978), by Janice Mirikitani, a third-generation Japanese American:

> if you're too dark
> they will kill you
> if you're too swift
> they will buy you
> if you're too beautiful
> they will rape you
> Watch with eyes open
> speak darkly
> turn your head like the owl
> behind you

Young Asian American writers have also been moved to portray the recent immigrant experience. In "Song for My Father" (1975), a poem by Jessica Tarahata Hagedorn, the narrator is caught between America, "the loneliest of countries," and the land of her father, islands of music and tropical fruits. In a satirical story titled "The Blossoming of Bongbong" (1975), Hagedorn, who emigrated from the Philippines at an early age, traces the experiences of a young Filipino immigrant in a hostile America.

Consciousness of cultural conflict is also a major theme in the work of the Korean immigrant writer Kichung Kim, whose short story, "A Homecoming" (1972), depicts the confusion of a young Korean who returns to his homeland after ten years in the United States. In Ty Park's *Guilt Payment* (1983), many of the Korean immigrant characters fail to escape the haunting memories of the life they left behind. Of the few works of fiction in English by refugees from Southeast Asia, most focus on Asia. The protagonist of Tran Van Dinh's *Blue Dragon White Tiger* (1983) is a Vietnamese who has lived in America, but the novel itself is set largely in Vietnam. *The Coffin Tree*, an important novel by Burmese immigrant writer Wendy Law Yone, tells the story of a female protagonist who moves from Burma to America, only to face a contrast so severe that she almost loses her mind.

Although familiar themes still dominate it, Asian American writing has followed Asian American experience in accommodating an ever-widening range of perspectives. The poetry of Mei Mei Berssenbrugge (*Random Possession* [1979]), Alan Chong Lau (*Songs for Jadina* [1980]), James Mitsui (*Crossing the Phantom River* [1978]), and John Yau (*Crossing Canal Street* [1976] and others) demonstrates that Asian American writers cannot be confined by "Asian American" themes or by narrow definitions of "Asian American" identity. Their writings are all the more "Asian American" because they contribute to the broadening of what that term means. The most effective poems in Cathy Song's *Picture Bride* (1983) are not the ones replete with images of jade sour plums; they are those that explore the relationship between the persona and her family, from whom she ventures forth and with whom she is eventually reconciled.

Asian American writers are stronger today than ever before, and they deserve greater recognition and support, particularly as they strive to explore aspects of Asian American experience that remain misunderstood and unappreciated. Meanwhile, as they continue to celebrate the complexity and diversity of Asian American experience, they will also contribute to the emerging mosaic of American literature and culture.

Note

1. Asian American literature is defined here as published creative writings in English by Americans of Chinese, Filipino, Japanese, Korean, and Southeast Asian (for now, Burmese and Vietnamese) descent about their American experiences.

Feminist Literary Criticism and Theory

Shari Benstock, Suzanne Ferriss, and Susanne Woods

In this chapter from their book A Handbook of Literary Feminisms *(2002), Benstock, Ferriss, and Woods trace the history of literary feminism from its initial emphasis on images of women in literature and popular culture to its later focus on women writers and a female literary tradition. As it developed, the theory met with criticism that it only spoke for middle-class, white, Western, heterosexual women. While a necessary corrective drew attention to concerns of race and gender, the authors suggest that the projects of black and lesbian critics more firmly rooted feminine identity in biology. With the introduction of poststructuralist theory, feminist literary criticism experienced a significant transformation; critics initially divided into two camps: those suspicious of theory and those who saw its potential. By the mid-1980s, feminist literary criticism and theory was firmly institutionalized, but it also took a variety of forms as it "was more inclusive and mindful of the differences among women and how such differences shaped both literature and our approaches to it" (p. 274). The authors close by noting the trend at the end of the twentieth century to move from the monolithic to the homogeneous, from the universal to the particular, and to contextualize by focusing on the contingent, tentative, and changing.*

Feminist literary criticism offers strategies for analyzing texts to emphasize issues related to gender and sexuality in works written by both men and women, but is particularly concerned with women's writing. Inherently interdisciplinary, it is not singular but plural, assuming a variety of forms and approaches to texts. Feminist literary analyses may examine:

- Images of women and representations of female experience in texts written by authors of either sex

- Women writers, including the specific qualities and concerns of female authorship and the creation of a female tradition or canon

- Women readers, focusing on the role gender plays in the reception of literary texts and the emergence of a distinct female readership

- Language, attempting to define a distinctly feminine mode of writing or *écriture féminine*

- Literary form, particularly the relationship between literary genre and gender

- Publication, noting the impact of the publishing system on the production and consumption of texts by women

From *A Handbook of Literary Feminisms* (New York: Oxford UP, 2002): 153–78.

In the early 1960s, feminist criticism and theory established itself as a distinct form of literary and cultural analysis. It emerged as part of the larger political movement for women's rights and was preceded by a long and rich tradition of literary criticism by women dating from the medieval period. The earliest critics, such as Aemilia Lanyer, Margaret Cavendish, and Aphra Behn, expressed the fundamental ambivalence of early female literary critics: faith in their powers of judgment but fear that expressing such conviction may be "unfeminine." Christine de Pisan appealed to the authority granted by her position as a woman: "in that I am indeed a woman, I can better bear witness on this aspect than he who has no experience of it." In the seventeenth and eighteenth centuries, women presiding over literary salons in France and England, such as the bluestocking circle, established themselves as judges of literary excellence and adjudicators of fame. With the rise of criticism as a separate literary establishment in the eighteenth century, women's contributions—like men's—became more formalized.

By the nineteenth century, the first wave of feminism—the push for access to equal education, the professions, and political institutions—challenged separate standards of appropriateness for female readers and high-lighted the connection between gender and genre, particularly in defense of the novel as a respectable literary form. In *Northanger Abbey* (1818), Jane Austen used Fanny Burney's novels to justify novels as works "in which the greatest powers of the mind are displayed, in which the most thorough knowledge of human nature, the happiest delineation of its varieties, the liveliest effusions of wit and humour are conveyed to the world in the best chosen language."

A century later Virginia Woolf again justified women's choice of the novel but with a difference, identifying a distinctly female literary tradition. She praised Austen and Emily Brontë for writing "as women write, not as men write." In *A Room of One's Own* (1928), Woolf noted the odd dichotomy between the "woman in fiction," as she is represented in the works of men, and the woman as author: "she pervades poetry from cover to cover; she is all but absent from history."

The second wave of feminist criticism that emerged in the early 1960s followed Woolf's lead in focusing on the place of women in literary history, creating a female canon and establishing forms of literary criticism that highlighted gender distinctions in writing, culture, and society. As a separate area of investigation, feminist literary criticism emerged in the late 1960s in the context of the contemporary women's movement and increased attention to civil rights in the United States, the intellectual revolutions undertaken by students and workers in France that toppled the government of President de Gaulle, and the Campaign for Nuclear Disarmament and the resurgence of Marxism and trade unionism in Britain. What distinguished contemporary feminist criticism from that of previous eras was the self-consciousness or self-awareness of its enterprise. Feminist literary criticism became institutionalized, conceiving itself as a collective endeavor of female writers and scholars engaged not only in the practice of literary criticism but also in establishing a tradition of women's literature and feminist critique.

Feminist Criticism 1963–71: Images of Women in Literature and Popular Culture

The publication of Betty Friedan's *The Feminine Mystique* in 1963 marked the emergence of contemporary feminist consciousness in America. Friedan's enormously popular work had resonance for many white middle-class housewives frustrated by their exclusion from the workforce and public life. The term "mystique" captured their vague feeling of dissatisfaction. Friedan questioned women's complicity in sustaining gender inequity and their passivity in accepting a narrowly defined domestic sphere of influence. She isolated the source for their indoctrination in popular depictions of femininity in women's magazines, advertisements, and popular fiction. She urged women to "raise their consciousness" through education and to recognize the stereotyped images on display in popular culture and literature.

This consciousness-raising activity was transferred to literature with the publication of Mary Ellmann's *Thinking about Women* (1968) and Kate Millett's *Sexual Politics* (1970) in America and Germaine Greer's *The Female Eunuch* (1970) in England. These early critics followed Friedan's lead in focusing on the images of women in texts by male authors. They saw literature as a manifestation of male power and an instrument of socialization. Feminist criticism exposed patriarchal constructs. Ellmann argued, for instance, that Western culture is pervaded by "thought by sexual analogy," that we tend to "comprehend all phenomena, however shifting, in terms of our original and simple sexual differences" (6). This sexual analogy reveals itself in literature in terms of 11 stereotypes of femininity; women are equated with qualities from passivity and compliance to irrationality and instability. Greer likewise argued that stereotypes of women in literature and popular culture derive from historical understandings of sexuality that equate the female with the "castrate," and found examples in the works of Blake, Strindberg, Marlowe, Shakespeare, Rabelais, and others. She took on Mailer in a debate at town hall in New York City over issues of "machoism" and male domination, as represented in his writing and in society at large.

Kate Millett's text was the most popular of these early works and hence the most influential for feminist literary criticism in the 1970s. As a result, Millett has been claimed as the "mother" of American feminist criticism. Begun as a doctoral thesis, *Sexual Politics* offered a vituperative attack on what she perceived as the misogyny of D. H. Lawrence, Norman Mailer, Henry Miller, and Jean Genet. Millett assumed that "however muted its present appearance may be, sexual dominion obtains nevertheless as perhaps the most pervasive ideology of our culture and provides its most fundamental concepts of power" (25).

These early examples of feminist criticism enhanced our understanding of both literature and gender, presenting literature as a product of culture and gender as a social construction, not a biological given. At the same time, however, they offered a reductive view of literature as an unmediated mirror of social reality, ignoring its fictional and imaginative qualities, and tended to confuse the author of the text with the characters within it. Millett, for instance, claimed that "Paul Morel is of course Lawrence himself" (246) and thus held the author accountable for the crimes of his creation. The attitudes of Lawrence and other male authors were evidence of a generalized, universal, unchanging patriarchal system of power, in which women are granted little individual possibility or potential for resistance. Almost exclusively focused on male texts, Millett, Greer, and Ellmann overlooked the position of women as authors and critics. As such, their texts have provided a problematic legacy.

Creating a Female Tradition: 1972–80

By the mid-1970s, feminist critics had turned their attention to texts written by women and shifted their focus to questions of authorship. They began recovering and creating a female literary tradition. Patricia Meyer Spacks's *The Female Imagination* (1976) examined "the ways the life of the imagination emerges in the work of women writing prose directly as women" (6–7), tracing the "themes that have absorbed female minds during the past three centuries as recorded in literature written in English." In *Literary Women* (1976), Ellen Moers identified women's writing as a "rapid and powerful" undercurrent beneath the male tradition (63). She noted, in particular, the interrelationship between women's texts—between George Eliot and Harriet Beecher Stowe, Emily Dickinson and Elizabeth Barrett Browning, and Charlotte Brontë and Harriet Martineau, tracing a distinctly female pattern of influence. According to Moers, Jane Austen "achieved the classical perfection of her fiction because there was a mass of women's novels, excellent, fair, and wretched, for her to study and improve upon. . . . The fact is that Austen studied Maria Edgeworth more attentively than Scott, and Fanny Burney more than Richardson; and she came closer to meeting Mme de Staël than she did to meeting any of the literary men of her age" (67). While Moers later claims there is no single female tradition, sensibility, or style in literature, she asserts that literary scholars have an obligation to pay their "humble toll of tribute to the great women of the past who did in fact break ground for literary women" (95). Moers's text is itself an example of the practice she describes, with chapters on "Female Realism," "Female Gothic," and an appended list of the "great" female authors. She defines literary feminism as "heroinism": women's texts featuring female protagonists "create a heroic structure for the female voice in literature" (187).

In *A Literature of Their Own* (1977), Elaine Showalter not only engaged in recovering a buried or suppressed feminine tradition but also sought to give it shape and direction. She organized English women's writing into three periods—Feminine, Feminist, and Female—divided not simply chronologically but in terms of their subject matter and their authors' conscious awareness of women's position in society and culture. During the "Feminine" period (1840–80), "women wrote in an effort to equal the intellectual achievements of the male culture, and internalized its assumptions about female nature" ("Toward," 137). Examples include George Eliot for the "distinguishing sign" of the male pseudonym, signalling women writers' desire to be accepted as the equivalent of men. Authors identified as "Feminist" (1880–1920) "reject the accommodating postures of femininity and . . . use literature to dramatize the ordeals of wronged womanhood" (138). The "purest" examples are the Amazon utopias of the 1890s, "fantasies of perfected female societies set in an England or America of the future" (138). Finally, authors of the "Female" period (1920–present) "reject both imitation and protest—two forms of dependency—and turn instead to female experience as a source of an autonomous art, extending the feminist analysis of culture to the forms and techniques of literature" (139). Showalter examined the work of Dorothy Richardson and, not surprisingly given her title's obvious allusion to *A Room of One's Own*, Virginia Woolf herself as evidence of a distinct and separate female tradition.

These early attempts to develop a history of women's literature high-lighted the politics implicit in creating the Western literary canon, arguing that this tradition was essentially a *male* tradition. Woolf, Spacks, Moers, Showalter, and others challenged the view of history as universal, convincingly demonstrating that literary history itself was influenced by the position and gender of its authors, that it was a sociocultural construction and not an unmediated reflection on the past. By drawing attention to neglected works written by women, they initiated a project that continues to this day, notably in the work of Dale Spender in Britain and Nina Baym in the United States.

The construction of a separate "female" canon has been criticized, however, for its tendency to fall into many of the errors it set out to address. Showalter's influential account of feminist literary history as divided into three historical moments presumes a progressive, linear development originating in the nineteenth century. This excludes women's writing prior to that period as well as texts that may not fit into one of its three categories. Owing to Showalter's emphasis on increasing feminist awareness, her account implicitly holds texts to twentieth-century standards. Creating a separate female canon further risks marginalizing the contributions of women writers who are considered only in relation to or reaction against the male standard. And, like the male tradition it seeks to reject, the female tradition is conceived of as comprehensive when it is in fact and necessarily partial, as is any history of literature. Take, for instance, Moers's claim that "Women poets do not complain of the power of love . . . they rejoice in love and boast of the transformation in themselves resulting from what Kate Chopin called 'The Awakening.' . . . There seems to be more fire than ice in women's love poetry" (256). Here she not only generalizes about women's love poetry but also argues that male poets, by contrast, "draw on the imagery of cold, because their beloved's resistance, denial, and betrayal are the principle occasions dramatized in their poems" (256). Certainly readers would be quick to take issue with such a simplistic distinction between female passion and male rationalism.

By the late 1970s, feminist criticism revealed a self-consciousness about the practice of feminist literary history and the feminist critical enterprise itself. In "Toward a Feminist Poetics" (1979), Showalter identified "two distinct varieties of feminist criticism." The first, "feminist critique," is focused on

> *woman as reader*—with woman as the consumer of male-produced literature, and with the way in which the hypothesis of a female reader changes our apprehension of a given text, awakening us to the significance of its sexual codes. . . . [I]t is a historically grounded inquiry which probes the ideological assumptions of literary phenomena. Its subjects include the images and stereotypes of women in literature, the omissions of and misconceptions about women in criticism, the fissures in male-constructed literary history. It is also concerned with the exploitation and manipulations of the female audience, especially in popular culture and film; and with the analysis of woman-as-sign in semiotic systems. (128)

Representative works of this form of critique included Kate Millett's *Sexual Politics* and Judith Fetterley's *The Resisting Reader* (1978). Fetterley contended that "American literature is male. To read the canon of what is currently considered classic American literature is perforce to identify as male" (564). She advocated, by contrast, that "the first act of the feminist critic must be to become a resisting rather than assenting reader and, by this refusal to assent, to begin the process of exorcising the male mind that has been implanted in us" (570).

Showalter's second type focused on *"woman as writer*—with woman as the producer of textual meaning, with the history, themes, genres, and structures of literature by women. Its subjects include the psychodynamics of female creativity, linguistics and the problem of a female language; the trajectory of the individual or collective female literary career; literary history; and, of course, studies of particular writers and works" (128). She termed this form "gynocriticism," adapted from the French term *la gynocritique.*

Despite Showalter's contention that "both kinds are necessary," the second—"woman as writer"—in fact predominated from the late 1970s and into the 1980s. Feminists emphasized not women's equality with, but their difference from, men, noting that such differences are not natural or essential but culturally determined. According to Stephen Heath:

> Difference . . . speedily comes round to an essence of woman and man, male and female, a kind of anthropologico-biological nature. But men and women are not simply given biologically; they are given in history and culture, in a social practice and representation that includes biological determinations, shaping and defining them in its process. The appeal to an "undeniable" biological reality as essential definition is always itself a form of social representation, within a particular structure of assumption and argument. (222)

For literary critics, the social construction of difference could potentially account for issues of female authorship and provide a framework for discussion of texts as distinctly feminine. Their critical claim clearly echoes Virginia Woolf's discussions of sexual difference and androgyny written decades earlier.

Sandra Gilbert and Susan Gubar's *The Madwoman in the Attic* (1979) offered at once a revisionist literary history focused on women authors of the nineteenth century and a theory of female literary creation derived from a feminist reinterpretation of the "anxiety of influence" Harold Bloom had traced in male authors. Bloom had argued that male authors suffer anxiety when confronted by the literary achievements of their predecessors; Gilbert and Gubar argued that the female artist faced a doubled anxiety, cowed not only by her male literary predecessors but also by strictures against feminine authorship. They asserted that the pen is a "metaphorical penis" and that traditional metaphors of authorship focus on the writer as "father" of his text. How can a woman thus pick up the pen? Further, they argued that "for the female artist the essential process of self-definition is complicated by all those patriarchal definitions that intervene between herself and herself" (17). Patriarchal texts have offered two competing visions of woman as the "eternal feminine"—the "angel in the house" who is passive, docile, and selfless—or as the monstrous creature, the "madwoman," who refuses this submissive role and asserts herself—in action and in writing.

Women writers of the nineteenth century, they argued, resolved this dilemma through duplicity and subversion:

> Women from Jane Austen and Mary Shelley to Emily Brontë and Emily Dickinson produced literary works that are in some sense palimpsestic, works whose surface designs conceal or obscure deeper, less accessible (and less socially acceptable) levels of meaning. Thus these authors

managed the difficult task of achieving true female literary authority by simultaneously conforming to and subverting patriarchal literary standards. (73)

In Dickinson's words, the woman writer would "Tell all the Truth but tell it slant." By such duplicity, according to Gilbert and Gubar, the female author could appear as an "angel" by ostensibly conforming to patriarchal conventions while in fact subverting them in her texts.

The result is a "female schizophrenia of authorship," the figure for which is the madwoman, such as Bertha Mason in Charlotte Brontë's *Jane Eyre*. She is the *"author's* double, an image of her own anxiety and rage." As such, the female writer's monster is a parody of patriarchal conventions:

> In projecting their anger and dis-ease into dreadful figures, creating dark doubles for themselves and their heroines, women writers are both identifying with and revising the self-definitions patriarchal culture has imposed on them. All the nineteenth- and twentieth-century literary women who evoke the female monster in their novels and poems alter her meaning by virtue of their own identification with her. For it is usually because she is in some sense imbued with inferiority that the witch-monster-madwoman becomes so crucial an avatar of the writer's own self. (79)

Gilbert and Gubar's readings of these texts served as a model of feminist literary criticism in which the reader is attentive to textual strategies, to subversions and parodies of traditional plots, images, and characters as a means of recuperating the female author and her text. This strategy of reading against the grain proved influential for feminist criticism in the 1980s.

Despite the obvious complexity and sophistication of their argument, Gilbert and Gubar's reading of women's literary history shared some of the same weaknesses of earlier models. Like Showalter, Gilbert and Gubar focused on the nineteenth century almost exclusively, although later they were to extend their argument to twentieth-century texts in their three-volume series *No Man's Land* (1988–1994) and, it could be argued, in *The Norton Anthology of Literature by Women*, first published in 1985. Critics of their work have objected to the image of the woman author as victim and her texts as documents of suffering. Others have noted the relatively small number of writers to which they apply their thesis, claiming that while it may well apply to the major writers of the late nineteenth century it cannot serve as a model for all writing by women.

Dialogue among feminist critics took place in the pages of journals, at conferences, and in the classroom, as women's studies programs developed on university campuses. Journals devoted to women's studies — such as *Signs: Journal of Women in Culture and Society, Tulsa Studies in Women's Literature, Women's Studies, Feminist Studies,* and *differences* — were established in the late 1970s and early 1980s. They fueled the conversation among feminist scholars and became an important means of supporting women's studies programs across the country and legitimating feminist scholarship in a wide variety of fields, including sociology, anthropology, biology, medicine, history, art, and literary studies. Teachers created classroom packets — syllabi, reading lists of primary works and secondary materials — which became the basis for establishing a textbook market for feminist studies across various disciplines. University presses at Columbia, Cornell, Indiana, and elsewhere distributed feminist journals and initiated series devoted to publishing individual and collective works of feminist criticism. Feminist literary studies in fact led the way by posing the types of questions that would guide other forms of feminist scholarship: Are women presented differently in texts written by women and men? Does a literary text written by a woman differ significantly from a text written by a man? Do female readers approach texts differently? Is there a link between gender and genre? How have the processes of production and canonization affected views of women's literature? Journals not specifically devoted to feminist scholarship produced special issues on feminist literary criticism and theory: *Diacritics*, *Critical Inquiry*, and *Modern Fiction Studies*, to name but a few. But as feminist criticism became increasingly institutionalized, it also came under fire — from within.

Resistances: Black, Lesbian, and Marxist Criticism, 1977–81

Feminist literary critics of the 1970s were taken to task for claiming to speak for all women when in fact they spoke largely for white, Western, heterosexual women of the middle class. Black feminists, such as Alice Walker, Barbara Smith, Deborah McDowell, bell hooks, Audre Lorde, and Susan Willis, argued that black women writers were doubly oppressed, ignored by both white feminists and black literary critics, who were predominantly male. Two important volumes published in the early 1980s collected essays originally published in feminist journals in the late 1970s that were critical of white, mainstream feminism and outlined plans of action for drawing attention to women of color: *This Bridge Called My Back: Writings by Radical Women of Color* (1981), edited by Cherríe Moraga and Gloria Anzaldúa, and *All the Women Are White, All the Blacks Are Men, But Some of Us Are Brave* (1982), edited by Gloria T. Hull, Patricia Bell Scott, and Barbara Smith. Both books gave impetus to creating a separate canon of works by women of color and defining critical approaches that would account for their differences from white women as well as from men.

A collection of essays, poems, and testimonials, *This Bridge Called My Back* gave voice to marginalized women of color:

> We are the colored in a white feminist movement.
> We are the feminists among the people of our culture.
> We are often the lesbians among the straight.

Deliberately heterogeneous and highly personal, the pieces in the volume reflected the contributors' "flesh and blood experiences to concretize a vision that can begin to heal our 'wounded knee.'" As the title suggests, the collection was an effort to "bridge" the emerging divide among feminists. It was a form of consciousness raising for both women of color and white middle-class women.

While *This Bridge Called My Back* did not explicitly outline a new feminist project, *But Some of Us Are Brave* set out to advance the cause of black women's studies, supplying reading lists and syllabi listing the literary works of black women. The collection also included Smith's influential essay, "Toward a Black Feminist Criticism" (1977). She contended, "Black women's existence, experience, and culture and the brutally complex systems of oppression which shape these are in the 'real world' of white and/or male consciousness beneath consideration, invisible, unknown" (168). Launching a savage attack on Showalter, Moers, and Spacks for overlooking black and Third World women, Smith outlined three principles for a black feminist literary criticism: (1) It would "work from the assumption that Black women writers constitute an identifiable literary tradition"; (2) it would be "highly innovative, embodying the daring spirit of the works themselves"; and (3) it would trace the "lesbian" subtext in black women's novels (174–75). Smith applied these principles in a highly personal reading of Toni Morrison's *Sula*. She sees Nel and Sula's friendship as "suffused with an erotic romanticism," a bond strengthened by race, as "Morrison depicts in literature the necessary bonding that has always taken place between Black women for the sake of barest survival" (176–77). In Smith's view, Nel falls prey to convention by marrying an unexceptional man, while Sula defies patriarchal values by rejecting heterosexual marriage. As such, "Sula's presence in her community functions much like the presence of lesbians everywhere to expose the contradictions of supposedly 'normal' life" (178). Although Sula has sex with men, she does so, according to Smith, only to delve further into herself. Instead, "the deepest communion and communication in the novel occurs between two women who love each other" (180). Thus, Morrison's novel is an "exceedingly lesbian novel" (180). Smith's own essay, she hoped, would "lead everyone who reads it to examine *everything* that they have ever thought and believed about feminist culture and to ask themselves how their thoughts connect to the reality of Black women's writing and lives" (183).

Smith's essay did provoke a response from Deborah McDowell, who agreed that black women writers were "disenfranchised" by white feminist critics and by black scholars, "most of whom are males." She pointed out, however, that Smith's articulation of a black feminist aesthetic raised difficulties of its own. McDowell noted that some of the key features of black women's texts could be found in male texts as well and pressed for greater attention to how such elements were used differently by women, a project later taken up by Susan Willis and others in the mid-1980s. She further asked, "Are there noticeable differences between the languages of Black females and Black males?" (189), anticipating the critical turn toward the examination of language that would characterize the 1980s. Finally, McDowell argued that Smith's definition of lesbianism was "vague and imprecise," that Smith had "simultaneously oversimplified and obscured the issue of lesbianism" and in so doing overlooked *Sula*'s "density and complexity, its skillful blend of folklore, omens, and dreams, its metaphorical and symbolic richness" (190). Following the example of author Alice Walker, who had begun to trace a tradition of black women writers in *In Search of Our Mother's Gardens* (1974), McDowell advocated a "contextual approach to Black women's literature" that would expose "the conditions under which literature is produced, published, and reviewed" (192).

Despite its limitations, Smith's essay drew attention to two distinctly marginalized groups within feminist literary criticism — women of color and lesbians — and focused on the identity of the female reader and author, not simply on the basis of her sex, but on her race and sexuality. Lesbian feminists argued that they, like black women, experienced a doubled oppression — sexism and homophobia. The neglect of lesbian authors and lesbian themes in literature was a serious oversight by feminists that seemed all the more striking given the role of lesbians in radical feminist politics in the late 1960s and early 1970s. Shulamith Firestone published *The Dialectic of Sex: The Case for a Feminist Revolution* in 1970, which argued that women had been oppressed on the basis of their reproductive capacity and advocated an end to "the tyranny of the biological family" through women's control of their reproductive functions and a return to a polymorphous sexuality. Ti-Grace Atkinson's *Amazon Odyssey* (1974) took Firestone's thesis a step further, contending that "love" was in fact an institution of heterosexual sex and that feminist revolutionary practice could be found in its rejection. Charlotte Bunch argued that true feminism was lesbianism. Poet Adrienne Rich's "Compulsory Heterosexuality and Lesbian Existence" (1980) outlined a lesbian continuum, a range of "woman-identified experience" from friendship to sexual intimacy.

The woman-identified woman should be a focus of feminist literary criticism, according to Bonnie Zimmerman. In "What Has Never Been: An Overview of Lesbian Feminist Criticism" (1981), she noted a profound absence of lesbian material in the anthologies and collections produced by influential American literary critics, including Moers, Spacks, Showalter, and Gilbert and Gubar. She sought to define a lesbian criticism or "world view" based on the assumption "that a woman's identity is not defined only by her relation to a male world and male literary tradition . . . , that powerful bonds between women are a crucial factor in women's lives, and that the sexual and emotional orientation of a woman profoundly affects her consciousness and thus her creativity" (201). The lesbian critic would be attentive to heterosexist assumptions and contribute to the development of a lesbian canon, a project initiated by Jeannette Foster in *Sex Variant Women in Literature* (1956) and extended by Jane Rule in *Lesbian Images* (1975) and Lillian Faderman in *Surpassing the Love of Men: Romantic Friendship and Love between Women from the Renaissance to the Present* (1981). According to Faderman,

> "Lesbianism" describes a relationship in which two women's strongest emotions and affections are directed toward each other. Sexual contact may be part of the relationship to a greater or lesser degree, or it may be entirely absent. By preference the two women spend most of their time together and share most aspects of their lives with each other. (17–18)

Based on this definition, the lesbian literary tradition would extend from Mary Wortley Montagu, Mary Wollstonecraft, Anna Seward, and Sarah Orne Jewett to the women of the "first self-identified lesbian feminist community in Paris" in the early twentieth century (Natalie Barney, Colette, Djuna Barnes, Radclyffe Hall, Renée Vivien, and peripherally Gertrude Stein). Analysis would focus on "the images, stereotypes, and mythic presence of lesbians in fiction by or about lesbians" as well as a lesbian literary style.

Critics attentive to race and sexuality introduced a necessary corrective by pointing out the dangers of taking gender alone as a lens for critical investigation and reminding feminists to take differences among women into account as they investigated images of women in literary texts and expanded the canon to include works by women. In many respects, however, the projects of black and lesbian critics shared, or perhaps augmented, the weaknesses of the mainstream feminism they criticized. Feminine identity was more firmly grounded in biology, given additional emphasis on race and sexuality. While the positive reconstruction of a group identity was strategically essential as a response to degrading and marginalizing cultural practices, the newly created categories of "black female" and "lesbian" risked becoming as monolithic as "woman."

As a result, feminist critics influenced by Marxist analyses of culture stressed attention to historical specificity, to the material conditions influencing the production of women's texts. In *Women's Oppression Today* (1979) Michèle Barrett argued that literary texts must be considered in relation to class structures and to the cultural institutions—including education and publishing—that support both economic and gender inequities. Taking Virginia Woolf as her example, she asked, "what are the consequences for the woman author of historical changes in the position of women in society?" (1). Her reading attended to Woolf's limited access to formal education and her domestic isolation as historical conditions affecting women that revealed themselves in Woolf's novels and criticism. The London-based Marxist-Feminist Literary Collective, whose members included Cora Kaplan and Mary Jacobus as well as Barrett, produced readings of Charlotte Brontë's *Jane Eyre, Shirley, Villette,* and Elizabeth Barrett Browning's *Aurora Leigh* that identified the marginal position of women writers in the mid-nineteenth century as part of the general exclusion of women "from the exercise of political power and their separation from production." Ironically, despite their attention to material conditions, such readings continued to privilege the works of a particular class, excluding texts by working-class women and women of color. Many women also argued that in their focus on historical determinism, Marxist feminists overlooked the role of the imagination or the psyche of the individual author in literary creation. These positions attentive to class, sexuality, and race were to reemerge in more complex and convincing forms in the mid-1980s and exert a profound influence on feminist literary studies throughout the 1990s and beyond.

Theory, Language, and Écriture Féminine: 1980–85

In the early 1980s ("around 1981," according to Jane Gallop) feminist literary criticism underwent a sea change with the introduction of post-structuralist theory. Broadly defined, post-structuralist theory is concerned with language in shaping identity and history, and its premises are drawn from philosophy. From deconstruction to psychoanalysis, post-structuralist theory challenged traditional intellectual categories and practices, calling into question the concept of the individual as a unified subject, the stability of meaning, and the "truth" of history.

Feminist critics were initially divided between those suspicious of theory's influence and those who recognized its potential for reinvigorating and enhancing feminist literary criticism. The debate split along lines of gender and nationality, with post-structuralist theory defined by its critics as male and French, "as manly and aggressive as nuclear physics — not intuitive, expressive, and feminine, but strenuous, rigorous, impersonal, and virile," in the words of Showalter ("Feminist Poetics," 140). Others were more open to possibility. In "Dancing through the Minefield: Some Observations on the Theory, Practice, and Politics of Feminist Literary Criticism" (1980), Annette Kolodny argued:

> In my view, our purpose is not and should not be the formulation of any single reading method or potentially Procrustean set of critical procedures nor, even less, the generation of prescriptive categories for some dreamed-of non-sexist literary canon. Instead, as I see it, our task is

to initiate nothing less than a playful pluralism, responsive to the possibilities of multiple critical tools and methods, but captive of none, recognizing that the many tools needed for our analysis will necessarily be
largely inherited and only partly of our own making. (161)

Early warnings of the dangerous influence of "white, male" theory on
feminist projects gave way as post-structuralist theory exerted its influence, enriching and extending feminist critique by drawing attention to another dimension of literature: language.

The first feminist theories influenced by post-structuralist philosophy emerged in France and came to be known collectively as "French
feminism" to Anglo-Americans. Contemporary French feminist thought,
however, derived from both Anglo-American and French feminist traditions. Virginia Woolf's own position as a literary stylist and experi-
menter led her to ponder the possibility of a distinctly feminine mode
of writing, to question what, if anything, distinguished women's writing
from men's. The same impulse can clearly be seen in attempts to define
écriture féminine (feminine writing). Feminists working in France were
also profoundly influenced by Simone de Beauvoir's *The Second Sex*
(1949), which applied existential philosophy to the position and condition of women. In her classic text, de Beauvoir argued that woman has
been defined as man's "Other," that she has been conceived of as an
object with no right to her own subjectivity. She notes that this is not a
natural condition, but a social and cultural construction: "One is not
born a woman; one becomes one." De Beauvoir sought to explain the
definition of woman as Other in biology, psychoanalysis, and Marxism,
emphasizing that women internalize their objectified status.

The works of the French feminists were first published in France in
the 1970s, but most Anglophone readers were introduced to them through
Elaine Marks and Isabelle de Courtivron's translations in *New French
Feminisms* (1980). As such their influence on feminist criticism and theory in Britain and the United States was felt in the mid- to late 1980s.

The "new" French feminists—most notably Hélène Cixous, Luce
Irigaray, and Julia Kristeva—emphasized that woman is constructed
as Other through language. In "The Laugh of the Medusa" (1976; "Le Rire
de la méduse," 1975), Cixous argued that "nearly the entire history of
writing is confounded with the history of reason. . . . It has been one with
the phallocentric tradition" (249). Consequently, "writing is precisely *the
very possibility of change*, that space that can serve as a springboard for
subversive thought, the precursory movement of a transformation of social and cultural structures" (249). The identification and practice of *écriture féminine* thus has the potential for undermining woman's position as
Other by establishing her as the subject of her own writing, and for transforming her position in culture and politics as well.

In asserting the primacy of language, Cixous borrowed from post-
structuralist thought, the deconstructive theory of Jacques Derrida,

and the psychoanalytic theory of Jacques Lacan. Derrida, following Martin Heidegger, offered a critique of Western metaphysics, arguing that Western thought is grounded in a series of binary oppositions: light/darkness, good/evil, soul/body, life/death, mind/matter, speech/ writing, and so on. The terms are not conceived of as equal, but exist in a hierarchical structure (light is privileged over darkness, good over evil, etc.). Fundamentally, Derrida argued, Western thought has privileged unity, identity, and immediacy, or presence, over absence (light is presence; darkness is its absence). In "Sorties" (1980; from *La Jeune née* [The Newly Born Woman], 1975), Cixous extended Derrida's argument by focusing on gender, contending that implicit in each binary opposition is a distinction between man/woman, masculine/feminine. Thus she accounted for woman's position in Western culture as Other: She is defined in opposition to, and in terms of, man. He is present; she is absent. He is associated with being, she is associated with death.

According to Derrida, such meanings are produced in language. The structural linguist Ferdinand de Saussure argued that the process of signification was characterized by difference. Meaning was produced not on the basis of the sign's relation to its referent (e.g., the word "cat" meaning the furry little animal). Instead, Saussure argued that the sign (word) was composed of two parts, the spoken or written word (signifier) and its mental concept (signified). The bond between the signifier and the signified was arbitrary; there is no natural connection, for instance, between the signifier "light" and idea of light itself. Meaning emerges only through the distinction of one signifier from another. We understand the signifier "light" only in opposition to the signifier "dark." We understand "light" as different not only from "dark" but also from other signifiers ("might," "bright," "tight"). Meaning also unfolds in time, along the chain of signification, the sequence of signifiers that unfolds in time as we speak (or read) words.

Derrida complicated this understanding—hence his theory is *post-structuralist*—by arguing that "within the system of language, there are only differences." The process of making meaning obviates the possibility of a sign bearing a stable, unified meaning. For instance, we understand the word "cat" in part because it is not "dog" or "hat." In the jazz world, "cat" refers not to the furry creature but to a human being, a "cool cat." Signification is not a static process, but a never-ending play of one signifier (that is present in language) against a series of others (that are absent). It is characterized not only by difference, but deferral, for meaning is deferred along the chain of signification, which never ends. Derrida's critique of Western thought focused, then, on how we have tended to stop the play of signification and arbitrarily privilege one meaning over other possible meanings.

In perhaps his most famous example, taken from Plato's *The Phaedrus*, Derrida examined the apparent contradiction between the two meanings of the Greek word "pharmakon" (from which the word "pharmacy" is derived). In Greek, "pharmakon" is an ambiguous term, meaning both poison and remedy. In *The Phaedrus*, Plato refers to writing as a "pharmakon," typically taken to mean that writing is poisonous, open to misinterpretation and misuse. Writing is seen to be dangerous, in the absence of the speaker who can confirm its meaning. Derrida, however, noting that "pharmakon" may also mean remedy, argues that writing may serve a positive role. It can enhance speech, aid memory, and serve as a record of history that lives on beyond the speaker. Writing, can, in fact, not be seen as either poison or remedy but as embodying both elements simultaneously. Deconstructive practice thus undermines or subverts the closure of the binary opposition. Derrida conceived of deconstruction as a two-stage process that first exposes binary thought in language and then demonstrates the continuing play of difference at work.

In "The Laugh of the Medusa," Cixous emphasized that writing has sustained the opposition between male and female. "Woman" has been defined in language, as a signifier defined in opposition to "man." Cixous advocated the deconstruction of this opposition:

> If woman has always functioned "within" the discourse of man, a signifier that has always referred back to the opposite signifier which annihilates its specific energy and diminishes or stifles its very different sounds, it is time for her to dislocate this "within," to explode it, turn it around, and seize it; to make it hers, containing it, taking it in her own mouth, biting that tongue with her very own teeth to invent for herself a language to get inside of. (257)

Defined in opposition to man, woman has been relegated to a subordinate position within language. Cixous proposed an alternative discursive practice—a *new insurgent* writing—as a means of unsettling the opposition that devalues the feminine. Writing, in this sense, means "working (in) the in-between, inspecting the process of the same and of the other without which nothing can live." Cixous capitalized on Derrida's assertion that Western thought is "phallogocentric," that its binary logic privileges the masculine, through the "transcendental signifier" of the phallus. The term "phallus" refers not simply to the male organ but to the power accrued to its possessor in language and in culture.

In her analysis of phallogocentrism, Cixous also relied on innovations in psychoanalytic theory. The French psychoanalyst Jacques Lacan traced the origins of patriarchal authority in the process of human maturation, transforming Freud's theory of psychosexual development by focusing on the acquisition and role of language. Lacan distinguished between the Imaginary and Symbolic orders: the Imaginary refers to the infant's early, preverbal relationship to the mother, the Symbolic to the order of language, an order associated with the father. Prior to acquiring language, the child experiences an imaginary unity with the mother's body and has no sense of itself as an independent being.

According to Lacan, separation of the infant from the mother begins during the mirror stage, normally when the child is six to eight months old. During this period, the child encounters its reflection—not necessarily in an actual mirror but even in its mother's eyes or the sight of another child—and thus perceives itself as separate from the mother's body. But what the child perceives is not the self, but an image of the self. It perceives itself as an independent entity when, in fact, it is still physically dependent on the mother for its survival. Hence the origin of the self emerges from a misrecognition that the child can stand on its own, move of its own volition, and control physical space. A radical split has been introduced between the projected mirror ideal and the actual self that perceives the image.

The psychological construction of selfhood begun during the mirror stage is only resolved during the Oedipal crisis. Following Freud, Lacan argued that the dyadic unity the child perceives between itself and the mother is broken by a third, the father, through the threat of castration. According to Freudian theory, the boy perceives his difference from his mother in the recognition that he possesses a penis, like the father, and that she does not. Forced, owing to the incest taboo, to repress his desire for the mother, the boy identifies with the father as the figure of authority and the law. In other words, while the physical manifestation of difference is the penis, the psychological manifestation is the power accorded to the father as head of the household. For girls, the Oedipal crisis is far more complicated, as Freud himself noted in his essay "On Femininity" (1932). He posited that the girl recognizes that she, like the mother, is already "castrated," that is, lacking in authority because she lacks a penis: "She makes her judgement and her decision in a flash. She has seen it and knows that she is without it, and wants to have it." She thus turns her desire from the "castrated" mother to the father.

Feminists from Charlotte Perkins Gilman to Kate Millett have mocked Freud's account, noting that by focusing on the presence or absence of the penis it emphasizes biological determinism. It institutes, in Gilman's words, "phallic worship" and reduces women to passivity and absence. Others, like Juliet Mitchell in *Psychoanalysis and Feminism* (1974), have noted that psychoanalysis is not a justification but an explanation, a description and not a prescription, for the privileging of masculinity in Western culture. Freudian theory has, in fact, potential value for feminist theory because it demonstrates that sexual definition is not innate or inborn, but constructed and precarious:

> Freud's writing shows that sexual difference is . . . a hesitant and imperfect construction. Men and women take up positions of symbolic and polarised opposition against the grain of a multifarious and bisexual disposition. . . . The lines of that division are fragile in exact proportion

to the rigid insistence with which our culture lays them down; they constantly converge and threaten to coalesce. (Rose 226–27)

Boys are taught at an early age not to cry, not to show weakness, not to reveal their emotions, to instead be competitive and independent. Girls learn to acquiese to authority, care for others, display their emotions and sexuality, and repress their independence and self-determination. As we acquire a sense of selfhood we are forced to take up a position on one side of the sexual divide between masculinity and femininity. Identifying the psychosocial processes that privilege masculinity may enable women to challenge and subvert them.

Lacan thus provided feminist theorists with an additional insight and opportunity, for he added to Freud's account that the development of a sense of self coincides with the acquisition of language, with entry into the Symbolic order. As we take up a subject position on one side of the sexual divide we also take up a position in language. When we identify ourselves as subjects, as "I," we define ourselves in terms of the Other; we are stating, in effect, that we are not "you" or any other available subject position. When we say "I am" we mean "I am she (or he)." Gender difference is the ground for identity. Lacan contended that the Symbolic realm is governed by the Law of the Father owing not simply to the incest taboo and threat of castration, but to the fact that in the definition of subjectivity, the phallus becomes the "transcendental signifier," the basis by which gender is determined and subject position assigned. The subject, however, is constructed through separation and denied imagined wholeness with the mother due to the intrusion of paternal law. As a result, woman is associated with lack and with the "repressed."

Feminists working in the Lacanian psychoanalytic tradition sought to subvert the position accorded woman in the phallogocentric symbolic order. As Cixous argued, "Their 'symbolic' exists, it holds power. . . . But we are in no way obliged to deposit our lives in their bank of lack. . . . We have no womanly reason to pledge allegiance to the negative" (255). Instead, she envisioned a feminine response in language, an *écriture féminine*:

It is by writing, from and toward women, and by taking up the challenge of speech which has been governed by the phallus, that women will confirm women in a place other than that which is reserved in and by the symbolic, that is, in a place other than silence. Women should break out of the snare of silence. They shouldn't be conned into accepting a domain which is the margin or the harem. (251)

She advocated the paradoxical action of making the silence speak, of giving voice to that which has been marginalized and repressed. The result would be revolutionary: "when the 'repressed' of their culture and their society returns, it's an explosive, *utterly* destructive, staggering return" (256).

Écriture féminine is associated with the pre-Oedipal stage of imagined wholeness with the maternal body:

> Women must write through their bodies, they must invent the impregnable language that will wreck partitions, classes, and rhetorics, regulations and codes, they must submerge, cut through, get beyond the ultimate reserve-discourse, including the one that laughs at the very idea of pronouncing the word "silence." (256)

Associated with the body, *écriture féminine* is characterized by its drives and rhythms, its suppleness and fluidity. It would inscribe women's sexuality, "its infinite and mobile complexity." Cixous further envisioned that, repressed within the symbolic, within writing, women's language exists in a "privileged relationship with the voice." An *écriture féminine* would thus capture the patterns of speech.

Cixous's idea of an *écriture féminine* was visionary, an outline of a practice that does not yet exist. She had encountered glimpses of it in the avant-garde practices of modernist texts written by male authors, in James Joyce's *Ulysses* when Molly Bloom affirms " . . . And yes," and in Jean Genet's *Pompes funèbres* when "he was led by Jean." If it did exist, it would resist definition:

> It is impossible to *define* a feminine practice of writing, and this is an impossibility that will remain, for this practice can never be theorized, enclosed, coded—which doesn't mean that it doesn't exist. But it will always surpass the discourse that regulates the phallocentric system; it does and will take place in areas other than those subordinated to philosophico-theoretical domination. (253)

Cixous challenges the primacy of philosophical categories and hierarchies, deliberately avoiding "rational" discourse in favor of a poetic style. Thus, Cixous—in an apparent contradiction—did not "define" *écriture féminine* but instead demonstrated its practice in her own writing. Her texts are not organized in a linear narrative, and frequent punning enacts the doubleness or multivalence of language. Cixous's assertion that "she writes in white ink," for instance, embodies the principles she outlines. "She" refers at once to woman, to the maternal, and to Cixous herself. Writing in "white" ink is a contradictory image of the feminine practice of making the silence speak. And white ink is a literary equivalent of mother's milk.

Luce Irigaray similarly defined feminine language in terms of the body, but rejected the association Cixous established with the maternal body as "a privileging of the maternal over the feminine," of accepting a male-derived definition of the "phallic maternal." Instead, Irigaray equated female language with "the multiplicity of female desire." In

"This Sex Which Is Not One" (1980; *Ce Sexe qui n'en est pas un*, 1977), she argued that "female sexuality has always been theorized within masculine parameters" (99). Psychoanalytic theory casts her fate as "one of 'lack,' 'atrophy' (of her gentials), and 'penis envy,'" since the penis is the only recognized sex organ of any worth" (99). The dominant phallic system privileges sight over touch and mono- (or phallic) sexuality over the multiplicity of female desire and defines sexuality according to a binary opposition where the "other sex" is "only the indispensable complement to the only sex" (103). As woman's desire has been repressed, so has her language: "Woman's desire most likely does not speak the same language as man's desire, and it probably has been covered over by the logic that has dominated the West since the Greeks" (101). Like Cixous, Irigaray resisted philosophical thinking and advocated a subversive, revolutionary practice in language, giving voice to woman's desire.

Within the binary logic of patriarchal culture, "she resists all adequate definition" (101). Irigaray argued that Western culture has privileged sight. This dominant economy of scopophilia has a double effect: Woman is reduced to an object of the male gaze as the eroticized female body becomes a "beautiful object." But "her sexual organ represents the horror of nothing to see" (101); it is not visible. Instead, Irigaray argued that feminine sexuality escapes scopophilic logic, as woman takes pleasure more from touching than from looking. Her desire evades masculine control for "she touches herself by and within herself directly, without mediation" (100).

To the argument that woman has no visible sex organ, Irigaray countered, "She has at least two of them, but they are not identifiable as ones. . . . Her sexuality, always at least double, is in fact *plural*," for "*woman has sex organs just about everywhere*" (102, 103). Resisting binary logic, Irigarary argued "*She is neither one nor two*" (101). Instead, "her pleasure is far more diversified, more multiple in its differences, more complex, more subtle, than is imagined" (103).

Feminine desire is reflected in language, which echoes its rhythms and pulsations:

> "She" is indefinitely other in herself. That is undoubtedly the reason she is called temperamental, incomprehensible, perturbed, capricious—not to mention her language in which "she" goes off in all directions and in which "he" is unable to discern the coherence of any meaning. Contradictory words seem a little crazy to the logic of reason, and inaudible for him who listens with ready-made grids, a code prepared in advance. In her statements—at least when she dares to speak out—woman retouches herself constantly. She just barely separates from herself some chatter, an exclamation, a half-secret, a sentence left in suspense—when she returns to it, it is only to set out again from another point of pleasure or pain. (103)

Irigaray, like Cixous, envisioned *écriture féminine* as nonlinear, characterized by repetition, incompletion, disruption, and resistance to reason.

Woman's position as subject of language, however, is complicated by her definition within the symbolic order. Defined as lack or absence, she is, in effect, not a subject in her own right but only defined in relation to the male subject. As such, she has two options, according to Irigaray: She can write/speak as a man, mimicking male discourse, or she can be relegated to silence, to the gaps and interstices, and deciphered only between the lines. In her own work, *Speculum of the Other Woman* (1985; *Speculum de l'autre femme*, 1974), Irigaray exhibits both positions. She offers a critique of Freud and Western philosophers from Plato to Hegel, situating her own commentary within their texts, often without distinguishing marks of punctuation. She simultaneously mimics their texts, presenting their words as her own, and disrupts them, insisting deliberately "upon those *blanks* in discourse which recall the places of her exclusion" (142). At various moments, for instance, she writes, "And as I, Freud, say . . . ," while in other places question marks inserted parenthetically or italicized words disrupt the seamless flow of Freud's argument and reveal the disruptive resistances of Irigaray's commentary:

> So you will now hear that "the further you go from the narrow sexual sphere"—constitutable then as a regional activity? compartmentalized? specialized? but in regard to what generality? totality? capital?—"the more obvious will the 'error of superimposition' become" (p.115) (an error to which recourse has been and will be made almost continuously, even as an effort is made to dissuade you yourselves from having recourse to it). "For certain women, with whom only men capable of showing themselves passively docile can manage to get along [?], may display, in many domains, tremendous activity." (17)

In this passage, Irigaray intersperses sentences from Freud's essay "On Femininity" with her own questions and comments to disrupt his apparently seamless argument regarding feminine sexuality. The feminine subject—precisely that which Freud's text relegates to passivity—asserts itself to subvert repressive notions of female sexuality. Irigaray thus agrees with Cixous that "a feminine text cannot fail to be more than subversive" (258). Perhaps inevitably, then, Irigaray's unorthodox psychoanalytic critique led to her immediate explusion from Lacan's *Ecole freudienne* because it challenged founding priniciples of Lacan's theory of gender identification.

Despite their resistance to and critique of binary opposition, Cixous and Irigaray have been criticized for accepting the sexual divide between male and female and simply reversing the hierarchy, privileging the feminine over the masculine. Further, it has been charged that their definitions of a complex, multiple feminine language rest uncritically on a simplistic equation of the feminine with the female, accepting traditional definitions of woman as biological essence, whether the maternal body, in the case of Cixous, or the sexualized female body, in the case of Irigaray. Their references to woman's multiplicity and heterogeneity paradoxically imply a simple, unified "she" that neglects the real differences in the material conditions of women. As Julia Kristeva argued in "Women's Time" (1981; *Le Temps des femmes*, 1979), "the term 'woman' . . . essentially has the negative effect of effacing the differences among the diverse functions or structures which operate beneath this word" (193).

For this reason, Kristeva found "highly problematic" the existence of a "woman's language." She agreed with Irigaray and Cixous that sexual difference is a product of the symbolic order:

> Sexual difference—which is at once biological, physiological, and relative to reproduction—is translated by and translates a difference in the relationship of subjects to the symbolic contract which is the social contract: a difference, then, in the relationship to power, language, and meaning. The sharpest and most subtle point of feminist subversion . . . will henceforth be situated on the terrain of the inseparable conjunction of the sexual and the symbolic, in order to try to discover, first, the specificity of the female, and then, in the end, that of each individual woman. (196)

Kristeva located the point of feminist subversion not in the female body per se but in the "semiotic," her term for the pre-Oedipal system of drives and pulsions that exists between the mother and the child and is "analogous to vocal or kinetic rhythm." Together these drives articulate what Kristeva terms the chora.

In *Revolution in Poetic Language* (1984; *La révolution du langage poétique*, 1974), Kristeva described the semiotic as a preverbal signifying system that "precedes and underlies" the symbolic order governed by the Law of the Father. The semiotic is "feminine" only to the extent that is marginalized by the patriarchal symbolic order. It is not a language, for since we are defined as subjects within the symbolic order, we can only speak or write within that order. In fact, according to Kristeva, the speaking subject is split between the semiotic and the symbolic, and language operates a dialectical process, not a monolithic system. Since our entry into the symbolic order results from repressing our unity with and desire for the mother, the semiotic—like the unconscious—can disrupt the symbolic order, revealing itself in language as ruptures, absences, and gaps in the text. As such, semiotic disruption of the symbolic is revolutionary, for it challenges the prescribed order of sexuality and language.

According to Kristeva, this revolutionary energy of the semiotic can best be seen in literature: literature reveals a certain knowledge and sometimes the truth itself about an otherwise repressed, nocturnal, secret, and unconscious universe . . . by exposing the unsaid, the uncanny (82). She cites as examples avant-garde works by Joyce, Céline, Artaud,

Mallarmé, and Lautréamont. Thus, revolutionary language is not identified as the product of female authors but can reveal itself as disrup-
tions of the patriarchal symbolic order in texts written by either sex.

Kristeva's interpretation of literary texts focused on the dialectic
between the semiotic and the symbolic to reveal a subversive practice
of "intertextuality." In "Psychoanalysis and the Polis" (1982) she examined the novels of Céline, finding semiotic disruption in his segmented
sentences and ellipses. Also, like Irigaray and Cixous, she herself exhibited the subversive practices she described and defined. In "Stabat
Mater" (1987; "Héréthique de l'amour," 1977), for example, she placed
an analysis of the cult of the Virgin Mary alongside an account of her
own pregnancy and experience of the maternal. The two texts, in differing typeface, are separated spatially on the page and further demarcated in terms of style, with fragmented, highly personal reflections on
one side and a narrative account of the Christian myths on the other.
Her personal reflections literally disrupt the text. Following a critique
of contemporary feminist attitudes to motherhood—which tend either
to idealize or to reject the maternal function—a journal entry announces, "FLASH—instant of time or of dream without time; inordi-
nately swollen atoms of a bond, a vision, a shiver, a yet formless,
unnameable embryo. Epiphanies" (162). Evocations of the specific, material experience of motherhood stand in relation to claims that the
Virgin came to become "that ideal totality that no individual woman
could possibly embody" and "the fulcrum of the humanization of the
West in general and of love in particular" (171). The effect is to undercut
or disrupt such totalizing impulses. By essay's end, the two texts have
become intertwined and interchangeable, with theoretical argument in
the space of personal reflection and elliptical, fragmentary sentences
in the place of the analytical.

Kristeva's theory emphasized marginality and subversion and
could be described as feminist to the extent that she argues the feminine has been devalued. However, since her account emphasized posi-
tionality, not essence—that the feminine is a subject position within
language that can be occupied by authors of either sex—some have
described her as "anti-feminist." At the same time, despite her emphasis on revolutionary literary practice, she has been accused of giving
slight attention to material conditions such as class and race, to the
lived differences among women in history and culture, as have Cixous
and Irigaray.

Feminist Legacy of Post-Structuralism
and French Feminism: 1980–90

Many feminist literary critics saw great potential in the poststructuralists' emphasis on language and the position of the speaking
subject. Much criticism of the mid-1980s is thus characterized by an

attentiveness to language. Following the French example, feminist literary critics engaged in close readings of texts by both male and female authors, locating the workings of the feminine in the gaps, silences, and fissures of the text. Associating the feminine with avant-garde practices meant that many of the most influential texts, such as Alice Jardine's *Gynesis* (1985) and Nancy Miller's *The Poetics of Gender* (1986), focused on women writing during the Modern period. Susan Gubar's " 'The Blank Page' and the Issues of Female Creativity" (1981) interprets a short story by Isak Dinesen as a metaphor for female creativity. Dinesen's story focuses on the defiance of a young princess, whose refusal to consummate her arranged marriage is visible to all in the absence of blood stains on the white sheets, traditionally displayed the following day as a sign of the bride's purity and acquiescence. The blank sheet, to Gubar, tells the tale of either her sexual experience (i.e., that she was not a virgin at marriage) or her refusal to give in to her husband's desires. It speaks in "the subversive voice of silence."

Employing the subversive strategy of deconstruction, Barbara Johnson offered a controversial reading of a poem by Gwendolyn Brooks in "Apostrophe, Animation, and Abortion" (1986). "The Mother" is typically read as an argument against abortion: "I have heard in the voices of the wind the voices of my dim killed children." Attentive to the poet's use of apostrophe (the poetic form of address that animates inanimate objects or forces), Johnson argued that the speaker humanizes the aborted children. Thus the poem can be seen as a more complex expression of a mother's grief. She further notes that, ironically, the speaker herself can only exist in language: she is a mother only by re-animating her dead children in the poem.

The influence of post-structuralist emphases on language and subjectivity was perhaps most evident in feminist investigations of autobiography. Literary critics stressed that female authors emphasized the complexities of subjectivity and self-definition. In their introduction to *Life/Lines* (1988), Bella Brodzki and Celeste Schenck argue that the masculine autobiographical tradition "had taken as its first premise the mirroring capacity of the autobiographer: *his* universality, *his* representativeness, *his* role as spokesman for the community" (1), and as such relied on a notion of the self as unified and transcendent. Female autobiographers, by contrast, take "as a given that self-hood is mediated" (1). As a result, "Autobiography localizes the very program of much feminist theory—the reclaiming of the female subject—even as it foregrounds the central issue of contemporary critical thought—the problematic status of the self" (1–2).

Feminist critical analyses of autobiography demonstrate that women's subjectivity is framed by definitions of femininity and conceptions of social class, racial identity, and ethnicity. In "Maxine Hong Kingston's *Woman Warrior*: Filiality and Woman's Autobiographical Storytelling" (1987), Sidonie Smith argues that Kingston's memoir challenges "the ideology of individualism and with it the ideology of gender" (150). In her text, Kingston demonstrates that identity emerges within a community. By focusing on the stories of her mother, herself, and other women in the Chinese American community of her past, Kingston demonstrates that her autobiography is shaped by the stories others tell—about her and about themselves. Thus, for Smith, Kingston's text is "an autobiography about women's autobiographical storytelling" (150).

Drawing on psychoanalytic insights into the imperfect and unstable construction of the subject, Shari Benstock argued in "Authorizing the Autobiographical" (1988) that male autobiographical texts tended to "seal up and cover over gaps in memory, dislocations in time and space, insecurities, hesitations, and blind spots" (20), offering instead a unified and coherent self as the "I" of the text. By contrast, women authors of the modern era—Djuna Barnes, Isak Dinesen, H. D., Mina Loy, Anaïs Nin, Jean Rhys, Gertrude Stein, and Virginia Woolf— emphasized the instability of the subject. In analyzing Woolf's *Moments of Being*, Benstock attends to the disparities among Woolf's memories as evidence of the "futility and failure of life writing" (27).

The Postmodern Turn

By the mid-1980s, feminist literary criticism and theory had established itself as a separate area of investigation, conscious of itself as a collective enterprise concerned with sexual difference in literature but equally aware that feminist criticism took a variety of forms and approaches. Collections and anthologies reflected these differences. *The New Feminist Criticism: Essays on Women, Literature, and Theory* (1985), edited by Elaine Showalter, incorporated essays by black feminists, lesbian critics, and feminist literary theorists—the same groups who had so potently challenged mainstream feminist criticism as white, middle class, and monolithic. The "new" feminist criticism was more inclusive and mindful of the differences among women and how such differences shaped both literature and our approaches to it. By the 1990s, critics self-consciously avoided references to "the" feminist criticism or theory (new or old), insisting instead on the plurality of feminist positions, on *feminisms*.

This self-consciousness emerged as a consequence of the "postmodern turn" in the social sciences. Postmodern theorists argue that the guiding assumptions of Western thought are not universal and unchanging but derive from a particular moment in intellectual history: the Enlightenment. The eighteenth century gave rise to a set of assumptions now considered "modern": the unity of humankind, the individual as the source of creativity, the inherent superiority of the West, the idea that scientific investigation leads to truth, and the belief that history is linear and leads inevitably to social progress. In *The Postmodern Condition* (1984), Jean-François Lyotard identified these theories as "metanarratives," explanations that presume an ahistorical, all-knowing, rational subject who has a "God's eye point of view" on history and society. He argued, instead, that the ideals of the Enlightenment emerged out of a particular moment in history and that the authors of key Enlightenment texts (Thomas Hobbes, Montesquieu, Condorcet, David Hume, Adam Smith) were themselves influenced by the historical and social conditions during the period in which they wrote, such as the rise of industrial capitalism, the development of liberal democracy, and the organization of knowledge into separate disciplines. As a result, Lyotard defines the "postmodern" as "incredulity toward metanarratives" (26). Postmodern theoretical practice delegitimizes the so-called foundational theories of modern thought in law, science, medicine, politics, economics, and social theory. Purporting to be privileged narratives capable of evaluating all other discourses, metanarratives are, in fact, historically derived and contingent, as postmodern critics reveal. Thus, the work of poststructuralists can be seen as part of the postmodern turn: We have already seen that Derrida exposed the binarism inherent in Western metaphysics and Lacan revealed the instability of the subject in language. (It is doubtful, however, that Derrida would endorse any notion of "the postmodern" given that the term itself appears totalizing, as Judith Butler points out in "Contingent Foundations: Feminism and the Question of 'Postmodernism'" [1990].)

Philosopher Michel Foucault described such work as evidence of the "local" character of criticism in its resistance to the "global" and totalizing theories that were the product of the Enlightenment. In *Power/Knowledge* (1972), he identified a "return of knowledge," or more forcefully "an insurrection of subjugated knowledge," those blocs of knowledge that were disqualified as illegitimate within the accepted hierarchy of science and knowledge, such as that of the psychiatric patient or even doctor against the word of the established scientist. Foucault called the rediscovery of these "local popular knowledges" a "genealogy." In his words, the genealogical project would "entertain the claims to attention of the local, discontinuous, disqualified, illegitimate knowledges against the claims of a unitary body of theory which would filter, hierarchise and order them in the name of some true knowledge and some arbitrary idea of what constitutes a science and its objects" (83). Such knowledges, Foucault contended, were opposed to the centralizing powers of institutionalized and organized scientific discourse. In works on insanity (*Madness and Civilization*, 1961), medicine (*The Birth of the Clinic*, 1963), the prison system (*Discipline and Punish*, 1975), and sexuality (*The History of Sexuality*, 1976, 1984), Foucault engaged in an "archaeology of knowledge," carefully reading the discourses and documents of the past to track the development of institutionalized knowledge to particular historical contexts and to disclose how competing discourses were silenced and elided.

In short, the thinkers loosely identified as postmodern resist all encompassing statements such as "man is this," "woman is that," or "society is such-and-such." Rather than working at the macro level of philosophy and science (common to the eighteenth century), these thinkers work at the micro level of highly specific investigations of human and social behavior. As Linda Hutcheon notes in *A Poetics of Postmodernism* (1988), "the local and regional are stressed in the face of mass culture and a kind of vast global informational village. . . . Culture (with a capital C and in the singular) has become cultures (uncapitalized and plural)" (12).

The connections between postmodernism and feminism are clear. Hutcheon argues that feminist theories helped to develop the postmodern focus on the "ex-centric," those discourses and aesthetic practices that have been marginalized in Western thought. Feminists have long argued that Enlightenment thought privileges male interests and values, asserting that claims about "humanity" have typically referred to men of a particular culture, class, and race. The project of recovering women's texts and contributions to history and society may also be seen as part of the "insurrection of subjugated knowledges" that Foucault describes. According to Hutcheon, "Feminist theory offers perhaps the clearest example of the importance of an awareness of the diversity of history and culture of women: their differences of race, ethnic group, class, sexual preference." Like the feminist critics of autobiography, Hutcheon takes Kingston's *The Woman Warrior* as a powerful example. She claims that Kingston's text "links the postmodern metafictional concerns of narration and language directly to her race and gender" (70). Kingston identifies the gendered nature of the Chinese language: "There is a Chinese word for the female *I*—which is 'slave'" (70). Yet, at the same time, she constructs her own sense of identity through language.

But as feminist criticism itself became institutionalized it opened itself to the same postmodern critique it practiced. Postmodernism challenged feminist critics to avoid generalizing statements about "women." American feminism, for instance, tended to be grounded in the truth of experience—"the personal is the political"—a statement that ironically denied the diversity of women's experiences by assuming that the personal was the same for all women, despite their real differences in race, class, and sexuality. As Nancy Fraser and Linda J. Nicholson describe, some feminist theories are themselves metanarratives: "They are insufficiently attentive to historical and cultural diversity, and they falsely universalize features of the theorist's own era, society, culture, class, sexual orientation, and ethnic, or racial group" (27). A postmodern feminist critique would be "attentive to differences and to cultural and historical specificity" (34). It would be (1) explicitly historical, (2) nonuniversalist, (3) comparativist, and (4) plural. According to Jane Flax, "Feminist theories, like other forms of postmodernism, should encourage us to tolerate and interpret ambivalence, ambiguity, and multiplicity as well as to expose the roots of our needs for imposing order and structure no matter how arbitrary and oppressive these needs may be" (56).

In "A Manifesto for Cyborgs" (1985), Donna Haraway offers a radical realization of such a theoretical project. She defines the cyborg as "a cybernetic organism, a hybrid of machine and organism, a creature of social reality as well as a creature of fiction" (191). As an invented creature, the cyborg is free from ties to history and culture. It prods us to think beyond traditional polarities—human/animal, animal/machine, physical/nonphysical, male/female, masculine/feminine, public/private— and thus may "suggest a way out of the maze of dualisms in which we have explained our bodies and our tools to ourselves" (223). As Haraway claims, "the cyborg is a creature in a postgender world; it has no truck with bisexuality, pre-Oedipal symbiosis, unalienated labor, or other seductions to organic wholeness" (192). The cyborg thus incarnates "the permanent partiality of feminist points of view" (192).

For many this represents a disturbing prospect, for it challenges the very foundations of feminism: the category of "woman," the female subject of literary criticism and theory, and the terms "sex" and "gender" themselves. At the end of the twentieth century, feminist criticism and theory was caught up in a significant shift, what Cornel West has termed the "new cultural politics of difference." The distinctive features of this critical turn are "to trash the monolithic and homogeneous in the name of diversity, multiplicity and heterogeneity; to reject the abstract, general and universal in light of the concrete, specific and particular; and to historicize, contextualize and pluralize by highlighting the contingent, provisional, variable, tentative, shifting and changing" (65).

Bibliography

Atkinson, Ti-Grace. *Amazon Odyssey*. New York: Links, 1974.

Barrett, Michèle. "Introduction." *Virginia Woolf: Women and Writing*. Ed. Michèle Barrett. New York: Harcourt Brace Jovanovich, 1979. 1–39.

Benstock, Shari. "Authorizing the Autobiographical." *The Private Self: Theory and Practice of Women's Autobiographical Writings*. Ed. Shari Benstock. Chapel Hill: U of North Carolina P, 1988. 10–13.

Brodzki, Bella, and Celeste Schenck, eds. *Life / Lines: Theorizing Women's Autobiography*. Ithaca: NY, London: Cornell UP, 1988.

Bunch, Charlotte. "Lesbians in Revolt." *Women and Values*. Ed. Marilyn Pearsall. Belmont, CA: Wadsworth, 1986. 129–131.

Butler, Judith. "Contingent Foundations: Feminism and the Question of 'Postmodernism.'" *The Postmodern Turn: New Perspectives on Social Theory*. Ed. Steven Seidman. Cambridge: Cambridge UP, 1994. 153–70.

Cixous, Helene. "The Laugh of the Medusa." *New French Feminisms*. Ed. Elaine Marks and Isabelle de Courtivron. New York: Schoken Books, 1981. 245–64.

————. "Sorties." *New French Feminisms*. Ed. Elaine Marks and Isabelle de Courtivron. New York: Schocken Books, 1981. 90–8. 179–87.

de Pisan, Christine. "Response to the Treatise on *The Romance of the Rose* by John of Montrevil." *Literary Criticism and Theory: The Greeks to the Present*. Ed. Robert Con Davis and Laurie Fink. New York: Longman, 1989.

Ellmann, Mary. *Thinking about Women*. New York: Harcourt, 1968.

Faderman, Lillian. *Surpassing the Love of Men: Romantic Friendship and Love between Women from the Renaissance to the Present*. New York: William Morrow, 1981.

Fetterley, Judith. "Introduction: On the Politics of Literature." 1978. *Feminisms: An Anthology of Literary Theory and Criticism*. Ed. Robyn R. Warhol and Diane Price Herndl. Rev. ed. New Brunswick, NJ: Rutgers UP, 1997. 564–73.

Firestone, Shulamith. *The Dialectic of Sex: The Case for Feminist Revolution*. New York: Morrow, 1970.

Flax, Jane. "Postmodenism and Gender Relations in Feminist Theory." *Feminism/Postmodernism*. Ed. Linda J. Nicholson. New York: Routledge, 1990. 39–62. [Originally published in *Signs* 12.4 (Summer 1987), pp. 621–43.]

Folger Collective on Early Women Critics, ed. *Women Critics 1660–1820: An Anthology*. Bloomington: Indiana UP, 1995.

Foster, Jeanette. *Sex Variant Women in Literature: A Historical and Quantitative Survey*. New York: Vantage P, 1956.

Foucault, Michel. *The Birth of the Clinic: An Archaeology of Medical Perception*. Trans. A.M. Sheridan Smith. New York: Vintage Books, 1975.

————. *Discipline and Punish: The Birth of the Prison*. Trans. Alan Sheridan. New York: Pantheon Books, 1977.

————. *The History of Sexuality, Volume 1: An Introduction*. Trans. Robert Hurley. New York: Vintage Books, 1978.

————. *Madness and Civilization: A History of Insanity in the Age of Reason*. Trans. Richard Howard. New York: Vintage Books, 1965.

————. *Power/Knowledge: Selected Interviews and Other Writings, 1972–1977*. Ed. and trans. Colin Gordon. New York: Pantheon Books, 1980.

Fraser, Nancy, and Linda J. Nicholson. "Social Criticism with Philosophy: An Encounter between Feminism and Postmodernism." *Feminism/Postmodernism*. Ed. Linda J. Nicholson. New York: Routledge, 1990. 19–38. [Originally appeared in *Communication* 10.3–4 (1998), pp. 345–66.]

Gilbert, Sandra M., and Susan Gubar. *The Madwoman in the Attic: The Woman Writer and the Nineteenth-Century Literary Imagination*. New Haven, CT: Yale UP, 1979.

————. *No Man's Land: The Place of the Woman Writer in the Twentieth Century*. 3 vols. New Haven, CT: Yale UP, 1988–94.

Greer, Germaine. *The Female Eunuch*. London: MacGibbon & Kee, 1970.

Gubar, Susan. "'The Blank Page' and the Issues of Female Creativity." In Showalter, *New Feminist Criticism*, 292–313. [Originally appeared in *Critical Inquiry* 8 (Winter 1981).]

Haraway, Donna. "A Manifesto for Cyborgs: Science, Technology, and Socialist Feminism in the 1980s." *Feminism/Postmodernism*. Ed. Linda J. Nicholson. New York: Routledge, 1990. 190–233. [Originally appeared in *Socialist Review* 80 (1985).]

Heath, Stephen. *The Sexual Fix*. New York: Schocken Books, 1984.

Hull, Gloria T., Patricia Bell Scott, and Barbara Smith, eds. *All the Women Are White, All the Blacks Are Men, But Some of Us Are Brave: Black Women's Studies*. Old Westbury, NY: The Feminist P, 1982.

Hutcheon, Linda. *A Poetics of Postmodernism: History, Theory, Fiction*. London: Routledge, 1988.

Irigaray, Luce. *Speculum of the Other Woman*. Trans. Gillian C. Gill. Ithaca, NY: Cornell UP, 1985.

———. "This Sex Which Is Not One." *New French Feminisms*. Ed. Elaine Marks and Isabelle de Courtivron. New York: Schocken Books, 1981. 99–106.

Jameson, Fredric. *Postmodernism, or, the Cultural Logic of Late Capitalism*. Durham: Duke UP, 1991.

Jardine, Alice A. *Gynesis: Configurations of Women and Modernity*. Ithaca: Cornell UP, 1985.

Johnson, Barbara. "Apostrophe, Animation, and Abortion." *Diacritics* 16 (Spring 1986): 29–39.

Kolodny, Annette. "Dancing through the Minefield: Some Observations on the Theory, Practice, and Politics of Feminist Literary Criticism." In Showalter, *The New Feminist Criticism*, 144–67. [Originally appeared in *Feminist Studies* 6 (1980).]

Kristeva, Julia. "Psychoanalysis and the Polis." *The Kristeva Reader*. Ed. Toril Moi. New York: Columbia UP, 1986. 302–20.

———. *Revolution in Poetic Language*. Trans. Leon S. Roudiez. New York: Columbia UP, 1984.

———. "Stabat Mater." *Tales of Love*. Trans. Leon S. Roudiez. New York: Columbia UP, 1987. 234–63.

———. "Woman's Time." *The Kristeva Reader*. Ed. Toril Moi. New York: Columbia UP, 1986. 187–213. [Originally appeared in *Signs* 7 (1981): 13–55.]

Lyotard, Jean-François. *The Postmodern Condition*. Minneapolis: U of Minnesota P, 1984.

McDowell, Deborah E. "New Directions for Black Feminist Criticism." In Showalter, *The New Feminist Criticism*, 186–99. [Originally appeared in *Black American Literature Forum* 14 (1980).]

Miller, Nancy K., ed. *The Poetics of Gender*. New York: Columbia UP, 1986.

Millett, Kate. *Sexual Politics*. London: Virago, 1977.

Mitchell, Juliet. *Psychoanalysis and Feminism*. New York: Pantheon Books, 1974.

Moers, Ellen. *Literary Women: The Great Writers*. New York: Doubleday, 1976.

Moi, Toril. *Sexual/Textual Politics: Feminist Literary Theory*. London: Methuen, 1985.

Moraga, Cherríe, and Gloria Anzaldúa. *This Bridge Called My Back*. Watertown, MA: Persephone P, 1981.

Rich, Adrienne. "Compulsory Heterosexuality and Lesbian Existence." *Blood, Bread, and Poetry: Selected Prose, 1979–1985*. New York: Norton, 1986. 23–75.

Rose, Jacqueline. *Sexuality in the Field of Vision*. London: Verso, 1986.

Rule, Jane. *Lesbian Images*. Garden City, NY: Doubleday, 1975.

Showalter, Elaine. *A Literature of Their Own*. Princeton, NJ: Princeton UP, 1977.

———. ed. *The New Feminist Criticism: Essays on Women, Literature, and Theory*. New York: Pantheon, 1985.

———. "Toward a Feminist Poetics." In Showalter, *The New Feminist Criticism*, 125–43.

Smith, Barbara. "Toward a Black Feminist Criticism." In Showalter, *The New Feminist Criticism*, 168–85. [Originally appeared in *Conditions: Two* 1.2 (October 1977).]

Smith, Sidonie. "Maxine Hong Kingston's *Woman Warrior*: Filiality and Women's Autobiographical Storytelling." *A Poetics of Women's Autobiography: Marginality and the Fictions of Self-Representation*. Ed. Sidonie Smith. Bloomington: Indiana UP, 1987. 150–73.

Spacks, Patricia Meyer. *The Female Imagination: A Literary and Psychological Investigation of Women's Writing*. London: George Allen & Unwin Ltd., 1976.

Todd, Janet. *Feminist Literary History: A Defence*. Cambridge: Polity P, 1988.

West, Cornel. "The New Cultural Politics of Difference." *The Postmodern Turn: New Perspectives on Social Theory*. Ed. Steven Seidman. Cambridge: Cambridge UP, 1994. 65–81. [Originally appeared in *October* 53 (1990).]

Zimmerman, Bonnie. "What Has Never Been: An Overview of Lesbian Feminist Criticism." In Showalter, *The New Feminist Criticism*, 200–24 [Originally appeared in *Feminist Studies* 7.3 (1981).]

Manhood, Class, and the American Renaissance

David Leverenz

Leverenz brings together a discussion of manhood and class as identity markers, arguing that class lines have been blurred in the United States because of the overwhelming triumph of the middle class. Thus, according to Leverenz, an emphasis was placed on manhood rather than class. Leverenz identifies three types of American manhood: patrician manhood based on "property, patriarchy, and citizenship" (p. 281), artisan manhood based on self-sufficiency, and the new manhood based on capitalist competition. Leverenz points to social historians and writers to support his contention that class tensions shaped notions of manhood and suggests that while patriarchy may reflect women's experience of men, it does not reflect men's relations with each other. In making his argument, Leverenz discusses texts such as Herman Melville's "Bartleby, the Scrivener" and Moby-Dick, *Nathaniel Hawthorne's* House of the Seven Gables *and* The Blithedale Romance, *and makes passing reference to Benjamin Franklin, Ralph Waldo Emerson, and Walt Whitman, among others. This essay appears in* American Literature, Culture, and Ideology *(1990), edited by Beverly R. Voloshin, but a fuller discussion may be found in Leverenz's book,* Manhood and the American Renaissance *(1989).*

From *American Literature, Culture, and Ideology: Essays in Memory of Henry Nash Smith*, ed. Beverly R. Voloshin (New York: Peter Lang, 1990): 79–92.

One of the most basic themes in American history has been the widely shared belief that the possibilities for individual upward mobility effectively blur class lines. Benjamin Franklin first gave mythic status to the rags-to-riches dream in his *Autobiography*. Elsewhere he emphasized the "happy mediocrity" of the American situation, so relatively free from class hierarchy and tyrannical aristocratic institutions. In the decades before the Civil War, especially in the Northeast, the idea of being self-reliant or a "self-made man"—a phrase apparently coined by Henry Clay in 1832—amounted to an obsession. Appropriately, Clay associates the phrase with the dominant values of American individualism. As he says during a lengthy speech defending tariffs, "In Kentucky, almost every manufactory known to me, is in the hands of enterprising and self-made men, who acquired whatever wealth they possess by patient and diligent labor."

In the last few years, various studies have suggested a middle-class frame for the paradoxes of American individualism. Its ethic of hard work, self-control, and material rewards rested on the presumption that everyone could be successful. The very term "middle class" came into use in the 1830s, replacing "the middling orders" or "the middling sort," to emphasize the paradoxical possibility of upward mobility for everyone.[1] Part of the reason class lines have been so blurred in America, I think, is that the triumph of middle class values and the economic system fostering them has been so overwhelming.

The triumph of the "new men" over the mercantile elite brought a preoccupation with manhood rather than class among men of the Northeast. The conflict was not a class war in conventional European terms, but an ideological tension felt in terms of gender. What did it mean to be manly? Did it mean a craftsman's independence and self-respect, or an entrepreneur's ability to best his competitors and exploit resources, human as well as material? Did a man's self-respect depend on a sense of being free and equal to any other man, or on a struggle to be dominant?

Here I will sketch three paradigms of American manhood. I think of them as akin to Max Weber's ideal types: conceptual categories never fully existing in the world, yet useful for studying more complicated social stresses. Their usefulness also extends to literary study, partly because writers such as Hawthorne and Melville employ similar stereotypes in their characterizations.

The patrician paradigm defined manhood through property, patriarchy, and citizenship. It was the ideology of a narrow elite: merchants, gentry, large landowners, lawyers—in old English as well as old Marxist perspective, the upper bourgeoisie. Its manly ideal of character and paternalism had much in common with older British aristocratic ideals of honor, a code which survived much longer in the South. So long as mercantile capitalism dominated economic production in the Northeast, this ideal of manhood held relatively comfortable sway.

The artisan paradigm defined manhood in Jeffersonian terms, as autonomous self-sufficiency. A man worked his land or his craft with integrity and freedom. Longfellow's "The Village Blacksmith" catches the myth:

> His brow is wet with honest sweat,
>   He earns whate'er he can,
> And looks the whole world in the face,
>   For he owes not any man.

As one can tell from the patrician paternalism of Jefferson and Long-fellow, this ideal of manhood worked well with mercantile capitalism, which depended for its raw materials on independent yeoman farmers, and whose characteristic mode of production was the small patriarchal village shop. The relationship between Colonel Henry "Manly" and his servant Jonathan in Royall Tyler's popular drawing-room comedy, *The Contrast* (1787), celebrates the triumph of true American manhood over quasi-British aristocratic manners, and presumes the harmony of master and servant.

In practice, many artisans shared the patriarchal emphasis on citizenship and the good of the whole. The result was what Nick Salvatore has called, in a different context, "deferential democracy." In the world that Eugene V. Debs grew up in, an artisan's sense of manhood was based primarily upon his work, and to a somewhat lesser extent on his role as father and husband. A man must provide for his family, and he must be "a model of industry and honesty." This code of manhood "also required an active political participation and the fulfillment of one's duty as a citizen." Such an ideal of work could deny existing class interests and stress a common purpose in part because it was such a small-town world. Ostensibly based on pride of craft, the "skilled worker's vision of manhood" also depended on what Salvatore calls "a fundamental cohesion within their society and culture."[2] In a larger, more amorphous marketplace world, where a man felt more and more like a hand, the already romanticized ideal of community could no longer be presumed as a frame for manly freedom and pride of craftsmanship. Skilled labor now seemed more like exploitation and oppression.

Faith in a patriarchal elite had its intimate counterpart in the patriarchy of the home. Though Jay Fliegelman's *Prodigals and Pilgrims* argues for a basic change from stern to benign fathering from 1750 to 1800, the assumption of father's primacy as father remains unquestioned.[3] Considerable psychological conflict roils under the surface of both paradigms, especially in the artisan model, where independence is uneasily yoked to filial deference. The classic text for the transition from artisan to patrician patriarchy is Franklin's *Autobiography*.

The real class tension came from the undeferential, ambitious entrepreneurs and speculators who challenged patrician modes of power.

Mary Kelley calls the victory of the new men the greatest social transformation in American history.[4] While that judgement may seem excessive, it catches some of the stress of the time, as men struggled to redefine for themselves what it meant to work. Lemuel Shaw, Melville's father-in-law, played a crucial role as Chief Justice of the Massachusetts Supreme Court in redefining the gentry ideal of property rights from an absolute end in itself to an instrumental means, thus allowing for corporate expansion. Traditional artisan ideals of manliness as independence, hard work, and pride in one's labor, the backbone of American rhetoric then and now, were also being challenged in a marketplace emphasizing competition, risk, and calculation, with all the instability attending the economic change to industrial capitalism. Instability itself, the sense of not knowing one's place, was another prime source for obsessive competitiveness.

Franklin himself was a ruthless entrepreneurial competitor, mixing wiles and pugnacity to dominate his rival printers, one of whom he drove to Barbados. He fell back on Deborah Read for a wife only after he failed to gain one with a £100 dowry. While he clothes the reality of his entrepreneurial success in the appearance of retrospective patrician mellowness, a newer generation would seek the main chance with less attentiveness either to self-image or civic usefulness.

The greatest paradox in the triumph of the capitalist middle class is that its collective success depended upon maximizing individual competition, which thrives on the zest for dominance and the fear of failure. What Mary Ryan has called the "ebullience of artisan culture" depended on a relatively stable village world with strong kinship ties. That world was giving way to a much more rivalrous, alienated, and uncertain market, with visions of greater gain and precipitous falls on every hand. As Melville puts it at the beginning of *Pierre*, the greatest of patriarchal families now "rise and burst like bubbles in a vat."

Mary Ryan's *Cradle of the Middle Class*, foremost among the recent social histories arguing for the growth of a new middle class during this period, finds a decisive change in the social expectations for adult men. As the role of father became more peripheral, or intermittent, the complementary myths of the self-made man and the cult of true American womanhood fostered a narrow intensity of will, work, and self-reliance in the man, while the family became the domestic cradle for nurturing little republicans of the future. Sons became strangers to their mothers at an early age. Joseph Kett's study of American adolescence also finds a striking change, in the 1840s, toward heightened expectations for boys to be hard working and self-disciplined.

Ryan also argues for a complementary paradox. If the intensified individualism of the new middle-class male was a response to heightened competition, it was also a response by families to protect their children. While "the fragmentation of the patriarchal household economy" led to much greater gender separation, the family remained as the basic survival unit. The goal of the family, according to Ryan, was not to be upwardly mobile so much as to maintain its middle-class status. Along with the fear of individual failure came the fear that their children might fall into the emerging working class. The legacy of such families to their children became education, not property, to give them the skills necessary for commercial or professional careers.[5]

There is a vitality and zest as well as risk and fear in the entrepreneurial spirit, to be sure. This was the age of "Go ahead!," of try, fail, land on your feet and try again. In particular, and here I differ from Ryan, the norm-setting entrepreneurs relished the struggle to gain some measure of dominance in the marketplace. Money was a means, a tangible yardstick of prowess. They experienced themselves much as George Stigler, a Nobel Prize–winning economist, so appreciatively describes them, as "men of force":

> The competitive industry is not one for lazy or confused or inefficient men: they will watch their customers vanish, their best employees migrate, their assets dissipate. It is a splendid place for men of force: it rewards both hard work and genius, and it rewards on a fine and generous scale.

Or as Vince Lombardi put it, in a phrase that has been widely misquoted, these are men for whom "Winning isn't everything, but wanting to win is."[6] Appropriating an artisan rhetoric of freedom, the entrepreneurial ideology of manhood veils a drive for competitive dominance in the language of equality.

Probably the first literary record of the self-made entrepreneur in the New World is Cotton Mather's fulsome praise of Governor William Phips, by all accounts except Mather's an Ahab of the second order. Kenneth Silverman calls him just a "choleric adventurer" who cursed up a storm, regularly knocked people down, and occasionally threw things at governors before he became one himself. Mather relishes stories of how Phips quelled mutinies on his ships and how he dominated people on ship and shore. The bookish clergyman, filled with a good measure of choleric feelings himself, had various reasons for making his celebration of Phips the lengthy coda to *Magnalia Christi Americana* (1702), including political gratitude. Beyond his political and psychological pleasure in depicting Phips's rise from obscure sheep-herder to great power, Mather presents Phips as the kind of man who can thrive in America: the exploitive, even brawling entrepreneur who seizes his chances and makes the most of them. The will to dominate is as fundamental to Mather's portrait as is the claim, almost a coinage of "self-made man," that Phips was "*A Son to his own Labours!*"[7]

A trickle of such men in the 1690s had become a torrent by the 1830s. True, these men of force, who gathered such great rewards from the economy they spurred, were not the ordinary men Ryan focuses on. As she argues, problematically, I think, middle-class boys were socialized not to become aggressive entrepreneurs but to aim for achievement and respectability.[8] Nonetheless, the bully-boys now set the pace and the norms for manhood in the marketplace. The social structure no longer restrained them. The artisan ideal now jostled with a new ideal of manhood, one previously accessible only to kings, court politicians, and great military leaders. Faced with a middle-class man of force, anyone on the other side of his dominance must have felt a little more fearful, a little less free. Sean Wilentz quotes an Irish artisan speaking at a New York labor rally in 1850: "'Even in this liberal country, the middle class stands above the workingmen, and every one of them is a little tyrant in himself, as Voltaire said.'"[9]

Emerson explicitly describes the new middle-class man in terms of ruthless power. In *Representative Men* (1850), he personifies the new middle class as Napoleon, the ultimate man of force. Napoleon, he says, represents "the class of business men . . . the class of industry and skill." He has all the virtues and vices of "the middle class of modern society; of the throng who fill the markets, shops, counting-houses, manufactories, ships, of the modern world, aiming to be rich." Utterly lacking in civilized generosity, "never weak and literary," "egotistic and monopolizing," "a boundless liar," Napoleon is always on stage to be seen and to manipulate his audience. He is "a monopolizer and usurper of other minds," to the end of exercising power and making "a great noise." Emerson's patrician disdain is clear. His admiration for Napoleon's force is also abundantly present. Many members of the elite had portrayed Andrew Jackson in much the same way.

It seems at least plausible, then, to see class tensions shaping the issue, What did it mean to be a man. Not only social historians but writers themselves, at least the best ones, sometimes dramatize social change with class-linked characterizations of manhood. Part of the dark comedy of Melville's "Bartleby, the Scrivener" is Bartleby's refusal to be categorized in the class niches assigned by the genteel narrator to Turkey, the down-at-the-heels deferential gentleman, and to Nippers, the young and ambitious if mechanical "new man" preoccupied with ward politics. If the narrator defines himself quite comfortably as an appendage of the old elite, prudent, unaggressive, safe and snug amid his legal briefs and Christian civilities, the story exposes him as a false self, unable to deal with anger and moral equality. The narrator starts to feel "unmanned," he says twice, at being dictated to by an underling. "'What earthly right have you to stay here?'" he finds himself expostulating. "'Do you pay any rent? Do you pay my taxes? Or is this property yours?'" He relies on traditional patrician conventions of self-controlled benevolence to evade his implicit connection to Bartleby's equally unexpressed anger. By the end he unwittingly becomes linked with Monroe Edwards, the "gentleman forger."[10] In Hawthorne's *Blithedale Romance*, too, the dispossessed elite become personified in Coverdale and Old Moodie, both narcissistic and shallow "men of show." They are ineffectual if meddling bystanders for the exploitive new Napoleons of power, Hollingsworth and Westervelt, or "western world."

Hawthorne's *House of the Seven Gables* also emphasizes class tensions. It begins with a lengthy, patronizing narration of Hepzibah's fall from leisured gentility into the prosaic necessity of running a shop. If the narrator makes fun of her at ponderous, ostensibly sympathetic length, he more unequivocally takes the side of hapless patrician Clifford against the apotheosis of the new man of power, Jaffrey Pyncheon. The real climax comes as the narrator circles slowly and vindictively around Jaffrey's ominous, threatening body, sitting motionless in a chair. The narrator's controlled glee at Jaffrey's death complements the out-of-control giddiness of Clifford's wild train ride. Yet Clifford's superficial release only exposes his permanent incapacity to be a man. The happy ending is left to Holgrave, the benign "new man" whose residual craftsman's integrity and patrician's chivalry rescue him from his Jaffrey-like inclinations toward heartless exploitation and dominance.

Despite path-breaking studies by Carolyn Porter, Myra Jehlen, and especially William Charvat, no analysis of classic American writing has come close to the brilliant Marxist synthesis that Raymond Williams's *Culture and Society* achieves for English literature.[11] The reason, I think, has to do with the relative prominence of gender issues over class consciousness in American self-perceptions. Perhaps that in turn has something to do with the relative absence of an empowered and leisured aristocracy. As Michel Chevalier concludes his *Society, Manners, and Politics in the United States* (trans. 1839), "The higher classes in the United States, taken as a whole and with only some exceptions, have the air and attitude of the vanquished; they bear the mark of defeat on their front."[12]

Partly because the middle class has come to be so diffusely triumphant, American men tend to define their self-respect much more stringently through their work than through any other aspect of their lives. Accordingly, the contradictions and intensities of gender ideology refract implicit class tensions subsumed in the workplace and the work ethic. Feminist descriptions of manhood as patriarchy quite rightly reflect women's experience of men at home, during this period. But patriarchy does not reflect men's experience of each other at work. Rather, it is associated with mercantile and artisan norms of manhood now being displaced by the new norm of capitalist competition.

The other side of a man's drive for dominance is his fear of humiliation. Melville's Ahab represents the extreme of both ends. He is at once the supreme entrepreneurial man of force and, toward the end of *Moby-Dick*, especially in "The Candles," a man who begs to be beaten by a stronger, even more heartless competitor. His drive for dominance stems neither from patriarchy nor from testosterone but from having been grossly humiliated, as he conceives of it, by a faceless competitor acting through the whale. *Moby-Dick* is really a gigantic suicide trip, as

Ahab becomes possessed by the new ideology of manhood, which for Melville is equivalent to the destruction of any kind of self.

"I hate to be ruled by my own sex," Miles Coverdale says to Zenobia in *The Blithedale Romance* (ch. 14, "Eliot's Pulpit"); "it excites my jealousy, and wounds my pride. It is the iron sway of bodily force which abases us, in our compelled submission." Despite such feelings, Coverdale seems on the verge of falling in love with Hollingsworth. Unlike Westervelt, this man of force also has a woman's capacity for tenderness. He makes the self-conscious narrator feel befriended and cared for rather than challenged in rivalry. "Hollingsworth's more than brotherly attendance gave me inexpressible comfort," Coverdale muses in chapter 6 ("Coverdale's Sick-chamber"). Most men, he continues, "have a natural indifference, if not an absolutely hostile feeling," toward the sick, the injured, and the weak, "amid the rude jostle of our selfish existence." This "ugly characteristic of our sex . . . has likewise its analogy in the practice of our brute brethren, who hunt the sick or disabled member of the herd from among them, as an enemy." Coverdale is astonished that Hollingsworth doesn't similarly turn on him, as any normal man would do.

However, when Hollingsworth appeals to Coverdale to join his cause, Coverdale reports his sensations as if he were being raped. It was "as if Hollingsworth had caught hold of my own heart, and were pulling it towards him with an almost irresistible force. . . . Had I but touched his extended hand, Hollingsworth's magnetism would perhaps have penetrated me with his own conception of all these matters." Coverdale's language eerily foreshadows Zenobia's fate, as Hollingsworth pokes a pole into her dead body.

The implicit rivalry between the two men is an allegory of class conflict as well as a psychodrama of homosexual fear. It ends with an ambiguous mixture of dominance and humiliation. Hollingsworth marries Priscilla, whom Coverdale suddenly announces he loves, yet Hollingsworth is deflated and defeated by his guilt for Zenobia. The man of force becomes a limp little boy, while the scared and skittish Coverdale can now smugly portray Hollingsworth's defeat and announce his love for the woman who tends his rival's humiliation.

Anyone preoccupied with manhood, in whatever time or culture, harbors fears of being humiliated, usually by other men. The sources for humiliation may be diverse, in parents or the loss of class position, in marketplace competition or other fears of being dominated. A preoccupation with manhood becomes a compensatory response. To adapt a term from John von Neumann's game theory, manhood becomes a way not of dominating, though that may be a by-product, but of minimizing maximum loss.[13] While the loss may be symbolized as castration, for instance in *Moby-Dick*, its roots lie not in the body but in a man's fear that other men will see him as weak, and therefore vulnerable to attack.

The new middle-class ideology of manhood intensifies fears of humiliation. Earlier ideologies of manhood link self-esteem to institutionalized social structures: class and patriarchy. The ideology of manhood emerging with entrepreneurial capitalism makes competition and power dynamics in the workplace the only source for valuing oneself. Manhood therefore becomes much more fundamental to a man's unconscious self-image.[14]

Seen in this context, classic male writers appear exceptionally self-conscious about their deviance from emerging business norms of manhood. The appendix to Lawrence Buell's fine recent study, *New England Literary Culture*, makes clear both the overwhelmingly elite origins of male writers and their search for careers other than in business. As covert acts of fight and flight, American Renaissance texts have received a very good press from twentieth-century academic critics, most of whom share these writers' alienation from business norms of manhood. The classic paradigms for canonized American texts presume victimization by bourgeois society as the inception of the writer's alienated imagination. We have the American Adam, a World Elsewhere of style, the Imperial Self, the prophetic and redemptive American Self, the Romance as a sacrifice of relation, the chaste marriage of wilderness males. Nina Baym has perceptively labelled these paradigms, all established by male critics, as "Melodramas of Beset Manhood."[15] The word "Melodramas," however, too easily dismisses the centrality of beset manhood to the texts these paradigms describe.

Male writers developed pre-modernist styles to explore their sense of being deviant from male norms emphasizing rivalry and exalting men of force. Women writers developed evangelical or more broadly moral narrations of domesticity to articulate the needs of a largely female reading public. As Alfred Habegger emphasizes, later writers such as Howells and James might accept with more equanimity the "sissy" role given to male writers in an industrializing middle-class society.[16] But from the 1820s through the 1850s, the writer's role and the male writer's audience were more uncertain. American Renaissance self-refashioning—of reader as well as writer—develops as a rhetorical strategy responsive to these social conditions.

Most strikingly, in ways I don't have space to show here, a common rhetorical pattern appears at the start of the diverse masterpieces of Thoreau, Melville, and Whitman. In *Walden*, *Moby-Dick*, and "Song of Myself," a "you" is accused and appealed to, as double and conventional man but also as potential convert and comrade for the self-refashioned "I." Male rivalry looms under the promise of fraternity, and the rivalry returns in the rhetoric of self-refashioning, along with fears of humiliation. My argument is the reverse, really the underside, of Leslie Fiedler's well-known claim that classic American literature expresses a mythic male bonding in the wilderness. Fiedler is certainly right to emphasize the myth.[17] Where he explains it as a fantasized flight from heterosexual anxiety, however, I see it as the wishful surface of fears about male rivalry and male deviance.

To focus on this literature as social rhetoric brings out issues of manhood, especially male rivalry and fears of humiliation. Such pre-occupations both express and mystify class conflicts, while also voicing and veiling more personal fears. Ultimately the effect of reading major texts this way, at least for me, is to demystify an enduring reverence for them as centerpieces of liberal and democratic values. As compensation, we can come to appreciate the writers' sensitivities to class and gender conflicts, in themselves as well as in their time.

Notes

1. Karen Halttunen, *Confidence Men and Painted Women: A Study of Middle-Class Culture in America, 1830–1870* (New Haven: Yale University Press, 1982), p. 29.
2. Nick Salvatore, *Eugene V. Debs: Citizen and Socialist* (Urbana: University of Illinois Press, 1982), pp. 10, 23–24. On the complexities of artisan culture, see Eric Foner's *Tom Paine and Revolutionary America* (New York: Oxford University Press, 1976); Charles G. Steffen, *The Mechanics of Baltimore: Workers and Politics in the Age of Revolution 1763–1812* (Urbana: University of Illinois Press, 1984); and Sean Wilentz, *Chants Democratic: New York City & the Rise of the American Working Class, 1788–1850* (New York: Oxford University Press, 1984). All of these studies stress the connections between artisan culture and the American rhetoric of social radicalism.
3. Jay Fliegelman, *Prodigals and Pilgrims: The American Revolution Against Patriarchal Authority, 1750–1800* (Cambridge: Cambridge University Press, 1982). On tensions between independence and filial deference, see Philip Greven's *Four Generations: Population, Land, and Family in Colonial Andover, Massachusetts* (Ithaca: Cornell University Press, 1970), and Robert Blair St. George, "Fathers, Sons, and Identity: Woodworking Artisans in South-East New England, 1620–1700," in *The Craftsman in Early America*, ed. Ian M. G. Quimby (New York: Norton, 1984), pp. 89–125.
4. Mary Kelley, *Private Woman, Public Stage: Literary Domesticity in Nineteenth-Century America* (New York: Oxford University Press, 1984), pp. 297, 392. Kelley is drawing on the work of Gordon Wood and Stowe Persons.
5. Mary P. Ryan, *Cradle of the Middle Class: The Family in Oneida County, New York, 1790–1865* (Cambridge: Cambridge University Press, 1981), pp. 236 (ebullience), 155 (roles), 220 (sons), 210 (fragmentation), 184 and 238 (fear of falling into lower class), 169–71 (education); Joseph F. Kett, *Rites of Passage: Adolescence in America 1790 to the Present* (New York: Basic Books, 1977). On the new middle class, see a fine review essay by Stuart M. Blumin, "The Hypothesis of Middle-Class Formation in Nineteenth-Century America: A Critique and Some Proposals," *American Historical Review*, 90 (April 1985), pp. 299–338.
6. Stigler is quoted, with relish, by Gary Hart, *A New Democracy* (New York: Quill, 1983), p. 46. On Lombardi, see a letter from Jerry James to *The New*

York Times (Sunday, September 28, 1986, section E), p. 24. "It's the only thing" was said by John Wayne, playing a football coach in "Trouble Along the Way."

7. Cotton Mather, *Magnalia Christi Americana*, ed. Kenneth B. Murdock (Cambridge, Mass.: Harvard University Press, 1977), pp. 273–359, quotation p. 279; Kenneth Silverman, *The Life and Times of Cotton Mather* (New York: Harper & Row, 1984), pp. 162–65.

8. Ryan, *Cradle of the Middle Class*, argues that mothers tried to socialize their children to reproduce petit-bourgeois traits and become cautious, prudent small-businessmen, not entrepreneurs. This argument confuses what mothers wanted with how their sons turned out. It also presumes strong maternal socialization, despite Ryan's demonstration that sons were removed quite early from maternal influence. See pp. 161 and 153 on the new imperative "of maximizing individual gain in a competitive market."

9. Wilentz, *Chants Democratic*, p. 380.

10. For a superb account of the story in its Wall Street setting, see Stephen Zelnick, "Melville's 'Bartleby': History, Ideology, & Literature," *Marxist Perspectives*, 2 (Winter 1979/80), pp. 74–92.

11. Raymond Williams, *Culture and Society 1780–1950* (Garden City: Anchor Books, 1960, 1st pub. 1958); Carolyn Porter, *Seeing and Being: The Plight of the Participant-Observer in Emerson, James, Adams, Faulkner* (Middletown, Ct.: Wesleyan University Press, 1981); Myra Jehlen, "New World Epics: The Novel and the Middle-class in America," *Salmagundi* (Winter 1977), 49–68, and also her *American Incarnation: The Individual, the Nation, and the Continent* (Cambridge, Mass.: Harvard University Press, 1986), which explores how rhetorical uses of the land incarnate a middle-class ideology of liberal individualism; William Charvat, *The Profession of Authorship in America, 1800–1870*, ed. Matthew J. Bruccoli (Columbus: Ohio State University Press, 1968), esp. pp. 61–64.

12. Michel Chevalier, *Society, Manners, and Politics in the United States: Letters on North America*, trans. T. G. Bradford, ed. John William Ward (Ithaca: Cornell University Press, 1961), pp. 418–19.

13. John von Neumann's "min-max" or minimax theory comes from his mathematical analysis of game strategy. It was popularized by others, who derived from it the idea that corporations function not to maximize profit but to minimize maximum loss. John von Neumann and Oskar Morgenstern, *Theory of Games and Economic Behavior* (Princeton: Princeton University Press, 1953), pp. 153–55.

14. My recent book, *Manhood and the American Renaissance* (Ithaca: Cornell University Press, 1989), explores all these issues at much greater length. For a more informal and personal exploration, see my essay, "Manhood, Humiliation, and Public Life: Some Stories," *Southwest Review*, 71 (Autumn 1986), 442–62.

15. Lawrence Buell, *New England Literary Culture from the Revolution to the Civil War* (Cambridge: Cambridge University Press, 1986); Nina Baym, "Melodramas of Beset Manhood: How Theories of American Fiction Exclude Women Authors," *American Quarterly*, 33 (1981), 123–39.

16. Alfred Habegger, *Gender, Fantasy, and Realism in American Literature* (New York: Columbia University Press, 1982).

17. Leslie Fiedler, *Love and Death in the American Novel*, rev. ed. (New York: Stein and Day, 1966).

Gender Studies

Michael Ryan

In this excerpt from the second edition of Ryan's Literary Theory *(2007),
he addresses the links between gender studies and gay/lesbian studies.
Ryan notes that gay and lesbian studies theorists seek to identify a tradition of homosexual writing while also questioning the notion of sexual
identity and the logic of gender categorization. Ryan discusses the role of
culture in creating and sustaining gender norms and points to gender's
performativity. Ryan closes with suggested readings of the Elizabeth
Bishop poems "Roosters," "In the Waiting Room," and "Exchanging Hats"
as well as the Henry James novel* The Aspern Papers.

Gender studies began as feminism and eventually became as well
gay, lesbian, bisexual, and transgender studies. Feminism came
into being as a school of literary and cultural study in the 1970s. Its
initial impetus as a scholarly project was to ask why women have
played a subordinate role to men in human history. It was concerned
with how women's lives have changed over time, and it asked what
about women's experience (including their writing) is different from
men's. Some feminists claimed that women's experience is the result of
an essential ontological or biological difference of identity, while others
contended that it is the result of historical imprinting and social construction. Either women think and act differently from men for biological reasons or they are made different by the fact that human culture
has always been male-dominated. Feminist literary criticism studies
literature by women for how it expresses the particularity of women's
lives. It studies the canon of male writers for how women have been
represented in it.

According to feminist anthropologists such as Gayle Rubin, the
subordination of women to men originated in early societies in which
women were used as tokens of exchange between clans. The rule against
incest forbade endogenous marriage, and exogenous marriages outside
one's clan became a way of fostering peaceful relations between groups
that might otherwise have been prone to conflict. The residues of such
ancient patriarchy are still palpable in our own societies. While women
occasionally become political or economic leaders, they are far outnum-
bered by the numerous men who run business, industry, and government. The assumed norm in many traditionalist societies in Africa, the
Middle East, the American "heartland," and Asia is for women to be in
charge of domestic labor while men do more public work. Moreover, the

From *Literary Theory: A Practical Introduction* 2nd Ed. (Malden: Blackwell
Publishers, 2007): 131–58.

pressure of what Adrienne Rich calls "compulsory heterosexuality" en-
sures that women have no other options than to submit to more economically powerful men.

Whatever its origin—nature or society—this situation of gender
inequality is sustained by culture. Most traditional religions such as
Catholicism, fundamentalist Protestantism, Islam, and Orthodox
Judaism assign women to secondary roles, and some forbid them from
participating in public activities with men. In mythology and philosophy, women are often associated with danger, uncontrolled bodily
urges, and madness, while men are linked to reason, courage, and independence. Even modern cultural forms such as film, because the industry is largely owned and controlled by men, foster assumptions that
further the subordination of women. Images of strong, publicly competent women are still hard to come by in film culture, while images of
women who are evil because they possess too much power are fairly
easy to find.

The French feminist philosopher Luce Irigaray argues that images
of frighteningly powerful, castrating women appear so frequently in
male-dominated culture because man's first relationship in the world
is with his mother. That mother is an overpowering being associated
with the threat of engulfment. Men compensate for this initial state of
powerlessness by engaging in an extreme rejection of the mother and
of all that she represents in terms of care and empathy. For men to have
an identity and to have power, the mother must be subordinated and
anything associated with her must be depicted as evil. That symbolic
early object in one's life gets transferred, of course, onto women in general. This would explain why in traditional societies women are often
made to appear under the total control of their husbands. They are
forced to live in confined interior spaces and forced to wear body-
covering clothing that marks them out as their husband's property.
That many women freely accede to such subordination is a sign of how
successful cultural conditioning can be even when it works against
one's interests.

American feminist scholars Sandra Gilbert and Susan Gubar add
important detail to this argument in *The Madwoman in the Attic*.
Women, they notice, are depicted either as monsters or angels in the
male literary tradition. They are often objects of fear. Irigaray's account
of how men compensate for the mother's early power over them helps
account for the angel ideal. Men, she contends, learn to abstract from
material life because it is associated with early experiences of union
with the mother's body. Such speculative abstractions push matter
away and keep it at a safe distance. Matter is replaced by spirit or ideal-
ity, a realm of pure mental abstraction that assures men of their ability
to control the physical world. The angel ideal that Gilbert and Gubar
study converts physical women into spiritual beings. In so doing, it

essentially kills them, since they are rendered immobile and inanimate and deprived of autonomy.

Gender studies also includes gay and lesbian studies, as well as the study of sexuality in general. Increasingly, gay and lesbian studies programs are called gay, lesbian, bisexual, and transgender studies programs. Gender became unfixed from the traditional heterosexual binary in the 1970s and 1980s. Gay and lesbian studies theorists became interested in unearthing the hidden tradition of homosexual writing and began to study the gender dynamics of canonical literature. The unearthing of a counter-tradition of homosexual writing was made difficult by the history of the closet. While there have been many gay writers, from Sappho to Tennessee Williams, few of them wrote openly about their lives and experiences. Heterosexual culture was intolerant of gay perspectives both on the streets and in books, and while strong women might be put in the attic for being "mad," gay people were put in jail for being "perverse" or "against nature." Oscar Wilde is the most famous example, but writers like Elizabeth Bishop and Henry James, who remained "in the closet" for most of their lives, were more common.

Gay critics interrogate the very notion of gender identity and question the logic of gender categorization. They especially cast doubt on the idea that there is a necessary relation between gender, physiology, and sexuality. The relation of such categories as masculine and feminine to such supposedly stable bodily and psychological identities as male and female is, they contend, contingent and historical. Not only do traits like masculine and feminine circulate quite freely in combination with biological realities and sexual choices, but also the meaning of each of the terms is highly variable across cultures and over time. There is no guarantee that what one is biologically will line up in a predictable and necessary way with particular sexual practices or psychological dispositions. The normative alignment in mainstream gender culture of male and female with heterosexual masculinity or femininity must therefore be seen as a political rather than a biological fact.

The variability of sexuality and of gender identity is quelled by the dominant discourse regarding gender, which enforces what it describes. By assuming that there are stable identities such as masculine and feminine or man and woman or heterosexual and homosexual that give rise to the discourses that describe them, mainstream gender ideology enforces the normativity of such identities. The possibility of a masculine female or of a feminine male comes to appear unnatural. One contingent style of sexuality—reproductive heterosexuality—becomes naturalized through constant repetition and rote learning. It comes to appear "normal" while all other gender and sexual possibilities are rendered marginal or subordinate. In this way, a gender regime that limits legitimate sexuality to reproductive heterosexuality comes to be mistaken for an originating ground that defines and determines the difference between norm and margin, acceptable and unacceptable. What is or what is assumed to be the only possibly normal way of being becomes "what should be." In reality, however, the normative ground is simply one among many diverse sex/gender possibilities, all of which have equal claim to legitimacy. There is a plurality of sex-gender possibilities—masculine lesbian, masculine heterosexual female, feminine gay male, feminine heterosexual male, etc. This plurality is subsumed to the binary heterosexual norm in mainstream culture, but its reality is evident throughout society.

If normative reproductive sexuality and the identities that accompany it are one among many possible modes and vectors of sexuality, then supposedly marginal forms of sexuality, rather than being perverse deviations from a norm, may be manifestations of the basic multiplicity of sexuality. The norm, in other words, is less a center that defines deviations than one deviation among many. There is no central form of sexuality that can be declared to be the normative standard that allows other forms of sexuality to be declared deviant. All sexuality, in a certain sense, is deviant. There is no norm; there is only a variety of possibilities both for gender identity and for sexual practice.

These theories focus attention on the role of culture in establishing and maintaining gender norms. They assume that gender is enforced by, as much as it is expressed in, culture. Culture privileges certain sexual object choices and psychological gender dispositions while denigrating others. In the 1950s in the US, for example, melodramas such as *Written on the Wind* routinely portrayed women who were interested in sex and wore raving red cocktail dresses in the middle of the day as deviant, wild, and dangerous to patriarchy. In contrast, women and men who dressed in accordance with demure heterosexual standards, honored the norms of reproductive sexuality, ignored their homosexual urges, and played it straight were rewarded with happiness and success. Gender theorists such as Judith Butler have focused attention on the way gender is "performed" into being. We assume cultural accouterments are expressions of a gender nature or ontology, but these theorists contend that the repetitive imitation of normative gender standards in fact generates a sense in humans of having a coherent gender identity that does not include "deviant" possibilities.

Why are the ruling heterosexual gender groups so interested in making sure their norms are enforced? Gender theorists argue that the contingency of gender—that we could in reality be anything we wish to be in regard to sexuality or gender identity because nothing is naturally mandatory—inspires panic in people whose sense of identity is inseparable from the sanctity of the reigning heterosexual gender norm. At the heart of heterosexual culture's antipathy to gays is a panic fear that heterosexuality is not in fact normative. Indeed, if heterosexuality and homosexuality are on a fluid continuum of diverse possibilities, none more normative or central than the next, then homosexuality is less an "other" that is outside heterosexuality than an "alter" that is one alternative along with heterosexuality in a range of diverse and equally weighted possibilities. This argument is made more compelling by gender theorists' attention to the "homosocial" dimension of female friendship and male alliance. Both of these "normal" kinds of behavior contain elements of homosexuality. Indeed, such homosexually tinged homosociality is a primary condition of the male alliances that subtend particular kinds of behavior (in the military, for example, or in right-wing politics) that are supposedly connected in a necessary way to highly masculine forms of heterosexuality. If one looks at the numerous homemade trailers for the film *Brokeback Mountain*, especially the *Top Gun* parody, this point becomes quite clear.

The panic at the heart of heterosexual culture is most palpable in its fear objects. Loss of power often gets metaphorized in male-centered culture as anal penetration, for example, and perhaps the most feared monster in male fantasy is the masculine woman. Such women are often associated with confusion in the realm of mental representation, an inability to establish the identity of objects. If male heterosexual identity is predicated on having a passive, feminine female other as guarantor of male identity, then the masculine female upsets all of the cognitive processes and psycho-sexual assumptions that underwrite that identity. If the object that lends one credibility as a heterosexual male subject can so easily flip into its opposite, then the object world itself becomes unstable and unpredictable. The response is often violence against those objects. In films like *Disclosure* and *Basic Instinct*, for example, which are about such heterosexual male panic, one of the crucial motifs is the inability to see straight, to mentally represent the world in such a way that objects are clearly identifiable and categorizable. But if women can be men and men women, that becomes a vexed and flawed undertaking.

What these insights suggest is that homosexuality is not an identity apart from and completely outside another identity called heterosexuality. This sealed box theory might be replaced by another, called the ocean current theory. According to this approach, the fact that at different moments of history and in different cultures, so-called homosexual practices were routinely engaged in by people who were supposedly heterosexual suggests that we all have gay potentials with us, even if we are practicing heterosexuals. In ancient Greece, boys spent an initiation period in a homosexual alliance with an older male before being admitted into public life. If everyone is potentially gay, then it is only the laborious imprinting of heterosexual norms by the cultures in which we live that cuts away those potentials and manufactures good, norm-honoring heterosexual subjects. Yet latent and suppressed homosexuality is queered into being in the various forms of homophilia that pop up everywhere in heterosexual culture, from "good old boy" butt-slapping to the varieties of love-crazed fandom. Sexual transitivity is stilled for the sake of species reproduction, but in the realms of cultural play, the excess of desire and identification over norm and rule testify to more plural possibilities. . . .

Exercise 7.2 Elizabeth Bishop, "Roosters," "In the Waiting Room," and "Exchanging Hats"

That one of the three expressly lesbian poems that Elizabeth Bishop wrote—"Exchanging Hats"—had to go unpublished (while one of the others—"The Shampoo"—was refused publication by Bishop's usual outlet, *The New Yorker*, because of its sexual allusions) says something about the problems faced by gay writers in the recent past.

"Roosters" might also be read as a lesbian poem, but I place it here more because it offers such a spectacular critique of male culture from a woman's perspective.

It will become clear fairly quickly—by line 3 at least—that by "roosters" Bishop means men. Notice how she uses a simple descriptive vocabulary to characterize male culture. What colors are used and why?

What is her attitude toward the roosters? How is it registered in description and choice of setting?

Why does she call their cries "traditional"?

What is the role of "wives" in all of this male display? And why are they characterized as "despised"?

Bishop eventually begins to lend thematic significance to the roosters. What do they mean in her eyes? What feelings do they evoke? And why does she associate them with "unwanted love, conceit, and war"?

She mocks their combativeness and seems to relish their deflation and death. But then she turns oddly away from her theme and begins what appears to be a reflection on the role of the rooster in Christian symbolism. She refers to the story of Christ's betrayal by Peter. Peter was told by Christ that he would betray him by the time the cock had crowed three times.

Why does Bishop turn to this story? What do you make of the lines that begin "There is inescapable hope, the pivot"? "Pivot" might refer to the way the cock on a weathervane turns on a pivot. But here the turn seems to have to do with Peter's sorrow over his sin of "spirit." How might the meaning of the cock change or be changed by Peter's story?

The final five stanzas seem to offer a different version of a morning that contrasts with the first one described in the opening stanzas of the poem. How is this morning different?

"In the Waiting Room" is a remarkable and debatable poem. Some read it as a story of a girl coming of age and realizing her identity. Others—myself included—read it as a story about a girl coming to realize that she is a lesbian.

When the poem was written, lesbians could not live openly. They were considered deviant, and it would have been a very troubling realization for a young girl to come to if she began to see herself as being more drawn to women than to men. Heterosexuality was compulsory at the time, and she would have been expected—unless she wished to be branded a "spinster" and considered odd—to grow up to marry a man. Her youth, one might say, would consist of being "in the waiting room" of heterosexuality. Now consider how heterosexual sex might appear to such a young woman. It might seem both violent and a violation, a source of pain rather than of pleasure, like going to the dentist. Quite literally, a man would have the right to poke around in one of your essential cavities, and you would have to grin and bear it.

The girl in the poem reads *National Geographic* while her Aunt Consuelo is inside with the dentist. Back then, this magazine often contained photographs of African women with exposed breasts, and it was one of the few places in the culture where one could see images of nakedness. It had a reputation as a form of mild pornography. Notice how the girl qualifies what she is doing—"(I could read)"—in parentheses that suggest a kind of inside that is parallel to the "inside" where the aunt is. This inside, one might say, is her inside self, and one senses that the poem will explore her psychology. What she describes, in other words, may be her own reactions to things as much as the things themselves.

Why would she "carefully" study the photographs? What does that word suggest about the quality of her attention? Imagine you are a young person seeing an image of a naked person for the first time. It would grab your attention probably, and it might light a fire of sexual interest in you. Notice what happens next to the girl—an exploding volcano, rivulets of fire. What do you make of that image?

The image that follows is of two explorers, one female, the other male, but you don't realize that immediately from the names. Why might the girl focus on how they are dressed? Can you tell which is male and which female?

The next image is troubling—a dead man slung on a pole. How might it fit in? "Long pig" is a very derogatory term. How might it be explained by a young lesbian girl's awakening hostility to compulsory heterosexuality?

A similar hostility might be said to inform the next images—women who seem bound to childbirth and child-rearing. Why the repetition here?

What do you make of the word "horrifying" applied to the girl's sense of their naked breasts? Given that her own reactions are so bound up with the things described, what about her reactions might provoke a feeling of horror in the girl? Are the breasts frightening, or are the feelings the breasts inspire frightening? And if so, why?

What do you make of the insistently reassuring quality of the following two lines—"I read it straight through. / I was too shy to stop"? There seems to be a small element of guilt here, as if she wanted to assure herself and readers that she didn't dawdle over the potentially erotically arousing photographs, taking pleasure from them. Notice that she implies that she wanted to stop to look longer, but she was "too shy" to do so.

She seems to seek even more reassurance in the lines that follow. By looking at the cover, she pushes the photographs (and her troubling reactions to them) inside. You might say, she represses the feelings they inspire by "covering" them. Notice the image of boundaries here—"margins"—as well as the punctuality of "date." In space and time, she wants to fix a boundary between herself and the feelings now safely "inside" the magazine.

All of this makes the next line striking and interesting—"Suddenly, from inside." Here "inside" refers or seems to refer to the dentist's inner room where Aunt Consuelo has gone and where the girl imagines her experiencing an "*oh!* of pain." That "oh" sounds like "O," and as in *King Lear*, it suggests the vaginal opening. If the dentist is a figure for a feared painful heterosexual experience the girl does not want to have, then that allusion would make sense. Compulsory heterosexual sex is pain for a lesbian.

What follows suggests that things are not clear-cut for the girl. She confuses herself with her aunt, but of course, that would be what a young girl trying to form her own identity from identifications with older relatives would be expected to do. Why would she begin this section by saying that she knew her aunt was "a foolish, timid woman"? If we generalize, what might that suggest about women who submit to a regime of compulsory heterosexuality that would turn them into beings like those in the magazine photographs, whose whole lives seem to be reduced to sex and child-rearing?

In the sentence "she was a foolish, timid woman," where do you think the stress falls? If it falls on "she," then the girl is marking out or trying to mark out a difference from her aunt. The girl knows SHE, meaning the aunt, may be timid and foolish, but she herself is not. Does that seem like a plausible reading?

If so, what do you make of her confusion of herself with the aunt? Why would she imagine that she is her foolish aunt? Is she imagining growing up to be like her aunt and wondering what that would mean? Or is her confusion more an expression of what we have noticed about her feelings in the previous stanza—an expression of preference for women over men?

That would seem to make a certain sense. After all, to be "like" someone in the sense of identifying with them in order to form one's own identity can easily be confused with to "like" them, as in having affection for them—just as in love we often mold our own identity on that of our love object. It all depends on how you read the line "Without thinking at all / I was my foolish aunt." Does she mean that she WAS her foolish aunt, but she didn't realize it? Or does she mean that she did not think she was her foolish aunt?

But why would the girl feel that they are "falling, falling" together, and why would their eyes be "glued" to the cover of the magazine? Does "fall" mean something like "caught in the act" and therefore "in sin"? Or is it more that the girl is falling back into the feelings awakened by the photographs in the magazine, disturbing lesbian sexual feelings, that make her yearn for the security and safety associated with a "cover," a boundary that seals off the dangerous affect somewhere inside?

Read the rest of the poem on your own. Take note of the interplay of identity and identification and notice how she uses "like" and "unlikely" in this regard. The black wave has to do, I would suggest, with the powerful affect released by the girl's awakening sense of herself as "unlike" others. If that is so, then the final stanza seems to re-evoke the possibility of some punctual, well-marked boundary where the danger both of the affect and for the girl of that realization can be controlled or concealed. Notice as well the odd configuration of inside and outside in that stanza, and think about how that might bear on this reading.

I will not say much about "Exchanging Hats," an unpublished poem about the fluidity of gender identity, other than to draw your attention to it and to say it is very interesting! You might take the trouble to look up "anandrous" and "avernal" and ask why she uses these words.

Exercise 7.3   Henry James, *The Aspern Papers*

The narrator of *The Aspern Papers* clearly adores Jeffrey Aspern, but does he love him? Is this a love story between men, one of whom is dead and remains accessible only through letters he wrote to a woman and one of whom is desperate to see the letters for purely "literary" reasons that seem to just barely conceal a much stronger passion?

Consider how Aspern's relations with women are characterized in the first chapter. How does the narrator describe those relations? You might look up the story of Orpheus to find out what that allusion means. To compare Aspern's female companions to Maenads is not flattering, since these followers of Dionysus were known for tearing people limb from limb. Notice how the narrator disparages women and asserts that Aspern was "not a woman's poet." Why does he seem so bent on diminishing the significance of Aspern's relations with women?

Do you get any sense of the narrator's sexuality in this chapter? He uses a sexual allusion to distance himself from the erotic attachment to women Aspern seems to have cultivated. The narrator says, "it struck me that he had been kinder and more considerate than in his place—if I could imagine myself in any such box—I should have found the trick of." It's a strangely convoluted way of saying something, and a psychoanalytic critic would latch on to that fact and suggest it is significant of a psychic conflict between desire and repression. Is the narrator imagining himself as Aspern or as one of Aspern's women? There are two sexual terms in the quoted passage—"box," a slang term for vagina, and "trick," a slang term for the sexual act. For the narrator to say that he can't imagine himself in any such box is a bit like saying he cannot imagine heterosexual sex. The name of his partner—"Cumnor"—also contains a sexual pun. To not "come" means to not ejaculate, and that might also be a symbolic signal of sexual detachment.

Are there other ways in which sexuality seems implied in the setting, action, and characterizations in the story?

Consider the discussion of the garden in chapter 2, for example. And there is another curious sexual pun at the end of that chapter. The narrator says of Juliana Bordereau that he "could pounce on her possessions and ransack her drawers." "Drawers" is an old slang term for women's underwear.

So what do you think the tale is about then—a man with sexual yearnings toward a maternal figure, or a man with negative feelings for women who clearly prefers other men?

Why do you think Juliana is described so negatively at the end of chapter 2? What significance does it lend her? What does it mean that the narrator seems to fear her so much?

Psychoanalytic theorists describe masochism as a process that converts pain into pleasure. In masochist fantasies, there always seems to be a strong, quasi-maternal figure who inflicts pain. Are there any indications that one aspect of the narrator's sexual make-up might be masochism? Notice how, at the beginning of chapter 4, he is described as "whimpering" in his friend's salon.

One of the more homoerotic moments in the text occurs in this chapter. The narrator imagines Aspern talking to him about being in Venice together in a "mystic companionship." Even the world seems to dissolve in an image of erotic bonding—"the marble of the palaces all shimmer and melt together."

Juliana's name contains a similar image of liquidity—"border" and "eau," which means "water" in French. If she is maternal and Aspern paternal in the fictional fantasy of which the narrator is the subject, then it is significant that she is associated with a dissolution of boundaries and with charged sexual imagery some of which focuses erotic energy on her. If a mother does not respect clear boundaries between herself and her male child, if she eroticizes his body through either inappropriate attentiveness or punitiveness, what results is very much like what one sees in the narrator. He idealizes and idolizes the paternal figure as an alternative, and he has strongly charged negative feelings toward the mother, some of which are erotic in character.

He imagines himself pelting her door with flowers, and the door "would have to yield." He has fantasies of her as someone characterized by "impenitent passion." And later, of course, the goal of his quest, the papers, will be hidden in her mattress, as symbolic a hiding-place as one could imagine.

What does Aspern represent? If Juliana is a death's mask who inspires fear and makes the narrator whimper, one should expect Aspern to offer a strong contrast. Notice the way he is characterized at the end of chapter 4. How is that significant in this context?

The relationship with Tina is tinged by expediency. It is also a kind of trial heterosexual relationship. The expediency works to remove any sincerity from the relation, and that would seem to confirm the gay theme by relieving the narrator of any responsibility, any sense that he really means this mock-heterosexual courtship. He is just playing for the sake of his more important goal—union in "mystic companionship" with Jeffrey Aspern. How does the narrator think through his motives regarding Tina? Do you detect signs of bad faith, of reasoning that excuses what should not be excused?

As the narrator nears the goal of his quest, the erotic imagery intensifies. He speaks of nearing the "climax of my crisis," and the papers are in a box in a mattress. He is close to being an object of Aspern's love, since the letters he seeks are written to a love object. Does the narrator want to be in Juliana's place in order to enjoy Aspern alone?

And what do you make of his intense feeling of shame upon being discovered? If his actions have the homoerotic meaning I have been attributing to them, the intensity of his shame would seem to be accounted for. What would a feminist critic say about how Juliana is characterized in this scene?

The final encounters with Tina are remarkable for the way they bring into direct relation the two gender-sexual strands at issue in the tale. The first would be compulsory heterosexuality, since that in part is what Tina represents. Juliana mocks the narrator for not being manly enough, and tries to push him into a heterosexual relationship with someone who moans with "ecstasy" when he takes her out on a date. The second would be the subcultural homosexuality whose name cannot be spoken in the culture of the late nineteenth century but which manifests itself latently and marginally in the narrator's quest for some connection, through the love letters, with a man he idealizes and loves. When Tina proposes marriage, notice how she characterizes the proposed gift of the papers. How does she eroticize them and suggest their sexual symbolism? She almost proposes playing doctor when she says "You could see the things—you could use them." How is the narrator's reaction significant? How does his homosexuality manifest itself at this moment? How does his connection with Aspern "save" him?

Finally, we've discussed the possibility of masochism. How might the ending be read as evidence of masochism?

CHAPTER

4

Considering the Geopolitical

In the age of New Historicism, it has become common practice to discuss texts within their sociohistoric contexts; however, it is also becoming more apparent that fully addressing American literature often necessitates crossing boundaries and enlarging our perspective. Thus more and more critics and instructors are asserting the need to consider the intersection of politics, geography, demography, and economics. At the most basic level, considering the geopolitical entails addressing geographic and political factors influencing a region. One common way to approach this task is to consider borders and border crossings and their impact on literature. Another popular avenue is to analyze the commonalities and differences between national literatures. An increasingly fashionable line of research involves the study of diasporas and linkages between the literature of an originally homogenous population that has been dispersed through forced or voluntary migration. The essays that follow provide a brief sampling of some of the very different avenues that a concern with the geopolitical might take.

In "America," Kirsten Silva Gruesz seeks to define *America*, taking into account geopolitical concerns by noting the multiple geographic and political connotations associated with the term. According to Gruesz, debates regarding the meaning of *America* reflect different ancestral claims to the Americas. In addition to exploring the shifting meanings of *America* through references to Walt Whitman and Phillis Wheatley, Gruesz discusses the American studies discipline and its relationship to the term.

Michael Warner's "What's Colonial about Colonial America?" also interrogates the notion of America, but in terms of its legacy of colonization. Warner follows the lead of historians who have moved away from a national narrative with regard to the colonial era and argues for literary critics to do the same. Noting that Anglo-American settlement did not look like typical colonialism, these early settlers came to think of themselves first as the locals and then as the colonized. Warner proposes a reading of colonial literature that assumes a distinctively American identity by pointing to such examples as John Winthrop and Benjamin Franklin.

Amy Kaplan's "Manifest Domesticity" takes the geopolitical notion of manifest destiny into the realm of gender. Kaplan complicates notions of separate private and public spheres by associating them on a national scale with the domestic and the foreign. Kaplan begins by asserting that the concept of foreign policy relies on a sense of the nation as a domestic space, while the idea of the foreign requires boundaries to distinguish the nation as home. Thus, Kaplan places women squarely in the middle of concerns regarding nationalism and foreign policy. She describes a mobile domesticity that both expands and contracts boundaries of home and nation, while producing variable notions of the foreign. Kaplan discusses such figures as Catherine Beecher, Sarah Josepha Hale, E. D. E. N. Southworth, and Harriet Beecher Stowe as she concludes that manifest domesticity turned "an imperial nation into a home" (p. 350).

In his essay, "American Literary Emergence as a Postcolonial Phenomenon," Lawrence Buell argues for the value of viewing the American Renaissance through the lens of postcolonialism. Noting the colonial influence of Britain, Buell invites readers to imagine the American Renaissance as an emergence from Britain's cultural authority. For example, Buell argues that Walt Whitman's 1855 preface to *Leaves of Grass* and Ralph Waldo Emerson's "The American Scholar" are at opposite ends of a continuum of the American Renaissance's literary nationalism, with Whitman envisioning a very different American voice, one that has repressed its international precedents, and Emerson presenting a vision of international tendencies within American Renaissance high culture. Although these are very different approaches, both continue a dialogue with Europe. Buell contends that American Renaissance writers wrote for both an American and a transatlantic audience. He concludes his essay by addressing various marks of postcolonialism in American Renaissance literature. In addition to Emerson and Whitman, Buell discusses James Fenimore Cooper, Herman Melville, Nathaniel Hawthorne, William Cullen Bryant, and Henry Thoreau in some detail.

The final essay, "The Hitchhiker's Guide to Ecocriticism" by Ursula K. Heise, offers a different inroad to the geopolitical through a concern with environmental issues. The essay provides an overview of the development of the field as it moved from the valuation of wild and rural places to a greater concern with people's interaction with their environment. Through this history, Heise traces the field's increased attention to women's and Native American literature and urban spaces. The field initially focused on nonfiction and nature poetry by such writers as Henry Thoreau, Ralph Waldo Emerson, Mary Austin, and Gary Snyder, but a second wave of publications emphasized women writers like Willa Cather, Adrienne Rich, and Terry Tempest Williams, as well as Native American writers such as Leslie Marmon Silko and Joy Harjo.

The essays collected here lay the groundwork for discussions regarding what constitutes American literature. A unit on the American Renaissance might be prefaced with texts on American identity, such as excerpts from Hector St. John de Crevecoeur's *Letters from an American Farmer*, Thomas Paine's *Common Sense*, and Thomas Jefferson's *Notes on the State of Virginia*, as well as Absalom Jones's "Petition of the people of Colour, free men . . . of Philadelphia," Tecumseh's *Speech of Tecumseh to Governor Harrison*, Margaret Fuller's *Woman in the Nineteenth Century*, and Sojourner Truth's "Speech to a Women's Rights Convention." Readings relevant to the development of an American literature include Edward Tyrell Channing's "On Models in Literature" and an excerpt from Cooper's *Notions on the Americans*. Readings from the American Renaissance can then be read and discussed in terms of how well they respond to the call for a national literature. Some texts that would be particularly well suited for this discussion include Emerson's "The American Scholar," an excerpt from Stowe's *Uncle Tom's Cabin*, Thoreau's "Resistance to Civil Government," Frederick Douglass's *Narrative of the Life*, Hawthorne's *The Scarlet Letter*, Melville's "Bartleby the Scrivener," excerpts from Whitman's *Leaves of Grass*, and a selection of Emily Dickinson's poetry.

America

Kirsten Silva Gruesz

In Keywords for American Cultural Studies *(2007), edited by Bruce Burgett and Glenn Hendler, Gruesz proffers a definition of* America. *She begins by noting the multiple connotations associated with America's geographic and political meanings. In presenting the history of the term, Gruesz notes the debates surrounding the naming of the continent and the meaning of the word. According to Gruesz, "this debate suggests that what's really at stake is not some etymological truth but a narrative of shared origins; each claim grants primacy and symbolic (if not literal)*

From *Keywords for American Cultural Studies*, ed. Bruce Burgett and Glenn Hendler (New York: New York UP, 2007): 16–22.

ancestry of the Americas to a different group" (p. 307). Gruesz observes that colonists initially avoided the term America *in favor of* New England, Nieuw-Amsterdam, *and* Nueva España; *however, the Civil War brought an upsurge of patriotic feeling that led to a greater sense of "Americanization." As she explores the shifting meanings of* America, *Gruesz refers to Walt Whitman's definition of* America *as "the race of races" (p. 306) and Phillis Wheatley's personification of* America *as* Columbia; *she concludes by exploring the American studies discipline's relationship to the term.*

"We hold these truths to be self-evident," begins the main body of the Declaration of Independence, and the definition of "America" may likewise seem utterly self-evident: the short form of the nation's official name. Yet the meaning of this well-worn term becomes more elusive the closer we scrutinize it. Since "America" names the entire hemisphere from the Yukon to Patagonia, its common use as a synonym for the United States of America is technically a misnomer, as Latin Americans and Canadians continually (if resignedly) point out. Given the nearly universal intelligibility of this usage, their objection may seem a small question of geographical semantics. But "America" carries multiple connotations that go far beyond its literal referent. In the statement "As Americans, we prize freedom," "American" may at first seem to refer simply to U.S. citizens, but the context of the sentence strongly implies a consensual understanding of shared *values*, not just shared passports; the literal and figurative meanings tend to collapse into each other. The self-evidence of "America" is thus troubled from the start by multiple ambiguities about the extent of the territory it delineates, as well as about its deeper connotations.

Seeking out the meaning of America might be said to be a national characteristic, if that proposition were not in itself tautological. The question prompts responses representing every conceivable point of view, from the documentary series packaged as *Ken Burns's America* (1996) to prizewinning essays by schoolchildren invited to tackle this hoary topic. Foodways, cultural practices, and even consumer products are readily made to symbolize the nation's essence ("baseball, hot dogs, apple pie, and Chevrolet," as a highly effective advertising campaign put it in the 1970s). Such metonyms gesture, in turn, at more abstract notions: Freedom, Liberty, Democracy. Whether implicit or explicit, such responses to the enigma of Americanness tend to obscure the conditions under which they were formulated. Who gets to define what "America" means? What institutions support or undermine a particular definition? Under what historical conditions does one group's definition have more or less power than another's? How does the continued repetition of such ideological statements have real, material effects on the ways people are able to live their lives? Without looking critically at these questions of nomenclature, "American" cultural studies cannot claim self-awareness about its premises or its practices.

Because the meaning of "America" and its corollaries—American, Americanization, Americanism, and Americanness—seems so self-evident but is in fact so imprecise, using the term in conversation or debate tends to reinforce certain ways of thinking while repressing others. In his slyly comic *Devil's Dictionary* (1911), pundit Ambrose Bierce defines the term only through its opposite: "un-American, *adj.* Wicked, intolerable, heathenish." "American" and "un-American," Bierce implies, shut down genuine argument by impugning the values of one's opponent. A less cynical example may be found in Walt Whitman's preface to *Leaves of Grass*, which in several pages seeks to define the essence of America: "The genius of the United States is not best or most in its executives or legislatures, nor in its ambassadors or authors or colleges or churches or parlors . . . but always most in the common people." "America is the race of races," he writes. "The Americans of all nations at any time upon the earth have probably the fullest poetical nature. The United States themselves are essentially the greatest poem" (Whitman 1855/1999, 4–5). Whitman's claims about America work toward his larger project of celebrating "the common people," the heterogeneous mixing of immigrants into a "race of races," and everyday, vernacular speech as the stuff of poetry. Each variant of his definition bolsters this larger ideology. Although Whitman seems to use "United States" and "America" interchangeably, elsewhere in the document Mexico and the Caribbean are included as "American"—a slippage from the *political* meaning to the *geographical* one that reveals the expansionist beliefs Whitman held at the time.

If the substitution of the name of its most powerful nation for the hemisphere as a whole is a mistake sanctified by the passage of time, the same may be said of the origins of the term "America." Against Columbus's insistence that the landmass he had "discovered" was Asia, the Italian explorer Amerigo Vespucci first dubbed it a "New World" in his treatise by that name. It was not Vespucci himself but a contemporary mapmaker, Martin Waldseemuller, who then christened the region "America," though it originally referred only to the southern continent. Later cartographers broadened the designation to include the lesser-known north—a further irony of history. The sixteenth-century Dominican priest Bartolomé de las Casas initiated an argument that raged across both Americas over whether Vespucci had usurped an honor rightly due Columbus; he proposed rechristening it "Columba."

To this day alternative theories of the naming of the continent flourish, finding new devotees on the Internet. Solid evidence links a British merchant named Richard Ameryk to John Cabot's voyages along the North Atlantic coast, leading to speculation that Cabot named "America" for his patron a decade or so before Waldseemuller's map.

Others have argued that the name comes from Vikings who called their Newfoundland settlement "Mark" or "Maruk"—"Land of Darkness." Still others have claimed, more circumstantially, that the root word derives from Phoenician, Hebrew, or Hindu terms, suggesting that one of these groups encountered America before Europeans did. Similar etymological evidence has been interpreted to show that the term ultimately stems from a word for show Moors or Africans, so that "America" really means "land of the blacks." "America" is thus a product of the same misunderstanding that gave us the term "Indian." Given this similarity, one final theory about the term's origins is particularly provocative. An indigenous group in Nicaragua had referred to one gold-rich district in their territory as "Amerrique" since before the Conquest, and Mayan languages of tribes further north use a similar-sounding word. These discoveries have led to the radical proposition that the name "America" comes from *within* the New World rather than being imposed on it. The continuing life of this debate suggests that what's really at stake is not some ultimate etymological truth but a narrative of shared origins; each claim grants primacy and symbolic (if not literal) ancestry of the Americas to a different group.

The fact that only one of these foundational fables of America's origin involves an indigenous name is revealing. Throughout the colonies, settlers tended not to refer to themselves as Americans, since the term then conveyed an indigenous ancestry—or at least the associated taint of barbarism and backwardness—they were (with certain romanticizing exceptions) eager to avoid. Instead, they called their home-spaces "New-England," "Nieuw-Amsterdam," "Nueva España," reminders of the homeland reflecting a local, rather than continental, identification. Until well into the nineteenth century, as the example from Whitman indicates, "America" and its analogues in Spanish, French, and other European languages designated something called "the New World," not necessarily "the United States." And during the early modern period in particular, it was persistently represented as female, using an iconography that ranged from the savage devourer to the desirable exotic. Following the same pattern of feminization, a poem published during the Revolutionary War by the African American celebrity Phillis Wheatley first personified the nascent country as Columbia, an invented goddess who lent a tinge of classical refinement to the nation-building project. The image and name were quite popular during the century that followed. Referring specifically to the United States, "Columbia" distinguished the nation from the hemisphere, but it also came to carry its own ideological baggage and can thus be seen as a kind of predecessor to the contemporary usage of "America." It prompted patriotic musings on the true meaning of "the Columbian ideal," and inspired events like the 1893 World's Columbian Exposition in Chicago, calculated to draw international attention to a nation that increasingly celebrated modernity and progress. In addition, "Columbia" had an iconographic presence that "America" no longer does; the figure of the goddess appeared on coins into the early twentieth century.

At what point, then, did "America" become synonymous with the USA, within the nation itself if not worldwide? "Americanism" and "Americanization" had entered common usage by the beginning of the nineteenth century, referring at first to evolving linguistic differences from the "mother tongue." Such changes are gradual, of course, but the Civil War marks one watershed. The war brought about not only an upsurge in patriotic feeling but a marked increase in centralized governmental power. A more unified vision of national identity seemed necessary to counteract the effects of sectionalism, followed by the perceived threat of the great surges of immigration at the end of the century. "Americanization" came to signify the degree to which those immigrants altered their customs and values in accordance with the dominant view of Americanness at the time.

Of the many figurative meanings that "America" has acquired over time, many involve notions of novelty, new beginnings, and utopian promise. The Mexican historian Edmundo O'Gorman influentially wrote in 1958 that America was "invented" before it was "discovered," demonstrating that Europeans had long imagined a mythical land of marvels and riches they then projected onto the unfamiliar terrain. This projection was not always positive. The common representation of a "virgin land" waiting to be explored, dominated, and domesticated relegates the natural world to the passive, inferior position then associated with the feminine. The French naturalist George Louis Leclerc de Buffon even argued in 1789 that since the region was geologically newer, its very flora and fauna were less developed than Europe's—a claim Thomas Jefferson took pains to refute. Nonetheless, the notion of the novelty of the Americas persisted, extending to the supposedly immature culture of its inhabitants as well.

Early debates over literature and fine arts in English, Spanish, and French America focused on the question of whether the residents of a land without history could cultivate a genuine or original aesthetic. Some Romantic writers tried on "Indian" themes, while others spun this "historylessness" in America's favor. The philosopher G. W. F. Hegel delivered an influential address in 1830 that claimed, "America is therefore the land of the future, where, in all the ages that lie before us, the burden of the World's History shall reveal itself—perhaps in a contest between North and South America. It is a land of desire for all those who are weary of the historical lumber-room of old Europe" (Hegel 1837/1956, 86). Here Hegel uses "America," as Whitman would a few decades later, to indicate the whole region, not just the United States. Claims about the New World's salvational role in global history, then, gestated from without as well as from within. Given this longstanding tendency to define America in mythic terms, we must be skeptical of the common boast that the United States is the only modern nation founded on an *idea*—democratic equality—rather than on a shared tribal or racial ancestry. Such a claim to exceptionalism is of course particularly appealing to intellectuals, who traffic in ideas. In the early years of American studies as an academic discipline, in the 1950s, the field's foundational texts located the essential meaning of America variously in its history of westward movement, in religious and philosophical individualism, or in the worship of progress and modernity. As the discipline has evolved, it now attempts to show how such mythic definitions arise in response to historically specific needs and conditions. When we go in search of what is most profoundly American, scholars now insist, we blinker our sights to the ways in which the actual history of U.S. actions and policies may have diverged from those expectations. Moreover, any single response to the prompt to define "America" tends to imply that this larger idea or ideal has remained essentially unchanged over time, transcending ethnic and racial differences. "America" has generally been used as a term of consolidation, homogenization, and unification, not a term that invites recognition of difference, dissonance, and plurality—all issues of crucial import in the post–civil rights movement era.

Such a recognition cuts to the heart of any Americanist pursuit, whether in historical, literary, or social studies, forcing scholars to confront fundamental questions of the field's scope and limits. Jan Radway's much-cited presidential address to the American Studies Association in 1998 repudiated the "imperial" arrogation by the United States of a name that originally belonged to an entire hemisphere, arguing that "American national identity is . . . constructed in and through relations of difference." She went so far as to suggest that the organization eliminate the term "American" from its name altogether in order to "reconceptualize the American as always relationally defined and therefore as intricately dependent on 'others' that are used both materially and conceptually to mark its boundaries" (Radway 2002, 54, 59).

Though her proposal to change the name of the organization was more a provocation than a promise, Radway's speech responded to challenges raised in preceding years by proponents of an "Americas" or "New World" cultural studies that would insist on a relational consideration of the United States within the larger context of the hemisphere. Inherently pluralistic, this transnational approach draws upon Latin American, Caribbean, and Canadian works and emphasizes their production within a history of U.S. imperial design. Rather than Alexis de Tocqueville and Michel Crèvecoeur, its canon of commentators on the meaning of America highlights lesser-known figures like the Cuban José Martí—who in an 1891 speech famously distinguished between "Nuestra" (Our) America, with its mestizo or mixed-race origins, and the racist, profit-driven culture he saw dominating the United States. Martí, like the later African American activist-writers W. E. B. Du Bois and C. L. R. James, was critical of the growing interventionist tendencies of the United States and sought to revive and provoke dissent and resistance. In addition to recovering such underappreciated figures, comparative Americanist work often locates its inquiry in spaces once relegated to the periphery of scholarly attention, such as the Spanish-speaking borderlands that were formerly part of Mexico. As contact zones between North and South, Anglo and Latino, such areas produce hybrid cultural formations that inflect mainstream U.S. culture with that of the "other" America.

"Americas" studies, capitalizing on the plurality of its name, seeks to relativize the status of the United States within the hemisphere and the world—and thus reaches well beyond matters involving Latin American and Latino cultures. Bell Gale Chevigny and Gari Laguardia, introducing their landmark essay collection *Reinventing the Americas* (1986, viii), write that "by dismantling the U.S. appropriation of the name 'America,' we will better see what the United States is and what it is not." The work of divorcing the name of the nation from the name of the continent has stumbled a bit on the lack of a ready adjectival form in English. A few scholars have recalled into service the neologism that Frank Lloyd Wright coined in the 1930s to describe his non-derivative, middle-class house designs: "Usonian." Others, like Chevigny and Laguardia, simply substitute "U.S." or "United Statesian" for "American," arguing that the very awkwardness of such terms has a certain heuristic value, recalling us to an historical moment before the pressure toward consensus and national unity became as pervasive as it is today.

Perhaps such consciousness-raising about the power of "self-evident" terms could begin the slow work of altering social relationships and structures of political power. On the other hand, pluralizing "America" to "Americas" does not in itself do away with imperial presumptions—indeed, some of its deployments may reiterate them. Proponents of the North American Free Trade Agreement (NAFTA), which took effect in 1994, argued that the treaty would open borders and promote cultural interchange—at the expense, many would contend, of subjecting Mexico's economy to tighter control by U.S.-based corporations than ever before. New proposals for a similarly structured "Free Trade Area of the Americas" could extend NAFTA to encompass thirty-four countries and some 800 million people. In this context, the plural term works opportunistically rather than critically, suggesting that in the future, the usage of "Americas" may require the same kind of critical scrutiny that we have just brought to "America."

Works Cited

Bierce, Ambrose. *Devil's Dictionary*, New York: Albert and Charles Boni, 1911.
Chevigny, Bell Gale, and Gari Laguardia, eds. *Reinventing the Americas: Comparative Studies of Literature of the United States and Spanish America.* New York: Cambridge University Press, 1986.

Hegel, G. W. F. *The Philosophy of History.* 1837. Reprint; translated by J. Sibree. New York: Dover, 1956.

Radway, Jan. "What's in a Name?" In *The Futures of American Studies*, edited by Donald Pease and Robyn Wiegman, 45–75. Durham, NC: Duke University Press, 2002.

Whitman, Walt. *Selected Poems 1855–1892: A New Edition.* 1855. Reprint, edited by Gary Schmidgall. New York: St. Martin's Press, 1999.

What's Colonial about Colonial America?

Michael Warner

Warner argues that discussions of colonial Anglo-America seldom occur within the context of colonialism due to a tendency to look at the literature of early America in terms of nation building. However, scholars are beginning to think in terms of "colonial literatures of the Atlantic world rather than of a future nation" (p. 313). After tracing different forms of colonialism, Warner notes the way in which white American settlers came to see themselves as the locals. He argues that the benign idea of settlement obscured the colonial history of British American colonies. In fact, rather than see themselves as colonizers, they saw themselves as colonized. Warner discusses this turn as the development of "creole nationalism" (p. 323). By questioning the distinctively American quality of early writers, Warner's thesis leads readers to question the perspective of such texts as John Winthrop's A Modell of Christian Charity, *which he maintains is neither American nor national in its use of "we."*

If we were to ask what was colonial about colonial Africa, the answers might be complex: different European powers behaved differently in different colonies, or at different times, and with a different mix of motives. But we would at least know that it meant something to ask the question. We would know that whatever the local variants, they were part of a larger pattern of domination in which the international nation-state system and world capitalism created imbalances of power and wealth that continue to this day, long after the formal arrangements of colonialism ended. We would know that any discussion of the subject would be frivolous if not engaged with the disastrous legacy of colonialism in the historical present. Discussions about colonial Anglo-America seldom have a perceptible relation to that context, despite the importance of the old Imperial school and a revival of transatlantic topics in recent historiography.[1] Among literary critics in particular, very few sentences about colonial America would be significantly

From *Possible Pasts: Becoming Colonial in Early America*, ed. Robert Blair St. George (Ithaca: Cornell UP, 2000): 49–70.

altered if the word "colonial" were simply replaced by the word "early."[2] At a time when historians have so much to say about the politics, economics, and everyday life of empire, the problem of colonialism in literary culture remains cloaked in banality—at least where American Indian relations are not explicitly thematic.

Historians can rely on the intrinsic interest of any aspect of the past; it is all history. But literary critics must ask questions of value and interest about what we study, not all of which is literature—at least not in the sense that inspires reading. Why, after all, does anyone want to read colonial Anglo-American literature? The standard and usually implicit answer is national. Early modern Atlantic writing is read because it is the cultural heritage of Americans. A nationalist impulse is an almost preinterpretive commitment of the discipline. In the first paragraph of *The Americans* (1958), for example, Daniel Boorstin quotes the famous "city on a hill" passage from John Winthrop's "Modell of Christian Charity." The text is given such prominence because "no one writing after the fact, three hundred years later, could have better expressed the American sense of destiny." This sense of destiny, Boorstin writes, is "the keynote of American history."[3]

Such arguments—and more generally the implicit assumption of national culture—motivate some people to read colonial texts. But not necessarily to read them very well. Boorstin was asking a national question and seeing a nation. In so doing he obscured most of what would now be interesting in Winthrop's text. In the time since Boorstin's book, historians have turned sharply away from the national narrative, having been preoccupied with the localism of early modern colonists, on one hand, and the transatlantic contexts of empire and trade, on the other. They would now be less inclined to let a member of the Massachusetts Congregational elite stand for all the colonies, to forget that some British American colonies remain colonies to this day, or to assume that colonial history had an inner propulsion toward modern nationalism. Given the complex picture of an early modern Atlantic world that historians have developed over the past two or three decades, Winthrop's text might seem to be marked less by the seeds of national destiny than by transitional narratives, a concern for discipline, the consciousness of a nascent imperial culture not fully recognizing itself as such, and a marked silence about those to be dispossessed.

When Winthrop says at the conclusion of his sermon, "Wee shall be as a Citty upon a Hill," the "we" is neither American nor national. He has been invoking a specific audience in the context of the previous paragraph—namely, church members in the Massachusetts Bay migration. Yet the sense of membership grows broader and more vague in the phrase "our selves and posterity." It grows broader still when Winthrop invokes the world-historical Protestant struggle ("wee shall be made a story and a by-word through the world"), with its fundamentally *transnational* self-understanding, or when he invokes an English national sense of audience through his use of the still novel term "New England." The whole passage is also marked by an uneasy yoking of geographies and temporalities: English traditionalism, the globalizing modernity of Protestant historical narrative, the timeless space of divine judgment, and the migratory spaces of empire and capital. None of this amounts to an "American sense of destiny," particularly as each of the final three paragraphs of the sermon ends rhetorically on a spectacle of failure: "the Lord will surely breake out in wrathe against us"; "we shall shame the faces of many of gods worthy servants, and cause theire prayers to be turned into Cursses upon us"; and "Wee shall surely perishe out of the good Land whither wee passe over this vast sea to possesse it." The nationalist reading papers over not only the implicit aggression of this anathematizing rhetoric but even its explicitly regulative intent. The language suggests not so much shared confidence as a will to authority, power, discipline, and restraint.[4]

These and other features of the text will stand out to any reader interested in colonial American history as a colonial history. But literary critics are only beginning to reimagine the literary history in general as one of a colonial culture. Nationalist criticism has always had a repertoire of themes by means of which colonial writing could be seen as essentially American: the wilderness, natural man, the social covenant, individualism, the rise of democracy and the self-made man, the revolt against Europe and the sublimity of new beginnings. These themes have been worked up with such mythic potency that undergraduates can reliably find them in colonial texts with practically no coaching—especially since the colonial archive has been anthologized to highlight them. There are almost no corresponding themes, in common currency, by which early modern writing might be seen as essentially colonial or Anglo-American. By asking new questions about colonial texts, scholars are currently moving to a new conception of the field—one of colonial literatures of the Atlantic world rather than of a future nation.[5] But when the glorious history of the nation is set aside, it remains to say what the story of colonial literatures in Anglo-America might be or how to read any given text in its colonial setting—let alone how to read it with pleasure. It is unlikely that any colonial themes will ever have the ego satisfactions of national belonging.

I.

We have only to pose the question seriously to see that the concept of "colonialism" is itself a problem. There have been many colonialisms, and any venture into postcolonial theory should begin with a comparative historical sense of their differences.[6] Historians sometimes distinguish between the "first" British Empire, to which the American colonies belonged, and a second empire that took shape partly in response to American independence. Even within the first empire there was enormous variation in British practice from one colony to another, as well as in the interaction of different peoples. Postcolonial critics often write in the singular of "colonialism," "the colonial condition," "colonial discourse," and "the colonial Other." Yet there are few constants in the history of colonialisms or even of European colonialisms in the early modern period. The northern white settler colonies of America only rarely used a native labor force for the extraction of wealth, and they never saw themselves as administering a native nation, as the British did in India and Africa. Many colonialisms were centrally defined by racism, but not all.[7] Some colonies involved settlement, others did not. Some colonies were driven by merchant capital, others were not. The English in North America tried settlement before they had more than a vague idea of transatlantic commerce, whereas the French developed a commercial policy that limited settlement.[8] Most of the great colonial powers—the Portuguese, the Dutch, the French, and the English, for example—had contrasting kinds of colonies at the same time, in some cases on opposite sides of the globe. They took slaves to some colonies but not to others. They used native labor in some but not in others. They conquered some at the outset, but others they first traded with as partners for long periods. Some they saw as savage and stateless; others, such as the Moghul Empire, were civilizations more advanced and complex than those of the Europeans, and the future colonizers found themselves dependent on the future colonized for financial and administrative systems.

Nor did Europeans act with one mind in relation to the same colonial venture. The Virginia Company inconsistently treated American Indians as wild savages and as feudal states, as when they sent a robe and crown with which to enthrone Powhatan as an ally, partly in imitation of a similar gesture made by Cortés to the Aztecs. Modern notions of race and nation took shape only gradually in colonial practice; they did not drive colonization consistently. It is not even easy to draw a sharp line between national ventures in colonialism and the practices of national unification that one historian has called "internal colonialism." Within England itself, the draining of the fens under Charles I gave rise to a state program of settlement "plantations" in East Anglia modeled directly on English colonialism in North America and Ireland.[9]

Even in the familiar context of English dispossession of Indians in America, recent scholarship has emphasized how misleading it is to speak of a direct conflict of two cultures. In cultural criticism, such scenes have been singled out for special attention since the Columbus quincentenary, and critics of Anglophone texts have done much to show how the racial and cultural divide organizes colonial writing.[10] But colonial culture is not simply racially bipolar. Neal Salisbury, for example, has shown how different tribal factions played out rivalries and conflicts with one another by adopting different relations with rival European groups; in his narrative, the most powerful effects of colonialism come not in a direct relation of force or domination between whites and Indians but in the transformation of Indian groups as they are drawn into an unequal economy. Richard White, tracing similar patterns, has given the name "the middle ground" to all the rites, negotiations, customs, and understandings that emerged neither from European nor from Indian culture but from these local interactions.[11]

In light of such scholarship, it becomes harder to reduce the conflicts of empire to simple scenes of the European and the Indian. And in the variety of colonialism that distinguishes the English mainland colonies—settlement plantation—the relation of settlers and indigenes does not take the visible form of super- and subordinate so much as of center and margin (that is, frontier). That is why Anglo-American settlement does not look like colonialism in the usual sense. Creole culture was able in general to ignore the context of dispossession. Unlike other white settlers in colonies such as Ulster or South Africa, white Americans did not leave in place a native majority to whom their colonial relation would be visibly troubling. Even in colonies with an imported slave population, the white Creoles learned to think of themselves as the locals. They learned to think of the story of their own entrenchment and expansion as the story of a developing local civilization. Indeed, the question of who gets to be local was always the brutally contested question of colonial American history.[12]

It would be helpful in this context to know more about the history of the territorial imagination in Anglo-American culture. In the case of the Spanish colonization of Mexico, a brilliant example of such work has been provided by Serge Gruzinski in *La colonisation de l'imaginaire*. Gruzinski painstakingly shows how Spanish administration, over a period of several generations, eroded and replaced Amerindian pictorial and narrative practices for representing space and time. Nothing of comparable sophistication has been done for Anglo America, though a similar colonization of the territorial imaginary was obviously at work at least as early as the Virginia Company's negotiations with Powhatan.[13] A history of that process would have to coordinate shifts in the imagination of land tenure, state administration of land, empiricist geography, and English relations to both Irish and Indian habits of territorialization. One of the most striking common threads between the Irish and American cases, for example, is the English insistence that the locals in each instance failed to possess the land fully. The Irish were "wild" because of the importance of transhumance in Irish land use. And the English frequently justified settlement by claiming that the Indians did not farm and possess the land, even though the same English circulated Théodor de Bry's engravings of Indian farming villages and depended on Indian agriculture for their own survival. In both cases the colonial project was linked to a restructuring of territorial thought, beginning with the surrender and regrant policy in Ireland in the 1540s and continuing in the long process of colonial charters, Indian treaties, and experiments in land appropriation.[14]

Cultural historians have a long-standing fondness for themes of wilderness, land, nature, settlement, and civilization in early Anglo-America. How would these themes be transformed if viewed as part of a complex but in important ways colonialist process of territorialization? Would it escape attention, for example, that William Byrd's works are structured by enterprises of surveying, conducted against a divided but constantly refreshed sense of metropolitan consciousness?[15] Or that Crèvecoeur's image of the yeoman farmer inescapably refers to the long process of possession, dispossession, the restructuring of land governance, and the struggle to be local? Or that the informational use of travel organizes so many colonial texts, from the early migrant histories to the narratives of Sarah Knight and Alexander Hamilton, captivity narratives, and the soldierly narratives of the imperial wars? Or, less literally, that a cosmopolitan sense of audience can be implicit even in some of the most local and private forms of writing, whenever that writing aspires to the politeness of belles lettres or the urbanity of the modern?

These patterns in the spatial imagination of colonial culture have tended to be ignored or distorted in nationalist criticism, partly because national culture has a different territorial imagination of its own. It demarcates American culture from the magical moment at which white folks begin inhabiting the future United States, which they are said to have "settled." The benign idea of settlement continues to be the main obstacle against recognizing the history of the British American colonies as a story of colonialism rather than of mere colonization. Settling is intransitive, or, if it has an object, the object is merely the land. The narrative of settlement was developed in British colonial theory before any serious colonizing efforts got under way and before North America was its principal site. In the context in which the British first understood themselves as colonial settlers, the natives were very much local, very willing to fight back, and very white. Settlement colonization was a deliberate political strategy for subduing ancient neighbors, the Irish. Not only does the English literature of America begin long before settlement of America; English *settlement* begins before settlement of America. "Settling" North America had not removed the white creoles from English imperial culture; it had made them part of that culture, and they sustained an awareness of the rest of the empire throughout the colonial period. Some of the North American colonies, of course, quickly began thinking of themselves as independent from London, but at their most independent—Massachusetts in the 1640s, for example—they were far from renouncing the English imperial project. They were still in the process of inventing it.

An imperial culture does not even require a political doctrine of empire. As late as 1782 the British House of Commons resolved that "to pursue schemes of conquest and extent of dominion, are measures repugnant to the wish, the honour, and the policy of this nation."[16] The ease of this disavowal shows how indirect and mediated colonial culture can be. In the American colonies the settlers often rejected political empire for their own reasons. But their struggle for autonomy, formerly much celebrated by nationalist historians, did not imply a rejection of what we might now call "the colonial project." Resisting political administration by the Crown and Parliament, they tended to envision an English Atlantic world held together by means of market, religion, and other cultural mediations—one that led equally to a future of English dominion. The nature of the empire was one of the principal subjects of conflict within the empire.

The challenge before us is to render the differences between versions of colonialism while still asking how the British American colonies were part of a larger British culture of colonialism and how that larger project informs creole culture in America despite the differences between American emigrants, creoles, and British colonials elsewhere. Because the objective economic structures and political administrations differ so much from one colony to another or from one period to another, we should be particularly attentive to the cultural patterns by which such disparate ventures were able to elaborate, for all their differences, a European colonial project, distinct from each of its manifestations but necessary to each.

One way to call attention to the colonialist pattern in these mediate areas of culture is to ascribe to them the integrity of *colonial discourse.*[17] But colonial discourse has no more unity than colonialism. To speak of it in the singular hypostatizes a political intention that belongs to no one. It is indeed sometimes possible to speak of a sharply delineated discourse. The sixteenth-century English literature of planting, for example, might be called the oldest branch of American literature in English. It produced the notion of emigrant settlement colonies oriented to trade, first for Ireland and then for the New World; in doing so it created an entirely different model of colonialism from the Iberian plan of armed conquest and the extraction of wealth from a native population. The literature of planting has a notable consistency of reference points, assumptions, and formal features. It is complex and varied, having to solve scientific problems of geography, new problems of economic theory, and unprecedented issues of national, racial, and Christian identity. It draws on sources in Roman history and Machiavelli, but in England and Scotland its major figures for the first century or so include the Hakluyts, Christopher Carleil, Sir Humphrey Gilbert, Edward Hayes, George Peckham, Sir Walter Ralegh, Thomas Hariot, Francis Bacon, Sir William Alexander, Richard Eburne, Thomas Mun, John White, Josiah Child, and the like.[18] It is a clear example of colonial discourse that is a discourse—an intertextual horizon, a way of talking and writing rather than simply some things said and written.

We can tell that resistance to this literature existed from the beginning because some pro-plantation tracts contain responses to common
objections. In addition, some cheap published ballads satirize it.[19] And
writers such as Hariot and Captain Smith vividly express their anxiety
about the reception of their works in London opinion circles. But the
objections to planting mostly remained unpublished. This second, ghost
discourse may have had some written expression, now mostly lost, and
it almost certainly had a wide, mercantile rather than exactly popular
circulation. It partly structures the published literature, as antithesis,
but does not occupy the same space. The dialogue between the two is
oblique and distorted. Printed speculations about cosmography and
colonies give a false appearance of unity to colonial discourse because
they have been pre-filtered by the ability and need to print. One might
want to define colonial discourse as both sides of this asymmetrical dialogue, including the asymmetry as one of its key discursive features.
But where does one discourse stop and another begin? Other texts or
kinds of language may prove to be ghosts in colonial discourse because
they elaborate colonial culture not so much through argument as through
narrative or fantasy; for example, literary romances such as Spenser's
Faerie Queene or Thomas Lodge's *A Margarite from America*.[20] But
then the meaning of colonial discourse has no unity *as a discourse*; it is
at best a retrospective mapping of sometimes overlapping but sometimes incommensurate contexts.

And because colonial culture is not a framework of shared meaning but multiple contexts of discourse in shifting relations, the indirect
mediations of empire sometimes have to be found far from official debate. Laura Brown and Felicity Nussbaum, for example, argue that
eighteenth-century narratives of women elaborate an imperial culture
not only through the obvious exoticization of "native" women but also
through the empire's growing concern with reproduction, population,
and domestic space.[21] In settler colonies, reproductive sexuality acquires
even more importance—and anxiety—than in the imperial home. (The
contrast between French and English practice in this regard could not
be sharper.) But the colonial context of sexuality has been best studied
only in the early period and very seldom with attention to the different
role of settlement in different places.[22]

Of all the mediating forms of Anglo-American colonialism, the market culture of the Atlantic may have been more responsible than anything else for the practical sense of belonging to an imperium. When the
Scotsman William Robertson wrote his *History of America* (1777), it
seemed natural to begin with an overview of "the progress of men, in
discovering and peopling the various parts of the earth." Robertson
thought that this progress should be credited less to empire than to
trade. With the spread of navigation and commerce, he wrote,

> The ambition of conquest, or the necessity of procuring new settlements,
> were no longer the sole motives of visiting distant lands. The desire of

gain became a new incentive to activity, roused adventurers, and sent them forth upon long voyages in search of countries whose products or wants might increase that circulation which nourishes and gives vigour to commerce. Trade proved a great source of discovery; it opened unknown seas, it penetrated into new regions, and contributed more than any other cause to bring men acquainted with the situation, the nature, and commodities of the different parts of the globe.[23]

In a way, Robertson was right. Some contemporary cultural critics have a tendency to speak of empire and capital as being the same. But from a very early point the commercial empire of Europe had exceeded the political empires of the European nations. Spain, which had pioneered the art of conquering and administering other lands across the ocean, had been surpassed by England, which in the words of Fernand Braudel was "the first territorial state to complete its transformation into a national economy or national market."[24] Merchants—as well as soldiers, settlers, and subjects—made the Atlantic world. The early modern economy had become, for the first time, a global economy. Cultural relations among different parts of the modern world increasingly took place through markets and commerce rather than through the administrators and courts of the state. Empire and commerce linked the world in different, sometimes incompatible ways. Colonists, constantly looking to get around the Navigation Acts, would never have confounded the two.

In 1986, Timothy Breen was still able to propose, as a controverted point, that export markets and luxury imports mattered to eighteenth-century colonists.[25] While it may be true that colonists became more market oriented after 1690, it is hard to believe that they were ever unrelated to transatlantic markets. More specifically, an asymmetrical core/periphery economy was central to English colonialism from the outset.[26] Wallerstein attributes much of the imperial crisis to a creole determination not to have the kind of asymmetrical economy that was already beginning to underdevelop much of the world. The structuring of the transatlantic economy as a colonial economy had deep consequences for almost every aspect of Anglo-American culture, from the routing of cultural and political life through London to the local politics of staple economies. Breen has shown how the structuring of colonial society as an imperial market underlay intercolonial relations and political consciousness. And David Shields has ably demonstrated the preoccupation of American poetry in the early eighteenth century with themes of imperial commerce.[27] The provincial relation to London can be observed in almost any piece of Anglo-American writing and certainly in any colonial newspaper or travel account.

It is in this indirect, provincial belonging to the world of the empire that Anglo-American commercial culture had its strongest links to the contrasting form of colonialism on the other side of the English imperial world. England's movement into America was in most ways parallel with its movement into India.[28] The East India Company (EIC), for example, was headed after its chartering in 1600 by Thomas Smythe, who also oversaw the Virginia Company. The first major English emissary to India was Sir Thomas Roe, who had earlier made three voyages for Ralegh to the Caribbean and whose letters to the EIC draw explicit analogies between what Abbé Raynal would later call "the two Indies."[29] For the remainder of the century, American and Indian ventures overlapped, just as they did earlier between America and Ireland. In many cases the investors were the same, as were some of the interlopers. The administrative problems were similar, and international imperial rivalries often made them equivalent—as in the Anglo-Dutch feuds of the 1630s or again in the 1660s, both times played out equally on the Hudson and in South Asia. Clive, before his death in 1774, was slated to quell American unrest following the Boston Tea Party; Cornwallis compensated for the loss of America by consolidating Bengal.

In other ways, of course, America and India are contrasting images of English colonial practice. The contrast was deliberately preserved by the English policy of bureaucratic rotation. (Burke, whose career neatly encapsulates the close relation of Ireland, America, and India, claimed that "the natives scarcely know what it is to see the grey head of an Englishman.")[30] Partly because of the deliberateness of this contrast, it is surprising how invisible India has been in the history of Anglo-American colonialism. Two world-historical ventures into colonialism: begun at the same time, by the same people, with the same infrastructures, elaborating the same world economy, contributing equally the intoxicating staples in the English drug empire (tea, coffee, sugar, tobacco, rum, opium), sources of the same city's metropolitan self-understanding, the same claims of imperial Crown sovereignty in relation to the English nation, linked by the same wars—in all these ways India and America were inescapably tied for merchants, generals, and statesmen. And American consumers were hardly unaware of their involvement in a world colonial system, even though the empire's goods came through London. For all the historical differences between America and India as examples of colonial practice, they were in many ways mutually defined, and Anglo-Americans were certainly part of the English culture of colonialism.

A kind of forgetfulness about this relation settled in during the early national period. The British American mainland colonies were the first to mount a critique of colonial administration and break away from it; yet the United States was also to become the last great colonial and imperial power—which of course it still is. The United States entered colonial relations with the rest of the world only after it became a nation (in 1803 by one reckoning, 1898 by another, but continuing through the present in any case). But how did all other arenas of colonialism manage to remain invisible in the anticolonial political writing of the Revolutionary period—so rich in anticolonial thought that

Thomas Paine would become a sacred name throughout Latin America? Americans had been aware of their place in a global English colonial project since before they were Americans. And the transatlantic debates about colonial regulation are full of comparisons between American and other colonies; usually these comparisons were made as arguments against independence. If we think about the so-called founding era as a moment of anticolonial critique, we will have to ask how such an opportunity passed from view, leaving scarcely a trace in the imperial century that followed.

This is not really surprising unless we try to identify the emergence of nationalism as a sharp break with colonial culture. White creoles in British America learned to think of themselves as colonized rather than as colonizers. But they were not colonized subjects in the sense intended by theories of colonial and postcolonial discourse.[31] The shift from British colonies to American nation was a shift mainly for white men: the Revolution is a poor period marker of decolonization. As Wallerstein puts it:

> This [eighteenth-century] "decolonization" of the Americas occurred
> under the aegis of their European settlers, to the exclusion not only of
> the Amerindian populations but also of the transplanted Africans, de-
> spite the fact that, in many of these newly sovereign states, Amerindians
> and Blacks constituted a substantial proportion (even a majority) of the
> population. . . . In any case, this decolonization differed strikingly from
> the second great "decolonization" of the modern world-system, that which
> occurred in the twentieth century, the difference being precisely in terms
> of the populations who would control the resulting sovereign states.[32]

Not only did the Americans fail to develop an anticolonial culture, but as Peter Marshall notes, Cornwallis's post-Yorktown triumphs in India were the turning point in British public opinion on empire. After the early 1790s, he writes, "British activities in India were never again, at least before the twentieth century, to be subjected to prolonged hostile scrutiny from within the mainstreams of British opinion."[33] If this change in British opinion seems like a willful deafness to the American critique, as well as to Burke's great speeches on both American and Indian issues, we should note that the American anticolonial theorists were just as deaf to anticolonial thought after independence. National culture began with a moment of sweeping amnesia about colonialism. Americans learned to think of themselves as living in an immemorial nation, rather than in a colonial interaction of cultures.[34]

II.

Colonial culture does not imply a unity of shared meaning or a will to dominate. It is a set of spatial and temporal hierarchies. The imperial culture of English America could therefore be experienced in many indirect ways—as an orientation to the modern, a spatial imagination, a moral language of civility, even as a prose style. Unequal economies of space and capital—including a territorial awareness that presupposed dispossession—were the condition both of colonial consciousness and of literary circulation. William Robertson's history might serve as an example. Robertson, though a Scot by birth, writes from the seat of empire. His prose rings with the confidence that he and his readers are its most informed and freely inquiring members. Only a commercial civilization such as the one Robertson describes could result in the erudition and polish of *History of America*, let alone provide it with a receptive audience. His is the voice of cosmopolitanism.

A different style is to be found in the journal of Sarah Knight, a Boston schoolteacher and shopkeeper of the early eighteenth century who had never been to Europe but was no less a subject of the British Empire. As she traveled the countryside she could not help dreaming: "The way being smooth and even, the night warm and serene, and the Tall and thick Trees at a distance, especially when the moon glar'd light through the branches, fill'd my Imagination with the pleasent delusion of a Sumpteous citty, fill'd with famous Buildings and churches, with their spiring steeples, Balconies, Galleries and I know not what: Granduers which I had heard of, and which the stories of foreign countries had given me the Idea of."[35]

Knight here longs for exotic sights and for a better context for her own consciousness. Her journal is filled with anecdotes of the boorish behavior of the colonials around her. Writing is her resource for survival. When the drunken provincials in the room next door will not shut up, she writes satiric verse about them. She does so to remind herself that there is a larger world than the one these locals know. The closest she can come to living there is to fill her journal with wit and poetry, manufacturing an urbane consciousness with the borrowed resources of a style she imported through reading. But she cannot escape the double bind of the colonial: because the style that makes her journal urbane is a borrowed one, it also makes her provincial. The metropolis of her imagination is a jumbled picture, full of indistinct balconies, galleries, "and I know not what."[36]

Twenty-five years before Knight wrote her journal, another Massachusetts Puritan named Mary Rowlandson wrote a famous narrative of her captivity among American Indians. Rowlandson had not returned to England since her infancy. Yet she interrupts her wild tale with a note of familiarity: "I saw a place where English Cattle had been. That was a comfort to me, such as it was. Quickly after that we came to an English path which so took with me that I thought I could have freely laid down and died. That day, a little after noon, we came to Squaukeag where the Indians quickly spread themselves over the deserted English fields, gleaning what they could find."[37]

This, too, is colonial language, and not just because of the value scale—English good, Indian bad. At a time when the English and Indians were at war over the right to the land, Rowlandson defines Englishness through evidence of settlement, glimpsed only in transit as the wild Indians ceaselessly move through unfelled forests. Cattle, path, and fields make Englishness local, even while they struggle to make local places English. These imprints on the countryside are the markers of Rowlandson's identity, and she unhesitatingly calls them English even though she had not been within three thousand miles of England in the time of her memory and would not talk this way about Englishness if she had.[38] Her captors tease her for the strength of her feeling: "What, will you love English men still?"[39]

Virtually every colonial writer looks both homeward to the seat of imperial culture and outward to the localities that would remain for them subordinate. They were also gradually developing their own patterns of culture. Already in the seventeenth century, English writers made sport of colonials in different regions. In Ned Ward's satirical sketches of Jamaica (1698) and New England (1699), in Aphra Behn's play about Virginia (1689), or in Ebenezer Cooke's satirical poem of Maryland (1708), colonials had come to be recognizable as comic types.[40] By 1705 Robert Beverley of Virginia could even embrace the stereotype with partial seriousness. "I am an *Indian*," he declared, though it may be doubted whether he ever meant to cast doubt on his own credentials as an Englishman.[41] Toward the middle of the eighteenth century, the word "American" began to appear more frequently in reference to white creole settlers rather than to Indians. Ironically, just as the English finally emerged the victors in the long struggle over North America, the sense of colonial identity had become strong enough to force a crisis in the imperial system. Colonial culture had begun to produce one of its least anticipated but most momentous effects: creole nationalism.

For the past two centuries, those colonists who happened to live in the future United States have been scrutinized for promising germs of Americanness; their provinciality has often been tactfully overlooked. Even Benjamin Franklin, regarded by many as the original American, spent twenty years of his life in London and as late as the 1760s fully intended to live there permanently as a happy Englishman. Portraits of him throughout most of his life show him in the powdered wig of a London gentleman. This is not the Franklin of nationalist criticism. But it is the Franklin who wrote most of the *Autobiography*. Later in life, particularly on his second trip to France, Franklin changed his image and played the American, a role he invented for the occasion.[42] It was such a successful performance that critics cannot always see past it to recover the English colonial author whose narrative of a transatlantic mercantile career is addressed to the royal governor of New Jersey.

Olaudah Equiano, by contrast, was dragged toward Englishness: he was taken from Africa to Montserrat and other West Indian islands, and from thence to Georgia, South Carolina, Pennsylvania, Virginia, and finally to London. There, renamed Gustavus Vassa, he began to write English prose. Equiano himself was now not only an author but an English subject, no longer fully African or American. His life history outstripped the labels of identity in a way that paradoxically makes him more typical of his world than those who had a more comfortable home in it. Equiano's long involuntary progress covered the full circuit of the commerce and colonies of the Atlantic rim. He saw and endured the force of its imperial order, perhaps more thoroughly than any other author in the period.

By the same token it would be a stretch to call Samson Occom a Native American. That term was coined much later, a conscious gesture designed to exploit the symbolic resonance of American nationalism. Occom was a Mohegan; in English terms, he was an Indian, an American, a Native. Only in the middle of his life did some Englishmen begin calling themselves American, and toward such disputes among the English as the Revolution he preferred to remain neutral. Toward English culture, however, he was far from neutral. He had made a significant break with most of his fellow Mohegans when he converted to Christianity and an even greater break when he pursued an English education and then traveled to England for two years. When he wrote a sketch of his own life, he began, "I was Born a Heathen and Brought up in Heathenism."[43]

Robertson, Knight, Rowlandson, Franklin, Equiano, and Occom—all occupied different positions in the same imperial culture. They might have had little else in common, but each writes in the language of England's dominion, and each invokes the reference points of empire, of the transatlantic economy, of Christendom, of modern history. In what sense was it the same culture? And was that culture colonial in the same sense in each case? I choose these examples to illustrate the variety of colonial settings. Not everyone in the period was swept up in the unfolding time of world history, like the ever modern Franklin; many lived in local worlds of less moment, relatively indifferent to markets, wars, printing, and other venues of the English Atlantic. No national identity really underlies these authors' writings. Indeed, as soon as we stop looking for Americanness, we see that none is aptly described as American. Most have conflicted, transitional identities. But these writers also illustrate some of the most prevalent patterns of early modern Anglo-American colonial writing: a struggle over identity, but also the dialectic of provincialism and cosmopolitanism, the remapping of space, and the experience of life against a background of world-historical time. For all but Rowlandson—and arguably for her as well—literary culture provides an indefinitely urbane sense of audience, a fundamentally extralocal imagination that, for each except Robertson, has to be poised somehow against the very local imagination of territorial possession and the invention of a creole community. This divided spatial attention has a distinctive tension in settlement colonialism, one that informs

Anglo-American writing not only in content but in style, voice, intertextual reference, and audience address.

III.

Literary culture has a highly conflicted place in the spatial and temporal hierarchies of colonial culture. Nationalist criticism blurs the issue insofar as it tries to view colonial writers as distinctively American. It sees them as consciously or unconsciously expressive of a larger, protonational culture. The difference between writers and nonwriters recedes from view. Literary culture is seen as representative rather than distinctive. A denationalized criticism of English Atlantic writing will need to pay special attention to the transatlantic arena of literary culture and the appeal it had for colonists, even when that arena is understood as, say, the community of the saints rather than as the secular audience of the imperial capital. Scholars have long noted the importance of writing in the development of empire, providing an informational and imaginative matrix for worlds that could not be experienced in any other way.[44] But the spatial imagination of the English Atlantic in turn underlies cultures of letters, giving writing an extralocal appeal.

A striking example is this 1619 letter from John Pory, then secretary of the Virginia Company in Jamestown:

> At my first coming hither the solitary uncouthnes of this place, compared with those partes of Christendome or Turky where I had bene; and likewise my being sequestred from all occurrents and passages which are so rife there, did not a little vexe me. And yet in these five monethes of my continuance here, there have come at one time or another eleven saile of ships into this river; but fraighted more with ignorance, then with any other marchandize. At length being hardned to this custome of abstinence from curiosity, I am resolved wholly to minde my busines here, and nexte after my penne, to have some good book alwayes in store, being in solitude the best and choicest company. Besides among these Christall rivers, and oderiferous woods I doe escape muche expense, envye, contempte, vanity, and vexation of minde. Yet good my lorde, have a little compassion upon me, and be pleased to sende mee what pampletts and relations of the Interim since I was with you, as your lordship shall thinke good, directing the same (if you please) in a boxe to Mr. Ralfe Yeardley, Apothecary (brother to Sir George Yeardley our governour), dwelling at the signe of the Hartychoke in great Woodstreet, to be sente to me by the first, together with his brothers thinges.[45]

Pory finds himself depending on London for material written goods; he also expresses a heightened self-consciousness about a broader cultural dependence. Like Sarah Knight, he looks to letters for a consciousness broader than his locale. Jamestown, he takes pains to say, is not completely savage: "Nowe that your lordship may knowe, that we are not the veriest beggers in the worlde, our cowekeeper here of James citty on Sundays goes accowtered all in freshe flaming silke; and a wife of one that in England had professed the black arte, not of a scholler, but of a collier of Croydon, weares her rough bever hatt with a faire perle hatband, and a silken suite thereto correspondent."[46] The urbane style of this sentence helps to place Pory in a map of the Jamestown streets through which this cowkeeper and this collier's wife parade, while equally placing him in relation to London and the Levant. Like the finery of his fellow colonists, Pory's style and humor invite us to see a progress in civilization. And this same geography of culture that makes Jamestown civilized, English, makes it provincial.

In his classic study *Savagism and Civilization*, Roy Harvey Pearce argued that the mixed uses of "civilization" in the colonial period gave way, shortly after the Revolution, to a racialized narrative legitimating dispossession.[47] "Civilization" came to be understood not as something that might exist in different versions but as Christianity, the wearing of clothing, table manners, or other positive contents of Englishness. Its implication of progress took on invidious implications for those whom it classed as "savage." Often it was used as synonymous with Christianity even by missionaries whose practice—aiming at conversion but not at literacy or refinement—implied a sharp distinction. And like so many normative concepts, it required a continual labor of ejecting from oneself all that is wild or savage—a labor that for the civilized person can produce what John Barrell calls "the psychopathology of empire." For these reasons, the narrative of civilization has often been seen as a prime example of colonialist thought.[48]

Yet in 1619, Pory does not see civilization as the defining identity of white Europeans (though this meaning is no doubt also available, on reserve). Writing makes him civilized. It also separates him from his fellow colonists. He has a clerk's sense of class. The civilization he craves is opposed not to savagism but to uncouthness. He sees it as remaining foreign to the settlers, at least compared with "those partes of Christendome or Turky where I had bene." Civilization, for him, is neither national nor racial. It is a marker of social identity shared with Turks, exactly because literary practice is said to supersede merely local forms of sociability; he seeks "best and choicest company" with "some good book." Books are resources that would allow a progress in self-culture. The "curiosity" that Pory values may be a defining ideal for the moral consciousness of an explorer and colonist; yet its promise of indefinite self-fashioning points elsewhere. For Pory it pointed to London, and he did not stay long in the Chesapeake.

The aspiration to civilization has contradictory meanings, each equally visible in Pory's letter and heightened by his dependence on his patron for print. Colonial writers are always inventing the meaning of civilization in this way. Even when the idea of civilization begins to afford the colonizer's sense of calling and destiny, it also separates the writer from the "solitary uncouthness" of his or her place. Its narrative assumption—human beings move from savagism to civility—leads, not inexorably, to the ideological perception of Indian cultures as inferior because primitive. But the same narrative orientation implies another possibility, powerfully expressed in Pory's letter, to which no modern reader of colonial texts can be altogether indifferent: a possibility of cumulative self-cultivation through the historical resources of arts and letters. Civilization at its most ideological is *also* a horizon of worldliness, a faraway port from which supplies can be recruited for a struggle against the "abstinence from curiosity" that is everyday local culture. Literate culture, in short, helped to define more than one cognitive geography. And because the stakes in the narrative of civilization were so high, the colonial writer could find him- or herself confronted with sweeping questions of value. Reflecting on the colonial project three years before Pory's letter, for example, John Smith was led to an extended meditation on what makes living interesting: "Then, who would live at home idly (or thinke in himselfe any worth to live) only to eate, drink, and sleepe, and so die?"[49] The writers of early modern Anglo-America had to map and narrate themselves in ways that could be more or less contradictory but were never without tensions.

Need it be added that this dialectic between colonial geographies and the critical inquiry of literate culture is also the context in which Anglo-American texts might now be reread?

Notes

1. For the Imperial school, see especially Charles Andrews, *The Colonial Period of American History*, 4 vols. (New Haven, 1934–38); Andrews, "On the Writing of Colonial History," *William and Mary Quarterly*, 3d ser., 1, no. 1 (1944): 27–48; George Louis Beer, *The Origins of the British Colonial System, 1578–1660* (New York, 1908); Laurence Henry Gipson, *The British Empire before the American Revolution*, 15 vols. (Caldwell, Idaho, 1936–70); Gipson, "The Imperial Approach to Early American History," in *The Reinterpretation of Early American History: Essays in Honor of John Edwin Pomfret*, ed. R. A. Billington (San Marino, Calif., 1966), pp. 185–200; and J. Holland Rose et al., eds., *The Cambridge History of the British Empire*, vol. 1, *The Old Empire, from the Beginnings to 1783* (Cambridge, 1929). For examples of a more recent focus on empire, see Ian K. Steele, *The English Atlantic* (New York, 1986); Stephen Saunders Webb, *The Governors-General: The English Army and the Definition of the Empire, 1659–1681* (Chapel Hill, 1979); David Hackett Fisher, *Albion's Seed: Four British Folkways in America* (New York, 1989); and Bernard Bailyn, ed., *Strangers within the Realm: Cultural Margins of the First British Empire* (Chapel Hill, 1991). D. W. Meinig, *The Shaping of America*, vol. 1, *Atlantic America, 1492–1800* (New Haven, 1986), goes far toward theorizing a transatlantic focus.

2. There are, of course, important exceptions, especially Myra Jehlen, "The Papers of Empire," in *The Cambridge History of American Literature*, ed. Sacvan Bercovitch (Cambridge, 1994), pp. 13–168. See also Gauri Viswanathan, "The Naming of Yale College: British Imperialism and American Higher Education," in *Cultures of United States Imperialism*, ed. Amy Kaplan and Donald Pease (Durham, N.C., 1993), pp. 85–108.

3. Daniel Boorstin, *The Americans: The Colonial Experience* (New York, 1958), pp. 3–4.

4. John Winthrop, "A Modell of Christian Charity" (1630), in *The Puritans*, ed. Perry Miller and Thomas H. Johnson, 2 vols. (New York, 1963), 1:197–99. For more on this passage and its subtexts, see Michael Warner, "New English Sodom," *American Literature* 64, no. 1 (March 1992): 19–47.

5. A somewhat similar point is argued by William C. Spengemann in his *A Mirror for Americanists: Reflections on the Idea of American Literature* (Hanover, N.H., 1989) and *A New World of Words: Redefining Early American Literature* (New Haven, 1994). Spengemann emphasizes the Britishness of American writing rather than colonial relations. For an example of how the study of colonial literature might include texts from the West Indies, Canada, and London itself, see Myra Jehlen and Michael Warner, eds., *The English Literatures of America, 1500–1800* (New York, 1997).

6. Anne McClintock, "The Angel of Progress: Pitfalls of the Term 'Post-Colonialism,'" *Social Text* 10, nos. 2–3 (1992): 84–98, reprinted in *Colonial Discourse and Post-Colonial Theory*, ed. Patrick Williams and Laura Chrisman (New York, 1994), pp. 291–304, argues that applying the term *postcolonial* to the United States not only fails to recognize the variety of colonialisms in modern history but also "actively obscures the continuities and discontinuities of US power around the globe." McClintock sees the United States as a "break-away settler colony," in which colonial control was transferred from the metropolis to the colony but where decolonization did not happen and is not likely to happen (p. 295). See also Vijay Mishra and Bob Hodge, "What is Post(-)colonialism?" in *Colonial Discourse*, ed. Williams and Chrisman, pp. 276–90.

7. J. G. A. Pocock argues for a history of the British Empire not driven by a unitary conception of empire, in "The Limits and Divisions of British History: In Search of the Unknown Subject," *American Historical Review* 87, no. 2 (1982): 311–36; see M. I. Finley, "Colonies—an Attempt at a Typology," *Transactions of the Royal Historical Society*, 5th ser., 26 (1976): 167–88. The Portuguese, for example, involved as they were in the slave trade, showed much more willingness than did other Europeans to use African and Indian languages, to interbreed, and to take on Indians and mixed-race offspring in administrative positions. The English were inconsistent on the degree of difference between themselves and the Irish, the Welsh, and the Scots. See J. H. Parry, *The Establishment of the European Hegemony: 1415–1715* (New York, 1966); Parry, *The Age of Reconnaissance: Discovery, Exploration, and Settlement, 1450 to 1650* (Berkeley, 1981); and Bailyn, *Strangers*.

8. On this point see Neal Salisbury, *Manitou and Providence: Indians, Europeans, and the Making of New England, 1500–1643* (New York, 1982), pp. 85–86, and W. L. Morton, *The Kingdom of Canada* (Toronto, 1963). An eloquent version of the contrast runs throughout Francis Parkman, *France and England in North America*, 2 vols. (New York, 1983).

9. See Michael Hechter, *Internal Colonialism: The Celtic Fringe in British National Development, 1536–1966* (Berkeley, 1975), and H. C. Darby, *The Draining of the Fens* (Cambridge, 1956).

10. Notably in Peter Hulme, *Colonial Encounters: Europe and the Native Caribbean, 1492–1797* (New York, 1986), and Anthony Pagden, *European Encounters with the New World* (New Haven, 1993). For similar studies of Anglophone writing see Larzer Ziff, "Conquest and Recovery in Early Writings from America," *American Literature* 68, no. 3 (1996): 509–26, and June Namias, *White Captives: Gender and Ethnicity on the American Frontier* (Chapel Hill, 1993).

11. Salisbury, *Manitou and Providence*; Richard White, *The Middle Ground: Indians, Empires, and Republics in the Great Lakes Region, 1650–1815* (New York, 1991).

12. Historians such as Michael Zuckerman and Timothy H. Breen have written eloquently of the "persistent localism" of English settlers, who built in the Caribbean the sharply pitched roofs ready to withstand the snows that never came. In part that localism represents the assertion of Englishness and in some colonies was accompanied by an extremely high rate of back migration in the first generation. But for those who stayed, the story is one of a developing territorial and cultural imagination that localized creole culture—to the disadvantage of both displaced natives and imported Africans. And this is localism in a different sense: not just the carrying over of English habits (which, as Zuckerman notes, was deliberately conservative rather than unreflectively traditional) but also the cultivation of a new version of the local, an imagination of space and identity that was at every moment political and transitive. The point about the roofs is Richard Dunn's, quoted in Michael Zuckerman, "Identity in British America," in *Colonial Identity in the Atlantic World, 1500–1800*, ed. Nicholas Canny and Anthony Pagden (Princeton, 1987), p. 135. See also Timothy H. Breen, *Puritans and Adventurers: Change and Persistence in Early America* (New York, 1980).

13. On territorial imagination, see Margarita Bowen, *Empiricism and Geographical Thought: From Francis Bacon to Alexander von Humboldt* (Cambridge, 1981), and Serge Gruzinski, *La colonisation de l'imaginaire* (Paris, 1988). A useful study in this context is Patricia Seed, *Ceremonies of Possession in Europe's Conquest of the New World* (Cambridge, 1995). See also David Grayson Allen, "*Vacuum Domicilium*: The Social and Cultural Landscape of Seventeenth-Century New England," in *New England Begins: The Seventeenth Century*, ed. Jonathan L. Fairbanks and Robert F. Trent, 3 vols. (Boston, 1982), 1:1–10.

14. Nicholas Canny, "The Ideology of English Colonization: From Ireland to America," *William and Mary Quarterly*, 3d ser., 30, no. 4 (1973): 575–98. See also Canny, "The Irish Background to Penn's Experiment," in *The World of William Penn*, ed. Richard S. Dunn and Mary Maples Dunn (Philadelphia, 1986), pp. 139–56. Howard Mumford Jones shows that perceptions of Natives and landscapes in America were framed by previous accounts of the Irish, in *O Strange New World* (New York, 1964), pp. 173–75. See also Kenneth R. Andrews et al., eds., *The Westward Enterprise: English Activities in Ireland, the Atlantic, and America, 1480–1650* (Detroit, 1979). David B. Quinn, *The Elizabethans and the Irish* (Ithaca, 1966), pp. 14–15. Canny, *The Elizabethan Conquest of Ireland* (New York, 1976).

15. See, for example, Wayne Franklin, *Discoverers, Explorers, Settlers: The Diligent Writers of Early America* (Chicago, 1979). An essential study of Byrd from this point of view is Norman S. Grabo, "Going Steddy: William Byrd's Literary Masquerade," *Yearbook of English Studies* 13 (1983): 84–96; see also the other essays on "colonial and imperial themes" in part 1 of this issue. See Michael Greenberg, "William Byrd II and the World of the Market," *Southern Studies* 16, no. 4 (1977): 429–56.

16. Quoted in Peter Marshall, "British Expansion in India," in Marshall, *Trade and Conquest: Studies on the Rise of British Dominance in India* (London, 1993), p. 31.

17. The term has not always been used to imply the integrity of discourse. Indeed, it seems to have gained its appeal initially from the way it pointed to mediated, or indirectly related, fields of culture. Edward W. Said, for instance, writes in *Culture and Imperialism* that "there was a commitment to [colonies] over and above profit, a commitment in constant circulation which, on the one hand, allowed decent men and women to accept the notion that distant territories and their native peoples *should* be subjugated, and, on the other, replenished metropolitan energies so that these decent people could think of the *imperium* as a protracted, almost metaphysical obligation to rule subordinate, inferior, or less advanced peoples" (*Culture and Imperialism* [New York, 1993], p. 10). This sense of imperial culture as metropolitan consciousness obviously could not be restricted to one discourse among others.

18. The literature on planting is summarized in Klaus E. Knorr, *British Colonial Theories, 1570–1850* (London, 1963). On sources, see David Quinn, "Renaissance Influences in English Colonization," in Quinn, *Explorers and Colonies* (London, 1990), pp. 97–118.

19. See, for example, "A West Country Man's Voyage to New England" (ca. 1632), in *English Literatures of America*, ed. Jehlen and Warner, or Richard Eburne, *A Plaine Pathway to Plantation* (London, 1624).

20. This is the subject of a fair amount of more recent scholarship. See, for instance, Jeffrey Knapp, *An Empire Nowhere* (Cambridge, Mass., 1989).

21. Laura Brown, *Ends of Empire: Women and Ideology in Early-Eighteenth-Century Literature* (Ithaca, 1993), and Felicity Nussbaum, *Torrid Zones: Maternity, Sexuality, and Empire in Eighteenth-Century English Narratives* (Baltimore, 1995).

22. For the early period, see Jonathan Goldberg, *Sodometries* (Stanford, 1992), or Richard Trexler, *Sex and Conquest: Gendered Violence, Political Order, and the European Conquest of the Americas* (Ithaca, 1995). See also Mary Beth Norton, *Founding Mothers and Fathers: Gendered Power and the Forming of American Society* (New York, 1996). There are also useful studies from different colonial contexts, such as Anne McClintock, *Imperial Leather* (New York, 1996), or Ann Stoler, "Carnal Knowledge and Imperial Power: Gender, Race, and Morality in Colonial Asia," in *Gender at the Crossroads of Knowledge: Feminist Anthropology in the Postmodern Era*, ed. Micaela di Leonardo (Berkeley, 1991), pp. 51–101.

23. William Robertson, *History of America*, 2 vols. (Dublin, 1777), 1:1, 4.

24. Fernand Braudel, *Civilization and Capitalism, Fifteenth–Eighteenth Century*, vol. 3, *The Perspective of the World*, trans. Siân Reynolds (New York, 1984), p. 51.

25. Timothy H. Breen, "An Empire of Goods: The Anglicization of Colonial America, 1690–1776," *Journal of British Studies* 25, no. 4 (1986): 467–99. See also Jean-Christophe Agnew, *Worlds Apart: The Market and the Theater in Anglo-American Thought, 1550–1750* (New York, 1986).

26. As described, for example, in Immanuel Wallerstein, *The Modern World-System: Capitalist Agriculture and the Origins of the European World-Economy in the Sixteenth Century* (New York, 1974); Wallerstein, *The Modern World-System II: Mercantilism and the Consolidation of the European World-Economy, 1600–1750* (New York, 1980); and Wallerstein, *The Modern World-System III: The Second Era of Great Expansion of the Capitalist World-Economy, 1730–1840s* (San Diego, 1989).

27. Wallerstein, *Modern World System*, pp. 335–40; Timothy H. Breen, "'Baubles of Britain': The American and Consumer Revolutions of the Eighteenth Century," *Past and Present*, no. 119 (1988): 73–104; David S. Shields, *Oracles of Empire* (Chicago, 1990).

28. Synoptic accounts since the Imperial school include Angus Calder, *Revolutionary Empire: The Rise of the English-Speaking Empires from the Fifteenth Century to the 1780s* (New York, 1981); C. E. Carrington, *The British Overseas: Exploits of a Nation of Shopkeepers* (Cambridge, 1968); and, from the English point of view, Linda Colley, *Britons: Forging the Nation, 1707–1837* (New Haven, 1992).

29. Abbé (Guillaume-Thomas) Raynal, *Histoire philosophique et politique des établissemens et du commerce des Européens dan les deux Indes*, 10 vols. (Geneva, 1780).

30. Quoted in Peter Marshall, "The Whites of British India, 1780–1830: A Failed Colonial Society?" in Marshall, *Trade and Conquest*, p. 75.

31. Lawrence Buell, "American Literary Emergence as a Postcolonial Phenomenon," *American Literary History* 4, no. 3 (Fall 1992): 411–42, esp. 434, describes American literature as "the first postcolonial literature." He acknowledges that this argument would seem to mystify the imperial direction of American culture and to blur the distinction "between the European settler as colonial and the indigene as colonial" (412). But he chooses to "bracket" such questions, he says, to show, borrowing from Ashis Nandy, how American literature "arose out of 'a culture in which the ruled were constantly tempted to fight their rulers within the psychological limits set by the latter'" (415). I take it that for Buell this condition *defines* the colonial relation. He argues, for example, that "the imperfectness of Cooper's break from Scott might be seen as a mark of the 'colonized mind'" (422). The rise of national culture in America, for Buell, was a process of decolonization. But if Cooper's mimicry of Scott is colonial, then the colonial is hard to distinguish from the merely provincial.

32. Wallerstein, *Modern World-System III*, p. 193.

33. Peter Marshall, "'Cornwallis Triumphant': War in India and the British Public in the Late Eighteenth Century," in Marshall, *Trade and Conquest*, p. 73.

34. For a beautiful illustration of this amnesia, see Alan Taylor's analysis of William Cooper's *Guide to the Wilderness*, in *William Cooper's Town: Power and Persuasion on the Frontier of the Early American Republic* (New York, 1996), esp. pp. 30–34.

35. "The Journal of Sarah Knight," in *The Puritans*, ed. Miller and Johnson, 2:430.

36. Ibid.
37. Mary Rowlandson, *The Soveraignty and Goodness of God, Together, with the Faithfulness of His Promises Displayed; Being a Narrative of the Captivity and Restauration of Mrs. Mary Rowlandson* (1682), in *Puritans Among the Indians: Accounts of Captivity and Redemption, 1676–1724*, ed. Alden T. Vaughan and Edward W. Clark (Cambridge, Mass., 1981), p. 45.
38. On this point see Benedict Anderson, "Exodus," *Critical Inquiry* 20, no. 2 (1994): 314–27.
39. Rowlandson, *Soveraignty and Goodness of God*, p. 36.
40. Ned Ward, *A Trip to Jamaica* (1698); Ward, *A Trip to New England* (1699); Aphra Behn, *The Widow Ranter; or, the History of Bacon in Virginia* (1689); and Ebenezer Cooke, *The Sot-Weed Factor* (1708) can all be found in *English Literatures of America*, ed. Jehlen and Warner.
41. Robert Beverley, *The History and Present State of Virginia, in Four Parts* (1705), ed. Louis B. Wright (Chapel Hill, 1947), p. 9.
42. Esmond Wright, "'The Fine and Noble China Vase, the British Empire': Benjamin Franklin's 'Love-Hate' View of England," *Pennsylvania Magazine of History and Biography* 111, no. 4 (1987): 435–64. See Alfred Owen Aldridge, *Franklin and His French Contemporaries* (New York, 1957).
43. Samson Occom, "A Short Narrative of My Life" (1768), in *The Elders Wrote: An Anthology of Early Prose by North American Indians, 1768–1931*, ed. Bernd Peyer (Berlin, 1982), p. 12.
44. Harold Innis, *Empire and Communication* (Oxford, 1950); J. Parker, *Books to Build an Empire: A Bibliographic History of English Overseas Interests to 1620* (Amsterdam, 1965); and Jehlen, "Papers of Empire."
45. Lyon G. Tyler, ed., *Narratives of Early Virginia* (New York, 1907; rpt., New York, 1952), p. 286.
46. Ibid., p. 285.
47. Roy Harvey Pearce, *Savagism and Civilization: A Study of the Indian and the American Mind* (Baltimore, 1953; rpt., Berkeley, 1988).
48. John Barrell, *The Infection of Thomas DeQuincey* (New Haven, 1991); Stanley Diamond, *In Search of the Primitive: A Critique of Civilization* (New York, 1974).
49. *A Description of New England*, in *The Complete Works of Captain John Smith (1580–1631)*, ed. Philip L. Barbour, 3 vols. (Chapel Hill, 1986), 1:344.

Manifest Domesticity

Amy Kaplan

Kaplan argues for a rethinking of domesticity that would "shift the cognitive geography of nineteenth-century separate spheres" (p. 333). Typically, when the domestic is considered a private realm, men and women are seen as inhabiting different domains. However, when domesticity is viewed in relation to the foreign, men and women share the same space, and people are divided not by gender, but by race. Kaplan further complicates the notion of the domestic by noting that domesticity is not only a static condition but also a process. Domestication in this sense would be related to "the imperial project of civilizing" (p. 334); thus, according to Kaplan, it both polices the borders between civilization and savagery and regulates the savage within. Noting the contemporaneous development of domestic discourse and Manifest Destiny, Kaplan suggests that these spatial configurations are linked in complex ways. In fact, Kaplan concludes that women's domestic narratives are inseparable from narratives of empire and nation. Kaplan's essay originally appeared in American Literature *in 1998.*

The "cult of domesticity," the ideology of "separate spheres," and the "culture of sentiment" have together provided a productive paradigm for understanding the work of white women writers in creating a middle-class American culture in the nineteenth century. Most studies of this paradigm have revealed the permeability of the border that separates the spheres, demonstrating that the private feminized space of the home both infused and bolstered the public male arena of the market, and that the sentimental values attached to maternal influence were used to sanction women's entry into the wider civic realm from which those same values theoretically excluded them. More recently, scholars have argued that the extension of female sympathy across social divides could violently reinforce the very racial and class hierarchies that sentimentality claims to dissolve.[1]

This deconstruction of separate spheres, however, leaves another structural opposition intact: the domestic in intimate opposition to the foreign. In this context *domestic* has a double meaning that not only links the familial household to the nation but also imagines both in opposition to everything outside the geographic and conceptual border of the home. The earliest meaning of *foreign*, according to the *OED*, is "out of doors" or "at a distance from home." Contemporary English speakers refer to national concerns as domestic in explicit or implicit contrast with the foreign. The notion of domestic policy makes sense only in opposition to foreign policy, and uncoupled from the foreign, national issues are never labeled domestic. The idea of foreign policy depends on the sense of the nation as a domestic space imbued with a sense of at-homeness, in contrast to an external world perceived as alien and threatening. Reciprocally, a sense of the foreign is necessary to erect the boundaries that enclose the nation as home.

Reconceptualizing domesticity in this way might shift the cognitive geography of nineteenth-century separate spheres. When we contrast the domestic sphere with the market or political realm, men and women inhabit a divided social terrain, but when we oppose the domestic to the foreign, men and women become national allies against the alien, and the determining division is not gender but racial demarcations of otherness.

Thus another part of the cultural work of domesticity might be to unite men and women in a national domain and to generate notions of the foreign against which the nation can be imagined as home. The border between the domestic and foreign, however, also deconstructs when we think of domesticity not as a static condition but as the process of domestication, which entails conquering and taming the wild, the natural, and the alien. Domestic in this sense is related to the imperial project of civilizing, and the conditions of domesticity often become markers that distinguish civilization from savagery. Through the process of domestication, the home contains within itself those wild or foreign elements that must be tamed; domesticity not only monitors the borders between the civilized and the savage but also regulates traces of the savage within itself.[2]

If domesticity plays a key role in imagining the nation as home, then women, positioned at the center of the home, play a major role in defining the contours of the nation and its shifting borders with the foreign. Those feminist critics and historians whose work has been fundamental in charting the paradigm of separate spheres, however, have for the most part overlooked the relationship of domesticity to nationalism and imperialism. Their work is worth revisiting here because their language, echoing that of their sources, inadvertently exposes these connections, which scholars have just recently begun to pursue. Jane Tompkins, for example, lauds Catherine Beecher's *Treatise on Domestic Economy* as "the prerequisite of world conquest" and claims of a later version that "the imperialistic drive behind the encyclopedism and determined practicality of this household manual . . . is a blueprint for colonizing the world in the name of the 'family state' under the leadership of Christian women."[3] As her title indicates, Mary P. Ryan's *Empire of the Mother: American Writing about Domesticity, 1830–1860* employs empire as a metaphor framing her analysis; yet she never links this pervasive imperial metaphor to the contemporaneous geopolitical movement of imperial expansion or to the discourse of Manifest Destiny. This blind spot, I believe, stems from the way that the ideology of separate spheres has shaped scholarship; until recently it has been assumed that nationalism and foreign policy lay outside the concern and participation of women. Isolating the empire of the mother from other imperial endeavors, however, runs two risks: First, it may reproduce in women's studies the insularity of an American studies that imagines the nation as a fixed, monolithic, and self-enclosed geographic and cultural whole; second, the legacy of separate spheres that sees women as morally superior to men can lead to the current moralistic strain in feminist criticism, which has shifted from celebrating the liberatory qualities of white women's writing to condemning their racism. In this essay I try instead to understand the vexed and contradictory relations between race and domesticity as an issue not solely of individual morality nor simply internal to the nation but as structural to the institutional and discursive processes of national expansion and empire building.[4]

My essay poses the question of how the ideology of separate spheres in antebellum America contributed to creating an American empire by imagining the nation as a home at a time when its geopolitical borders were expanding rapidly through violent confrontations with Indians, Mexicans, and European empires. Scholars have overlooked the fact that the development of domestic discourse in America is contemporaneous with the discourse of Manifest Destiny. If we juxtapose the spatial representations of these discourses, they seem to embody the most extreme form of separate spheres: the home as a bounded and rigidly ordered interior space is opposed to the boundless and undifferentiated space of an infinitely expanding nation. Yet these spatial and gendered configurations are linked in complex ways that are dependent upon racialized notions of the foreign. According to the ideology of separate spheres, domesticity can be viewed as an anchor, a feminine counterforce to the male activity of territorial conquest. I argue, to the contrary, that domesticity is more mobile and less stabilizing; it travels in contradictory circuits both to expand and contract the boundaries of home and nation and to produce shifting conceptions of the foreign. This form of traveling domesticity can be analyzed in the writings of Catherine Beecher and Sarah Josepha Hale, whose work, despite their ideological differences as public figures, reveals how the internal logic of domesticity relies on, abets, and reproduces the contradictions of nationalist expansion in the 1840s and 1850s. An analysis of Beecher's *A Treatise on Domestic Economy* demonstrates that the language of empire both suffuses and destabilizes the rhetoric of separate spheres, while an analysis of Hale's work uncovers the shared racial underpinnings of domestic and imperialist discourse through which the separateness of gendered spheres reinforces the effort to separate the races by turning blacks into foreigners. The essay concludes with suggestions about how understanding the imperial reach of domestic discourse might remap the way we read women's novels of the 1850s by interpreting their narratives of domesticity and female subjectivity as inseparable from narratives of empire and nation building.

Domesticity dominated middle-class women's writing and culture from the 1830s through the 1850s, a time when national boundaries were in violent flux; during this period the United States doubled its national territory, completed a campaign of Indian removal, fought its first prolonged foreign war, wrested the Spanish borderlands from Mexico, and annexed Texas, Oregon, and California. As Thomas Hietala has shown, this convulsive expansion was less a confident celebration of Manifest Destiny than a response to crises of confidence about national unity, the expansion of slavery, and the racial identity of citizenship—crises that territorial expansion exacerbated.[5] Furthermore, these movements evoked profound questions about the conceptual border between the domestic and the foreign. In the 1831 Supreme Court decision, *Cherokee*

Nation v. the State of Georgia, for example, Indians were declared members of "domestic dependent nations," neither foreign nationals nor United States citizens.[6] This designation makes the domestic an ambiguous third realm between the national and the foreign, as it places the foreign inside the geographic boundaries of the nation. The uneasy relation between the domestic and the foreign can also be seen in the debates over the annexation of new territory. In the middle of the Mexican War President Polk insisted that slavery was "purely a domestic question" and not a "foreign question" at all, but the expansion he advocated undermined that distinction and threatened domestic unity by raising the question of slavery's extension into previously foreign lands.[7] In debates about the annexation of Texas and later Mexico, both sides represented the new territories as women to be married to the U.S.; Sam Houston, for example, wrote of Texas presenting itself "to the United States as a bride adorned for her espousals"; and President Taylor accused annexationists after the Mexican War of trying to "drag California into the Union before her wedding garment has yet been cast about her person."[8] These visions of imperial expansion as marital union carried within them the specter of marriage as racial amalgamation. While popular fiction about the Mexican War portrayed brave American men rescuing and marrying Mexican women of Spanish descent, political debate over the annexation of Mexico hinged on what was agreed to be the impossibility of incorporating a foreign people marked by their racial intermixing into a domestic nation imagined as Anglo-Saxon.[9] One of the major contradictions of imperialist expansion was that while it strove to nationalize and domesticate foreign territories and peoples, annexation incorporated nonwhite foreign subjects in a way perceived to undermine the nation as a domestic space.

My point here is not to survey foreign policy but to suggest how deeply the language of domesticity suffused the debates about national expansion. Rather than stabilizing the representation of the nation as home, this rhetoric heightened the fraught and contingent nature of the boundary between the domestic and the foreign, a boundary that breaks down around questions of the racial identity of the nation as home. If we begin to rethink woman's sphere in this context, we have to ask how the discourse of domesticity negotiates the borders of an increasingly expanding empire and a divided nation. Domestic discourse both redresses and reenacts the contradictions of empire through its own double movement to expand female influence beyond the home and the nation while simultaneously contracting woman's sphere to police domestic boundaries against the threat of foreignness both within and without.

At this time of heightened national expansion, proponents of a "woman's sphere" applied the language of empire to both the home and women's emotional lives. "Hers is the empire of the affections," wrote

Sarah Josepha Hale, influential editor of *Godey's Lady's Book*, who opposed the women's rights movement as "the attempt to take woman away from her empire of home."[10] To educational reformer Horace Mann, "the empire of the Home" was "the most important of all empires, the pivot of all empires and emperors."[11] Writers who counseled women to renounce politics and economics, "to leave the rude commerce of camps and the soul hardening struggling of political power to the harsher spirit of men," urged them in highly political rhetoric to take up a more spiritual calling, "the domain of the moral affections and the empire of the heart."[12] Catherine Beecher gives this calling a nationalist cast in *A Treatise on Domestic Economy* when, for example, she uses Queen Victoria as a foil to elevate the American "mother and housekeeper in a large family," who is "the sovereign of an empire demanding as varied cares, and involving more difficult duties, than are exacted of her, who wears the crown and professedly regulates the interests of the greatest nation on earth, [yet] finds abundant leisure for theaters, balls, horse races, and every gay leisure."[13] This imperial trope might be interpreted as a compensatory and defensive effort to glorify the shrunken realm of female agency, in a paradox of what Mary Ryan calls "imperial isolation," whereby the mother gains her symbolic sovereignty at the cost of withdrawal from the outside world.[14] For these writers, however, metaphor has a material efficacy in the world. The representation of the home as an empire exists in tension with the notion of woman's sphere as a contracted space because it is in the nature of empires to extend their rule over new domains while fortifying their borders against external invasion and internal insurrection. If, on the one hand, domesticity draws strict boundaries between the home and the world of men, on the other, it becomes the engine of national expansion, the site from which the nation reaches beyond itself through the emanation of woman's moral influence.

The paradox of what might be called "imperial domesticity" is that by withdrawing from direct agency in the male arena of commerce and politics, woman's sphere can be represented by both women and men as a more potent agent for national expansion. The outward reach of domesticity in turn enables the interior functioning of the home. In her introduction to *A Treatise on Domestic Economy*, Beecher inextricably links women's work at home to the unfolding of America's global mission of "exhibiting to the world the beneficent influences of Christianity, when carried into every social, civil, and political institution" (12). Women's maternal responsibility for molding the character of men and children has global repercussions: "To American women, more than to any others on earth, is committed the exalted privilege of extending over the world those blessed influences, that are to renovate degraded man, and 'clothe all climes with beauty'" (14). Beecher ends her introduction with an extended architectural metaphor in which women's agency at home is predicated on the global expansion of the nation:

> The builders of a temple are of equal importance, whether they labor on
> the foundations, or toil upon the dome. Thus also with those labors that
> are to be made effectual in the regeneration of the Earth. The woman who
> is rearing a family of children; the woman who labors in the schoolroom,
> the woman who, in her retired chamber, earns with her needle, the mite
> to contribute for the intellectual and moral elevation of her country; even
> the humble domestic, whose example and influence may be molding and
> forming young minds, while her faithful services sustain a prosperous
> domestic state;—each and all may be cheered by the consciousness that
> they are agents in accomplishing the greatest work that ever was commit-
> ted to human responsibility. It is the building of a glorious temple, whose
> base shall be coextensive with the bounds of the earth, whose summit
> shall pierce the skies, whose splendor shall beam on all lands, and those
> who hew the lowliest stone, as much as those who carve the highest capi-
> tal, will be equally honored when its top-stone shall be laid, with new re-
> joicing of the morning stars, and shoutings of the sons of God. (14)

One political effect of this metaphor is to unify women of different social classes in a shared project of construction while sustaining class
hierarchy among women.[15] This image of social unity both depends
upon and underwrites a vision of national expansion, as women's varied labors come together to embrace the entire world. As the passage
moves down the social scale, from mother to teacher to spinster, the
geographic reach extends outward from home to schoolroom to country,
until the "humble domestic" returns back to the "prosperous domestic
state," a phrase that casts the nation in familial terms. Women's work
at home here performs two interdependent forms of national labor; it
forges the bonds of internal unity while impelling the nation outward
to encompass the globe. This outward expansion in turn enables the
internal cohesiveness of woman's separate sphere by making women
agents in constructing an infinitely expanding edifice.

Beecher thus introduces her detailed manual on the regulation of
the home as a highly ordered space by fusing the boundedness of the
home with the boundlessness of the nation. Her 1841 introduction
bears a remarkable resemblance to the rhetoric of Manifest Destiny,
particularly to this passage by one of its foremost proponents, John L.
O'Sullivan:

> The far-reaching, the boundless future will be the era of American great-
> ness. In its magnificent domain of space and time, the nation of many
> nations is destined to manifest to mankind the excellence of divine prin-
> ciples; to establish on earth the noblest temple ever dedicated to the
> worship of the most high—the Sacred and the True. Its floor shall be a
> hemisphere—its roof the firmament of the star-studded heavens, and its
> congregation an Union of many Republics, comprising hundreds of happy
> millions, calling, owning no man master, but governed by God's natural
> and moral law of equality.[16]

While these passages exemplify the stereotype of separate spheres (one describes work in the home and the other work of nation building), both use a common architectural metaphor from the Bible to build a temple coextensive with the globe. O'Sullivan's grammatical subject is the American nation, which is the implied medium in Beecher's text for channeling women's work at home to a Christianized world. The construction of an edifice ordinarily entails walling off the inside from the outside, but in both these cases there is a paradoxical effect whereby the distinction between inside and outside is obliterated by the expansion of the home/nation/temple to encompass the globe. The rhetorics of Manifest Destiny and domesticity share a vocabulary that turns imperial conquest into spiritual regeneration in order to efface internal conflict or external resistance in visions of geopolitical domination as global harmony.

Although imperial domesticity ultimately imagines a home co-extensive with the entire world, it also continually projects a map of unregenerate outlying foreign terrain that both gives coherence to its boundaries and justifies its domesticating mission. When in 1869 Catherine Beecher revised her *Treatise* with her sister, Harriet Beecher Stowe, as *The American Woman's Home*, they downplayed the earlier role of domesticity in harmonizing class differences while enhancing domesticity's outward reach. The book ends by advocating the establishment of Christian neighborhoods settled primarily by women as a way of putting into practice domesticity's expansive potential to Christianize and Americanize immigrants both in Northeastern cities and "all over the West and South, while along the Pacific coast, China and Japan are sending their pagan millions to share our favored soil, climate, and government." No longer a leveling factor among classes within America, domesticity could be extended to those conceived of as foreign both within and beyond American national borders: "Ere long colonies from these prosperous and Christian communities would go forth to shine as 'lights of the world' in all the now darkened nations. Thus the Christian family and Christian neighborhood would become the grand ministry as they were designed to be, in training our whole race for heaven."[17] While Beecher and Stowe emphasize domesticity's service to "darkened nations," the existence of "pagans" as potential converts performs a reciprocal service in the extension of domesticity to single American women. Such Christian neighborhoods would allow unmarried women without children to leave their work in "factories, offices and shops" or their idleness in "refined leisure" to live domestic lives on their own, in some cases by adopting native children. Domesticity's imperial reach posits a way of extending woman's sphere to include not only the heathen but also the unmarried Euro-American woman who can be freed from biological reproduction to rule her own empire of the mother.

If writers about domesticity encouraged the extension of female influence outward to domesticate the foreign, their writings also evoked anxiety about the opposing trajectory that brings foreignness into the home. Analyzing the widespread colonial trope that compares colonized people to children, Ann Stoler and Karen Sánchez-Eppler have both shown how this metaphor can work not only to infantilize the colonized but also to portray white children as young savages in need of civilizing.[18] This metaphor at once extends domesticity outward to the tutelage of heathens while focusing it inward to regulate the threat of foreignness within the boundaries of the home. For Beecher, this internal savagery appears to threaten the physical health of the mother. Throughout the *Treatise*, the vision of the sovereign mother with imperial responsibilities is countered by descriptions of the ailing invalid mother. This contrast can be seen in the titles of the first two chapters, "Peculiar Responsibilities of American Women" and "Difficulties Peculiar to American Women." The latter focuses on the pervasive invalidism that makes American women physically and emotionally unequal to their global responsibilities. In contrast to the ebullient temple building of the first chapter, Beecher ends the second with a quotation from Tocqueville describing a fragile frontier home centered on a lethargic and vulnerable mother whose

> children cluster about her, full of health, turbulence and energy; they are true children of the wilderness; their mother watches them from time to time, with mingled melancholy and joy. To look at their strength, and her languor one might imagine that the life she had given them exhausted her own; and still she regrets not what they cost her. The house, inhabited by these emigrants, has no internal partition or loft. In the one chamber of which it consists, the whole family is gathered for the night. The dwelling itself is a little world; an ark of civilization amid an ocean of foliage. A hundred steps beyond it, the primeval forest spreads its shade and solitude resumes its sway. (24)

The mother's health appears drained not by the external hardships inflicted by the environment but by her intimate tie to her own "children of the wilderness," who violate the border between home and primeval forest. This boundary is partially reinforced by the image of the home as an "ark of civilization" whose internal order should protect its inhabitants from the sea of chaos that surrounds them. Yet the undifferentiated inner space, which lacks "internal partition," replicates rather than defends against the boundlessness of the wilderness. The rest of the treatise, with its detailed attention to the systematic organization of the household, works to "partition" the home in a way that distinguishes it from the external wilderness.[19]

The infirmity of American mothers is a pervasive concern throughout the *Treatise*, yet its physical cause is difficult to locate in Beecher's text. Poor health afflicts middle-class women in Northeastern cities as much as women on the frontier, according to Beecher, and she sees both cases resulting from a geographic and social mobility in which "everything is moving and changing" (16). This movement affects women's health most directly, claims Beecher, by depriving them of reliable domestic servants. With "trained" servants constantly moving up and out, middle-class women must resort to hiring "ignorant" and "poverty-stricken foreigners," with whom they are said in *American Woman's Home* to have a "missionary" relationship (332). Though Beecher does not label these foreigners as the direct cause of illness, their presence disrupts the orderly "system and regularity" of housekeeping, leading American women to be "disheartened, discouraged, and ruined in health" (18). Throughout her *Treatise* Beecher turns the absence of good servants—at first a cause of infirmity—into a remedy; their lack gives middle-class women the opportunity to perform regular domestic labor that will revive their health. By implication, their self-regulated work will also keep "poverty-stricken foreigners" out of their homes. Curiously, then, the mother's ill health stems from the unruly subjects of her domestic empire—children and servants—who bring uncivilized wilderness and undomesticated foreignness into the home. The fear of disease and of the invalidism that characterizes the American woman also serves as a metaphor for anxiety about foreignness within. The mother's domestic empire is at risk of contagion from the very subjects she must domesticate and civilize, her wilderness children and foreign servants, who ultimately infect both the home and the body of the mother.[20]

This reading of Beecher suggests new ways of understanding the intricate means by which domestic discourse generates and relies on images of the foreign. On the one hand, domesticity's "habits of system and order" appear to anchor the home as a stable center in a fluctuating social world with expanding national borders; on the other, domesticity must be spatially and conceptually mobile to travel to the nation's far-flung frontiers. Beecher's use of Tocqueville's ark metaphor suggests both the rootlessness and the self-enclosed mobility necessary for middle-class domesticity to redefine the meaning of habitation to make Euro-Americans feel at home in terrain in which *they* are initially the foreigners. Domesticity inverts this relationship to create a home by rendering prior inhabitants alien and undomesticated and by implicitly nativizing newcomers. The empire of the mother thus shares the logic of the American empire; both follow a double compulsion to conquer and domesticate the foreign, thus incorporating and controlling a threatening foreignness within the borders of the home and the nation.

The imperial scope of domesticity was central to the work of Sarah Josepha Hale throughout her half-century editorship of the influential *Godey's Lady's Book*, as well as to her fiction and history writing. Hale has been viewed by some scholars as advocating a woman's sphere more thoroughly separate from male political concerns than Beecher did.[21] This withdrawal seems confirmed by the refusal of *Godey's* even to mention the Civil War throughout its duration, much less take sides. Yet when Hale conflates the progress of women with the nation's Manifest Destiny in her history writing, other scholars have judged her as inconsistently moving out of woman's sphere into the male political realm.[22] Hale's conception of separate spheres, I will argue, is predicated on the imperial expansion of the nation. Although her writing as editor, essayist, and novelist focused on the interior spaces of the home, with ample advice on housekeeping, clothing, manners, and emotions, she gave equal and related attention to the expansion of female influence through her advocacy of female medical missionaries abroad and the colonization of Africa by former black slaves. Even though Hale seems to avoid the issue of slavery and race relations in her silence about the Civil War, in the 1850s her conception of domesticity takes on a decidedly racial cast, exposing the intimate link between the separateness of gendered spheres and the effort to keep the races apart in separate national spheres.

In 1846, at the beginning of the Mexican War, Hale launched a campaign on the pages of *Godey's Lady's Book* to declare Thanksgiving Day a national holiday, a campaign she avidly pursued until Lincoln made the holiday official in 1863.[23] This effort typified the way in which Hale's map of woman's sphere overlaid national and domestic spaces; *Godey's* published detailed instructions and recipes for preparing the Thanksgiving feast, while it encouraged women readers to agitate for a nationwide holiday as a ritual of national expansion and unification. The power of Thanksgiving Day stemmed from its center in the domestic sphere; Hale imagined millions of families seated around the holiday table at the same time, thereby unifying the vast and shifting space of the national domain through simultaneity in time. This domestic ritual, she wrote in 1852, would unite "our great nation, by its states and families from the St. John to the Rio Grande, from the Atlantic to the Pacific."[24] If the celebration of Thanksgiving unites individual families across regions and brings them together in an imagined collective space, Thanksgiving's continental scope endows each individual family gathering with national meaning. Furthermore, the Thanksgiving story commemorating the founding of New England—which in Hale's version makes no mention of Indians—could create a common history by nationalizing a regional myth of origins and imposing it on the territories most recently wrested from Indians and Mexicans. Hale's campaign to transform Thanksgiving from a regional to a national holiday grew even fiercer with the approach of the Civil War. In 1859 she wrote, "If every state would join in Union Thanksgiving on the 24th of this month, would it not be a renewed pledge of love and loyalty to the Constitution of the United States?"[25] Thanksgiving Day, she hoped, could avert civil war. As a national holiday celebrated primarily in the home,

Thanksgiving traverses broad geographic circuits to write a national history of origins, to colonize the western territories, and to unite North and South.

The domestic ritual of Thanksgiving could expand and unify national borders only by also fortifying those borders against foreignness; for Hale, the nation's borders not only defined its geographical limits but also set apart nonwhites within the national domain. In Hale's fiction of the 1850s, Thanksgiving polices the domestic sphere by making black people, both free and enslaved, foreign to the domestic nation and denying them a home within America's expanding borders. In 1852 Hale reissued her novel *Northwood*, which had launched her career in 1827, with a highly publicized chapter about a New Hampshire Thanksgiving dinner showcasing the values of the American republic to a skeptical British visitor. For the 1852 version Hale changed the subtitle from "A Tale of New England" to "Life North and South" to highlight the new material on slavery she had added.[26] Pro-union yet against abolition, Hale advocated African colonization as the only means of preserving domestic unity by sending all blacks to settle in Africa and Christianize its inhabitants. Colonization in the 1850s had a two-pronged ideology, both to expel blacks to a separate national sphere and to expand U.S. power through the civilizing process; black Christian settlers would thereby become both outcasts from and agents for the American empire.[27]

Hale's 1852 *Northwood* ends with an appeal to use Thanksgiving Day as an occasion to collect money at all American churches "for the purpose of educating and colonizing free people of color and emancipated slaves" (408). This annual collection would contribute to "peaceful emancipation" as "every obstacle to the real freedom of America would be melted before the gushing streams of sympathy and charity" (408). While "sympathy," a sentiment associated with woman's sphere, seems to extend to black slaves, the goal of sympathy in this passage is not to free them but to emancipate white America from their presence. Thanksgiving for Hale thus celebrates national coherence around the domestic sphere while simultaneously rendering blacks within America foreign to the nation.

For Hale, colonization would not simply expel black people from American nationality but would also transform American slavery into a civilizing and domesticating mission. One of her Northern characters explains to the British visitor that "the destiny of America is to instruct the world, which we shall do, with the aid of our Anglo-Saxon brothers over the water.... Great Britain has enough to do at home and in the East Indies to last her another century. We have this country and Africa to settle and civilize" (167). When his listener is puzzled by the reference to Africa, he explains, "That is the greatest mission of our Republic, to train here the black man for his duties as a Christian, then free him and send him to Africa, there to plant Free States and organize

Christian civilization" (168). The colonization of Africa becomes the goal of slavery by making it part of the civilizing mission of global imperialism. Colonization thus not only banishes blacks from the domestic union, but, as the final sentence of *Northwood* proclaims, it proves that "the mission of American slavery is to Christianize Africa" (408).

In 1852 Hale published the novel *Liberia*, which begins where *Northwood* ends, with the settlement of Liberia by freed black slaves.[28] Seen by scholars as a retort to *Uncle Tom's Cabin*, *Liberia* can also be read as the untold story of Stowe's novel, beginning where she ends, with former black slaves immigrating to Africa.[29] Although the subtitle, "Mr. Peyton's Experiment," places colonization under the aegis of white males, the narrative turns colonization into a project emanating from woman's sphere in at least two directions. In its outward trajectory, the settlement of Liberia appears as an expansion of feminized domestic values. Yet domesticity is not only exported to civilize native Africans; the framing of the novel also makes African colonization necessary to the establishment of domesticity within America as exclusively white. While Hale writes that the purpose of the novel is to "show the advantages Liberia offers to the African," in so doing it construes all black people as foreign to American nationality by asserting that they must remain homeless within the United States. At the same time, Hale paints a picture of American imperialism as the embodiment of the feminine values of domesticity: "What other nation can point to a colony planted from such pure motives of charity; nurtured by the counsels and exertions of its most noble and self-denying statesmen and philanthropists; and sustained, from its feeble commencement up to a period of self-reliance and independence, from pure love of justice and humanity" (iv). In this passage America is figured as a mother raising her baby, Africa, to maturity; the vocabulary of "purity," "charity," "self-denial," and "love" represents colonization as an expansion of the values of woman's separate sphere.

The narrative opens with a threat to American domesticity on two fronts. The last male of a distinguished Virginia family is on his death bed, helpless to defend his plantation from a rumored slave insurrection; the women of the family, led by his wife, "Virginia," rally with the loyal slaves to defend their home from an insurrection that never occurs. Thus the novel opens with separate spheres gone awry, with the man of the family abed at home and white women and black slaves acting as protectors and soldiers. While the ensuing plot to settle Liberia overtly rewards those slaves for their loyalty by giving them freedom and a homeland, it also serves to reinstate separate spheres and reestablish American domesticity as white.

When the narrative shifts to Africa, colonization has the effect not only of driving black slaves out of American nationhood but also of Americanizing Africa through domesticity. A key figure in the settlement is the slave Keziah, who has nursed the white plantation owners.

She is the most responsive to Peyton's proposal for colonization because of her desire both to be free and to Christianize the natives. Her future husband, Polydore, more recently arrived from Africa and thus less "civilized," is afraid to return there because of his memory of native brutality and superstition. This couple represents two faces of enslaved Africans central to the white imagination of colonization: the degenerate heathen represented by the man and the redeemed Christian represented by the woman. Keziah, however, can only become a fully domesticated woman at a geographic remove from American domesticity. When Keziah protects the plantation in Virginia, her maternal impulse is described as that of a wild animal—a "fierce lioness." Only in Africa can she become the domestic center of the new settlement, where she establishes a home that resembles Beecher's Christian neighborhood. Keziah builds a private home with fence and garden, and civilizes her husband while expanding her domestic sphere to adopt native children and open a Christian school.

Keziah's domestication of herself and her surroundings in Africa can be seen as part of the movement in the novel noted by Susan Ryan, in which the freed black characters are represented as recognizably American only at the safe distance of Africa.[30] Once banished from the domestic sphere of the American nation, they can reproduce themselves for readers as Americans in a foreign terrain. The novel not only narrates the founding of Liberia as a story of colonization, but Hale's storytelling also colonizes Liberia as an imitation of America, replete with images of an open frontier, the Mayflower, and the planting of the American flag. A double narrative movement at once contracts American borders to exclude blacks from domestic space and simultaneously expands U.S. borders by recreating that domestic space in Africa. The novel thus ends with a quotation that compares the Liberian settlers to the Pilgrims and represents them as part of a global expansion of the American nation:

> I do not doubt but that the whole continent of Africa will be regenerated, and I believe the Republic of Liberia will be the great instrument, in the hands of God, in working out this regeneration. The colony of Liberia has succeeded better than the colony of Plymouth did for the same period of time. And yet, in that little company which was wafted across the mighty ocean in the *May Flower*, we see the germs of this already colossal nation, whose feet are in the tropics, while her head reposes upon the snows of Canada. Her right hand she stretches over the Atlantic, feeding the millions of the Old World, and beckoning them to her shores, as a refuge from famine and oppression; and, at the same time, she stretches forth her left hand to the islands of the Pacific, and to the old empires of the East. (303)

African slaves are brought to America to become Christianized and domesticated, but they cannot complete this potential transformation until they return to Africa.

Hale's writing makes race central to woman's sphere not only by excluding nonwhites from domestic nationalism but also by seeing the capacity for domesticity as an innate, defining characteristic of the Anglo-Saxon race. Reginald Horsman has shown how by the 1840s the meaning of Anglo-Saxonism in political thought had shifted from a historical understanding of the development of republican institutions to an essentialist definition of a single race that possesses an innate and unique capacity for self-government.[31] His analysis, however, limits this racial formation to the male sphere of politics. Hale's *Woman's Record* (1853), a massive compendium of the history of women from Eve to the present, establishes woman's sphere as central to the racial discourse of Anglo-Saxonism; to her, the empire of the mother spawns the Anglo-Saxon nation and propels its natural inclination toward global power.[32] In her introduction to the fourth part of her volume on the present era, Hale represents America as manifesting the universal progress of women that culminates in the Anglo-Saxon race. To explain the Anglo-Saxon "mastery of the mind over Europe and Asia," she argues that

> if we trace out the causes of this superiority, they would center in the moral influence, which true religion confers on the female sex. . . . There is still a more wonderful example of this uplifting power of the educated female mind. It is only seventy-five years since the Anglo-Saxons in the New World became a nation, then numbering about three million souls. Now this people form the great American republic, with a population of twenty three millions; and the destiny of the world will soon be in their keeping! Religion is free; and the soul which woman always influences where God is worshipped in spirit and truth, is untrammeled by code, or creed, or caste. . . . The result before the world—a miracle of advancement, American mothers train their sons to be men. (564)

Hale here articulates the imperial logic of what has been called "republican motherhood," which ultimately posits the expansion of maternal influence beyond the nation's borders.[33] The Manifest Destiny of the nation unfolds logically from the imperial reach of woman's influence emanating from her separate domestic sphere. Domesticity makes manifest the destiny of the Anglo-Saxon race, while Manifest Destiny becomes in turn the condition for Anglo-Saxon domesticity. For Hale domesticity has two effects on national expansion: It imagines the nation as a home delimited by race and propels the nation outward through the imperial reach of female influence.

Advocating domesticity's expansive mode, *Woman's Record* includes only those nonwhite women whom Hale understood to be contributing to the spread of Christianity to colonized peoples. In the third volume, Hale designates as the most distinguished woman from 1500 to 1830 an American missionary to Burma, Ann Judson, a white American (152). The Fourth Era of *Woman's Record* focuses predominantly on

American women as the apex of historical development. In contrast to the aristocratic accomplishments of English women, "in all that contributes to popular education and pure religious sentiment among the masses, the women of America are in advance of all others on the globe. To prove this we need only examine the list of American female missionaries, teachers, editors and authors of works instructive and educational, contained in this 'Record'" (564). While Anglo-Saxon men marched outward to conquer new lands, women had a complementary outward reach from within the domestic sphere.

For Hale, African colonization can be seen as part of the broader global expansion of woman's sphere. In 1853 Hale printed in *Godey's Lady's Book* "An Appeal to the American Christians on Behalf of the Ladies' Medical Missionary Society," in which she argued for the special need for women physicians abroad because they would have unique access to foreign women's bodies and souls.[34] Her argument for the training of female medical missionaries both enlarges the field of white women's agency and feminizes the force of imperial power. She sees female medical missionaries as not only curing disease but also raising the status of women abroad: "All heathen people have a high reverence for medical knowledge. Should they find Christian ladies accomplished in this science, would it not greatly raise the sex in the estimation of those nations, where one of the most serious impediments to moral improvement is the degradation and ignorance to which their females have been for centuries consigned?" (185). Though superior to heathen women in status, American women would accomplish their goal by imagining gender as a common ground, which would give them special access to women abroad. As women they could be more effective imperialists, penetrating those interior feminine colonial spaces, symbolized by the harem, that remain inaccessible to male missionaries:

> Vaccination is difficult of introduction among the people of the east, though suffering dreadfully from the ravages of small-pox. The American mission at Siam writes that thousands of children were, last year, swept away by this disease in the country around them. Female physicians could win their way among these poor children much easier than doctors of the other sex. Surely the ability of American women to learn and practice vaccination will not be questioned, when the more difficult art of inoculation was discovered by the women of Turkey, and introduced into Europe by an English woman! Inoculation is one of the greatest triumphs of remedial skill over a sure loathsome and deadly disease which the annals of Medical Art record. Its discovery belongs to women. I name it here to show that they are gifted with genius for the profession, and only need to be educated to excel in the preventive department.
>
> Let pious, intelligent women be fitly prepared, and what a mission-field for doing good would be opened! In India, China, Turkey, and all over the heathen world, they would, in their character of physicians, find access to the homes and harems where women dwell, and where the good

seed sown would bear an hundredfold, because it would take root in the
bosom of the sufferer, and in the heart of childhood. (185)

In this passage the connections among women circulate in many directions, but Hale charts a kind of evolutionary narrative that places
American women at the apex of development. Though inoculation was
discovered by Turkish women, it can only return to Turkey to save
Turkish children through the agency of English women transporting
knowledge to Americans, who can then go to Turkey as missionaries
and save women who cannot save themselves or their children. While
Hale is advocating that unmarried women be trained as missionaries,
the needs of heathen women allow female missionaries to conquer
their own domestic empire without reproducing biologically. Instead,
American women are metaphorically cast as men in a cross-racial
union, as they sow seeds in the bosom of heathen women who will bear
Christian children. Through the sentiment of female influence, women
physicians will transform heathen harems into Christian homes.

My reading of Hale suggests that the concept of female influence so
central to domestic discourse and at the heart of the sentimental ethos
is underwritten by and abets the imperial expansion of the nation.
While the empire of the mother advocated retreat from the world-
conquering enterprises of men, this renunciation promised a more thorough kind of world conquest. The empire of the mother shared with the
American empire a logical structure and a key contradiction: Both
sought to encompass the world outside their borders; yet this same
outward movement contributed to and relied on the contraction of the
domestic sphere to exclude persons conceived of as racially foreign
within those expanding national boundaries.

Understanding the imperial reach of domesticity and its relation to the
foreign should help remap the critical terrain upon which women's domestic fiction has been constructed. We can chart the broader international and national contexts in which unfold narratives of female
development that at first glance seem anchored in local domestic
spaces. We can see how such narratives imagine domestic locations in
complex negotiation with the foreign. To take a few well-known examples from the 1850s, Susan Warner's *The Wide, Wide World* sends its
heroine to Scotland, while the world of Maria Cummins's *The Lamplighter* encompasses India, Cuba, the American West, and Brazil. In
E. D. E. N. Southworth's *The Hidden Hand*, the resolution of multiple
domestic plots in Virginia relies on the participation of the male characters in the Mexican War, while the geographic coordinates of *Uncle
Tom's Cabin* extend not only to Africa at the end but also to Haiti and
Canada throughout.[35] Such a remapping would involve more than
just seeing the geographic settings anew; it would turn inward to the
privileged space of the domestic novel—the interiority of the female

subject—to find traces of foreignness that must be domesticated or expunged. How does this struggle with foreignness within "woman's sphere" shape the interiority of female subjectivity, the empire of the affections and the heart? While critics such as Gillian Brown, Richard Brodhead, and Nancy Armstrong have taught us how domestic novels represent women as model bourgeois subjects,[36] my remapping would explore how domestic novels produce the racialized national subjectivity of the white middle-class woman in contested international spaces.

Many domestic novels open at physical thresholds, such as windows or doorways, that problematize the relation between interior and exterior; the home and the female self appear fragile and threatened from within and without by foreign forces. These novels then explore the breakdown of the boundaries between internal and external spaces, between the domestic and the foreign, as they struggle to renegotiate and stabilize these domains. This negotiation often takes place not only within the home but also within the heroine. The narrative of female self-discipline that is so central to the domestic novel might be viewed as a kind of civilizing process in which the woman plays the role of both civilizer and savage. Gerty in *The Lamplighter*, for example, like Capitola in *The Hidden Hand*, first appears as an uncivilized street urchin, a heathen unaware of Christianity whose anger is viewed as a "dark infirmity" and whose unruly nature is in need of domesticating. We later learn that she was born in Brazil to the daughter of a ship captain, who was killed by malaria, the "inhospitable southern disease, which takes the stranger for its victim."[37] To become the sovereign mother of her own domestic empire, Gerty must become her own first colonial subject and purge herself of both her origin in a diseased uncivilized terrain and the female anger identified with that "dark" realm. This split between the colonizer and the colonized, seen here within one female character, appears in *Uncle Tom's Cabin* racially externalized onto Eva and Topsy.[38]

My point is that where the domestic novel appears most turned inward to the private sphere of female interiority, we often find subjectivity scripted by narratives of nation and empire. Even at the heart of *The Wide, Wide World*, a novel usually understood as thoroughly closeted in interior space, where the heroine disciplines herself through reading and prayer, her favorite book is the popular biography of George Washington, the father of the nation. Her own journey to live with her Scottish relatives can be seen as a feminized reenactment of the American revolution against the British empire. Similarly, in *The Hidden Hand*, the most inner recess of woman's sphere is conjoined with the male sphere of imperial conquest. While the American men in the novel are invading Mexico, in Virginia, a bandit, significantly named "Black Donald," invades the heroine's chamber and threatens to rape her. To protect the sanctity of her home and her own chastity, Capitola performs a founding national narrative of conquest. She drops the rapist through a trap door in her bedroom into a deep pit dug by the original owner in order to trick the Indian inhabitants into selling their land. The domestic heroine thus reenacts the originating gesture of imperial appropriation to protect the borders of her domestic empire and the inviolability of the female self.

Feminist criticism of *Uncle Tom's Cabin* has firmly established that the empire of the mother in Stowe's novel extends beyond the home to the national arena of antislavery politics. This expansive movement of female influence, I have been arguing, has an international dimension that helps separate gendered spheres coalesce in the imperial expansion of the nation by redrawing domestic borders against the foreign. In light of my reading of Hale's *Liberia*, we might remap the critical terrain of Stowe's novel to ask how its delineation of domestic space, as both familial and national, relies upon and propels the colonization of Africa by the novel's free black characters. Rather than just focusing on their expulsion at the end of the novel, we might locate, in Toni Morrison's terms, "the Africanist presence" throughout the text.[39] Africa appears as both an imperial outpost and a natural embodiment of woman's sphere, a kind of feminized utopia, that is strategically posed as an alternative to Haiti, which hovers as a menacing image of black revolutionary agency. The idea of African colonization does not simply emerge at the end as a racist failure of Stowe's political imagination; rather, colonization underwrites the racial politics of the domestic imagination. The "Africanist presence" throughout *Uncle Tom's Cabin* is intimately bound to the expansionist logic of domesticity itself. In the writing of Stowe and her contemporary proponents of woman's sphere, "Manifest Domesticity" turns an imperial nation into a home by producing and colonizing specters of the foreign that lurk inside and outside its ever shifting borders.

Notes

I wish to thank the organizers of the conference "Nineteenth-Century American Women Writers in the Twenty-First Century" (Hartford, May 1996) for inviting me to present my first formulation of the ideas in this essay. Special thanks to Susan Gillman, Carla Kaplan, Dana D. Nelson, and Priscilla Wald for their helpful and encouraging readings at crucial stages.

1. Influential studies of this paradigm by historians and literary critics include Barbara Welter, "The Cult of True Womanhood," *American Quarterly* 18 (summer 1966): 151–74; Kathryn Kish Sklar, *Catherine Beecher: A Study in American Domesticity* (New Haven: Yale Univ. Press, 1973); Nancy Cott, *The Bonds of Womanhood: "Woman's Sphere" in New England, 1780–1835* (New Haven: Yale Univ. Press, 1977); Ann Douglas, *The Feminization of American Culture* (New York: Knopf, 1977); Nina Baym, *Woman's Fiction: A Guide to Novels by and about Women in America, 1820–1870* (Ithaca, N.Y.: Cornell Univ. Press, 1978); Mary P. Ryan, *Cradle of the Middle Class: The Family in Oneida County, New York, 1790–1865* (Cambridge,

Eng.: Cambridge Univ. Press, 1981), and *Empire of the Mother: American Writing about Domesticity, 1830–1860* (New York: Institute for Research in History and Haworth Press, 1982); Mary Kelley, *Private Woman, Public Stage: Literary Domesticity in Nineteenth-Century America* (New York: Oxford Univ. Press, 1984); Jane Tompkins, *Sensational Designs: The Cultural Work of American Fiction, 1790–1860* (New York: Oxford Univ. Press, 1985); Gillian Brown, *Domestic Individualism: Imagining Self in Nineteenth-Century America* (Berkeley and Los Angeles: Univ. of California Press, 1990); and the essays in *The Culture of Sentiment: Race, Gender, and Sentimentality in Nineteenth-Century America*, ed. Shirley Samuels (New York: Oxford Univ. Press, 1992). See also the useful review essay by Linda K. Kerber, "Separate Spheres, Female Worlds, Woman's Place: The Rhetoric of Women's History," *The Journal of American History* (June 1988): 9–39.

2. On the etymology of the word *domestic* and its relation to colonialism, see Karen Hansen, ed., *African Encounters with Domesticity* (New Brunswick, N.J.: Rutgers Univ. Press, 1992), 2–23; and Anne McClintock, *Imperial Leather: Race, Gender, and Sexuality in the Colonial Contest* (New York: Routledge, 1995), 31–36. On the uses of domesticity in the colonial context, see Vicente L. Rafael, "Colonial Domesticity: White Women and United States Rule in the Philippines." *American Literature* 67 (December 1995): 639–66.

3. Tompkins, *Sensational Designs*, 143, 144. Despite Tompkins's well-known debate with Ann Douglas, both critics rely on imperial rhetoric. While Tompkins applauds the imperialist impulse of sentimentalism, Douglas derides sentimental writers for a rapacious reach that extends as far as the "colonization of heaven" and the "domestication of death" (240–72).

4. Even recent revisionist studies that situate woman's sphere in relation to racial and class hierarchies often overlook the international context in which these divisions evolve. In the important essays in *Culture of Sentiment*, for example, many of the racialized configurations of domesticity under discussion rely on a foreign or imperial dimension that remains unanalyzed. To take a few examples, Laura Wexler's analysis of Hampton Institute makes no mention of its founding by influential missionaries to Hawaii ("Tender Violence: Literary Eavesdropping, Domestic Fiction, and Educational Reform," 9–38); Karen Halttunen's analysis of a murder trial revolves around the uncertain identity of a white woman's foreign Spanish or Cuban lover ("'Domestic Differences': Competing Narratives of Womanhood in the Murder Trial of Lucretia Chapman," 39–57); Lynn Wardley ties domesticity's obsession with detail to West African fetishism ("Relic, Fetish, Femmage: The Aesthetics of Sentiment in the Work of Stowe," 203–20). Several essays note comparisons of slavery to the oriental harem, including Carolyn Karcher on Lydia Maria Child's antislavery fiction ("Rape, Murder, and Revenge in Slavery's Pleasant Homes: Lydia Maria Child's Antislavery Fiction and the Limits of Genre," 58–72) and Joy Kasson's analysis of Hirams's *The Greek Slave* ("Narratives of the Female Body: *The Greek Slave*," 172–90). The only essay to treat the imperial dimensions of domesticity is Lora Romero's "Vanishing Americans: Gender, Empire, and New Historicism" (115–27).

5. Thomas R. Hietala, *Manifest Design: Anxious Aggrandizement in Late Jacksonian America* (Ithaca, N.Y.: Cornell Univ. Press, 1985).

6. *Cherokee Nation v. the State of Georgia*, in *Major Problems in American Foreign Policy: Documents and Essays*, ed. Thomas G. Paterson, 2 vols. (Lexington, Mass.: Heath, 1989), 1:202.

7. Quoted in Walter La Feber, *The American Age: United States Foreign Policy at Home and Abroad* (New York: Norton, 1989), 112.

8. Quoted in George B. Forgie, *Patricide in the House Divided: A Psychological Interpretation of Lincoln and His Age* (New York: Norton, 1979), 107–08.

9. On popular fiction of the Mexican War, see Robert W. Johannsen, *To the Halls of the Montezumas: The Mexican War in the American Imagination* (New York: Oxford Univ. Press, 1984), 175–204.

10. Sarah Josepha Hale, "Editor's Table," *Godey's Lady's Book*, January 1852, 88.

11. Quoted in Ryan, *Empire of the Mother*, 112.

12. From "The Social Condition of Woman," *North American Review*, April 1836, 513; quoted in Annette Kolodny, *The Land Before Her: Fantasy and Experience of the American Frontiers, 1630–1860* (Chapel Hill: Univ. of North Carolina Press, 1984), 166.

13. Catherine Beecher, *A Treatise on Domestic Economy* (Boston: Marsh, Capen, Lyon, and Webb, 1841), 144. Subsequent references to this work are cited parenthetically in the text.

14. Ryan, *Empire of the Mother*, 97–114.

15. Kathryn Kish Sklar is one of the few scholars to consider Beecher's domestic ideology in relation to nation building. She analyzes the *Treatise* as appealing to gender as a common national denominator, and as using domesticity as a means to promote national unity to counterbalance mobility and conflicts based on class and region. Sklar fails to see, however, that this vision of gender as a tool for national unity is predicated upon the nation's imperial role (*Catherine Beecher*). Jenine Abboushi Dallal analyzes the imperial dimensions of Beecher's domestic ideology by contrasting it with the domestic rhetoric of Melville's imperial adventure narratives in "The Beauty of Imperialism: Emerson, Melville, Flaubert, and Al-Shidyac" (Ph.D. diss., Harvard University, 1996), chap. 2.

16. John L. O'Sullivan, "The Great Nation of Futurity," in *Major Problems in American Foreign Policy*, ed. Paterson, 1:241.

17. Catherine Beecher and Harriet Beecher Stowe, *The American Woman's Home* (Hartford, Conn.: J. B. Ford, 1869), 458–59.

18. Karen Sánchez-Eppler, "Raising Empires like Children: Race, Nation, and Religious Education," *American Literary History* 8 (Fall 1996): 399–425; Ann Stoler, *Race and the Education of Desire: Foucault's "History of Sexuality" and the Colonial Order of Things* (Durham, N.C.: Duke Univ. Press, 1995), 137–64.

19. Although the cleanliness and orderliness of the home promises to make American women healthier, Beecher also blames a lack of outdoor exercise for American women's frailty, suggesting that the problematic space outside the home—the foreign—can both cause and cure those "difficulties peculiar to American women."

20. This generalized anxiety about contamination of the domestic sphere by children may stem from the circulation of stories by missionaries who expressed fear of their children being raised by native servants or too closely identifying with native culture. Such stories circulated both in popular mission tracts and in middle-class women's magazines such as *Godey's* and *Mother's Magazine*; see, for example, Stoler, *Race and the Education of Desire*; and Patricia Grimshaw, *Paths of Duty: American Missionary Wives in Nineteenth-Century Hawaii* (Honolulu: Univ. of Hawaii Press, 1989), 154–78. The licentiousness of men was also seen as a threat to women's health within the home. For example, in "Life on the Rio Grande" (*Godey's Lady's Book*, April 1847), a piece celebrating the opening of public schools in Galveston, Texas, Sarah Josepha Hale quotes a military officer who warns that "liberty is ever degenerating into license, and man is prone to abandon his sentiments and follow his passions. It is woman's high mission, her prerogative and duty, to counsel, to sustain—as to control him" (177). On the borderlands, women have the role of civilizing savagery in their own homes, where men's passions appear as the foreign force to be colonized.

 In general, domesticity is seen as an ideology that develops in middle-class urban centers (and, as Sklar shows, in contrast to European values), and is then exported to the frontier and empire, where it meets challenges and must adapt. It remains to be studied how domestic discourse might develop out of the confrontation with foreign cultures in what has been called the "contact zone" of frontier and empire.

21. Sklar, *Catherine Beecher*, 163; Douglas, *Feminization of American Culture*, 51–54.
22. Nina Baym, "Onward Christian Women: Sarah J. Hale's History of the World," *New England Quarterly* 63 (June 1990): 249–70.
23. Sarah J. Hale, "Editor's Table," *Godey's Lady's Book*, January 1847, 53.
24. Sarah J. Hale, *Godey's Lady's Book*, November 1852, 303.
25. Ruth E. Finley, *The Lady of Godey's, Sarah Josepha Hale* (Philadelphia: Lippincott, 1931), 199.
26. Sarah J. Hale, *Northwood; or, Life North and South: Showing the True Character of Both* (New York: H. Long and Brother, 1852). See Hale's 1852 preface, "A Word with the Reader," on revisions of the 1827 edition. Further references to *Northwood* will be cited parenthetically in the text.
27. On the white ideological framework of African colonization, see George Fredrickson, *The Black Image in the White Mind: The Debate on Afro-American Character and Destiny, 1817–1914* (New York: Harper and Row, 1971), 6–22, 110–17; Susan M. Ryan, "Errand into Africa: Colonization and Nation Building in Sarah J. Hale's *Liberia*," *New England Quarterly* 68 (December 1995): 558–83.
28. Sarah J. Hale, *Liberia; or Mr. Peyton's Experiment* (1853; reprint, Upper Saddle River, N.J.: Gregg Press, 1968).
29. On *Liberia* as a conservative rebuff to Stowe, see Thomas F. Gossett, *"Uncle Tom's Cabin" and American Culture* (Dallas, Tex.: Southern Methodist Univ. Press, 1985), 235–36.
30. Susan Ryan, "Errand into Africa," 572.
31. Reginald Horsman, *Race and Manifest Destiny: The Origins of American Racial Anglo-Saxonism* (Cambridge: Harvard Univ. Press, 1981), 62–81.

32. Sarah J. Hale, *Woman's Record* (New York: Harper & Brothers, 1853).

33. Linda K. Kerber, *Women of the Republic: Intellect and Ideology in Revolutionary America* (Chapel Hill: Univ. of North Carolina Press, 1980).

34. Sarah J. Hale, "An Appeal to the American Christians on Behalf of the Ladies' Medical Missionary Society," *Godey's Lady's Book*, March 1852, 185–88.

35. Susan Warner, *The Wide Wide World* (1850; reprint, New York: Feminist Press, 1987); Maria Susanna Cummins, *The Lamplighter* (1854; reprint, New Brunswick, N.J.: Rutgers Univ. Press, 1988); E. D. E. N. Southworth, *The Hidden Hand; or, Capitola The Madcap* (1859; reprint, New Brunswick, N.J.: Rutgers Univ. Press, 1988); Harriet Beecher Stowe, *Uncle Tom's Cabin* (1852; reprint, New York: Viking Penguin, 1981).

36. Nancy Armstrong, *Desire and Domestic Fiction: A Political History of the Novel* (New York: Oxford Univ. Press, 1987); Brown, *Domestic Individualism*; Richard Brodhead, "Sparing the Rod: Discipline and Fiction in Antebellum America," in *The New American Studies: Essays from "Representations,"* ed. Philip Fisher (Berkeley and Los Angeles: Univ. of California Press, 1991).

37. Cummins, *The Lamplighter*, 63, 321. On the male characters' involvement in imperial enterprises in India in *The Lamplighter*, see Susan Castellanos, "Masculine Sentimentalism and the Project of Nation-Building" (paper presented at the conference "Nineteenth-Century Women Writers in the Twenty-First Century," Hartford, May 1996).

38. On this split, see Elizabeth Young, "Topsy-Turvy: Civil War and *Uncle Tom's Cabin*," chap. 1 of *A Wound of One's Own: Gender and Nation in American Women's Civil War Writing* (forthcoming).

39. Toni Morrison, *Playing in the Dark: Whiteness and the Literary Imagination* (Cambridge: Harvard Univ. Press, 1992), 6.

American Literary Emergence as a Postcolonial Phenomenon

Lawrence Buell

Initially published in American Literary History *(1992), Buell's essay attempts to use the lens of postcolonial literatures to perform a retrospective reading of the mid-nineteenth century's American Renaissance. Buell seeks to examine American literary emergence in light of the cultural colonization of the thirteen American colonies by Britain. One aspect of his argument is a consideration of the non-American implied reader of American Renaissance texts; he suggests that American writers imagined a transatlantic audience in addition to an American one. Buell also points to several marks of postcolonialism in the writing of the American Renaissance, such as semi-Americanization of the language, cultural hybridization, the*

From *American Literary History* 4.3 (1992): 411–42.

*belief that artists are agents of national liberation, the confrontation of
neocolonialism, the issue of "alien genres" (p. 370), and pastoralism.*

1

As the first colony to win independence, America has a history that
Americans have liked to offer as a prototype for other new nations,
yet which by the same token might profitably be studied by Americans
themselves in light of later cases. In the field of American literary history, however, such a retrospective rereading has rarely been tried.
This essay attempts precisely that: to imagine the extent to which the
emergence of a flourishing national literature during the so-called
Renaissance period of the mid-nineteenth century can be brought into
focus through the lens of more recent postcolonial literatures. This is a
project I have come to as an Americanist by training who has since
turned to studying Anglophone writing on a more global scale. Although this body of writing and the critical commentary that has
arisen to frame it interest me mainly for their own sake, as an Americanist I have also found that they have caused me to rethink what I
thought I already knew.

If my approach seems strange, as I hope it will, the reasons should
be clear. Some formidable barriers inhibit Americanists from analogizing between this country's literary emergence and even that of Canada
or Australia, let alone West India or West Africa—barriers both of ignorance and of principle. Most Americanists know little about those
other literatures, nor am I much beyond my novitiate. As to the barrier
of principle, even mildly liberal academics will suspect the possible hypocrisy of an exercise in imagining America of the expansionist years
as a postcolonial rather than proto-imperial power, as if to mystify modern America's increasingly interventionist role in world affairs. All the
more so is my study subject to such suspicions given the ease with
which it is possible to slide from thinking about America as the first
new nation to thinking about America as the model for other new nations. And all the *more* so if the analogizing also risks, as mine will,
blurring the distinction between the European settler as colonial and
the indigene as colonial. I shall return to these issues at the end of my
essay but shall bracket them for now.

A more discipline-specific barrier is that American literary study
has tended to focus so overwhelmingly on American texts as to reduce
the internationalist (usually European) quotient within its field of vision. This foreshortening of vision can happen as easily to scholars of
cosmopolitan erudition as to Americanists who in fact know little more
than American literary history. In Harold Bloom's theory of American
poetic succession, for example, no foreign power disrupts the symposium once Emerson enters it; British and American literary histories
are kept rigorously distinct, though presumably Bloom is quite aware

that until well into the twentieth century the "strong" American poets read Anglo-European masters more attentively than they read each other. Of course, American literary scholarship always has and probably always will recognize the legitimacy of monographs on Emerson and Carlyle, Fuller and Goethe, and so forth, but such influence studies implicitly occupy a minor niche in the larger scheme of things, the equivalent of the prefatory section on the zeitgeist or background influences in a large-scale thematic study.

Up to a point, there is certainly nothing strange or amiss about focusing the study of American letters on America. Studies of all national literary histories commit the same reductionism. A problem more particular to American literary studies arises, however, when the restriction of focus to the national field is regulated in terms of notions of American cultural distinctiveness used to sort authors and texts in or out according to a criterion of emerging indigenousness that fails to take account of such factors as the interpenetration of the "indigenous" and the "foreign," the extent to which the former is constructed by the latter, and consequently the extent to which the sorting of individual authors in or out of the American canon by this criterion (Hawthorne in, Longfellow out) is arbitrary and quixotic. But precisely this has been the tendency since the establishment of American literature as a scholarly subfield in the 1920s, which also (by no coincidence) marked the point at which literary historiography began to be practiced in the climate of major thesis books about the coherence of the American literary tradition, for example, in the pioneering work of D. H. Lawrence, William Carlos Williams, Lewis Mumford, and Vernon L. Parrington. One of the reasons F. O. Matthiessen's *American Renaissance* continues to endure as a landmark study is that it was the last major precontemporary book on the era to be informed by a profound appreciation for Anglo-American intertexts: how his five figures saturated themselves in the rhetorics of Shakespeare, Milton, metaphysical poetry and prose, neoclassicism, and Romanticism. Since Matthiessen, however, the study of American literary emergence has evolved around assumptions about the coherence of the American canon formed in the image of such myths of American distinctiveness as Puritan inheritance or Adamic innocence, generic patterns like the jeremiad or the captivity or the romance considered as national artifacts, as well as particular lineal succession stories like from Edwards to Emerson, Emerson to Whitman, Whitman to Stevens, and so on. Through these devices the unity, the density, and (of course) the respectability of the specialization gets consolidated. These are indeed important reference points; the problem lies not so much in the scholarship that has established them as in its unintended consequence of prompting ever-more-intensive refinements of the map of American letters.

Thus we find ourselves practicing de facto a kind of cisatlantic hermeticism. This starts with our experience as students in American literature courses, when we are socialized (for instance) into forgetting that except for Thoreau's debt to Emerson no American Renaissance writer can confidently be said to have formed his or her style chiefly from native influences, nor with the exception of Melville's essay on Hawthorne is there a clear case on record of one canonical American Renaissance writer insisting that another ranks with the great world authors. We form the habit of picturing Hawthorne as leading to Melville rather than to, say, George Eliot, even though nothing in the Melville canon follows a Hawthornian pretext more faithfully than *Adam Bede* follows *The Scarlet Letter* (see Mills 52–71). We then find ourselves perpetuating the same aesthetic order in American Renaissance courses.

Today, we are better able than in the recent past to combat such parochialisms. Feminist and African-Americanist critiques of the American canon as it crystallized between the 1920s and the 1960s have begun to inspire a pervasive reflexivity about all our instruments of classification, including our conception of literary genealogy, and have in some instances prodded us into thinking transatlantically, as with Henry Louis Gates's exposition of the permutations of Eshu in *The Signifying Monkey* or the image of a Euro-American community of nineteenth-century women writers implicit in feminist criticism of Emily Dickinson since Gilbert and Gubar's *The Madwoman in the Attic*.[1] A small but growing number of Americanists have even taken Anglo-American or Euro-American literary interrelations as their main subject: for example, Jonathan Arac (*Commissioned Spirits*), Leon Chai (*The Romantic Foundations of the American Renaissance*), Nicolaus Mills (*American and English Fiction in the Nineteenth Century*), Larry Reynolds (*European Revolutions and the American Literary Renaissance*), Robert Weisbuch (*Atlantic Double-Cross*), and William Spengemann (*A Mirror for Americanists*), not to mention monographs on single figures like George Dekker's *James Fenimore Cooper: The American Scott* and Jeffrey Rubin-Dorsky's study of Irving, *Adrift in the Old World*.[2]

This work, however, has not yet seriously affected the way Americanists conduct business as usual. The pedagogy and criticism if not the personal conviction of literary Americanists still for the most part give the appearance of being driven, as Spengemann put it, by "the idea that an appreciation of American writing depends upon our keeping it separate from the rest of the world" (141). Spengemann seems to believe this holds for all eras of American literary historiography. Maybe so; but I confine myself here to the period of literary emergence, not only because I know it best but also because the compartmentalizing seems more customary than in the study of, say, literary modernism or the early colonial period. We continue to think much more about how he might have read Scott, more about how Whitman's prosodic experimentalism might have been encouraged by Emerson or Poe than by Keats or Tennyson. We know much more about how American writers of woman's fiction relate to each other than how they related to Dickens or other popular British sentimentalists of either sex. The average article or monograph therefore projects a vision of nineteenth-century American literary history far more autotelic than that of the writers themselves except in their wildest cultural nationalist dreams. This is probably not so much because American literary scholarship continues to be passionately attached to the idea of American distinctiveness at this late date, as because the familiar procedure of grouping American writers together is so ingrained. The effect is to perpetuate at the level of literary commentary the utopian fantasy of American literary autonomy cherished during the early national period, and to abet, in consequence, an American exceptionalist mentality that may without our fully realizing it reinforce in us—or in those who listen unwarily to us—an insularity of perspective that is hazardously inaccurate. It is striking, for example, that for all its critical sophistication, the New Historicist critique of the ideological duplicity of classic American Renaissance texts (their ostensible radicalism versus their actual centrism) has not seriously challenged the assumption that these texts can be adequately understood as an internally coherent and nationally distinctive series.

My own approach to resisting Americanist centripetalism, for which I hold myself as accountable as anyone, will be to reexamine the notion of American literary emergence itself. I do not intend to argue that the American Renaissance never happened, but rather that its achievement, and by extension the "native" literary traditions it helped to create or sustain, cannot be understood without taking into account the degree to which those traditions arose out of "a culture in which the ruled were constantly tempted to fight their rulers within the psychological limits set by the latter," to appropriate Ashis Nandy's diagnosis of the intellectual climate of colonial India (3). To transpose from the colonial to the postcolonial stage of the first half of the American nineteenth century, we need only substitute cultural authority for political/military authority as the object of resistance. Although the thirteen American colonies never experienced anything like the political/military domination colonial India did, the extent of cultural colonization by the mother country, from epistemology to aesthetics to dietetics, was on the whole much more comprehensive—and partly because of the selfsame comparative benignity of the imperial regime.

2

For most students of the American Renaissance, the phenomenon of American writers' cultural dependence has come increasingly to look like a side issue and, after about 1830, a virtual nonissue. Especially since the intensification of Puritan legacy studies, the seeds of an indigenous culture have come to seem so early planted and so deeply rooted as to assure its full flowering eventually if not immediately, so as to make America's continuing imbrication in old-world culture seem uninterestingly epiphenomenal. This mentality has conduced to the view that postcolonial dependency was merely a virus that infected the juvenilia of the great canonical writers of the antebellum era. I dare-say many of us who teach nineteenth-century American literature have set up our courses by using British reviewer Sydney Smith ("In the four quarters of the globe, who reads an American book?") as a straw man for our syllabi to refute rather than as an ever-present anxiety and constituent shaping force.

If so, consider the case of Henry T. Tuckerman, whose *America and Her Commentators* (1864), a self-consciously monumental and monumentally self-conscious synopsis of the history of transatlantic views of America, is still a useful sourcebook. Tuckerman asserts that Smith's dictum is "irrelevant and impertinent to-day" (286): "In history, poetry, science, criticism, biography, political and ethical discussions, the records of travels, of taste, and of romance, universally recognized and standard exemplars, of American origin, now illustrate the genius and culture of the nation" (285–86); but his project refutes him, preoccupied as it is with expounding upon how America has been anatomized as literary object rather than reborn as literary force. The idea of America's emerging culture elicits Tuckerman's patriotism, but what commands his awe is the conviction that "never was there a populous land whose inhabitants were so uniformly judged *en masse*" (444). Tuckerman's argument that Americans are no longer mere culture consumers is quixotic and halfhearted. "The statistics of the book trade and the facts of individual culture prove that the master minds of British literature more directly and universally train and nurture the American than the English mind," argues Tuckerman ingeniously (287–88). This glosses over the statistics themselves (as late as 1876, the ratio of American book imports to exports stood at 10 to 1) and the consumer mentality that Tuckerman gamely tries to make the best of: namely that from the "distance that lends enchantment" as well as the diffusion of general education, "Shakespeare and Milton, Bacon and Wordsworth, Byron and Scott have been and are more generally known, appreciated, and loved, and have entered more deeply into the average intellectual life, on this than on the other side of the Atlantic" (288). In short, American cultural autonomy is proven by the fact that more copies of the English classics are bought and avidly read in America than in Britain. Tuckerman's book is itself a kind of vade mecum for the discriminating book importer.

Tuckerman does not draw a connection between how British classics "enchant" American readers and his efforts throughout his assiduous compendium to resist the enchantment of foreign travelers' representations of America. Yet his book, by its mere existence, dramatizes that the authority of European letters was felt to extend itself to the form of an extensive discourse of America that the American writer had to reckon with. Although scholars have been studying this body of travelers' reports for more than half a century, and some of its most distinguished examples are well known (notably Alexis de Tocqueville's *Democracy in America*), the significance of this "occidentalist" writing emerges more fully in light of recent studies of colonial discourse.[3] During what is now called our literary renaissance, America remained for many foreign commentators (especially the British), albeit diminishingly, the unvoiced "other"—with the predictable connotations of exoticism, barbarism, and unstructuredness. This notwithstanding America's legislative innovations and growing economic potency, notwithstanding that no racial barrier separated most travelers from the dominant American racial group, and notwithstanding that European travelers were very well aware that *these* natives had the will and the technology to answer them back publicly in a European language. Indeed, American sensitiveness to foreign opinion was proverbial, and several travelers commented that this severely diminished the frankness with which they could write or speak. Still, it is clear that many nineteenth-century Americans considered themselves to be treated as a minor power by foreign visitors, like the politician who complained to British geologist Charles Lyell that "you class us with the South American republics; your embassadors [sic] to us come from Brazil and Mexico to Washington, and consider it a step in their advancement to go from the United States to . . . some second-rate German court" (1: 226).

For this there was much evidence. Foreign visitors denied America refinement (the want of which was, for Frances Trollope in *Domestic Manners of the Americans*, the greatest American defect). Nineteenth-century travelers on the notorious American practice of tobacco chewing and spitting, for instance, sound like V. S. Naipaul on Indian shitting.[4] European travelers acknowledged American skill at practical calculation (deprecating it as part of the apparatus of American materialism) but tended to depict Americans as more irrational than rational, as an unphilosophical culture whatever its legislative genius, as hasty and slapdash nation builders. They regularly denied America a voice in a culturally substantial sense à la mode Sydney Smith. ("If the national mind of America be judged of by its legislation, it is of a very high order. . . . If the American nation be judged by its literature, it may be pronounced to have no mind at all" [Martineau 2: 200–01].) They even denied the Americans language in the spirit of Rudyard Kipling's remark that "the American has no language," only "dialect, slang, provincialism, accent, and so forth" (24).[5]

It was common for foreign travelers to frame their accounts as narratives of disillusionment, to stress that they started with hopeful, even utopian, expectations of finding a model nation-in-the-making only to discover a cultural backwater. Dickens is a notable case in point, since his *American Notes* avoids stating his disillusionment overtly but proceeds to narrativize it more dramatically than most, as if this were a spontaneous deposition. Starting exuberantly with a stimulating visit to Boston, Dickens gradually sours amid New York slums, Washington rowdiness, and an arduous trip to the interior that reaches a positively Conradian moment during a steamboat voyage down the Ohio River. Dickens luridly evokes the dreary solitude ("For miles, and miles, and miles . . . unbroken by any human footstep"), the sudden ugly rent in the forest for a primitive cabin and straggling field ("full of great unsightly stumps, like earthy butchers'-blocks"), and the malevolent tangle of fallen trees in the current ("their bleached arms start out . . . and seem to try to grasp the boat, and drag it under water") (*American Notes* 159–60). This is merely the travel-book version, the equivalent of Conrad's Congo diaries. For purposes of Martin Chuzzlewit's ill-fated venture to "Eden," the *Heart of Darkness* equivalent, the phantasmagoria is heightened:

> On they toiled through great solitudes, where the trees upon the banks grew thick and close; and floated in the stream; and held up shrivelled arms from out the river's depths; and slid down from the margin of the land, half growing, half decaying, in the miry water. On through the weary day and melancholy night: beneath the burning sun, and in the mist and vapour of the evening: on, until return appeared impossible, and restoration to their home a miserable dream. (375)

Both Dickens and Tocqueville, in their separate ways, reckoned America a country of the future; but Tocqueville's estimate (that America represented the vanguard of the inevitable democratization of modern society that was afoot, willy-nilly, in Europe also) was less typical than Dickens's estimate of America as a crudely vigorous young country still a long way from maturity. Not surprisingly, Tuckerman lauded Tocqueville and deplored Dickens's "superficial and sneering" manner (130–31, 221). Yet Tocqueville himself exhibits perhaps the single most condescending occidentalist gesture, also a hallmark of Orientalism: the overbearing confidence with which occidental traits are generalized. "Americans of all ages, all conditions, and dispositions constantly form associations"; "the Americans are much more addicted to the use of general ideas than the English and entertain a much greater relish for them"; "the love of wealth is . . . to be traced, as either a principal or an accessory motive, at the bottom of all that the Americans do" (2: 114, 15, 240). Tocqueville's many shrewd hits should not blind us to the arrogance of this rhetoric of the imperial generalization. One wonders, as when reading Foucault, whether Tocqueville felt a need to make magisterialism compensate for his theory of individual powerlessness at the level of his sociohistorical vision. The imperial generalization, in any case, is a time-honored device for formulating natives, as Albert Memmi and others have pointed out.[6]

3

The Americans encapsulated in nineteenth-century European travelers' reports were thus by no means wholly like Africans or Asians: They were, after all, mostly Anglo-Saxon, as well as being energetic entrepreneurs of burgeoning economic and military potency, impressive for their efforts at general education if not for their high culture. But as a civilization, America was still comparatively barbarous, the frontier hinterland its dominant reality and its gentry (as Francis Grund stressed in *Aristocracy in America*) pathetic cardboard Europhiles. A thriving oral culture existed, but with exceptions most travelers could count on the fingers of one hand, literary culture did not, and the most visible approximation to a literary class were American journalists, a disreputable lot. Though an American businessman would not have found this composite portrait especially daunting, an aspiring writer would have felt almost as marginalized by it qua writer as Caliban contemplated by Prospero.

With this as our backdrop, we can better understand the terms under which Whitman sought to give voice to American poetry in *Leaves of Grass*. The 1855 Preface starts with the magisterial image of America as the calm witness to the corpse of European tradition being "slowly borne from the eating and sleeping rooms of the house" (709). Because Whitman craftily adopts a pose of impassivity here, and because we are taught to classify this document firmly within the success story of American literary independence, it takes an effort of will to realize that what he has actually done is to make grotesque a trope from the traditional repertoire of Eurocentrism, the *translatio studii*—the transfer of art and learning from the Old World to the New—a trope that had been invoked to underwrite colonization efforts and subsequently the hegemony of the late colonial gentry. It is a figure Whitman uses not just once but repeatedly, for example, in the 1871 "Song of the Exposition," which noisily summons the Muse to "migrate from Greece and Ionia," to "Placard 'Removed' and 'To Let' on the rocks of your snowy Parnassus," and envisions her wafting her way amid the "thud of machinery and shrill steam-whistle undismay'd," "Bluff'd not . . . by drainpipe, gasometers, artificial fertilizers, / Smiling and pleas'd with palpable intent to stay, / . . . install'd amid the kitchen ware!" (196, 198). The calculated tackiness that subverts old-world decorums while nominally observing them seems more pointed if we see it as akin to, for example, modern West Indian inversions of the Prospero-Caliban trope, as in George Lamming's autobiographical essays *The Pleasures of Exile* and Aimé Cesaire's dramatic redaction *A Tempest*, or (analogously) the Crusoe-Friday inversion in Derek Walcott's play *Pantomime*. For what Whitman has done in these passages I have cited is in effect to Calibanize *translatio studii*, to render it hairy and gross and thereby to reveal America's ongoing struggle to extricate its forms of thought from old-world categories, meaning not just rhetorical figures but also social figurations like the Americans-as-barbarians stereotype. To see this, however, one needs to know what the prototypes of struggle have been. Even if we know something about the history of *translatio studii*, we Americanists tend not to think this far, because we think of *translatio studii* as a motif that America left behind soon after the turn of the nineteenth century; and we have lately grown accustomed to thinking of Caliban as a figure elevated to hero status by third-world, particularly Caribbean, intellectuals, over against a Eurocentrism that includes America as well as the earlier imperial powers. Yet as the most articulate West Indian proponent of Caliban as "our symbol" sheepishly admits, Caliban appears to have been associated with Yankeedom before Latin Americans thought to canonize him (Fernández Retamar 10). Whitman himself, in fact, was likened in one British review to "Caliban flinging down his logs, and setting himself to write a poem"—the reviewer's proof text being the "barbaric yawp" passage (qtd. in Murphy 60). Whitman proceeded to select this among the other excerpts to append as promotional material for the 1856 edition of *Leaves of Grass*.

As the Caliban analogy suggests, Whitman's rewriting of *translatio studii* anticipates one of the major modern postcolonial strategies. Indeed, *Leaves of Grass* as a whole makes the same move on a much vaster scale, with its bending and breaking of epic tradition (McWilliams 218–37). This rewriting process reflects a resistance-deference syndrome that artists and scholars alike have found it hard to talk about without hypocrisy. Whitman by turns sought to eradicate old-world myth and to reinstate it ("Old Brahm I, and I Saturnius am" [443]). The critic for whom the narrative of national differentiation is primary is tempted to identify the former posture as more "authentic" or "progressive" than the latter, when in fact it was the creative irritant of their interaction that produced their unique result, an interaction in which the "imperial" epic model figures as part of the empowerment as well as an object of resistance.

Another case that will help to clinch this point is James Fenimore Cooper's Leatherstocking. No vernacular hero has been more influential in all of American literary history, with the possible exception of Huckleberry Finn, for whom Natty Bumppo probably helped to prepare the way. Yet Bumppo was not, strictly speaking, an indigenous figure, though he can be traced to "real-life" frontiersman prototypes, so much as the result of a rewriting of the trope of the genteel protagonist cum vernacular comic sidekick in Scott's Waverley novels (e.g., Henry Morton and Cuddie Headrigg in *Old Mortality*), a characterological pattern that indeed dates from the very beginnings of the "modern" novel (in *Don Quixote*). Cooper's inversion of this pattern was of landmark significance, providing American literature's first compelling model of the common unlettered person as hero. Yet this breakthrough did not come easily to Cooper; he seems to have discovered his desire to upend the Scottian hierarchy only during the process of composing *The Pioneers*, which begins squarely focused upon the Oliver Edwards–Judge Temple melodrama and only gradually discovers that Bumppo is a much more interesting character than either. Even at that, Cooper continues to require a Waverley figure as a concomitant and to labor over the proper mimetic level at which to peg Bumppo, whose speech, as Richard Bridgman remarks, "wobbles from one realm of usage to another," from racy slang to grand-manner cliché (67). As if to hold his incipient populism in check, Cooper sees to it that Bumppo retains his vassal status through the first four Leather-stocking tales; only after Cooper has reinvented him at his most decorous, in *The Deerslayer*, does Bumppo finally cease playing the factotum.

The imperfectness of Cooper's break from Scott might be seen as a mark of the "colonized mind." Natty's genteel charges, like Oliver Edwards and Duncan Uncas Middleton of *The Prairie*, are indeed pathetic residues of Cooper's classism, as is the savagist machinery that motors Chingachgook, Bumppo's Indian companion. But why expect a clean break in the first place, and why indeed should one even long to find one when the hierarchicalized genteel hero/folk companion pattern proved to be so productive of innovation? Cooper's achievement looks more substantial when considered as a hard-won new-world adjust-ment of a transcontinental intertext than either as a homespun inven-tion compromised by the pollution of foreign mannerisms, or (see Green 129–50) as another avatar of old-world conquest narrative.[7]

A third exhibit to set beside Whitman and Cooper is Emerson's "The American Scholar," "our intellectual declaration of independence," as twentieth-century American scholars (following Oliver Wendell Holmes) still like to call it. Its exordium contains Emerson's most fa-mous literary nationalist aperçu: "Our day of dependence, our long ap-prenticeship to the learning of other lands, draws to a close" (52). But when we examine the two specific signs of this, deferred until the end of the discourse, we find them presented as European-instigated trends only now on the verge of coming to fruition in the New World: the valo-rization of the humble and the familiar ("This idea has inspired the genius of Goldsmith, Burns, Cowper, and, in a newer time, of Goethe, Wordsworth, and Carlyle" [68]) and the renewed respect accorded the individual person—which Emerson makes a point of emphasizing has not yet trickled over to America ("We have listened too long to the courtly muses of Europe. The spirit of the American freeman is already suspected to be timid, imitative, tame" [69]). Emerson seeks, para-doxically, to shame his nation into celebrating common life and self-sufficiency by reminding his countrymen that they are living in "the age of Revolution" (67). Unlike Tocqueville, Emerson makes no claim that America is already in the vanguard of this international move-ment, although nothing would have been easier given the nature of the occasion than for him to do so; it is as if he has chosen to create his national history in the image of his own belated intellectual emergence, for which Coleridge helped much more than any American thinker to provide the scaffolding. Perhaps this helps explain why the whole literary nationalist theme, as "The American Scholar" handles it, is so comparatively muted and so belated. The bulk of the discourse is taken up with expounding the scholar's triad of resources—nature, books, and action—which in principle can be seen as a distinctly "new-world" recipe (the argument being to devalue classical education, indeed formal study in general, and to aggrandize direct noncosmopolitan experience and pragmatic application) yet which does not explicitly define this regimen as a cultural nationalist program. One further lesson that might be drawn from this silence, a lesson that much of Whitman's poetry teaches also, is that the whole issue of cultural distinctiveness versus internationalism is not equally pressing throughout a writer's canon, or even throughout the space of an individual work. Perhaps because he was addressing one of the most Anglophile audiences in America, but more likely because he himself was too cosmopolitan (and too honest) to restrict the scholar solely to American influences or to exerting a solely American influence, Emerson kept his cultural nationalist rhetoric to a minimum: a few mandatory flourishes at start and close. Self-reliance clearly interested Emerson far more than national self-sufficiency.

Altogether, "The American Scholar" and Whitman's 1855 Preface might be taken as the two poles between which the literary nationalism of American Renaissance high culture tends to oscillate: On the one hand, Emerson's vision of cultural emergence catalyzed by auspicious international tendencies that emergence might be expected to develop further; on the other hand, Whitman's vision of a scandalously different American voice whose international precedents have been repressed, although by no means deleted, out of self-mystification and dramatic effect. In either case, "Europe" plays a weighty, conflict-producing role, measured by citation or elision, as the case may be.

4

Intimately related to the question of the models underlying literary practice is the question of the audience to which writing is implicitly directed. This has been a major subject of debate in the study of so-called newer English literatures, which appear, in some interpretations, to represent national culture with international audiences in mind. For a sense of what is at stake, consider this short passage toward the start of Chinua Achebe's *Things Fall Apart*, the first third-world novel accepted into the Anglophone canon. "Okoye said the next half a dozen sentences in proverbs. Among the Ibo the art of conversation is regarded very highly, and proverbs are the palm-oil with which words are eaten" (10). Such expository rhetoric, common in African Anglophone writing, immediately raises such questions as: For whom is this passage written? Do Ibos need to hear it? Do even Yoruba and

Hausa readers need to hear it? Is Achebe mainly addressing a Euro-American audience, then? (Achebe denies this but also declares that "my audience is not limited to Nigeria. Anybody who is interested in the ideas I am expounding is my audience" [Egejuru 17].)[8] The rhetoric of this passage, anyhow, carefully negotiates the insider-outsider dualism by explicating ethnic custom with anthropological lucidity while casting the explanation in Ibo form, as a proverb.

A comparable instance from classic American literature might be this passage from an early chapter in Herman Melville's *White-Jacket*: "Owing to certain vague, republican scruples, about creating great officers of the navy, America has thus far had no admirals; though, as her ships of war increase, they may become indispensable. This will assuredly be the case should she ever have occasion to employ large fleets; when she must adopt something like the English plan . . ." (20).

Americanists do not usually read American Renaissance texts as if the implied reader were other than American; yet on reflection we know that is nonsense: Actually, American writers keenly desired to be read abroad. Melville himself voyaged to England in order to market *White-Jacket* and sometimes made (or consented to) substantive revisions in the interest of British readers. Indeed, the very first words of Melville's first book (the preface to *Typee*) were got up with British readership in mind, and that narrative is strategically sprinkled with familiarizing English place references (Cheltenham, Stonehenge, Westminster Abbey, etc. [96, 154, 161]).[9] In the passage from *White-Jacket*, the expository elaborateness and the obliquity with which it edges toward the narrator's outspoken antiauthoritarianism become more understandable if we take them as studiously devious in anticipation of being read by both patriotic insiders and Tory outsiders, whether literal foreigners or Yankee Anglophiles. We know from Melville's letters and criticism that he was acutely aware of the problem of negotiating between ideologically disparate readerships, but no one thinks much about the possibility that his doctrine that the great writer communicates to his ideal reader through double meanings which philistine readers are intended to miss might have been brought into focus partly by his position as a postcolonial writer.

The textual consequences of anticipating transcontinental readership are admittedly harder to establish than the impact of foreign literary influences. Open-and-shut cases like the diplomatically vacillating chapter on European travelers' accounts of America in Irving's *The Sketch Book* are rare. Direct evidence is usually limited to textual variants for which the responsibility is unclear (Did the author devise? advise? consent? reluctantly agree to delegate?), or to ex cathedra statements (like Cooper's to a British publisher that *The Prairie* "contains nothing to offend an English reader" [1: 166]) which do not in themselves prove that the work would have been written differently had the author designed it for an American readership alone. What we can assert more positively is this. First, that some of the most provincially embedded American Renaissance texts bear at least passing direct witness to anticipating foreign readers, like Thoreau's *Walden*, which (in keeping with its first "publication" before the Concord lyceum) begins by addressing fellow townspeople but ends by musing as to whether "John or Jonathan will realize all this" (333). And second, that the hypothesis of Americans imagining foreign as well as native opinion, whatever their conscious expectation of literal readership, makes luminous some otherwise puzzling moments in American Renaissance literature. One such moment is Whitman's abrupt reconception of his persona between 1855 and 1856 as coextensive not simply with America but with the world (e.g., in "Salut au Monde!"). Another is the oddly extended sequence in *Moby-Dick* reporting the gam between the *Pequod* and the *Samuel Enderby*, and its aftermath (chs. 100–01).

James Snead remarks that Achebe's novels "provide an unexpectedly tricky reading experience for their western audience, using wily narrative stratagems to undermine national and racial illusions," such as "the almost casual manner in which they present African norms" to international readers: glossary apparatus that seems deliberately incomplete, interjection of reminders of the Western reader's outsidership in the course of a cozily familiar-seeming, European-style realist narrative (241). For example, the guidebook dimension of the passage quoted above creates a deceptive degree of transparency for the Western reader, inasmuch as its "we have a saying" formula is a common introductory formula in Ibo proverbial statement not remarked upon as such; the passage, then, maintains a certain covertness despite, indeed because of, its forthrightness. Melville uses narrative geniality and cross-culturalism somewhat similarly in the sequence under view so as to sustain the young-America-style jauntiness with which *Moby-Dick* customarily treats old-world cultures, but without the kind of bluntness used against "the Yarman," for instance (Melville, *Moby-Dick* 351–60).

The gam with the *Samuel Enderby* reworks a cross-cultural comparison repeatedly made by British travelers to America: that Americans were grim workaholic zealots with no time for small talk. The chapter is obviously framed with national stereotypes in mind. Melville initially sketches the encounter between Ahab and Captain Boomer, or rather the interruptive byplay between Boomer and the ship's surgeon, so as to make the Englishmen seem like patronizing boobies. Yet it is Ahab's truculence that finally comes off as more disturbing and that makes English joviality (itself an American stereotype) seem healthy by comparison. The last emotion to be expressed is the good-humored British captain's honest astonishment. In the ensuing chapter ("The Decanter") Ishmael aligns himself with that same spirit of comic banter (long since identified as an Ishmaelite trait) and pays a mock-heroic homage to the whole firm of Enderby, which in fact turns out to have dispatched the first ships ever to hunt the sperm whale in the Pacific, the waters the *Pequod* is about to enter. Ishmael then proceeds, in what first looks like a complete digression, to report a later, more convivial and rousing gam with the *Samuel Enderby* in which he partook, a drunken feast "at midnight somewhere off the Patagonian coast" (444).

Ishmael's reinstitution of good fellowship with his English counterparts "atones" ex post facto for Ahab's bad manners and "validates" the English captain's good-humored bewilderment at Ahab's stormy departure. Yet through this dexterous maneuver, Melville is given license to laugh at the cliché version of British thickheadedness not once but twice—first apropos Ahab's tragedy, then apropos the farce of sailorly roistering—thereby propitiating American cultural nationalism without offending British readers. It is testimony both to Melville's wiliness and to his deference that the vigorous in-house censorship upon which his British publishers insisted, of religiously and culturally offensive matter in the manuscript of *The Whale* (resulting in the deletion of chapter 25 on British coronation procedures, for instance), left chapters 100–01 untouched (Melville, *Moby-Dick* 681–83).[10]

5

The marks of postcolonialism in American Renaissance writing are far more numerous than a short article can hope to discuss. Here is a brief checklist of some of the most salient.

1. *The semi-Americanization of the English language.* What language shall we speak? American settlers did not face this question in its most radical form, as put by Ngugi wa Thiong'o in *Decolonizing the Mind*, which argues that African literature should be written in the indigenous languages. But the weaker version of the argument (namely how to creolize and neologize American English so that it spoke a voice of the culture distinct from the standardizing mother tongue) does certainly link Cooper and Emerson and Whitman and Twain with Amos Tutuola, Gabriel Okara, and Raja Rao, whose work sheds light on such subissues as the inextricability of "naturalness" and "artifice" in Whitman's diction and the inextricability of idealization and caricature in Cooper's vernacular heroes like Natty Bumppo. Bill Ashcroft, Gareth Griffiths, and Helen Tiffin remark that postcolonial literatures are "always written out of the tension between the abrogation of the received English which speaks from the center, and the act of appropriation which brings it under the influence of a vernacular tongue" (39). That is a duality crucial to American literary emergence as well. In the early national period, we see it especially in texts that counterpoint characters who speak dialect (who are always comic) with characters who speak Standard English, for example, Colonel Manly versus his servant Jonathan in Royall Tyler's *The Contrast* and Captain Farrago versus his servant Teague O'Reagan in Hugh Henry Brackenridge's *Modern*

Chivalry. At this stage, the vernacular is still clearly a national embarrassment to be indulged only obliquely, through satire. "Vulgarity," as Bridgman puts it, "had to be fenced in with quotation marks" (7). This is the American equivalent of, say, the colloquial dramatic monologues of Indo-Anglian poet Nissim Ezekiel:

> I am standing for peace and non-violence
> Why world is fighting fighting
> Why all people of world
> Are not following Mahatma Gandhi
> I am simply not understanding. (22)

By the time of Thoreau and Whitman, the American inventiveness with language, through individual neologizing and provincial variant usages, that Tocqueville (and others) considered one of the most "deplorable" consequences of democratization had become positive aesthetic values (Tocqueville 2: 71). Thus without any hint of parody, in section 5 of "Song of Myself," Whitman could allow the sublime vision following from the persona's possession by his soul to come to rest on "the mossy scabs of the worm-fence" (33)—the latter an American coinage never used in poetry before, referring to a characteristic motif of American agricultural construction that foreign visitors often singled out as particularly wasteful and ugly (Mesick 161–62). The "mossy scabs" metaphor makes it absolutely clear, if further proof be needed, that Whitman seeks to fashion the sublime from the positively vulgar. Not that he was prepared to forgo literary English. His position—almost quintessentially postcolonial in this respect—was to justify an Americanization of English expression as the poetic way of the future on the ground that English itself was remarkable for its engraftment of other linguistic strains (Warren 5–69).

2. *The issue of cultural hybridization*. Another recurring motif in American Renaissance texts is their fondness for cross-cultural collages: Whitman's composite persona; Thoreau's balancing between the claims of post-Puritan, Greco-Roman, Native American, and Oriental mythographies in *A Week* and *Walden*; Melville's multimythic elaboration of the whale symbol in tandem with the *Pequod* as a global village; Cooper's heteroglossic tapestry of six or seven different nationalities in *The Pioneers*. David Simpson argues, respecting Cooper, that Templeton's polyglot character, each resident speaking his or her own peculiar dialect (except for the Temple family, of course), registers the social fissures of still-experimental nationhood (149–201); and I think we might further understand this phenomenon by thinking of it in reference to (for example) composite national-symbol characters like Salman Rushdie's Saleem Sinai (in *Midnight's Children*) and G. V. Desani's Mr. Hatterr, or the syncretism of Wole Soyinka's interweave between Yoruba and Greek mythology. What Lewis Nkosi says of modern African

Anglophone poetry's quest to define its path applies beautifully to the world of Cooper's *Pioneers*: "[T]he first requirement . . . was precisely to articulate the socio-cultural conditions in which the modern African writer had to function, the heterogeneity of cultural experiences among which the poet had to pick his or her way" (151).[11]

3. *The expectation that artists be responsible agents for achieving national liberation*, which in turn bespeaks a nonspecialized conception of art and an ambivalence toward aestheticism that threatens to produce schizophrenia. Soyinka calls attention to the pressure upon the postcolonial African writer to "postpone that unique reflection on experience and events which is what makes a writer—and constitute himself into a part of that machinery that will actually shape events" (16). Emerson wrestles with a very similar looking public/private dilemma in "The American Scholar" and later attempts at political interventions like the first Fugitive Slave Law address. Anozie's statement that "[t]here seemed to exist a genetic struggle between a romantic pursuit of art for its own sake and a constantly intensive awareness of the social relevance of art" could apply equally well to Soyinka and Emerson, though in fact it refers to Nigerian poet Christopher Okigbo (175), the closest approximation to a "pure aesthete" among the major figures of the illustrious first contemporary generation of Nigeria's Anglophone literati but later killed as a soldier in the Biafran war.

4. *The problem of confronting neocolonialism*, the disillusionment of revolutionary hopes, which threatens to turn the artist against the audience that was prepared to celebrate him or her as symptomatic of cultural emergence. Postcolonial Africa, for instance, has inspired an oppositional literature that both helps to explain American Renaissance oppositionalism as a predictable postrevolutionary symptom and to define its limits. Thoreau as individualistic civil disobedient both is and is not the counterpart of Ngugi's revolutionary socialism.

5. *The problem of "alien genres"*: Eurocentric genres that carry authority but seem not to be imitable without sacrifice of cultural authenticity. There is a striking semicorrespondence here between the critique of the protagonist-centered realist novel by third-world intellectuals and complaints by nineteenth-century American fictionists from Cooper to Hawthorne to James that the novel was not transplantable to American soil. Conversely, some genres have seemed not only transplantable with great ease but precisely tailored for American and other new-world contexts. A prime example is my next and last rubric, which I should like to unfold at somewhat greater length than the others.

6. *New-world pastoral*. "Pastoralism" in the broadest sense of a recurring fascination with physical nature as subject, symbol, and theater in which to act out rituals of maturity and purification has long

been seen as a distinctive American preoccupation, but without it being grasped how this can be generalized. Mutatis mutandis the same can be said of Canadian and Australian writing, although their versions of nature are (and for more complicated reasons than just geography) less benign than ours; and a version of the same can be said of third-world writing as well, despite manifest differences between white-settler pastoral and nonwhite indigene pastoral. Here the obvious analogue is negritude, as well as other forms of cultural nationalism that hold up a precolonial ideal order as a salvific badge of distinctiveness. Retrospective pastoralization of ancient tribal structures occurs in the American Renaissance as well: particularly in the more sentimental treatments of Puritan heritage and the old plantation order, not to mention the even more vicarious sort of nostalgia represented by Anglo-American savagist fantasies like Longfellow's *Song of Hiawatha*. Perhaps this explains why Thoreau became simultaneously addicted to nature and to New England antiquities. *Walden* and *The Scarlet Letter* are predictable complements in their mutual preoccupation with cultural origins.

But to stay with pastoral at the level of physical nature, what Americanists tend to miss, and what recent postcolonial critiques have been helpful in pointing out (e.g., Amuta 49), is the extent to which the conception of naturism as a mark of cultural independence needs to be countered by the conception of naturism as a neocolonial residue. Thomas Jefferson's *Notes on the State of Virginia*, which contains the classical statement of the American pastoral ideal, shows this clearly. Jefferson recommends that the new country follow the agrarian way in the explicit awareness that that will mean dependence on European manufactures. The preservation of national virtue, which he associates with rurality, he considers worth the cost. Some, even today, would argue that it is. But my point here is the lacuna in Jefferson's earlier thinking: his belief that moral self-sufficiency can coexist with economic dependence. Some years later, as Leo Marx shows in *The Machine in the Garden* (139), Jefferson changed his mind about America industrializing. What Marx does *not* diagnose is the status of Jefferson's original position as the intellectual artifact of a late-colonial intellectual. Marx shows, of course, that the conception of America as a pastoral utopia originates in Europe, but he ceases to think of European antecedence as important once pastoral thinking becomes naturalized in America by the mid-eighteenth century, and this in turn keeps him from beginning to approach figures like Jefferson and Thoreau in the light of being driven against their conscious intent by an ideological mechanism set in place to appropriate the New World in the interest of the Old — the antithesis of the state both men saw themselves as promoting.

Nothing could have been more natural than for the American Romantics to valorize physical nature as a central literary subject (whether benign, as in Transcendentalism, or ominous, as in *Moby-Dick* or the forest sequence in *The Scarlet Letter*), for this was an obvious way of turning what had often been deemed a cultural disadvantage into a cultural asset. But this same move, which capitalized upon an aesthetic value of international Romanticism as well as an established old-world image of the New World, was not without its risks. A text that illustrates these is the well-known sonnet addressed by William Cullen Bryant in farewell to his friend the painter Thomas Cole, bound for Europe.

> Thine eyes shall see the light of distant skies:
>   Yet, Cole! thy heart shall bear to Europe's strand
>   A living image of thy native land,
> Such as on thy own glorious canvass lies;
> Lone lakes—savannahs where the bison roves—
>   Rocks rich with summer garlands—solemn streams—
>   Skies, where the desert eagle wheels and screams—
> Spring bloom and autumn blaze of boundless groves.
> Fair scenes shall greet thee where thou goest—fair,
>   But different—every where the trace of men,
>   Paths, homes, graves, ruins, from the lowest glen
> To where life shrinks from the fierce Alpine air.
>   Gaze on them, till the tears shall dim thy sight,
>   But keep that earlier, wilder image bright!

Bryant's valedictory tribute affirms a nationalist vision of America as nature's nation (lakes, savannahs, rocks, skies), over against a European scene that everywhere bears "the trace of men." Bryant rightly credits Cole's American landscape paintings with having registered this sense of the American difference. Like Whitman, Bryant revises *translatio studii*, charging Cole to bear an American aesthetic gospel to Europe, but the poem's cautionary ending betrays a postcolonial anxiety as to whether Cole will keep the faith. That very significant and well-warranted anxiety is, however, a telling moment, the only moment that the poem begins to acknowledge the extent to which Bryant and Cole have in fact always already been affected by the European gravitational field whether consciously or not. Cole, like other self-consciously American landscape painters of his day, had been deeply influenced by the tropes of European Romantic landscape (and in his case also history) painting (Novak 226–73). As for Bryant, although his poem is replete with distinctively American references (such as bison, eagle, and the fall colors that regularly amazed European travelers), what strikes a modern reader much more strongly is its bondage to old-world language and form: "savannahs" as a cosmopolitan synonym for "prairies"; the placement of the eagle in a generic, symbolic "desert"; "Alpine" as a surrogate for the sublimity of American mountains; and above all, Bryant's unconsciously ironic choice of sonnet—a hypercivilized form if ever there was one—as the vehicle for enjoining his gospel of the "wilder image." In short, the authentic insider's view of America Bryant/Cole have to offer Europe as new-world cultural evangelists is at most a slightly nuanced version of the view that their position as Euro-American settlers has prepared them for.

In an excellent recent study of American landscape representation in the Revolutionary era, Robert Lawson-Peebles discusses this effect under the heading of "the hallucination of the displaced terrain."[12] Lawson-Peebles points out that cultural nationalist visions of a pastoralized America pulled "towards Europe and away from the facts of the American continent. Even the writers who attended closely to those facts shaped them so that they answered European criticisms, and in doing so they collaborated in a dream-world" (57). Bryant is a clear case in point: it is almost as if "the American Wordsworth" had set out with the intention of playing back to Coleridge an image of America just slightly (but not alarmingly) more feral than Coleridge had entertained thirty years before in *his* sonnet on "Pantisocracy," which envisions a rural valley purified of nightmare and neurosis, where "Virtue" dances "to the moonlight roundelay" and "the rising Sun" darts "new rays of pleasaunce trembling to the heart" (68–69).

In stressing the postcolonial basis of American pastoral visions like Bryant's, I do not mean to discredit them; on the contrary, I am convinced they potentially have great power even today as mimetic and ideological instruments. No doubt, for example, the American pastoral tradition helps account for the high degree of public environmental concern that now obtains in America, despite notorious slippages between doctrine and daily practice, between law and implementation. But in order to understand the potentially formidable continuing power of pastoral as a cultural instrument, we need also to understand the element of mimetic desire that has historically driven the pastoralizing impulse.

In Naipaul's autobiographical narrative, *The Enigma of Arrival*, he remembers how

> as a child in Trinidad I had projected everything I read onto the Trinidad landscape, the Trinidad countryside, the Port of Spain streets. (Even Dickens and London I incorporated into the streets of Port of Spain. Were the characters English, white people, or were they transformed into people I knew? A question like that is a little like asking whether one dreams in color or in black and white. But I think I transferred the Dickens characters to people I knew. Though with a half or a quarter of my mind I knew that Dickens was all English, yet my Dickens cast, the cast in my head, was multiracial.) (169–70)

The resemblance to Thoreau's projective creation of Walden is quite close. During the first summer's Walden journal, Thoreau sustains his high excitement by repeatedly imagining his experience in epic and pastoral terms, ancient Greece connoting for him, as for other Romantics, the morning of Western culture: the pastoral moment of the race. This carries over into the book itself, especially the "Visitors" and the "Reading" chapters. In the encounter with the woodchopper, particularly, Thoreau plays the kind of game Naipaul describes: loving and believing in the magnification that he halfway allows himself to realize is a game. This awareness is manifested elsewhere too in "The Ponds" chapter in his reference to his locale as "my lake country." His first descriptive encapsulation of the pond environment stresses that "for the first week, whenever I looked out on the pond it impressed me like a tarn high up on the side of a mountain" (86): Walden as Alpine lake. In order for Thoreau's spirit to accompany his body to the literal spot, or rather in order for the Thoreauvian persona to re-present the pond in a serious work of American literature, he must approach this bit of Yankee real estate as the image of some more resonantly romantic elsewhere.

For both Naipaul and Thoreau, the game of animating the provincial quotidian with imagery from the repertoire of metropolitan culture is of course class-specific (the elegant recreation of the cultivated person for whom Euroculture is the touchstone for local knowledge), but in either case this type of consciousness entails not simply a limitation of vision but an access of vision also, vision indeed of two types (both of the ordinary object, now seen luminously, and of oneself, of one's own imagination's tricks and needs). Their visions should not, then, be seen as nothing more than false consciousness. But they invite that interpretation (in Thoreau's case, for example) if we begin from the premise that his pastoralizing ought to be read as American Adamism deployed against Euroculture, rather than simply a development within the latter camp.

6

The case of Thoreau, whose art is patently more homegrown than Bryant's, raises the question of when, if at all, the postcolonial moment in American literary history ended or at what point "postcolonialism" ceases to become a meaningful category of analysis. To settle the point with respect to this, the first postcolonial literature, might be especially helpful in orienting discussion of later instances as well as the American one. The beginning of an answer is to recognize that no clear answer can be given. On the one hand, "postcolonial" is from the start an objectionably reductive term since it coerces us to look at everything within the indigenous cultural field as old-world driven. On the other hand, American culture can be said to remain at least vestigially postcolonial as long as Americans are impressed by the sound of an educated British accent—or (to take a more pertinent example) as long as D. H. Lawrence's *Studies in Classic American Literature* remains an iconic text for American literary studies. American scholarship has, ironically, absorbed Lawrence's wilderness-romance–oriented paradigm of American literature as obsessed with rebellion against civilized structures while largely deleting the Lawrentian premise that gave rise to it, that is, the vision of America as a postcolonial society caught in a state of cultural adolescence because still caught in the same escapist impulse that originated in the desire to flee from the motherland.[13] This diagnosis reflects, of course, the uses to which Lawrence himself put aboriginal America (Cowan 1–12, 124–28)—Lawrence being a Coleridgean dreamer who really acted out his dreams.

It could be argued that once "civilization" becomes imaginatively localized within America instead of placed across the Atlantic as in Bryant's sonnet, then American pastoral becomes for all practical purposes fully Americanized—although of course this happened for different writers at different times, and for some nineteenth-century American writers, like Henry James, it never happened at all. Another criterion might be the rise in the nineteenth century of what is now called American imperialism. One might argue that by the time Mark Twain, in *The Connecticut Yankee*, could imagine an American state of military and political superiority to an archaized Britain (reversing the British traveler's report of a generation earlier), or when Melville could imagine a Yankee entrepreneurialism roughly homologous to a decadent Spanish imperialism in "Benito Cereno," the American postcolonial moment was over, or at least evanescent. This, however, raises another fundamental question as to the link between American postcolonialism and American imperialism. Such a link there seems indeed to be. Captain Frederick Marryat, who as naval officer and as author of juvenile fiction helped to underwrite British expansionism, was told during his visit to America that Britain need not exult over its continuing superiority as an imperial power because America would soon pick up some colonies for itself (*A Diary in America*).

In the literary sphere, Cooper and Whitman are interesting test cases. The anxious patriotic hubris that generated the Whitmanesque "I" can never rest until it circles the globe in massive retaliatory overcompensation. Cooper played the postcolonial to the extent that he deferred to Scott's plot forms, but he played the imperialist to the extent that his own narratives reflected and perpetuated the romance of American expansionism. It begins to appear, then, that the old-world tropes whose ingestion by the new-world citizen marks his or her cultural subordination can in turn become reactivated, whether on the frontier within one's own borders or on the frontiers beyond (e.g., bwana Hemingway in East Africa), to reproduce new versions of cultural subordination. This, again, is not the sole or inevitable consequence of postcolonialism, only the most disturbing, but it is by the same token the most dramatic reminder of the quixotism of positing a firm boundary between a postcolonial era and what follows it.

Notes

Preliminary versions of this essay were delivered as lectures at Texas A & M University, Columbia University, Brown University, and the American Antiquarian Society. I am most grateful for comments and suggestions received on all four occasions.

1. Gilbert and Gubar may be credited with establishing "I think I was enchanted" (593)—a reflection upon the influence of Elizabeth Barrett Browning—as central to the Dickinson canon (647–48; Gilbert 33–37). An interesting test case of the larger consequences of this placement of Dickinson among a Euro-American sisterhood, as opposed to the Edwards-Emerson tradition, is the shifting interpretation of "He fumbles at your soul" (315). Before 1980, the generally preferred approach—still sometimes espoused (e.g., Phillip. 179–80)—was to read the "He" as bullying preacher or perhaps deity (Duchac 149–51). Feminist revisionism ensured the currency of a more specifically gendered reading of the "he" as "the pure energy of the *idea* of the masculine" (Dobson 81). The two readings can of course be conflated (e.g., Rich 56–57), but in practice a critical emphasis on gender tends to run counter to a "New England mind"–oriented reading. This may also be the place to comment on my almost total concentration in the balance of this essay, seemingly ironic in light of my honorific citation of feminist and African-Americanist revisionism, upon white male writers. My choice reflects these two hypotheses: that the main symptom of "colonization" in antebellum African-American discourse arises from the pressure on black writers to write in "white" genres and rhetorical forms, and, secondly, that women writers of the period were less troubled about extricating themselves from the shadow cast by Europe than were their male counterparts, partially though not exclusively for the reason advanced by Gilbert and Gubar (i.e., that pre-modern women writers were not mutually competitive, anxious for rather than repressed by their female precursors). These concerns, which require further research, I intend to pursue on another occasion.

2. I have profited from all of these works. Spengemann presents the most outspoken theoretical/historical argument for considering Anglo-American writing as part of English literature generally. Arac, Chai, Reynolds, and Mills provide more specific, less polemical case studies: Arac, of literature as social prophecy in the nineteenth century; Chai, of tendencies in international Romanticism; Reynolds, of American responses to 1848. Mills undertakes specific book-to-book comparisons of American and English authors. All these writers focus on intertextual and intercultural influences or connections with minimal attention to American cultural dependence as a (post)colonial event. Weisbuch comes closest to my approach in a series of somewhat Bloomian studies of American writers reacting against British precursors, set in the context of a defensive-antagonistic model of Anglo-American literary relations. This leads to results that are very illuminating and provocative, although I think the variability of American attitudes toward European culture (including extreme deference and total insouciance, as well as rivalry and antagonism, sometimes all of these commingling in the same person or text) needs to be taken more greatly into account. In addition to the studies of broad scope just

mentioned, a growing number of significant monographs on individual authors address issues of postcolonialism without necessarily conceptualizing them as such: e.g., Rubin-Dorsky and Dekker.

3. My term "occidentalism" designedly echoes Said's use of "Orientalism." Some differences between the two discourses are noted below. My lowercase "o" registers another: "occidentalism" is my neologism, not a term of European usage, much less of the long-established field of academic research Said's *Orientalism* was written to critique. (The academic field of American studies is of course the obverse of Orientalism in having been constituted in the US and still largely dominated by American scholars.) Yet Said's larger argument, that Europeans formulated a condescending discourse of the "other" region as a fascinating but inferior civilization, also applies to antebellum travel narratives, and even more exactly to American perceptions of how they were viewed by these. "*Orientalism*," writes Said, "is premised upon exteriority, that is, on the fact that the Orientalist, poet or scholar, makes the Orient speak, describes the Orient, renders its mysteries plain for and to the West. . . . What he says and writes, by virtue of the fact that it is said or written, is meant to indicate that the Orientalist is outside the Orient, both as an existential and as a moral fact" (20–21). This is largely true for what I am calling "occidentalism" as well. In focusing on America as the object of "occidentalist" discourse, it should, of course, not be forgotten that (Euro-)Americans were at the same time themselves "Orientalists"; see, for example, Baird 3–80.

4. Naipaul: "Indians defecate everywhere. They defecate, mostly, beside the railroad tracks. But they also defecate on the beaches; they defecate on the river banks; they defecate on the streets; they never look for cover" (*Area* 74). Dickens: "In the courts of law, the judge has his spittoon, the crier his, the witness his, and the prisoner his; while the jurymen and spectators are provided for, as so many men who in the course of nature must desire to spit incessantly" (*American Notes* 112–13). In this way both writers, with nervous/sardonic intensity, put the former colony under the sign of filth.

5. The pervasiveness of these and other motifs of commentary are conveniently summarized by Tuckerman; Mesick; and Berger.

6. See Memmi: "Another sign of the colonized's depersonalization is what one might call the mark of the plural. The colonized is never characterized in an individual manner; he is entitled only to drown in an anonymous collectivity ('They are this.' 'They are all the same.')" (85). Of course it would be rash to say that Tocqueville and other generalizers thought they actually knew America thoroughly, to the core. On the contrary, America often seemed mysterious to them; its inchoate ungraspability inspired a range of vertiginous sensations in the observer, both painful and pleasurable. Indeed, American mysteriousness and the will to explicate it through clarifying generalization were opposite sides of the same coin: see Tocqueville on "that strange melancholy which often haunts the inhabitants of democratic countries in the midst of their abundance" (2: 147). Additional light is shed on this fusion of opposites by Conrad's study of British travelers from Frances Trollope to Christopher Isherwood. Conrad shows that they resolutely created America in the image of their own fantasies, but that the fantasies often sprang from their own baffled malaise (e.g., 7–15).

7. Green oversimplifies in diagnosing the Leatherstocking saga as "the next great stage," after the Daniel Boone myth, "of the WASP adventure tale and adventure hero" (133), but he is right to place Cooper in the context of the history of the imperial adventure tale. The limitation of Green's approach to Cooper is that he does not apply to Cooper his good insight concerning Scott's ambivalence toward the absorption of Scotland into Great Britain: "If anyone could have written the serious novel of adventure, it probably would have been a Scotsman, because of the mode of Scots participation in the Empire—the disengagement (compared to England) despite the deep involvement" (121). Cooper manifests, it seems to me, even deeper reservations about the march of civilization than Scott; indeed, this note of reservation seems to me to be one of the motifs Cooper took over from Scott and extended.

8. Egejuru is not justified in concluding from this and other statements that "the African writer is very much controlled by an external audience whose existence he consciously tries to erase" (36), but it is clear that the writers she interviewed were somewhat hard-pressed to reconcile their Africanist commitments with the fact of being published and (often) more widely read abroad. Part of their dilemma must be political, part the result of the impossibility of bringing unconscious motives to full consciousness. Nineteenth-century American writers faced a similar if less intense set of pressures.

9. My thanks to Eric Haralson for first calling my attention to signs of dual audience consciousness in *Typee*.

10. Though they seldom raise the issue as a subject of direct remark, American writers of the Renaissance period must have been acutely aware of being vulnerable to both European and nativist scrutiny and criticism whenever they penned a scene that suggested a value judgment one way or another on national traits. In *Martin Chuzzlewit*, Dickens registers both sensitivities at once in his caricature of the egregious Mrs. Hominy, the American "literary" person who builds her reputation by purveying jingoistic cliché. Mrs. Hominy is the Tocquevillean democratic writer, the "independent" American constrained to speak in the voice of the majority; Dickens's narrator is the cosmopolitan Britisher recoiling against American boorishness. Postcolonial writers in other cultures have experienced similar pressures. Rajan wittily remarks on an Indian counterpart to Mrs. Hominy: "Countries which are newly independent can attach undue importance to the image of themselves which their literatures present, thus degrading the writer into a public relations officer. 'You have been unfair to the South Indian mother-in-law,' a critic told me indignantly at a railway station. It was well that I restrained my inclination to laugh. He was deadly serious and not unrepresentative in his seriousness" (84).

11. Nkosi proceeds to quote from Abioseh Nicol's "African Easter," which begins with a nursery rhyme ("Ding, dong bell") and juxtaposes this with "matin bells," the cry of the muezzin, and "pagan drums" (qtd. in 151–52). An intercultural salad considerably more diverse than Cooper's Templeton.

12. Lawson-Peebles borrows this term from art critic Harold Rosenberg (23).

13. Leslie Fiedler and Wright Morris have both written rather severely about American pastoralism as a form of cultural immaturity, in *Love and Death*

in the American Novel and *The Territory Ahead*, respectively (Fiedler in particular being indebted to Lawrence), but formulating their position as a critique of social pathology without regard to America's postcolonial history.

Works Cited

Achebe, Chinua. *Things Fall Apart.* 1958. Greenwich, CT: Fawcett, 1959.

Amuta, Chidi. *The Theory of African Literature.* London: Zed, 1989.

Anozie, Sunday. *Christopher Okigbo: Creative Rhetoric.* London: Evans, 1972.

Ashcroft, Bill, Gareth Griffiths, and Helen Tiffin. *The Empire Writes Back: Theory and Practice in Post-Colonial Literatures.* London: Routledge, 1989.

Baird, James. *Ishmael: A Study of the Symbolic Mode in Primitivism.* New York: Harper, 1956.

Berger, Max. *The British Traveler in America, 1785–1835.* New York: Columbia UP, 1922.

Bridgman, Richard. *The Colloquial Style in America.* New York: Oxford UP, 1966.

Bryant, William Cullen. "Sonnet—to an American Painter Departing for Europe." *The Norton Anthology of American Literature.* Ed. Nina Baym, et al. 3rd ed. Vol. 1. New York: Norton, 1989. 893–94. 2 vols.

Coleridge, Samuel Taylor. *The Poems of Samuel Taylor Coleridge.* Ed. Ernest Hartley Coleridge. London: Oxford UP, 1931.

Conrad, Peter. *Imagining America.* New York: Oxford UP, 1980.

Cooper, James Fenimore. *Letters and Journals.* Ed. James Franklin Beard. 6 vols. Cambridge: Belknap-Harvard UP, 1960–68.

Cowan, James C. *D. H. Lawrence's American Journey.* Cleveland: P of Case Western Reserve U, 1970.

Dickens, Charles. *American Notes and Pictures from Italy.* London: Oxford UP, 1957.

———. *Martin Chuzzlewit.* London: Oxford UP, 1966.

Dobson, Joanne A. "'Oh, Susie, it is dangerous': Emily Dickinson and the Archetype." *Feminist Critics Read Emily Dickinson.* Ed. Suzanne Juhasz. Bloomington: Indiana UP, 1983. 80–97.

Duchac, Joseph. *The Poems of Emily Dickinson: An Annotated Guide to Commentary Published in English.* Reference Publication in Literature. Boston: Hall, 1979.

Egejuru, Phanuel. *Towards African Literary Independence: A Dialogue with Contemporary African Writers.* Contributions in Afro-American and African Studies 53. Westport, CT: Greenwood, 1980.

Emerson, Ralph Waldo. *The Collected Works of Ralph Waldo Emerson.* Ed. Robert E. Spiller and Alfred R. Ferguson. Vol. 1. Cambridge: Belknap-Harvard UP, 1971. 4 vols. 1971–87.

Ezekiel, Nissim. *Latter-Day Psalms.* Delhi: Oxford UP, 1982.

Fernández Retamar, Roberto. *Caliban and Other Essays.* Trans. Edward Baker. Minneapolis: U of Minnesota P, 1979.

Gilbert, Sandra M. "The Wayward Nun beneath the Hill: Emily Dickinson and the Mysteries of Womanhood." *Feminist Critics Read Emily Dickinson.* Ed. Suzanne Juhasz. Bloomington: Indiana UP, 1983. 22–44.

Gilbert, Sandra M., and Susan Gubar. *The Madwoman in the Attic: The Woman Writer and the Nineteenth-Century Literary Imagination.* New Haven: Yale UP, 1979.

Green, Martin. *Dreams of Adventure, Deeds of Empire.* New York: Basic, 1979.

Kipling, Rudyard. *American Notes.* New York: Arcadia, 1950.

Lawrence, D. H. *Studies in Classic American Literature.* 1923. Garden City, NY: Doubleday, 1951.

Lawson-Peebles, Robert. *Landscape and Written Expression in Revolutionary America: The World Turned Upside Down.* Cambridge: Cambridge UP, 1988.

Lyell, Charles. *A Second Visit to the United States of North America.* 3 vols. New York, 1849.

McWilliams, John P., Jr. *The American Epic: Transforming a Genre: 1770–1860.* Cambridge Studies in American Literature and Culture. Cambridge: Cambridge UP, 1989.

Martineau, Harriet. *Society in America.* 2 vols. New York, 1837.

Marx, Leo. *The Machine in the Garden: Technology and the Pastoral Ideal in America.* New York: Oxford UP, 1964.

Melville, Herman. *Moby-Dick.* Ed. Harrison Hayford, Hershel Parker, and G. Thomas Tanselle. Evanston: Northwestern UP; Chicago: Newberry Library, 1988.

———. *Typee.* Ed. Harrison Hayford, Hershel Parker, and G. Thomas Tanselle. Evanston: Northwestern UP; Chicago: Newberry Library, 1968.

———. *White-Jacket.* Ed. Harrison Hayford, Hershel Parker, and G. Thomas Tanselle. Evanston: Northwestern UP; Chicago: Newberry Library, 1970.

Memmi, Albert. *The Colonizer and the Colonized.* Trans. Howard Greenfield. Boston: Beacon, 1965.

Mesick, Jane Louise. *The English Traveler in America, 1836–1860.* New York: Columbia UP, 1922.

Mills, Nicolaus. *American and English Fiction in the Nineteenth Century: An Antigenre Critique and Comparison.* Bloomington: Indiana UP, 1974.

Murphy, Francis, ed. *Walt Whitman: A Critical Anthology.* Baltimore: Penguin, 1970.

Naipaul, V. S. *An Area of Darkness.* New York: Vintage, 1964.

———. *The Enigma of Arrival: A Novel in Five Sections.* New York: Viking, 1987.

Nandy, Ashis. *The Intimate Enemy: Loss and Recovery of Self Under Colonialism.* Delhi: Oxford UP, 1983.

Ngugi wa Thiong'o. *Decolonizing the Mind: The Politics of Language in African Literature.* London: Currey, 1986.

Nkosi, Lewis. *Tasks and Masks: Themes and Styles of African Literature.* Essex: Longman, 1981.

Novak, Barbara. *Nature and Culture: American Landscape and Painting, 1825–1875.* New York: Oxford UP, 1980.

Phillips, Elizabeth. *Emily Dickinson: Personae and Performance.* University Park: Pennsylvania State UP, 1988.

Rajan, Ballachandra. "The Indian Virtue." *Journal of Commonwealth Literature* 1 (1965): 79–85.

Rich, Adrienne. "Vesuvius at Home: The Power of Emily Dickinson." *Parnassus* 5 (1976): 49–74.

Said, Edward W. *Orientalism.* New York: Vintage, 1978.

Simpson, David. *The Politics of American English, 1776–1850.* New York: Oxford UP, 1986.

Snead, James. "European Pedigrees/African Contagions: Nationality, Narrative, and Communality in Tutuola, Achebe, and Reed." *Nation and Narration.* Ed. Homi K. Bhabha. London: Routledge, 1990. 231–49.

Soyinka, Wole. *Art, Dialogue and Outrage: Essays on Literature and Culture.* Ed. Biodun Jeyifo. Ibadan, Nigeria: New Horn, 1988.

Spengemann, William C. *A Mirror for Americanists: Reflections on the Idea of American Literature.* Hanover, NH: UP of New England, 1989.

Thoreau, Henry David. *Walden.* Ed. J. Lyndon Shanley. Princeton: Princeton UP, 1973.

Tocqueville, Alexis de. *Democracy in America.* Trans. Henry Reeve. Ed. Phillips Bradley. 2 vols. New York: Vintage, 1945.

Tuckerman, Henry T. *America and Her Commentators.* New York, 1864.

Warren, James Perrin. *Walt Whitman's Language Experiment.* University Park: Pennsylvania State UP, 1990.

Whitman, Walt. *Leaves of Grass.* Ed. Harold W. Blodgett and Sculley Bradley. Comprehensive Reader's Ed. New York: New York UP, 1965.

The Hitchhiker's Guide to Ecocriticism

Ursula K. Heise

Heise provides a detailed overview of the development of ecocriticism, *which is also referred to as* environmental criticism, literary environmental studies, literary ecology, literary environmentalism, *and* green cultural studies. *She begins by noting that unlike feminist criticism or those fields related to other social movements of the 1960s and 1970s, ecocriticism did not develop as the academic wing of a political movement but instead was part of a large field of overlapping projects. Heise attributes the different names of the field to this diversity, and she suggests that the 1990s offered a more conducive environment for the investigation of the relation between nature and culture. Ecocriticism began with a focus on the valuation of wild and rural places, self-sufficiency, a sense of place, local knowledge, and alternative spirituality, but gradually moved its inquiry to more social-ecological positions, which recognized that the transhistorical ideal of wilderness did not consider the displacement of Native Americans. According to Heise, this shift was prompted in part by challenges to the field regarding what was "socially excluded, historically erased, and textually forgotten" (p. 387). These challenges led to greater attention to women's and Native American literature as well as more interest in urban spaces. Heise concludes by detailing various strands of ecocriticism. The essay originally appeared in a 2006 issue of* PMLA.*

From *PMLA* 121.2 (2006): 503–16.

The Emergence of Ecocriticism

The first few frames of the belgian comic-strip artist Raymond
Macherot's work "Les Croquillards" (1957) provide a shorthand for
some of the issues that concern environmentally oriented criticism,
one of the most recent fields of research to have emerged from the rapidly diversifying matrix of literary and cultural studies in the 1990s. A
heron is prompted to a lyrical reflection on the change of seasons by a
leaf that gently floats down to the surface of his pond (see the next p.):
"Ah! the poetry of autumn . . . dying leaves, wind, departing birds. . . ."
This last thought jolts him back to reality: "But—I'm a migratory bird
myself! . . . Good grief! What've I been thinking?" And off he takes on
his voyage south, only to be hailed by the protagonists, the field rats
Chlorophylle and Minimum (the latter under the spell of a bad cold),
who hitch a ride to Africa with him. "Are you traveling on business?" he
asks his newfound passengers. "No, for our health," they answer.

The scene unfolds around two conceptual turns relevant to ecocriticism. The speaking animal, a staple of comic strips, is credited with an
aesthetic perception of nature that relies on the long Western tradition
of associating beauty with ephemerality: autumn's appeal arises from
its proximity to death, decay, and departure, a beauty the wind will
carry away in an instant. But ironically this Romantic valuation of nature separates the heron from his innate attunement to its rhythms: the
falling leaf makes him sink into autumnal reverie and forget to seek out
warmer latitudes. As soon as he takes flight, however, Macherot once
again twists the idea of seasonal migration by turning the heron into a
sort of jetliner on bird wings transporting what might be business or
leisure travelers. What is (or should be) natural for the bird is not so for
the rats, whose illness hints at another type of failure to adapt to seasonal rhythms. On one hand, this comic strip humorously raises the
question whether an aesthetic appreciation of nature brings one closer
to it or alienates one from it; on the other, it highlights the tension between bonds to nature that are established by innate instinct, those
that arise through aesthetic valuation, and those that are mediated by
modern-day travel. The heron's flight remains comically suspended between the vocabularies of nature, art, and international business. In
what ways do highly evolved and self-aware beings relate to nature?
What roles do language, literature, and art play in this relation? How
have modernization and globalization processes transformed it? Is it
possible to return to more ecologically attuned ways of inhabiting nature, and what would be the cultural prerequisites for such a change?

This is a sample of issues that are often raised in ecocriticism, a
rapidly growing field in literary studies. The story of its institutional
formation has been told in detail and from several perspectives (Cohen
9–14; Garrard 3–15; Glotfelty, "Introduction" xvii–xviii, xxii–xxiv; Love
1–5; Branch and Slovic xiv–xvii)[1]: scattered projects and publications

Figure 1.

involving the connection between literature and the environment in the 1980s led to the founding of ASLE, the Association for the Study of Literature and the Environment, during a convention of the Western Literature Association in 1992. In 1993 the journal *ISLE: Interdisciplinary Studies in Literature and Environment* was established, and in 1995 ASLE started holding biennial conferences. Seminal texts and anthologies such as Lawrence Buell's *The Environmental Imagination* (1995), Kate Soper's *What Is Nature?* (1995), and Cheryll Glotfelty and Harold Fromm's *Ecocriticism Reader* (1996) followed, as well as special journal issues (Murphy, *Ecology; Ecocriticism*). At the same time, newly minted ecocritics began to trace the origins of their intellectual concerns back to such seminal works in American and British literary studies as Henry Nash Smith's *Virgin Land* (1950), Leo Marx's *The Machine in the Garden* (1964), Roderick Nash's *Wilderness and the*

American Mind (1967), Raymond Williams's *The Country and the City* (1973), Joseph Meeker's *The Comedy of Survival* (1974), and Annette Kolodny's *The Lay of the Land* (1975). ASLE membership grew rapidly, topping a thousand in the early years of the new century, and offspring organizations in Australia-New Zealand, Korea, Japan, India, and the United Kingdom were founded, as was, most recently, the independent European Association for the Study of Literature, Culture and Environment (EASLCE).

Given the steadily increasing urgency of environmental problems for ever more closely interconnected societies around the globe, the explosion of articles and books in the field may not strike one as particularly surprising. But what is remarkable about this burst of academic interest is that it took place at such a late date; most of the important social movements of the 1960s and 1970s left their marks on literary criticism long before environmentalism did, even though environmentalism succeeded in establishing a lasting presence in the political sphere. Why this delay?

The main reason lies no doubt in the development of literary theory between the late 1960s and the early 1990s. Under the influence of mostly French philosophies of language, literary critics during this period took a fresh look at questions of representation, textuality, narrative, identity, subjectivity, and historical discourse from a fundamentally skeptical perspective that emphasized the multiple disjunctures between forms of representation and the realities they purported to refer to. In this intellectual context, the notion of nature tended to be approached as a sociocultural construct that had historically often served to legitimize the ideological claims of specific social groups. From Roland Barthes's call in 1957 "always to strip down Nature, its 'laws' and its 'limits,' so as to expose History there, and finally to posit Nature as itself historical" (*Mythologies* 175; trans. mine) to Graeme Turner's claim in 1990 that "Cultural Studies defines itself in part . . . through its ability to explode the category of 'the natural'" (qtd. in Hochman 10), the bulk of cultural criticism was premised on an overarching project of denaturalization. This perspective obviously did not encourage connections with a social movement aiming to reground human cultures in natural systems and whose primary pragmatic goal was to rescue a sense of the reality of environmental degradation from the obfuscations of political discourse.

By the early 1990s, however, the theoretical panorama in literary studies had changed considerably. New Historicism had shaded into American cultural studies, which styled itself antitheoretical as much as theoretical, signaling not so much the advent of a new paradigm as the transition of the discipline into a field of diverse specialties and methodologies no longer ruled by any dominant framework. Ecocriticism found its place among this expanding matrix of coexisting projects, which in part explains the theoretical diversity it has attained in a mere dozen years. But this diversity also results from its relation to the sociopolitical forces that spawned it. Unlike feminism or postcolonialism, ecocriticism did not evolve gradually as the academic wing of an influential political movement. It emerged when environmentalism had already turned into a vast field of converging and conflicting projects and given rise to two other humanistic subdisciplines, environmental philosophy and history. This diversity resonates in the different names by which the field has been identified: *ecocriticism* has imposed itself as a convenient shorthand for what some critics prefer to call *environmental criticism, literary-environmental studies, literary ecology, literary environmentalism,* or *green cultural studies* (see Buell, *Future* 11–12).

Changes in the perceived cultural relevance of biology also helped to open up the conceptual space for ecocriticism. Sociobiological approaches that had been rejected in the 1970s reentered debate in the 1990s as genetic research and biotechnologies began to shed new light on old questions about innate and acquired behavior. While many of these questions have remained intensely controversial among scientists and humanities scholars and while many ecocritics are highly critical of sociobiology and evolutionary psychology, there can be no doubt that the 1990s offered a climate very different from that of earlier decades for investigating the relation between nature and culture. This is not to say that the early 1990s marked an altogether welcoming moment for the articulation of an environmentalist perspective on culture. The so-called science wars, brewing since the 1980s, came to a head with Paul Gross and Norman Levitt's polemical repudiation of constructivist approaches to science in their book *Higher Superstition* (1994). The physicist Alan Sokal's faux-poststructuralist essay on quantum mechanics in the journal *Social Text* in 1996 took the confrontation between scientists and their critics to a new level of ferocity as well as public awareness. Ecocriticism, with its triple allegiance to the scientific study of nature, the scholarly analysis of cultural representations, and the political struggle for more sustainable ways of inhabiting the natural world, was born in the shadow of this controversy. Even though the grounds of the debate have shifted since then, the underlying issues of realism and representation that informed the science wars continue to pose challenges for ecocritical theory.

Because of the diversity of political and cross-disciplinary influences that went into its making, ecocriticism is not an easy field to summarize. Even if ecocritics, perhaps more than other academic scholars, still long for a sense of community and shared holistic ideals, the reality is that they diverge widely in their views. Recent vigorous critiques and ripostes are healthy signs of a rapidly expanding field. Somewhat like cultural studies, ecocriticism coheres more by virtue of a common political project than on the basis of shared theoretical and methodological assumptions, and the details of how this project should translate into the study of culture are continually subject to challenge and revision. For this reason, ecocriticism has also become a field whose complexities by now require the book-length introductions that have appeared over the last two years: Greg Garrard's *Ecocriticism* (2004), Buell's *The Future of Environmental Criticism* (2005), and, shorter and sketchier, Walter Rojas Pérez's *La ecocrítica hoy* (2004).

Environmentalism and the Critique of Modernity

Like feminism and critical race studies, ecocriticism started with a critical reconceptualization of modernist notions of human psychological identity and political subjecthood. The ecocritical attempt to think beyond conceptual dichotomies that modernity, the Enlightenment, and science were thought to have imposed on Western culture—the separation of subject and object, body and environment, nature and culture—articulated itself, as it did in other fields, through the combination of analytic modes of academic discourse with more experientially based forms of writing that Scott Slovic has called "narrative scholarship" ("Ecocriticism"). But ecocriticism in its first stage differed sharply from other forms of "postmodern" thought in that it sought to redefine the human subject not so much in relation to the human others that subjecthood had traditionally excluded as in relation to the nonhuman world. Environmentalism and ecocriticism aim their critique of modernity at its presumption to know the natural world scientifically, to manipulate it technologically and exploit it economically, and thereby ultimately to create a human sphere apart from it in a historical process that is usually labeled "progress." This domination strips nature of any value other than as a material resource and commodity and leads to a gradual destruction that may in the end deprive humanity of its basis for subsistence. Such domination empties human life of the significance it had derived from living in and with nature and alienates individuals and communities from their rootedness in place.

Projected alternatives to this kind of modernity extend from deep ecology to social ecology. Deep ecology foregrounds the value of nature in and of itself, the equal rights of other species, and the importance of small communities. Social ecology, by contrast, tends to value nature primarily in its human uses and has affinities with political philosophies ranging from anarchism and socialism to feminism. Deep ecology, associated often with a valuation of wild and rural spaces, self-sufficiency, a sense of place, and local knowledge and sometimes with an alternative spirituality, played an important part in the early stages of ecocriticism. Especially for Americanists, this philosophy resonated with writers from Thoreau (in a certain reading of his work) to Wendell Berry, Edward Abbey, and Gary Snyder. From the late 1990s on, however, the field gradually moved to the more social-ecological positions that dominate ecocriticism today (Buell, *Future* 97–98).

This shift was prompted in part by the sheer numerical expansion of the field, which led scholars from a wide variety of intellectual backgrounds to bring their interests to bear on environmental issues. In part it also emerged under the pressure of explicit challenges to the field: like other areas of cultural theory, ecocriticism saw its initial assumptions questioned for what they had socially excluded, historically erased, and textually forgotten (or refused) to account for.[2] The historicization of the wilderness concept by the environmental historian William Cronon is undoubtedly one of the most important critiques. Unlike ecological movements in other parts of the world, Cronon argues, environmentalism in the United States tends to hold up an ideal of landscapes untouched by human beings as the standard against which actual landscapes are measured. But this standard is problematic in its relation to past and future. It conceals the fact that the apparently transhistorical ideal of *wilderness* only acquired connotations of the sublime and sacred in the nineteenth century and that the cultural valuation of pristine and uninhabited areas led to the displacement of native inhabitants and in some cases to the creation of official parks. Far from being nature in its original state, such wildernesses were the product of cultural processes. The wilderness concept makes it difficult for a political program to conceptualize desirable forms of human inhabitation, relying as it does on the categorical separation of human beings from nature.

For ecocritics, who had often referred to statements such as Thoreau's "In wildness is the preservation of the world" as touchstones, Cronon's critique prompted a reexamination of established environmental authors as well as a broadening of the canon. Greater attention to women's and Native American literature shifted the emphasis to more communal engagements with a natural world conceived as always intertwined with human existence.[3] But greater inclusiveness also brought more challenges, since not all minority literatures proved as easy to assimilate into ecocritical concerns as Native American texts, many of whose authors had long been active in the environmental movement. African American literature, for example, as Michael Bennett and others have shown, is difficult to address with standard ecocritical vocabulary, since African American authors tend to associate rural life and sometimes even wild places with memories of slavery and persecution rather than with peaceful refuge (see Wallace and Armbruster). "[O]f what use is ecocriticism if the culture under consideration has a different relationship with pastoral space and wilderness than the ideal kinship that most nature writers and ecocritics assume and seek?" Bennett asks, and he emphasizes that "even the most inviting physical environment cannot be considered separately from the sociopolitical structures that shape its uses and abuses" (195, 201).

Critiques such as these led to increased emphasis on urban spaces (Bennett and Teague; Dixon; MacDonald) as well as on issues of social inequality that environmental problems often overlap. From the turn of the millennium, environmental-justice criticism increasingly influenced the field by drawing attention to social and racial inequalities in both access to natural resources and exposure to technological and ecological risk (Martínez-Alier; Adamson, Evans, and Stein). "Aesthetic appreciation of nature has not only been a class-coded activity, but the insulation of the middle and upper classes from the most brutal effects of industrialization has played a crucial role in environmental devastation," T. V. Reed argues in his call for an ecocriticism that fuses concerns for natural preservation with those for distributive justice (151). Along with the emergence of a fully post-structuralist ecocriticism (about which more later on), this critical agenda has opened up the full gamut of concepts and methods from cultural studies for environmental criticism.

The shift to a more in-depth engagement with the sociopolitical framing of environmental issues has also fundamentally, if not always explicitly, altered the way in which most ecocritics view the relation between modernity and nature. In earlier types of environmental scholarship, nature tended to be envisioned as a victim of modernization but also as its opposite and alternative; nature is now more often viewed as inextricably entwined with modernity—both as a concept and in the material shape in which we experience it today. More than that, environmentalists and ecocritics have begun to see how their search for a more authentic relation to nature is itself a product of modernization. The geographer David Harvey points out that

> the problem of authenticity is itself peculiarly modern. Only as modern industrialization separates us from the process of production and we encounter the environment as a finished commodity does it emerge. . . . The final victory of modernity . . . is not the disappearance of the non-modern world, but its artificial preservation and reconstruction. . . . The search for an authentic sense of community and of an authentic relation to nature among many radical and ecological movements is the cutting edge of exactly such a sensibility. (301–02)

Understanding itself in this way, as both derived from and resistant to modernity, may also help ecocriticism develop modes of critique of the modern that are less dependent than they have been so far on recourse to premodern forms of inhabitation and culture.

Scientific Intersections

Ecocriticism's engagement with modernization has been partly shaped by environmentalists' ambivialence toward scientific inquiry (see Heise). On one hand, science is viewed as a root cause of environmental deterioration, both in that it has cast nature as an object to be analyzed and manipulated and in that it has provided the means of exploiting nature more radically than was possible by premodern means. On the other hand, environmentalists are aware that the social legitimation of environmental politics and their own insights into the state of nature centrally depend on science. In ecocriticism, this ambivalence has translated into divergent perceptions of how the sciences should inform cultural inquiry.

At one end of the spectrum, a small number of ecocritics, such as Joseph Carroll and Glen Love, would like to make the life sciences in general and evolutionary theory in particular the foundation of literary study, following E. O. Wilson's idea of "consilience." Starting from the idea that culture is based on the human "adapted mind"—that is, "a biologically constrained set of cognitive and motivational characteristics" (Carroll vii)—this group seeks to explain cultural phenomena in terms of what they accomplish for human adaptation and survival. Many scholars in the humanities almost instinctively recoil in horror from such a sociobiological agenda, associating it with social Darwinism or Nietzschean ideology and the legitimations they have historically provided for various forms of political hegemony. But, in fairness, Darwinian theory should not simply be conflated with such ideological appropriations: Carroll categorically dismisses social Darwinism as a value-laden misinterpretation of evolutionary theory (xiv).

The more crucial question is what contribution an adaptationist approach, with its concept of human nature as a "universal, species-typical array of behavioral and cognitive characteristics" (vii), might be able to make to a discipline that has recently invested most of its theoretical capital in historical and cultural diversity. One answer is that there is no compelling reason why cultural inquiry has to focus on cultural differences rather than similarities. Fair enough—literary criticism certainly used to be more interested in universals than it has been in the last three decades. If the adaptationist approach can produce an analysis of cultural and literary universals that is descriptive rather than normative and that does not rely on the values of one particular culture dressed up as human nature (as was usually done in earlier attempts to define universals), it deserves to be heard as part of a full theory of culture. Obviously, an important part of such an analysis would have to be a careful examination of the terms used to describe the object of study: words such as *literature*, *aesthetics*, *narrative*, and *culture* itself have complex cultural histories and cannot be taken for granted in a biologically based approach.

What is less clear is how such an adaptationist understanding might inflect the vast areas of literary study that are concerned with historically and culturally specific phenomena. Human anatomy and physiology have not changed substantially over the last few thousand years, whereas cultural forms have varied enormously over the same time period. While a biological perspective might provide a general background, it seems at present unlikely to transform the study of such variations in the near future. In this sense, literary Darwinism offers not so much a competing theoretical approach as the outline of a different research area (culture, in its most abstract and universally human dimensions and evolutionary functions) that only partially overlaps with what most cultural scholars focus on today (cultures, in their historically and locally specific dimensions and social functions).

Most ecocritical work is shaped by science in a more indirect but no less important way. Ecology, for many environmentalists a countermodel against "normal" analytic science, has opened the way for a holistic understanding of how natural systems work as vast interconnected webs that, if left to themselves, tend toward stability, harmony, and self-regeneration. A fully mature ecosystem, the climax community of classical ecology, consists of a set of animals and plants ideally adapted to their environment. With such a standard in mind, science can be easily associated with a set of ideal values and a code of ethics: "Ecology . . . seemed to be a science that dealt with harmony, a harmony found in nature, offering a model for a more organic, cooperative human community" (Worster 363). Understood in this way, science can help determine what kinds of human interventions into the natural world are acceptable and what types of cultures are to be considered superior or inferior, and it can help ecocriticism evaluate texts that engage with nature. A powerful image behind an important social movement, the idea of holistic, self-regenerating ecosystems has catalyzed political, legal, and cultural changes that have unquestionably benefited the environment and human welfare (340–87).

But by the time ecocriticism emerged in the 1990s, this idea had already been exposed as no longer in accord with the state of knowledge in ecological science. Even by the 1960s, ecology had become a more analytic, empirical, and mathematical field than it was at its emergence in the late nineteenth century. Holistic notions of universal connectedness, stability, and harmony had lost much of their credibility among ecological scientists, for the most part engaged in specialized research (372–79). As environmental historians realized, ecology no longer offered a general foundation for "morality and causality": "Historians thought ecology was the rock upon which they could build environmental history; it turned out to be a swamp" (White 1113, 1114). The biologist Daniel Botkin's popular scientific book *Discordant Harmonies* (1990) brought such insights to a broader public by presenting a different and more complex image of ecosystems as dynamic, perpetually changing, and often far from stable or balanced: "We have tended to view nature as a Kodachrome still-life, much like a tourist-guide illustration . . . but nature is a moving picture show" (6).

This idea is taken up in the first book-length critique of ecocriticism, Dana Phillips's *The Truth of Ecology* (2003), which lambasts environmental scholars for adhering to an obsolete notion of ecological science and for transferring ecological terms to literary study by means of mere metaphor (42–82). Phillips is certainly right in cautioning eco-critics against undue metaphorization, moralization, or spiritualiza-tion of scientific concepts and in calling for more up-to-date scientific literacy — a literacy that, one should mention, would minimally require some training in quantitative methods that does not to date form part of cultural scholars' education. Yet a comprehensive alternative model for linking ecology and ecocriticism does not emerge from his analysis. Perhaps, given the varied and controversial nature of current connec-tions between the humanities and sciences, such a model would be a rather tall order. Nevertheless, because of the importance of ecological science for environmentally oriented criticism, Garrard is surely right that defining their relation more clearly is one of the key challenges for ecocritical scholarship (178).

Those ecocritics who situate their work at the poststructuralist end of the spectrum would go one step further than Phillips by not only criticizing particular ideas about the environment wrongly be-lieved to derive from science but also exposing the concept of the envi-ronment itself as a cultural construct. In his study of antebellum American literature, for example, David Mazel emphasizes that his analysis

> is not . . . about some myth *of* the environment, as if the environment were an ontologically stable, foundational entity we have a myth *about*. Rather, the environment is *itself* a myth, a "grand fable," a complex fic-tion, a widely shared, occasionally contested, and literally ubiquitous narrative. . . . [T]his study treats the environment as a discursive con-struction, something whose "reality" derives from the ways we write, speak, and think about it. (xii)

Mazel examines how early America's self-definition as "Nature's Na-tion" generates environmental discourses that end up bolstering con-servative social agendas despite their professed progressive politics (xii). This resolutely constructivist and politically oriented argument is quite familiar from New Historicism and cultural studies. To the ex-tent that a scientific view of nature forms part of the analysis at all, it is to study science's role in the emergence of a socioculturally grounded conception of the environment. Most ecocritics have been reluctant to go as far as Mazel in reducing nature to a discursive reality, but he illustrates one extreme of the theoretical spectrum: while literary Darwinists subordinate cultural phenomena to scientific explanation, ecopoststructuralists subordinate material reality and its scientific ex-planation to cultural analysis. Ecocritical inquiry, most of which adopts a more dialectical perspective on the relation between culture and sci-ence, plays itself out in the tension between these two extremes.[4]

Realisms: Perception and Representation

This tension between realist and constructivist approaches crucially involves questions about how our perception of the environment is culturally shaped and how that perception is mediated through language and literature. One strand of ecocriticism critical of modernist thought has tended to privilege philosophies and modes of writing that seek to transcend divisions between culture and nature, subject and object, and body and environment. The European phenomenological tradition has provided some of the most powerful impulses for thinking beyond such dichotomies. The German philosopher Martin Heidegger's notion of "dwelling" as part of human essence and as a form of existence that allows other forms of being to manifest themselves (160–64) has been interpreted as proto-environmentalist by some. The French phenomenologist Maurice Merleau-Ponty's emphasis on bodily experience, and especially the erotic metaphor that undergirds the "embrace of the flesh of the world," spelled out in his *Le visible et l'invisible*, (188–95, 302–04), has been taken up by some ecocritics as a way of envisioning the physical interrelatedness of body and habitat. The Norwegian philosopher Arne Naess's "deep ecology," finally, itself influenced by Heidegger, portrays environmentalism as the realization of a self that encompasses both the individual and the cosmos (171–76).

The influence of these phenomenological approaches makes itself felt in numerous literary works and critical analyses that focus on the importance of a "sense of place," on "dwelling," "reinhabitation" (Snyder), or an "erotics of place" (T. Williams). Sometimes this cognitive, affective, and ethical attachment to place is envisioned in terms of epiphanic fusions with the environment: Edward Abbey describes in *Desert Solitaire* how after a prolonged solitary stay in the wilderness, he began to perceive a leaf when he looked at his hand (251); Snyder's "Second Shaman Song" and one of Aldo Leopold's sketches feature similar experiences of total immersion.[5] This emphasis on interrelatedness had led some ecocritics to revise assumptions of conventional rhetoric—for example, the pathetic fallacy, which "is a fallacy only to the ego clencher," as Neil Evernden puts it: "There is no such thing as an individual, only . . . individual as a component of place, defined by place" (101, 103). Since metaphor is a particularly easy way of establishing such connections between mind, body, and place, it is not surprising that ecocriticism has engaged poetry more than other schools of criticism have in recent decades.[6]

The interest in modes of thought and language that reduce or nullify the distance between the experiencing body and experienced environment has been productive for ecocriticism and set it apart from other theoretical approaches. Yet the difficulties of such a perspective are also quite obvious. In the pursuit of physical connectedness between body and environment, language and texts might initially function as mediating tools but can in the end be little more than obstacles—as they are for Macherot's lyrically minded waterfowl (see also Phillips 11–20). Physical closeness also usually refers to the individual's encounter with nature, but some feminist and indigenous perspectives understand this encounter as a fundamentally communal one. Phenomenological approaches tend not to offer clear models for mediated and collective experiences of nature; neither do they provide the means for explaining how the authenticity of natural encounters is itself culturally shaped. To the extent that this postulation of authenticity relies on the assumption that all modern subjects are alienated from nature, it is difficult to describe the particular forms of alienation suffered by socially disenfranchised groups.

This is not to say that attention to the real differences that class, gender, and race make in the experience of nature does not come with its own set of representational problems. As Buell has convincingly shown, many instances of "toxic discourse"—accounts of pollution, health threats, and the displacement of native inhabitants—that at first sight look realistic rely in fact on tropes and genres with long traditions in American literary history (*Writing* 35–54). The rhetorical power of such accounts derives precisely from their reliance on such traditions. To give one well-known example, Rachel Carson's influential indictment of pesticide overuse in *Silent Spring* (1962) skillfully uses tropes of the pastoral, biblical apocalypse, nuclear fear (in her comparisons of chemical contamination with radioactive fallout), and 1950s anti-Communism ("a grim specter has crept upon us almost unnoticed" [3]; Killingsworth and Palmer 27–32). Problems of textuality and literariness therefore surface at both ends of the ecocritical spectrum, in phenomenologically informed explorations of the encounter between body and environment as well as in politically oriented approaches to the disjunctions between body, community, and nature that result from environmental pollution and social oppression.

Poststructuralists circumvent such difficulties by presenting nature as a purely discursive construction. But like feminists and race theorists who emphasized the cultural rather than biological grounding of their objects of study, these critics must face the objection that such a view plays into the enemy's hand by obfuscating the material reality of environmental degradation. This problem may be a minor one for academic cultural theory, which surely stands to be enriched by the poststructuralist approach, as Mazel argues (xv), but it is serious for green politics. In the end, it seems likely that strong constructivist positions will be less convincing to ecocritics, many of whom are also green activists, than weak constructivist ones that analyze cultural constructions of nature with a view toward the constraints that the real environment imposes on them (see Hayles; Soper 151–55). This would also seem the most promising theoretical ground from which to pursue the analysis of environmental literature in its relation to cultural and rhetorical traditions, on one hand, and social as well as scientific realities, on the other.

Thinking Globally

Along with its theoretical diversity and interdisciplinarity, the rapid expansion of its analytic canon is one of the most striking features of ecocriticism. British Romanticism and twentieth-century American literature initially proved the most fertile fields of inquiry, as two cultural moments with a decisive influence on current conceptions of nature. Jonathan Bate's *Romantic Ecology* (1991) and *Song of the Earth* (2000) as well as Karl Kroeber's *Ecological Literary Criticism* (1994) blazed the environmental trail in studies of Romanticism; Slovic's *Seeking Awareness in American Nature Writing* (1992) and Buell's *Environmental Imagination* foregrounded the importance of nature writing for the American literary canon. Slovic's and Buell's efforts were accompanied by a multitude of other studies of American literature, often with a focus on nonfiction and nature poetry by such writers as Thoreau, Emerson, John Muir, Mary Austin, Robinson Jeffers, Edward Abbey, Gary Snyder, Wendell Berry, Annie Dillard, and Barry Lopez. A second wave of publications placed greater emphasis on women writers, from Willa Cather and Adrienne Rich to Terry Tempest Williams and Karen Tei Yamashita, and on Native American literature, from Leslie Marmon Silko to Simon Ortiz, Linda Hogan, and Joy Harjo. This shift in themes and authors was accompanied by a broadening of the generic horizon. Science fiction came into view as a genre with important environmental dimensions, as did film and computer games. At the same time, ecocritics have developed analyses of cultural institutions and practices outside the arts, from landscape architecture and green consumerism to various forms of tourism and the national park system.

Critics such as Patrick Murphy and Slovic have also made sustained efforts to spread ecocritical analysis to the study of other cultures and languages, though their success has been limited. Ecocriticism has achieved fairly good coverage of Australian, British, Canadian, and United States literatures, but ecocritical work on languages other than English is still scarce,[7] and some of it is not well connected to scholarship in English. Murphy's monumental anthology *Literature of Nature: An International Sourcebook* (1998) represents a first heroic effort to put ecocriticism on a truly comparatist and global basis. Yet its coverage remains uneven, not only because there are more essays on anglophone than on other literatures but also because essays on some countries cover several hundred years (India), others only one literary period (Taiwan), and yet others a single author (Brazil). The surprising selectiveness of the bibliographies in some of these essays is symptomatic of broader international disjunctures.[8] Works on British or American environmental literature tend to refer to one another but not to work like Jorge Marcone's and Candace Slater's on Latin American texts or Axel Goodbody's and Heather Sullivan's on German literature, even though much of this work is available in English. Critical anthologies are usually not received by anglophone ecocritics when their focus of study lies outside English-based literatures.[9] Ecocriticism is a good deal more international than cultural studies was initially, but its geographic scope is not evident in most of the published work. Obviously, part of the problem is linguistic: monolingualism is currently one of ecocriticism's most serious intellectual limitations. The environmentalist ambition is to think globally, but doing so in terms of a single language is inconceivable — even and especially when that language is a hegemonic one.

Precisely because ecocritical work encompasses many literatures and cultures, it would also stand to gain from a closer engagement with theories of globalization (Garrard 178).[10] To date, environmental-justice ecocriticism is the only branch of the field that has addressed globalization issues in any depth. To put it somewhat simplistically, this type of ecocriticism rejects economic globalization, which it understands to be dominated by transnational corporations, but welcomes cultural border crossings and alliances, especially when they are initiated by the disenfranchised in the current economic world order. The interdependencies of these two forms of globalization, however, deserve closer theoretical scrutiny. Ecological issues are situated at a complex intersection of politics, economy, technology, and culture; envisioning them in their global implications requires an engagement with a variety of theoretical approaches to globalization, especially, for ecocritics, those that focus on its cultural dimensions. With such a theoretical framework to link together the pieces of its international and interdisciplinary mosaic, ecocriticism promises to become one of the most intellectually exciting and politically urgent ventures in current literary and cultural studies.

Notes

1. See also the useful typology of ecocriticism in Reed 148–49.
2. See Cohen for a more chronological account of these challenges.
3. Space constraint makes it impossible for me to give a detailed account of the role of ecofeminism here, whose intellectual trajectory and complexity deserve an essay of their own.
4. As Levin sums it up, "Much recent [ecocritical] work can be divided into two competing critical camps: realists, who advocate a return to nature as a means of healing our modern/postmodern alienation, and social constructionists, who see that nature as a discursive strategy and adopt a more skeptical stance with regard to its alleged healing properties. . . . [T]he dialectical critics from the two different camps appear to have more in common with each other than the more and less sophisticated representatives of the same camp" (175).

5. On Snyder, see Buell, *Environmental Imagination* 166–67; on Leopold, see Berthold-Bond 23–24.
6. Admittedly, the emphasis has been on fairly conventional forms of poetry from Romanticism to the present. More recently, however, experimental poetry has come into focus, from the founding of the journal *Ecopoetics*, in 2001, to Cooperman's work on Olson, Hart's on Eigner, and Fletcher's on Ashbery (175–224).
7. Research by Americanists outside the United States includes work by Hollm; Mayer; and Suberchicot. In her 2004 presidential address to the American Studies Association, Shelley Fisher Fishkin foregrounded the importance of more sustained attention to such research in American studies at large (35–40).
8. Even in single national traditions, some of the omissions are surprising: the essay on Brazil does not refer to Soares's critical anthology *Ecologia e literatura* (1991), and none of the four pieces on Japan in Murphy's anthology mentions Colligan-Taylor's *The Emergence of Environmental Literature in Japan* (1990).
9. For example, Larsen, Nøjgaard, and Petersen's *Nature: Literature and Its Otherness* (1997).
10. Guha's critique of American environmentalism and Guha and Martínez-Alier's *Varieties of Environmentalism* provide good starting points for such an inquiry.

Works Cited

Abbey, Edward. *Desert Solitaire: A Season in the Wilderness*. New York: Ballantine, 1968.

Adamson, Joni, Mei Mei Evans, and Rachel Stein, eds. *The Environmental Justice Reader: Politics, Poetics, and Pedagogy*. Tucson: U of Arizona P, 2002.

Armbruster, Karla, and Kathleen R. Wallace, eds. *Beyond Nature Writing: Exploring the Boundaries of Ecocriticism*. Charlottesville: U of Virginia P, 2001.

Barthes, Roland. *Mythologies*. Paris: Seuil, 1957.

Bate, Jonathan. *Romantic Ecology: Wordsworth and the Environmental Tradition*. London: Routledge, 1991.

———. *The Song of the Earth*. London: Picador, 2000.

Bennett, Michael. "Anti-pastoralism, Frederick Douglass, and the Nature of Slavery." Armbruster and Wallace 195–210.

Bennett, Michael, and David W. Teague, eds. *The Nature of Cities: Ecocriticism and Urban Environments*. Tucson: U of Arizona P, 1999.

Berthold-Bond, Daniel. "The Ethics of 'Place': Reflections on Bioregionalism." *Environmental Ethics* 22 (2000): 5–24.

Botkin, Daniel B. *Discordant Harmonies: A New Ecology for the Twenty-First Century*. New York: Oxford UP, 1990.

Branch, Michael P., and Scott Slovic, eds. *The ISLE Reader: Ecocriticism, 1993–2003*. Athens: U of Georgia P, 2003.

Buell, Lawrence. *The Environmental Imagination: Thoreau, Nature Writing, and the Formation of American Culture*. Cambridge: Harvard UP, 1995.

———. *The Future of Environmental Criticism: Environmental Crisis and Literary Imagination*. Oxford: Blackwell, 2005.

————. *Writing for an Endangered World: Literature, Culture, and Environment in the U.S. and Beyond*. Cambridge: Harvard UP, 2001.

Carroll, Joseph. *Literary Darwinism: Evolution, Human Nature, and Literature*. New York: Routledge, 2004.

Carson, Rachel. *Silent Spring*. Boston: Houghton, 1962.

Cohen, Michael P. "Blues in the Green: Ecocriticism under Critique." *Environmental History* 9 (2004): 9–36.

Colligan-Taylor, Karen. *The Emergence of Environmental Literature in Japan*. New York: Garland, 1990.

Cooperman, Matthew. "Charles Olson: Archaeologist of Morning, Ecologist of Evening." Tallmadge and Harrington 208–28.

Cronon, William. "The Trouble with Wilderness; or, Getting Back to the Wrong Nature." *Uncommon Ground: Rethinking the Human Place in Nature*. Ed. Cronon. New York: Norton, 1995. 69–90.

Dixon, Terrell, ed. *City Wilds: Essays and Stories about Urban Nature*. Athens: U of Georgia P, 2002.

Ecocriticism. Spec. issue of *New Literary History* 30.3 (1999): 505–716.

Evernden, Neil. "Beyond Ecology: Self, Place, and the Pathetic Fallacy." Glotfelty and Fromm 92–104.

Fishkin, Shelley Fisher. "Crossroads of Cultures: The Transnational Turn in American Studies." *American Quarterly* 57 (2005): 17–57.

Fletcher, Angus. *A New Theory for American Poetry: Democracy, the Environment, and the Future of Imagination*. Cambridge: Harvard UP, 2004.

Garrard, Greg. *Ecocriticism*. London: Routledge, 2004.

Glotfelty, Cheryll. "Introduction: Literary Studies in an Age of Environmental Crisis." Glotfelty and Fromm xv–xxxvii.

Glotfelty, Cheryll, and Harold Fromm, eds. *The Ecocriticism Reader: Landmarks in Literary Ecology*. Athens: U of Georgia P, 1996.

Goodbody, Axel. "Deutsche Ökolyrik: Comparative Observations on the Emergence and Expression of Environmental Consciousness in West and East German Poetry." *German Literature at a Time of Change, 1989–1990: German Unity and German Identity in Literary Perspective*. Ed. Arthur Williams, Stuart Parkes, and Roland Smith. Bern: Lang, 1991. 373–400.

————. "'Es stirbt das Land an seinen Zwecken': Writers, the Environment and the Green Movement in the GDR." *German Life and Letters* 47 (1994): 325–36.

Gross, Paul R., and Norman Levitt. *Higher Superstition: The Academic Left and Its Quarrels with Science*. Baltimore: Johns Hopkins UP, 1994.

Guha, Ramachandra. "Radical American Environmentalism and Wilderness Preservation: A Third World Critique." *Environmental Ethics* 11 (1989): 71–84.

Guha, Ramachandra, and Joan Martínez-Alier. *Varieties of Environmentalism: Essays North and South*. London: Earthscan, 1997.

Hart, George. "Postmodernist Nature/Poetry: The Example of Larry Eigner." Tallmadge and Harrington 315–32.

Harvey, David. *Justice, Nature and the Geography of Difference*. Oxford: Blackwell, 1996.

Hayles, N. Katherine. "Constrained Constructivism: Locating Scientific Inquiry in the Theater of Representation." *Realism and Representation: Essays on the Problem of Realism in Relation to Science, Literature, and Culture*. Ed. George Levine. Madison: U of Wisconsin P, 1993. 27–43.

Heidegger, Martin. "Bauen Wohnen Denken." *Vorträgeund Aufsätze.* Ed. Friedrich-Wilhelm von Herrmann. Frankfurt am Main: Klostermann, 2000. 145–64.

Heise, Ursula K. "Science and Ecocriticism." *American Book Review* 18 (1997): 4–6.

Hochman, Jhan. *Green Cultural Studies: Nature in Film, Novel, and Theory.* Moscow: U of Idaho P, 1998.

Hollm, Jan. *Die angloamerikanische Ökotopie: Literarische Entwürfe einer grünen Welt.* Frankfurt am Main: Lang, 1998.

Killingsworth, M. Jimmie, and Jacqueline S. Palmer. "Millennial Ecology: The Apocalyptic Narrative from Silent Spring to Global Warming." *Green Culture: Environmental Rhetoric in Contemporary America.* Ed. Carl G. Herndl and Stuart C. Brown. Madison: U of Wisconsin P, 1996. 21–45.

Kolodny, Annette. *The Lay of the Land: Metaphor as History and Experience in American Life and Letters.* Chapel Hill: U of North Carolina P, 1975.

Kroeber, Karl. *Ecological Literary Criticism: Romantic Imagining and the Biology of Mind.* New York: Columbia UP, 1994.

Larsen, Svend Eric, Morten Nøjgaard, and Annelise Ballegard Petersen, eds. *Nature: Literature and Its Otherness / La littérature et son autre.* Odense, Den.: Odense UP, 1997.

Levin, Jonathan. "Beyond Nature? Recent Work in Ecocriticism." *Contemporary Literature* 43 (2002): 171–86.

Love, Glen A. *Practical Ecocriticism: Literature, Biology, and the Environment.* Charlottesville: U of Virginia P, 2003.

MacDonald, Scott. "Ten+ (Alternative) Films about American Cities." Branch and Slovic 217–39.

Macherot, Raymond. "Les croquillards." *Chlorophylle à Coquefredouille.* N.p.: Le Lombard, 1998. 7–52.

Marcone, Jorge. "De retorno a lo natural: *La serpiente deoro*, la 'novela de la selva' y la crítica ecológica." *Hispania* 81 (1998): 299–308.

———. "Jungle Fever: Primitivism in Environmentalism: Rómulo Gallegos's *Canaima* and the Romance of the Jungle." *Primitivism and Identity in Latin America: Essays on Art, Literature, and Culture.* Ed. Erik Camayd-Freixas and José Eduardo González. Tucson: U of Arizona P, 2000. 157–72.

Martínez-Alier, Joan. "'Environmental Justice' (Local and Global)." *The Cultures of Globalization.* Ed. Fredric Jameson and Masao Miyoshi. Durham: Duke UP, 1998. 312–26.

Marx, Leo. *The Machine in the Garden: Technology and the Pastoral Ideal in America.* New York: Oxford UP, 1964.

Mayer, Sylvia. *Naturethik und Neuengland-Regionalliteratur: Harriet Beecher Stowe, Rose Terry Cooke, Sarah Orne Jewett, Mary E. Wilkins Freeman.* Heidelberg: Winter, 2004.

Mazel, David. *American Literary Environmentalism.* Athens: U of Georgia P, 2000.

Meeker, Joseph. *The Comedy of Survival: Literary Ecology and a Play Ethic.* 3rd ed. Tucson: U of Arizona P, 1997.

Merleau-Ponty, Maurice. *Le visible et l'invisible: Suivi de notes de travail.* Ed. Claude Lefort. Paris: Gallimard, 1964.

Murphy, Patrick D., ed. *Ecology in Latin American and Caribbean Literature.* Spec. issue of *Hispanic Journal* 19.2 (1998): 199–342.

————, ed. *Literature of Nature: An International Source-book.* Chicago: Fitzroy Dearborn, 1998.

Naess, Arne. *Ecology, Community and Lifestyle: Outline of an Ecosophy.* Trans. David Rothenberg. Cambridge: Cambridge UP, 1989.

Nash, Roderick. *Wilderness and the American Mind.* New Haven: Yale UP, 1967.

Phillips, Dana. *The Truth of Ecology: Nature, Culture, and Literature in America.* Oxford: Oxford UP, 2003.

Reed, T. V. "Toward an Environmental Justice Ecocriticism." Adamson, Evans, and Stein 145–62.

Rojas Pérez, Walter. *La ecocrítica hoy.* San José, Costa Rica: Aire Moderno, 2004.

Slater, Candace. *Entangled Edens: Visions of the Amazon.* Berkeley: U of California P, 2002.

Slovic, Scott. "Ecocriticism: Storytelling, Values, Communication, Contact." *ASLE Related Conferences and Abstracts.* 7 Dec. 2005 <http://www.asle.umn.edu/conf/other_conf/wla/1994/slovic.html>.

————. *Seeking Awareness in American Nature Writing: Henry Thoreau, Annie Dillard, Edward Abbey, Wendell Berry, Barry Lopez.* Salt Lake City: U of Utah P, 1992.

Smith, Henry Nash. *Virgin Land: The American West as Symbol and Myth.* Cambridge: Harvard UP, 1950.

Snyder, Gary. "Reinhabitation." *A Place in Space: Ethics, Aesthetics, and Watersheds.* Washington: Counterpoint, 1995. 183–91.

Soares, Angélica. *Ecologia e literatura.* Rio de Janeiro: Tempo Brazileiro, 1992.

Sokal, Alan D. "Transgressing the Boundaries: Toward a Transformative Hermeneutics of Quantum Gravity." *Social Text* 46–47 (1996): 217–52.

Soper, Kate. *What Is Nature? Culture, Politics and the Non-human.* Oxford: Blackwell, 1995.

Suberchicot, Alain. *Littérature américaine et écologie.* Paris: Harmattan, 2002.

Sullivan, Heather I. "Organic and Inorganic Bodies in the Age of Goethe: An Ecocritical Reading of Ludwig Tieck's 'Rune Mountain' and the Earth Sciences." *ISLE* 10.2 (2003): 21–46.

Tallmadge, John, and Henry Harrington, eds. *Reading under the Sign of Nature: New Essays in Ecocriticism.* Salt Lake City: U of Utah P, 2000.

Wallace, Kathleen R., and Karla Armbruster. "The Novels of Toni Morrison: 'Wild Wilderness Where There Was None.'" Armbruster and Wallace 211–30.

White, Richard. "Environmental History, Ecology, and Meaning." *Journal of American History* 76 (1990): 1111–16.

Williams, Raymond. *The Country and the City.* New York: Oxford UP, 1973.

Williams, Terry Tempest. "Yellowstone: The Erotics of Place." *An Unspoken Hunger: Stories from the Field.* New York: Pantheon, 1994. 81–87.

Wilson, Edward O. *Consilience: The Unity of Knowledge.* New York: Knopf, 1998.

Worster, Donald. *Nature's Economy: A History of Ecological Ideas.* 2nd ed. Cambridge: Cambridge UP, 1994.

CHAPTER

5

Approaches in the Classroom

I have found that I get my best teaching ideas from other instructors. In fact, I have a file called, "Other People's Class Stuff." This file contains syllabi, assignments, handouts, and various resources. When I came across someone's great idea, I used to say something along the lines of, "That sounds great, let me have a copy, so I can steal that for my class." I have been a blatant thief, but I have now turned over a new leaf and, rather than stealing unabashedly from my colleagues, I engage in a process known as "sharing best practices." (I must thank my former dean, Toby Parcel, for passing along this phrase—it sounds so much nicer than the outright thievery I had practiced.) Sharing best practices allows teachers to learn from the trials, errors, and successes of others.

The essays collected here represent some instructors' best practices, providing concrete, practical examples of activities that teachers can use in their classrooms. For example, Margaret Faye Jones's essay, "Bringing New Historicism into the American Literature Survey," provides both a definition of New Historicism and practical advice regarding how to use it in the classroom. Jones discusses the value of parallel reading of literary and nonliterary texts, using Benjamin Franklin's *Autobiography* and diary entries by Anne Shippen Livingston as examples. She notes that diaries and letters are particularly effective because they give students a glimpse into the private side of a particular subject. Other valuable nonliterary sources include legal and government documents, speeches, and newspapers.

William J. Scheick provides insight into teaching poetry in his essay, "Early Anglo-American Poetry: Genre, Voice, Art, and Representation."

Scheick helps students understand poetry by first addressing issues of genre, voice, and art before discussing issues of representation. Scheick notes that his approach is designed to allow students to understand contextual implications, artistic techniques, and subtextual subtleties, as well as conceptual limitations.

"Portrait of the Artist as a Young Slave: Douglass's Frontispiece Engravings" by Ed Folsom is an excellent example of using New Historicism in the classroom. Folsom describes having his students "read" the 1845 frontispiece portrait alongside Frederick Douglass's narrative. He then compares the Douglass portrait to Walt Whitman's engraving from the first edition of *Leaves of Grass* and Douglass's later engraving included with *My Bondage and My Freedom*, both published in 1855. Folsom contends that Douglass's portraits reveal the relationship between the author and the slave.

Martha Nell Smith's "Enabling Undergraduates to Understand Advanced Humanities Research: Teaching with the *Dickinson Electronic Archives*" offers instructors very specific ways to incorporate this online resource into their courses. Smith is particularly encouraging to those who may not consider themselves technologically savvy by making it clear that the teacher is the starting point. Her examples point to exciting possibilities for approaching Dickinson's poetry.

"From Gilded Garden to Golden Anniversary: Teaching Hurston's 'The Gilded Six-Bits'" by Margaret D. Bauer presents an interesting approach to teaching Hurston's story as a revision of the Adam and Eve story. After introducing students to the notion of the *felix culpa*, or "fortunate fall," Bauer suggests that Joe, not Missie May, was first tempted by Slemmons, the Satan figure. Bauer also points to possible connections between Hurston's story and Nathaniel Hawthorne's "Young Goodman Brown," which depicts the New World as a new Eden.

In "Asking Ecocritical Questions," SueEllen Campbell illustrates how to approach literature of nature and the environment. She discusses ecocritics' assumptions and how these assumptions inform discussion questions she creates for her classes. Campbell also explains how she gets her students to create "good thinking questions" (p. 455). Campbell gives examples from teaching Henry Thoreau's *Walden*, but her discussion techniques are not limited to ecocritical subjects.

Each of the foregoing essays provides wonderful examples of exercises that can be used as described or adapted to suit particular class settings. I expect to make use of many of them in my own teaching. I frequently teach "The Gilded Six-Bits," but have never approached it in relation to the Adam and Eve story, so I look forward to seeing how Bauer's approach works with my students. I also wonder how Campbell's questions might lead to a different reading of texts such as Langston Hughes's "The Negro Speaks of Rivers," as I have never thought of the rivers as characters or personas. Jones's essay reinforces my own thoughts about the value of using nonliterary texts in literature classes, and I do a good bit of dabbling with New Historicism in my classes already. For example, I often discuss the relationship between Harlem Renaissance writers and their white patrons; it would be interesting to have students read correspondence between Langston Hughes and his patron Carl Van Vechten, which is collected in *Remember Me to Harlem: The Letters of Langston Hughes and Carl Van Vechten, 1928–1964*, edited by Emily Bernard. Scheick and Folsom not only provide specific examples of how to approach particular texts, they also provide a road map for instructors to use in their discussions of other works. For example, instructors who find Folsom's discussion of portraiture valuable might expand on this idea and pair literature with artwork of the period. Finally, while many teachers are turning to the Internet to expand their teaching toolkit, whether it be through clips of author interviews or poetry readings, Smith suggests another realm of technological innovation via digital humanities. Resources such as the *Dickinson Electronic Archives* provide students with a different view of literary texts. Whether one thinks of utilizing the ideas included here as thievery or as sharing best practices, they are clearly a great resource for teachers.

Bringing New Historicism into the American Literature Survey

Margaret Faye Jones

Jones begins her Introduction to American Literature course by asking "What does it mean to be an American?" as a means of illustrating that "American-ness" is not as clear-cut as one might think. In an attempt to provide a fuller answer to this question, she utilizes a modified New Historicism in her class. Jones notes that she follows Peter Barry's definition of New Historicism as a parallel reading of literary and nonliterary texts rather than as merely providing historical context for literature. She finds that students are often particularly interested in the nonliterary texts when they relate to their interests or majors. Jones provides specific examples of her teaching of Benjamin Franklin's Autobiography *alongside diary entries by Anne Shippen Livingston to illustrate her methods in the classroom. She also suggests other possible approaches before addressing student and faculty concerns related to the incorporation of nonliterary texts. Jones's essay was published in 2000 in* Teaching English in the Two-Year College.

From *Teaching English in the Two-Year College* 28.2 (2000): 186–91.

Introduction

"What does it mean to be an American?" I ask this question of students at the first class meeting of an Introduction to American Literature course. The answers are usually predictable and positive: "Being an American means we care about people's rights and freedoms." "We believe in educating everyone and that all people with motivation can succeed in this country." "We're the greatest country in the world." "Family and God are what we care the most about." Occasionally, the responses are not so complimentary: "All we care about is money." "We're too superficial and materialistic." "Americans want to take over the world."

That first class period, I simply record the responses on the board and ask students to write them down in their notebooks. I return to that same question frequently during the semester and ask the students to reconsider and modify, if necessary, any of their initial responses. The goal is to help them see that U.S. literary history consists of many voices, voices that may contradict some of their perceived impressions about what it means to be an American, voices that may have been silenced or diminished during the country's history. I don't belittle the students' definitions or the works of the canonical figures we read; I simply want the students to understand that the issue of "American-ness" is not as straightforward as they (and numerous politicians) sometimes believe. If they critique their own definitions of what it means to be an American, I believe the students will come to a deeper understanding of their literary and cultural heritage. Therefore, I construct the syllabus purposefully to include voices from a variety of ethnic groups and social classes during each of the historical periods we study.

However, I have never quite been able to meet my goal of inclusion when teaching eighteenth-century American literature, especially in regard to women. Of course, the textbook anthology (Baym, et al.) includes Mary Rowlandson and Phillis Wheatley, but the emphasis remains on men and political writings that preceded and followed the American Revolution. Because I wanted the students to get a fuller picture of the time period, I decided to use a modified New Historicism by adding the private journals and letters of eighteenth-century women.

New Historicism

In his very useful overview of modern critical theory, Peter Barry defines New Historicism as a "method based on the *parallel* reading of literary and nonliterary texts, usually of the same time period" (172). While many of us provide historical backgrounds to the texts students read for our courses, that is not the same as "doing" New Historical work. New Historicism does not "privilege" the literary work over the nonliterary one (Barry 172). The two texts work off each other equally and provide a larger cultural picture of the historical period.

Aram Veeser lists some assumptions which underlie New Historicism's heterogeneous practices:

1. Every expressive act is embedded in a network of material practices;

2. Every act of unmasking, critique, and opposition uses the tools it condemns and risks falling prey to the practice it exposes;

3. Literary and nonliterary "texts" circulate inseparably;

4. No discourse, imaginative or archival, gives access to unchanging truths nor expresses inalterable human nature; and

5. A critical method and a language adequate to describe culture under capitalism participate in the economy they describe (xi).

New Historicism recognizes that all writings take place within specific historical periods and that literary artists and their texts can no more escape being affected and influenced by that culture than can the authors of more "prosaic" writings such as legal documents, letters, travel books, etc. Therefore, by looking at literary works in juxtaposition with these other texts, it becomes easier to find those underlying cultural influences. However, New Historicism reminds us that we (readers and critics) also work within a cultural milieu that we cannot shed to examine these texts with objectivity.

Using New Historicism in the classroom has benefits for both instructor and student. New Historical criticism is often much more accessible and interesting than some other theoretical approaches (Barry 178). New Historical practices also work well in conjunction with other theoretical approaches such as Marxist, feminist, postcolonial, and cultural studies. Finally, students often find this sort of analysis interesting because the nonliterary texts—such as business, legal and scientific writings—can relate to their own interests or majors.

Classroom Activities

The major canonical text I teach for the eighteenth-century is Benjamin Franklin's *Autobiography*. I choose Franklin for several reasons. Students are familiar with him and usually like him. He also appeals to the working class and working students by being a self-made man. Finally, his work is a good example of what Larzer Ziff calls "the represented self as representative history" (118). As Ziff points out, Franklin's aim in this work is not to correct misconceptions or necessarily to present the "truth" about his past. The incidents in his life have been carefully chosen as lessons for his readers. Franklin's chief message in *The*

Autobiography is that individuals have the ability to determine what kind of people they will be, and this ability is not due to intelligence or natural abilities, but learning specific habits (119). It certainly can be argued that Franklin single-handedly developed the American myth of the rags-to-riches potential of anyone who is willing to work hard enough to achieve success. It is an appealing myth, and many if not most of the students accept it.

We start by looking at the way Franklin carefully develops his persona. We discuss the incidents he chooses to relate. I point out his use of the term "errata" to refer to his mistakes (a printing term that implies correction). We pay special attention to the section where he develops his thirteen virtues and shares his daily schedule with the reader (90–96). After this discussion, I ask students to consider whether Franklin is truly representative of the American experience, and we move into a discussion of the lives of others during Franklin's time.

I bring to class some diary entries by Anne Shippen Livingston that were written in 1783. She was a woman who had fallen in love with a Frenchman but was persuaded by her father into a more economically providential match with an American, Colonel Henry Beekman Livingston. The marriage was a disaster, and after her husband turned abusive, she moved back in with her family. Her father ordered her to send her daughter to live with her in-laws for a time so that the child's inheritance would be assured. The diary entries deal with this ordeal, and it was also during this time that she made a list of "Some Directions Concerning a Daughter's Education" (Harris 64).

These directions seem to provide a parallel to Franklin's list of virtues. Some typical directions include the following:

> *6th* Observe strictly the little seeds of reason in her & cultivate the first appearance of it diligently.
> *13th* Seem not to admire her wit, but rather study to rectify her judgment.
> *18th* Show her the deformity of anger and rage.
> *25th* Particularly inform her in the duties of a single & married state.
> *28th* Discreetly check her desires after things pleasant & use her to frequent disappointments.
> *35th* Use her to rise betimes in the morning & set before her in the most winning manner an order for the whole day. (in Harris 67–68)

After reading this entry, we compare it to Franklin's *Autobiography*. First, we focus on the similarities. Both are types of autobiographical writing; both believe that by assuming certain types of behaviors, life can be successful (Franklin) or at least manageable (Livingston). Both also exhibit a typically eighteenth-century belief in reason. In a way, they are both didactic works. Franklin's purpose is to be a role model for his reader, to provide an example that the reader can emulate. Livingston is also concerned with teaching, but she limits herself to listing directions for her daughter.

Next, we discuss the differences between the two works. Students quickly point out that Franklin's is a public document; Livingston never had any idea that her entries would be read by anyone but herself. Then I ask the students how we can be sure of this. As Suzanne Bunkers points out, the locked diary is a twentieth-century invention. In previous centuries, women sometimes wrote diaries in collaboration. Other diaries were kept as family records (17). Therefore, we can't assume the private intentions of any diary writer, and as a class, we explore the possible purposes of Livingston. (Of course, at this point, I also point out the difficulty of ever knowing for sure an author's intention. What we consider is how the style and content of a work may change due to the writer's perception of an audience.)

Second, Franklin's remembrances of the past are told with a certain detachment, if with some regret about his "errata." Of course, he wrote years after the events had occurred and with a clear didactic purpose. Confession was not his major goal. Livingston's entries, on the other hand, are immediate and full of anguish at the likely loss of her daughter and her inability to have any power or voice in the decision. Students also discover quickly that Franklin's text, while specifying hard work and good morals, has a sense of freedom and autonomy about it. Livingston's directions for raising her daughter have a much more circumscribed feel to them.

However, for me, the most important thing about this exercise is that students begin to realize that no single text can represent any time period of a culture and that sometimes you have to look beyond literary works to see a truer picture and put canonical works into context.

Diaries and personal letters work well for this sort of project. Students like them because they provide a private side to the public world they are studying. Women's issues of childcare, spousal abuse, and financial concerns are often a surprise to the students. Some of the younger ones have a hard time believing that women haven't always had choices. Some of the more conservative are a little nonplused to discover that these were women's issues long before modern times.

The brevity of the diary entries and letters is an advantage as well. There is only one survey course in our curriculum, so we have to cover everything from Native American creation myths to John Updike in fifteen weeks. Time is always an issue, and shorter works take less course time. Students also tend to feel overwhelmed by the amount of reading they must do for the course. A diary entry or letter can have a great impact because it requires only a small investment of students' time.

Obviously, there are many texts that would work just as well, depending on the instructor's purpose. Sometimes, we read Deborah Read

Franklin's letters to her husband in conjunction with his autobiography. These almost illiterate texts can be quite instructive. Not only do students make the contrast between the writing styles, they also see the difference in opportunities between the sexes. Furthermore, these letters also give modern readers a glimpse into the responsibilities of the eighteenth-century housewife. It can also be instructive to compare sections from autobiographies of members from various marginalized groups, such as Samson Occam's story of his life as a Native American preacher (Baym, et al. 286) or Olaudah Equiano's *Interesting Narrative* (Baym, et al. 343).

An instructor can also move out of narrative form altogether and bring in legal documents, speeches, newspaper articles, and government reports from the same time period. All of these work well in the classroom. Once again, using Franklin as an example, his *Autobiography* can be compared to a speech by Benjamin Rush on the education of women (*The Microbook*) or business letters from women.

Finally, students can be assigned to find such documents as part of research projects. In a recent class, a student brought in a report on almshouses by a state committee in Massachusetts in the 1850s as a counterpoint to a Mary Wilkins Freeman story, "Sister Liddy," which is set in a poorhouse. By looking at these texts together, students started to understand that there has been a debate in this country from its very beginning about what to do with the poor. I don't claim that any major insights were gained here, but I do believe some students came away from that class with the idea that the poverty question is older and more complicated than they first realized.

Student and Faculty Concerns

While most students enjoy looking at documents that correlate with the texts in the anthology, occasionally they express some concern. The first has to do with a perception of political correctness on my part, and the second relates to the definition of literature in the first place.

When I use journals and letters in the classroom, sometimes a question indicates that a student believes I have a political agenda by bringing in these works. I try to deal with this issue by explaining at the beginning of the semester that everyone is influenced by some sort of theory or agenda, that there is no such thing as an objective and dispassionate study of literature. I also explain that all literature takes place within a culture and history that simply can't be removed from the text. Therefore, the more we know about that history and culture, the better we can interpret and appreciate literary works in general. I also make it clear that I am not making any claims for superior aesthetic qualities of some of these works, but I also point out how hard it is to decide exactly what makes something aesthetically superior.

Even after those explanations, some student will still ask in a puzzled tone after we have read a diary entry or letter, "Is this literature?" I actually welcome the question because it gives the class an opportunity to reflect on what exactly can be considered literature. We brainstorm together, and many of the suggestions return to aesthetic concerns. Then we look up the definition of "literature" in a dictionary. For example, in *The American Heritage Dictionary*, the first definition is "imaginative or creative writing." Students quickly note that this definition doesn't help them very much. Then I read from the preface of Larzer Ziff's *Writing in the New Nation*. "In that day [the late 1700s], most who thought about the matter defined literature as all of written knowledge, which is to say that belles lettres constituted a very small part of what they regarded as literary" (ix). Students can then see that the definition of literature itself (just like judging the quality of literary works) changes according to the needs and wants of the time and the cultures doing the defining.

The very fact that students ask these questions and we discuss them in class shows them, I hope, that literature is a living field of study and one that is relevant to them as individuals and citizens.

Some instructors have concerns about using New Historicism in their literature classrooms. These concerns include not being trained as a historian, not having time to do the amount of historical preparation necessary, and finding nonliterary texts that are accessible to the students and relevant to the subject. While trying a new theoretical technique always requires time and energy, these obstacles are not insurmountable.

First, most instructors of American and British literature survey courses are already quite knowledgeable about the general historical periods. What is really necessary is the willingness to critique and question the values of a literary work in juxtaposition to nonliterary texts.

Second, finding appropriate nonliterary texts does require forethought and planning. However, there are numerous resources to help. Colleagues from the history department and librarians can provide useful ideas. In the field of early American literature, many works by marginalized groups have been published. *The World Turned Upside Down*, edited by Colin Calloway, provides a variety of Native American voices, including speeches, myths, letters, autobiographies, treaties, deeds, and wills. Sharon Harris's *American Women Writers to 1800* provides many short excerpts from the writings of a variety of women in early America. One especially helpful resource is *The Microbook Library of American Civilization*, which is a microfiche collection of materials relating to American life and literature from the country's beginnings to the beginning of World War I. Materials include poetry, fiction, autobiography, biography, pamphlets, periodicals, as well as rare books that are often unavailable elsewhere. Using this resource, I have found an eighteenth-century informational handbook for Germans considering moving to the United States, a self-help book for new wives, and letters from a European monarch commanding that the native peoples be treated well.

Conclusion

Throughout the history of America, certain groups have been marginalized and denied full access to the publishing world that would have allowed their voices to be heard in a public arena. Such nonliterary writing that gives us a picture of these marginalized groups and their lives is appropriate material for the classroom. These works provide a wider context that will allow readers a new sense of the cultural milieu in which texts are written and read. By studying these works in conjunction with the ones in their course anthologies, students can begin to learn that literature is not a dead art with no relevance to them, but a living cultural artifact that arises out of the conflicts and contexts of people's lives.

Works Cited

Barry, Peter. *Beginning Theory: An Introduction to Literary and Cultural Theory.* Manchester: Manchester UP, 1995.

Baym, Nina, et al. eds. *The Norton Anthology of American Literature: Shorter 5th ed.* New York: Norton, 1999.

Bunkers, Suzanne. "Diaries: Public and Private Records of Women's Lives." *Legacy* 7.2 (1990): 17–26.

Calloway, Colin G., ed. *The World Turned Upside Down: Indian Voices from Early America.* Boston: Bedford, 1994.

Franklin, Benjamin. *The Autobiography.* 1791. Ed. Louis Masur. Boston: Bedford, 1993.

Harris, Sharon M. *American Women Writers to 1800.* New York: Oxford UP, 1996.

Livingston, Anne Shippen. Journal Entry. Harris 65–68.

The Microbook Library of American Civilization. Chicago: Library Resources, 1972.

Veeser, H. Aram. ed. *The New Historicism.* New York: Routledge, 1989.

Ziff, Larzer. *Writing in the New Nation: Prose, Print, and Politics in the Early United States.* New Haven: Yale UP, 1991.

Early Anglo-American Poetry: Genre, Voice, Art, and Representation

William J. Scheick

Originally appearing in 1999 in Teaching the Literatures of Early America, *edited by Carla Mulford, Scheick's essay argues that the diversity of early Anglo-American poetry requires "attention to historical context and*

From *Teaching the Literatures of Early America*, ed. Carla Mulford (New York: MLA, 1999): 187–99.

such notions as the chain of being, universal order, sin, common sense, and reason" (p. 410). As an instructor, his goal is gradually to deepen his students' understanding of verse by addressing issues of genre, voice, art, and representation. Scheick notes that the order of these perspectives is immaterial with the exception of representation, which he views as a counterbalance to the others and is thus reserved for last. Scheick illustrates his approach to each of these issues through a diverse selection of poetry such as Edward Taylor's meditations, Anne Bradstreet's "To My Dear Children," Philip Freneau and Hugh Henry Brackenridge's A Poem on the Rising Glory of America, Gaspar Pérez de Villagrá's Historia de la Nueva México, and Phillis Wheatley's "On Being Brought from Africa to America." Scheick's essay is particularly helpful for instructors seeking to have students make connections among poets.

The subject and cultural matter of British American poetry from Anne Bradstreet's *The Tenth Muse* (1650) to Phillis Wheatley's *Poems on Various Subjects, Religious and Moral* (1773) is diverse. This matter, ranging from late-Renaissance and Reformed traditions to Neoclassical standards, necessitates attention to historical context and such notions as the chain of being, universal order, sin, common sense, and reason. Brief books by E. M. W. Tillyard and Peter Gay are helpful in introducing students to this pertinent information. Of course, even as a pedagogical prop any historical approach is at best contingent, one version among alternatives (White). So from time to time I mention problems inherent in all acts of historicizing, including several indeterminacies in my own approach to early Anglo-American poetry.

I present these poems in terms of a tiered axis of chronological perspectives, including genre, voice, art, and representation, capped with some poststructural considerations. The order of these perspectives is not crucial to my goal of incrementally deepening my students' perspectives on this verse, except for representation, which I position last because it provides a cautionary counterbalance to the other three.

Genre

That many students can identify various genres is one advantage to the literary-model approach. Selecting a representative type of early American verse is difficult, and the choice is often determined by what has previously succeeded with students. Since I have found the elegy, a complex form rich for pedagogical purposes, to be unappealing even to graduate students, I tend to prefer the meditative poem. Meditative verse does not evince a single pattern, for its European antecedents are many; but in general, and as practiced by the Puritans, it focuses on a religious topic germane to the interior spiritual drama of the poet (Martz).

The richest examples of early colonial meditative poetry show the influence of the emblem tradition, such as exhibited in the English verse of Francis Quarles and George Herbert. Images (candles, wings, skulls, hearts, children) from Quarles's seventeenth-century bestseller *Emblems* and from a hieroglyphic poem such as Herbert's "Easter-Wings" (which visually converts the fallen-over hourglass of mortality into a butterfly of redemptive ascent) show that meditative verse often expresses religious concepts through verbal pictures. Such a poem may focus on the sea to represent humanity's helplessness in a turbulent world, as in Philip Pain's *Daily Meditations*, or on trees and rivers to represent, respectively, humanity's former Edenic posture and present temporal condition, as in Anne Bradstreet's frequently reprinted "Contemplations." In the unusual instance of "Meditation 2.3" Edward Taylor presents his own face as an emblem of mortality; students, urged to discern the fifty-one-year-old poet's facial features as well as the significance of these features in the poem, detect such details as his hirsute cheeks, blemished skin, and graying blond hair. This poem, related to early Puritan emblematic interpretations of human names and bodies, dramatizes how intensely personal meditative verse is.

Emblems such as these are concrete instances of how Puritans read nature as *liber mundi* (creation as a divinely inspired text that reiterates Scripture). Emblems tend to have layers of signification, and so students with some knowledge of the Bible might be encouraged to think further about verticality (the trees) and horizontalness (the river) in "Contemplations." In this poem, with the same number of stanzas as Christ's age at his crucifixion, the two natural types of river and trees emblematically suggest the intersection of the divine (eternal) and the human (temporal) on Christ's cross (Scheick). Similarly, Taylor's often anthologized "Meditation 1.8" offers such emblems as a caged bird, which represents, at the microcosmic level, the famished soul confined within the body and, at the macrocosmic level, inept humanity confined beneath the dome of nature. The proliferation of natural and domestic types in Taylor's poem—horizon, cage, barrel, bread loaf, inverted bowl—at first seems free-associative; but all share the emblematic shape of the half circle. After students recall the traditional symbolism of the circle (unity, perfection) and its religious significance, I ask them to consider the value of the half circle for the poet, who laments that he can only write crookedly (produce marred meditations) because he is in the dark while the sun (Son, i.e., Christ) is beyond the arched horizon. Exemplifying how Puritans viewed nature emblematically, the half-circle natural types in Taylor's late-seventeenth-century meditation intimate the scriptural prophecy of Christ's second coming.

If such types give Taylor hope rather than assurance concerning his own personal redemption, a century later similar images usually convey a far more secular and presumptive prophecy. During the eighteenth century's revival of classical aesthetic models meditation lost its status as a predominant cultural art form. The epic, narrative verse in elevated style celebrating episodes historically and prophetically important to a people, became a popular classical mode in the new republic, dating from such early epic gestures as *A Poem, on the Rising Glory of America* by Philip Freneau and Hugh Henry Brackenridge. The epic traces in this work refer to Columbus's discovery of America, the settlers' feats, and the heroes' sacrifices during the French and Indian War—each embedded in another classical type, the dialogic pastoral mode celebrating agriculture.

As students contrast the imagery of this 1772 poem with the late-seventeenth-century emblems in Bradstreet's "Contemplations" and Taylor's "Meditation 1.8," they can be directed toward the following observations. Rather than symbolize scriptural meanings in the Christian *liber mundi* tradition, the natural types in *Rising Glory* reinforce historical meanings in the British imperial tradition. Whereas the meditative poets a century earlier rehearse the scriptural version of human events in the hope that the divine prophecies include them as individuals, Freneau and Brackenridge collapse the millennial prediction of the Book of Revelation into a rehearsal of Western history and recent New World settlement. They announce, at least in this youthful phase of their careers, that America, the "final stage" of empire, is destined to fulfill Old World history. In *Rising Glory* nature symbolizes not spiritual admonition but secular fulfillment, specifically fortune through commodification: "Much wealth and pleasure agriculture brings"; "Nor less from golden commerce flow the streams / Of richest plenty on our smiling land" (lines 356, 374–75).

When concluding the comparison I ask students whether a Puritan meditator would likely have written in the manner of the later poem. Most say no, but several indicate that certain images and the sentiment of the 1772 poem could have been meditatively applied to the imagined regenerative state of the elect in heaven. This point reminds students that the religious energy of the Puritan meditation and the secular energy of the later dialogic pastoral are subtly related despite evident generic differences.

Voice

In contrasting the seventeenth-century meditation and the eighteenth-century epic-pastoral, including their nature imagery, my students are often quick to notice a related difference concerning voice. They are struck by the apparent loneliness of the Calvinistic meditative authors, who write as if no fellow human being could help them satisfy their primary spiritual desires. They detect Bradstreet's attraction to the beauty of nature in "Contemplations" and her affection for her spouse and children in such poems as "A Letter to Her Husband" and "Upon My Son Samuel." But they also acknowledge her isolation as "[s]ilent alone" her life follows "pathless paths" in a world that is at best a "lonely place, with pleasures dignifi'd" (lines 50–51, 144). Students likewise observe that in "Meditation 1.8" Taylor stands alone beneath the night sky, which is as beautiful to him as are the woods to Bradstreet and as insufficient to meet his spiritual needs. Like Bradstreet, Taylor presents nature, however much its splendor and plenitude fill his eyes, as "[a]n Empty Barrell": the "Creatures field" (nature) provides "no food for Souls" (14–16).

For meditative poets like Bradstreet and Taylor the beauty of nature does not invite proto-Romantic sentiment. This beauty, instead, is a divine goad indicting them as fallen descendants of Adam and Eve. Musing on the grandeur of nature as the artwork of the Logos, Bradstreet is struck "mute," her poem virtually discontinued after stanza 9; and Taylor, dizzy from starvation (the lack of Eucharistic manna), struggles with "puzzled thoughts" virtually depleted, "pore[d]" out, in the first stanza of his poor and porous poem (line 5). At such points, typical of Puritan meditative manner, both poets turn away from the book of nature, which only reminds them of what humanity has lost, and toward Holy Writ, as collective Christian memory, to recall the Old Testament account of the fall from grace and the New Testament gospel of redemption. Taylor's meditation ends with an authorized fantasy of his conceivable election to salvation; and Bradstreet's meditation ends with *memento mori* devices, including an allusion to the heavenly antithesis of the gravestone, designed to counter her vanity, a personal proclivity she confesses in "To My Dear Children." Neither meditator presumes redemption; indicted by nature, each remains a humble voice actively disposed to wait passively for the revelation of divine will after death.

Transatlantic comparisons may help students understand this unfamiliar attitude toward voice. While the meditative poem reveals a Renaissance ancestry, especially in its display of verbal agility, the Reformed version practiced by the Puritans downplays the value of the self, especially in typological terms. Typology, the correspondence between foreshadowing Old Testament matter and consummating New Testament matter, might or might not include the meditator, and that has considerable consequences concerning a poet's voice. When, for example, Herbert's Low Anglican "Aaron" is matched with Taylor's Congregationalist "Meditation 2.23," some students notice that the English poet concludes with a confident and affirmative sense of his share in the Old Testament high priest's fulfillment in Christ, whereas the New England poet (who occasionally alludes to Herbert's verse) finds no comfort in the Aaron type and instead only hopes that he might somehow be found worthy of redemption as one of the high priest's cups. Similar comparisons can be made between Herbert's "Affliction V" (on Noah's ark) and "The Altar" (on the Hebrew sacrificial table) and Taylor's "Meditation 2.29" and "Meditation 2.82." Here my students have seen, without much prompting, that Herbert's orderliness and neat resolution are in distinct contrast to Taylor's apparent disorder and irresolution.

Nearly a century later the swains in *Rising Glory* provide an even greater contrast. Their dialogic exchange and celebration of the common good (at least as they understood it) demonstrate an appreciation of community not evident in the meditative monologues. The voices of these country youths convey self-possession, not helplessness, and in nature they find incentive to speak rather than indictment and curtailment of speech. They share the meditators' regard for the rich plenitude of nature, but they do not draw biblical parallels from natural signs. They express a millennial and utilitarian vision of a "Paradise a new" where the commodification of natural riches fulfills human aspirations (line 754).

Sometimes a few students seem supportive of this essentially Deistic, exuberant voice prophesying the domination of nature for human benefit. I ask them to compare the sentiment of *Rising Glory* and Gaspar Pérez de Villagrá's seventeenth-century epic *Historia de la Nueva México*, which the class sampled earlier in the semester. Since students usually criticize Villagrá's celebration of unmitigated conquest, the comparison encourages a fuller awareness of the social and environmental implications of the 1772 poem.

My students even more often prefer the optimism of *Rising Glory* over the self-deprecation of Calvinistic meditations. On such occasions I ask them to determine which voice exhibits a greater appreciation of beauty. The ensuing debate touches on the question of what we mean by beauty, but finally students delve again into the poems. I consider the debate particularly successful if certain subtleties emerge — when, say, someone argues that the meditators' sense of dispossession increased their valuation of nature's beauty whereas the pastoralists' relentless stress on utilization and commodification may have blinded them to that perception.

However, this differentiation of voice risks the suggestion that seventeenth- and eighteenth-century authors were either strict Calvinists or implicit Deists. Phillis Wheatley's late-eighteenth-century verse, especially the widely available "On Being Brought from Africa to America," counters this misperception effectively because it mingles a Congregationalist sensitivity to the Bible and an Enlightenment awareness of politics. To highlight Wheatley's regard for personal liberty and her esteem for Holy Writ, I ask students to interpret the elliptical last two lines: "Remember, *Christians, Negroes*, black as *Cain* / May be refin'd, and join th' Angelic train" (lines 7–8). Some read the lines as "Remember, *Christians*, [that] *Negroes*," whereas others read them as "Remember [that] *Christians*, [and] *Negroes*." Does the final line refer only to intellectual and aesthetic refinement, such as the poet's careful management of metrics and rhyme, or does it also possibly refer to the management of the ambiguous syntax of the preceding line to imply the equality of both races as mutually "benighted soul[s]" (line 2)? To ask these related questions is to inquire into Wheatley's religiopolitical voice, which performs and proves her argument that an African American can be taught to understand the refinements of both religion and art. Advanced students might further be asked to consider whether the final line tactfully alludes to images from Isaiah, the poet's favorite prophetic scriptural book, specifically Isaiah 6.1 and 48.10. If so, then her voice simultaneously defers to scriptural authority (like the seventeenth-century meditative poets) while it subtly asserts its authority (like the eighteenth-century epic-pastoral poets) by making an unprecedented racial application of two biblical passages.

Art

Wheatley's poem is basically an encomium, the classical verse of praise revived by the eighteenth-century English authors she admired. In typical neoclassical manner, her poem is presented in rhymed couplets of nearly perfect iambic pentameter. In comparison to such model precision, the slight irregularities of the last two lines, including the ambiguous syntax and possible truncated allusions, appear to draw attention to themselves, particularly since they are emphatically introduced by the direct address "Remember." Are these irregularities the product of the young author's cunning or her lack of skill? Students who see these effects as intentional tend to value the poet's voice as empowered in its Enlightenment insistence on social revision. Students who see these effects as unintentional tend to assess her voice as inherently alienated from the religious and cultural paradigms it unsuccessfully attempts to assimilate and mimic.

Questions concerning intention apply as well to Puritan meditative verse. Bradstreet's "Contemplations," for instance, breaks into uneven units: stanzas 1–9 (on the book of nature), stanzas 10–20 (on biblical history), 21–23 (on human life in New Testament terms), 24–28 (on emblematic birds and fish), and 29–33 (on the mariner soul in the prone vessel of the body). Oddities occur, such as the echo of the first unit at the start of the third; and the fourth unit is structurally more a lateral swelling than a linear development of the gist of the poem, which is perhaps why some anthologists delete it. Is such fragmentation the product of Bradstreet's amateurishness or of her humility? Does it express her artistic refusal to vainly construct a poetic monument to herself in a world defined by time's "fatal wrack," which (as the poet observes) crumbles "into th' dust" all "sumptuous monuments" (lines 225, 229)?

Taylor's meditations, seemingly so free-associative and nonsequential, are likewise open to questions concerning intention. Does Taylor consciously revise the patterns of such metaphysical poets as Herbert, or is he a pale, inept version of them? Possibly Taylor practices a "decorum of imperfection," a poetic mode that recognizes the depravity of art, the impropriety of celebrating human life, and the human inability to glorify God (Mignon). As we saw in "Meditation 1.8," beneath the surface chaos of a poetic voice that presents itself as benighted, malnourished, feverish, sick, and maladroit, there is a semicircle emblem that engenders hope by intimating a divine order potentially encompassing and redeeming the poet's temporal disorder. Taylor's concern with salvation affects his art in another manner: He vacillates between despair and presumption just as the soul-bird in "Meditation 1.8" is depicted in various postures of fall and ascent. The Puritan meditative poet usually tries neither to presume nor to despair but to await disclosure of divine will; hence the series of poem-suspending questions in the penultimate stanzas of "Meditation 1.8" and "Meditation 2.3," which both end with a hope for redemption rather than with an optimistic personal redress typical of, say, Herbert's poetry.

For Wheatley, as students should see by now, salvation is far more imminent, not only spiritually but politically, especially regarding abolition. For Freneau and Brackenridge, personal salvation lies in the utilization of natural and human resources, in the temporal and secular fulfillment of American millennial prospects, "richly stor'd with all / The luxuries of life" (line 787). *Rising Glory* includes religious tradition and imagery, such as the poets' wish for Isaiah's power of prophecy and their claim that the star of Bethlehem now shines on America. But in contrast to Wheatley's presentation of religious and historical matters as integral concerns, Freneau and Brackenridge's religious allusions are hollow reeds, mere stage properties, in an ebullient secular forecast. Students readily sense that *Rising Glory*, unlike Puritan meditative verse and Wheatley's poetry, emphasizes the surfaces of life, at least overtly. If the 1772 poem does not quite replicate the catalogs of earlier New World advertisements (Richard Rich's poem *Newes from Virginia*, for example), it delights in the material world as commodity. Even the pronunciation of the names of things is delightful, as if artfully fashioned words were physical objects rather than representations.

Representation

At this point I urge my class to delve beneath the surface representations and the design of *Rising Glory* to discover less evident features of the poem and the colonial enterprise it celebrates. If time permits, the sanguine vision of this poem can be instructively compared with the jaundiced satire of Ebenezer Cook(e)'s *The Sot-Weed Factor*. Or students can focus on the admission in *Rising Glory* that "the mysteries of future days" are unknowable, which remark may stimulate class scrutiny of the limitations in the author's awareness (line 594). My students, many of them Hispanic, notice the poem's chauvinism, including its anti-Spanish sentiment. Some notice that the iterated claim that "merciful" Britain did not, like "cruel Spain," shed "seas of Indian blood" is challenged when the poem elsewhere mentions "heroes" "from Canada / To

Georgia" who slew "Indian hosts" (lines 51–52, 259–60). I then ask whether the poem's silence about the future presence of Native Americans implicitly participates in the racial displacement and extermination overtly depicted in Villagrá's epic. Some hesitate to make that indictment, but others sense how cultural oversights and silence can also be powerful instruments of suppression.

Students may need more help detecting still other problems in these poems, such as how the derivativeness of *Rising Glory* undermines its authors' claims for a new American art or how the diffusion of its focus—it nervously flits from one thing to another as if fearful of looking too closely—fails to impart a substantial identity to the colonies. In this poem America seems more a reification of abundant energy than the momentous culmination of history. In short, the poem accidentally somewhat reflects the instability of the polymorphous society of late-eighteenth-century America. *Rising Glory* omits more than a future for Native Americans; it is also silent about slaves, who Wheatley knew were not "by freedom blest" (line 787). But is Wheatley's nuanced representation of herself as a religiously and spiritually refined person who politely raises Cain similarly compromised? I urge students to consider the potential cost of the poet's burying the resistant aesthetics of "Being Brought"—its possible appropriation of ministerial authority in suggesting unprecedented racial readings of Isaiah's prophesies—beneath an outward acquiescence to conventional religious and literary authorization. Even if Wheatley hoped to instill her revisionary message deep within the reader's mind, does her positioning of her resistance below the conventional surface merely reenact the slave's daily experience of oppression? Class responses tend to be sharply divided.

Some students argue that the Puritan meditative poets were reenacting a form of enslavement too, particularly through an early Calvinistic devaluation of human capability, the very capacity Freneau and Brackenridge later exalt. Although, as I said, my students prefer the optimism of *Rising Glory* to the self-deprecation of Calvinistic meditations, they tend to distrust as exaggeration Freneau and Brackenridge's representation of "America" and to trust as genuine the Puritans' representation of their humble submission to divine authority. When they do I ask them to differentiate between the preoccupation with the personal fulfillment that is prophesied in *Rising Glory* and the preoccupation with personal salvation featured in the Puritan meditations.

I also remind students that the meditators assumed personae in a culturally authorized sinner-saint drama, not only by envisaging redemption but also by addressing specific audiences (Hammond). Moreover, if Bradstreet and Taylor practiced a decorum of imperfection, then they composed and evaluated their verse in relation to a humanly constructed paradigm. Therefore they valued their art, even if only as an expression of their incapability, potentially blurring the boundary between humility and pride.

In, say, Bradstreet's 1666 poem on the burning of her house and in Taylor's 1683 poem on a sweeping flood, both of which seesaw between resentment toward and acceptance of divine will, my students encounter other indications that submission to divine authority might not have been easy for Puritans. Bradstreet interrupts the recollection of lost prized material possessions with "Adieu, Adieu; All's Vanity" (line 36), a safe, conventional ventriloquising of Ecclesiastes 1.14. I ask my students, since there is no personal poetry in this formulaic line, no detail, does Bradstreet's declaration inhabit the same emotion-laden, well-furnished house as the previous lines of the poem? Does the disruptiveness of this line signal her flight from a potentially rebellious sentiment, as if the house of her emotion-filled verse were also dangerously on fire? Here, as throughout my effort, I am content if students plumb such questions from various angles and discover diverse, even antithetical, grids of *represented* meanings.

Although my approach privileges depth over breadth of perception, it is designed to enlarge student appreciation of contextual implications, artistic techniques, subtextual subtleties, and finally conceptual limitations. This last goal—acknowledging the enigmatic elusiveness of certainty and hence viewing resolute determination skeptically—is personally important to me. To appreciate the persistence of mystery at the edge of human understanding is implicitly to urge a profound communal humility and tolerance.

Works Cited

Primary Works

Bradstreet, Anne. *The Works of Anne Bradstreet*. Ed. Jeannine Hensley. Cambridge: Harvard UP, 1967.

Cook(e), Ebenezer. *The Sot-Weed Factor*. 1708. *Colonial American Poetry*. Ed. Kenneth Silverman. New York: Hafner, 1968. 282–301.

Freneau, Philip, and Hugh Henry Brackenridge. *A Poem, on the Rising Glory of America*. 1772. *Colonial American Poetry*. Ed. Kenneth Silverman. New York: Hafner, 1968. 423–43.

Herbert, George. *The Works of George Herbert*. Ed. F. E. Hutchinson. Oxford: Clarendon, 1941.

Pain, Philip. *Daily Meditations*. 1668. Excerpted in *American Poetry of the Seventeenth Century*. Ed. Harrison T. Meserole. University Park: Pennsylvania State UP, 1985. 287–91.

Quarles, Francis. *The Complete Works of Francis Quarles*. Ed. A. B. Grosart. 3 vols. New York: AMS, 1967.

Rich, Richard. *Newes from Virginia*. 1610. *American Garland*. Ed. Charles A. Firth. Oxford: Clarendon, 1915. 9–16.

Taylor, Edward. *The Poems of Edward Taylor*. Ed. Donald E. Stanford. New Haven: Yale UP, 1960.

Villagrá, Gaspar Pérez de. *Historia de la Nueva México*. 1610. Excerpted in *The Heath Anthology of American Literature*. Ed. Paul Lauter. Vol. 1. Lexington: Heath, 1998. 163–72.

Wheatley, Phillis. *Phillis Wheatley and Her Writings*. Ed. William H. Robinson. New York: Garland, 1984.

Secondary Works

Gay, Peter. *The Age of Enlightenment*. New York: Time-Life, 1966.

Hammond, Jeffrey A. *Sinful Self, Saintly Self: The Puritan Experience of Poetry*. Athens: U of Georgia P, 1993.

Martz, Louis. *The Poetry of Meditation: A Study of English Literature in the Seventeenth Century*. New Haven: Yale UP, 1962.

Mignon, Charles W. "Edward Taylor's *Preparatory Meditations:* A Decorum of Imperfection." *PMLA* 83 (1968): 1423–28.

Scheick, William J. *Design in Puritan American Literature*. Lexington: UP of Kentucky, 1992.

Tillyard, E. M. W. *The Elizabethan World Picture*. London: Chatto, 1943.

White, Hayden. *Metahistory: The Historical Imagination in Nineteenth-Century Europe*. Baltimore: Johns Hopkins UP, 1973.

Portrait of the Artist as a Young Slave: Douglass's Frontispiece Engravings

Ed Folsom

When teaching Douglass's narrative, Folsom asks his students to "read" the 1845 frontispiece portrait and to consider how it functions as part of Douglass's text. He argues that engraved portraits were particularly well suited to opening slave narratives because of "their emphasis on the process of creating verisimilitude, [and] their habit of incorporating in the same image various stages of composition (from rough sketch to finished portrait) . . ." (p. 425). These attributes made them "more effective vehicles than photographs or paintings would have been in representing identity as an act of labor and artistry" (p. 425). Folsom compares Douglass's portrait with the 1855 engraving of Walt Whitman from the first edition of Leaves of Grass. *Throughout his career, Whitman "coordinated illustrations of himself with the song of himself" (p. 425). Also in 1855, Douglass published* My Bondage and My Freedom, *illustrated with a different engraving. Folsom concludes that Douglass's portraits work to illustrate the relationship between the author and the slave. This essay originally appeared in* Approaches to Teaching Narrative of the Life of Frederick Douglass *(1999), edited by James C. Hall.*

I most often teach *Narrative of the Life of Frederick Douglass, an American Slave, Written by Himself* in an advanced undergraduate course on the literature and culture of nineteenth-century America.

From *Approaches to Teaching* Narrative of the Life of Frederick Douglass, ed. James C. Hall (New York: MLA, 1999): 55–65.

After students have completed their reading of the *Narrative* and we have spent at least one class period talking about the historical and political issues surrounding Douglass's text, I begin the next class by projecting a slide of the 1845 frontispiece portrait (Fig. 1). I tell the students I'd like them to *read* this portrait, to view it not only as a key physical element of the *book* that appeared in 1845 but also as an important component of the *text*, an image that has meaning in relation to the patterns of verbal imagery in Douglass's narrative. How, I ask my students, does this visual representation of Douglass correspond to his verbal self-representation in the narrative proper? How, in fact, does it function as part of the narrative? The portrait, I remind them, would have been very much a part of the original readers' experience of the text—the first representation of Douglass that they would have encountered and one that they no doubt returned to as they read and thought about the book. I quote Douglass's own statements about the importance of visual art: "Man is the only picture making and picture appreciating animal in the world," he wrote, going on to observe that visual art spans our individual lifetimes ("for childhood delights in pictures") and our history (art rises "with the first dawnings of [. . .] civilization, lifting the thoughts and sentiments of men higher by every one of its triumphs") and thus must be "diligently cultivated" (qtd. in Wheat [iii]). Douglass, then, would have been keenly aware of the impact the frontispiece picture of himself would have on readers.

I show my class a few slides of other examples of contemporary authors' portraits—Lowell and Whittier and Emerson and Longfellow (I save Whitman for later)—all of them framing the head and shoulders only, all of them presenting the author in formal dress, as the exemplar of decorum. These are portraits of the artist as a privileged man. Then I show the class some of the painful J. T. Zealy daguerreotypes of slaves taken in 1850—naked or half-naked, stripped of their right to dignity even as their eyes register defiance, the very emblems of violated civilized decorum. I explain to my students that few contemporary visual representations exist of individual slaves and that these Zealy portraits were taken to serve as specimens to support the scientist Louis Agassiz's racist polygenesis theories.[1]

Coming back to Douglass's portrait, I ask my students what they see now and how what they see relates to what they've read, and then I stand back and let the responses come. Someone always mentions the clothes, how the dress and fashion seem too formal for a former slave and affiliate him too closely with the privileged white authors. If I'm lucky, someone else will respond that that's just what some white people in the mid-nineteenth century said about Douglass's manner of speaking and manner of writing—that it was too "white," too "learned" and refined to sound authentic. One abolitionist friend told Douglass he needed "a little of the plantation speech" in his writing to give it a realistic edge: "it is not best that you seem too learned" (qtd. in Foner, *Frederick*

Figure 1. Frontispiece engraving of Frederick Douglass for *Narrative of the Life of Frederick Douglass, an American Slave, Written by Himself.* Boston: Anti-slavery Office, 1845.

Douglass 59). And it was not only whites who felt this way: Douglass recalled that Sojourner Truth always considered it "her duty [. . .] to ridicule my efforts to speak and act like a person of cultivation" (qtd. in McFeely 97).

Questions follow: Could part of the impact of Douglass's portrait, then, be a shock of recognition for white readers, a sudden and surprising realization that an African American could assume the status and dress (and voice) of the privileged white author? Is the portrait a conservative gesture that tries to reassure a white readership by portraying Douglass as safe and familiar (a black man certifying white dominance by playing at being white), or is it a radically disorienting gesture that makes Douglass seem dangerously insurgent (a black man essentially altering the power hierarchy by claiming an identity previously reserved for whites)? Has the institution of white authorship usurped Douglass and co-opted his identity, or has Douglass, the black slave, invaded and undermined the all-white establishment of privileged authorship? Could the portrait have functioned for antebellum readers as a kind of optical illusion, at one moment comforting them with an image of assimilation, at the next challenging them with an image of inversion and invasion?

I try to raise questions that broaden the discussion into issues of cultural identity: What range of possibilities for identity formation do the visual representations we've looked at suggest for people living in mid-nineteenth-century America? Do the Zealy portraits of South Carolina slaves and the various portraits of America's successful white male authors in some way set the poles of social identity in America — from the powerless to the powerful, from those denied any education to those who enjoy the privileges of a Harvard education, from those whose portraits were made for "scientific" categorizing and who thus remain nameless or recalled only with a first name to those whose portraits were signs of their fame, familiar faces that accompanied their famous names? If these are the poles of identity in antebellum America, how far could a black man travel from the Zealy slave portraits toward the Boston Brahmin portraits? Does Douglass make the complete journey?

Some students will note that while at first glance Douglass's portrait looks more like those of the successful authors than like those of the slaves, his portrait actually unsettles the bipolar sense of separate and even opposite identities that one assumes when looking at the two sets of images. Douglass's portrait seems to enact an impossible melding of the slave portrait with the successful author portrait. His face and hair join him to the slave portraits, but his clothing and his manner and his firm and elegant signature — the sign of his self-authoring — tie him to the author portraits. It's as if Douglass was demonstrating the fluidity of self-fashioning, literally posing the possibility that one's race could no longer prevent an ascent to cultural power and influence.

I ask students to consider, too, the way this portrait fits into the developing notions of cultural celebrity. The 1840s were the period of America's first celebrity authors, the decade that marked the appearance of what Michael Newbury has called "the mixed feelings about celebrity and exposure in the cultural sphere that simultaneously gave prominent figures power over while leaving them vulnerable to" their new fans (182). Newbury discusses the ways that "celebrity-as-slave figurations" (162) appear at this time, as celebrities become not those who produce commodities but instead commodities themselves. Douglass's striking portrait makes him the first "slave-as-celebrity," and his fame made him identifiable on the street, an obviously dangerous result for an escaped slave. In the warped mirror world of slavery, even celebrity was distorted: America's first celebrity stalkers may have been slave catchers. Douglass's growing celebrity, in fact, led him to flee the country for England, where he purchased his freedom. But by becoming a freed man he entered a new kind of enslavement, an enslavement to a fetishized image of himself that the portrait helped create. That problematic developing dynamic of former-slave/current-celebrity suggests some promising approaches to reading Douglass's 1892 *Life and Times of Frederick Douglass*, where we see the author struggling with what fame has brought and made him.

At this point I invite my class to examine the portrait even more closely. I tell them the 1845 engraving was based on an oil portrait of Douglass completed in the early 1840s by an unidentified artist (Voss 22). The anonymous engraver managed to stiffen and strengthen the gentler face that appears in the painting, but the major change the engraver made was to empty out or half-erase the bottom half of the portrait. Instead of making an engraving that pretended to be a copy of the oil portrait, the engraver emphasized (rather than disguised) the artificial and constructed nature of his steelcut image. While the engraving renders Douglass's face in photographic detail, its intensity of realistic detail quickly fades as our eyes descend; verisimilitude evaporates and we're left with a rough sketch. The total effect of the portrait emerges, then, from an intriguing tension between a half-sketched quality that emphasizes the artificial, constructed nature of the image and a finished, highly detailed quality that approaches photographic realism. I ask students to think about the implications of this oddly bifurcated image.

I explain that the emphasis on process, on the artifice of constructing detailed identity out of initial bare sketches, is part of the tradition of portrait engraving. Most portrait engravings in the nineteenth century emphasize to some extent the artifice of the engraving by leaving some part of the image unfinished or barely sketched in. The Douglass engraving, however, exaggerates this convention of having a detailed portrait arise out of a rough sketch; from the shoulders down Douglass is represented only by a bare, primitive line drawing, while from the shoulders up he emerges suddenly into a fully realized presence. Peter Dorsey describes the engraving as representing "a disappearing body" (445), but the dynamics of this portrait (mirroring the narrative) actually make it a self in the process of *appearing*. Like all visual art for Douglass, this portrait is about "lifting the thoughts and sentiments of men higher" by "rising" from the primitive to the "cultivated" (qtd. in Wheat [iii]).

At this point, students can begin to draw the connections between visual text and written text and to see how such a portrait enhances the pattern of Douglass's narrative, where Douglass the successful author and orator emerges from a slave who is prevented from having any access to his own personal history, whose ability to learn and form an identity is stunted by slavery's restrictions on movement and education.

Douglass's book traces his rise from a generic "American slave" with an empty identity to "Frederick Douglass," a newly named and fully realized individual who has taken control of his life and is now the agent of his narrative instead of a faceless product of the slavery system, a servant in someone else's master narrative. His ability to gain access to writing and reading, to learn to "write by himself," brings his past under his own guidance and control, and his signature under his half-sketched, half-realized portrait is ink affirming a literacy that creates and verifies identity; for a significant part of Douglass's life, that signature was impossible, because the name and the ability to sign it were absent. His page was blank; his narrative is the story of learning to sign his name, at first literally and later figuratively, and to fill the blank pages with his identity. His book is his signature, and it ends with the act of signing his name, a full circle back to the frontispiece page. The visual emblem of himself imitates his emergence from blank, absent, or sketchy beginnings into a distinctive and distinguished selfhood.

If we look at the title page that appears opposite the portrait in the 1845 *Narrative*, we can see that the placement of the words underscores the significance of the portrait: The words "Frederick Douglass" appear in large type across from the singular, fully delineated face, while, in smaller type, "American Slave" appears opposite the part of the portrait that is not fleshed out. The words "Written by Himself" appear opposite Douglass's verifying signature. The pattern of words on the title page mirrors the portrait. Douglass's barely visible hands resting on the single line of his leg form the fade-out lower border of the portrait, but those hands are affirmed as active by the signature, which appears clearly just below and which is, along with the entire narrative, the visible work of those hands. A student once suggested that in reading "up" the portrait, we move from a nondescript outline of a body through more fully realized imitative clothing—the white man's uniform of success—and on up to the most detailed and individualized part of the portrait—the face and hair that distinguish this from all previous portraits of authors. The imitativeness (of dress, style, manner, voice) ultimately yields distinction, and the portrait emphasizes the irony of cultural identity that one must embrace imitation to emerge as an individual. As Dorsey notes in his fine study of Douglass's "self-fashioning process," any attempt at "acquiring mastery—whether of human material, or textual resources— presupposes mimesis." Thus, Dorsey says, "Douglass emphasizes that resistance to oppression requires a degree of imitation; to change their position, the oppressed must at some level copy the metaphors, the behaviors, and even the thought processes of the oppressor"—only through such imitation can the oppressed gain "access to political exchanges that can alter social structures" (436–37).

Engraved portraits, then, served as particularly appropriate openings to slave narratives, a genre centered on confirmations of identity and celebrations of free individuals emerging from an institution that strove to keep such individuality invisible, blank, and unformed. Engravings—with their emphasis on the process of creating verisimilitude, their habit of incorporating in the same image various stages of composition (from rough sketch to finished portrait)—were thus more effective vehicles than photographs or paintings would have been in representing identity as an act of labor and artistry.

After the class finishes discussing the 1845 image, I show students another slide, this one of Walt Whitman, the writer we will study after Douglass. All the effects we've talked about in portrait engravings are famously captured in Samuel Hollyer's 1855 frontispiece engraving of Whitman for the first edition of *Leaves of Grass* (Fig. 2). (I discuss this portrait in more detail and compare it with Douglass's 1845 portrait in Folsom 135–45. I offer a summary of that discussion here.)

All through his poetic career, Whitman carefully coordinated illustrations of himself with the song of himself: every portrait, he once noted, "has some relation to the text" (Traubel 2: 536); "the portrait," Whitman said, "in fact is involved as part of the poem" (Kennedy 248). For Whitman the inclusion of his portrait was not a decoration or badge but, rather, a challenge to the reader to work, to struggle for meaning, to respond. As with Douglass's portrait, it was as essential a part of the book as the written text was and demanded the same kind of involvement from the reader, who was required to actively interpret not only the words but the visual images as well.

This 1855 frontispiece portrait has become the most familiar of all the images of Whitman—hat on, shirt open, head cocked, arm akimbo. Early reviewers often commented on Whitman's oddly *un*cultivated self-presentation: "The damaged hat, the rough beard, the naked throat, the shirt exposed to the waist, are each and all presented to show that the man to whom these articles belong scorns the delicate art of civilization" (Leaves of Grass *Imprints* 42). The 1855 portrait makes its point in a number of ways: It is in sharp contrast to the expected iconography of authors' portraits, portraits that conventionally emphasized formality and the face instead of this rough informality where arms, legs, and body diminish the centrality of the head. Authors' portraits in the nineteenth century indicated that writing was a function of the intellect, a formal business conducted in book-lined rooms where ideas fed the head through words. Whitman, of course, was out to undermine this conception, to move poetry to the streets, to deformalize it, to yank it away from the authority of tradition, and to insist that poetry emerges from the heart, lungs, genitals, and hands, as much as from the head. He wanted the representative democratic poet to speak in his poems, and the absence of his own name from the title page allowed the representative portrait to speak to authorship. These were poems written by a representative democratic person living life in the world and experiencing life through the five senses—a self that found authority in experience, that doffed its hat to no one, that refused to follow the decorum of

Figure 2. Frontispiece engraving of Walt Whitman for *Leaves of Grass*. Brooklyn, 1855.

removing one's hat indoors or even in books. Just as the appearance of Douglass's name in large type and his signature in a firm hand was crucial for the identity formation Douglass needed to represent, so is the absence of these nominal signs crucial for Whitman's quite different needs. As a white man speaking for the culture as a whole, Whitman could luxuriate in the absorption of his individual self into the communal identity of "America."

The engraved portrait, in one sense, works very much like Douglass's 1845 portrait. While Hollyer's engraving renders Whitman's face and upper torso in photographic detail, the intensity of its realistic detail fades toward the bottom of the image; Whitman's legs are rendered with less and less detail until they diminish to simple sketch lines, then fade into the blankness of the paper itself. The image advertises its constructedness. As with Douglass's portrait, Whitman's emerges from an intriguing tension between a rough, half-sketched quality that emphasizes the artificiality of the image and a finished, highly detailed quality that imitates the verisimilitude of the original daguerreotype on which it is based. It is as if Hollyer (and Whitman) want to underscore the process, the labor involved in making ink turn into identity, in making lines turn into humanity, in making a book turn into a man.

Whitman was familiar with Douglass's work, and the poems of the 1855 *Leaves* were in some ways based on what Whitman learned from slave narratives like Douglass's. Whitman's 1855 poems in fact incorporate a slave narrative, from the "runaway slave [who] came to my house and stopped outside" and "staid with me a week, before he was recuperated and passed north, / I had him sit next me at the table" (36) to the moments when Whitman speaks as the slave: "I am the hounded slave . . . . I wince at the bite of the dogs" (65) and "I hate him that oppresses me, / [. . .] How he informs against my brother and sister and takes pay for their blood, / How he laughs when I look down the bend after the steamboat that carries away my woman" (*Complete Poetry* 113). Whitman appropriated aspects of slave narratives to make concrete the expression of desire for freedom and equality in his poetry. Like a slave narrative, *Leaves* was the record of a human being seeking a new name, an unfettered identity, an open road that would lead away from all forms of enslavement—whether social conventions, literary traditions, or actual institutions of slavery.

Fittingly, Whitman's frontispiece portrait echoes certain aspects of Douglass's even as it differs from Douglass's in other ways: For Douglass, the escape was from work clothes to formal clothing, a change that signaled success and the acquisition of education and manners; for Whitman, the escape was in the opposite direction. Whitman, the white man, seeking democratic expression, could profitably fashion himself *down*, could take on the garb of the worker and seek to imaginatively identify with the slave's experience; Douglass, the black man, seeking cultural authority, had to fashion himself *up*, discovering identity in an escape from slavery. The same social conventions that marked an achievement of identity for Douglass threatened identity for Whitman. An African American posing as a distinguished writer was every bit as singular in the culture of mid-nineteenth-century America as a white poet posing as a day laborer. Just as Douglass's portrait undermined the generally expected image of a slave, Whitman's portrait undermined the expectations that his readers would have brought to an engraving of an author.

The same year that Whitman's *Leaves of Grass* appeared, Douglass published *My Bondage and My Freedom* and included a new frontispiece portrait, by J. C. Battre (Fig. 3). At the end of our class discussion about *Narrative*, I show my students a slide of this engraving. Like Whitman's portrait, Douglass's 1855 engraving was based on a daguerreotype, and an intense photographic realism is apparent in this image. True to the engraving tradition, however, the lower part of the

Figure 3. Frontispiece engraving of Frederick Douglass for *My Bondage and My Freedom*. New York: Miller, Orton, and Mulligan, 1855.

portrait fades into simple lines, though the rough-to-finished effect is much more subtle than in the 1845 frontispiece. Here Douglass's clothes—more elegant and formal than those in the earlier engraving—are emphasized even more and given a finish that the clothing in the 1845 image lacked. Also emphasized is Douglass's rigid bearing: It is not a formal rigidity so much as stiff discomfort, as if the clothes are forcing a manner on a body that resists it. As in the 1845 image, Douglass's hands are muted, faded, but unlike the earlier portrait, here they are fisted and tensed. Douglass's narration of his life moves from his use of his fists to enforce his freedom and "rekindle in [his] breast the smouldering embers of liberty" (246) to his discovery of how to use words as his weapons of freedom. In *My Bondage and My Freedom*, Douglass apologizes for the roughness of his physical fight with Covey and the roughness of his writing about the fight — "undignified as it was, and as I fear my narration of it is" (246) — but at the same time he expands his description of the encounter. He is both beyond that roughness and essentially formed by it, and his portrait captures this quality precisely. The faded but fisted hands are subdued but still visible and are vital parts of Douglass's newer, more refined identity: The fully realized face, intelligent and serious and black, unites the clothes and the fists and gives coherence to the author and the slave. Peter Dorsey observes:

> The title of *My Bondage and My Freedom* [. . .] contains the poles of a metaphorical equation: a self inevitably bound by the figures he and others used but simultaneously liberated from those chains, not just by the realization that he was (and is) always more than the metaphors attached to him but by his own mastery of the possibilities of self-figuration. (447)

So, too, Douglass's title serves as a fitting caption for his frontispiece image. His pose and his costume represent both his bondage and his freedom, the brute physicality of his slave past and the straitened refinement of his celebrity present. In his bondage Douglass found freedom, and in his freedom he finds other kinds of bondage. His frontispiece portraits, read as textual images, represent these tensions and ambiguities and serve as visual analogues of Douglass's narratives. By 1855, Douglass had become, as William L. Andrews says, "an accomplished man of letters, a sophisticated journalist as well as orator" (*To Tell* 218), but this accomplishment and erudition rose from and remained attached to a life that began in denial of accomplishment and learning. Douglass's portraits manifest these tensions of origin and result, of what Dorsey calls "becoming the other" (435). When a reporter for the *Herald of Freedom* in 1844 tried to describe Douglass's "impressive speech," his analysis breaks at the seams of these very tensions:

> It was not what you could describe as oratory or eloquence. It was sterner, darker, deeper than these. It was a storm of insurrection. [. . .] He stalked to and fro on the platform, roused up like the Numidian lion. [. . .] There was great oratory in his speech. [. . .] He was not up as a speaker, performing. He was an insurgent slave, taking hold on the right of speech, and charging on his tyrants the bondage of his race. [. . .] He is a surprising lecturer. I would not praise him, or describe him; but he is a colored man, a slave, of the race who can't take care of themselves — our inferiors, and therefore to be kept in slavery. [. . .] He is one of the most impressive and majestic speakers I have ever heard. [. . .] I have never seen a man leave the platform, or close a speech, with more real dignity, and eloquent majesty. (qtd. in Foner, *Frederick Douglass* 58)

Here once again is Douglass as a maddening, shifting optical illusion —
not an orator, a great orator; not eloquent, majestically eloquent; a wild
animal, a dignified man; an ignorant slave, an accomplished speaker.
Douglass's emergence into eminence and accomplishment and fame always carried with it the ragged and rugged delineations of his past. His
portraits are always about the relationship of the author to (and as) the
young slave.

Note

1. Instructors can make slides of the Douglass portraits from public-domain
copies of the 1845 *Narrative* and the 1855 *My Bondage and My Freedom*,
available in the special collections departments of many public and university libraries. (The illustrations for this essay are from the University of
Iowa Special Collections.) The portraits are reproduced in several modern
editions of Douglass's work and are also available in Dorsey and in Voss.
The Zealy daguerreotypes are in the Peabody Museum at Harvard University, and several are reproduced and discussed by Trachtenberg (52–60), in
Reichlin, and in Wallis.

Works Cited

Andrews, William L. *To Tell a Free Story: The First Century of Afro-American
Autobiography, 1760–1865.* Urbana: U of Illinois P, 1986.
Dorsey, Peter A. "Becoming the Other: The Mimesis of Metaphor in Douglass's
My Bondage and My Freedom." *PMLA* 111 (1996): 435–50.
Douglass, Frederick. *My Bondage and My Freedom*. New York, 1855.
Folsom, Ed. "Appearing in Print: Illustrations of the Self in *Leaves of Grass*."
The Cambridge Companion to Walt Whitman. Ed. Ezra Greenspan. Cam-
bridge: Cambridge UP, 1995. 135–65.
Foner, Philip S. *Frederick Douglass.* New York: Citadel, 1969.
Kennedy, William Sloane. *The Fight of a Book for the World.* West Yarmouth:
Stonecroft, 1926.
Leaves of Grass Imprints. Boston, 1860.
McFeely, William S. *Frederick Douglass.* New York: Norton, 1991.
Newbury, Michael. "Eaten Alive: Slavery and Celebrity in Antebellum Amer-
ica." *ELH* 61 (1994): 159–87.
Traubel, Horace. *With Walt Whitman in Camden.* Vols. 1–3. 1906–14. New
York: Rowman, 1961.
Voss, Frederick S. *Majestic in His Wrath: A Pictorial Life of Frederick Douglass.*
Washington: Smithsonian, 1995.
Wheat, Ellen Harkins, ed. *Jacob Lawrence: The "Frederick Douglass" and
"Harriet Tubman" Series of 1938–1940.* Seattle: U of Washington P, 1991.
Whitman, Walt. *Complete Poetry and Collected Prose.* New York: Lib. of Amer.,
1982.

Enabling Undergraduates to Understand Advanced Humanities Research: Teaching with the *Dickinson Electronic Archives*

Martha Nell Smith

Smith encourages instructors to use technology in the classroom through her practical, hands-on guide to using the Dickinson Electronic Archives. *She considers Dickinson an ideal subject for teaching students to think about how a poem comes to be because Dickinson left poems unfinished for conventional publication and poems in various versions. As an example, she points to "Safe in their Alabaster Chambers"—is it a two-stanza poem with four different second stanzas, a three-stanza poem, or five one-stanza poems? The* Dickinson Electronic Archives *provides digital replicas of documents surrounding the poem's publication as well as drafts of the poem. This online resource also allows students to consider how editorial decisions are made as different editors viewing the same material come to different conclusions. The essay, which appeared in* Teaching Literature and Language Online *(2009), edited by Ian Lancashire, provides exciting ideas for teaching and scholarly publishing.*

Today, I cannot imagine offering a successful course—whether a small graduate seminar or a large lecture course—bereft of thoughtful application of technology. The possibilities for use are various: peer-to-peer information exchange through which students can develop scholarly projects; digital repositories of literature, art, history, and music that can profoundly augment lectures and seminar discussions; blogs enabling daily critical responses to works under study; wikis enabling a class to collaborate on critical responses in ways unimagined even after the creation of the World Wide Web in the early 1990s. Though I am a strong advocate of using these tools for both research and teaching, I am not a technological expert. In other words, though I founded and directed the Maryland Institute for Technology in the Humanities (MITH; www.mith2.umd.edu) and am founder and executive editor of the *Dickinson Electronic Archives* (www.emilydickinson.org), I do not build software, I am not an advanced specialist in text encoding, and, contrary to what some technophiles in our profession have argued, I do not think one needs to be either of those things to use technology, and use it well, in teaching and research. My hope is that sharing some stories about my experiences will prove valuable for others, especially those who will neither darken the door of an institute for technology in the humanities nor build an online archive.

From *Teaching Literature and Language Online*, ed. Ian Lancashire (New York, MLA, 2009): 278–89.

If you now holding this book in hand fit the above criteria, please do not put this wonderful machine, the primary means for knowledge transmission for the last several hundred years, down. You too can use new technologies to profound effect in the classroom. In fact, the fanciest computational software can do nothing, nothing interesting at all, unless directed and engaged by the most important software of all — that proffered by the human touch, by you. Teachers have been thoughtfully applying technologies in their instruction praxes long before the invention of the Internet, the computer, the typewriter, the pencil, even before AD and BC marked the accounting of time. Therefore, though some of my colleagues have said that there is no more important development for humanities knowledge production than that of digital studies, I respectfully disagree. Our knowledge building would be important whether we had digital tools or not. Smart classrooms, immense digital archives, speedier-than-the-blink-of-an-eye communications, and all the other amazing tools at our disposal are not interesting in and of themselves, and they cannot produce knowledge by themselves; it is what we make of them that matters.

In this instance of storytelling, I extend points made elsewhere describing and analyzing how using digital resources in my research and teaching has changed the way I work (see Smith, "Computing," "Democratizing"). At this point, reflecting on the humanities and their contribution to society and culture at large is important. The humanities are vital to the educational system Thomas Jefferson saw as necessary for achieving democracy. In fact, Americans' inalienable right to the pursuit of happiness depends on knowledge. For Jefferson, the two primary facets of education, and of learning to make knowledge, were subject matter, or the knowledge required to obtain a level of happiness, and subject method, or the processes by which knowledge is made.

Even while working as a teaching assistant, I integrated the research of my dissertation into my courses, but my methods have changed dramatically over the years. For more than a decade, I have shared my research through the *Dickinson Electronic Archives* projects, where I have been able to show rather than merely describe the signs Emily Dickinson inscribed in her manuscripts, signs that open up her exquisite poetry to unanticipated textual conditions. By 2006, I had been working online for more than a decade and a half, first through the e-mail connections that scholars on the science side of the University of Maryland had taught me about and then through the World Wide Web, which has become increasingly flexible as its use has expanded from a forum for research exchange and knowledge transfer for physicists and other scientists to knowledge exchange at all levels (from prekindergarten to institutes for advanced study), not to mention its use as a place for transactions of news, entertainment, politics, finances, families, enemies, and friends. Through these new tools, access to views I had only had in the reading rooms and special collections of exclusive academic libraries has been made possible. Though mediated through digitization, the access to those views by any student or teacher or reader with a Web browser is a very big deal. The possibility of making those views available to anyone interested in studying the writings of Dickinson (rather than relying on detailed linguistic reporting of them) was the first technological advance that profoundly influenced my teaching.

Years before I even thought of using a computer, much less of using one in the classroom as a teacher of poetry, I asked my students, "How did the poems, or rather texts, you see on the book leaf page come into being? Who made those texts?" The eager students, first stunned by the question itself, would quizzically answer, "Emily Dickinson" (or whichever poet we were reading). I pointed to the copyright and permissions page and gave a brief overview of the editors that had worked to move the handwritten works of Dickinson to the printed page. Students found this process interesting but usually dismissed it as my especial research concern rather than anything of real use or significance to them and their education. For them, there was no educational relevance in learning how and why particular books or versions of books come into being and others do not (they tended to make assumptions about a kind of magical meritocracy of authorial talent that always prevailed) or in learning how texts travel from writers' manuscript pages to the printed pages of anthologies and poetry collections.

The case of Dickinson provides a perfect opportunity for teaching students to look beyond the surface of any bibliographic page. Though she prepared at least forty manuscript volumes of her poems, Dickinson did not prepare volumes for print. She did not, therefore, see her poems through the usual stages of submission to publisher, acceptance, responses to readers' reports, final manuscript preparation, proofreading for final publication, and so forth. She left thousands of manuscripts behind for others to usher into print. Dickinson left poems in compositional stages not finished for conventional publication and in versions featuring variant words without any marked as clearly her preference. She sent others in apparently finished forms to correspondents but chose to send different versions of those finalized poems to different audiences or to record a different version in her manuscript books. Her work offers telling examples of poems in progress or of poems in conditions that appear markedly different from what readers are accustomed to seeing on the pages of an anthology or a book of printed poetry. When I started the *Dickinson Electronic Archives*, I was well aware of these facts (see Smith, *Rowing*). Since the dynamic, multimedia space of the online resource offered many more opportunities than the few halftones my publisher allowed to show rather than primarily tell and since it also made possible the kind of interactive editing I had imagined in *Rowing in Eden*, developing its possibilities was clearly the next step in both my research and teaching. In the mid-1990s, I confronted another challenge—many humanities colleagues were very suspicious of the World Wide Web and were not persuaded by the passionate arguments of pioneers such as Jerome McGann. Surprisingly, many students, even those comfortable with online gaming and other activities, were equally skeptical.

To show how the new online resources might be used, I decided to design digital samplers, or online articles, showing what can be made visible with digital tools that is not available in print. I decided to use the very familiar about Dickinson to coax readers to venture into unknown (online) territory and chose to focus on popular misconceptions about America's most well known poet. Even those only casually acquainted with Dickinson usually think they know certain facts about her: that she worked in solitude; that she tended to be morbid (and so was not particularly funny); and that she wrote little poems that, situated on the page, were surrounded by far more white space than type. These three supposed facts dictated the shape of the samplers or digital articles: "Emily Dickinson Writing a Poem," the oldest section of the *Dickinson Electronic Archives*, shows the poet at work, responding to the criticisms of her dear friend and confidante Susan Dickinson, as she writes her famous poem "Safe in their Alabaster Chambers," a poem she arguably never finished. "Dickinson, Cartoonist" shows that the poet long rumored to be morbid was in fact quite witty, even silly at times, and produced drawings and cutouts that bordered on the slapstick. "The Letter-Poem, a Dickinson Genre" shows that the poet's writings were not what most of her readers are accustomed to think of them as — pristine, clearly numbered, discrete units, easily identifiable as lyric poems. Instead, they are much more difficult to identify than her variorum and reader's editions leave one to believe.

Using "Emily Dickinson Writing a Poem," I was able to demonstrate that the identity of "Safe in their Alabaster Chambers" — any theory about its being, what the text is generically — is debatable. The poem, much circulated since the volumes of poetry were printed in the 1890s and printed during Dickinson's lifetime in the local *Springfield Republican*, is not fixed in its being. The versions that readers have encountered of the poem are not so clearly defined as those many publications of and about the poem would lead them to believe. Questions I had asked before were profoundly rejuvenated when posed in an environment of digital surrogates. How isolated was Dickinson in her writing practices, really? Is the poem under consideration by Emily and her friend Susan a two-stanza poem with four different second stanzas, as their writings and the contemporaneous printing that Dickinson saw suggest? Or is it a three-stanza poem, as rendered in its 1890 posthumous printing? Or is it five one-stanza poems? "Safe in their Alabaster Chambers" is one of four poems that Dickinson enclosed when she initiated a correspondence with the famous editor Thomas Higginson. Why might she have chosen a particular version in response to his *Atlantic Monthly* lead article "Letter to a Young Contributor"? One can see that those questions, even flattened out on the page, are important. But if you leave the page you hold now in hand and go to the online exhibition or sampler in "Emily Dickinson Writing a Poem," you will find that the questions themselves are linked to digital surrogates of the documents that inspire them, including Higginson's article. The textual conditions and situations of these writings and questions online differ from those presented in the pages of a book.

Considering the identity of the poem by using this online exhibition of the documents, readers are able to enlarge, for closer inspection, images of the marks Dickinson and others made, examine the printing of the poem in the *Springfield Republican*, and compare the handwriting in various versions to ponder for themselves whether the drafts Dickinson made are final or provisional and are properly dated. The online resource thus provides interaction, navigation, and simulation not possible in the pages of a book. Simulation of an editor at work is especially possible in the "Interactive Explorations" section of "Emily Dickinson Writing a Poem." There, through the *Virtual Lightbox*, even beginning scholars (at the undergraduate and even the secondary or elementary levels) can simulate the work of advanced researchers to determine the relation of texts to one another poetically, chronologically, and ontologically. The *Virtual Lightbox* enables any reader to arrange and rearrange the printing Dickinson saw during her lifetime, as well as all the known manuscripts related to "Safe in their Alabaster Chambers," and thereby evaluate the meanings of individual documents and their relations to one another and to one of Dickinson's most popular and written-about poems (see also Smith and Vetter). Through the many exercises made possible by this dynamic, flexible, manipulable display of primary documents, students since the mid-1990s, working at all levels of critical inquiry, have come to understand some of the ways in which poems (and other literary artifacts) are made.

Using "The Letter-Poem, a Dickinson Genre," particularly "Morning / might come / by Accident," augments the function of literary objects as social products—made by writers, editors, compositors, copyeditors, and proofreaders working collaboratively—by showing how editors looking at the same material artifact can draw different conclusions about what they see on the manuscript page and also how predetermined notions about genre influence conclusions drawn about what is seen on the page. Editing the document that lies in the Dickinson Collection in the Houghton Library, at Harvard, to increase its general circulation in print, scholars have drawn very different conclusions about what they are seeing on these manuscript pages: Martha Dickinson Bianchi did not flatly state whether this "penciled message" is a poem or a letter but laid it out as a one-stanza poem when she quoted it in 1924 (87). Thomas H. Johnson edited it as a letter but laid all the lines including and following "Show me Eternity" as if at least part of the document was a poem (Johnson and Ward 830). Forty years after Johnson, R. W. Franklin took the lines Johnson had laid out as a poem and placed them, removed from the other lines on the physical document, in his edition of the poems (1452). Since all lines of the document are choreographed similarly, my coeditor Ellen Louise Hart and I edited the entire work as poetic and used Susan Dickinson's nomenclature "letter-poem" to describe its type (256–57). Understanding what these editors were seeing that made them draw such different conclusions would not have been possible without photographic representation of the original document, and online distribution has made this access much more widely available than would a very expensive facsimile edition in book form housed in a few libraries.

The examples recounted make clear how new media can enhance, enrich, and extend subject matter by increasing access. Even more powerful, however, is access to the other facet that Jefferson identified as a key to education, subject method. When humanists began working to produce digital scholarly editions, there were clear models for producing scholarly editions of integrity but no clear models for producing them for or with new media. Using digital media, the scholarly editions can be made perpetually updatable in ways that a book cannot. What were the implications when scholars imported into electronic editions those criteria and standards that had been established for bibliographic editions? Understanding bibliographic editions requires understanding the type of technology that the book is, inhabits, or deploys. Just before the World Wide Web became part of our daily lives, Donna Haraway observed:

> Technologies and scientific discourses can be partially understood as formalizations, i.e., as frozen moments, of the fluid social interactions constituting them, but they should also be viewed as instruments for enforcing meanings. (164)

Books record frozen social relations, points in time of critical understandings, including those regarding editorial matters.

Ron Rosenbaum's book, *The Shakespeare Wars*, recounts how scholars invest deeply in particular versions of the bard's plays, labeling some authentic and others not. A similar state of affairs exists in Dickinson studies, which some, such as Betsy Erkkila, are calling the Dickinson wars. (Elsewhere I have critiqued at length why "war" is such a wildly inappropriate term for describing critical dissensus [Smith, "Public, Private Spheres"]). Some critics are so deeply entrenched in their positions of what and how texts count as literary that they have argued that all matters about how Shakespeare and Dickinson and other writers' manuscripts are understood must be settled. Such a position claims that the social relations in and around any text must be frozen to be understood, at least to determine textual identity. Scholarly methods conceived from this perspective necessarily aim to define the authentic to produce the definitive and to do so must unnecessarily limit the authoritative. Dickinson herself wrote that "Publication—is the Auction" (Franklin 742), and many have pointed out that these critical debates, entangled as they are in the frozen social relations of bibliographic technologies, are in part created by academic capitalism that for centuries has been circulating its valuables in books. Another editorial interpretation of writings in which powerful institutions (in these instances Oxford and Harvard) have produced authoritative editions may seem burdensome, distracting, or frightening. Such reactions are not surprising when one has been accustomed to compare critical judgments in the exchange structures created by books and their production technologies. The report of judgments in print cannot be changed or substantively augmented without costly (in time, energy, money) corrected reprintings or the equivalent. From this standpoint, it is no wonder that some scholars are tempted to liken well-informed and principled editorial dissensus to war, where there must be winners and losers and some standard must prevail. In these intellectual horizons, some scholars declare that electronic editions place too much burden on the reader, who might be distracted from the poetic by paying excess attention to the trivial.

Yet recent literary criticism reveals that assumption to be a product of critical preference for the frozen social relations of the definitive edition. The access to more views of Dickinson's writings created first by a major facsimile printing in 1981 and then expanded by the *Dickinson Electronic Archives* in the 1990s appears to have liberated many readers, creating new insights, different textual pleasures, and critiques that would not have been possible without the additional views provided by these new delivery mechanisms (which can be perpetually expanded and improved). Recently, questions unthinkable when access to Dickinson's manuscripts was limited have been eloquently and generatively posed by Virginia Jackson: "Can a text not intended as a lyric become one? Can a text once read as a lyric be unread? If so—then what is—or what was—a lyric?" (6). In other words, what is and what is not an Emily Dickinson poem? Or, what kinds of poetry was Dickinson really writing? Social relations are key to Jackson's critical perspective, since she situates her speculations about Dickinson in the social relations of literary history and collaborates with new media productions. Haraway's observations about the social relations between tools and knowledge are useful to keep in mind. Technologies are formalizations or frozen social relations, but in their use, relations can be unfrozen, information unbound, and new tools developed:

> The boundary is permeable between tool and myth, instrument and concept, historical systems of social relations and historical anatomies of possible bodies, including objects of knowledge. Indeed, myth and tool mutually constitute each other. (164)

Knowledge and the tools we use to access, talk about, reflect on, distribute, and build it mutually constitute each other.

Social relations result in a book such as *The Poems of Emily Dickinson*, which is distinct from *The Letters of Emily Dickinson*. Their mutual existence demonstrates that scholars are already working collaboratively and consent to be bound by bibliographic codes. The social nature of texts has been a key concern for theorists for several decades, and, before online research archives and teaching instruments, students have understood textual sociologies to varying degrees. Yet many in literary studies have understood the sociologies of texts to be an area of critical inquiry reserved for specialists. I have found, however, that using this online resource has deepened and expanded the various classroom inquiries about texts and their ontologies so that students understand the questions previously reserved for specialists and go right to the heart of knowledge production. Without online resources, I have not been able to take students at all different levels of education this far.

The technology of self-consciousness required by viewing images of primary texts on a screen produces a healthy self-consciousness about what Jay David Bolter and Richard Grusin describe as "remediation" and what Bruno Latour and Steve Woolgar describe as "black-boxing," which occurs when one "renders items of knowledge distinct from the circumstances of their creation" (259n). In black-boxing, critical opinion becomes fact; more often than not, amnesia sets in after that factual instantiation, and, having been effectively black-boxed, fact becomes truth. The linguistic reporting on the manuscript of "Morning / might come" in the printings that made it a one-stanza poem, a letter, a letter with a poem, and a letter-poem constitutes a sort of black-boxing. Print editions cannot help black-boxing their decision-making processes. Those digital surrogates of manuscripts are obviously remediated—as printed volumes of the original writings remediate and refashion them into print objects, so electronic presentations remediate and refashion both the originals and their print translations.

As I tell my students, ways in which the remediations of new technologies unsettle our sureties about both the scholarly matters and the scholarly methods of education can be effectively exploited. But doing so requires successful application of the most important software of all—human inquiry. As I talked about plans for the *Dickinson Electronic Archives* with my colleagues and students, I concluded that two paths were before me: adopt the old paradigm and work for years developing a digital scholarly edition behind the curtain, where it would be unavailable to audiences until it was perfect. The dynamic edition would be developed following the protocols by which books are made. The alternative was to develop the digital scholarly edition publicly, sharing the production process with audiences and using that transparency as part of the critical review process. That second method, the one I used, is a new paradigm in the humanities, one that builds on the guidelines for scholarly editing established by the MLA's Committee on Scholarly Editions. Using this paradigm can reveal the processes of knowledge work to students and prompt them to ask, "How do our items of knowledge come into being, who made them, and for what purposes?"

The paradigm shift from print to digital edition will change the old truisms of scholarly publishing, the ones entangled in and by the social relations of the book:

> An author's work is best when presented in a single, most authoritative scholarly edition.
> Scholarly editions subsequent to such an edition are corrections and supplant what has come before.
> Editors working on a single edition probably agree with one another. In any disagreement, one party is right and all others are wrong, or at least one party is "better than" all others.
> Readers and users of such editions need not be bothered with the details of judgment that went into determining what to exclude and what to include, in what order.

As far as editorial work goes, such assumptions lead to critical games of "gotcha" among editors and critics and suppress the creation and validity of different versions, which may allow that both, neither, or either might all be true. Neither faultfinding as an end in itself nor hiding the processes that determined final products is healthy for knowledge production and critical understanding.

Moving beyond the idea that scholarly conclusions can only be authentic, authoritative, and reliable when determined by a single expert or group makes it possible to bring in keen insights from people with different levels of expertise, such as the middle school teachers and students who, inspired by Dickinson's reworkings of "Safe in their Alabaster Chambers" that they studied in the *Dickinson Electronic Archives*, wrote poems of their own that extended a metaphor, just as Dickinson did in "'Hope' is the thing with feathers" and contributed them to the *Contemporary Youth's Companion* site ("Debbie").

What new methods of editing and understanding texts might, with diligent application of human software, be created in a dynamic electronic environment? Or, what lessons from and for the classroom have been described here?

> An author's work does not need to be normalized; diverging views of its identity should not be excised.
> Multiple authorities can be included for scholars and students of all levels to process and analyze instead of a single authoritarian view dictating what is seen and known.

> Scholarly editions produced over time are not so much corrections as they are genealogical markers of what audiences could see and understand in different intellectual eras.
>
> Editors working on a single edition need not agree with one another. Each can report what he or she sees, and audiences benefit from multiple viewpoints and levels of expertise, from critical dissensus.
>
> Users of such editions can benefit from exposure to the details of judgment that went into determining what was worthwhile to include and can contribute to the decision-making process.

Using new media to share research findings among scholars and in the classroom enables distribution of humanities research in more interactive, rigorous, and accountable ways than traditional training leads one to think possible. It not only enables students to understand advanced humanities research but often turns them into researchers, even as the teachers and primary researchers become students. A digital environment opens up to beginners those research territories hitherto reserved for the most advanced researchers and makes use of intellectual and social networks.

Works Cited

Bianchi, Martha Dickinson. *Life and Letters of Emily Dickinson.* Boston: Houghton, 1924. Print.

Bolter, Jay David, and Richard Grusin. *Remediation: Understanding New Media.* Cambridge: MIT P, 2000. Print.

"Debbie A. Smith's Seventh Grade Class." *Contemporary Youth's Companion.* Maintained by Lara Vetter, Jarom McDonald, and Tanya Clement. Dickinson Electronic Archives, 10 Mar. 2008. Web. 6 Jan. 2009.

"Dickinson, Cartoonist." Ed. Martha Nell Smith. Maintained by Lara Vetter, Jarom McDonald, and Tanya Clement. *Dickinson Electronic Archives.* Dickinson Electronic Archives, 1999. Web. 6 Oct. 2006.

"Emily Dickinson Writing a Poem." Ed. Martha Nell Smith. Maintained by Lara Vetter, Jarom McDonald, and Tanya Clement. *Dickinson Electronic Archives.* Dickinson Electronic Archives, 1999. Web. 6 Oct. 2006.

Erkkila, Betsy. "Dickinson and the Art of Politics." *A Historical Guide to Emily Dickinson.* Ed. Vivian Pollak. Oxford: Oxford UP, 2004. 133–74. Print.

Franklin, R. W., ed. *The Poems of Emily Dickinson: Variorum Edition.* Cambridge: Belknap-Harvard UP, 1998. Print.

Haraway, Donna. "A Cyborg Manifesto: Science, Technology, and Socialist-Feminism in the Late Twentieth Century." *Simians, Cyborgs, and Women: The Reinvention of Nature.* New York: Routledge, 1991. 149–81. Print.

Hart, Ellen Louise, and Martha Nell Smith, eds. *Open Me Carefully: Emily Dickinson's Intimate Letters to Susan Huntington Dickinson.* Ashfield: Paris P, 1998. Print.

Jackson, Virginia. *Dickinson's Misery: A Theory of Lyric Reading.* Princeton: Princeton UP, 2005. Print.

Johnson, Thomas H., and Theodora Ward, eds. *The Letters of Emily Dickinson.* Cambridge: Belknap-Harvard UP, 1958. Print.

Latour, Bruno, and Steve Woolgar. *Laboratory Life: The Construction of Scientific Facts.* 2nd ed. Princeton: Princeton UP, 1986. Print.

"The Letter-Poem, a Dickinson Genre." Ed. Martha Nell Smith. Maintained by Lara Vetter, Jarom McDonald, and Tanya Clement. *Dickinson Electronic Archives.* Dickinson Electronic Archives, 1999. Web. 6 Oct. 2006.

Rosenbaum, Ron. *The Shakespeare Wars: Clashing Scholars, Public Fiascoes, Palace Coups.* New York: Random, 2006. Print.

Smith, Martha Nell. "Computing: What's American Literary Study Got to Do with IT?" *American Literature* 74.4 (2002): 833–57. Print.

———. "Democratizing Knowledge." *Humanities: The Magazine of the National Endowment for the Humanities* Sept.–Oct. 2005: 12–15. Web. 15 Oct. 2006.

———. "Public, Private Spheres: What Reading Emily Dickinson's Mail Taught Me about Civil Wars." *Companion to Emily Dickinson.* Ed. Smith and Mary Loeffelholz. Malden: Blackwell, 2008. 58–78. Print.

———. *Rowing in Eden: Rereading Emily Dickinson.* Austin: U of Texas P, 1992. Print.

Smith, Martha Nell, and Lara Vetter, eds. *Emily Dickinson's Correspondences: A Born-Digital Inquiry.* U of Virginia P, 2008. Web. 21 July 2009.

From Gilded Garden to Golden Anniversary: Teaching Hurston's "The Gilded Six-Bits"

Margaret D. Bauer

Bauer presents an approach to teaching Zora Neale Hurston's "The Gilded Six-Bits" as a revision of the Adam and Eve story with Adam/Joe being tempted first. After pointing out the paradise-like setting featuring a couple patterned after Adam and Eve, she introduces the concept of the fortunate fall: humans are better off due to Adam and Eve's expulsion from Eden. Bauer then establishes Joe's temptation by Slemmons/Satan by drawing students' attention to his admiration for Slemmons's appearance and worldliness. Bauer also provides suggestions for reading the story alongside Nathaniel Hawthorne's "Young Goodman Brown," which shows "the Puritan perception of the New World as a new Eden" (p. 446). The essay originally appeared in John Lowe's Approaches to Teaching Hurston's *Their Eyes Were Watching God and Other Works (2009).*

"The Gilded Six-Bits," first published in 1933 in *Story*, is now among the most often anthologized of Zora Neale Hurston's works. Robert Bone considers it "representative of [Hurston's] principal achievement in the short story form" (144). I suggest that part of Hurston's

From *Approaches to Teaching Hurston's* Their Eyes Were Watching God *and Other Works*, Ed. John Lowe (New York: MLA, 2009): 164–70.

achievement with this story is how she recasts in it perhaps the oldest short story of all: the story of Adam and Eve.[1] Teaching it, therefore, offers an opportunity to demonstrate resisting reading that reenvisions texts traditionally presented from a patriarchal perception.[2] In addition, this Hurston short story is an excellent avenue for explaining to students the concept of the *felix culpa*.

Toward both these goals, I try to coax students from their usual initial response to Missie May's affair with Otis D. Slemmons as an unforgivable betrayal of her husband, Joe, to a more compassionate response to this young woman's fall. I begin class discussion by asking students to note the parallels between Hurston's story and the story of Adam and Eve, and then I ask them to identify the major difference: in Hurston's story Adam/Joe is tempted first.

First, we discuss the story's paradisiacal setting and Adam-and-Eve-like couple. The story's opening sentence, which notes the setting to be "a Negro yard around a Negro house in a Negro settlement" (86), suggests that the inhabitants of this home are separated from the racial conflict and oppression we know to have existed in Hurston's day. We discuss the playfulness of the two characters, which begins with Joe's tossing his week's pay in the door and culminates with this scene: "For several minutes the two were a furious mass of male and female energy. Shouting, laughing, twisting, turning, tussling, tickling each other in the ribs" (87). The reference to "male and female energy" suggests that the couple's horseplay has led to sexual relations, but we note that the sexual activity is described in terms of play. Hurston is thereby emphasizing the couple's youth: even in their lovemaking, Joe and Missie May play like children. Students recognize that this couple seems relatively carefree, like Adam and Eve in Eden.

I call to the students' attention the line "It was this way every Saturday afternoon" (87). On the positive side, this sentence tells us that Joe receives regular wages and that he makes enough money for the young couple to get by comfortably, which is also supported by Hurston's earlier idyllic description of their home, by the absence of any reference to Missie May working outside the home, and by the very substantial Saturday dinner Missie May makes and the extra money Joe has for chocolate kisses and ice cream.[3] On the more negative side, the sentence just quoted also emphasizes the sameness of the couple's day-to-day life. I ask students to consider how long such sameness would be enjoyable to them; eventually, wouldn't they get bored with any routine, week after week, no matter how pleasant? Here I introduce the concept of the *felix culpa*, or "fortunate fall," to students: humans are better off for Adam and Eve's having been expelled from Eden. Even Eden would have become boring after a while. Indeed, isn't Joe showing signs of dissatisfaction with the status quo?

In response to this question about Joe, students note his admiration for the worldliness and appearance of the new man in town, which Joe contrasts with his own limited experience and self-image. Examining what Joe says about Slemmons during his conversation with Missie May over dinner leads students to recognize Joe as the first to be tempted by the serpent that has entered this garden.[4] Missie May, in contrast, admires Joe's appearance ("Ah'm satisfied wid you jes lak you is, baby. God took pattern after a pine tree and built you noble" [90]) and is suspicious of Slemmons's stories about his various adventures and accomplishments ("Ah hates to see you so dumb. Dat stray nigger jes' tell y'all anything and y'all b'lieve it" [90]).

Slemmons as dissembler confirms his role as the story's Satan figure. His apparent success and prosperity appeal first to Joe, as Eve was first attracted to Satan's promises of the divine knowledge that would be hers if she ate of the forbidden fruit. The forbidden fruit that Slemmons dangles is his gold jewelry, which he claims was given to him by white women. Slemmons is thereby implying that he has cuckolded the white man—certainly a reason to be admired by black men. One might here recall the association that Joe made earlier between Slemmons and the white man—his build "make 'm look lak a rich white man" (89)—which was meant to be a compliment, despite the white man's role as oppressor in the black man's history.[5]

During the discussion of Slemmons's association with the white man—his reference to receiving gifts from white women as well as Joe's comparison of Slemmons's build to that of a prosperous white man—I have students ponder the significance of Slemmons's use of the word *forty* as an adjective for anything he perceives as being valuable (as in, "Dat wife of yours is jes' thirty-eight and two. Yessuh, she's forte!" [91]). I challenge students to recall various biblical references to the number forty: the forty days and nights of rain sent to wash the earth clean, sparing only Noah and his family; the forty years that the Hebrews had to wander in the desert because of Moses's lack of faith; and the forty days that Jesus fasted in the desert and was tempted by Satan. These examples give the number forty negative connotations, as does a reference to forty in African American history: the forty acres and a mule that were promised to slaves after the Civil War. The allusion to that unfulfilled promise of Reconstruction days reminds us that Slemmons has come south from Chicago, like a carpetbagger,[6] and therefore prepares us for the later discovery that his gold buttons are fake. This allusion also points out to us that the Edenic setting of the story is probably as falsely paradisiacal as the intentions for the Reconstruction South. Together with the presence of the clueless white store clerk at the story's end and the references Joe and Slemmons make to white men within the story, the allusion to the forty acres reminds us of the racial conflict that exists in the world surrounding this domestic scene. Thus the reader is ultimately disturbed by Slemmons's appeal to Joe and Joe's wish to show Missie May off, apparently to get Slemmons's approval.

Sadly, despite Missie May's early perception of Slemmons's spe-
ciousness, she, like Adam, is ultimately tempted as well—but like
Milton's Adam in *Paradise Lost*, who succumbed to temptation in order
to be banished from Eden with Eve rather than remain without her,
Missie May falls more because of her love for Joe than because of her
own ambition. Before Missie May even sees Slemmons's gold, Hurston
foreshadows this fall and prepares us to understand why Missie May
cuckolds Joe—even as she questions Joe's admiration of Slemmons and
reminds Joe of his own appeal: "Youse a pretty man, *and if Ah knowed
any way to make you mo' pretty still Ah'd take and do it*" (90; my emphasis). But after Missie May and Joe have been to the ice cream parlor,
while Missie May is still not that impressed with Slemmons ("He'll do
in case of a rush" [91]), she is now quite enchanted with the gold money
and covets it for Joe: "Dat's de first time Ah ever seed gold money. It
lookted good on him sho nuff, but it'd look a heap better on you" (91).

Oddly, on returning from their first evening at the ice cream parlor,
Joe, in contrast, is no longer so wishful for himself as he was when he
first brought Slemmons up to Missie May; now, in response to *her* reaction to the gold, he says, "Don't be so wishful 'bout me. Ah'm satisfied de
way Ah is" (91). Ironically, it is just before Joe catches Missie May in bed
with Slemmons that Hurston confirms Joe's dissipated ambition to be
like the seemingly more prosperous man. On his way home early to his
wife that ill-fated night, Joe ponders his life and reveals to the reader
that, instead of being tired of the routine of his married life, he thought

> [t]hat was the best part of life—going home to Missie May. Their white-
> washed house, the mock battle on Saturday, the dinner and ice cream
> parlor afterwards, church on Sunday nights when Missie out-dressed
> any woman in town—all, everything was right. (92)

How do we account for this change in Joe? I ask students. We note how
this role reversal reestablishes the traditional domestic hierarchy: Joe
becomes the voice of reason ("Who, me? Missie May youse crazy! Where
would a po' man lak me git gold money from?" [91]), while Missie May,
who had earlier chastised Joe for being so gullible, now fantasizes about
the gold ("Us might find some goin' long de road some time" [91]). The
stage is now set for Missie May's fall.

When Joe walks into the bedroom, prepared to defend Missie May
from some uninvited intruder, and finds Slemmons struggling to get
into his pants, Hurston writes, "The great belt on the wheel of Time
slipped and eternity stood still" (93). Note that Hurston says *"eternity
stood still"*—this event marks the end of their lives in Eden, where
human beings had no awareness of death and thus of time.[7] In discussing the significance of this line, I propose to students a more secular
reading of the story of the Garden of Eden than they are perhaps accustomed to: Adam and Eve were mortals and were thus going to die

someday whether they ate the fruit or not; but until they ate of the forbidden tree, they (like most children) did not understand what mortality—what death—meant. Considering again Hurston's description of the childlike behavior of Missie May and Joe, we understand that their relationship was still in its honeymoon phase before this tragic event: it had not yet been tested. I bring up again the concept of the *felix culpa* and ask students what might be fortunate about Missie May's fall. I quote from *Paradise Lost* regarding God's explanation for giving human beings free will when he knew they would fail the test: "Not free, what proof could they have given sincere / Of true allegiance, constant Faith or Love" (3.103–04). The point is to show students how the love between Missie May and Joe is not certain until it is tested. Returning to the line referring to the wheel of time, the revelation of Missie May's betrayal of her marriage banishes the couple from Eden and into the realm of time, and the rest of the story will either support the cliché "Time heals all wounds" or reveal that their love is not strong enough to withstand Missie May's mistake.

Whereas students are usually disgusted with Missie May for messing up the paradisiacal situation Hurston had set up in the story's opening frame, I note to them that the injured party, Joe, does not so quickly condemn his wife. We discuss his very adult response to the betrayal: while he cannot forgive her instantly, he does not send her away, leave her, or even chastise her outright. One might argue that his leaving the gilded coins around as payment for sexual relations later in the story is at least a subconscious act of retaliation for the pain she has inflicted on him. Whether subconscious or intentional cruelty, this act serves to humanize Joe, since he otherwise handles himself and the situation with more maturity than most people would be able to summon under such circumstances.

Considering again how Joe was the first to be tempted by the signs of Slemmons's prosperity, perhaps Joe recognizes his part in Missie May's sin.[8] He certainly seems to understand that her infidelity was motivated by her love for him. Turning to Missie May, then, we contrast her development with Joe's: earlier in the story, Joe seemed to be the one dissatisfied with himself; Missie May had not yet reached a stage of wanting more out of life. By the time that Missie May's head is turned by the gold jewelry, Joe seems to have made some adjustment in his values: perhaps having contrasted his wife with Slemmons's jewelry, he has realized that he is the richer man. Both points of contrast suggest that Joe is slightly more mature than his wife, which prepares us for Missie May's naïveté regarding the consequences of an affair. Like Adam and Eve—or any child who has not yet committed a serious transgression—how was she to understand the consequences of such behavior, not yet having experienced any threat to her blissful life?

The compassionate, pensive Joe we see after his discovery of his wife's infidelity is more admirable than the bombastic Joe in the first few pages of the story—which brings us to another reason that the couple's fall can be viewed as fortunate. The class discusses how, once Joe and Missie May know that their marriage can withstand one of the hardest tests of a relationship, they are in a better place than they were before, Joe's awareness of which is reflected in the increased number of candy kisses he buys for Missie May at the story's end. While he resumes the ritual to indicate to his wife that everything is going to be all right, the students agree that Hurston does not mean to indicate that the couple will go back to the status quo; quite the contrary, since by this time they have a baby to take care of.[9] Adults now, rather than two children playing house, they are more ready for this new responsibility than they were before Missie May's affair.

"The Gilded Six-Bits" can be read along with other American retellings of the fall, like Nathaniel Hawthorne's "The Maypole of Merry Mount" and "Young Goodman Brown." Thus, in an American literature survey course, the students see evidence of the continued influence of the Puritan perception of the New World as a new Eden. And in a general introduction to literature or a short story class, the students see how the very earliest stories continue to influence literature throughout time.

In "The Maypole of Merry Mount," two of the maypole revelers are married during the festivities. Immediately following their vows, the two become pensive. Hawthorne's description of their apparent—and mature—recognition of the possible consequences of love reminds us of the postlapsarian Joe and Missie May:

> No sooner had their hearts glowed with real passion than they were sensible of something vague and unsubstantial in their former pleasures, and felt a dreary presentiment of inevitable change. From the moment that they truly loved they had subjected themselves to earth's doom of care and sorrow and troubled joy, and had no more a home at Merry Mount. (45)

Indeed, following their recognition, the merrymakers are interrupted by Endicott and his fellow Puritans, who prepare to punish them for their hedonistic behavior. While in this story, as in his other works, Hawthorne exposes the cruelty of his Puritan ancestors that belied their Edenic analogies of the New World, at the same time, he, like Hurston, reveals the positive side of living in a fallen world. He begins by noting that "never had their [the newlyweds'] youthful beauty seemed so pure and high as when its glow was chastened by adversity" (51), thus also suggesting that virtue must be tested to be assessed. The story proceeds with the husband and then the wife pronouncing their willingness to die for the other. The Puritans recognize the couple's genuine virtue and recruit rather than punish them, and Hawthorne concludes that the couple "returned to [the maypole] no more" and that their lives subsequently led them "heavenward supporting each other along the difficult path which it was their lot to tread" (52).

Reading Hurston's story along with this Hawthorne story reveals the development of Hurston's characters' relationship from an immature, falsely paradisiacal love to a mature love that has withstood a serious test and will thus probably last through the couple's golden anniversary (hence my title for this essay). Hurston's story can also help students see the pride of the title character of "Young Goodman Brown" as the greatest sin, which Hawthorne condemns here. Once students forgive Missie May for her very human mistake and understand Joe's heroism in forgiving her, they are better able to understand Goodman Brown's culpability (whereas they are usually distracted from such understanding by the "devil worshipping" that took place in the woods, much as they are initially compelled to condemn Missie May). Brown, like Joe, is the first to be tempted into the woods, while his wife, Faith, pleads with him to stay with her. But unlike Joe, after finding that his wife, too, has succumbed to temptation (or might have—the whole experience may have been a dream), Brown is not so forgiving. When on emerging from the woods he sees Faith, he "looked sternly and sadly into her face and passed on without a greeting," and we are told that in the years that followed, "often, awaking suddenly at midnight, he shrank from the bosom of Faith, and at morning or eventide when the family knelt down at prayer he scowled and muttered to himself and gazed sternly at his wife and turned away" (71). Brown, unlike Joe, is not able to forgive his wife for succumbing to that which tempted him as well. In contrast to Joe, who seems self-aware, Brown must have determined from his experience in the woods not that he is one among many sinners but that he is the only one in his community who is not a sinner. The "stern ... sad ... darkly meditative ... distrustful ... man" (71) who emerges from the woods is starkly different from the last we see of Hurston's playful and content, wise and compassionate Joe, returning to his wife and new son with candy kisses.

Notes

1. Bone (149) and Lillie P. Howard (263) have also noted Edenic parallels in the story.
2. See *The Resisting Reader*, in which Judith Fetterley argues that "the first act of the feminist critic must be to become a resisting rather than an assenting reader and, by this refusal to assent, to begin the process of exorcizing the male mind that has been implanted in us" (xxii).
3. In their article on this story, Nancy Chinn and Elizabeth E. Dunn refer to its Depression-era setting. They also take note of Joe's steady job, but not without pointing out that the couple owns no luxuries, nothing beyond basic necessities (778).
4. Cheryl A. Wall (15), Gayl Jones (162), and Chinn and Dunn (788) also recognize that Joe is the first to have his head turned by Slemmons's apparent prosperity, but other critics overlook this detail. Bone, for example, focuses on how "*the woman* functions as a pivot between two value systems" in the

story: "the one urban and 'sophisticated,' the other rural and elemental. At *first she* chooses falsely" (149; emphasis added). Bone's reference to Missie May as "the woman" and his later reference to Edenic parallels ("As the story opens, Joe and Missie May frolic in prelapsarian innocence" [149]) suggest that his reading of this story is influenced by Milton's emphasis on Eve's culpability.

5. As Hildegard Hoeller has also pointed out, Otis D. Slemmons anticipates Hurston's Joe Starks of *Their Eyes Were Watching God* (778). Hoeller also notes a comparison between "Gilded Six-Bits" and "Now Cooking with Gas," another Hurston story that examines "the relations between race, money, and sexuality" (779).

6. Chinn and Dunn also discuss "Slemmons's inventive use of the word 'forte,'" calling it "pure big-city talk" and relating it to his having "sloughed off all that was Southern, rural, and black while he was in the North." His "alien language and habits fascinate *first* Joe and then Missie May," they note, anticipating their reading of the story's conflict emerging when the two main characters "allow corrupt desires to replace their innocent acceptance of their native cultural values" (780; emphasis added).

7. I tell my students how my professor of Milton at the University of Southwestern Louisiana, Albert Fields, called prelapsarian human beings "divine pets"; to explain this appellation, I compare Adam and Eve before the fall to my own cats, sleeping the day away with no awareness that they only have a limited time on this earth and thus have no need to seize the day. We discuss how the older we get, the more aware we become of the brevity of life, and thus the more we are driven to make the best use of that time.

8. In his examination of how comedy and tragedy are "intertwined" in this story (75), John Lowe points out Joe's role in Missie May's betrayal: "We readers know . . . (and surely Joe does too, eventually) that he had much to do with it in his oft-expressed yearning for money and power" (77).

9. Howard reads the ending similarly: "The marriage has come full circle, but it will never be the same. The carefree innocence which characterized the early marriage has been replaced by painfully-gained maturity and knowledge. The lesson has been costly but because the foundation upon which the marriage was built has been strong, the marriage has survived" (264). Rosalie Murphy Baum writes, "The birth of their son . . . and Joe's efforts to sort and control his overwhelming feelings create a new basis for a less innocent but perhaps deeper relationship" (98).

Works Cited

Baum, Rosalie Murphy. "The Shape of Hurston's Fiction." Glassman and Seidel 94–109.

Bone, Robert. *Down Home: A History of Afro-American Short Fiction from Its Beginnings to the End of the Harlem Renaissance*. New York: Putnam, 1975. Print. New Perspectives on Black America Ser.

Chinn, Nancy, and Elizabeth E. Dunn. "'The Ring of Singing Metal on Wood': Zora Neale Hurston's Artistry in 'The Gilded Six-Bits.'" *Mississippi Quarterly* 49.3 (1996): 775–90. Print.

Fetterley, Judith. *The Resisting Reader: A Feminist Approach to American Fiction*. Bloomington: Indiana UP, 1978. Print.

Glassman, Steve, and Kathryn Lee Seidel, eds. *Zora in Florida*. Orlando: U of Central Florida P, 1991. Print.

Hawthorne, Nathaniel. "The Maypole of Merry Mount." *Twice-Told Tales*. London: Standard, 1931. 41–52. Print.

———. "Young Goodman Brown." *Mosses from an Old Manse*. London: Standard, 1931. 59–72. Print.

Hoeller, Hildegard. "Racial Currency: Zora Neale Hurston's 'The Gilded Six-Bits' and the Gold-Standard Debate." *American Literature* 77.4 (2005): 761–85. Print.

Howard, Lillie P. "Marriage: Zora Neale Hurston's System of Values." *College Language Association Journal* 21 (1977): 256–68. Print.

Hurston, Zora Neale. "The Gilded Six-Bits." 1933. Hurston, *Complete Stories* 86–98.

Jones, Gayl. "Breaking Out of the Conventions of Dialect." Wall, *"Sweat"* 153–68.

Lowe, John. *Jump at the Sun: Zora Neale Hurston's Cosmic Comedy*. Urbana: U of Illinois P, 1994. Print.

Milton, John. *Paradise Lost. Complete Poems and Major Prose*. Ed. Merritt Y. Hughes. New York: Macmillan, 1985. 173–454. Print.

Wall, Cheryl A. Introduction. Wall, *"Sweat"* 3–19.

Asking Ecocritical Questions

SueEllen Campbell

In her essay regarding how to approach literature of nature and the environment, Campbell's premise is that "it matters how questions are constructed, how we ask them, [and] how we teach students to develop their own" (p. 450). She asks typical questions about character, plot, point of view, imagery, and theme, but she also asks about inanimate characters, such as the Missouri River, and animal characters. Campbell notes that ecocritics assume that places are more than just settings or sources of imagery. Over the course of the essay, she provides examples of the questions she uses to address both generalizations and textual details that allow her to "zoom in and zoom out" (p. 455). Campbell also discusses how she has students create what she terms "good thinking questions," which are "text-based and text-directed, open-ended, challenging questions, mixed (optionally) with bits of data, speculations and thinking" (p. 455). The essay refers to Henry Thoreau's Walden *and other texts with ecocritical themes. Campbell's essay originally appeared in* Teaching North American Environmental Literature *(2008), edited by Laird Christensen, Mark C. Long, and Fred Waage.*

From *Teaching North American Environmental Literature*, Eds. Laird Christensen, Mark C. Long, and Fred Waage (New York, MLA 2008): 215–22.

As an ecocritically minded teacher of literature, I begin with the premise that the environment matters. Then, borrowing tactics from many kinds of criticism, I ask all sorts of questions about the texts I read, and I teach my students to do the same.

Of course all questions are not equally productive: some dead-end quickly, some evaporate into the vast spaces of speculation; some are not really questions at all but are disguised as arguments, rants, or emotional reactions; some require information that is hard to come by in a classroom; some are too easy. So it matters how questions are constructed, how we ask them, how we teach students to develop their own. If questions are carefully handled, I have learned, even the simplest ones will open up into layered mazes of complications—and into unexpected illuminations.

What I offer here is a sample set of the questions I explore with my classes on the literature of nature and the environment. Some of these questions are what I see as necessary basics; others open into current ecocritical issues. Because all questions (and their key terms) can and should be qualified, modified, and elaborated for specific texts and contexts, and because when they are asked about particular texts they expand quickly, in this essay I have simplified them and made them generic, though I have occasionally gestured toward well-known and potentially productive examples. With a little coaching and thoughtful, talkative students at any college or graduate level, each paragraph below can easily fill a class period and provoke several term papers.

Beginning with the Text

In recent years I have found myself returning to the classic formalist questions about character, plot, point of view, imagery, theme, and so forth. These simple but potentially incisive questions can cut equally well through the smooth and nearly invisible surface of a book like Aldo Leopold's *Sand County Almanac*, the charismatic shield of a book like Edward Abbey's *Desert Solitaire*, and the challenging complexities of something like Henry David Thoreau's *Walden*. They are tools that help students grasp the basic structure and ideas of texts and also what the writer might have wanted to accomplish—two things I think it is important to consider from the start.

What kind of character is the person or narrator whose "voice" we are "hearing" as we read? What is this voice like? What kinds of sentence structures, words, images does the speaker use? What is his or her rhetorical stance? (Abbey's stance in *Desert Solitaire* is very different from Rachel Carson's in *Silent Spring*: but exactly how, and so what?) What is the primary grammatical point of view, and does it change? How is this technical choice connected to the conceptual (or perceptual) point of view? Anthropologists often act as participant observers, a concept that fits much environmental literature. Is the narrator an outsider-observer, an insider-participant, or both? In what proportions? (Compare Columbus with Lewis and Clark: where do they observe? where do they participate?) Does the narrator's conceptual point of view change through the text?

What other characters are important? Are some of them nonhuman, even inanimate? Is the setting a character, and, if so, how? Can a rock be a character? Can a blizzard? Can a farm? How about Walden Pond? the Missouri River, the Mississippi, the Colorado? How does each character add to the text? How does the narrator relate to these characters? How does the narrator filter what we learn about other characters?

How are animal characters perceived, described, and valued? As stimulus-response machines? As products of evolution, fighting to survive? As objects of our scientific inquiry? As servants to humans, or as imitation humans? Does the author personify or anthropomorphize animals? With what purposes and results? Does the text see animals as beings equal in value to humans, partly like us and partly different — partly mysterious? Consider Abbey's dancing snakes, John Muir's dog Stickeen, Barry Lopez's wolves or polar bear, Diane Ackerman's bats and penguins: how do these authors talk about these animals, why, and to what effects?

What is the basic structure of the text? Is it an almanac, journal, journey, rant, quest, physical or mental exploration, jeremiad, meditation, something else? Compare Leopold's almanac with the winter-to-winter time frame of Annie Dillard's *Pilgrim at Tinker Creek* or *Walden*'s summer through spring: their structures are similar but not the same, and their differences are interesting. What if we think about Meriwether Lewis's and William Clark's journals as a quest narrative? And what about a more complicated book like Terry Tempest William's *Red* or Dillard's *For the Time Being*?

How many plots are there? Can we distinguish, say, an event plot (what happens when), a telling plot (how the story unfolds), and a thematic plot (so what?)? Are there layers of plots? Is there a story behind the story? Do the climaxes of all the plots coincide? If not, why? If the text has chapters or subsections, how are they related to each other and to the plot? Does each part have its own plot, or are they, rather, installments in a book-long plot, or both? Is there an exterior plot and an interior plot, a physical one in the landscape, a second emotional or conceptual one in the narrator's mind? If so, does one direct the other? How else are they related?

Thinking about the Landscape

Environmental literature typically (or perhaps by definition) foregrounds the landscape, and ecocritics typically do the same thing in any text we read: that is, we assume at least as a hypothesis that places operate as more than just background settings and sources of imagery.

When we consider the land itself as a critical factor, we most clearly distinguish ecocriticism from other current modes of literary study, but we also share with other current critical approaches an interest in human cultural, social, and political issues. These subjects are extremely difficult to separate, of course, and there are often excellent reasons not to try.

What kinds of nature and environment are of interest in this text? How does the author define these terms (explicitly or implicitly), and how useful are these definitions? What kinds of landscapes (wild, agricultural, toxic, restored, domestic, urban, suburban, feral, garden, etc.) are important, and how? (Contrast the desert wilderness of *Red* with the urban alleys of Robert Sullivan's *Rats*, the woodlot retreat of *Walden* with Leopold's farm.) What are the text's attitudes toward these landscapes? Do these attitudes challenge those held by the larger culture at the time the text was written? Now?

How intimately, how thoroughly, and in what ways does the author-narrator know these places? How many kinds of lenses are used to look at a place? How involved are the author-narrator's body, senses, imagination, heart, memory, curiosity, intellect, passion?

How aware is the author of the other living things in this place and how they relate to one another? How much does she or he think about what is not visible to a human observer, at this time? Is the human history of this place considered? Its environmental history? How it is (and has been) linked to other places through commerce, politics, ecology? Disturbing things about the place, such as pollutants and extinction? How the place has changed, recently and over deep time? What relations are visible in this text among the local, regional, and global? Are these categories understood in terms of bioregions, human cultures, political boundaries, watersheds, economics, ecosystems, worldwide forces (like climate change), something else?

What kinds of scientific information are present? How are facts framed and used? What scientific assumptions and models underlie them? What understanding of issues like evolution, environmental change, ecological relations, and so forth? How much faith in science is visible? How much is the information provided by science integrated with cultural information? What kinds of research has the author done? How much scientific literacy—or knowledge of the history of the natural sciences—do we need to be good readers of this text? What different things should we know to read William Bartram and David Quammen, and what is it like to read Bartram from the time of Quammen?

How might we describe the text's environmental politics? Is the author-narrator an environmental fundamentalist or a relativist? Is he nostalgic for something that has been lost? If so, is that nostalgia sentimental or robust? What is her attitude toward contemporary life—globalization, multinational corporations, sport-utility vehicles, virtual reality, shopping malls, agribusiness, consumer capitalism, other forces and issues of our time? If the text is older, what is its attitude toward the comparable issues of its own time? Is the text subversive or resistant to dominant forces and patterns? What alternatives does its response suggest?

When human desires (for jobs; mobility; prosperity; children; moving to richer, safer countries) conflict with other environmental values, how does the author-narrator choose? How concerned is the text with climate change, species extinction, habitat loss, toxic pollutants, resource depletion, population increase, warfare, desertification, disease, hunger, and so forth? What kinds of solutions does the text offer, if any? Are these solutions nostalgic? Misanthropic? Idealistic? What are their conceptual and practical implications? Is the author or the text activist? How? Compare Thoreau with Carson or with Rick Bass: what kinds of politics and activism does each enact?

What seem to be the author's religious, spiritual, moral, and ethical values, beliefs, and emotions? Does she or he regard the land (all or just parts?) as sacred, and, if so, how might we describe that vision of sacredness and its cultural contexts? Does the text use religious language or refer to specific religious beliefs or stories? (Dillard, Williams, and Gary Snyder speak overtly about religious ideas; how do their investigations compare with the ethical questions asked by Leopold or Kathleen Dean Moore?) How does the author understand the human position on the planet, our responsibilities to the rest of its occupants? What vision of happiness, fulfillment, or a good life does the text offer? (Think about the zest for life that is so evident in Thoreau's and Muir's books. What is its source?) What balance does the text offer between prohibitions (don't do this) and encouragements (do this)?

In what ways does the text deal with human cultural issues of identity, race, ethnicity, class, gender, sexuality, power, justice, and so on? Are race and ethnicity foregrounded, or not? Is this author conscious of the effects of his or her ethnic, racial, and class positions and their cultural histories? Does the author accept or resist these effects? Does the author's gender and sexual orientation affect the text? (How should we read Abbey's comments about women?) Does the text have anything to say about masculinity or femininity, about gender and sexual identity, perception, and behavior? (Compare Gretchen Legler's *All the Powerful Invisible Things* with Williams's *Red.*) What human power relations are evident, either present or past? Are some of them colonial or imperialistic? Are they economic, or class-based? What is the stance of the text toward these topics?

With these issues, does the text seem to be retrograde, old-fashioned, conventional, progressive, inventive, quirky? What connections does the text make or suggest between these human issues and the land, or between these issues and human relationships with the land? Is identity conceived of as partly, or significantly, ecological? Is place, or natural environment, seen as part of what creates identity? (Consider the work of Gary Paul Nabhan, Gary Snyder, Leslie Marmon Silko, or Keith Basso.) What is the author's or narrator's attitude toward other people on the land sharing the same place? What cultural issues beyond those directly connected to land are present in this text? Are they linked to land issues or seen as separate?

Carrying on the Conversation

Like other literary critics, ecocritics are interested in the cultural work done by texts and in the conversations that develop in communities of writers, books, and readers. The following questions address, in different ways, these conversations.

In what genres or subgenres is this text? What conventions does it make use of? Into what literary traditions does the author seem to be entering? (Think about what Robert Sullivan does with the model of *Walden* in his *Meadowlands* and *Rats*.) Does the text change, challenge, stretch, alter any significant conventions or traditions? Does it cross boundaries of genre, subgenre, literary tradition, or academic discipline? How, why, and so what? (What can we make of a highly unconventional book like Dillard's *For the Time Being*?) In what historical and current conversations—about what issues—is this text taking part? What are its contributions to these conversations? (What happens to the literary tradition of solitary encounters with wild nature when a writer like Kathleen Dean Moore has her children with her on river trips?) What elements of the author's life and historical circumstances seem important in shaping these contributions?

As readers, we're part of these conversations, too: what is the text's relationship to us? What does the author seem to want from us? What kind of reader does the text seem to want us to be, at least for a while? What if we are that kind of reader or can imagine ourselves to be? What if we aren't and can't or won't? What kinds of (ironic, skeptical, critical, historical) distances might we have as readers from the narrator's position? Can we try to read two ways at once, from our own assumptions and values and from those of the writer? What imaginative work does it take for us to see through the eyes of Christopher Columbus or Mary Rowlandson?

What are the main questions the author is exploring in this text? How overt or how subtle are these questions? (Some books foreground their questions—Rebecca Solnit's *Savage Dreams*, Dillard's *For the Time Being*, Thoreau's *Walden*, and Moore's *Pine Island Paradox* are excellent examples. But all texts can be seen as asking them.) Are they common questions or startling ones? Concrete and specific or giant and cosmic? No single person, much less a single text, can ask all questions or consider all possible answers. To which questions is this text blind? Which questions does the author simply choose not to consider in this text? What does the text do with the questions it asks? Does it offer answers?

Possibilities? Illuminations and insights? Does it simply embody, enact, or elaborate the questions? Does it see some questions as unanswerable?

What does this text help us understand about the world? about other people's perceptions of it, their ways of being in it? about all the other beings that share it with us? about our own perceptions, values, curiosities, passions? about actions we might wish to take? about our own possible places in the world? about the kinds of lives we wish to live?

Using These Questions in Classrooms

I use questions like these in two main ways. I ask them of myself as I read and prepare for class; they help me make sense of new texts and challenge me to think about familiar ones in fresh ways. I think about which are the most important, discussable, and incisive ones to ask about each text, and I revise and tailor them to focus on the issues I want to cover in class. Then I pose them to my students to start and continue class discussions. I also very often assign them as homework. That is to say, I ask students to write their own "good thinking questions"—clusters of focused, text-based and text-directed, open-ended, challenging questions, mixed (optionally) with bits of data, speculations, and thinking. (I typically ask upper-level undergraduates to bring to each class meeting two to four clusters of roughly 250 words each.) Then I'll have them use these questions to direct whole- and small-group conversations. This assignment takes a couple of weeks of intensive training at the beginning of the term and then runs itself.

In all the ensuing discussions, we mix big with small, giant generalizations with textual details; we zoom in and zoom out. We balance simplifications with complications. And we resist premature answers; if someone has a good answer, we try to build another question on that answer. I discourage questions like, will we ever learn to treat animals well? I ask instead that we think about what the author at hand might have to say about this "world question." I find that our discussions stay much more focused and that we do end up talking about the world issues anyway, just indirectly. I think often of an article I once read that suggested metaphors for kinds of class discussions. Some discussions, this article said, are like body-building or beauty contests, with each student parading his or her ideas before the rest of the class, whose job it is to admire and judge. Some are like wrestling matches, in which the best argument pins the weaker ones to the mat. And some are like barn raisings and quilting bees: everyone contributes a little something (a nail, a bit of stitching), and the product is truly communal. Classrooms full of questions, I believe, produce barns and quilts—or, to drop the metaphor, they produce students who can themselves recognize, create, and pursue good questions. I hope, in courses on environmental literatures, this may also mean that they produce good environmental citizens who will help create a healthy future.

Additional Readings

Alberti, John. *The Canon in the Classroom: The Pedagogical Implications of Canon Revision in American Literature.* New York: Garland, 1995.

Allen, Paula Gunn. *Studies in American Indian Literature: Critical Essays and Course Designs.* New York: MLA, 1983.

Ammons, Elizabeth, and Susan Belasco. *Approaches to Teaching Stowe's* Uncle Tom's Cabin. New York: MLA, 2000.

Amory, Hugh, and David D. Hall, *The History of the Book in America.* New York: Cambridge UP, 1999.

Anderson, Danny J., and Jill S. Kuhnheim. *Cultural Studies in the Curriculum: Teaching Latin America.* New York: MLA, 2003.

Aranda, José, Jr. *When We Arrive: A New Literary History of Mexican America.* Tucson: U of Arizona P, 2003.

Augenbraum, Harold, and Margarite Fernández Olmos. *U.S. Latino Literature: A Critical Guide for Students and Teachers.* Westport, CT: Greenwood P, 2000.

Baker, Houston A., Jr. *Three American Literatures: Essays in Chicano, Native American, and Asian-American Literature for Teachers of American Literature.* New York: MLA, 1982.

Baym, Nina. *Feminism and American Literary History: Essays.* Piscataway, NJ: Rutgers UP, 1992.

Beach, Richard. *A Teacher's Guide to Reader-Response Theories.* Urbana, IL: NCTE, 1993.

Bennett, Paula Bernat, et al. *Teaching Nineteenth-Century American Poetry.* New York: MLA, 2007.

Bercovitch, Sacvan. *The American Jeremiad.* Madison: U Wisconsin P, 1980.

———, Sacvan, ed. *The Cambridge History of American Literature.* 8 vols. New York: Cambridge UP, 1997.

Brogan, Martha L., and Daphnée Rentfrow. *A Kaleidoscope of Digital American Literature.* Washington, D.C.: Council on Library and Information Resources Digital Library Federation, 2005.

Brooker, Jewel Spears. *Approaches to Teaching Eliot's Poetry and Plays.* New York: MLA, 1988.

Burt, Daniel S. *The Chronology of American Literature: America's Literary Achievements from the Colonial Era to Modern Times.* Boston: Houghton Mifflin, 2004.

Cahalan, James M., and David B. Downing, eds. *Practicing Theory in Introductory College Literature Courses.* Urbana, IL: NCTE, 1991.

Dimock, Wai Chee, and Michael T. Gilmore, eds. *Rethinking Class: Literary Studies and Social Formations.* New York: Columbia UP, 1994.

Earhart, Amy E., and Andrew Jewell, eds. *The American Literature Scholar in the Digital Age.* Ann Arbor: U of Michigan P, 2011.

Eddins, Dwight, ed. *The Emperor Redressed: Critiquing Critical Theory.* Tuscaloosa: U of Alabama P, 1995.

Fast, Robin Riley, and Christine Mack Gordon. *Approaches to Teaching Dickinson's Poetry.* New York: MLA, 1989.

Fiedler, Leslie. *Love and Death in the American Novel.* First Dalkey Archive ed. Normal, IL: Dalkey Archive, 1998.

Fisher, Dexter, and Robert B. Stepto, eds. *Afro-American Literature: The Reconstruction of Instruction.* New York: MLA, 1979.

Foley, John Miles. *Teaching Oral Traditions.* New York: MLA, 1998.

Gerster, Carole, and Laura W. Zlogar. *Teaching Ethnic Diversity with Film: Essays and Resources for Educators in History, Social Studies, Literature and Film Studies*. Jefferson, NC: McFarland & Company, 2006.

Goebel, Bruce A., and James C. Hall. *Teaching a "New Canon"?: Students, Teachers, and Texts in the College Literature Classroom*. Urbana, IL: NCTE, 1995.

Graff, Gerald. *Beyond the Culture Wars: How Teaching the Conflicts Can Revitalize American Education*. New York: Norton, 1992.

Graff, Gerald, and Michael Warner, eds. *The Origins of Literary Studies in America: A Documentary Anthology*. New York: Routledge, 1989.

Graham, Maryemma, et al. *Teaching African American Literature*. Oxford: Routledge, 1998.

Haggerty, George, and Bonnie Zimmerman, eds. *Professions of Desire: Lesbian and Gay Studies in Literature*. New York: MLA, 1995.

Hall, James C. *Approaches to Teaching* Narrative of the Life of Frederick Douglass. New York: MLA, 1999.

Hoeveler, Diane Long, and Tamar Heller. *Approaches to Teaching Gothic Literature: The British and American Traditions*. New York: MLA, 2003.

Hoffmann, Leonore, and Deborah Rosenfelt. *Teaching Women's Literature from a Regional Perspective*. New York: MLA, 1982.

Hoffmann, Leonore, and Margo Culley. *Women's Personal Narratives: Essays in Criticism and Pedagogy*. New York: MLA, 1985.

Holifield, E. Brooks. *Era of Persuasion: American Thought and Culture, 1521–1680*. Woodbridge, CT: Twayne, 1989.

Hune, Shirley, et al., eds. *Asian Americans: Comparative and Global Perspectives*. Pullman: Washington State UP, 1991.

Kalaidjian, Walter, ed. *The Cambridge Companion to American Modernism*. Cambridge: Cambridge UP, 2005.

Knight, Denise D., and Cynthia J. Davis. *Approaches to Teaching Gilman's "The Yellow Wallpaper" and* Herland. New York: MLA, 2003.

Knippling, Alpana Sharma. *New Immigrant Literatures in the United States: A Sourcebook to Our Multicultural Literary Heritage*. Westport, CT: Greenwood P, 1996.

Koloski, Bernard. *Approaches to Teaching Chopin's* The Awakening. New York: MLA, 1988.

Kummings, Donald D. *Approaches to Teaching Whitman's* Leaves of Grass. New York: MLA, 1990.

Landsman, Ned C. *From Colonials to Provincials: American Thought and Culture, 1680–1760*. Woodbridge, CT: Twayne, 1997.

Lauter, Paul. *Canons and Contexts*. New York: Oxford UP, 1991.

Leonard, James S., ed. *Making Mark Twain Work in the Classroom*. Durham, NC: Duke UP, 1999.

Levander, Caroline F. *Where Is American Literature?* West Sussex: John Wiley & Sons, 2013.

Lewis, R. W. B. *The American Adam: Innocence, Tragedy, and Tradition in the Nineteenth Century*. Chicago: U Chicago P, 1959.

Lim, Shirley Geok-lin. *Approaches to Teaching Kingston's* The Woman Warrior. New York: MLA, 1991.

Lim, Shirley Geok-lin, and Amy Ling. *Reading the Literatures of Asian America*. Philadelphia: Temple UP, 1992.

Maitino, John R., and David R. Peck, eds. *Teaching American Ethnic Literatures*. Albuquerque: U of New Mexico, 1996.

Martín-Rodríguez, Manuel M. *Life in Search of Readers: Reading (in) Chicano/a Literature*. Albuquerque: U of New Mexico P, 2003.

Matthews, Jean. *Toward a New Society: American Thought and Culture, 1800–1830*. Woodbridge, CT: Twayne, 1991.

Mayberry, Katherine J. *Teaching What You're Not: Identity Politics in Higher Education.* New York: New York UP, 1996.

McDowell, Deborah E., and Arnold Rampersad. *Slavery and the Literary Imagination.* Baltimore: Johns Hopkins UP, 1989.

Michaels, Walter Benn, and Donald E. Pease. *The American Renaissance Reconsidered.* Baltimore: Johns Hopkins UP, 1989.

Miller, Perry. *Errand into the Wilderness.* Cambridge, MA: Belknap, 1975.

Mulford, Carla. *Teaching the Literatures of Early America.* New York: MLA, 2000.

Napier, Winston, ed. *African American Literary Theory: A Reader.* New York: New York UP, 2000.

Palumbo-Liu, David, ed. *The Ethnic Canon: Histories, Institutions, and Interventions.* Minneapolis: U of Minnesota P, 1995.

Papke, Mary E., ed. *Twisted From the Ordinary: Essays on American Literary Naturalism.* Knoxville: U of Tennessee P, 2003.

Poey, Delia. *Latino American Literature in the Classroom: The Politics of Transformation.* Gainesville: UP of Florida, 2002.

Reising, Russell. *The Unusable Past: Theory and the Study of American Literature.* New York and London: Methuen, 1986.

Richter, David H. *Falling into Theory: Conflicting Views on Reading Literature.* Boston: Bedford/St. Martin's, 2000.

Rooney, Ellen, *The Cambridge Companion to Feminist Literary Criticism.* Cambridge: Cambridge UP, 2006.

Rose, Anne C. *Voices of the Marketplace: American Thought and Culture, 1830–1860.* Woodbridge, CT: Twayne, 1997.

Ruoff, A. LaVonne Brown, and Jerry W. Ward, Jr., eds. *Redefining American Literary History.* New York: MLA, 1990.

Saldívar, José David. *Border Matters: Remapping American Cultural Studies.* Berkeley: U of California P, 1997.

Schneider, Richard J. *Approaches to Teaching Thoreau's* Walden *and Other Works.* New York: MLA, 1996.

Selden, Raman. *Practicing Theory and Reading Literature: An Introduction.* Lexington: UP of Kentucky, 1989.

Shalhope, Robert. *The Roots of Democracy: American Thought and Culture, 1760–1800.* Woodbridge, CT: Twayne, 1990.

Shirley, Carl R., and Paula W. Shirley. *Understanding Chicano Literature.* Columbia: U of South Carolina P, 1988.

Showalter, Elaine. *Teaching Literature.* Malden, MA: Blackwell, 2002.

Smethurst, James Edward. *The Black Arts Movement: Literary Nationalism in the 1960s and 1970s.* Chapel Hill: U of North Carolina P, 2005.

Smith, Henry Nash. *Virgin Land: The American West as Symbol and Myth.* Cambridge, MA: Harvard UP, 1971.

Stevenson, Louise L. *The Victorian Homefront: American Thought and Culture, 1860–1880.* Woodbridge, CT: Twayne, 1991.

Sundquist, Eric, *American Realism: New Essays.* Baltimore: Johns Hopkins UP, 1982.

Taylor, Alan. *American Colonies: The Settling of North America.* New York: Penguin, 2002.

Tompkins, Jane. *Sensational Designs: The Cultural Work of American Fiction, 1790–1860.* New York: Oxford UP, 1986.

Weinstock, Jeffrey Andrew, and Tony Magistrale, eds. *Approaches to Teaching Poe's Prose and Poetry.* New York: MLA, 2008.

Wright, Louis B. *The Cultural Life of the American Colonies.* Mineola, NY: Dover, 2002.

Yancey, Kathleen Blake. *Teaching Literature as Reflective Practice.* Urbana, IL: NCTE, 2004.

About the Volume Editor

Venetria K. Patton is Director of African American Studies and Associate Professor of English at Purdue University. Prior to her appointment at Purdue, Dr. Patton was an Associate Professor of English and African American Studies at the University of Nebraska–Lincoln, where she won two teaching awards: the Annis Chaiken Sorensen Distinguished Teaching Award in the Arts and Humanities and the College of Arts and Sciences Distinguished Teaching Award. She is the author of *The Grasp That Reaches Beyond the Grave: the Ancestral Call in Black Women's Texts* (2013) and *Women in Chains: The Legacy of Slavery in Black Women's Fiction* (2000), the co-editor of *Double-Take: A Revisionist Harlem Renaissance Anthology* (2001), and editor of the first and second editions of *Background Readings for Teachers of American Literature* (2006 and 2014, respectively).

About the Contributors

Margaret D. Bauer is the editor for the *North Carolina Literary Review*, which won the Parnassus Award for Significant Editorial Achievement in 2007. The journal is published jointly by the North Carolina Literary and Historical Association and East Carolina University, where Bauer is a professor of English and Rives Chair of Southern Literature. Her research interests encompass Southern literature, literature by women, and American literature. Her books include *Understanding Tim Gautreaux* (2010) and *William Faulkner's Legacy: "what shadow, what stain, what mark"* (2005).

Shari Benstock earned her Ph.D. from Kent State University in 1975, when she began publishing on literary modernism. She held academic appointments at the University of Tulsa (1982–1986), serving as the Director of the Tulsa Center for the Study of Women's Literature and the editor of *Tulsa Studies in Women's Literature*. At the University of Miami, where Benstock taught from 1986 to 2004, she was the founding director of the program in Women's Studies, later serving as Chair of the English Department and Associate Dean for Faculty Affairs in the College of Arts and Sciences. She has published several texts, including *Women of the Left Bank* (1987), *The Private Self: Theory and Practice of Women's Autobiographical Writing* (1988), *Feminist Issues in Literary Scholarship* (1987), and *On Fashion* (with Suzanne Ferriss, 1994). In 2004 Benstock took a leave of absence for health reasons. She has since retired.

Lawrence Buell is the Powell M. Cabot Professor of American Literature at Harvard University where he has been teaching since 1990. He completed his undergraduate degree at Princeton University and received his Ph.D. from Cornell University. Buell's extensive academic research over the past two decades has resulted in numerous published articles and five books, including *Ecocriticism: Some Emerging Trends* (2012), *Emerson* (2003), and *Writing for an Endangered World: Literature, Culture, and Environment in the United States and Beyond* (2001).

Marta Caminero-Santangelo is a professor of English at the University of Kansas, where she has been teaching since 1997. Her first book, *The Madwoman Can't Speak: Or Why Insanity Is Not Subversive* (1998), was named Outstanding Academic Title by *Choice*. Her second book, *On Latinidad: U.S. Latino Literature and the Construction of Ethnicity* (2009), explores issues of external, panethnic Latino/a identity construction. Her manuscript in progress, *Documenting the Undocumented: Narrative, Nation, and Social Justice in the Gatekeeper Era*, extends this inquiry to representations of Latin American undocumented immigrants in contemporary American literature.

SueEllen Campbell is co-editor of *Under the Sign of Nature*, an ecocritical book series published by the University of Virginia Press. Her books, *The Face of the Earth: Natural Landscapes, Science, and Culture* (2011); *Even Mountains Vanish: Searching for Solace in an Age of Extinction* (2003); and *Bringing the Mountain Home* (1996) coincide with her interests in environmental literature. Campbell is co-director of Changing Climates, a multidisciplinary project focused on education and community outreach at Colorado State University, where Campbell is a professor of English.

Emory Elliott, formerly a University Professor in the University of California system, directed the UC Riverside Center for Ideas and Society. Elliott also taught for seventeen years at Princeton, where he was awarded for distinguished service. He co-edited the *Columbia Literary History of the United States* (1988), which won the American Book Award. Elliott, who died in 2009, is known for his work in advancing multiculturalism in American literature.

Suzanne Ferriss, who received her Ph.D. from the University of Miami, is a professor in the humanities department of Florida's Nova Southeastern University. Her research interests range from romantic literature to "chick flicks" to fashion. Ferriss has published several books, including *On Fashion* (with Shari Benstock, 1994), *Chick Lit: The New Woman's Fiction* (with Mallory Young, 2005), and *Motorcycle* (with Steven E. Alford, 2008).

Philip Fisher received his Ph.D. from Harvard University and currently teaches in the English department there. His academic interests include the American novel, the English novel, cultural theory, modernism, and American art and its cultural institutions. Fisher has published several books on these topics, such as *Making and Effacing Art* (1991) and *New American Studies* (1991).

Ed Folsom is the Carver Professor of English at the University of Iowa. He has edited the *Walt Whitman Quarterly Review* since 1983 and has published several books on the poet, including *Re-Scripting Walt Whitman* (2005), *Whitman East and West* (2002), and *Walt Whitman and the World* (1995). Folsom co-directs the *Walt Whitman Archive*; his work has been supported by the National Endowment of the Humanities and the Guggenheim Foundation.

Jason Gladstone, an assistant professor at Ball State University, received his M.A. and Ph.D. at Johns Hopkins. Gladstone's research interests include postwar, nineteenth-century, and twentieth-century American literature and culture; media theory; and literary aesthetic. With Daniel Worden, Gladstone co-edited a special issue of *Twentieth Century Literature*, called *Postmodernism, Then* (2011). He is working on the book manuscripts *Lines in the Dirt: American Postmodernism and the Failure of Technology* (which explores the effects of technological failure in relation to American art, literature, and theory) and, with Andrew Hoberek and Daniel Worden, *Postmodern / Postwar—And After*.

Kirsten Silva Gruesz is a professor and undergraduate program director at the University of California, Santa Cruz. Her research interests include Latino/a literature and nineteenth-century American literature. These interests have led Gruesz to direct the Latino Literary Cultures Project at UCSC and serve as program chair of C19: The Society of Nineteenth-Century Americanists from 2010 to 2012. Her book, *Ambassadors of Culture: The Transamerican Origins of Latino Writing* (2001), traces Latino literary history in the United States.

Trudier Harris served as the J. Carlyle Sitterson Professor of English at the University of North Carolina at Chapel Hill until her 2009 retirement. She received her M.A. and her Ph.D. from Ohio State University and, years later, the university presented her with its first annual Award of Distinction for the College of Humanities. Harris is a specialist on African American literature and folklore and has lectured throughout the United States as well as in Europe, Jamaica, and Canada. She has published numerous articles and books, including *Black Women in the Fiction of James Baldwin* (1985), which received the College Language Association Creative Scholarship Award. In 2003 Beacon Press published her memoir, *Summer Snow: Reflections from a Black Daughter of the South*. Harris, who is working on a book about Martin Luther King Jr. and African American literature, is currently teaching at the University of Alabama.

Ursula K. Heise is an English professor at the University of California, Los Angeles. She earned her Ph.D. at Stanford, and taught there from 1993 to 2012. In 2011 she was named a Guggenheim Fellow. Her research interests include environmental culture, globalization, science and literature, and digital humanities. Heise's book *Sense of Place and Sense of Planet: The Environmental Imagination of the Global* was published in 2008. She is currently working on a project called *Where the Wild Things Used to Be: Narrative, Database, and Biodiversity Loss*.

Maureen Honey received her M.A. and her Ph.D. from Michigan State University and upon graduating accepted a job at the University of Nebraska, where she continues to teach English and women's studies. She has been interviewed on women's roles in World War II by national media giants such as PBS, NPR, CNN, NBC, the *Wall Street Journal*, and *U.S. News and World Report*. Harris has published a book on the subject entitled *Creating Rosie the Riveter: Class, Gender, and Propaganda during World War II* (1984). Her other research interests include twentieth-century multicultural women writers and the Harlem Renaissance. Honey co-edited the book *Double-Take: A Revisionist Harlem Renaissance Anthology* (2001) with Venetria K. Patton.

Gregory S. Jay received his Ph.D. in English from the State University of New York in Buffalo. He has authored three books, entitled *American Literature and the Culture Wars* (1997), *America the Scrivener: Deconstruction and the Subject of Literary History* (1990), and *T. S. Eliot and the Poetics of Literary History* (1983). He has also edited several books and published many essays and articles. Jay currently teaches English at the University of Wisconsin, where he offers his students helpful writing tips such as "Be more or less specific" and "Exaggeration is a billion times worse than understatement."

Margaret Faye Jones was born in England and spent much of her childhood in rural Alabama. She has two master's degrees, in education and in English, and she received her Ph.D. in English from Indiana University of Pennsylvania. Since 1987 she has taught at Nashville Community College, and in January 2005 she was named dean of learning resources. Faye Jones's main academic interest is British and American working women of the Victorian age.

Amy Kaplan received her Ph.D. from Johns Hopkins University. She is the English Department Chair at the University of Pennsylvania, where she teaches courses on the culture of imperialism; comparative perspectives on the Americas; and mourning, memory, and violence. Kaplan wrote *The Social Construction of American Realism* (1988) and *The Anarchy of Empire in the Making of U.S. Culture* (2002). A cultural critic, Kaplan has published essays on September 11th, and Guantanamo Bay. Her essay *Manifest Domesticity* won the Norman Forster Prize for the best essay in American literature in 1988.

AnaLouise Keating spent much of her early life in Chicago. After receiving her M.A. and Ph.D. from the University of Illinois, Keating left for the southwest and a job at Eastern New Mexico University. She is currently a professor and doctoral program director in the department of women's studies at Texas Woman's University, where she continues to break new ground teaching and researching transformative multiculturalism. Keating has been published extensively in various books and journals. In 1996 her book *Women Reading Women Writing: Self-Invention in Paula Gunn Allen, Gloria Anzaldúa, and Audre Lorde* was selected as an outstanding academic book.

Elaine H. Kim teaches Asian American studies at the University of California at Berkeley, where she received her Ph.D. Kim is the co-founder of Asian Women United of California, Asian Immigrant Women Advocates, and the Korean Community Center. She produced the documentaries *Labor Women* (2002), *Art to Art* (1993), *Sa-I-Gu: From Women's Perspectives* (1993), and *Slaying the Dragon: Asian Women in U.S. Television and Film* (1988), and wrote and directed the sequel *Slaying the Dragon: Reloaded* (2010). In addition, Kim has published many books and articles on Asian American studies. In 2012, Kim received the San Francisco Asian Pacific American Heritage Lifetime Achievement Award.

David Leverenz, a professor emeritus in the University of Florida English department, received his M.A. and Ph.D. from the University of California at Berkeley. His major publications include *Manhood and the American Renaissance* (1989), *Paternalism Incorporated: Fables of American Fatherhood* (2003), and *Honor Bound: Race and Shame in America* (2012). Leverenz is the father of four children who, he asserts, helped to raise him.

David Palumbo-Liu is professor of comparative literature at Stanford University. He completed both his undergraduate and graduate work at the University of California at Berkeley, receiving his Ph.D. in 1988. Palumbo-Liu helped establish the Asian American Studies Department at Stanford University and is the author of several books and articles concerning Asian American pedagogy. His books include *The Ethnic Canon: History, Institutions, Interventions* (1995); *Asian / American: Historical Crossings of a Racial Frontier* (1999), and *The Deliverance of Others: Reading Literature in a Global Age* (2012). Palumbo-Liu is the founding editor of the journal *Occasion: Interdisciplinary Studies in the Humanities* and writes blogs for *Truthout's* Public Intellectual Project and *Arcade*.

A. LaVonne Brown Ruoff is a professor emerita of English at the University of Illinois in Chicago and a pioneer in Native American studies. Her personal relationships (her former husband was Menominee and her adopted daughter is Ojibwe) sparked her interest in Native American literature, which she began teaching thirty years ago. Her work in the field led to the publication of *American Indian Literatures: An Introduction, Bibliographic Review, and Selected Bibliography* (1990) and the Lifetime Scholarly Achievement Award of the Modern Language Association in 2002. In 2005, the journal *Studies in American Indian Literatures* published a special issue to honor Ruoff and her ground-breaking research.

Michael Ryan was born in Ireland and came to America in 1960. Ryan teaches in the Department of Film and Media Arts at Temple University. His books include *Marxism and Deconstruction: A Critical Articulation* (1982), *Politics and Culture: Working Hypotheses for a Post-Revolutionary Society* (1989), and the first and second editions of *Literary Theory: A Practical Introduction* (1999 and 2007, respectively). Ryan is currently writing a history of American film, which will be published online as an open-source textbook.

William J. Scheick, a professor emeritus at the University of Texas, edited *Texas Studies in Literature and Language* from 1975 to 1992. He also founded and edited *The Society of Early Americanists Newsletter* from 1989 to 2006. His extensive list of publications includes creative work, professional articles, horticultural essays, and book reviews. He was awarded the Pushcart Prize for creative writing, the Choice Award for Outstanding Academic Book, and the Center for Humanities Research Prize in literary and cultural studies. Scheick's other interests include gardening, creating stained-glass panels, and photographing flowers for local and statewide publications.

Daniel Joseph Singal grew up in Boston and graduated from Harvard University. He received his M.A. and Ph.D. from Columbia University and began his teaching career at Tulane University. In 1980 he joined the faculty of Hobart and William Smith College, where he teaches American historiography and political history. His books include *The War Within: From Victorian to Modernist Thought in the South* (1982) and *William Faulkner: The Making of a Modernist* (1997). Singal is currently at work on a book that explores modernist culture in the United States from the late nineteenth century to the 1970s.

Martha Nell Smith, a renowned Dickinson scholar and digital humanist, began the *Dickinson Electronic Archives* in 1997. Smith served as the founding director of the Maryland Institute of Technology in the Humanities. Her research interests are revealed in her publications, such as the books *Open Me Carefully: Emily Dickinson's Intimate Letters to Susan Dickinson* (1998), *Comic Power in Emily Dickinson* (1993), *Blackwell's Companion to Emily Dickinson* (with Mary Loeffelholz, 2008), and *Emily Dickinson, A User's Guide* (2010). In 2008 Smith co-edited with Lara Vetter *Emily Dickinson's Correspondence: A Born-Digital Textual Inquiry*, which allows scholars to filter letters by such features as date or genre. Smith currently teaches at University of Maryland.

Cecelia Tichi is the William R. Kenan Jr. Professor of English at Vanderbilt University. She completed her undergraduate work at Penn State University, and received her master's degree from Johns Hopkins and her Ph.D. from the University of California at Davis. Her primary academic focus is on the nineteenth- and twentieth-century American novel, but her interests encompass everything from technology and the environment to country music. Tichi's diverse interests are evident in her published articles and books, which include *Civic Passions: Seven Who Launched Progressive America (and What They Teach Us)* (2009); *Reading Country Music: Steel Guitars, Opry Stars, and Honky-Tonk Bars* (1998); and *Exposés and Excess: Muckracking in America* (2004). In 2006, Tichi was appointed to Chair of Modern Culture at the Library of Congress John W. Kluge Center.

Michael Warner is a professor of American studies and former chair of the English department at Yale University. His research interests include early American literature, social movements, new media, and, most recently, secularism, which led to his book *Varieties of Secularism in a Secular Age* (2010), co-edited with Craig Calhoun and Jonathan VanAntwerpen. His other books include *The Portable Walt Whitman* (2003), *The Trouble with Normal* (1999), and *American Sermons* (1999).

Susanne Woods taught at Brown University from 1972 to 1995, during which time she served as Associate Dean of Faculty, Director and Chair of the Executive Committee for the Women's Writer's Project, and Director of Graduate Studies. Woods has published books and essays about feminist theory, women's writing and vocation, and English versification, and she was co–general editor of the series *Women Writers in English, 1350–1850*. After serving as provost at Wheaton College from 1999 to 2006, Woods became a distinguished visiting scholar at University of Miami and an independent higher education consultant.

Daniel Worden's first book, *Masculine Style: The American West and Literary Modernism* (2011), won the 2012 Thomas J. Lyon Book Award in Western American Literary and Cultural Studies. His research interests run the gamut from gender and sexuality in literature to American modernism, documentary film, globalization, and even comic books. Worden, an assistant professor at the University of New Mexico in Albuquerque, co-edited a special issue of *Twentieth Century Literature*, called *Postmodernism, Then* (2011).

Acknowledgments *(continued from p. ii)*

Marta Caminero-Santangelo. "Introduction: Who Are We?" pp. 1–35, from *On Latinidad: U.S. Latino Literature and the Construction of Ethnicity* by Marta Caminero-Santangelo. Copyright © 2007 Gainesville: University Press of Florida. Reprinted with permission of the University Press of Florida.

SueEllen Campbell. Reprinted by permission of copyright owner, Modern Language Association of America from "Asking Ecocritical Questions," *Teaching North American Environmental Literature*, pages 215–22.

Emory Elliott. "1670—The American Jeremiad" by Emory Elliott, reprinted by permission of the publisher from *A New Literary History of America*, edited by Greil Marcus and Werner Sollors, pp. 40–44, Cambridge, Mass.: The Belknap Press of Harvard University Press. Copyright (c) 2009 by the President and Fellows of Harvard College.

Philip Fisher. Reprinted by permission of copyright owner, Modern Language Association of America from "American Literary and Cultural Studies Since the Civil War," *Redrawing the Boundaries: The Transformation of English and American Literary Studies*, pages 232–50.

Ed Folsom. Reprinted by permission of copyright owner, Modern Language Association of America, from "Portrait of the Artist as a Young Slave: Douglass' Frontispiece Engravings," *Approaches to Teaching Narrative of the Life of Frederick Douglass*, pages 55–65.

Jason Gladstone and Daniel Worden. "Introduction: Postmodernism, Then" from *Twentieth-Century Literature* 57.3 & 57.4, Fall/Winter 2011. Copyright © 2011. Reprinted by permission.

Kirsten Silva Gruesz. "America" by Kirsten Silva Gruesz from *Keywords for American Cultural Studies*, edited by Bruce Burgett and Glenn Hendler. Copyright © 2007 by New York University. Reprinted by permission of New York University Press.

Trudier Harris. "African-American Literature: A Survey" by Trudier Harris from *Africana Studies: A Survey of Africa and the African Diaspora*, *3/e*, edited by Mario Azevedo. Copyright © 2005. Reprinted by permission of Carolina Academic Press.

Ursula K. Heise. Reprinted by permission of copyright owner, Modern Language Association of America, from "The Hitchhiker's Guide to Ecocriticism" PMLA (2006): pp. 503–16.

Gregory S. Jay. "The End of 'American' Literature: Toward a Multicultural Practice" from *College English* 3 (1991). Copyright © 1991 by the National Council of Teachers of English. Reprinted with permission.

Margaret Faye Jones. "Bringing New Historicism into the American Literature Survey" from *Teaching English in the Two-Year College*, 28:2, December 2000. Copyright © 2000 by the National Council of Teachers of English. Reprinted by permission.

Amy Kaplan. "Manifest Domesticity" by Amy Kaplan from *American Literature*, Vol. 70, No. 3, September 1998, pp. 581–606. Copyright © 1998 by Duke University Press. All rights reserved. Republished by permission of the copyright holder, Duke University Press. www.dukeupress.edu

AnnLouise Keating. "Interrogating 'Whiteness,' (De)Constructing 'Race'" by AnnLouise Keating from *College English*, Vol. 57, No. 8, December 1995. Copyright © 1995 by the National Council of Teachers of English. Reprinted by permission.

Elaine H. Kim. "Asian American Literature" by Elaine H. Kim from *Columbia Literary History of the United States*, edited by Emory Elliott. Copyright © 1988 by Columbia University Press. Reprinted with permission of the publisher.

David Leverenz. "Manhood, Class, and the American Renaissance" from *American Literature, Culture, and Ideology: Essays in Memory of Henry Nash Smith*, edited by Beverly R. Voloshin. American University Studies Series Xxiv, American Literature (Book 8). Copyright © 1990 by Peter Lang Publishing, Inc., New York. Reprinted with permission of the publisher.

David Palumbo-Liu. "Assumed Identities" from *New Literary History*, 31:4 (Autumn 2000), 765–780. Copyright © 2000 by New Literary History, The University of Virginia. Reprinted with permission of Johns Hopkins University Press.

Venetria K. Patton and Maureen Honey. "Revisioning the Harlem Renaissance." Excerpt from *Double Take: A Revisionist Harlem Renaissance Anthology*. Copyright © 2002 by Rutgers, The State University. Reprinted by permission of Rutgers University Press.

A. LaVonne Brown Ruoff. Reprinted by permission of copyright owner, Modern Language Association of America, from "Introduction to American Indian Literatures," *American Indian Literatures: An Introduction, Bibliographic Review, and Selected Bibliography*, pages 1–19.

Michael Ryan. Excerpts from "Gender Studies" from *Literary Theory: A Practical Introduction, 2/e* by Michael Ryan. Copyright © 1999, 2007 by Michael Ryan. Reproduced with permission of John Wiley and Sons in the format Republish in a book via Copyright Clearance Center.

William J. Scheick. Reprinted by permission of copyright owner, Modern Language Association of America, from "Early Anglo-American Poetry: Genre, Voice, Art, and Representation," *Teaching the Literatures of Early America*, pages 187–99.

Daniel Joseph Singal. "Towards a Definition of American Modernism" from *American Quarterly* 39:1 (Spring 1987), 7–26. Copyright © 1987 by The American Studies Association. Reprinted with permission of Johns Hopkins University Press.

Martha Nell Smith. Reprinted by permission of copyright owner, Modern Language Association of America, from "Enabling Undergraduates to Understand Advanced Humanities Research: Teaching with the Dickinson Electronic Archives," *Teaching Literature and Language Online*, pages 278–89.

Cecelia Tichi. Reprinted by permission of copyright owner, Modern Language Association of America, from "American Literary Studies to the Civil War," *Redrawing the Boundaries*, pages 209–31.

Michael Warner. "What's Colonial about Colonial America" by Michael Warner from *Possible Pasts: Becoming Colonial in Early America*, edited by Robert Blair St. George. Copyright © 2000 by Cornell University. Used by permission of the publisher, Cornell University Press.